AF877599

Centre-State Financial Relations in India

1870 to 2010

140 Years of Indian Federal Finance

Centre-State Financial Relations in India
1870 to 2010

A Comprehensive Introduction on Centre-State Financial Relations in India during the Pre- and Post-Independence Periods with Summary and Commentary on each of the Reports of the Finance Commissions from First Finance Commission to Twelfth Finance Commission

M.M. Sury

INDIAN TAX FOUNDATION
New Delhi, India

in association with

New Century Publications
New Delhi, India

NEW CENTURY PUBLICATIONS
4800/24, Bharat Ram Road,
Ansari Road, Daryaganj,
New Delhi - 110 002 (India)

Tel.: 011 – 2324 7798, 4358 7398, 6539 6605
Fax: 011 – 4101 7798
E-mail: indiatax@vsnl.com
www.newcenturypublications.com

Editorial office:
34, Gujranwala Town, Part-2,
Delhi - 110 009

Tel.: 27247805, 27464774

Copyright © 2008 by the author

All rights reserved. No part of this book may be reproduced, stored in a retrieval system, or transmitted in any form or by any means, mechanical, photocopying, recording, or otherwise without the prior written permission of the publisher.

First Published – **July 2008**

ISBN: **978-81-7708-168-8**

Published by New Century Publications and printed at Salasar Imaging Systems, New Delhi

Cover Design: W & P Graphics Pvt. Ltd., New Delhi

PRINTED IN INDIA

About the Book

India's present fiscal structure is the result of a gradual evolution, along decentralised lines, dating back to December 14, 1870 when the resolution of Lord Mayo, Viceroy of India, was issued. The Mayo resolution explained the scheme by which the Government of India envisaged enlargement of the powers and responsibilities of the Provinces. The process of decentralisation of functions and finances in India will complete 140 years with the termination of the recommendations of the Twelfth Finance Commission in March 2010. This book traces the developments in the federal structure of India over this period.

Fiscal fcdcralism is a subject of topical interest in India in view of some recent developments of historical importance. With the passage of the Constitution (Seventy-third Amendment) Act, 1992, a uniform structure of *panchayats* has emerged throughout the country. Similarly, the passage of the Constitution (Seventy-fourth Amendment) Act, 1992 was a landmark in the history of municipal administration in India. As a result of these amendments, *panchayats* and municipalities are now constitutional bodies forming the third tier of the federal polity of India.

Furthermore, the Constitution (Eightieth Amendment) Act, 2000, significantly changed the manner of distribution of Central tax collections between the Central and State Governments. Prior to this amendment, income tax and Union excise duties were the only taxes shared with the States. This amendment altered the pattern of sharing of Central taxes between the Centre and the States by providing for the sharing of the net proceeds of all Union taxes and duties with the States. Still further, the Constitution (Eighty-eighth Amendment) Act, 2003 has included 'taxes on services' under entry 92C in the Union List (List I) in the Seventh Schedule of the Constitution.

This work provides a detailed description and analysis of the evolution and the present nature of Centre-State financial relations in India. It explains the existing constitutional arrangements for intergovernmental financial transfers and the role of the Finance Commission and the Planning Commission in effecting these transfers. The book consists of 27 chapters which explain different dimensions of fiscal federalism in India. There are 8 appendices which provide supplementary information related to Centre-State financial relations in India. Besides, it contains time-series data (1950-51 to 2007-08) on India's public finances. It also includes a glossary of fiscal terms.

This reference work is useful for teachers and students of economics, commerce, public administration, and management. It will also serve the needs of legislators, government functionaries and those in industry and trade.

Author's Profile

M.M. Sury received his B.A. (Hons.), M.A., and Ph.D. degrees in economics from the University of Delhi. He taught economics in the same university for 42 years. Specialising in fiscal economics, he has published extensively on Indian fiscal system in recognised national and international journals, such as *Small Industry Bulletin for Asia and the Pacific* (United Nations, Bangkok), *Bulletin for International Fiscal Documentation* (International Fiscal Association, Amsterdam), *Asian-Pacific Tax and Investment Bulletin* (Singapore), *Journal of the Indian School of Political Economy* (Pune), *Indian Economic Journal* (Bombay), and *Margin* (New Delhi).

Dr. Sury was a Visiting Fellow at the International Bureau of Fiscal Documentation, Amsterdam (May 1989), a Fellow at the Indian Institute of Advanced Study, Shimla (1991-92) and a Visiting Fellow in the Department of Law and Management, University of Mauritius, Mauritius (September-October, 2000). He was Economic Adviser, Delhi State Finance Commission (1996-97). He is President of the Indian Tax Foundation (ITF), New Delhi.

Indian Tax Foundation

Indian Tax Foundation was started in June 2000 by a team consisting mainly of teachers and researchers of the University of Delhi and Indira Gandhi National Open University, New Delhi. It is an independent, non-profit, non-governmental research organisation devoted to the study of Indian taxation and allied subjects. It records and reviews tax policy developments in India and examines their impact on different sectors of the economy. It undertakes its own and contractual research in these areas. It also provides consultancy and database services on Indian taxation. Publications of the Foundation, authored by experts/research teams contain both theoretical and empirical analysis. Occasionally, the Foundation also brings out special reports on subjects of topical interest concerning Indian economy.

Results of research conducted at the Foundation are given wider dissemination through its publications to create public awareness, update information and improve ideas. The Foundation provides facilities for knowledge on taxation to meritorious students and researchers, irrespective of caste, creed, sex or religion.

Indian Tax Foundation, based in Delhi, is registered with the Registrar of Societies, Delhi under the Indian Societies Registration Act (XXI) of 1860.

Registration No.: S 37728	Date of Registration: 24th August 2000

Preface

A federal set up creates a dual polity based on divided governmental functions and powers. Fiscal federalism, as a branch of public finance, deals with financial arrangements and their working in a federal polity.

Finance is the life blood of a government. Arrangements for finance are more complicated in a federal set up than in a unitary form of government. Imbalances often (rather invariably) arise between functional responsibilities and financial resources at different layers of the government. This is so because revenue-raising capacities and revenue needs of various federating units are different. This is a characteristic feature of all federations, particularly of those whose economies are more dynamic. Even in older federations (like the US, and Canada) financial conflicts persist between national and sub-national governments and their once-for-all solution is unachievable.

The mismatch between functions and financial powers occurs partly because of changing responsibilities of different tiers of government and partly due to the dominant position of the national government in regard to taxation powers, which is often by design. Therefore, vertical imbalances of resources and expenditure responsibilities emerge between different levels of the government, calling for transfer of resources from the higher level of government to lower level of government. Thus, intergovernmental transfers are an inherent part of a multi-level fiscal system. This is a familiar problem of federal finance.

India's present fiscal structure is the result of a gradual evolution, along decentralised lines, dating back to December 14, 1870 when the resolution of Lord Mayo, Viceroy of India, was issued. The Mayo resolution explained the scheme by which the Government of India envisaged enlargement of the powers and responsibilities of the Provinces.

The next landmark in the history of Centre-State financial relations was the Montague-Chelmsford Report on Constitutional Reforms which led to the passing of the Government of India Act, 1919. This Act sought to secure for the Provinces a greater degree of financial independence by abolishing the *divided heads* and effecting a complete separation between the Central and Provincial heads of revenue.

The Government of India Act, 1935 was a watershed in the evolution of Centre-State financial relations. The Act was a step towards consolidation and enhancement of Provincial autonomy in matters of resources and functions. It laid the foundations for the structure of Centre-State relations as incorporated in the present Constitution of India.

The partition of the country gave rise to new problems of financial adjustments, particularly in relation to the divided Provinces of Bengal and Punjab.

Drafting of the Constitution of independent India provided another opportunity to review the financial relations between the Centre and the States. For the purpose of incorporating financial provisions in the Draft Constitution, the President of the Constituent Assembly constituted an Expert Committee of three members under the chairmanship of Shri N.R. Sarker.

Prior to Independence in 1947, Princely States had remained outside the fiscal and financial system of the rest of the country except for certain arrangements entered into with them by the Government of India regarding such matters as maritime customs, central excises, posts and telegraph and railways. The Scheme of the Government of India Act, 1935, contemplated the accession of these States to the Indian federation. Under it, the Princely States were to accede in regard to foreign relations, defence and communications, with an option to accede in regard to other Central subjects also. This followed an extensive examination of the problems connected with the assimilation of States of varying sizes and having different kinds of relationship with the Centre into a workable system of financial relations with the proposed federation. As it happened, the provisions of the Government of India Act, 1935, relating to federation never came into operation.

During the period between the achievement of Independence and the framing of the Constitution, a great step forward was taken in the unification of the country by the integration of Princely States. Within less than two years from the date of Independence, all the Princely States had been either formed into sizeable units, or merged in the neighbouring Provinces or constituted into separate Centrally administered Chief Commissioners' Provinces.

Recognising the fact that the financial resources of the States may prove inadequate for undertaking welfare, maintenance, and development activities, the framers of India's Constitution did make elaborate, *albeit* complex, arrangements relating to flow of funds from the Centre to the States. The disequilibrium between proliferating functional responsibilities of the States and their own resources is corrected by Central transfers effected through Finance Commission and the Planning Commission.

The Constitution of India, operative since 1950, has shown flexibility towards changing needs and aspirations of the people. The passage of the Constitution (Seventy-third Amendment) Act, 1992 marked a milestone in the history of modern India. With this amendment, a uniform structure of *panchayats* emerged throughout the country. Similarly, the passage of the Constitution (Seventy-fourth

Amendment) Act, 1992 was a landmark in the history of municipal administration in India. As a result of these amendments, *panchayats* and municipalities are now constitutional bodies forming the third tier of the federal polity of India. India's decentralisation initiative in the form of Seventy-third and Seventy-fourth amendments poses challenges and offers opportunities.

Furthermore, the Constitution (Eightieth Amendment) Act, 2000, significantly changed the manner of distribution of Central tax collections between the Central and State Governments. Prior to this amendment, income tax and Union excise duties were the only taxes shared with the States. This amendment altered the pattern of sharing of Central taxes between the Centre and the States significantly by providing for the sharing of the net proceeds of all Union taxes and duties with the States.

Still further, the Constitution (Eighty-eighth Amendment) Act, 2003 has included 'taxes on services' under entry 92C in the Union List (List I) in the Seventh Schedule of the Constitution.

It was in the 1950-51 budget speech that the Finance Minister announced the constitution of the First Finance Commission, an epoch-making arrangement for the evolution of sound fiscal federalism in India. The First Finance Commission was set up in November 1951 and it submitted its report in December 1952 for the period 1952-57. Since then eleven more Finance Commissions have submitted their reports, the last being the Twelfth Finance Commission which submitted its report on November 30, 2004 for the period 2005-10. The Thirteenth Finance Commission was constituted under the Chairmanship of Dr. Vijay L. Kelkar on November 13, 2007. The Commission shall make recommendations covering a period of five years commencing on the April 1, 2010. It is expected to submit its report in October 2009.

Recommendations of the Finance Commission constitute the core of fiscal federalism in India. Finance Commission is a unique feature of the Indian Constitution without parallel in the existing federal constitutions of the world. Reports of the Finance Commissions provide glimpses of the events, challenges, problems and their solutions in the highly complex area of Centre-State relations in India during the last 55 years. These Reports highlight contemporary issues in Centre-State relations and record measures suggested by the Finance Commissions, from time to time, to solve them. They are an authentic and reliable source for the study of post-Independence economic history of India.

This work provides a detailed description and analysis of the evolution and the present nature of Centre-State financial relations in India. It explains the existing constitutional arrangements for intergovernmental financial transfers, the role of the Finance Commission and the Planning Commission in effecting these transfers, particularly the principles followed by these agencies to reduce vertical and horizontal imbalances in the availability of resources to various tiers of government in India.

Delhi
July 6, 2008

M. M. Sury

Contents

List of Tables in the Text

Key to Numeration

1 lakh	=	0.1 million
10 lakh	=	1.0 million
1 crore	=	10.0 million
100 crore	=	1.0 billion

Exchange Rate

The unit of currency in India is Indian Rupee

As on March 7, 2008

1 US Dollar	= 40.51 Rupees
1 UK Pound	= 81.73 Rupees
1 Euro	= 62.41 Rupees

Fiscal Year

Fiscal year in India runs from April 1 to March 31 of the following year

anna = 1/16th of a rupee before the introduction of the metric system of currency in India from April 1, 1957

Naya paisa = 1/100th of a rupee after the introduction of the metric system of currency.

1

Centre-State Financial Relations: Theoretical Framework

This chapter examines the principal theoretical issues involved in financial relations between different layers of the government in a federal set up.

1.1 Federal Polity: Meaning and Essential Features

A federal set up crcatcs a multiple polity based on divided functions and powers among central, state and local governments. Fiscal federalism deals with financial arrangements and their working in a federal polity. Federal system of government is a mixed blessing. It has the advantage of economic integration which promotes industrial and defence capabilities of a nation. However, a country cannot reap fully the economies of scale if provision for public goods is decentralised.

According to the traditional classification followed by political scientists, constitutions are either unitary or federal. A federation means a union of several states brought about by the instrument of a treaty or agreement. The modern concept of federalism is associated with the establishment of American federation in 1787. Since there is no agreed definition of a federal state, the model of the US is often taken as the reference point.

Federalism is a dynamic and not a static concept. It can best be understood in terms of its essential features. The consensus of opinion is that a federal system involves the following essential features.

1.1.1 Dual Government: In a unitary state, there is only one Government, namely the national government. However, in a federal state, there are two layers of government: the union government and the state governments. A component state has no right to secede from the federation. This distinguishes a federation from a confederation.

1.1.2 Distribution of Powers: A federal state involves a division of authority between the federal government and the states. The method of distribution may not be alike in different federal constitutions.

1.1.3 Supremacy of the Constitution: A federal state derives it existence from the constitution. Every power (executive, legislative, or judicial) whether it belongs to the Union or to the State is subordinate to and controlled by the constitution.

1.1.4 Authority of Courts: As already noted, the legal supremacy of the constitution is essential to the existence of a federal system. There should be no violation of the provisions of the constitution by any tier of government. This is secured by vesting in the courts a final power to interpret the constitution.

1.1.5 Doctrine of Harmonious Construction: Harmonious construction means that different entries in different lists are so interpreted that a conflict between them is avoided. It must be accepted that the Constitution does not want to create conflict and make any entry nugatory. Hence, whenever there appears to be a conflict between two entries in the two different lists, the two entries should be so interpreted that each of them is given effect. For this purpose, the scope and meaning of one may be restricted so as to give meaning to the other.

1.1.6 Doctrine of Pith and Substance: In a federal set up, the central and the state governments should keep themselves within the respective domain assigned to them. In other words, no government should trespass into the legislative powers reserved for the other. A law made by a government which encroaches upon the field assigned to the other government is invalid. However, before a law is declared invalid, the courts should apply the rule of pith and substance.

The rule of pith and substance means that a law enacted by a legislature which is competent to enact it shall not become invalid merely because it incidentally touches a matter outside the competence of that legislature. It often happens that a legislation intending to deal with a subject in one list touches also upon a subject in another list. Blind adherence to a strict interpretation would result in a large number of statutes being declared invalid. Thus, where such overlapping occurs, it is asked what in 'pith and substance' is the effect of the enactment in question and in which list is the true character to be found.

1.1.7 Rule of Repugnancy: Repugnancy or inconsistency between two pieces of legislation means that conflicting results are produced when both the laws are applied to the same facts. Repugnancy between two legal provisions can arise in a number of ways.

A. Tests of Repugnancy

1. An obvious case of repugnancy arises when one statute says 'do it' and the other statute says 'do not do it'. In such a case there is clear and direct inconsistency between the two Acts and the situation is absolutely irreconcilable.
2. Even if there is no apparent conflict between the two statutes, yet there may be repugnancy because both cover the same field. For example, when a statute describes an offence already created by another statute, and imposes a different punishment, repugnancy arises between the two.
3. When two statutes pertain to the same subject mater, but when Parliament

intends to make its enactment a complete code and cover the whole field. In such a case, the State law whether passed before or after would be overruled on the ground of repugnancy.

1.2 Economic Basis of Decentralisation

Devolution of funds follows devolution of functions. The financing pattern of a government can be examined and decided only in the light of functions assigned to it. In fact, two factors determine the level of expenditure of a government: (a) its functional jurisdiction and (b) the standard at which its different functions are to be performed.

How should the responsibilities for providing public goods and services be shared between the central, state and local governments? According to the theory of fiscal federalism, functions which involve national interest, economies of scale, lumpy investments, and substantial spatial externalities (spill overs) should be left to the national government. Defence services are a case in point. Functions the benefits of which largely confine to regional jurisdictions and which are subject to heterogeneous preferences should be assigned to the state governments. Sanitation, street lightning, fire safety are services the benefits of which are localised and hence should be assigned to and performed by local governments (e.g. municipalities). In short, expenditure and service responsibilities should be assigned according to the benefit area of each service.

1.3 Advantages of Decentralised Decision-making

Decentralised decision-making meets the politico-economic aspirations of the people at the sub-national level.

Decentralisation of political and administrative powers is a virtue because it institutionalises the participation of those affected by local decisions. Following are the main advantages of decentralisation in a democratic set up.

1. Decentralisation of governmental functions allows better matching of public goods supply to local needs, tastes and preferences and hence increases social welfare.
2. State/local governments are more responsive and accountable to people than national government. Linkages between the decision to spend and that to raise resources improve fiscal discipline.
3. Mobilisation of resources at the state/local level reduces dependence and strain on the finances of national government.

1.3.1 Tiebout Hypothesis: According to Charles Tiebout, competition among local governments ensures efficiency in the supply of public goods, just as competition among firms ensures efficiency in the supply of private goods. He has argued that competition among local governments will result in these governments supplying the goods and services individuals want and producing these goods in an efficient manner. [1]

1.4 Problems of Multi-level Finance: Vertical and Horizontal Fiscal Imbalances

Although a federal system provides for divided governmental functions and powers, imbalances often (rather invariably) arise between functional responsibilities and financial resources at different layers of the government. This is so because revenue-raising capacities and revenue needs of various federating units are different. This is a characteristic feature of all federations, particularly of those whose economies are more dynamic. Even in older federations (like the United States, and Canada) financial conflicts persist between the national and sub-national governments and their once-for-all solution is unachievable.

The mismatch between functions and financial powers occurs partly because of changing responsibilities of different tiers of government and partly due to the dominant position of the national government in regard to taxation powers, which is often by design. Therefore, vertical imbalances of resources and expenditure responsibilities emerge between different levels of the government, calling for transfer of resources from the centre to the states. This is the familiar problem of federal finance. Financial imbalances at the vertical level (centre versus states), and at the horizontal level (among the states) are sought to be removed/reduced through constitutional arrangements, and in some countries through political bargaining as well.

1.5 Financing Pattern

1.5.1 Taxes: Tax revenue is generally the main source of financing public expenditure at different levels of the government. In most democratic countries, taxation powers of central, state and local governments are mentioned in the constitution itself. Taxation powers of the government at different levels may be mutually exclusive or overlapping. For example, most tax fields in Canada are jointly occupied by the federal and provincial governments. Personal income tax, corporation income tax, general sales tax, and consumption taxes (excise duties) are levied by the federal as well as provincial governments in that country. Customs duties which belong exclusively to the federal government are the only notable exception. The joint occupancy of tax fields has often caused friction not only between the federal and provincial governments but also among the provinces themselves. Mark Krasnick, a Canadian fiscal expert, observed, "The fact that both the federal government and the provinces occupy the lucrative income and commodity tax fields implies that in addition to any competition or conflict that may exist among the provinces, competition also exists between the federal government and the provinces. This conflict concerns the manner in which the tax capacity of a particular tax base is shared between the two levels; or, to use the common jargon, the way in which tax room is apportioned." [2]

In India, the centre and the states have no concurrent powers of taxation. Taxes with inter-state base and those in the case of which all-India uniformity in rates is desirable, to facilitate industry and trade, are vested in the central government. Taxes which are location-specific and relate to subjects of local consumption are with the states. Broadly speaking, taxes on production are levied by the centre and taxes on sale and purchase by the state governments. The absence of joint occupancy of tax fields has successfully minimised double taxation, tax rivalry between the centre and the states, and duplicate tax administration.

A. Assignment of Taxes: Assignment of a tax means transfer of taxation power from a higher level to a lower level of government. Taxation power includes the following: the right to levy the tax, collect the tax, and appropriate the proceeds from the tax. Thus, there can be three interpretations of assignment of a tax. In the first case, the higher level government may levy and collect a tax but handover the entire proceeds to a lower level government. Taxes levied by the Government of India under Article 269 of the Constitution are a case in point. [3] Secondly, the higher level government may levy a tax but allow the lower level government to collect it and retain fully the proceeds therefrom. Taxes levied by the Government of India under Article 268 of the Constitution fall under this category. [4] Finally, the higher level government may transfer a tax to a lower level government lock, stock and barrel, a situation which defines assignment of a tax in its strictest sense.

Assignment of taxes should not be unconditional. Along with the determination of tax domain for a state, the central government ought to prescribe conditions so that the underlying purpose of assignment is adequately served. Thus, it should be obligatory on the part of a state to levy the tax assigned to it. Not only this, the state should not have powers to alter the basic structure of the assigned tax. The state may enjoy flexibility in fixing the tax rates within a minimum and maximum range prescribed by the central government. Tax exemptions/concessions should be minimum because a state is not expected to serve national objectives through its tax policy. As at other levels, tax default through disputes should be discouraged by requiring full payments prior to disputing an assessment.

1.5.2 Transfers: Transfers (tax sharing and grants) are used to correct vertical fiscal imbalances. However, before such transfers are effected, it should be ensured that taxes, duties, and levies assigned to the lower level government are being optimally tapped. Thus, tax effort, if not a pre-condition, should at least form part of the formula for transfers.

A. Need for Transfers: The need for transfers arises because the own revenues of a lower level government are generally insufficient to meet the expenditure required for providing services allotted to it. Very often central government retains with it elastic revenue sources such as income tax, excise levies, and customs duties. Contrarily, inelastic sources of revenue (such as sales tax, excise on liquor, and motor vehicle tax) are allotted to state governments. The gap between 'own resources' and expenditure needs indicates the degree of dependence of state governments on the central government.

The theory of fiscal federalism justifies intergovernmental transfers on the following grounds.

1. **Fiscal Gap Correction:** Fiscal gap occurs when there is a mismatch between the expenditure needs and revenue means of a state. Fiscal capacity and fiscal needs differ because geographical and climatic conditions are more favourable in some areas as compared to others. Hence, the access to revenue base varies from region to region. Similarly, per unit cost of services (e.g. supply of drinking water) varies depending upon the nature of terrain, and density of population. Sometimes fiscal gap may occur due to inappropriate assignment of revenue sources and functional responsibilities.
2. **Minimum Standard of Services:** Transfers from the centre to the states may be needed to upgrade the existing level of services to ensure a common minimum standard across regions. For example, the central government may provide grants to states to ensure a national standard in the provision of some public services (say 70 litres of drinking water per person per day).
3. **Inter-jurisdictional Spill Overs:** Spill overs (or spatial externalities) occur where the benefits of a locally provided service spread to persons who are not legally required to contribute to costs of the service. Services the benefits of which generally spill over to neighbouring jurisdictions include public transport, subsidised educational and medical facilities, anti-pollution measures, parks and recreational facilities. Inter-governmental grants are a major and often the most practical way of correcting for spill over effects.
4. **Performance of Agency Functions:** Central government may use the services of state governments to implement certain schemes of national importance, e.g. disease control, preserving ecological balance, propagation of research and improved technology. Funds (often in the form of grants) are provided to state governments to perform such agency functions.

B. Forms of Transfers: Transfers from the higher level to a lower level of government are made in the form of (a) tax sharing, (b) grants and (c) loans. The first two items generally account for the bulk of transfers on the revenue account.

1. **Tax Sharing:** Formula-based tax sharing is a predictable source of revenue and the state governments automatically gain from the buoyancy of the shared central taxes. There are two types of tax sharing mechanism. Under the first method (called global sharing), the whole of the central tax revenue forms a pool for sharing with the state governments. A certain percentage of the total tax revenue of the centre is allocated to the state governments. The second method (called scheduler or itemised sharing) involves sharing of revenue from individual central taxes. Tax sharing may take the form of a fixed amount or a fixed proportion of tax revenue. Central government should share at least one buoyant tax (e.g. income tax) with state governments.
2. **Grants:** Grants have the advantage of being targeted towards fiscally disadvantaged states to reduce horizontal fiscal imbalances. They can also be made conditional regarding their utilisation. Grants are given mainly for the purpose of equalisation, though they are often given to promote the objectives and priorities of the central government. It is noteworthy that while a state cannot be denied a part of a shared central tax even if it has no demonstrated financial need, grants are given upon genuine financial needs of a state. It is possible that even before tax devolution from the centre, some high-income states have surplus in their revenue account.

Keeping in mind the criteria of fiscal equity and efficiency, three types of grants may be given by the central government to states.

- General purpose (or unconditional) grants are given to offset fiscal disadvantages arising from lower taxable capacity and/or higher unit cost of the services provided (due to bad terrain etc.). Such equalising grants have to be general and their basic purpose is to enable different states to come up to a minimum standard of services provided.
- Specific purpose (or conditional) grants are tied to the achievement of specific objectives. They may be with or without matching requirements. They are used to ensure minimum levels of specified public services to be provided by state governments. Such grants are justified also where services have spill over effects. Thus, afforestation, slum improvement and literacy drives create benefits not only to local residents but also to community as a whole. Such schemes should preferably be financed through grants from the centre to the states.
- The incentive grants are given for the purpose of encouraging states to streamline their operations. These grants should depend on the measures

taken by the states to strengthen their financial position.

3. **Loans:** Financial resources from the higher level of government to lower level of government also flow in the form of loans. These loans are generally given for capital projects

C. Principles of Transfers: The designing of a sound system of transfers is of vital importance in the context of financial discipline and promotion of local initiatives. Central government may keep in mind the following broad principles so that amount transferred is equitably distributed among the states.

1. The scheme of transfers should be based on well-defined objective criteria so that financially weak states are adequately assisted. These may include size of population, level of economic development, availability of infrastructure, and minimum service standards.
2. The system of transfers should be so designed that states are not discouraged to mobilise resources on their own. Contrarily, the system should contain in-built mechanism to promote internal mobilisation of resources and their judicious management. For this purpose, the following additional criteria may be adopted and given due weightage: tax effort, adoption of sound financial management, innovations in the provision of public services, and economy in expenditure.
3. The amount and frequency of transfers should be reasonably predictable. They should be pre-determined rather than being open-ended. Transparency, through explicit and identifiable budget entries, should also be ensured.

1.5.3 Borrowings: Long-term borrowings by a government are justified when the benefits of a capital project undertaken by it are likely to be reaped over a long period of time, i.e. by more than one generation of taxpayers. The financing of such projects should place the repayment burden on the present as well as future generations. If long-term capital projects are financed out of current revenues and/or short-term borrowings, the future generations would enjoy free riding. Thus, it is both fair and efficient that projects with long-term benefits are financed through long-term borrowings.

Access to long-term borrowings by a lower level government though desirable is hindered by a variety of factors. Generally, central government imposes restrictions on the borrowing powers of the state governments which, in turn, impose restrictions on the borrowing powers of the local bodies under them. Since borrowings by the lower level government are guaranteed, in most case, by the higher level government, the latter has a right to impose such restrictions. These restrictions apply to (a) the type of debt, (b) amount of debt, (c) term of the debt, (d) rate of debt, and (e) use of debt funds. Approval of the higher level government, often cumbersome, is needed before the debt is floated.

Moreover, capital markets in underdeveloped countries are not fully developed. As in the developed West, bond markets cannot be successfully introduced in the absence of institutional set up in place. Besides, the track record of state/local governments as borrowers is rather poor. Till they establish their credit worthiness, and financial intermediaries come of age, borrowings by lower level governments in developing countries are unlikely to be important.

1.6 Earmarking of Revenue

Earmarking is a fiscal practice under which revenue from one or more sources is pooled into a separate independent fund which is used to finance a pre-determined public service.

The purpose of earmarking is to ensure stable funding for important public activities. Another objective of earmarking is to introduce market prices into the budgetary process. In this context, earmarked taxes represent market prices charged indirectly for rendering public services.

1.6.1 Conditions for Successful Earmarking: For successful earmarking, the following conditions need to be satisfied.

A. Expenditure Specificity: Expenditure to be financed through earmarked revenue should be well-defined and specific, i.e. the taxpayers should be able to identify its obvious benefits.

B. Tight Linkage: The linkage between earmarked revenue (e.g. motor vehicle tax) and pre-determined expenditure (e.g. construction of a flyover) should be tight. If the amount earmarked is substantially less than the amount spent on the designated function, earmarking will be less effective.

C. Strong Benefit Linkage: There should be a close correspondence between the tax levied and the benefit received. Preferably, the tax should take the form of a direct user charge, e.g. a toll.

Traditionally, financing of expenditure on construction and maintenance of municipal roads and bridges from out of tolls, motor vehicle taxes, and fuel taxes has been considered an activity with strong economic rationale for earmarking. Similarly, airport tax is levied to meet expenditure on airport maintenance. The principle of earmarking could be applied to such municipal services as water supply and sewage disposal through water and sewer charges, using the base for property tax. However, earmarking should not be applied indiscriminately because too many funds created under it would be difficult to manage.

1.7 Nature of Indian Federation

The very first Article of the Constitution defines India as a Union of States. Though the word federation has been deliberately avoided in the Indian

Constitution, the fiscal structure created under it is essentially federal in nature.

The political system introduced by India's constitution possesses all the essentials of a federal polity.

India's constitution is the supreme organic law of our land. Both the Centre and State Governments derive their authority from the constitution. The States are not allowed to secede from the union.

There is a division of legislative, administrative and financial powers between the Union and the State Governments. These are elaborated in lists I, II and III of the Seventh Schedule of the constitution. List I (Union List) describes the functions and powers of the Union Government. List II (State List) mentions the functions and powers of the State Governments. List III (Concurrent List) describes the subject matter on which both the Union and the State Governments can legislate.

The Supreme Court stands at the head of our judiciary to guard this distribution of powers and to invalidate any action which violates the limitations imposed by the Constitution.

According to Article 254 of the Constitution of India, if any provision of a State law is repugnant to any provision of a Central law, then the Central law shall prevail and the law made by the State shall be void to the extent of repugnancy.

The most common application of Article 254 arises when both the Central and State Governments enact legislation on the same matter contained in List III (Concurrent List) of the Seventh Schedule of the Constitution. In such a situation, if there is repugnancy then Central law prevails over the State law.

It is, of course, true that the Indian constitution has a strong Central bias. The financial powers of the Central Government are overwhelming. According to some scholars the constitution of India is neither purely federal nor purely unitary but is a combination of both. India's constitution is sometimes described as federal in times of peace and unitary in times of war.

Notes

1. For more on Tiebout hypothesis, see 1. Harvey S. Rosen and Ted Gayer, *Public Finance* (New York: MacGraw Hill), International Eighth Edition (2008), pp. 511-514. 2. Joseph E. Stiglitz, *Economics of the Public Sector* (New York: W.W. Norton and Company) Third Edition, 2000, pp. 735-737.

2. Mark Krasnick, *Fiscal Federalism* (Toronto: University of Toronto Press, 1986), p. 6.

3. These taxes are: (a) taxes on the sale or purchase of goods other than newspapers, where such sale or purchase takes place in the course of inter-State trade or commerce, and (b) taxes on the consignment of goods where such consignment takes place in the course of inter-State trade or commerce. These taxes correspond to entries 92A and 92B in the Union List in the Seventh

Schedule of the Constitution. It is noteworthy that out of these two taxes only one is being levied at present, viz. inter-State sales tax (entry 92A).

4. These are duties of excise on medicinal and toilet preparations containing alcohol, and stamp duties, and correspond respectively to entries 84, and 91 of the Union List with corresponding qualification of entry 51 of the State List in the Seventh Schedule of the Constitution.

2

Pre-Independence Developments and Post-Partition Financial Adjustments

This chapter surveys the course of Centre-State fiscal relations in India from 1870 through 1947, the year of Independence. The pre-1947 arrangements for intergovernmental financial transfers had a strong bearing on the framing of Indian constitution, operative since 1950. Post-partition financial adjustments are also discussed in this chapter.

The present fiscal structure of India is the result of a gradual evolution over the last 140 years. Although it is desirable to look back at the historical developments of a subject to understand its current features, the situation is different in the present case. The political and economic scene in India is greatly different today from what existed during British rule. Before 1947, India was a dependency of the United Kingdom and consisted of British India, and the Princely States. It encompassed the entire area which now forms the four countries of India, Pakistan, Burma, and Bangladesh. The Princely States enjoyed internal financial autonomy and therefore did not form part of the public finances. They had separate budgets and separate sources of revenue. Neither there was any plan of economic development nor was there any attempt to build a welfare society.

Presently, India is an independent country and it includes the former Princely States but excludes the other three countries mentioned above. Due to changed circumstances there is lack of continuity and comparability of information and data. Still, a look back at the pre-1947 intergovernmental financial relations is necessary because they had a bearing on the framing of the Constitution of independent India.

2.1 Mayo Scheme, 1870

After the events of 1857, the British Crown assumed sovereignty over India from East India Company in 1858. The British had realised that governance of so vast and diverse a country of sub-continental size through centralisation of all power was difficult and some degree of decentralisation of authority to Provinces (or States) was necessary. [1] Prior to 1871, the administration of the country was rigidly centralised, characterised by absolute imperial control over Provincial revenues and expenditures. Provinces were entirely dependent on annual cash assignments from the Centre for the maintenance of their administration.

The first beginning towards decentralisation of finances was made when the resolution of Lord Mayo was issued on December 14, 1870. The Mayo resolution explained the scheme by which the Government of India envisaged enlargement of the powers and responsibilities of the Provinces. Thus, services like jails, police, education, medical, roads and civil works were transferred to the administrative control of the Provinces and to meet their costs, the departmental receipts under these heads were also assigned to them. This was done to encourage their interest in collections as well as to induce economy in expenditure. This arrangement came to be known as *Provincial Financial Settlements*. However, due to the inadequacy of these new heads of revenue, the existing system of fixed grants from Central revenues also continued. To quote, "The system of decentralisation was welcomed by the Provinces, because friction with the Central Government was thereby obviated and much useless correspondence avoided. But it did not give adequate resources to the Provinces nor provide conditions for the progressive administration of the services transferred to them. The only consideration which really weighed with the Government of India was that of administrative convenience." [2]

Satisfied with the Mayo scheme, the Government decided to carry it further and the next step towards decentralisation was taken in 1877 when subjects like land revenue, and general administration were transferred to the Provinces. The Mayo settlements were subject to revision annually but from 1882, they were made on quinquennial basis. Over the period 1882 to 1904, these settlements gave rise to the system of *divided heads of revenue.* Under the system, the Centre retained the entire profits of the commercial departments and the proceeds of revenue whose locale was no guide to its true incidence, such as the net receipts from customs, salt and opium. As the income derived from these sources was not sufficient to cover the central expenditure, other sources of revenue including income-tax were divided between the Central and Provincial Governments. The Central Government retained a proportion—fixed in the case of each Province, but not uniform as between the Provinces—of the proceeds of the main heads of revenue collected in the Provinces, based on an assessment of the respective needs of the Provinces. In practice, since no definite standards of needs had been evolved, allocations to the Provinces were largely a result of history. The revenue from *divided heads*, being insufficient to meet the needs of the Provincial Governments, was supplemented by means of fixed cash assignments, recurring as well as non-recurring, which continued to remain an important feature of the system.

In 1904, the settlements were made quasi-permanent and in 1911 began the period of permanent settlements. As the Indian Taxation Enquiry Committee (1924-25) observed, "The intention of the Government in adopting this change was on the one hand to give more elasticity to the settlements and more freedom to Local Governments in working them, and, on the other hand, to protect the general taxpayer of India against possible mismanagement in any particular province, and to put an end to the frequent and undesirable controversies over the adequacy of the existing settlements." [3]

2.2 Government of India Act, 1919

The next landmark in the history of Centre-State financial relations was the Montague-Chelmsford Report on Constitutional Reforms which led to the passing of the Government of India Act, 1919. The Act sought to secure for the Provinces a greater degree of financial independence by abolishing the *divided heads* and effecting a complete separation between the Central and Provincial heads of revenue. Thus, revenue heads like income tax, non-alcoholic excises including salt, customs, currency and mint, and contributions from railways, and post and telegraph came to the share of Central Government while relatively inelastic sources of revenue like land revenue, alcoholic excises, irrigation charges, judicial stamps, forest receipts, and registration fee were assigned to the Provinces. These arrangements enabled the Provinces to run their administration with the help of revenue raised by themselves. The Provincial budgets were separated from that of the Government of India and each Province presented its own budget and levied taxes assigned to it. With revenue heads distributed on these lines, it was estimated in the Report that there would remain a large deficit in the Government of India budget. It was, therefore, proposed in the Report that the Provinces should make contributions to the Central budget.

2.2.1 Meston Settlement, 1920: The Financial Relations Committee presided over by Lord Meston was appointed to advise on the amounts of provincial contributions, and also on the claims of Bombay to a share of the proceeds of income tax. The Meston Committee reported in March 1920.

While recognising that it would not be possible permanently to exclude Provincial Governments from some form of direct taxation upon the industrial and commercial earnings of their people, the Committee advised against the division of income tax with the Provinces. They recommended that general stamps be made provincial for financial and administrative reasons.

The Committee proposed a scheme of initial contributions and of standard contributions to be attained over a period of 7 years. The standard contributions, which were based on the relative taxable capacity of the Provinces and other economic factors, never came into operation. The initial contributions were computed on the increased spending power of each Province resulting from the new scheme of distribution, i.e. the additional income which each Province would acquire on the separation of the sources of revenue. The scheme of contributions was subjected to criticism from various quarters. Some Provinces disliked the initial contributions, others the standard contributions, and industrial Provinces like Bombay were opposed to the whole basis of the revised scheme.

The Joint Select Committee of Parliament on Draft Rules made under the Government of India Act, 1919, suggested a gradual reduction of the aggregate contribution of all Provinces and underlined the idea that contributions should cease at the earliest possible moment.

The Committee was opposed to provincialising income tax but recommended that some share in the growth of revenue from taxation of income should be granted to all Provinces in so far as that growth was attributable to an increase in the amount of incomes assessed in each Province. The scheme of financial arrangements contained in the Report on Indian Constitutional Reforms, as modified on the recommendations of the Joint Select Committee on Draft Rules, was incorporated in the Devolution Rules under the Government of India Act, 1919, which were promulgated in December 1920.

The recommendations of the Joint Select Committee relating to income tax provided that a Province should receive 3 pies in each rupee of the amount by which the assessed income of any year exceeded that of the year 1920-21. Inasmuch as collection might not accurately reflect the income tax revenue due to the economic activity of a Province, some ad hoc adjustments were made on account of industrial units located in a Province different from the Province in which they were assessed to income tax. The operation of the rule gave unequal results as between Provinces. It did not lead, on the whole, to any significant accretion to provincial revenues and, in particular, virtually failed to secure for the larger industrial Provinces a share in the yield of income tax. The rule, however, represented a slight departure in principle from the scheme of complete division of sources originally proposed, and thus marked the beginning of the use of income tax as a balancing factor.

From the very beginning, the scheme of *provincial contributions* came in for sharp criticism from various quarters, particularly from the Provinces themselves. The trends in the Central and Provincial budgets in the early 1920s vindicated the stand of critics and the demand for abolition of contributions grew still more persistent with the result that contributions were abolished from 1928-29. Provincial contributions under the Meston Settlement during the 1920s provide, perhaps, the only example of transfer of funds from the Provinces to the Centre in the long history of fiscal federalism in India.

There were some important lessons to be learnt from the Reforms of 1919. According to the Fourth Finance Commission, "The failure of the system of a rigid division between the Central and Provincial heads of revenue introduced by the Government of India Act of 1919 could not be prevented by the Meston award and the ultimate result was unsatisfactory both to the Centre and to the units. The experience of the nineteen-twenties led, however, to the emergence of the idea that the authority most suited for discharging a particular governmental function need not necessarily be the authority most suited to raise the financial resources required to discharge the function. The taxes on income had already been recognized before 1919 as a balancing factor and it continued to be recognized as such after 1935. But it also came to be recognized that other taxes could appropriately be levied and collected by the Central Government and distributed, wholly or partly, to the Provinces or States. The Government of India Act of 1935 recognised this principle and the Constitution adopted in 1950 made clear provision for (i) the assignment of the taxes raised by the Union Government under article 269 wholly to the States, (ii) for the obligatory division of the income-tax proceeds between the Union and the States, and (iii) for the division, with the approval of Parliament, of the proceeds of the Union excise duties." [4]

However, the framework of fiscal federalism set up in 1919 remained unaltered, by and large, till the Government of India Act, 1935 came into operation. The period covered by the Government of India Act, 1919, was marked by frequent discussions on the structure of financial relations between the Centre and the units. A principal objective of these discussions was to equip the Provincial Governments with greater financial resources. The inadequacy of the existing resources, both of the Centre and the units, and a search for fresh avenues of taxation, also represented a thread running through the discussions.

2.3 Indian Taxation Enquiry Committee, 1924-25

In the meantime, the Indian Taxation Enquiry Committee (President: Sir Charles Todhunter), 1924-25 examined, *inter alia*, the division of sources of revenue between the Centre and the Provinces. It recommended that the excise duty on country-made foreign liquor, excise on opium, and general stamps should be transferred to the Centre. The recommendation regarding said excises on liquor and opium was rejected by the Government in view of administrative difficulties involved. Similarly, owing to stiff opposition from the Provinces, the proposal to centralise general stamps was dropped and only duties on documents of commercial nature were transferred to the Central Government. The proposal of the Committee to give the provinces a small share of the receipts of the corporation tax was also rejected by the Government.

A major recommendation of the Committee pertained to the distribution of income tax revenue between the Centre and the Provinces. Prior to 1919, income tax was a *divided head* of revenue. However, the Montague-Chelmsford Reforms resulted in a complete separation of Central and Provincial finances, and income tax became a part of the Central revenues.

The Todhunter Committee expressed itself against giving the Provinces power to levy and administer an income tax as well as against the imposition by the Centre of surcharges for the benefit of the Provinces. It suggested that the most appropriate solution for this problem was the assignment to the Provinces of a share of the tax. In regard to its distribution, the Committee proposed that this should be based primarily on the principle of domicile. It proposed to give the Province the proceeds of a basic rate on personal incomes, graduated proportionally to the general rate. Under its scheme, collection on incomes not pertaining to residents in particular Provinces (such as the tax on undistributed dividends of companies or on incomes of persons resident outside the Province or the country) and the whole of super tax would be retained by the Centre. In addition to the allotment made on the basis of personal incomes, the allocation of which would be based entirely on domicile, the Committee also recommended a partial recognition of the principle of origin by assigning to each Province a small portion of the receipts of the corporation profits tax. It contemplated that this might be distributed on the basis of the collections of each Province

In short, the Todhunter Committee opined that in the event of any division of taxes between the Centre and the Provinces, the choice of income tax as the main balancing factor was inevitable. The Government of India Act, 1935, did assign to the Provinces a part of the net proceeds of income tax levied by the Centre. **For pre-Independence history of income tax in India, see Appendix 1 of this book.**

2.4 Indian Statutory Commission, 1930

In its report submitted in 1930, this Commission accepted the general principles of the scheme drawn up by its Financial Assessor, Sir Walter Layton, for the divisions of resources between the Central and Provincial Governments. Layton envisaged the use of income tax as the main balancing factor in the reallocation of revenues between the Centre and the Provinces. He suggested that in order to meet the claims of the industrial Provinces a substantial part of the revenue from income tax should be assigned to the Provinces. He endorsed the general method of division proposed by Todhunter Committee and recommended that one-half of the income tax paid by residents of a Province (including tax on dividends received by them from companies carrying on operations outside the Province) be assigned to the Province concerned. Super tax would remain entirely Central, subject to reconsideration after 10 years. The Provincial Governments were also to have the option of levying a surcharge on tax collected on the incomes of residents in the Province limited to half the tax transferred to them, i.e. one-fourth of the total tax. Significantly, the Commission also suggested that the exemption of agricultural incomes from income tax should be abolished by definite stages and the whole of the proceeds of the taxation of these incomes should be assigned to the Province of origin.

Sir Layton further recommended that a Provincial Fund be formed out of the proceeds of certain new excises on such commodities as cigarettes and matches and, when the centre budgetary position permitted, the duty on salt, for distribution among the Provinces on a per capita basis. The Commission endorsed this proposal.

2.5 Peel Committee I, 1931

The Federal Structure Committee of the Second and Third Round Table Conferences appointed two sub-committees to consider the problem of allocation of resources between the Centre and the Provinces. Both the sub-committees were presided over by Viscount Peel. The first sub-committee (Peel Committee I) submitted its report in 1931. Report of the second sub-committee (Peel Committee II) came in 1932. In between these two reports was submitted in 1932 the report of an Expert Committee presided over by Lord Percy.

Peel Committee I suggested that all income tax proceeds should be transferred to the Provinces with collection and administration being in federal hands. It suggested, though obliquely, that federal tax revenues should be mostly derived from indirect taxation. Any resultant federal deficit could be met from provincial contributions which would be gradually terminated over a 10 to 15 year period. Later, if any permanent federal surplus were to materialise, the federal government should be free to allocate the surplus to the Provinces as an alternative preferable to reduction of taxation. The Committee suggested that it was desirable that the Constitution itself should lay down the proportions in which funds thus available should be divided among the Provinces, whether according to respective revenues or to population or to some other criteria. It recommended that an expert committee should advise on this aspect as well as on the criteria by which the proceeds of income tax should be allocated among the Provinces.

2.6 Percy Committee, 1932

Accordingly, the Percy Committee was appointed to examine the issues raised by Peel Committee I. The basis of distribution of income tax among the Provinces was considered in detail by Percy Committee. It held that a proper basis of distribution of income tax receipts should satisfy the following three tests:

- It should be simple, easily understood and administratively workable.
- It should give results likely to be accepted as fair between Province and Province.
- It should be compatible with the idea of a federation of autonomous units.

It opined that an allocation on the basis of collections would lead to gross injustice as between Province and Province and ruled it out. While distribution by population had equally no scientific basis it could be adopted with advantage for the distribution of taxes on certain forms of income not easily assignable to any locality. Theoretically, the basis of origin had much to commend it, but it would be administratively unworkable unless the allocations were made on arbitrary lines. Hence, the Committee did not recommend the adoption of this basis. Finally, it expressed itself in favour of the basis of residence in one of two forms, either the basis of personal income assessed or assessable in each Province or the amount of income tax attributable to each Province.

As regards the question of distribution of income tax between the Centre and the Provinces, the Percy Committee expressed the view that if the entire proceeds of income tax were transferred, the Centre would be faced with a substantial deficit. It, therefore, proposed the following scheme:

- Corporation tax (super tax on companies), tax paid by residents in federally administered areas and tax paid on salaries of federal officers should be retained by the Centre.
- Of the remainder of the net proceeds, a Province should receive the amount of personal super tax on the basis of collections from residents, an estimated amount of personal income tax creditable to it, and a share on the basis of population of the tax on non-residents and undistributed profits of companies, both to be taken as an estimated percentage of the total collections.

In order to ensure stability of provincial budgets, it suggested that the share of income tax due to the Provinces should not be altered from year to year even if the data for this were readily available on the basis suggested by it. Instead, it should be fixed for a term of years, subject to revision every 5 years in the light of data of personal income tax for the previous quinquennium. The federal government would have the power to impose a surcharge, for its own purposes, on any tax levied by it for the benefit of the Provinces. Federal grants, if and when they became feasible, should be made on population basis as the Committee believed that the surplus would arise mostly from taxes on consumption.

2.7 Peel Committee II, 1932

It proposed a two-fold division of the proceeds of taxes on income: (a) share which would be assigned as a permanent constitutional arrangement to the federal government and (b) share which would be assigned as a permanent constitutional arrangement to the Provinces. The federal government would be entitled to a share based on the proceeds of heads of tax which were not derived solely from the residents in British India, such as corporation tax, tax on federal officers, tax in federal areas, tax on Government of India securities and taxes on the incomes of persons not resident in British India. The whole of the remaining proceeds from income tax were to be assigned to the Provinces. However, the federal government should retain a block amount out of the provincial share of income tax until sufficient time had elapsed for the development of new sources of revenue. The Committee was in favour of the federal government having the power to levy for its own purposes a surcharge on the heads of income tax permanently assigned to the Provinces. Most of the members of the Committee were also agreed that the Provinces should have a right to levy a surcharge on the personal tax levied on its residents under the heads permanently allocated to the Provinces, subject to a maximum of 12.5 per cent. The Committee also proposed subventions from the Centre to deficit Provinces in approved cases and on certain conditions, to enable them to balance their budgets on the basis of providing for bare necessities.

2.8 White Paper on Indian Constitutional Reforms, 1931

The White Paper issued by Government in December 1931 contemplated that a prescribed percentage, not being less than 50 per cent nor more than 75 per cent, of the net revenue derived from taxes on income, other than agricultural income, except taxes on the income of companies should be assigned to the Provinces on a prescribed basis. It also proposed that the federation should retain for the first 3 years a prescribed sum out of the provincial share which would continue to be retained for a further period of 7 years with a reduction of one-eighth of the original sum in each successive year. Both the federation and the Provinces were to have power to levy surcharges on income tax for their own purposes.

Proposals contained in the White Paper introduced two new features into the plan for the division of sources of revenue. Firstly, the federal legislature was to be empowered by a law to assign to the units the whole or part of the yield of salt duties, excise duties, other than those specifically assigned to the units, and export duties. Secondly, it also suggested that in respect of certain taxes, including terminal taxes and death duties, while the power to levy the tax would be vested solely in the federation, the proceeds would be distributed to the Provinces. However, the federation would have the right to impose a surcharge for federal purposes. **For pre-Independence history of excise duties in India, see Appendix 2 of this book.**

2.9 Joint Parliamentary Committee on Indian Constitutional Reforms, 1934

This Committee was, by and large, in agreement with the proposals contained in the White Paper. It left the provincial share of income tax to be prescribed by an Order-in-Council, but could not visualise any prospect of the Provinces' share of income tax exceeding half of the net revenue from the source. The Committee did not favour the proposal to empower the Provinces also to impose surcharges on personal income tax. The modified proposals relating to income tax and other matters were incorporated in the Government of India Act, 1935.

It is noteworthy that the idea of devolving the whole of income tax to the Provinces leaving the Centre to cover the consequent deficit by provincial contributions was abandoned, and a measure of elasticity in the distribution of income tax was introduced by limiting the provincial share to a part of the net proceeds and giving the Centre power to retain, for a transitional period, a fixed amount out of the provincial share to give it time to adjust its finances.

2.10 Government of India Act, 1935

The Government of India Act, 1935 was a watershed in the evolution of Centre-State financial relation. To quote, "While under all the previous Government of India Acts, the Government of India was unitary, the Act of 1935 prescribed a federation, taking the Provinces and the Indian States (i.e. Princely States) as Units. But it was optional for the Indian States to join the federation; and since the Rulers of the Indian States never gave their consent, the Federation envisaged by the Act of 1935 never came into being." [5] Nevertheless, the Act was a step towards consolidation and enhancement of Provincial autonomy in matters of resources and functions. It laid the foundations for the structure of Centre-State relations as incorporated in the present Constitution of India. The Act divided taxation heads into the following three broad categories.

1. Taxes levied by and meant exclusively for the Central Government.
2. Taxes levied by and meant exclusively for Provincial Governments.

3. Taxes levied by the Centre but shared with the Provinces or completely assigned to them.

The Act also provided for grants-in-aid from the Centre to the Provinces in need of assistance.

The main provisions of the Act of 1935 relating to the subject under study were as follows.

1. Agricultural income tax was included in the list of Provincial subjects.
2. Provision was made under Section 138 of the Act for the assignment to Provinces of a percentage of the net proceeds of taxes on income other than agricultural income.
3. Section 140 of the Act provided that duties on salt, Central duties of excise, and export duties, while levied and collected by the Centre would, if an Act of Central legislature so provided, be assigned wholly or in part to the Provinces.
4. Under Section 142 provision was made for the payment of grants-in-aid of the revenues of such Provinces as might be in need of assistance.
5. The Act also provided for the levy by Central legislation of duties in respect of succession to property other than agricultural land, stamp duties, terminal taxes on goods and passengers carried by railway or air and taxes on railway fares and freights, and for the distribution of net proceeds to the Provinces.

2.10.1 Indian Financial Enquiry Report, 1936: Fiscal arrangements of the Act of 1935 left several questions to be decided and Sir Otto Niemeyer was appointed to make recommendations on matters which under Sections 138 (1) and (2), 140 (2) and 142 of the Act had to be prescribed or determined by Order-in-Council and on certain other ancillary matters. The scope of the enquiry was made comprehensive by a supplementary reference which enabled it to be extended to cover a review of the existing liabilities of the Provincial Governments to the Centre.

In respect of income tax, having regard to the dual considerations of the necessity of safeguarding the financial stability of the Centre and the obvious future needs of the Provinces, Sir Otto Niemeyer felt it was desirable that the maximum practicable distribution should be achieved. He recommended that 50 per cent of the net proceeds of income tax should be assigned to the Provinces.

As regards the distribution of the provincial share, he expressed the view that the mere accident of place of collection was an unsuitable guide and that the residence of the individual though it might be a convenient practical dividing line for the avoidance of double taxation between separate political units, was not in itself a very scientific criterion, particularly in a federation. Even supposing it were practicable to ascertain to what part of the country particular fractions of income and the incidence of the taxation burden properly adhered, it was, he pointed out, still arguable that in a federation other considerations also were involved, particularly if the benefits and incidence of other forms of common taxation were unequally divided as between the various partners.

After a consideration of the various elements of the problem, he came to the conclusion that substantial justice would be done by fixing the scale of distribution partly on residence and partly on population. He recommended distribution among the Provinces according to the fixed percentages given in Table 2.1.

Table 2.1: Distribution of Provinces' Share in Income Tax among the Provinces Recommended by Sir Otto Niemeyer

Province	**Per cent**
Madras	15
Bombay	20
Bengal	20
United Provinces	15
Punjab	8
Bihar	10
Central Provinces	5
Assam	2
North-West Frontier Province	1
Orissa	2
Sind	2
Total	**100**

Source: *Report of the Finance Commission,* 1952, p. 20.

Sir Otto Niemeyer also recommended that the Centre should retain for the first 5 years out of the provincial money a sum equivalent to the amount by which the central share plus the contribution from Railways fell short of Rs. 13 crore a year and that the amount retained from the provincial share should be surrendered to the Provinces over a further period of 5 years. As part of the assistance he contemplated for the jute-growing Provinces, Sir Otto Niemeyer recommended that the provinces' share of the jute export duty be raised by 12.5 per cent to 62.5 per cent of the net proceeds of the duty.

In short, his main recommendations as contained in the Indian Financial Enquiry Report 1936 were the following.

1. That 50 per cent of the net proceeds of income tax should be assigned to the Provinces.
2. That the share of jute-growing Provinces in the jute export duty be raised by 12.5 per cent to 62.5 per cent of the net proceeds of the duty.
3. The outstanding debts (to the Centre) of Bengal, Bihar, Assam, North-West Frontier Province, and Orissa, contracted prior to April 1, 1936 be cancelled, and the outstanding debt of the Central Provinces be reduced.
4. Annual grants of varying amounts were also recommended for United Provinces, Assam, North-West Frontier Province, Orissa, and Sind (Table 2.2).

Table 2.2: Annual Grants to the Provinces Recommended by Sir Otto Niemeyer

(Rs. lakh)

United Provinces	25 for a fixed period of 5 years
Assam	30
North-West Frontier Province	100 subject to consideration at the end of 5 years.
Orissa	40 with Rs. 7 lakh additional in the first and Rs. 3 lakh additional in each of the next 4 years.
Sind	105 for 10 years, with Rs. 5 lakh additional in the first year, and thereafter falling until the grant ceased in about 45 years time

Source: *Report of the Finance Commission,* 1952, p. 21.

The aforesaid recommendations were accepted by the authorities and embodied in the Government of India (Distribution of Revenues) Order, 1936. This Order, subject to a change made in 1940, continued to regulate the allocation of resources between the Centre and the units until the partition of the country in August 1947.

Following the outbreak of Second World War, and the increasing expenditure it entailed on the Centre, steps had to be taken to strengthen Central finances. It was decided that for the duration of the war, the Centre should be permitted to retain a fixed sum of Rs. 4.5 crore out of the provincial share of income tax. The Order-in-Council was amended accordingly to secure this and the modified provision regulated the distribution of the tax from 1940-41 to 1945-46. In each of the next 4 years the sum retained by the Centre from the provincial share was reduced by Rs. 75 lakh a year over the previous year, and the full provincial share was restored to the Provinces in 1950-51.

2.11 Financial Adjustments after the Partition: Deshmukh Award

The partition of the country gave rise to new problems of financial adjustments. Though the scheme of distribution of both income tax and jute export duty, as suggested by Sir Otto Niemeyer, were retained, the shares of the divided Provinces of Bengal, and Punjab were reduced in proportion to population while the shares of Sind, and North-West Frontier Province were pooled for distribution so far as income tax was concerned. Regarding jute export duty, the Provincial share was reduced from 62.5 per cent to 20 per cent, roughly in proportion to the jute growing area which went to the share of Pakistan.

2.11.1 Income Tax: Since a Finance Commission could not be appointed immediately after the commencement of the Constitution, the States' share of income tax and the payment of grants-in-aid had to be regulated by the Order of the President during the intervening period. Also, some of the States were not happy with the arrangements regarding the allocation of income tax and the jute export duty made by the Government immediately after the partition. It was, therefore, decided to refer these matters to an impartial authority for reconsideration. Accordingly, Mr. C.D. Deshmukh was requested to enquire into and decide these matters. Deshmukh enquiry confined itself to the reallocation of the percentages released as a result of the partition from the share of the divided Provinces and the Provinces wholly included in Pakistan.

Table 2.3 records the percentage distribution among the States of their share of income tax before the partition, immediately after the partition, and under the Deshmukh award. The Deshmukh award came into operation from April 1, 1950 and remained in force till March 31, 1952.

2.11.2 Grants-in-aid in Lieu of Jute Export Duty: It was in 1916 that jute export duty was first levied and became divisible with the jute-growing Provinces only under the Government of India Act, 1935. The question of giving the jute-growing Provinces a share of the export duty on jute and jute products was considered during the constitutional discussions preceding the enactment of the Government of India Act, 1935. The Act in Section 140(2), provided that "one half or such greater proportion as His Majesty in Council may determine of the net proceeds in each year of any export duty on jute or jute products shall not form part of the revenues of the federation, but shall be assigned to the Provinces or federated States in which jute is grown in proportion to the respective amounts of jute grown therein". Sir Otto Niemeyer who was asked to make recommendations regarding the proportion of the export duty to be assigned to the Provinces recommended that the provincial share be increased to 62.5 per cent of the net proceeds and this recommendation was embodied in the Government of India (Distribution of Revenues) Order, 1936.

Table 2.3: Percentage Distribution among the States of Their Share of Income Tax

Province	Pre-partition share	Share under Government of India allocation	Share under Deshmukh award
Madras	15	18	0.5
Bombay	20	21	21.0
West Bengal	20*	12	13.5
Uttar Pradesh	15	19	18.0
Punjab	8*	5	5.5
Bihar	10	13	12.5
Madhya Pradesh	5	6	6.0
Assam	2*	3	3.0
Orissa	2	3	3.0

* relates to the undivided Provinces
Source: *Report of the Finance Commission,* 1952, p. 25.

Consequent upon the division of Bengal and Assam on the partition of the country in 1947, roughly 70 per cent of the jute growing area of undivided India got included in Pakistan, necessitating the reconsideration of the allocation of the duty made in the Government of India Act, 1935, particularly as the basis of distribution between the Provinces was the amount of jute grown in them.

When the Government of India Act, 1935, was adapted at the time of the transfer of power, the provision in Section 140 about the proportion of the jute export duty allocable to the Provinces was amended and the provincial share was left to be prescribed by Order of the Governor General. In the altered circumstances the Government of India decided that the share of the jute export duty allocable to the Provinces should be reduced from 62.5 per cent of the net proceeds to 20 per cent, the basis of allocation among the Provinces continuing to be the amount of jute grown in them. The necessary Order was made by the Governor General from year to year prescribing this percentage. This reduction in the share of the jute export duty led to protests from certain jute-growing States. The difficulty created for the Government of West Bengal by the loss of revenue from this source was recognised by the Government of India which sanctioned ad hoc grants of Rs. 40 lakh in 1947-48 and Rs. 50 lakh in each of the years 1948-49 and 1949-50.

The Expert Committee on the Financial Provisions of the Constitution of Independent India held that export duties were unsuitable for sharing with the

Provinces and recommended that these should be entirely Central. They, however, proposed that the Provinces which were receiving a share of the export duty on jute and jute products should be compensated for the loss of this item of revenue. They suggested following grants for the four States: West Bengal (Rs. 100 lakh), Assam (Rs. 15 lakh), Bihar (Rs. 17 lakh) and Orissa (Rs. 3 lakh).

The Constitution made no provision for the sharing of export duties. The principle of compensation, for a transitional period, to the four jute-growing States was incorporated in Article 273. The sums to be paid were not, however, specified but were left to be prescribed by the Order of the President. After a Finance Commission have been constituted, the President is required to make the Order after considering the recommendations of the Commission. In November 1949 the Government of India requested Shri C.D. Deshmukh to determine the grants-in-aid payable to the four States mentioned above. Shri Deshmukh held that the grants-in-aid payable to these States must necessarily be related to the sums actually received in the past by the States concerned, viewed as part of their revenue, and could not be related to any estimates of the net proceeds in future years of the export duty. He decided that, until the Finance Commission proposed any revision, the following annual grants-in-aid should be paid to these States: West Bengal (Rs. 105 lakh), Assam (Rs. 40 lakh), Bihar (Rs. 35 lakh and Orissa (Rs. 5 lakh). These grants-in-aid were paid in 1950-51 and 1951-52.

2.12 Expert Committee on Financial Provisions of the Constitution, 1947

Drafting of the Constitution of independent India provided another opportunity to review the financial relations between the Centre and the States. For the purpose of incorporating financial provisions in the Draft Constitution, the President of the Constituent Assembly constituted an Expert Committee of three members under the chairmanship of Shri N.R. Sarker. This Committee recommended that the whole of income tax, including corporation tax and income tax on federal emoluments, should be shared between the Centre and the States except to the extent of the tax attributable to Centrally administered areas. It suggested that the provincial share should be fixed at 60 per cent and allocated among the Provinces in the following manner: 20 on the basis of population and 35 on the basis of collection, the remaining 5 being used for mitigating hardships that might arise as a result of the application of the other two criteria.

As regards the jute export duty, the Committee recommended that the existing arrangements for the sharing of the net proceeds with the Provinces should be terminated as, in their view, export duties were unsuitable for sharing with the Provinces. However, in order to avoid hardship to the four jute-growing Provinces which were receiving a share of the duty it proposed that fixed grants-in-aid of Rs. 1 crore to West Bengal, Rs. 15 lakh to Assam, Rs. 17 lakh to Bihar and Rs, 3 lakh to Orissa be given every year as *compensation* for a period not exceeding 10 years or till the export duties on jute were abolished.

Another recommendation of the Committee related to central excise duties. The Committee remarked that the Provincial Governments had been almost unanimous in demanding some share of excises and considered the problems being not only one of finding more resources for the units but also one of imparting a better balance to their revenue structure. The Committee suggested that the Provincial Governments should be given a share of one of the important central excises on a commodity not receiving tariff protection, viz. tobacco, and accordingly recommended that 50 per cent of the net proceeds of the excise duty on tobacco be distributed to the Provinces on the basis of estimated consumption.

Following the recommendations of the Committee, export duties were made exclusively Central under the Constitution. Provision was made for the payment of grants-in-aid to the States of West Bengal, Bihar, Assam and Orissa in lieu of their share of the jute export duty; the amounts were, however, left to be prescribed by the President. The Committee also suggested that a Finance Commission should be set up to deal, among other things, with matters connected with the division of revenues between the Centre and the States and the distribution among the States of their shares.

In short, the main recommendations of the Expert Committee were as follows.

1. The whole of income tax, including corporation tax, should be shared between the Centre and the States in the ratio of 40:60.
2. The existing arrangements for the sharing of the net proceeds of jute export duty with the Provinces should be terminated.
3. Provincial Governments should be given some share of Central excise duties so as to impart a better balance to their revenue structure.
4. That a Finance Commission should be set up to deal with matters connected with the division of revenues between the Centre and the States and the States *inter se*.

2.13 Financial Integration of Princely States

Prior to Independence in 1947, Princely States had remained outside the fiscal and financial system of the rest of the country except for certain arrangements entered into with them by the Government of India regarding such matters as maritime customs, central excises, posts and telegraphs and railways. The scheme of the Government of India Act, 1935, contemplated the accession of these States to the Indian federation. Under it the Princely States were to accede in regard to foreign relations, defence and communications, with option to accede in regard to other Central subjects also. This followed an extensive examination of the problems connected with the assimilation of States of varying sizes and having different kinds of relationship with the Centre into a workable system of financial relations with the proposed federation. As it happened, the provisions of the Government of India Act, 1935, relating to federation never came into operation.

During the period between the achievement of Independence and the framing of the Constitution, a great step forward was taken in the unification of the country by the integration of Princely States. Within less than two years from the date of Independence, all the Princely States had been either formed into sizeable units, or merged in the neighbouring Provinces or constituted into separate Centrally administered Chief Commissioners' Provinces.

2.14 Indian States Finances Enquiry Committee, 1948

The political integration of Princely States had to be followed by financial integration with the Centre. This Committee (Chairman: Shri V.T. Krishnamachari) was set up to consider this problem. The Committee was asked to examine and report on the following matters.

- Desirability and feasibility of integrating federal finance in the Princely States and Unions of States with the rest of India.
- Extent to which the process of integration should be gradual and the manner in which it ought to be brought about.
- Results of a policy of integration upon the finances of the States and the Unions of States and the consequential financial adjustments between the Governments of these States and Unions of States and the Government of India.
- Measures necessary to revise the structure of *provincial* finance and the levels and sources of *provincial* revenue in these States and Unions of States.

While the scope of this Committee's work was limited to what were called Part B States, it was also requested to advise on similar problems arising out of the merger of Baroda with Bombay. The recommendations of the Committee were accepted by the Government of India and the Governments of the States concerned, with certain agreed modifications, and embodied in agreements entered into by the Government of India with them.

The broad features of these agreements which affected the allocation of resources between the Centre and the States were as follows.

As a result of the integration, the Centre took over from these States the subjects and services falling in the Union List of the Constitution with the related assets and liabilities.

In the context of the distribution of subjects adopted by the Constitution, some of the States had, in effect, been financing services falling in the State field from the surplus from Union subjects. Some form of financial assistance thus became necessary to enable them to meet the dislocation caused by the disappearance from their budgets, following integration, of the revenue and expenditure relating to Union subjects. It was, therefore, agreed that the Centre should make good to such States, for a transitional period, the difference between the revenue lost to them from Union subjects and the expenditure saved to them on Union subjects and services as a result of financial integration. The payments made to these States under this arrangement, generally called *revenue gap grants*, were guaranteed in full for the first 5 years and on a gradually diminishing scale for a further period of 5 years.

After integration all the Part B States became entitled to a share in divisible sources of Central revenue (like income tax) on the same footing as the Part A States.

Notes

1. It may be noted that Princely States enjoyed internal financial autonomy and therefore did not form part of the structure of public finances of British India. They had separate budgets and separate sources of revenue. After Independence, the former Princely States were integrated into the fiscal and financial system of the country.

2. Gyan Chand, *The Essentials of Federal Finance: A Contribution to the Problem of Financial Re-adjustment in India* (Humphrey Milford, Oxford University Press, 1930), p. 42.

3. Government of India, *Report of the Indian Taxation Enquiry Committee*, 1924-25, Vol. I (President: Sir Charles Todhunter), p. 372.

4. *Report of the Fourth Finance Commission*, 1965, pp. 6-7.

5. Durga Das Basu, *Introduction to the Constitution of India* (New Delhi: Prentice-Hall of India Pvt. Ltd., 1987), p. 9.

3

Financial Relations under the Constitution and the Roles of Planning Commission and Finance Commission

This chapter explains the complex nature of constitutional provisions pertaining to Centre-State financial relations in India, including arrangements regarding taxation powers of different tiers of government in India. It also examines the role of the Finance Commission and the Planning Commission in effecting financial transfers from the Centre to the States.

3.1 India: A Federal Polity

The Constitution of India adopted on November 26, 1949, became operative on January 26, 1950. It provides for two layers of Government, one at the Central level, and the other at the level of the States. A federal polity of this kind requires division of powers and responsibilities between the Centre and the States and generally brings in its wake problems and conflicts in Centre-State relations. Other important countries of the world with federal set up of government are: US, Canada, Australia, Brazil, and Nigeria.

Why did the framers of the Constitution opt for a federal set up? Answering this question, the Commission on Centre-State Relations, 1988, observed, "In a country too large and diverse for a unitary form of Government, they envisaged a system which would be worked in co-operation by the two levels of government —national and regional—as a common endeavour to serve the people. Such a system, it was conceived, would be most suited to Indian conditions as it would at once have the advantages of a strong unified central power, and the essential values of federalism." [1]

The Constitution describes in detail the legislative powers and functions of the two tiers of Government. Under Article 246 read with Seventh Schedule of the Constitution, these powers have been defined through precise entries in the three lists in the Schedule. Thus, the Centre has exclusive powers to legislate in respect of matters contained in List I (Union List) such as defence, foreign affairs, citizenship, railways, posts and telegraph, telephones, broadcasting, airways, banking, coinage and currency. Entries 82 to 92C of this list pertain to taxation powers. Similarly, the States enjoy the power to legislate on matters mentioned in List II (State List) such as public order, police, public health, local government, agriculture and fisheries. Entries 45 to 63 of this list relate to taxation powers of the States. The Parliament and the State Legislatures have concurrent powers to make laws on any matters in List III (Concurrent List). The framers of the Constitution recognised that there was a category of subjects of common interest which could not be allocated exclusively either to the Union or the States. Some of the items included in the Concurrent List are: marriage and divorce, forests, economic and social planning, population control and family planning, legal, medical, and other professions. This list does not contain any head of taxation which means the Centre and the States have no concurrent powers of taxation. Residuary powers of legislation including taxation belong to the Centre as per Entry 97 of List I.

The foregoing three-fold division of subjects of legislation rests on the ground that matters of national concern are placed in the Union List and those of purely State or local significance in the State List. Matters of common Centre-State interest are included in the Concurrent List.

3.2 Centrally Biased Constitution and its Justification

From its very inception, the Constitution is loaded in favour of the Centre. Constitutional amendments effected subsequently have tilted the balance further in favour of the Centre. The concept of a strong Centre has been incorporated in the anatomy of the Constitution through a variety of devices, among which the following are noteworthy.

3.2.1 Supremacy of Union Legislative Power: Article 246 (2) and (3), and Article 254 (1) establish the supremacy of Union legislative power. Thus, where with respect to a matter, there is irreconcilable conflict or overlapping as between the three lists of the Seventh Schedule, the legislative power of the States must yield to that of the Union. This is how the non-obstante provisions of clauses (1) and (2) of Article 246 are interpreted. Similarly, Article 254 (1) states that a law made by a State legislature, repugnant to a law made by the Parliament or an existing law applicable in that State, in regard to any matter enumerated in the Concurrent List, shall be void to the extent of repugnancy.

3.2.2 Union Control over State Legislation: Articles 200 and 201 establish control of the Union executive over State legislation. Article 200 provides that a Bill passed by a State Legislature shall be presented to the Governor who may give his assent, withhold his assent or return the same for reconsideration by the legislature. However, if it is again passed by the State legislature, with or without amendment, he shall not withhold his assent. The Governor may also reserve the Bill for consideration of the President (in effect the Union Council of Ministers) who may in turn signify his assent, withhold the same or return it for reconsideration. However, in contrast to the position of the Governor, the President need not give his assent when such a Bill is returned with or without amendment after reconsideration by the legislature of the State (Article 201).

3.2.3 Emergency Provisions: Articles 352 and 360 provide for certain emergency provisions. Article 352 provides for proclamation by the President of a grave emergency whereby the security of India is threatened by war or external aggression or armed rebellion. When such a proclamation is in operation, the Union may assume for its organs all the legislative and executive powers of the States. A proclamation of emergency has the effect of converting the State List into Concurrent List and, therefore, if the Parliament legislates on any subject in the State List, the State laws, to the extent of repugnancy, shall be null and void and the law made by the Parliament shall prevail.

Article 360 envisages yet another type of emergency, i.e. financial emergency. If the President is satisfied that a situation has arisen whereby the financial stability or credit of India or of any part of its territory is threatened, he may proclaim a financial emergency. When such an emergency is in operation, the executive authority of the Union extends to directing any State for the purpose of securing observance of canons of financial propriety.

3.2.4 Restrictions on Taxation Powers of the States: Constitution also imposes certain restrictions on the taxation powers of the States. Although a State legislature enjoys the power to levy any of the taxes mentioned in List II, in the case of certain taxes, this power is subject to restrictions imposed by substantive provisions of the Constitution. Some examples of these restrictions are as follows.

1. The power to impose taxes on the sale or purchase of goods other than newspapers belongs to the States vide entry 54 of List II. However, Article 286 ensures that sales taxes imposed by the States do not interfere with imports and exports or inter-State trade and commerce which are matters of national importance. In view of this, Article 286 places the following restrictions on the power of the States to enact sales tax legislation.

(a) No law of a State shall impose a tax on the sale or purchase of goods where such sale or purchase takes place (i) outside the State; or (ii) in the course of import into or export out of the territory of India; (b) with regard to inter-State trade, there are two restrictions (i) the power to tax sales taking place in the course of inter-State trade and commerce belongs to the Union vide entry 92A of List I in the Seventh Schedule, and (ii) the sales tax on intrastate sales of 'declared goods' (i.e. goods of special importance in inter-State trade) is subject to certain restrictions in terms of the nature of the levy and the rate of tax.

2. A State legislature is empowered to levy a tax on professions, trade, calling

or employment vide entry 60 of List II. However, the total amount payable in respect of any one person to the State by way of such tax is not to exceed Rs. 2,500 per annum [Article 276(2)].

3.2.5 Restrictions on Borrowing Powers of the States: Under Article 292 the executive power of the Centre extends to borrowing, either within or outside India, upon the security of the Consolidated Fund of India, within such limits, if any, as may from time to time be fixed by Parliament. However, the borrowing power of a State (Article 293) is subject to a number of restrictions: (i) it cannot borrow outside India; (ii) it can borrow within the territory of India subject to the following conditions (a) limitations as may be imposed by the State Legislature, (b) consent of the Union Government to raise fresh loan if the Union has guaranteed an outstanding loan of the State, (c) consent of the Union to raise fresh loan if a Union loan to the State remains outstanding. Since all the States are in debt to the Centre, they have to obtain Centre's permission for raising loans. These restrictions are meant to avoid uncontrolled borrowings by the States and thus to prevent the possibility of any State becoming defaulter or insolvent.

3.2.6 President's Rule: Lastly, there is the controversial Article 356. According to it, if the President on receipt of a report from the Governor of a State, or otherwise, is satisfied that a situation has arisen in which the Government of the State cannot be carried on in accordance with the provisions of the Constitution, he may by proclamation assume to himself all or any of the functions of the State Government. He may also declare that the powers of the Legislature of the State shall be exercised by or under the authority of the Parliament.

In view of the above provisions of the Constitution, some experts call it unitary in extraordinary situations, such as war (or emergency), and federal in normal times. It is also called as a quasi-federal Constitution.

Similarly, a scrutiny of the taxation powers contained in the Union List and the State List reveals that major and elastic sources of tax revenue belong to the Centre while relatively inelastic sources of revenue come under the purview of State Governments. Moreover, the Centre enjoys almost unlimited powers to borrow from internal and external sources while the borrowing powers of the States are subject to various restrictions.

Why is there a need for a strong Centre? According to the Commission on Centre-State Relations, 1988, "The primary lesson of India's history is that, in this vast country, only that polity or system can ensure and protect its unity, integrity and sovereignty against external aggression and internal disruption, which ensures a strong Centre with paramount powers, accommodating, at the same time, its traditional diversities. This lesson of history did not go unnoticed by the framers of the Constitution. Being aware that, notwithstanding the common cultural heritage, without political cohesion, the country would disintegrate under the pressure of fissiparous forces, they accorded the highest priority to the ensurance of the unity and integrity of the country." [2] Moreover, the founding fathers were aware that several regions or areas of India were economically and industrially far behind in relation to others, a situation which exists even today. Revenue-raising capacities and revenue needs of various States also differ. To reduce these economic disparities, a policy of regional balanced development was necessary, and which could be effectively implemented by a financially and otherwise strong Centre.

3.3 Constitutional Provisions Pertaining to Taxes

The Constitution makes elaborate and complex arrangements relating to the distribution, between the Union and the States, of taxes, the power of borrowing, and provision for grants-in-aid by the Union to the States. The underlying philosophy of these arrangements is to place at the disposal of the two tiers of Government adequate financial resources to enable them to discharge their respective responsibilities under the Constitution.

3.3.1 Distribution of Taxation Powers: Article 265 of the Constitution specifically states that no taxes shall be levied or collected except by the authority of law. Entries 82 to 92B of List I in the Seventh Schedule refer to the taxation powers of the Union Government (Table 3.1). Entries 45 to 63 of List II in the same Schedule specify the taxation powers of the State Governments (Table 3.2). List III does not contain any head of taxation which means the Union and the States have no concurrent powers of taxation. The absence of joint occupancy of tax fields is meant to avoid duplication in tax administration, and minimise tax rivalry between the Centre and the States, and among the States themselves. [3] The residual powers of taxation, as in general legislation, belong to the Union vide entry 97 of List I in the Seventh Schedule. For example, gift tax (abolished in 1998) was imposed by the Union Government under these residual powers. Similarly, prior to the Constitution (Eighty-eighth Amendment) Act, 2003, service tax was imposed under these residual powers.

The Constitution does not provide for any taxation powers to local governments. However, the implication of Article 276 is that the taxes on professions, trades, callings or employment are for the benefit of a State or of a municipality, district board, local board or any other local authority. The States on their own may assign any of the taxes in the State List to the local bodies. The taxes generally assigned to local governments are property taxes, octroi, and taxes on vehicles.

Table 3.1: Taxes within Union Jurisdiction as Enumerated in List I in the Seventh Schedule of the Constitution of India

S. No.	Entry No. in List I	Description of the tax/duty
1.	82	Taxes on income other than agricultural income.
2.	83	Duties of customs including export duties.
3.	84	Duties of excise except on alcoholic liquors and narcotics but including medicinal and toilet preparations containing alcohol.
4.	85	Corporation tax.
5.	86	Taxes on the capital value of assets, exclusive of agricultural land, of individuals.
6.	87	Estate duty in respect of property other than agricultural land.
7.	88	Duties in respect of succession to property other than agricultural land.
8.	89	Terminal taxes on goods and passengers carried by railway, sea or air; taxes on railway fares and freights.
9.	90	Taxes other than stamp duties on transactions in stock exchanges and future markets.
10.	91	Rates of stamp duty in respect of bills of exchange, cheques, promissory notes, bills of lading, letters of credit, policies of insurance, transfer of shares, debentures, proxies, and receipts.
11.	92	Taxes on the sale or purchase of newspapers and on advertisements published therein.
12.	92A*	Taxes on the sale or purchase of goods other than newspapers, where such sale or purchase takes place in the course of inter-State trade or commerce.
13.	92B**	Taxes on the consignment of goods (whether the consignment is to the person making it or to any other person), where such consignment takes place in the course of inter-State trade or commerce.
14.	92C***	Taxes on services
15.	97	Any tax not enumerated in List II or List III of the Seventh Schedule.

* Inserted by the Constitution (Sixth Amendment) Act, 1956.
** Inserted by the Constitution (Forty-sixth Amendment) Act, 1982.
*** Inserted by the Constitution (Eighty-eighth Amendment) Act, 2003.
Source: Government of India, Ministry of Law, Justice and Company Affairs, *The Constitution of India,* Seventh Schedule, List I.

Table 3.2: Taxes within State Jurisdiction as Enumerated in List II in the Seventh Schedule of the Constitution of India

S. No.	Entry No. in List II	Description of the tax/duty
1.	45	Land revenue.
2.	46	Taxes on agricultural income.
3.	47	Duties in respect of succession to agricultural land.
4.	48	Estate duty in respect of agricultural land.
5.	49	Taxes on lands and buildings.
6.	50	Taxes on mineral rights subject to any limitations imposed by Parliament by law relating to mineral development.
7.	51	Duties of excise on alcoholic liquors and narcotics manufactured or produced in the State but not including medicinal and toilet preparations containing alcohol.
8.	52	Taxes on the entry of goods into a local area for consumption, use or sale therein.
9.	53	Taxes on the consumption or sale of electricity.
10.	54*	Taxes on the sale or purchase of goods other than newspapers, subject to the provisions of Entry 92A of List I.
11.	55**	Taxes on advertisements other than advertisements published in the newspapers (and advertisements broadcast by radio or television)
12.	56	Taxes on goods and passengers carried by road or on inland waterways.
13.	57	Taxes on vehicles, whether mechanically propelled or not, suitable for use on roads, including tram-cars subject to the provisions of Entry 35 of List III.
14.	58	Taxes on animals and boats.
15.	59	Tolls.
16.	60***	Taxes on professions, trades, callings and employment.
17.	61	Capitation taxes.
18.	62	Taxes on luxuries, including taxes on entertainment, amusements, betting and gambling.
19.	63	Rates of stamp duty in respect of documents other than those specified in the provisions of List I with regard to rates of stamp duty.

*Substituted by the Constitution (Sixth Amendment) Act, 1956: ** The words 'and advertisements broadcast by radio or television' inserted by the Constitution (Forty-second Amendment), Act, 1976: *** The scope of these taxes is spelt out in Article 276, the clause (2) of which fixes the amount payable by a person on account of these taxes.

Source: Government of India, Ministry of Law, Justice and Company Affairs, *The Constitution of India,* Seventh Schedule, List II.

The property of the Centre is exempt from State taxation under Article 285(1). Likewise, the property and incomes of the States are exempt from Union taxes [Article 289 (1)], except that Parliament may by law provide for Central taxation of any trading activities of a State which are not incidental to the ordinary functions of Government [Article 289(2)]. As regards Union Territories, the Parliament has the power to impose any tax included in the State List.

3.3.2 Restrictions on the Taxation Powers of the States: see section 3.2.4 of this chapter.

3.3.3 Rationale for Constitutional Arrangements: Constitutional division of taxation powers between the Union and the States rests on economic and administrative considerations. Taxes with an inter-State base, and those in the case of which uniformity in rates is desirable, are vested in the Central Government. Also, taxes which the taxpayer can evade by shifting his habitat, or where the place of residence is not a correct guide to the true incidence of the tax, belong to the Centre. Taxes which are location-specific and relate to subjects of local consumption are with the States. Broadly speaking, taxes on production, with some exceptions, are levied by the Centre, and taxes on sales by the State Governments. The distribution of taxation powers between the Centre and the States is meant to minimise tax problems in a federal set up such as double taxation, tax rivalry among States, duplicate tax administration, and tax evasion.

Commenting upon the soundness of the constitutional arrangements regarding division of taxation powers, the Commission on Centre-State Relations, 1988, observed, "A well balanced distribution of heads of taxation based on economic and administrative rationale between the Union and the States and adequate arrangements for sharing of resources is vital for the proper functioning of the two-tier polity. We are of the firm view that the basic scheme of the Constitution dividing the field of taxation between the Union and the States and incorporating adequate arrangements for sharing of resources between them, is sound and no major modifications in it are called for." [4]

Similarly, the Sixth Finance Commission made the following observations in this regard, "We must bear in mind that the country as a whole and every part thereof has gained significantly from the maintenance of a vast unified market within which there is free movement of goods and men. Having regard to the trends all over the world even for independent political entities to come together to forge closer economic links in the form of common markets and economic groupings, our best hopes of accelerated economic development lie in the further strengthening of our national market and in the promotion of fiscal arrangements that are most conducive to the effective functioning of this market. Given this basic fact, there can be no room for argument that the levy and administration of taxes with wide economic base such as income tax, corporation tax, Union excise duties and of course also import and export duties will have to remain with the Union Government. In fact the architects of our Constitution drew on the experience of some of the other federations in which the assignment of taxes with wide economic base to units had led to intractable problems of conflicting tax jurisdictions. They wisely averted the possibility of such conflicts by assigning such taxes right from the beginning to the Union Government. At the same time, the framers of our Constitution rightly allocated to the States' subjects such as agriculture, education, medical care, public health, irrigation and law and order that touch intimately the lives of the people. These can be efficiently administered in a vast country only by the State Governments which are closer to the people and are more keenly alive to their problems and needs. The heads of revenue and responsibilities were distributed on the basis of whether the Centre or the State was better equipped to deal with the particular head." [5]

3.3.4 Sharing of Central Taxes: Although the taxation powers allocated to the Union and the States are mutually exclusive, all the taxes and duties levied by the Union are not meant entirely for the purpose of the Union. Revenues from certain taxes and duties leviable by the Union are totally assigned to or shared with the States to supplement their revenues in accordance with their needs. It is a tribute to the foresight of the founding fathers that they realised that the sources of revenue allocated to the States may not prove sufficient in view of their growing welfare, maintenance, and developmental activities. Hence, specific provisions were made to set apart a portion of Central revenues for the benefit of States. These provisions indicate the flexibility of India's Constitution in terms of distribution of financial resources between different layers of the Government. They also make a distinction between the legislative power to *levy* a tax and the power to *appropriate* the proceeds of a tax so levied.

Prior to the eightieth amendment of the Constitution, two main Central taxes were shared with the states, namely income tax other than corporation tax and the Union excise duties. The sharing of the income tax was mandatory under Article 270 while that of the Union excise duties was discretionary under Article 272. There were also two tax rental arrangements with the States, where the Union Government collected the tax on behalf of the States and then distributed the proceeds among the States on the basis of criteria recommended by the Finance Commission. These were (i) additional duties of excise in lieu of sales tax on textiles, tobacco and sugar and (ii) grant in lieu of tax on railway passenger fares.

The Constitution (Eightieth Amendment) Act, 2000, significantly changed the manner of distribution of Central tax collections between the Central and State Governments. Following this amendment, all central taxes were brought into a shareable pool and it became mandatory to assign a share from each central tax to the States. The amended article 270 provided for the sharing of all central taxes except taxes under Articles 268 and 269, earmarked cesses, and surcharges under Article 271. Only *net proceeds* are to be shared, and as such *cost of collection* has to be deducted to obtain the net proceeds as prescribed under Article 279. The proceeds are to be distributed among the States where the central taxes are *leviable* in *that year*. Article 269 was also amended and it now contains only central sales tax and consignment tax, which is not levied.

The objective of the Constitution (Eightieth Amendment) Act, 2000 was to construct a pool of all central taxes for sharing so that a holistic view can be taken and both sides could share in the aggregate buoyancy of the central tax revenues.

Furthermore, Constitution (Eighty-eighth Amendment) Act, 2003 placed service tax under the Union List in the Seventh Schedule and was brought under the purview of Article 268A which provides as follows:

"(1) Taxes on services shall be levied by the Government of India and such tax shall be collected and appropriated by the Government of India and the States in the manner provided in clause (2).

(2) The proceeds in any financial year of any such tax levied in accordance with the provisions of clause (1) shall be

(a) collected by the Government of India and the States;

(b) appropriated by the Government of India and the States;

in accordance with such principles of collection and appropriation as may be formulated by Parliament by law."

Thus, Article 268A specifies that the principles of collection and appropriation of taxes on services will be determined by Parliament. Prior to Eighty-eighth Amendment, the Central Government levied the service tax on specific services under its residual powers (vide entry 97 of List I in the Seventh Schedule). The sharing of this revenue was on the basis of the recommendations of the Finance Commission, as applicable to other central taxes. However, revenue from taxation of services which are taxed by the centre under article 268A rather than under article 270 is now excluded from the purview of the Finance Commission. In this connection, the Twelfth Finance Commission remarked, "With service taxes having been excluded from the ambit of the recommendations of the finance commission, the idea of an overall shareable pool of central taxes appears to be in the process of being reversed. While service taxes are likely to prove highly buoyant in the near future, these will not be subjected to sharing with the states under the Constitution, although other statutory arrangements can be made, which can include sharing as well as assignment. It may be noted that hitherto items under articles 268 and 269 were subjects that were generally of inter-state nature with limited revenue importance. These were wholly assigned to the states. In this context, it needs to be stressed that any legislation passed by Parliament with respect to appropriation of service tax proceeds must take care to ensure that the revenue accruing to the states through any proposed changes should not be less than the share that would accrue to them, had the entire service tax proceeds been part of the shareable pool." [6]

After the Constitution (Eighty-eighth Amendment) Act, 2003, the Central taxes can be classified into the following categories.

Duties Levied by the Union but Collected and Appropriated by the States (Article 268): These include duties of excise on medicinal and toilet preparations containing alcohol, and stamp duties on bills of exchange etc. as mentioned in entries 84 and 91 of the Union List respectively.

Service Tax Levied by the Union and Collected and Appropriated by the Union and the States (Article 268A).

Taxes Levied and Collected by the Union but Assigned to the States (Article 269): These are: taxes on the sale or purchase of goods other than newspapers, where such sale or purchase takes place in the course of inter-State trade or commerce, and taxes on the consignment of goods (whether the consignment is to the person making it or to any other person), where such consignment takes place in the course of inter-State trade or commerce. These taxes correspond to entries 92A and 92B in the Union List. [7]

Taxes Levied and Distributed Between the Union and the States (Article 270): All taxes and duties referred to in the Union List shall be levied and collected by the Government of India and shall be distributed between the Union and the States with the following exceptions: (a) duties and taxes referred to in Articles 268 and 269, (b) surcharge on taxes and duties referred to in Article 271 and (c) any cess levied for specific purposes under any law made by Parliament.

3.3.5 Philosophy of Articles 268 and 269: Taxation arrangements under Articles 268 and 269 of the Constitution are of special importance. They place under the charge of the Union the taxes and duties which have inter-State character and require uniformity in rate structure for the smooth conduct of business and trade activities throughout the country. These two Articles mention taxes/duties which shall be levied by the Centre but assigned completely to the States within which they are leviable.

A. Duties under Article 268: Article 268 mentions duties which shall be levied by the Union but collected and appropriated by the States within which they are leviable. These are duties of excise on medicinal and toilet preparations containing alcohol, and stamp duties, and correspond respectively to entries 84, and 91 of the Union List with corresponding qualification of entry 51 of the State List in the Seventh Schedule of the Constitution. The Eighth Finance Commission was asked for the first time to examine the scope for enhancing revenues from these duties.

Duties on medicinal and toilet preparations are imposed under the Medicinal and Toilet Preparations (Excise Duties) Act, 1955. It includes a range of medicinal items which are important from the viewpoint of public health policy. They have inter-State significance and therefore uniformity in regard to taxation is in larger national interest. Since the rates of duty on these preparations were increased in 1982 (the year in which the Commission was constituted), the Commission did not find any scope for enhancing this duty at that time.

Stamp duties are leviable on bills of exchange, cheques, promissory notes, bills of lading, letters of credit, policies of insurance, transfer of shares, debentures, proxies, and receipts. These documents are executed in the course of business and trade and they find place in the Union List to ensure uniformity of rates throughout the country for the smooth conduct of commercial and related transactions. Inter-State disparities in their rates and tax regulations can hinder, and even disrupt, the free flow of trade and commercial activities. The levy and collection of stamp duty is governed by the Indian Stamp Duty Act, 1899 which was last amended in 1976 when rates of stamp duty on certain instruments were revised.

After ascertaining the views of States and other relevant agencies, the Eighth Finance Commission did not think it desirable to raise the rates of stamp duty on bills of exchange, promissory notes, life insurance policies, transfer of shares, debentures, proxies, and receipts. Raising duty on these instruments was considered to be detrimental to the growth of trade and industry. The Commission also disfavoured reimposition of stamp duty on cheques. [8] However, the Commission opined that scope for raising the rates of duty exists in respect of bills of lading, letters of credit, and policies of general insurance.

B. Taxes and Duties under Article 269: Article 269 mentions taxes which shall be levied and collected by the Union but assigned completely to the States, in which they are leviable. These taxes are: (a) taxes on the sale or purchase of goods other than newspapers, where such sale or purchase takes place in the course of inter-State trade or commerce, and (b) taxes on the consignment of goods where such consignment takes place in the course of inter-State trade or commerce. These taxes correspond to entries 92A and 92B in the Union List in the Seventh Schedule of the Constitution. It is noteworthy that out of these two taxes only one is being levied at present, viz. inter-State sales tax (entry 92A).

3.3.6 Taxes and Duties in the Union List not being Levied at Present:

These taxes/duties are discussed below individually along with the logic for retaining them with the Centre.

A. Entries 87 and 88: These two entries pertain to estate duty, and succession duty in respect of property other than agricultural land respectively. Since the incidence of both estate duty, and succession duty is on the same object, viz. property passing on the death of the owner to his successors, they are essentially similar in nature. However, while in the case of the estate duty, the value of the whole estate, even if situated in more than one State, is the base for taxation, the succession duty is relatable to the value of individual shares (i.e. parts of an estate) passing on to the successors.

The desirability of retaining both these duties with the Centre is self-evident. An individual may have properties located in more than one State and a total assessment of his estate can better be undertaken by the Union Government. Similarly, if succession duty is levied by the States, the persons inheriting properties in different States will have to deal with different tax rates and procedures. Moreover, if estate/succession duties are levied by the States, it may trigger unhealthy competition among the States, resulting into harassment of the assessees and hence litigation. On efficiency criterion (i.e. cost of collection) also it is desirable if these duties are levied and administered by the Union, thus avoiding duplication of tax administration. Moreover, the Union has better access to information and otherwise also it is in larger national interest to ensure uniformity with respect to these duties. It may be noted that estate duty was first imposed in India in 1953 when the Estate Duty Act of that year imposed a duty on the capital value of all property passing on the death of any person on or after October 15, 1953. It was abolished with effect from March 16, 1985.

B. Entry 89: It relates to terminal taxes on goods and passengers carried by railway, sea or air. However, by virtue of entry 52 of List II, States are competent to impose octroi (terminal tax) on entry of goods into a local area for consumption, use or sale. Likewise, under entry 56 of List II, States are empowered to levy taxes on goods and passengers carried by road or on inland waterways. Thus, the taxation powers in regard to the services of the major means of transport rest with the Union.

In a developing and diversifying economy like India, the importance of transport sector is self-evident. The growth of this vital infrastructure enlarges the size of the market and determines, *inter alia*, the level of private enterprise. Lest the free flow of inter-State trade should be hampered by differential State levies, the taxation of transport services is, by and large, with the Union Government. The Fifth and the Eighth Finance Commissions examined the scope for levying these taxes but expressed themselves against their imposition on grounds of administrative difficulties and meagre revenue potential. It is noteworthy that there already exists a terminal tax on passengers carried by railway from or to certain places of pilgrimage or where fairs or exhibitions are held. The proceeds of the tax are credited to the Consolidated Fund of the concerned States. The tax is restrictive and limited in scope and not a general terminal tax on passengers carried by railways to all places.

Entry 89 also refers to taxes on railway fares and freights. The Eighth Finance Commission favoured levying tax on railway passenger fares but not until the present arrangement of giving grants in lieu of such a tax continues to exist.

C. Entry 90: It pertains to 'taxes other than stamp duties on transactions in stock exchanges and future markets.' Since stock exchanges and future markets [9] are at a formative stage and have an inter-State character therefore it is desirable to retain these taxes with the Union. The Eighth Finance Commission did not think it advisable to levy taxes on transactions in stock exchanges and future markets.

D. Entry 92: It refers to 'taxes on the sale or purchase of newspapers and on advertisements published therein.' This tax is retained with the Union to protect the freedom of the press, and avoid undue tax burden on newspaper industry, particularly the regional language newspapers. Since newspaper reading habit is not sufficiently developed and widespread in the country, it is not desirable to impose a tax on the sale or purchase of newspapers.

Both the Fifth and the Eighth Finance Commissions did not recommend a tax on the sale or purchase of newspapers. However, both the Commissions opined that there was scope for tax on advertisements published in newspapers. The Eighth Commission cautioned that a tax on advertisement, if levied, should be borne by the advertisers themselves and not passed on to the newspapers and journals.

3.3.7 Freedom as to Payment of Taxes for Promotion of any Particular Religion: According to Article 27 of the Constitution of India, "No person shall be compelled to pay any taxes, the proceeds of which are specifically appropriated in payment of expenses for the promotion or maintenance of any particular religion or religious denomination."

3.4 Centralisation of Revenues and the Need for Transfers

Constitutional provisions regarding taxation and borrowing powers of the Centre and the States, place the former in a commanding position. Not only the major sources of tax revenue belong to the Centre, its borrowing (internal and external) powers are also unlimited. Moreover, the Central Government enjoys the exclusive right to print currency. Budget estimates for the year 2006-07 showed total tax collections at the all-India level at Rs. 6,99,135 crore of which Central taxes (gross) accounted for Rs. 4,42,153 crore (63.2 per cent). The remaining Rs. 2,56,982 crore (36.8 per cent) was shown the share of all the States put together. In the case of non-tax revenue of Rs. 1,13,532 crore at the all-India level for the same year, the shares of Centre and the States were Rs. 75,964 crore (66.9 per cent) and Rs. 37,568 crore (33.1 per cent) respectively. Similarly, total revenue collections (tax plus non-tax) at the all-India level were projected at Rs. 8,12,667 crore with shares of the Centre and the States standing at Rs. 5,18,117 crore (63.8 per cent) and Rs. 2,94,550 crore (36.2 per cent) respectively (Table 3.3). These figures show the degree of centralisation of revenues, size of the vertical fiscal gap and hence the need to transfer resources from the Centre to the States.

Table 3.3: Centralisation of Tax and Non-tax Revenues in India, 2006-07*

(Rs. crore)

Total Tax Collections (All-India)	6,99,135 (100.0)
Centre's Tax Collections (before Transferring States' Share)	4,42,153 (63.2)
States' Tax Collections	2,56,982 (36.8)
Total Non-tax Revenue (All-India)	1,13,532 (100.0)
Centre's Non-tax Revenue	75,964 (66.9)
States' Non-tax Revenue	37,568 (33.1)
Total Revenue (All-India)	8,12,667 (100.0)
Total Revenue Raised by the Centre	5,18,117 (63.8)
Total Revenue Raised by the States	2,94,550 (36.2)

*Budget estimates.

Figures in parentheses indicate percentages of the respective totals.

Source: Rearranged data from Government of India, Ministry of Finance, *Indian Public Finance Statistics*, 2006-2007, Tables 1.7, 2.2 and 3.2.

3.5 Mechanism of Central Transfers to the States

Though the Constitution creates a dual polity based on divided governmental powers and functions, this division is not watertight. As the Administrative Reforms Commission, 1968, observed, "Exact correspondence of resources and functions is not possible to secure in any federal situation but in India the balance is tilted rather heavily in favour of the Centre and the outstanding feature of the financial relationship between the Centre and the States consequently is that the former is always the giver and the latter the receivers. The favourable position given to the Centre in regard to financial resources reflects the strong-centre theme running through the Constitution and many feel that this has been an important factor in keeping the country united." [10]

Emergence of imbalances between functional responsibilities and financial resources of different tiers of government is a characteristic feature of all federations, particularly of those whose economies are more dynamic. Even in older federations (like the United States, and Canada), financial conflicts between the national and sub-national governments persist and their once-for-all solution is difficult to find. The mismatch between functions and taxation powers occurs partly because of changing responsibilities of governments at different levels and partly because of the dominant position of federal government in regard to taxation powers, which is often by design. Therefore, vertical imbalances in terms of resources and expenditure responsibilities emerge between different levels of government calling for transfer of resources from the Centre to the States. This is the familiar problem of federal finance.

Thus, intergovernmental transfers are an inherent part of a multi-level fiscal system. Such transfers are justified on horizontal equity considerations.

Recognising the fact that the financial resources of the States may prove inadequate for undertaking welfare, maintenance, and development activities, the framers of India's Constitution did make elaborate, *albeit* complex, arrangements relating to flow of funds from the Centre to the States. The disequilibrium between proliferating functional responsibilities of the States and their own resources is corrected by Central transfers effected through three main channels.

1. Statutory transfers through the Finance Commission.
2. Plan transfers through the Planning Commission.
3. Discretionary transfers for Centrally Sponsored Schemes, relief from natural calamities, and relief and rehabilitation of displaced persons.

Apart from these direct transfers, resources also flow to the States indirectly through the following channels.

1. Establishment/expansion of Central public sector enterprises.
2. Subsidised lending by banking and financial institutions.
3. Subsidised borrowing by the States from the Central Government and the banking system.

These may be called invisible transfers or subterranean transfers

3.6 Transfer of Resources through the Finance Commission

Transfers routed through the Finance Commission pertain to sharing of certain Central taxes, and grants-in-aid of revenues of the States. In other words, although the taxation powers allocated to the Centre and the States are mutually exclusive yet all the taxes and duties levied by the Centre are not meant entirely for the Centre. In fact, revenues from certain taxes and duties leviable by the Centre are totally assigned to or shared with the States to supplement the revenues of the States in accordance with their needs.

The architects of the Constitution probably realised that even with a share in the proceeds of divisible taxes, some States might still need financial assistance. Accordingly, they made provision for annual grants-in-aid of revenues under Article 275(1) to such States as may be in need of assistance. Also, the Centre is required to give grants-in-aid to the States for the welfare of Scheduled Tribes and for raising the level of administration in Scheduled Areas and separately for Assam. These provisions which set apart a portion of Central revenues for the benefit of States indicate flexibility of India's Constitution in terms of distribution of financial resources between the Centre and the States.

3.6.1 Finance Commission: Although the Constitution provides for Central transfers, it neither indicates the share of the States in the divisible taxes nor prescribes any principles for the distribution of States' share among the States themselves. Framers of the Constitution consciously avoided permanent formulae in this regard in view of expected changes in the spheres of taxation and public expenditure. Thus, the precise manner of sharing taxes and the actual determination of grants is left to the deliberations of the Finance Commission which is appointed by the President (under Article 280) every quinquennium, or earlier if necessary. [11] The Finance Commission, consisting of a chairman and four members, recommends to the President, *inter alia*, the principles of distribution between the Union and the States of the proceeds of taxes and the allocation among the States of the shares of such proceeds. The recommendations of Finance Commissions are based on a detailed assessment of the financial position of the Central and State Governments. For this purpose, the Commissions visit the State Capitals and hold discussions with government leaders and officials. Discussions are also held with public finance experts and studies are commissioned on specific topics.

A. Powers and Procedure: Under sub-clause (2) and (4) of Article 280 of the Constitution, the qualifications which shall be requisite for appointment as Members of the Commission and the manner in which they shall be selected have to be determined by Parliament by law and the Commission shall have such powers in the performance of their functions as Parliament may by law confer on them.

The Constitution authorises the Commission to determine their procedure, while the Finance Commission (Miscellaneous Provisions) Act, 1951, has conferred on the Commission all the powers of a Civil Court under the Code of

Civil Procedure, 1908. The Commission have also been empowered to require any person to furnish information on such points or matters as, in the opinion of the Commission, may be useful for, or relevant to, any matter under the consideration of the Commission. The powers conferred on the Commission are set out in detail in Section 8 of the Act mentioned earlier.

As the Sixth Finance Commission remarked, "The purpose of Finance Commission, as envisaged in the Constitution, is primarily to facilitate a periodical assessment of the fiscal needs of the States and the formulation on an objective basis of proposals for transfer of resources from the Centre to the States through devolution of taxes and grants-in-aid. But an incidental and by no means insignificant advantage of the appointment of a Finance Commission has generally been to rekindle interest in issues pertaining to financial relations between the Centre and the States and to promote an enlightened national debate on the several facets of our federal fiscal set up." [12]

Under Article 281 of the Constitution, the report of the Finance Commission, together with the Explanatory Memorandum on the action taken on the recommendations of the Commission, is laid on the Table of the House by the Government. Though the President is not bound to accept the recommendations of the Finance Commission, they are generally accepted in view of the quasi-judicial nature of the Commission. [13] By and large, the Finance Commissions have worked independently and some of them, particularly the recent ones, have been quite assertive. Award of a Finance Commission generates considerable interest in issues pertaining to financial relations between the Centre and the States. Twelve Finance Commissions have reported since the commencement of the Constitution. The work of the Thirteenth Finance Commission is under way. The years of establishment, years of reporting, periods of award, and the names of Chairmen of various Finance Commissions are given in Table 3.4.

Finance Commission is a unique feature of the Indian Constitution having no parallel in the existing federal constitutions of the world. As the Commission on Centre-State Relations, 1988 observed, "Unlike the Commonwealth Grants Commission of Australia, the Indian Finance Commission is a Constitutional body and the objectivity in its role has been facilitated by keeping it outside the Union executive. Compared with its Australian counterpart, the Indian Finance Commission has a greater scope inasmuch as it recommends sharing of tax proceeds also, besides the grants-in-aid, and advises on other matters referred to it in the interest of sound finance. The absence of clear Constitutional provisions for revenue sharing created many problems in other federations and they had to evolve a variety of arrangements to overcome them. For example, in Canada, tax-rental arrangements were resorted to. In Australia, the Australian Commonwealth

Grants Commission was set up to consider allocation of grants among the claimant States. Specific purpose grants, with strict enforcement conditions, came into existence in countries like USA." [14]

Table 3.4: Chronology of Finance Commissions in India

Finance Commission	Year and month of establishment	Year and month of reporting	Period of award	Name of the chairman
First	November 1951	December 1952	1952-53 to 1956-57	K.C. Neogy
Second	June 1956	September 1957	1957-58 to 1961-62	K. Santhanam
Third	December 1960	December 1961	1962-63 to 1965-66	A.K. Chanda
Fourth	May 1964	August 1965	1966-67 to 1968-69	P.V. Rajamannar
Fifth	February 1968	July 1969	1969-70 to 1973-74	Mahavir Tyagi
Sixth	June 1972	October 1973	1974-75 to 1978-79	K. Brahmananda Reddy
Seventh	June 1977	October 1978	1979-80 to 1983-84	J.M. Shelat
Eighth	June 1982	April 1984	1984-85 to 1988-89	Y.B. Chavan
Ninth	June 1987	July 1988* and December 1989#	1989-90* and 1990-91 to 1994-95#	N.K. P. Salve
Tenth	June 1992	November 1994	1995-96 to 1999-00	K.C. Pant
Eleventh	July 1998	July 2000	2000-01 to 2004-05	A.M. Khusro
Twelfth	November 2002	November 2004	2005-06 to 2009-10	C. Rangarajan
Thirteenth	November 2007	October 2009 (Expected)	2010-11 to 2014-15	Vijay Kelkar

* First Report; #Second Report

Source: *Finance Commission Reports.*

The Australian Commonwealth Grants Commission recommends special purpose grants to the claimant States, but the general grants are determined largely on the basis of negotiations at the political level. In India, the Finance Commission has replaced political bargaining by objective criteria in regard to devolution of resources, ensuring at the same time flexibility in revenue-sharing.

What is a Finance Commission expected to achieve? Its first task is to evolve a scheme of transfer of financial resources from the Centre to the States so as to ensure financial equilibrium at the two levels of Government during the period of its award. Secondly, it is to design formulae to allocate resources so transferred among the States.

The task of the Finance Commission consists of the following.

1. Forecasting resources and expenditure of the Central Government to determine the volume of resources to be transferred to the States during the ensuing five years.
2. Forecasting own current revenues of the States and non-Plan current expenditures.
3. Devising formula for distribution of States' share among the States themselves.
4. Filling the post-devolution projected gaps with grants between the non-Plan current expenditures and current revenues.

The task of a Finance Commission is by no means easy as it has to judge the conflicting claims, needs, and resources of the Centre and the States and evolve a scheme of transfers which would balance the needs and resources of the two layers of the Government.

Broadly speaking, the procedure adopted by the Finance Commission to fulfil its duties is as follows: On the basis of the trends in the finances of Central and State Governments, it prepares estimates of revenue and expenditure for the period of its award. It then decides the total amount of transfers from the Centre to the States so as to maintain the desired equilibrium in the finances of the two tiers of the Government. Thereafter, the total amount of transfers is broken down into devolution and grants-in-aid among the States. Transfer of resources from the Centre to the States is designed to correct vertical imbalances while the distribution of resources among the States (with wide differentials in fiscal capabilities and needs) aims at correcting horizontal imbalances.

Should Central transfers to the States through the Finance Commission be examined in their totality or item-wise? For a better understanding of the nature and role of these transfers, it is necessary to examine them from both angles. The total approach is significant to understand adjustments in vertical financial imbalances while item-wise approach reveals adjustments in horizontal financial imbalances. It is noteworthy that various items included in the aggregate transfers are not alike and therefore have different importance for different States.

Commenting upon the working of the Indian federal polity, the Sixth Finance Commission observed, "Among the various federal polities in the world today, the Indian federal fiscal system whether one views it as federal or quasi-federal, is undoubtedly among the few that have demonstrated remarkable resilience in coping satisfactorily with the new demands made on it from time to time. The provisions of the Constitution concerning financial relations between the Centre and the States seem to have been designed with great care and circumspection so as to forestall precisely the kind of difficulties that even the older federations do not appear to have overcome in securing closer correspondence between resources and functions of the different layers of Government. These observations should not be construed as implying that the present matrix of financial relations between the Centre and the States does not admit of improvement or simplifications. All that we would like to stress is that the financial provisions of our Constitution give enough room for reconciling such conflicts of interest as may arise from time to time between the Union and the constituent units. If despite these well conceived provisions of the Constitution, some signs of dissatisfaction are discernible in the actual conduct of financial affairs between the Centre and the States, the reasons are to be found partly in the stresses and strains which the national economy as a whole has had to face in recent years and also perhaps in the spirit in which the provisions of the Constitution have sometimes been worked." [15]

3.6.2 From Itemised Sharing to Global Sharing: The most important development in the field of Centre-State financial relations pertains to the new system of sharing Central taxes with the State Governments.

Prior to Constitution (Eightieth Amendment) Act, 2000, income tax and Union excise duties were the only taxes shared with the States, apart from the grants given in lieu of passenger tax, and the collections from additional excise duty in lieu of sales tax sugar, tobacco and textiles. Taxes on income and Union excise duties were shared with States under Article 270 and 272 respectively. The aforesaid amendment altered the pattern of sharing of Central taxes between the Centre and the States significantly. It substituted a new Article for Article 270 and omitted the old Article 272. The new Article 270 provides for the sharing of the net proceeds of all Union taxes and duties with the States. However, the surcharge levied for purposes of the Union under Article 271 is excluded from the divisible pool.

Eleventh Finance Commission was the first to make recommendations in accordance with the new provisions of the Constitution.

3.7 Economic Planning in India

Economic development of India over the last six decades is unique in several ways. After Independence in 1947, the founding fathers adopted the middle course of a mixed economy, assigning a pivotal role to public sector and economic planning. This new approach to socio-economic growth was set within a framework of parliamentary democracy guaranteeing universal franchise.

Vide entry 20 of List III (Concurrent List) of the Constitution of India, economic and social planning is a subject in which the Centre as well as the States are interested and have to work in unison. The Centre has certain emergency powers, but normally coordination of policies is effected through mutual consultation. This system of consultation and of formulation of policies on the basis of over-all national requirements is ensured in the interests of planning. Care is taken to see that the plan is implemented throughout the country as a single coordinated whole. The National Development Council is intended to secure this result. It is obvious that without complete coordination of policies and timely, concerted action, there is danger of waste and misdirection of effort, which may have consequences extending far beyond the area of responsibility of any single authority, and this places special responsibilities on the Centre. In short, planning is a matter of common interest to the Central and the State Governments.

3.7.1 Establishment of the Planning Commission: Economic development of India over the last six decades is unique in several ways. In an innovative effort the founding fathers adopted the middle course of a mixed economy, assigning a pivotal role to public sector and economic planning. This new approach to socio-economic growth was set within a framework of parliamentary democracy guaranteeing universal franchise.

The Planning Commission was set up in March 1950 by a resolution of the Government of India which defined the scope of its work in the following terms:

"The Constitution of India has guaranteed certain Fundamental Rights to the citizens of India and enunciated certain Directive Principles of State Policy, in particular, that the State shall strive to promote the welfare of the people by securing and protecting as effectively as it may a social order in which justice, social, economic and political shall form all the institutions of the national life, and shall direct its policy towards securing, among other things:

(a) that the citizens, men and women equally, have the right to an adequate means of livelihood;

(b) that the ownership and control of the material resources of the community are so distributed as best to subserve the common good; and

(c) that the operation of the economic system does not result in the concentration of wealth and means of production to the common detriment.

Having regard to these rights and in furtherance of these principles as well as of the declared objective of the Government to promote a rapid rise in the standard of living of the people by efficient exploitation of the resources of the country, increasing production and offering opportunities to all for employment in the service of the community,

The Planning Commission will:

(1) make an assessment of the material, capital and human resources of the country, including technical personnel, and investigate the possibilities of augmenting such of these resources as are found to be deficient in relation to the nation's requirements;

(2) formulate a Plan for the most effective and balanced utilisation of the country's resources;

(3) on a determination of priorities, define the stages in which the Plan should be carried out and propose the allocation of resources for the due completion of each stage;

(4) indicate the factors which are tending to retard economic development, and determine the conditions which, in view of the current social and political situation, should be established for the successful execution of the Plan;

(5) determine the nature of the machinery which will be necessary for securing the successful implementation of each stage of the Plan in all its aspects;

(6) appraise from time to time the progress achieved in the execution of each stage of the Plan and recommend the adjustments of policy and measures that such appraisal may show to be necessary; and

(7) make such interim or ancillary recommendations as appear to it to be appropriate either for facilitating the discharge of the duties assigned to it; or, on a consideration of the prevailing economic conditions, current policies, measures and development programmes; or on an examination of such specific problems as may be referred to it for advice by Central or State Governments."

In July 1951, the Planning Commission presented a Draft Outline of a plan of development for the period of five years from April 1951 to March 1956. The Draft Outline was addressed to the country for general discussion and comments in the following words:

"Planning in a democratic State is a social process in which, in some part, every citizen should have the opportunity to participate. To set the patterns of future development is a task of such magnitude and significance that it should embody the impact of public opinion and the needs of the community. We have, therefore, felt it necessary, before presenting our proposals in complete detail, to offer a Draft Outline of the Plan. The Draft is intended to be a document for the widest possible public discussion. We hope to have further consultations with the Central Ministries, State Governments and our own Advisory Board and Panels, and also to obtain the views of Members of Parliament before we finalise the Plan."

3.7.2 Establishment of National Development Council: It was set up in August 1952 with the following objectives.

1. To review the working of the National Plan from time to time.
2. To consider important questions of social and economic policy affecting national development.
3. To recommend measures for the achievement of the aims and targets of the National Plan.

The Planning Commission prepares the blueprint of economic plans in consultation with the States and in accordance with the guidelines provided by the National Development Council (NDC) which consists of the Prime Minister (chairman), Central Cabinet Ministers, Chief Ministers of the States, and Members of the Planning Commission. After the draft plan is approved by the NDC and finalised by the Central Government, it is implemented, to a substantial extent, through the state machinery. Apparently, successful execution of a plan presupposes co-operation between the Central and the State Governments.

NDC, being the apex body for economic matters, takes all final decisions as regards the size, contents, objectives, and strategies of the Plan. The Planning Commission functions as an advisory body to NDC.

3.7.3 Objectives of Economic Planning in India: The objectives of economic planning in India have been stated and reiterated in various plan documents. Ever since the launching of the First Five Year Plan in 1951, these objectives have remained, by and large, the same with varying degree of emphasis on them. Broadly speaking, the earlier Plans stressed the need to develop heavy industries, the later Plans have emphasised self-reliance and anti-poverty programmes. The long-term broad objectives of economic planning are the following:

A. Rapid Economic Growth: The basic objective of economic planning is to ensure high rate of economic growth, i.e. increase in real per capita income. This is possible only when the rate of growth of real national income is more than the rate of growth of population. Various plans have attended to the development of crucial sectors of the economy such as agriculture, industry, transport and communications. On the average, the growth target of plans has hovered around 5 to 6 per cent annual increase in real national product. Making a significant departure from the past practice, the Tenth Five Year Plan (2002-07) fixed a target of 8 per cent rate of growth.

B. Removal of Poverty and Unemployment: Poverty and unemployment are the two most formidable problems of the Indian economy. Population explosion after Independence has compounded the task of planners to ensure a reasonable standard of living for every citizen. The massive additions to the existing labour force have increased the backlog of job seekers. In spite of the various poverty-alleviation and employment generation schemes launched from time to time, these two inter-related problems are showing no signs of solution.

C. Reduction of Economic Inequalities: In tune with the Directive Principles of State Policy enunciated in the Constitution of India, the Five Year Plans have emphasised the need for a more equitable distribution of income and wealth. In the earlier phase of economic planning, great stress was laid on the establishment of a socialistic pattern of society. The removal of poverty is partly dependent on a better distribution of economic power.

D. Self-reliance: Excessive dependence on external assistance for financing the earlier plans created uncertainty and interference in the implementation of the plans. Starting from Third Five Year Plan (1961-66), self-reliance came to be accepted as a desirable objective of planning process. In the Indian context it has a special meaning, viz. avoidance of undue dependence on foreign aid for financing the plans. In other words, the endeavour should be to make investments from out of domestic savings to the greatest possible extent.

E. Regional Balanced Development: Uneven development during British rule left many States of the country much backward as compared to certain other States. To ensure that benefits of development planning flow to all parts of the country, regional balanced development has all along been accepted as an important objective of economic planning. Federalism is not only a unifying but also a levelling up force. Considerable economic inequalities exist among different States of India and their reduction is an argument in favour of centralisation of resources. No doubt, priority has been given in the plans to the development of notified backward areas.

F. Employment Generation: Employment generation has been an important objective of development planning in India. Though employment opportunities have increased over the years, growth of population and labour force has aggravated the unemployment problem year after year. Fulfilment of this objective is nowhere in sight.

The objectives of economic planning in India are laudable. However, these objectives have been met to a limited extent during the last 55 years. Millions of people still live below the poverty line and there is widespread unemployment.

More distressingly, there is no hope of the two formidable problems of poverty and unemployment being solved in the near future. In the Preface itself, the Tenth Five Year Plan (2002-07) document mentioned the unemployment problem being aggravated, much less mitigated, during the Plan period and thereafter.

Although India has invested enormous amounts of financial and real resources in successive Plans, the benefits resulting from development of the economy have not been evenly distributed either among various regions or among different economic classes in the country. Growing inter-regional and inter-personal disparities have caused migration of labour from relatively poorer States to economically better off States, causing social and political tensions.

Moreover, there has been a lack of consensus and understanding among various political parties as regards the philosophy and contents of a particular Plan. There are instances of ongoing Plans being rolled up with the change of government at the Centre. Such disruptions caused huge losses because the ongoing schemes/programmes were either truncated or completely discontinued. This highlights the need for a national approach to a Plan and its objectives.

3.7.4 Financing of the Plan: Resources for the plans are assessed separately for the public and private sector plans based on the estimates of savings and consumption in the economy. While only a broad estimate of investment is attempted for the private sector, a detailed exercise is undertaken for estimating resources for the public sector plan. The latter is done in terms of (a) internal resources, and (b) external resources. The internal resources pertain to (i) budgetary surpluses on current account, (ii) surplus of public enterprises, (iii) market borrowings, (iv) additional resource mobilisation (ARM) and (v) deficit financing. For the States' plans, estimates are made of the States' own resources and Central plan assistance.

A. Internal Resources: Internal resources include the following:

- **Balance from Current Revenues:** Surplus on revenue account of the Central budget represents a measure of Government savings. Till the year 1978-79, it was almost customary that Central budgets recorded surplus on revenue account. However, beginning with the year 1979-80, the revenue account has registered regular and growing deficits. If these deficits are to be converted into surpluses then increased reliance will have to be placed on taxation, particularly direct taxation of the affluent classes. It is also necessary to augment non-tax revenue of the Government. To generate surplus on revenue account, control of non-Plan revenue expenditure is inescapable.
- **Surpluses of Public Enterprises:** Public sector enterprises contribute to plan financing by transferring surpluses to the general budget (non-tax revenue)

and thereby helping public savings in the form of balance from current revenues. The retained profits of public sector undertakings and deposits accepted from the public represent internal and extra-budgetary resources of public sector. Unfortunately, the number of enterprises which contribute to general budget is small.

- **Market/Internal Borrowings:** The rising trend in Government's internal liabilities is definite and marked the scope for additional resources from this source is also limited. The increased reliance on borrowings and the enhanced interest rates paid thereon have directly multiplied the debt servicing liabilities of the Government. Experts have warned of internal debt trap, a situation in which borrowings have to be resorted to just to keep up with the servicing of debt.
- **Additional Resource Mobilisation (ARM):** It means resources raised through additional efforts such as raising the tax rates.
- **Deficit Financing:** After exhausting all other sources, the Government is left with inflationary manner of raising resources which include borrowings from RBI against the sale of treasury bills (deficit financing) and hikes in administered prices which get reflected in the increased profits or reduced losses of public sector enterprises.

B. External Assistance: The external sector does not hold much prospects for plan financing in view of deteriorating balance of payments situation, low foreign exchange reserves, and rising debt-servicing ratio. United States and other donor countries are shying away from future investments in Asia and looking for greener pastures in Eastern Europe. As a solution to external debt problem, the developing countries should make concerted efforts at rescheduling and writing off of loans. It is also necessary to curb effectively inessential imports so that valuable foreign exchange could be released for the import of critical raw materials and capital goods.

3.8 Transfer of Resources through the Planning Commission

The Planning Commission, which for all practical purposes is a political body, makes an assessment of the existing resources of the individual States and the country as a whole and sets objectives in various fields and formulates plans for economic development in the light of requirements of each State. Article 282 of the Constitution of India provides that the Centre or a State may make grants for any public purpose. With the establishment of the Planning Commission in 1950, the Central Government invoked Article 282 for making grants to the States for plan purposes. Ever since the launching of the First Five Year Plan, these grants have occupied an important place in Central financial transfers to the States. It is noteworthy that under Article 293, the Central Government may grant loans to the States or give guarantees in respect of loans raised by them. The permissive nature of this provision is obvious.

Grants given under Article 282 are a subject matter of controversy. These grants were intended by the Constitution makers to meet unforeseeable emergencies (like droughts, famines, and other natural calamities) and were not envisaged as part of normal Centre-State financial relations. Thus, Central grants to States to help settle persons displaced as a result of the partition of the country was a typical example of the purpose contemplated by Article 282. These grants, meant for emergency purposes, were kept outside the purview of the Finance Commission which otherwise was entrusted with all the major questions of Centre-State financial relations.

Some experts feel that the Planning Commission is an unintended channel for transferring resources to the States because the founding fathers envisaged a pre-eminent role for the Finance Commission in dealing with problems of fiscal federalism. They never anticipated the rise of the Planning Commission and the National Development Council with enormous powers in the matter of allocation of resources to the State Governments. In view of the dominant role of the Planning Commission, the effectiveness of the Finance Commission has been circumscribed, its role being restricted to non-Plan expenditure of State budgets. Therefore, it is often suggested that for healthy intergovernmental financial relations, the Finance Commission should decide grants-in-aid to each State under Article 282 of the Constitution. The Planning Commission should assist the Finance Commission by drawing up a priority list of projects, their costs, locational feasibility and other technical matters. If this is to happen, the task of the Finance Commission will become still more difficult and the oft-repeated suggestion that Finance Commission should be transformed from a quinquennial to a permanent body, will gain strength. Such a permanent arrangement will ensure continuity in the work of the Finance Commission and make mid-term readjustments in its recommendations possible.

3.8.1 Gadgil Formula: What is the basis for allocating Central assistance for State Plans? During the first three Five Year Plans and the three Annual Plans thereafter, the distribution of Central assistance was not based on any clear-cut principles, giving the Planning Commission considerable discretion in allocating funds. In view of demand from the States for the adoption of a well-defined formula, the entire issue was discussed on the eve of the formulation of the Fourth Five Year Plan (1969-1974). The deliberations resulted in the adoption of a formula which later became known as the Gadgil Formula (named after the then

Deputy Chairman of the Planning Commission, Shri D.R. Gadgil). The formula, approved by the NDC, was as follows.

1. Requirements of Special Category States should first be met out of the total pool of Central assistance.
2. The balance of assistance should be distributed among the remaining 14 States on the basis of the following criteria:

- 60 per cent on the basis of population,
- 10 per cent on the basis of per capita State income of those States the per capita income of which is below the national level,
- 10 per cent on the basis of tax effort, determined on the basis of individual State's per capita tax receipts as percentage of the State's per capita income,
- 10 per cent on the basis of major irrigation and power projects which were to continue during the Fourth Plan and
- 10 per cent for special problems of individual States (Table 3.5).

Central Plan assistance during the Fourth and the Fifth Plans was distributed in accordance with the provisions of the Gadgil formula. Adoption of Gadgil formula reduced the discretion of Planning Commission and instead introduced objectivity and transparency in the allocation of Plan assistance to the States.

Table 3.5: Original, Modified, and Revised Gadgil Formula for Central Plan Assistance to States

Weight (per cent)

S. No.	Criterion	Original formula (Fourth and Fifth Plans)	Modified formula (Sixth and Seventh Plans)	Revised formula (Eight and subsequent Plans)
1.	Population	60	60	60
2.	Per capita income below the national average (deviation)	10	20	25*
3.	Per capita tax effort	10	10	--
4.	Outlay on continuing irrigation and power projects	10	--	--
5.	Performance	--	--	7.5
6.	Special problems	10	10	7.5
	Total	100	100	100

*5 per cent was allocated to all the States on distance method.

Sources: *Report of the Commission on Centre-State Relations*, Part I, 1988, p. 277, and decisions of the National Development Council reported in the Press.

Gadgil formula was modified on the eve of the formulation of the Sixth Plan to make it more progressive for the benefit of economically backward States. The modified formula, approved by the NDC in 1980, and applied for the Sixth and the Seventh Plans, was different from the original formula in following respects.

The 10 per cent weightage given to ongoing irrigation and power projects in the original formula was dropped. The weightage to per capita income below the national average (backwardness factor) was increased from 10 per cent to 20 per cent (Table 3.5).

The tug-of-war among the States for Central assistance continued as each State suggested a formula which best suited its interests. This led to further modifications in the Gadgil Formula. The Revised Gadgil Formula, meant for the Eighth Plan, was discussed and approved by the NDC at its meeting held on December 23-24, 1991. It had the following components (Table 3.5).

1. The weightage assigned to population factor was retained at 60 per cent.
2. The weightage given to per capita income factor was increased from 20 per cent to 25 per cent. Out of this 25 per cent, 20 per cent was allocated to States whose per capita income was below the national level. The remaining 5 per cent was allocated to all the States on the distance method.
3. The earlier tax effort factor with 10 per cent weightage was discarded.
4. A new factor called *performance* was introduced with 7.5 per cent weightage. It consisted of tax effort, fiscal management, national priorities including population, literacy, female welfare programmes, and land reforms.
5. The weightage given to special problems was reduced from 10 per cent to 7.5 per cent. The element of discretion associated with funds earmarked for special problems was considerably reduced with the identification of the following seven special problem areas in the Revised Formula: coastal areas, special environment issues, flood and drought prone areas, exceptionally sparse or thickly populated areas, special financial difficulties for achieving minimum reasonable Plan size, desert problems, and slums in urban areas.

Thus, since 1969 the Central assistance for the State Plans has been distributed to the States as per the Gadgil formula. Some marginal changes have been made in this formula from time to time but the emphasis has always been on channelising larger Central assistance to the backward States. The formula was last amended in 1991-92. As per the existing formula, after setting apart the funds required for Externally Aided Projects (EAPs) and reasonable amounts for Special Area Programmes, 30 per cent of the balance is earmarked for ten Special Category States. The balance amount is distributed among Non-special Category States on the basis of criteria and weightage shown in Table 3.5.

3.8.2 Nature of Plan Transfers: Plan transfers by the Planning Commission are made under a set of clearly laid out objective criteria approved by the National Development Council and are subject to review by it. Therefore, it would be wrong to call Plan transfers as discretionary, as is believed by some experts. Even in the case of *other transfers* (for natural calamities etc.) there are standardised procedures as recommended by the Seventh and the Eighth Finance Commissions. It is, of course, true that though Plan assistance to States is formula-based, the total amount of such assistance to be transferred to the States each year is determined by the Centre.

As regards the nature of Plan transfers, the Commission on Centre-State Relations, 1988, observed, "The Plan and other transfers which are labelled *discretionary* do not amount to subversion of the Constitutional scheme. They cannot be considered either unreasonable or discretionary in a literal sense as their allocation follows predetermined criteria, or is tied to meet the specific requirements of the States. The large magnitude of Plan transfers should not pose any controversy in this regard as the framers of the Constitution could not anticipate the extent of development resource-needs under the Plans of the States. The significant growth of Central assistance to States for planned development is, indeed, a natural response to such needs. The crux of the matter is that the States' participation in the planning process should be such that the Plan transfers are treated by them as part of a commonly agreed programme for the deployment of the nation's resources." [16] The Commission further observed that the controversy regarding statutory versus discretionary transfers was more theoretical than realistic in nature.

3.9 Centrally Sponsored Schemes

A contentious issue related to Plan assistance pertains to Centrally Sponsored Schemes. In view of their national importance, these schemes are launched by the Centre and implemented by the State Governments with Central assistance. The Central Ministries concerned propose and formulate these schemes which are approved by the Planning Commission. The States execute these schemes under the technical guidance and supervision of the Centre which also issues guidelines regarding the contents, coverage, expenditure pattern, and staffing of such schemes. The assistance given for these schemes on a matching basis is over and above the assistance given for State Plans and the provision for it is made in the budgets of the Central Ministries. For example, in the agricultural sector, these schemes pertain to propagation of research and improved technology, disease control, preserving ecological balance, support to specific crops like pulses, cotton, jute etc.

The States are generally unhappy with their inadequate involvement in the formulation of Centrally sponsored schemes which mainly pertain to subjects included in the State List. Sponsoring of these schemes by the Centre is also considered an intrusion into subjects reserved for States. In this connection, the Administrative Reforms Commission opined, "The intrusion is not, technically, unconstitutional for it is protected by Article 282 but it is a question whether, with the help of financial carrot such intrusion is desirable and conducive to the growth of healthy federal relationship." [17]

The States have also complained against Centrally sponsored schemes on the ground that the system of matching grants involved in the schemes favours the richer States because they are better placed to provide matching funds to avail Central assistance. Such schemes induce the States to divert their limited resources to areas which may occupy low priority in the investment scheme of a State. As regards the magnitude of Centrally sponsored schemes, the Ninth Finance Commission observed, "Centrally sponsored schemes have grown in volume and number over the years. As of April 1985, the schemes under implementation were as many as 262. The outlay of Rs. 18,000 crore approximately of these schemes accounted for about 80 per cent of Central assistance provided for the State Plans during the Seventh Five Year Plan. This has happened despite States' objection to their proliferation and the decision of NDC in 1979 to roll them back to the level of 1/6th of the Central assistance for States' Plans by hacking away schemes costing a total of Rs. 2,000 crore. More recently, the NDC after considering the Ramamurti Committee Report in November 1985 had set up a Committee headed by the then Union Minister for Human Resources Development to go into this matter. This Committee had in turn constituted a group of officials whose recommendations favour retention of most of the schemes." [18]

The confrontation between the Centre and the States on this issue was considerably reduced when at the December 23-24, 1991 meeting of the NDC it was decided to transfer 113 sponsored schemes to the States along with the allocations being made for these schemes.

Government's policy regarding Centrally sponsored schemes was made clear in the 1996-97 budget speech of the Finance Minister, "...it is our desire that most Centrally-sponsored schemes should be transferred to the control of the State Governments. In the meantime, States will be given greater flexibility in the implementation of these programmes. Provisions available under all other schemes will be pooled and the basic entitlement ratio will be worked out for each State. The States will be free to select for implementation, within their annual entitlement, such schemes that are more suited to their needs." [19]

3.10 Size and Pattern of Central Transfers

Regarding the magnitude of Central transfers to the States, it is natural to expect claims and counter claims by the two levels of the Government. The States have often complained that resources allocated to them are inadequate to enable them to discharge their responsibilities. They complain against widening gap between their own resources and needs, a trend indicating their increasing dependence on the Centre for resources. They assert that their resources should be commensurate with their obligations and responsibilities. Similarly, the Centre also feels constrained at the widening gap between its resources and needs, as reflected in the budgetary deficits. Since the early 1980s, the Centre has been running considerable deficit on its revenue account. Its commitments towards defence, subsidies, and interest payments claim a major chunk of its resources and there is little hope of any respite on these accounts in the near future.

Table 3.6 shows the magnitude and the composition of financial resources transferred from the Centre to the State in the 2008-09 budget.

Table 3.6: Financial Resources Transferred from the Centre to the States: Budget 2008-09

(Rs. crore)

1.	States' share of taxes and duties	1,78,765
2.	Non-Plan grants and loans	43,383
3.	Central assistance for State Plans	59,858
4.	Assistance for Central and Centrally sponsored schemes	25,620
5.	Gross resources transferred (1+2+3+4)	3,07,626
6.	Less: recovery of loans and advances	2,666
7.	Net resources transferred (5-6)	3,04,960

Source: Government of India, Ministry of Finance, *Budget at a Glance*, 2008-09.

To conclude, the Central Government raises the major part of combined resources and a significant part of that is transferred to the States to ensure vertical equity in the distribution of resources. Centralisation of revenues and adjustments thereafter is a characteristic feature of most federations of the world. Hence, to view Central transfers to the States as indicative of the latter's dependence on the former is erroneous because a significant part of the transfers takes place under constitutional provisions and in accordance with predetermined formulas. To the question whether the Centre has been making adequate transfers to the States, the Commission on Centre-State Relations, 1988 opined, "The Union Government is thus already transferring substantial resources to the States.

Under the present circumstances, there is need to pay attention to structural change in transfers for which there is apparently greater economy." [20]

3.11 Commission on Centre-State Relations, 1988

Government of India appointed in 1983 a Commission on Centre State Relations under the Chairmanship of Mr. Justice R.S. Sarkaria, a retired judge of the Supreme Court. The Commission was set up to review the whole gamut of Centre-State relations in their legislative, administrative, and financial aspects.

The monumental report of the Commission, submitted in 1988, basically accepted the existing framework of the Constitution. It disfavoured any major changes in the provisions of the Constitution including the financial arrangements. It stood for a strong Centre to preserve the unity and integrity of the country.

An important recommendation of the Commission pertained to the residuary power of legislation under the Constitution. Article 248 read with entry 97 of List I (Union List) of the Seventh Schedule vests in Parliament the residuary powers of legislation with respect to any matter not enumerated in List II (State List) or List III (Concurrent List). Such residuary powers include the power of making any law imposing a tax not mentioned in these Lists.

Regarding residuary powers of legislation, the Commission recommended, "that residuary power of legislation in regard to taxation should advisedly remain with Parliament. But, the residuary field other than that of taxation may be transferred to the Concurrent List....The Constitution may be suitably amended to give effect to this recommendation." [21]

Thus, the Commission recommended partial transfer of entry 97 to the Concurrent List. Unfortunately, no action has been taken so far to implement this recommendation of the Commission.

As regards financial relations between the Centre and the States, the Commission recommended as follows.

1. The Commission disfavoured any major modification in the basic scheme of the Constitution dividing the fields of taxation between the Centre and the States.
2. It rejected almost all the suggestions to shift the taxation powers of the Centre to the States. Such suggestions pertained mainly to the shifting of terminal taxes on goods and passengers carried by railways, estate duty, and banking etc.
3. The Commission was not in favour of making the devolution of funds from the Centre to the States automatic. In its view the existing division of functions between the Finance Commission and the Planning Commission

was reasonable and must continue.

4. In its opinion the terms of reference of the Finance Commission should be drawn up in consultation with State Governments.
5. Significantly, the Commission recommended the sharing of corporation tax between the Centre and the States. Most other suggestions for enlarging the divisible pool were turned down.
6. It recommended legislation to levy consignment tax and constitutional amendment to enable levy of tax on advertisements in broadcasting.
7. As regards agricultural income tax, the Commission observed that as opinions are divided the matter should be examined further in depth.
8. The Commission recommended the setting up of an expert committee to examine taxation reforms and resource mobilisation.
9. Some other recommendations of the Commission included: review of the royalty paid to the States, modernisation of treasury systems, making available foreign borrowings by States from the banks, the issue of tax free municipal bonds, and assistance for natural calamities, shifting of additional excise duty from fabric to yarn, and setting up of special courts for economic offences.

Notes

1. Government of India, *Report of the Commission on Centre-State Relations* (Chairman: Justice R. S. Sarkaria) Part I, 1988, p. 8.

2. *Ibid.*, p. 7.

3. Concurrent taxation powers are a characteristic feature of federal set up in USA, Canada, and Australia. Most tax fields in these countries are jointly occupied by the federal and provincial governments. The overlapping taxation powers have often caused frictions not only between the federal and provincial governments but also among the provinces *inter se.* Tax problems owing to joint occupancy of tax fields are solved through tax rental and tax sharing negotiations and agreements.

4. *Report of the Commission on Centre-State Relations*, Part I, 1988, op. cit., p. 271.

5. *Report of the Sixth Finance Commission*, 1973, p. 5

6. Report of the Twelfth Finance Commission (2005-10), November 2004, pp. 15-16.

7. Prior to the Eightieth Amendment of the Constitution, provisions of Article 269 were as follows.

Taxes Levied and Collected by the Union but Assigned to the States (Article 269): These were: (a) duties in respect of succession to property other than agricultural land, (b) estate duty in respect of property other than agricultural land, (c) terminal taxes on goods or passengers carried by railway, sea or air, (d) taxes on railway fares and freights, (e) taxes other than stamp duties on transactions in stock exchanges and future markets, (f) taxes on the sale or purchase of newspapers and on advertisements published therein, (g) taxes on the sale or purchase of goods other than newspapers, where such sale or purchase takes place in the course of inter-State trade or commerce, and (h) taxes on the consignment of goods (whether the consignment is to the person making it or to any other person), where such consignment takes place in the course of inter-State trade or commerce. These taxes corresponded to entries 87, 88, 89, 90, 92, 92A and 92B in the Union List.

8. Stamp duty was payable on cheques prior to 1927 but was withdrawn in that year.

9. Future trading refers to contracts for sale and purchase of goods at a future date primarily with a view to avoid price fluctuations. Presently, future trading is allowed at specific centres in respect of four commodities, viz. jute products, paper, turmeric, and *gur*.

10. Administrative Reforms Commission, *Report of the Study Team on Centre-State Relationships*, Vol. I, 1968, p. 15.

11. Since the President is guided in all his decisions by the advice of the Central Council of Ministers (Article 74), the appointment of the Finance Commission and the determination of its terms of reference becomes the prerogative of the Central Government for all practical purposes. This prerogative of the Centre is often criticised because the Centre itself is a party to the *dispute* between the Centre and the States regarding sharing of financial resources, and the role of the Finance Commission is that of an arbiter.

12. *Report of the Sixth Finance Commission*, 1973, p. 5.

13. Article 280(3) requires the Finance Commission to make recommendations to the President who is to lay the same under Article 281 before each House of Parliament. It is nowhere laid down in the Constitution that recommendations of the Commission shall be binding upon the Government of India. They are, therefore, non-justiciable. However, to safeguard the interests of the States in the Union taxes which are divisible, the Constitution provides (Article 274) that no bill or amendment which (i) varies the rate of tax in which the States are interested; (ii) affects the principles on which moneys are distributable or (iii) imposes any surcharge on any such tax for the purpose of the Union, shall be introduced or moved in the Parliament except on the recommendation of the President.

The Centre has generally accepted the major recommendations of the Finance Commissions though there are some instances of partial acceptance of such recommendations. For example, the Centre did not accept the entire set of recommendations of the Eighth Finance Commission relating to the first year (1984-85) of the five year period covered by it. The Centre held the view that by the time the report was submitted (April 30, 1984), the Central and the State budgets had been passed and it was late to reopen the estimates. However, it was widely felt that this decision of the Government was in violation of the spirit of Article 280 of the Constitution.

14. *Report of the Commission on Centre-State Relations*, Part I, 1988, op. cit., p. 254.

15. *Report of the Sixth Finance Commission*, 1973, p. 5

16. *Report of the Commission on Centre-State Relations*, Part I, 1988, op. cit., p. 279.

17. Administrative Reforms Commission, *Report of the Study Team on Centre-State Relation-ships*, Vol. I, 1968, op. cit., p. 122.

18. *First Report of the Ninth Finance Commission*, 1988, p. 24.

19. Government of India, *Budget papers 1996-97: Speech of the Finance Minister*, Part I, p. 16.

20. *Report of the Commission on Centre-State Relations*, Part I, 1988, op. cit., p. 281.

21. *Report of the Commission on Centre-State Relations*, Part I, *1988*, op. cit., p. 31.

4

Trends in Combined (Centre and States) Tax Revenues

4.1 Trends in Tax-GDP Ratio

In 1950-51, total tax collections in India were a mere 6.31 per cent of GDP. With the launching of the Five Year Plans in 1951, and expansion in administrative and welfare activities of the Government at different levels, the need for revenue increased and it was met mainly by additional tax efforts. Consequently, tax-GDP ratio started increasing from decade to decade, being 7.86 per cent in 1960-61, 10.40 per cent in 1970-71 and 13.80 per cent in 1980-81. [1] It stood at 15.43 per cent in 1990-91 and after that it declined to as low as 13.38 per cent in 1998-99. Lately, an upward trend is noticeable in tax-GDP ratio (Table 4.1).

The slippage in tax-GDP ratio was noted by the Twelfth Finance Commission. To quote, "Taking the 15-year period from 1987-88 to 2001-02, and comparing three-year averages at both ends, that is for 1987-90 and 1999-2002, we note that the tax-GDP ratio fell from a level of about 16 per cent relative to GDP by 1.6 percentage points to reach an average level of 14.4 per cent of GDP." [2] Stating the reasons for the slippage, the Commission noted, "As a result of tax reforms, the indirect taxes relative to GDP started coming down whereas that of direct taxes started increasing. But the magnitude of increase in the direct taxes was less than the fall in indirect taxes. In consequence, the overall tax-GDP ratio fell from its peak in 1987-88 to 14.4 per cent in 2001-02." [3] It is noteworthy that rates of excise and customs duties have gradually been lowered during the post-1991 period. Emphasising the need to increase tax-GDP ratios, the Commission suggested ratios for the year 2009-10 (Table 4.2).

4.2 Trends in the Relative Significance of Direct and Indirect Taxes

There is no legal definition of direct and indirect taxes in India. Taxes under the charge of Central Board of Direct Taxes are direct taxes while those administered by the Central Board of Excise and Customs are indirect taxes. The classification adopted in this book is the same as followed in the documents of the Government of India. In 1950-51, direct taxes accounted for a sizeable 36.8 per cent of total tax collections: Rs. 231 crore out of Rs. 627 crore. Within a span of 35 years the proportionate share dropped to less than half at 14.4 per cent in 1985-86, and stood at 13.1 per cent in 1987-88.

Table 4.1: Combined Tax Revenue as Per Cent of GDP: 1990-91 to 2006-07

(Rs. crore)

Year	Combined tax revenue*	Col. 2 as % of GDP
1	2	3
1990-91	87,722	15.43
1991-92	1,03,198	15.80
1992-93	1,14,166	15.26
1993-94	1,21,961	14.19
1994-95	1,47,849	14.60
1995-96	1,75,259	14.75
1996-97	2,01,056	14.69
1997-98	2,20,659	14.49
1998-99	**2,33,017**	**13.38**
1999-00	2,74,583	14.02
2000-01	3,05,320	14.49
2001-02	3,14,535	13.79
2002-03	3,56,277	14.54
2003-04	4,14,084	15.00
2004-05	4,94,370	15.81
2005-06	5,95,350	16.69
2006-07	6,99,135	16.95

* Total tax revenue of the Central and State Governments.

2005-06= Revised estimates; 2006-07 = Budget estimates

Note: The ratios of GDP since 1950-51 are with reference to new series GDP (Base: 1993-94) at current market prices.

Source: Rearranged data from Government of India, Ministry of Finance, *Indian Public Finance Statistics*, 2006-2007, Tables 1.7 and 1.8.

Table 4.2: Tax-GDP Ratios Suggested by the Twelfth Finance Commission for the Year 2009-10

	2004-05	2009-10
Combined tax revenue	15.6	17.6
Centre's gross tax revenue	9.7	10.9
States' own tax revenues	5.9	6.8

Source: Report of the Twelfth Finance Commission (2005-10), November 2004, Tables 4.12 and 4.13 (excerpted).

The declining trend of direct taxes led to a rising share of indirect taxes. The ratio between direct and indirect taxes which stood at 36.8:63.2 in 1950-51 worsened with every passing decade, recording 29.8:70.2 in 1960-61, 21.2:78.8 in 1970-71, 16.5:83.5 in 1980-81 and 13.1:86.9 in 1987-88. [4] The declining share of direct taxes was not consistent with the norms of tax theory. It is well-known that as an economy experiences modernisation, diversification, and expansion of corporate sector, the scope for direct taxes widens. [5]

It is customary to explain the limited role of direct taxes in developing countries in terms of their peculiar circumstances which include large agricultural sector of subsistence nature, small-scale industrial activities, lack of monetisation and accounting practices, and low levels of income. Even a modest exemption limit of personal income tax keeps the vast majority of income earners outside the income tax net. In addition to these underlying reasons, a host of specific factors also contributed to the reduced role of direct taxes. These included:

- Scaling down rates of direct taxes.
- Plethora of exemptions/concessions.
- Abolition of estate duty in 1985.
- Large-scale tax evasion.

The declining share of direct taxes caused concern in Government circles and this feeling was expressed in official documents. The Long Term Fiscal Policy (LTFP) while seeking to correct the imbalance maintained, "While the predominance of indirect taxes in the present situation is unavoidable, it cannot be gainsaid that a certain balance has to be maintained between direct and indirect taxes. Taxes like the personal income tax have an important role in the tax structure and cannot be substituted by taxes on commodities. It is not easy to tailor commodity taxes to the circumstances of the taxpayers in the same way as is possible with the personal income tax. Hence, although reliance on indirect taxation cannot be avoided in the foreseeable future, it is necessary to make a transition to a system whereby income tax makes a larger contribution to revenue. Such transition is not possible without a distinct improvement in the buoyancy of the income tax in response to growth in incomes. An important objective of fiscal policy must be to reverse the decline in the share of direct taxes over the long term." [6]

4.2.1 Reversal of Roles: After the tax reforms initiated in 1991, the decline in the relative share of direct taxes has not only been arrested but reversed. The ratio between direct and indirect taxes which stood at 14.0:86.0 in 1990-91 was estimated at 30.4:69.6 in the budget estimates for 2006-07 (Table 4.3).

Table 4.3: Combined Tax Revenue, Breakdown between Direct and Indirect Taxes with Percentage Shares: 1990-91 to 2006-07

(Rs. crore)

Year	Combined tax revenue* (3+4)	Direct taxes	Indirect taxes	Col. 3 as % of Col. 2	Col. 4 as % of Col. 2
1	2	3	4	5	6
1990-91	87,722	12,260	75,462	14.0	86.0
1991-92	1,03,198	16,657	86,541	16.1	83.9
1992-93	1,14,166	19,387	94,779	17.0	83.0
1993-94	1,21,961	21,713	1,00,248	17.8	82.2
1994-95	1,47,849	28,878	1,18,971	19.5	80.5
1995-96	1,75,259	35,777	1,39,482	20.4	79.6
1996-97	2,01,056	41,061	1,59,995	20.4	79.6
1997-98	2,20,659	50,538	1,70,121	22.9	77.1
1998-99	2,33,017	49,119	1,83,898	21.1	78.9
1999-00	2,74,583	60,864	2,13,719	21.4	78.6
2000-01	3,05,320	71,762	2,33,558	23.5	76.5
2001-02	3,14,535	73,108	2,41,427	23.2	76.8
2002-03	3,56,277	87,365	2,68,912	24.5	75.5
2003-04	4,14,084	1,09,546	3,04,538	26.5	73.5
2004-05	4,94,370	1,37,093	3,57,277	27.7	72.3
2005-06	5,95,350	1,73,214	4,22,136	29.1	70.9
2006-07	6,99,135	2,12,804	4,86,331	30.4	69.6

* Total tax revenue of the Central and State Governments.
2005-06 = Revised estimates; 2006-07 = Budget estimates.
Source: Rearranged data from Government of India, Ministry of Finance, *Indian Public Finance Statistics*, 2006-2007, Table 1.7. Columns 5 and 6 calculations own.

Stating the reasons for fall in the share of indirect taxes and increase in the share of direct taxes, the Tenth Five Year Plan (2002-07) observed, "The reasons for this steep fall in the indirect tax revenue are obvious. The structural and administrative reforms in the Indian tax system during the Nineties characterised by scaling down of the tax rate, reduction in number of slabs, introduction of modified value added tax system, etc, among others, were not necessarily aimed at raising revenue productivity. Rather, the purpose was to improve efficiency in production and trade by removing market distortion. The analysis of data in the post -reform period exposes several issues worth mentioning. First, the value of imports has not responded to tariff reduction in equal proportion, i.e. import elasticity with respect to tariff has not been very high. Second, a host of tariff exemptions still exists on substantial proportion of imports ranging from 60 per cent to 80 per cent. Third, the excise duty has not been structured to lead to a revenue-neutral tax system under MODVAT/CENVAT. Fourth, the tax base for excise revenue (manufacturing sector) is gradually shrinking as a proportion of GDP. Our projections of the tax buoyancy for the Tenth plan have considered all these issues.

The improvement in direct tax collection, which has been experienced despite the scaling back of income tax rates in India during the post-reform period, could be attributed to expansion in the tax base through introduction of innovative schemes, extension of the base for tax deduction at source and improvement in direct tax administration etc. Continuous efforts towards improvement in the direct tax administration and its re-structuring, and introduction of information technology on a large scale to facilitate tax administration are expected to further enhance revenue collection under direct tax." [7]

4.2.2 Equity Implications: Though, of late, the share of direct taxes has increased, they are still far below the contribution made by indirect taxes. The subdued role of direct taxes or the dominance of indirect taxes in India's tax structure has serious equity implications. Indirect taxes do not allow considerations for personal circumstances of taxpayers as do direct taxes. It is not possible to grant exemptions or allow deductions or to have a progressive rate schedule, e.g. in the case of excisable goods. Commodity taxes are borne in relation to consumption expenditure which constitutes a higher percentage of income for lower income groups than for persons in higher income brackets.

Moreover, a substantial amount of indirect taxes is paid by the Government to itself. Broadly speaking, public expenditure at all levels forms one-fourth of the total spending in India. Customs duties, excise levies, and sales taxes and the hikes in them entail additional expenditure on the part of Central and State Governments to maintain their existing command over real resources of the economy. Commodities like motor vehicles, petrol, air conditioners, water coolers, and steel furniture are favourite items for heavy and additional taxation and these are also the items extensively used by civil and defence establishments of the Government. Therefore, a substantial part of indirect tax revenue including the additional tax effort is merely a book transfer and does not reflect increase in real resources at the command of the Government. This argument can also be extended to increase in the prices of goods produced by public sector enterprises. Any such increase and the resultant additional proceeds may improve the finances of an individual public enterprise but not necessarily of the Government of India because the various Ministries and Departments will be required to spend more to purchase the same volume of goods and services from the concerned enterprise. Thus, in any reform of indirect tax structure it is important to emphasise, apart from quantity, the quality of revenue, i.e. who pay the taxes to the Government.

With the growth of corporate sector and the rise in income levels, India is showing signs of modernisation, reflecting increased scope for direct taxes. For widening the direct tax base, effective measures are needed to tap the unincorporated industrial sector and the affluent agricultural class.

Notes

1. See Table 1 on page 551 of this book.
2. *Report of the Twelfth Finance Commission* (2005-10), November 2004, p. 22.
3. Ibid., p. 63.
4. See Table 1 on page 551 of this book.
5. According to a study conducted by Raja Chelliah and others for a group of 47 developing countries for the average of the period 1969-71, the average share of indirect taxes was 64 per cent of the total tax revenue. As for developed economies, the share of indirect taxes ranged between 45-50 per cent of the total tax revenues. [See R.J. Chelliah, H.J. Bass, and M.R. Kelly, "Tax Ratios and Tax Efforts in Developing Countries, 1969-71", *I.M.F. Staff Papers,* Volume 22, No. 1, March 1975, Table 2]. It is noteworthy that in India the proportion of indirect taxes stood at 78.8 per cent in 1970-71, much higher than the international average of the developing world.
6. Government of India, Ministry of Finance, *Long Term Fiscal Policy* (December 1985), p.23.
7. Government of India, Planning Commission, *Tenth Five Year Plan* (2002-07), Vol. I, p. 61.

5

Trends in Central Taxes

Central taxes account for about two-thirds of total tax collections in India. [1] The relative significance of various taxes in Central revenues has undergone major changes since Independence. Income tax and wealth tax are the direct taxes while excise levies and customs duties are the indirect taxes of the Central Government.

5.1 Central Taxes as Per Cent of GDP

In 1950-51, gross central taxes accounted for 4.08 per cent of GDP. With the widening and deepening of the tax net to raise resources for development projects, the percentage started increasing with every passing decade. It increased to 5.21 in 1960-61, to 7.02 in 1970-71 and stood at 9.17 in 1980-81. [2]

In 1990-91, when the process of economic reforms was initiated, gross central taxes accounted for 10.12 per cent of GDP. However, as a result of tax reforms introduced since then, this percentage started falling and it became as low as 8.20 in 2001-02. Stating the reasons for this fall of more than 2 percentage points, the Twelfth Finance Commission noted, "The impact of these reforms on direct and indirect taxes was diametrically opposite. While the direct taxes showed, even with the lower rates, a rising tax-GDP ratio, this ratio for the indirect taxes kept sliding down. The indirect taxes had a larger share in the total tax revenues of the centre and the fall in the indirect tax to GDP ratio could not be compensated by a rise in the direct taxes. As a result, the overall central tax-GDP ratio fell." [3]

Of late, however, recovery is noticeable in the tax-GDP ratio at the level of Central Government (Table 5.1).

5.2 Direct and Indirect Taxes

As in the case of combined (Centre and States) tax revenues, tax structure at the Central level also evolved around indirect taxes during the post-Independence period. The ratio between direct and indirect taxes in gross central taxes declined from 43.4:56.6 in 1950-51 to 32.6:67.4 in 1960-61, to 27.1:72.9 in 1970-71 and to 22.7:77.3 in 1980-81. [4] Resultantly, indirect taxes came to occupy a dominant place in Central finances.

In the wake of reforms initiated in the early 1990s, rates of both corporate and personal income tax were substantially reduced. Following better compliance, the decline in the relative share of direct taxes has been reversed. Direct taxes as a percentage of Centre's total tax collections rose from 19.2 per cent in 1990-91 (pre-reform period) to 34.7 per cent in 1997-98. The figure stood at 46.7 per cent in the 2006-07 budget (Table 5.2). In the 2008-09 budget, the ratio between direct and indirect taxes was estimated at 53.1:46.9 (Table 5.3).

Table 5.1: Gross Central Taxes as per cent of GDP: 1990-91 to 2006-07

(Rs. crore)

Year	Gross Central taxes*	Col. 2 as % of GDP
1	2	3
1990-91	57,577	10.12
1991-92	67,361	10.31
1992-93	74,636	9.97
1993-94	75,742	8.82
1994-95	92,297	9.11
1995-96	1,11,224	9.36
1996-97	1,29,762	9.48
1997-98	1,39,220	9.14
1998-99	1,43,797	8.26
1999-00	1,71,752	8.77
2000-01	1,88,603	8.95
2001-02	1,87,060	8.20
2002-03	2,15,905	8.81
2003-04	2,54,348	9.21
2004-05	3,04,957	9.75
2005-06	3,70,141	10.38
2006-07	4,42,153	10.72

* Before transferring States' share in Central taxes.
2005-06 = Revised estimates; 2006-07 = Budget estimates.
Note: The ratios of GDP since 1950-51 are with reference to new series GDP (Base: 1993-94) at current market prices.
Source: Rearranged data from Government of India, Ministry of Finance, *Indian Public Finance Statistics*, 2006-2007, Tables 1.7 and 1.8.

5.3 Composition of Direct Taxes

5.3.1 Income Tax: In 1950-51, personal income tax accounted for almost one-third (32.7 per cent) of Central tax collections. However, the relative contribution declined over the years and was less than one-tenth (9.3 per cent) in 1990-91. After the tax reforms initiated since early 1990s, the share of personal income tax in gross tax revenues of the Central Government increased sharply. In the 2008-09 budget, it was estimated at 20.1 per cent (Table 5.3). In the case of corporation tax, the relative contribution was 9.9 per cent in 1950-51 while in 1990-91 it was 9.3 per cent. In the intervening period, however, moderate changes are noticeable in the proportionate share of corporation tax. As in the case of personal income tax, the proportionate share of corporation tax in Centre's gross tax revenues has increased sharply during the post-1991 period. In the 2008-09 budget, it was estimated at 32.9 per cent (Table 5.3).

Table 5.2: Gross Central Taxes, Breakdown between Direct and Indirect Taxes with Percentage Shares: 1990-91 to 2006-07

(Rs. crore)

Year	Gross Central taxes*(3+4)	Direct taxes	Indirect taxes	Col. 3 as % of Col. 2	Col. 4 as % of Col. 2
1	2	3	4	5	6
1990-91	57,577	11,030	46,547	19.2	80.8
1991-92	67,361	15,353	52,008	22.8	77.2
1992-93	74,636	18,140	56,496	24.3	75.7
1993-94	75,742	20,299	55,443	26.8	73.2
1994-95	92,297	26,973	65,324	29.2	70.8
1995-96	1,11,224	33,564	77,660	30.2	69.8
1996-97	1,29,762	38,898	90,864	30.0	70.0
1997-98	1,39,220	48,282	90,938	34.7	65.3
1998-99	1,43,797	46,601	97,196	32.4	67.6
1999-00	1,71,752	57,960	1,13,792	33.7	66.3
2000-01	1,88,603	68,305	1,20,298	36.2	63.8
2001-02	1,87,060	69,197	1,17,863	37.0	63.0
2002-03	2,15,905	83,363	1,32,542	38.6	61.4
2003-04	2,54,348	1,05,091	1,49,257	41.3	58.9
2004-05	3,04,957	1,32,183	1,72,774	43.3	56.6
2005-06	3,70,141	1,67,341	2,02,800	45.2	54.8
2006-07	4,42,153	2,06,687	2,35,466	46.7	53.3

* Before transferring States' share in Central taxes.
2005-06 = Revised estimates; 2006-07 = Budget estimates.
Source: Rearranged data from Government of India, Ministry of Finance, *Indian Public Finance Statistics*, 2006-2007, Tables 1.7. Columns 5 and 6 calculations own.

It is noteworthy that both personal and corporate income taxes were rationalized as part of the package of economic reforms initiated in 1991. The number of rate categories, as well as the marginal income tax rates, was substantially reduced.

5.3.2 Wealth Tax: This so-called capital tax of the Central Government is without much revenue significance. .

Table 5.3: Trends in the Level and Composition of Gross Tax Revenues* of the Central Government: Selected Years

(Rs. crore)

Central taxes	1950-51	1960-61	1970-71	1980-81	1990-91	2000-01	2008-09#
A+B Gross tax revenues	404 (100.0)	888 (100.0)	3,206 (100.0)	13,179 (100.0)	57,576 (100.0)	1,88,603 (100.0)	6,87,715 (100.0)
A. Direct taxes of which	174 (43.1)	290 (32.6)	870 (27.1)	3,004 (22.8)	11,025 (19.1)	68,306 (36.2)	3,65,000 (53.1)
1. Corporation tax	40 (9.9)	11 (12.5)	371 (11.6)	1,310 (9.9)	5,235 (9.3)	35,696 (18.9)	2,26,361 (32.9)
2. Personal income tax	132 (32.7)	166 (18.7)	473 (14.8)	1,506 (11.4)	5,371 (9.3)	31,764 (16.8)	1,38,314 (20.1)
3. Other taxes**	2 (0.5)	13 (1.5)	26 (0.8)	188 (1.4)	319 (0.5)	846 (0.5)	325 (0.1)
B. Indirect taxes of which	229 (56.7)	599 (67.5)	2,337 (72.9)	10,175 (77.2)	46,552 (80.9)	1,20,297 (63.8)	3,22,715 (46.9)
1. Customs duties	157 (38.9)	170 (19.1)	524 (16.3)	3,409 (25.8)	20,644 (35.8)	47,542 (25.2)	1,18,930 (17.3)
2. Union excises	68 (16.8)	414 (46.6)	1,759 (54.9)	6,500 (49.3)	24,514 (42.6)	68,526 (36.3)	1,37,874 (20.1)
3. Service tax	-	-	-	-	-	-	64,460 (9.4)
4. Other taxes***	4 (1.0)	15 (1.7)	54 (1.7)	266 (2.0)	1,394 (2.4)	4,229 (2.2)	1,451 (0.2)

* Before transferring States' share in Central taxes; # Budget estimates.

** These are wealth tax and some other taxes of minor revenue significance.

*** These are State excise duties, taxes on vehicles, sales tax, octroi, duties on electricity, stamp and registration, entertainment tax (all from Union Territories without legislature) and foreign travel tax.

Figures in parentheses are corresponding percentages of total tax collections.

Sources: Government of India, Ministry of Finance, *Explanatory Memorandum on the Budget of the Central Government*
(various years); *Receipts Budget* (various years); and *Budget at a Glance*, 2008-09.

5.4 Composition of Indirect Taxes

5.4.1 Union Excise Duties: In the post-Independence period (1950-70), a major change in the Indian tax system pertained to the phenomenal rise in the relative revenue significance of Union excise duties. In 1950-51, excise revenue accounted for a modest 16.8 per cent of total Central tax collections: Rs. 68 crore out of Rs. 404 crore. Within a span of 20 years, the proportionate share shot up to 54.9 per cent in 1970-71. It declined to 49.3 per cent in 1980-81. In 1990-91 it was recorded at 42.6 per cent. In the 2008-09 budget, the contribution of excise duties in gross tax revenues of the Centre was estimated at 20.1 per cent (Table 5.3). The relative contribution of excise revenue has declined due to reduction in the average tax rates without a compensatory rise in the tax base, evasion, and litigation.

5.4.2 Service Tax: In view of the need for additional resources and the rising contribution of service sector to GDP, a modest effort was made in the 1994-95 budget when a 5 per cent tax was imposed on the services of telephones, non-life insurance, and stock brokers with effect from July 1, 1994. Since then the coverage of service tax has been extended to a host of other services and it is considered as the tax of the future. In the 2008-09 budget, the contribution of service tax in gross tax revenues of the Centre was estimated at 9.4 per cent (Table 5.3).

5.4.3 Customs Duties: During pre-Independence days and even during the early post-Independence period, customs duties formed the mainstay of Central tax revenues. However, the relative share of customs duties started declining from early 1950s in view of a protective trade policy and dwindling foreign exchange reserves. The share of customs revenue in Centre's total tax collections dropped from 38.9 per cent in 1950-51 to as low as 16.3 per cent in 1970-71. After that customs revenue maintained an upward swing, accounting for 35.8 per cent of Central taxes in the year 1990-91. This upward trend was attributable to a changed emphasis from physical to fiscal controls to regulate imports, a policy reiterated in the Long-Term Fiscal Policy of December 1985. However, during the post-liberalisation period, a sharp fall is noticeable in the relative share of customs duties in gross tax revenues of the Central Government. This is due to drastic reductions in the tariff rates across the rate categories including the peak rate in the wake of WTO commitments and to become globally competitive. In the 2008-09 budget the share of customs revenue was estimated at 17.3 per cent (Table 5.3).

Notes

1. Tax collections (or gross tax revenues) of the Central Government are different from its

net tax revenues because a part of the proceeds from taxes is transferred to State Governments under tax sharing arrangements of the Constitution.

2. See Table 2 on page 553 of this book.
3. *Report of the Twelfth Finance Commission* (2005-10), November 2004, p. 31.
4. See Table 2 on page 553 of this book.

6

Trends in State Taxes

From a modest amount of Rs. 222 crore in 1950-51, revenue from States' taxes has grown consistently over the years and was estimated at Rs. 2,56,982 crore in the 2006-07 budgets of the State Governments. The relative significance of State taxes has changed over the years since Independence in 1947. Land revenue, which contributed 22.1 per cent to State taxes in 1950-51, has almost disappeared. In the 2006-07 budgets of the State Governments, the share of land revenue was estimated at 1.3 per cent. Conversely, sales tax, which contributed 26.1 per cent to State taxes in 1950-51, has become the mainstay of State finances. In the 2006-07 budgets of the State Governments, the share of sales tax in State taxes was estimated at 58.8 per cent (Table 6.3). Apart from sales taxes, other important state level taxes are state excise duties, motor vehicle tax, stamp duties and registration fees, entertainment tax, and electricity duties.

6.1 State Taxes as Per Cent of GDP

In 1950-51, state taxes accounted for 2.23 per cent of GDP. This percentage started increasing with every passing decade with the growth of tax bases allocated to the states under the Constitution. The percentage increased to 2.65 in 1960-61, to 3.38 in 1970-71 and to 4.64 in 1980-81. [1]

On the eve of initiation of economic reforms, state taxes accounted for 5.30 per cent of GDP in 1990-91. The percentage fell to a low of 5.12 in 1998-99, owing to tax competition among the States. Of late, the percentage has improved and was estimated at 6.23 in the 2006-07 budgets of the State Governments (Table 6.1). This improvement is chiefly attributed to agreement among the States to implement floor rates of sales tax and to reduce and rationalize various exemptions and concessions.

6.2 Direct and Indirect Taxes

States' own tax revenue has increasingly relied upon indirect taxes during the post-Independence period. The ratio between direct and indirect taxes at the State level dropped from 24.8:75.2 in 1950-51 to 24.2:75.8 in 1960-61, to 9.0:91.0 in 1970-71 and further down to 4.1:95.9 in 1980-81. [2]

During the post-reforms period, the ratio between direct and indirect taxes worsened further. It declined from 4.1:95.9 in 1990-91 to 2.4:97.6 in 2006-07

(Table 6.2). Presently, there is no direct tax of revenue significance at the level of States. This highly unbalanced tax structure is a cause for concern.

Table 6.1: States' Own Taxes as Per Cent of GDP: 1990-91 to 2006-07

(Rs. crore)

Year	States' own taxes	Col. 2 as % of GDP
1	2	3
1990-91	30,145	5.30
1991-92	35,837	5.49
1992-93	39,530	5.28
1993-94	46,219	5.38
1994-95	55,552	5.49
1995-96	64,034	5.39
1996-97	71,294	5.21
1997-98	81,439	5.35
1998-99	89,220	5.12
1999-00	1,02,831	5.25
2000-01	1,16,717	5.54
2001-02	1,27,475	5.59
2002-03	1,40,372	5.73
2003-04	1,59,736	5.79
2004-05	1,89,413	6.06
2005-06	2,25,209	6.31
2006-07	2,56,982	6.23

2005-06 = Revised estimates; 2006-07 = Budget estimates.

Note: The ratios of GDP since 1950-51 are with reference to new series GDP (Base: 1993-94) at current market prices.

Source: Rearranged data from Government of India, Ministry of Finance, *Indian Public Finance Statistics*, 2006-2007, Tables 1.7 and 1.8.

6.2.1 Composition of Direct Taxes: There is no direct tax which can claim a prominent place in the tax systems of the States.

A. Land Revenue: Land revenue (entry 45 in List II in the Seventh Schedule of the Constitution) which formed the bulwark of States' tax revenue during the pre-Independence period and even in the early post-Independence years has declined in importance over the years (Table 6.3). In some States, land revenue has been abolished altogether.

B. Agricultural Income Tax: Agricultural income tax (entry 46 of List II in the Seventh Schedule of the Constitution) which could have been an important source of revenue for the States has remained negligible till date. .

Table 6.2: States' Own Taxes, Breakdown between Direct and Indirect Taxes with Percentage Shares: 1990-91 to 2006-07

(Rs. crore)

Year	States' own taxes (3+4)	Direct taxes	Indirect taxes	Col. 3 as % of Col. 2	Col. 4 as % of Col. 2
1	2	3	4	5	6
1990-91	30,145	1,230	28,915	4.1	95.9
1991-92	35,837	1,304	34,533	3.6	96.4
1992-93	39,530	1,247	38,283	3.2	96.8
1993-94	46,219	1,414	44,805	3.1	96.9
1994-95	55,552	1,905	53,647	3.4	96.6
1995-96	64,034	2,213	61,822	3.5	96.5
1996-97	71,294	2,163	69,131	3.0	97.0
1997-98	81,439	2,256	79,183	2.8	97.2
1998-99	89,220	2,518	86,702	2.8	97.2
1999-00	1,02,831	2,904	99,927	2.8	97.2
2000-01	1,16,717	3,457	1,13,260	2.9	97.1
2001-02	1,27,475	3,911	1,23,564	3.1	96.9
2002-03	1,40,372	4,002	1,36,370	2.8	97.2
2003-04	1,59,736	4,455	1,55,281	2.8	97.2
2004-05	1,89,413	4,910	1,84,503	2.6	97.4
2005-06	2,25,209	5,873	2,19,336	2.6	97.4
2006-07	2,56,982	6,117	2,50,865	2.4	97.6

2005-06 = Revised estimates; 2006-07 = Budget estimates.
Source: Rearranged data from Government of India, Ministry of Finance, *Indian Public Finance Statistics*, 2006-2007, Tables 1.7. Columns 5 and 6 calculations own.

C. Professions Tax: A tax on professions (entry 60 of List II in the Seventh Schedule of the Constitution) is levied as a fixed amount per person per year on professions. It is a kind of licence fee to practice a profession. The tax is levied irrespective of the income derived by a person from the profession practiced by him. The scope of this tax is spelt out in Article 276, the clause (2) of which fixes the amount payable by a person on account of this tax. Presently, the total amount payable in respect of any one person to the State by way of such tax is not to exceed Rs. 2,500 per annum.

6.2.2 Composition of Indirect Taxes:

A. Sales Tax: An outstanding development in the sphere of State finances since Independence has been the precipitous growth in the relative revenue significance of sales tax levied under entry 54 of List II in the Seventh Schedule of the Constitution. It has grown considerably in depth and coverage, and forms the mainstay of States' tax revenue. It is levied not only on consumer goods but also on raw materials and capital goods. In 1950-51, the relative share of sales tax was 26.1 per cent: Rs. 58 crore out of a total collection of Rs. 222 crore from States' taxes. In the budget estimates for 2006-07, this share stood at 58.8 per cent (Table 6.3).

Prior to tax reforms initiated in early 1990s, sales tax was characterised by a multiplicity of tax rate and exemptions, lack of uniformity across States, large number of exemptions and concessions, and differing procedures for tax collection. In mid-1990s, most states had agreed to phase out the incentive related exemptions and implement floor rates of sales tax. As part of the nation wide efforts to redesign commodity taxation and the implementation of CENVAT at the level of the Centre, many States have modified their sales tax regimes to launch a state level VAT under the scheme prepared by the Empowered Committee for this purpose.

B. State Excises: Under entry 51 of List II in the Seventh Schedule of the Constitution, the States are empowered to levy, "duties of excise on (a) alcoholic liquors for human consumption; (b) opium, Indian hemp and other narcotic drugs and narcotics; but not including medicinal and toilet preparations containing alcohol or any substance included in sub-paragraph (b) of this entry". The revenues accrue to the states in the form of licence duties from the vendors as well as the tax, which can be specific or ad valorem.

After sales tax, State excise duties (on liquors and other narcotics) are the most important source of States' own tax. revenues. Though second in importance, their relative revenue significance has declined over the years from 21.6 per cent in 1950-51 to 11.5 per cent in 2006-07 (B.E) [Table 6.3]. This has happened mainly because of the policy of prohibition adopted in some States from time to time. However, it is difficult to totally prohibit the consumption of alcohol in the states. Attempts at full prohibition lead to illegal production and export of the tax base to the neighboring states.

It is noteworthy that while in Western countries the main objective of duties on intoxicants is revenue collection, in India the overriding consideration in imposing these duties is to discourage consumption of intoxicants as a matter of public policy. Since demand for alcoholic beverages is generally price-inelastic, this tax provides a case for keeping high tax rates for controlling the level of consumption. In fact, high tax rates yield both high revenues and greater control on consumption.

Table 6.3: Trends in the Level and Composition of Revenue from States' Own Taxes: Selected Years

(Rs. crore)

State taxes	1950-51	1960-61	1970-71	1980-81	1990-91	2000-01	2006-07#
A+B Revenue from States' taxes	222 (100.0)	455 (100.0)	1,546 (100.0)	6,665 (100.0)	30,145 (100.0)	1,16,717 (100.0)	2,56,982 (100.0)
A. Direct taxes of which	55 (24.8)	110 (24.2)	140 (9.0)	271 (4.1)	1,230 (4.1)	3,457 (3.0)	6,117 (2.4)
1. Land revenue	49 (22.1)	97 (21.3)	113 (7.3)	145 (2.2)	607 (2.0)	1,377 (1.2)	3,332 (1.3)
2. Agricultural income tax	3 (1.3)	10 (2.2)	10 (0.6)	46 (0.7)	169 (0.6)	76 (0.0)	36 (0.0)
3. Other taxes*	3 (1.3)	3 (0.6)	17 (1.1)	80 (1.2)	454 (1.5)	2,004 (1.7)	2,749 (1.1)
B. Indirect taxes of which	167 (75.2)	345 (75.8)	1,406 (91.0)	6,394 (95.9)	28,915 (95.9)	1,13,260 (97.0)	2,50,865 (97.6)
1. Sales tax	58 (26.1)	158 (34.7)	755 (48.8)	3,887 (58.3)	16,476 (54.6)	68,386 (58.6)	1,51,099 (58.8)
2. State excises	48 (21.6)	53 (11.6)	194 (12.5)	824 (12.4)	4,798 (15.9)	15,825 (13.6)	29,668 (11.5)
3. Taxes on vehicles	7 (3.2)	33 (7.2)	104 (6.7)	415 (6.2)	1,535 (5.1)	6,506 (5.6)	13,617 (5.3)
4. Stamps and registration fees	26 (11.7)	43 (9.4)	122 (7.9)	425 (6.4)	2,089 (6.9)	9,343 (8.0)	27,843 (10.8)
5. Other taxes**	28 (12.6)	58 (12.7)	231 (14.9)	843 (12.6)	4,017 (13.3)	13,200 (11.3)	28,638 (11.1)

#Budget estimates.

*Profession tax, surcharge on cash crops and urban immovable property tax.

**Taxes on passengers and goods, electricity duty, entertainment tax and cess on sugarcane etc.

Figures in parentheses indicate corresponding percentages of the total revenue from States' own taxes.

Sources: Reserve Bank of India, *Report on Currency and Finance,* Vol. II, (various years); and Government of India, Ministry of Finance, *Indian Public Finance Statistics*, 2006-2007, Tables 1.7 and 3.2.

C. Taxes on Motor Vehicles: Under entry 57 of List II in the Seventh Schedule, State Governments enjoy the power to levy taxes on vehicles suitable for use on roads. These are levied for registration, permits, driving licences etc. and are based on the type of vehicle (truck, bus, car, scooter etc.). In the 2006-07 budgets, taxes on vehicles accounted for 5.3 per cent of tax revenue from States' own taxes (Table 6.3). In most states a compounded system of motor vehicle tax exists, where a one time levy is paid for the life of the vehicle. This arrangement has saved the taxpayers from the hassle of interacting with the tax department every year.

D. Entertainment Tax: Under entry 62 of List II in the Seventh Schedule of the Constitution, States are empowered to levy taxes on entertainment. Such taxes are levied on the price charged for admission to any place of entertainment such as a circus, cinema, theatre, exhibition, variety show, etc. The bulk of revenue from this tax is provided by the cinema shows. Though the tax is collected from the exhibitors, the ultimate burden is borne by the cinegoers. According to Tenth Five Year Plan (2002-07), "The tax rates in the entertainment industry are among the highest in the world. Though some State Governments are waiving entertainment tax on multiplex theatres for periods ranging from three to ten years, on the whole tax on film theatres continues to be high. Lowering of these rates will not only benefit the entertainment industry, which has an annual turnover of Rs. 400 crore, but will also promote real estate development in the form of theatres in cities, towns and even villages." [3]

In recent times, entertainment tax has lost its importance due to proliferation of means of home-based entertainments.

E. Stamp Duty and Registration Fees: Under entry 63 of List II in the Seventh Schedule of the Constitution, Stamp duty is levied on the registration of property or other conveyances. In the 2006-07 budgets of the State Governments, the share of stamp duty and registration fees in revenue from own taxes of the States was estimated at 10.8 per cent (Table 6.3).

Till recently, the stamp duty rates were quite high in most states and the procedures for evaluating the conveyances were also complicated. In this context, the Tenth Five Year Plan (2002-07) remarked, "Stamp duty needs to be paid on all documents which are registered and the rate varies from state to state. With stamp duty rates of 13 per cent in Delhi, 14.5 per cent in Uttar Pradesh and 12.5 per cent in Haryana, India has perhaps one of the highest levels of stamp duty. Some states even have double stamp incidence, first on land and then on its development. In contrast the maximum rate levied in most developed markets whether in Singapore or Europe is in the range of 1-2 per cent. Even the National Housing and Habitat Policy, 1998, recommended a stamp duty rate of 2-3 per cent. Most of the methods to avoid registration are basically to avoid payment of high stamp duty.

Another fall out of high stamp duty rates is the understatement of the proceeds of a sale. This is also linked to payment of income tax and capital gains tax. When registration has not been effected, a transfer is not deemed to have taken place and hence capital gains tax can be totally avoided. Thus, the present provisions in various laws and their poor implementation have led to a situation where there is considerable financial loss to the exchequer on account of understatement of sale proceeds, non-registration and consequent non-payment of stamp duty and avoidance of capital gains tax." [4]

Of late, states have undertaken reforms by reducing the duty rates and streamlining procedures for evaluation of property. After the reduction of rates, the general experience has been revenue-augmenting due to improved compliance of law.

F. Electricity Duty: Under entry 53 of List II in the Seventh Schedule of the Constitution, the electricity duty is charged to consumers along with the electricity consumption rates. The rates are meant for the providers of electricity (electricity boards) while the electricity duty is meant for the state treasury.

G. Octroi: Octroi, an important source of revenue for local bodies, is a tax on the entry of goods into a local area from other areas for the purpose of consumption or sale. It is mentioned in entry 52 of List II (State List) in the Seventh Schedule. Industry and trade circles have criticised the continuation of octroi and termed it as a retarding factor in the growth of business and commerce in the country. By obstructing the free movement of vehicles carrying goods, the levy of octroi causes delays and thus hampers industrial progress. Therefore, it is suggested that octroi should be replaced by some other form of taxation, e.g. surcharge on sales tax. Unfortunately, State Governments are not favourably disposed to these suggestions and prefer to continue with the controversial levy.

H. Land and Buildings: Under entry 49 of List II in the Seventh Schedule of the Constitution, States are empowered to impose taxes on land and buildings, popularly known as property tax or house tax. State Governments generally assign this tax to municipal bodies.

Property tax is charged by the municipal authorities for the upkeep of basic civic services in the city. Generally, the property tax is levied on the basis of reasonable rent at which the property might be let from year to year. The reasonable rent can be actual rent if it is found to be fair and reasonable. In the case of un-let properties, the rental value is to be estimated on the basis of letting rates in the locality.

6.3 Local Finance

The Constitution does not reserve any taxes for the local bodies. Since local government is a State subject (entry 5 of List II), State Governments may assign any of the taxes in the State List, wholly or partially, to urban local bodies. Taxes usually assigned to local bodies are property taxes, octroi and taxes on professions. Property tax (house tax) is an important source of revenue for local bodies.

Assigning taxes enables State Governments to exercise a degree of supervision and control over the affairs of city corporations, municipalities, district boards, and other local bodies. These local bodies provide certain public services like basic health and education, construction and maintenance of local roads, sanitation, street lighting, and parks. Local governments also receive grants-in-aid from State Governments and earn non-tax revenue from enterprises operated by them.

Notes

1. See Table 5 on page 559 of this book.
2. See Table 5 on page 559 of this book.
3. Government of India, Planning Commission, *Tenth Five Year Plan* (2002-07), Vol. II, p. 835.
4. Ibid., pp. 833-834.

7

Sales Tax and State Level VAT

In India, sales tax in its modern form was levied for the first time by the Government of Central Provinces (now Madhya Pradesh) in 1938. Since then, the levy has proved an outstanding development in the sphere of State finances. It has grown considerably in depth and coverage, and forms the mainstay of States' tax revenue. It is levied not only on consumer goods but also on raw materials and capital goods. In 1950-51, the relative share of sales tax was 26.1 per cent: Rs. 58 crore out of a total collection of Rs. 222 crore from States' taxes. Recording a precipitous growth in relative revenue significance, sales tax was estimated to contribute 58.8 per cent to States' own tax revenues in the 2006-07 budgets of the State Governments (Table 7.1).

Table 7.1: Trends in the Relative Share of Sales Tax in States' Own Taxes: Selected Years

(Rs. crore)

State taxes	1950-51	1960-61	1970-71	1980-81	1990-91	2000-01	2006-07#
A+B Revenue from States' own taxes	222 (100.0)	455 (100.0)	1,546 (100.0)	6,665 (100.0)	30,145 (100.0)	1,16,717 (100.0)	2,56,982 (100.0)
A. Direct taxes	55 (24.8)	110 (24.2)	140 (9.0)	271 (4.1)	1,230 (4.1)	3,457 (3.0)	6,117 (2.4)
B. Indirect taxes of which	167 (75.2)	345 (75.8)	1,406 (91.0)	6,394 (95.9)	28,915 (95.9)	1,13,260 (97.0)	2,50,865 (97.6)
Sales tax	58 (26.1)	158 (34.7)	755 (48.8)	3,887 (58.3)	16,476 (54.6)	68,386 (58.6)	1,51,099 (58.8)

#Budget estimates.
Figures in parentheses indicate corresponding percentages of the total revenue from States' own taxes.
Sources: Reserve Bank of India, *Report on Currency and Finance,* Vol. II, (various years); and Government of India, Ministry of Finance, *Indian Public Finance Statistics*, 2006-2007, Tables 1.7 and 3.2.

7.1 Different Forms of Sales Tax

Sales tax is normally an *ad valorem* levy imposed on the seller with reference to the transaction of sale. On the basis of the stage of collection, sales tax is classified into (a) multi-point sales tax, and (b) single-point sales tax.

7.1.1 Multi-point Sales Tax: As a multi-point levy, sales tax may be applied at two or more stages of production and distribution and becomes akin to a turnover tax applicable at each transaction of purchase and sale. Multi-stage sales tax is politically expedient. A given amount of revenue can be raised at a lower rate of taxation which also reduces the temptation for tax evasion.

The chief demerit of multi-point sales tax is its encouragement to vertical integration of production and distribution processes. Thus, it discriminates against non-integrated firms. Producers of finished products prefer to produce their own materials and components, and this tendency harms the interest of independent suppliers, particularly small ones. Furthermore, multi-point sales tax discriminates against those goods, and their consumers, which have to pass through numerous transactions. In view of these disadvantages, John Due has opined, "On administrative as well as economic and equity grounds the objections to the multi-stage form are so great as to suggest its complete rejection, regardless of circumstances." [1]

7.1.2 Single-point Sales Tax: A single-point sales tax applies to one stage, either at the manufacturing, or the wholesale, or the retail level. At the manufacturing level, sales tax applies to the sale by manufacturer of finished product and is similar to excise duty. At the wholesale level, the tax applies to the last wholesale transaction, i.e. purchase by retailer. The retail sales tax applies to the final sale which means sale to the consumer.

The main advantage of single-point sales tax is that it does not discriminate against non-integrated firms as does multi-point sales tax. It, thus, discourages vertical integration and promotes horizontal integration. As regards the stage of its imposition, the retail stage is considered the most satisfactory due to the following reasons.

1. Sales tax at the retail stage is collected when final sale to the consumer takes place. Thus, it avoids what economists call the cascading or pyramiding effect of a tax. The contention is that middlemen apply fixed percentage mark ups to purchase prices and if the purchase price include taxes (as is the case if sales tax is imposed at manufacturer's, or wholesaler's level), the mark ups will be applicable to the tax component of the purchase prices as well, a situation which must be avoided in the interest of the consumers.
2. A given revenue can be realised by applying a lower tax rate at the retail stage as compared to other stages because the margins of all middlemen are included at the final stage of sale, meaning thereby the enlargement of the tax base at the retail stage.
3. The desired change in the ratio of tax to consumer expenditure can be

achieved more effectively in case of retail-stage sales tax. This will be difficult at 'other stages' because the margins of dealers on various goods, besides being applied to the tax component of the purchase prices, may differ significantly.

4. Sales tax at the retail stage can be shown separately from the price and thus made known to the purchaser, increasing tax consciousness among the taxpayers.
5. Expected changes in the rates of retail sales tax do not lead to changes in inventory position of the firms. Anticipated changes in the rates of sales tax at 'other stages' may influence inventory decisions of the firms causing dislocation in trade circles.

However, retail-stage sales tax has its own problems, the chief being the large number of taxpayers in the form of small shopkeepers and scattered retail outlets. In developing countries, the problem of tax administration is more acute in view of widespread illiteracy, lack of monetisation, and poor accounting practices. From administrative viewpoint, this form of taxation is costlier and cumbersome, offering ample scope for tax evasion and corruption.

Sales tax at manufacturing or wholesale stage is administratively preferable because the number of taxpayers is small and readily identifiable. However, the problem of 'cascading' will reappear. In fact, the farther we move from the retail level, the more serious the problem of 'cascading' becomes. In short, the problem boils down to a trade off between economic rationale and administrative efficiency. The relative weightage to competing objectives depends on political judgement and the economic circumstances under which the sales tax system has to operate.

7.2 Pre-Constitution Developments

Entry 48 of List II in the Seventh Schedule of the Government of India Act, 1935, vested in the Provinces the power to levy 'taxes on the sale of goods and on advertisements'.

The Government of the Central Provinces (now Madhya Pradesh) was the first to take advantage of this provision when it levied a retail sales tax on motor spirit and lubricants in 1938. This so-called 'petrol tax' was a selective sales tax imposed through the Central Provinces and Berar Sales of Motor Spirit and Lubrication Taxation Act, 1938.

In 1939, Madras levied a general multi-point sales tax through the Madras General Sales Tax Act, 1939. The tax levied at the rate of half per cent was ostensibly meant to compensate the loss of revenue resulting from the policy of prohibition.

7.2.1 Initial Legal Hurdles: Since its very inception, sales tax has been a controversial levy embroiled in legal wranglings. Thus, soon after its enactment, the Central Provinces Act referred above was challenged by the Central Government as unconstitutional. It may be recalled that entry 45 of List II in Seventh Schedule of the Government of India Act, 1935 had given the Central Government the power to levy excise on tobacco and other goods manufactured or produced in India. Hence, the Central Government maintained that sales tax on motor spirit and lubricants by Central Provinces was *ultra vires* because the power to levy excise on such products belonged to it (Central Government). Deciding in favour of the Provincial Government, the Federal Court observed that such taxes were in no way connected with the production or manufacture of goods, but were imposed on their sale.

In another legal battle, the Central Government contested the Madras General Sales Tax Act, 1939 referred to above. Being a multi-point sales tax, it covered sales by manufacturers also which was challenged by the Central Government. Once again, the Federal Court decided in favour of the Provincial Government and held that it had the power to tax sales of every kind, including sales by a manufacturer or producer.

The above two judicial pronouncements made it clear that the Provinces were competent to tax sales of any commodity and at any stage. In other words, a clear-cut distinction was drawn between the two, excise to be a tax on the act of production or manufacture, and the sales tax to be a levy on the act of sale.

Initial legal squabblings over, sales tax gained rapid popularity among the Provinces with the beginning of 1940s. Bengal adopted a single-point general sales tax levied at retail level in 1941. In the same year, Punjab introduced a general sales tax broadly based on the multi-point model of Madras. A general sales tax on the lines of single-point system of Bengal was introduced by Bihar in 1944 and by Bombay in 1946. Other Provinces followed suit and by 1948, all of them were operating sales tax in one form or the other with the notable exception of Jammu and Kashmir. This State was the last to introduce sales tax in 1962.

7.2.2 Beggar-my-neighbour Policies: There was no provision in the Government of India Act, 1935, to restrict or prohibit the Provinces from levying sales tax on inter-State transactions. In other words, the Act did not require the Provinces to levy sales tax only on those transactions which exclusively took place in their respective territories.

Taking advantage of this loophole in the Act, almost all the Provincial legislatures enacted sales tax laws which enabled them to tax goods exported from one State to another. These practices led to multiple taxation of the same transaction by different Provinces. As one scholar remarked, "Perhaps, the most important problem relating to sales taxation in the pre-Constitution period was the taxation of inter-State sales. All the Provinces, with the exception of West Bengal, were collecting sales tax on goods being sent to other Provinces and were, in effect, indulging in 'beggar-my-neighbour policies." [2]

In order to sort out these problems and to ensure all-India co-ordination, the Government of India convened a conference of the Finance Ministers of States in October, 1948. At this conference, attempts were made to achieve some degree of uniformity in the taxation of inter-State sales. However, these attempts failed in view of the widespread disagreement among the States. In particular, States which produced important raw materials/ manufactured goods were opposed to changes that would result in the exclusion of inter-State trade from the purview of their sales tax laws. In short, the system of sales tax during the pre-Constitution period was arbitrary and bereft of national considerations.

7.3 Constitution of India and the Provisions for the Regulation of Taxation of Inter-State Sales

The problems relating to taxation of inter-State sales were considered by the Drafting Committee of the Constituent Assembly. It proposed incorporation of provisions in the Constitution restricting the powers of the State Governments in respect of the levy of sales tax in the course of foreign trade, inter-State trade, and on essential commodities. In spite of opposition from some States, these provisions were finally incorporated in the Constitution as Article 286 (described below).

Under entry 54 of List II (State List) in the Seventh Schedule of the Constitution, the States were given the power to levy "a tax on sales or purchases of goods other than newspapers". This provision was quite similar to entry 48 of List II in the Seventh Schedule of the Government of India Act, 1935. However, under the Constitution, the States' power to levy sales tax was subject to a number of restrictions. These restrictions on the sale or purchase of goods as mentioned in Article 286 of the Constitution were the following.

1. No law of a State shall impose a tax on the sale or purchase of goods where such sale or purchase takes place: (a) outside the State, or (b) in the course of import of goods into, or export of goods out of, the territory of India.
2. Except in so far as the Parliament may by law otherwise provide, no law of a State shall impose a tax on the sale or purchase of any goods where such sale or purchase takes place in the course of inter-State trade or commerce.
3. No law made by the legislature of a State imposing a tax on the sale or purchase of any such goods as have been declared by Parliament by law to be essential for the life of the community, shall have effect unless it has been

reserved for the consideration of the President and has received his assent.

In simple words, the States were prevented from taxing the following transactions: 1. Sales or purchases in the course of foreign trade. 2. Sales of goods delivered in another State for consumption purpose. 3. Sales in the course of inter-State trade and commerce. Furthermore, the power of States to levy the tax on commodities declared to be 'essential' by the Parliament was made subject to the prior approval of the President.

7.3.1 Consequences of Constitutional Restrictions on Sales Tax: The first restriction resulted in considerable loss of revenue to States, which were levying sales tax on exports. The main losers in this category were Bombay, Bihar, Madhya Pradesh, Orissa, and Assam. Nevertheless, this was the least controversial provision of Article 286.

The second and third restrictions, the benefits of which applied equally to registered dealers, unregistered dealers, and consumers, led to large scale evasion and avoidance of tax and hence loss of revenue to the States in general. As the Taxation Enquiry Commission, 1953-54, observed, "Traders in one State started to sell direct to unregistered dealers and consumers in another. Similarly, consumers of valuable commodities tried to get these from dealers in another State rather than buy the articles from their local dealers. The practice grew for sales of goods within a State itself to be shown in the books of accounts as having been made to fictitious dealers outside the State and the goods having then been resold by those dealers to consumers within the State. For valuable commodities like motor vehicles, jewellery, watches, etc. this practice became very common. On transactions that could be shown to be in the course of inter-State trade, the 'exporting' State was prohibited under Article 286 from levying the sales tax; and if the goods delivered as a result of these transactions were shown to be received by individual consumers or unregistered dealers neither could any tax be levied on them by the 'importing' State. Thus, many of these transactions escaped sales tax altogether." [3]

The loss of revenue was more for States with single-point system as compared to States having multi-point sales taxation. This was so because the restriction was not applicable to sales in the State prior to the last point of sale for export to another State.

The constitutional restrictions led to uneconomic diversion of trade and production centres. The problems which the constitutional provisions sought to solve got further compounded *albeit* with a different nature. To quote, "The constitutional restrictions on sales taxation greatly increased the scope for evasion. While the problem before the Constitution had been multiple taxation (by different States) on the same act of inter-State sale, the problem after the

Constitution was that inter-State sales frequently escaped taxation altogether." [4]

7.3.2 Essential Goods Act, 1952: As already noted, in addition to the above restrictions, Article 286 also prevented the States from levying tax on sales or purchases of goods declared by the Parliament to be essential for the life of the community, except with the previous assent of the President. For this purpose, the Parliament enacted the Essential Goods (Declaration and Regulation of Tax on Sale or Purchase) Act, 1952, and various commodities were declared as essential including cereals and pulses, fresh and dried fruits, fresh milk, meat, fish, salt, hides and skins, iron and steel, coal, fertilisers, petroleum products, and books.

As to the desirable purpose of the Act, the Taxation Enquiry Commission, 1953-54, noted, "It is obvious that the object of restricting the power of the states to levy a tax on the sale or purchase of 'essential goods' is to achieve some degree of uniformity in the tax burden on those goods, and not necessarily or in all cases to eliminate altogether the sales tax on such goods. When the Bombay Government sought the assent of the President to tax some of the 'essential goods' under their new multi-point tax system, the assent was given on condition that the tax burden on these goods should not in any event exceed the previous tax burden under the single-point system. This seems to indicate that the policy underlying the restriction is one of freezing the existing tax levied on these goods and of ensuring that new proposals to tax them are confined within reasonable limits." [5]

In spite of its desirable objectives, the enactment of the Essential Goods Act, 1952, led to various problems and criticism from some State Governments. Since the legislation was not retrospective, the States which had been levying sales tax on 'essential goods' prior to the passage of the Essential Goods Act, continued to levy the tax. However, those States which sought to levy the tax after the passage of the Act had to obtain the consent of the President. This evoked sharp resentment among the State Governments.

The resentment among the States was further fuelled by the fact that the Central Government itself was levying relatively high rates of excise/customs duties on some of the so-called 'essential goods'.

7.4 Constitution (Sixth Amendment) Act, 1956

In view of the problems arising from constitutional restrictions on the taxation of inter-State sales, the Taxation Enquiry Commission, 1953-54, recommended as follows, "In essence, the sales tax must continue to be a State tax. However, power and responsibility of the State must end and that of the Union begin when the sales tax of one State impinges administratively and fiscally on the consumers of another State. Inter-State sales tax should be the concern of the Union." [6]

Consequently, the Constitution was amended by the Sixth Amendment Act of 1956. Under this Amendment, the Parliament was empowered to impose 'taxes on the sale or purchase of goods other than newspapers, where such sale or purchase takes place in the course of inter-State trade or commerce'. This new provision in the Constitution was made by inserting entry 92A in List I (Union List) in the Seventh Schedule. Simultaneously, entry 54 in List II (State List) was made subject to the provisions of the new entry 92A of List I. Also, Article 269 of the Constitution was amended which added a new clause (1)(g) which permitted taxes on the sale or purchase of goods in the course of inter-State trade to be levied and collected by the Government of India but assigned to the States. [7] Again, clauses (2) and (3) of Article 286 of the unamended Constitution were substituted by new clauses to make it read as follows.

(1) No law of a State shall impose or authorise the imposition of a tax on the sale or purchase of goods where such sale or purchase takes place (a) outside the State, or (b) in the course of import of goods into or export of goods out of the territory of India.

(2) Parliament may by law formulate principles for determining when a sale or purchase of goods takes place in any of the ways mentioned in clause (1).

(3) Any law of a State shall in so far as it imposes or authorises the imposition of a tax on the sale or purchase of goods declared by Parliament by law to be of special importance in inter-State trade or commerce, be subject to such restrictions and conditions in regard to the system of levy, rates and other incidents of the tax as Parliament may by law specify.

The new Article 286(2) gave Parliament the powers to define a sale outside a State. The new Article 286(3) is different from the old 286(3) in the following respect: In the old provision, Parliament had the authority to restrict State taxation of commodities declared by Parliament to be 'essential for the life of the community'. In the new provision, Parliament is empowered to restrict State taxation of goods declared to be of special importance in inter-State trade only. [8]

7.5 Central Sales Tax (CST) Act, 1956

Consequent upon the Constitution (Sixth Amendment) Act, 1956, the Central Sales Tax (CST) Act was passed in 1956. The following three main objectives of the CST Act were stated in the Preamble: 1. To formulate principles for determining when a sale or purchase of goods takes place in the course of inter-State trade or in the course of import into or export from India. 2. To provide for the levy, collection, and distribution of taxes on sale of goods in the course of inter-State trade or commerce. 3. To declare certain goods to be of special importance in inter-State trade and specify the restrictions to which State laws imposing taxes on the sale and purchase of such goods of special importance shall be subject.

7.5.1 Main Provisions of CST Act: The regulations contained in the CST Act provide, *inter alia,* for a degree of uniformity by prescribing a maximum rate of sales tax on certain goods considered important for the whole country. According to Section 3 of the CST Act, a sale or purchase of goods is deemed to take place in the course of inter-State trade if it (a) occasions the movement of goods from one State to another, or (b) is effected by a transfer of documents of title to the goods during their movement from one State to another.

Section 14 of the Act declares certain goods to be of special importance in inter-State trade and commerce. These are: coal, cereals, cotton, cotton yarn, cotton fabrics, crude oil, hides and skins, iron and steel, jute, oilseeds, pulses, rayon and artificial silk fabrics, sugar, tobacco, woollen fabrics. The list of 'declared goods' originally covered by the Act in 1956 was expanded twice, once in 1957 to include textiles, sugar, and tobacco, and again in 1976 to include cereals (like wheat, paddy, rice etc.), crude oil, and pulses.

Section 15 of the Act lays down the rate structure. The rates are different depending upon the classes of goods and the status of the person to whom the goods are sold. Thus, goods are either 'declared goods' (goods of special importance) or 'non-declared goods' while a person may be a registered or a non-registered dealer. Based on these classifications, the rates of sales tax are prescribed by the Central Government though the tax is administered (i.e. assessed, collected and appropriated) by the State Governments by virtue of the powers delegated to them by the Central Government under Article 258(1) of Constitution.

The maximum prescribed rate of sales tax on 'declared goods' inside a State is 2 per cent of the sale price and is not leviable at more than one stage. [9] Thus, although sales tax on intrastate sales is levied by the States, taxation of intrastate sales of 'declared goods' (goods of special importance) is subject to certain restrictions in terms of the nature of the levy (not to be levied at more than one stage) and the rate of tax (not more than 2 per cent).

In the case of inter-State sale of such goods to registered dealers, the rate of tax is the same as applicable to the sale of such goods inside the exporting State. In respect of sale of 'declared goods' to non-registered dealers (including consumers) the CST is chargeable at twice the rate applicable to the same goods inside the State, i.e. 8 per cent. Where 'non-declared' goods are sold in the course of inter-State trade to a registered dealer, the ceiling rate is 4 per cent [10] or the rate applicable to internal sales of the concerned goods, whichever is lower. [11]

However, on inter-State sale of non-declared goods to non-registered dealers, the rate of CST is 10 per cent or the rate applicable to the sale of such goods inside the exporting State, whichever is higher. [12]

The Act further specifies that when a sales tax has been levied inside a State on any declared goods and such goods are sold in the course of inter-State trade, the tax so levied shall be refunded. Provision also exists that goods which are generally and unconditionally exempt from the sales tax within a State will also be exempt from CST in the course of inter-State trade.

7.5.2 Working of CST Act: It is clear as to why some kind of Central control is necessary on sales tax for larger national interest. Had Punjab, and Haryana been free to levy sales tax on foodgrains at will, the people of food deficit States would have suffered. Similarly, uncontrolled imposition of sales tax by West Bengal, and Bihar on iron and steel, and coal would have impeded the growth of engineering industry in Gujarat and Maharashtra.

CST Act authorises a State to tax residents of other States. Lest this power should be misused to export undue tax burden to the other States, the original scheme devised in 1956 kept the rate of CST low at 1 per cent ensuring some reasonable revenue for the exporting States. However, over the years the rate of CST has been raised by stages to 4 per cent. This trend has benefited industrially advanced States (like Maharashtra, Gujarat, Tamil Nadu, and West Bengal) at the cost of industrially backward States. Since manufactures are the main items of inter-State trade, the developed States are able to export a part of their taxation to other States. In effect, it amounts to transfer of financial resources from poorer States to well off States, much against the declared objective of regional balanced development and equitable distribution of resources among the States. Moreover, the high rate of CST hinders the free flow of trade and commerce within the country.

It may be suggested that the rate of CST should be reduced to the original level of 1 per cent to safeguard the interests of poorer States. Furthermore, the Central Government should declare some more inputs as goods of special importance in inter-State trade to restrict the power of the States to tax such goods. However, these suggestions have met with stiff resistance from most State Governments. At the New Delhi Conference of Chief Ministers held on September 16-17, 1980, there was a unanimous opinion that the rate of CST should not be brought down from 4 per cent to 1 per cent. However, it was agreed to constitute a panel of Chief Ministers to consider, *inter alia*, additions to the list of 'declared goods'. The Conference also expressed unanimity over the need for uniform sales tax laws in the country because various variants of the sales tax pose problems for the collecting authorities as well as for the taxpayers. The

Chief Ministers' Conference decided to request the Law Commission to undertake, on a high priority basis, the drafting of a model sales tax law for consideration by the States.

7.6 Additional Duties of Excise (Goods of Special Importance) Act, 1957

Another landmark in the evolution of sales tax in India was the year 1956 when, following a voluntary agreement between the Centre and the States at a meeting of the National Development Council (NDC) held in December, 1956, it was decided to replace sales tax on textiles, tobacco, and sugar by additional duties of excise and to distribute revenues derived therefrom among the States. **For more details, see chapter 11 of this book.**

7.7 Constitution (Forty-sixth Amendment) Act, 1982 and Consignment Tax

Consequent upon the Sixth Amendment of the Constitution, the Central Sales Tax (CST) Act was passed in 1956. Section 14 of the Act declares certain goods to be of special importance in inter-State trade while section 15 of the Act lays down the rate structure.

However, the CST Act left out of its ambit the consignments (or despatches or stock-transfers) from a company to its branch located in a different State. Since no sale is involved, it is called in-house transaction by a company. The loophole has come in handy for unscrupulous parties to evade sales tax by showing virtual sales as consignments from one State to another. By this method, the payment of CST is avoided. Only local sales tax becomes payable. Therefore, through the Constitution (Forty-sixth Amendment) Act, 1982, the Parliament was empowered to levy `taxes on the consignment of goods (whether the consignment is to the person making it or to any other person), where such consignment takes place in the course of inter-State trade or commerce.' This was done by inserting entry 92B in List I of the Seventh Schedule and simultaneously amending Article 269 by inserting sub-clause 269(1)(h). Consignment tax is a levy on inter-State transfer of goods.

Ever since, the States have been pressing the Centre to levy the tax, the net proceeds of which are entirely assignable to States under Article 269. The proposed tax is intended to check avoidance of CST. The Commission on Centre-State Relations, 1988, also impressed upon the Government to "bring in suitable legislation in this regard without further loss of time." [13]

7.7.1 Issues Related to Consignment Tax: Though the necessary legislation is still to be enacted, industrial and commercial circles have expressed grave concern about the deleterious effects of the impending levy. Trade circles maintain that consignments become necessary in view of seasonal fluctuations in the demand for goods as well as frequent transport bottlenecks. Commercial practices like 'branch transfer' or 'transfer on consignment basis' also help manufacturer-supplier to reduce avoidable costs of holding high levels of inventory.

What will be the impact of consignment tax on prices? What should be the rate of tax? Who shall have the exemption powers? How will it affect the location of industries? How will the proceeds of this tax be shared among the States? These are some of the issues to be sorted out.

The impact of the consignment tax on prices will depend on the rate of the new levy and the commodities covered under its ambit. Since the new levy will be in addition to CST leviable at 4 per cent, it is bound to push up prices. To minimise the inflationary potential, the rate of the new levy may preferably be fixed at a low level of 1 per cent. It may be recalled that in 1956 when the CST Act was passed the rate was fixed at 1 per cent. However, over the years the rate of CST has been raised by stages to the present level of 4 per cent. Thus, the rate of proposed consignment tax should be low and pegged to that level through constitutional provisions to avoid frequent hikes as in the case of CST.

Furthermore, to lessen the adverse impact on prices, it is necessary to grant exemptions to items of mass consumption. To achieve this, it would be desirable that the power to grant exemptions from the proposed levy be concurrently enjoyed by the Centre and the States. The concurrent power of exemption would enable the Centre to ensure uniformity of taxation of goods of national importance, particularly those which are subject to the scheme of administered prices.

The levy of consignment tax may encourage lopsided industrial development of the country. Producers in States which are self-sufficient with respect to raw materials and the market for goods manufactured out of them will remain unaffected by the consignment tax. Conversely, the entrepreneurs in States which import raw materials from other States and also market their manufactures in other States will be doubly taxed, once on the raw materials and then on the manufactured goods. Under such circumstances, prospective entrepreneurs would be tempted to opt for self-sufficient States to enjoy price advantage on the final product, negating in the process the national policy of regional balanced development.

As regards the sharing of tax proceeds, it is apparent that producer-States like Maharashtra, and Gujarat would like the proceeds to accrue to the respective States in full. Contrarily, the backward States would prefer to see a higher proportion of the proceeds distributed among the States through the Finance Commission. At a conference of the Chief Ministers held in February 1989, it was agreed that 50 per cent of the proceeds of the consignment tax would be retained by the collecting States and the remaining 50 per cent would flow into a divisible pool from which the amount would be distributed among the States in accordance with the formula devised by the Finance Commission. At the same Conference, the Government announced its decision to introduce a Bill in this regard in the monsoon session of Parliament of that year. Since then nothing has been heard about this legislation.

Sales tax system has already played havoc with internal freedom of industry and trade. Enjoying their constitutional right, different State Governments levy sales tax on a wide range of commodities at different rates with different procedures and rules for its collection. In a scenario like this, the introduction of consignment tax will further confound the existing confusion about commodity taxation at the State level. The imposition of consignment tax would discourage free movement of goods from one State to another. Restricting movement of goods across State borders through tax practices runs counter to the needs of a growing and diversifying economy. Moreover, in view of the current experiment with MODVAT at the Central level to save industry of the cumulative effects of excise duty, the introduction of consignment tax would hinder the process of rationalisation of commodity taxation. Ideally, imposition of consignment tax should be avoided. In case it is unavoidable, a cautious approach is necessary keeping in view the national interest.

7.8 Present Nature of Sales Tax

Under the Constitution, the right to levy sales tax belongs to the State Governments. Each State is, therefore, empowered to collect tax on the sale of goods within its territory according to the rules framed by it. Thus, different State Governments levy sales tax on a wide range of commodities at different rates with diverse procedures and rules for its collection. The Central Government also enters the field in so far as it prescribes the ceiling rate of sales tax on goods in inter-State trade. In the case of three important commodities, viz. textiles, sugar, and tobacco, additional duties of excise are imposed in lieu of sales tax, the proceeds of which are distributed among the States.

Different States have adopted different variants of the sales tax due to a number of reasons including administrative convenience, ad hoc measures to increase tax revenues, and to attract enterprise in their respective areas. Sales tax in a State may take the form of a single point, double-point and/or multi-point levy. However, single-point is the main type of sales tax imposed on most commodities in all States. In most States a significant part of sales tax revenue originates from first-point levy, i.e. at the manufacturer's level. Some States also levy surcharges on sales tax as an ad hoc measures to augment their resources.

The rate structure of sales tax is further complicated in view of different lists of exemptions/concessions, numerous nominal rate categories, and different administrative procedures in each of the States. These variations have caused disparities in the effective rate of sales tax on similar commodities in different States. Agricultural commodities like cereals and pulses are either exempt or bear low rate of sales tax ranging from 2 to 3 per cent. For most commodities, the rate of single-point levy varies between 4 to 8 per cent. However, in the case of luxury items like motor cars, refrigerators, and VCRs, the rate may go up to even 15 per cent in some States. The rate of multi-point levy hovers around 4 per cent.

7.9 Problems Created by Sales Tax

Perhaps no other tax impinges on so large a number of interests as sales tax. Firstly, it hurts the consumers who ultimately bear its burden. Next, there are the dealers from whom it is collected, and in many cases the producers also come in its ambit in case it is levied at the manufacturer's level. Then there are the State Governments, always anxious to extend its scope and retain their hold on it. Furthermore, the Central Government decides the rate of sales tax on goods of special importance in inter-State trade. Consequently, the operation of sales tax creates a host of problems which may be summarised as follows.

1. Sales tax is a levy on commodities which, in most cases, are also subject to excise duties. As excise duty and sales tax are levied by different layers of Government, it becomes difficult to determine judiciously the impact of these levies on production, investment, and the consumers. No attempt to rationalise commodity tax system can succeed if the Centre and 25 States act independently without co-ordination among themselves.

2. A closely related problem is the taxation of inputs and capital goods, by the Central and State Governments, through excise duties and sales tax respectively. Apart from generating cascading effect, sales taxation of inputs benefits the comparatively richer States at the cost of poorer States. To quote, "The (sales) taxation of inputs also means that its burden falls on consumers outside the State. While procedures exist for refund of excise duties on a product when it is exported outside the country, the sales tax paid on inputs is not rebated. In consequence, the more developed States which have attained high levels of agricultural or industrial production are able to derive additional resources, by taxing consumers in other States, while the resource mobilisation capacity of the less developed States, which have to depend on most of their needs being met by imports from other States, is weakened." [14] This reverse flow of funds is further strengthened by the frequent hikes in the rate of Central sales tax.

Originally at 1 per cent, the Central sales tax rate has steadily increased to 4 per cent, thereby imposing undue burden on the importing States and defeating, in the process, the very objective of Central Sales Tax Act of 1956.

To tackle the problem of cascading effect associated with the taxation of intermediate goods, recent reforms at the Central level provide instant credit of excise duty paid on inputs under the MODVAT scheme. Although State laws do provide relief through exemptions in regards to sales tax when inputs are sold to manufacturers, such concessions are limited and lack uniformity. This lacuna in the sales tax system has hindered reform of indirect tax system in India.

3. In order to attract trade and industry to their respective areas, some States have been indulging in a kind of 'rate war' (competitive reductions in sales tax rates). It is true that some States lack infrastructural facilities and to compensate for that sales tax concessions come handy to attract industries, but this shortcut erodes the resource-base of the States, so vital for the development of infrastructure which alone guarantees their speedy development on permanent footing.

Differential rates of sales tax on the same set of commodities in different States often lead to uneconomic diversion of trade as well as production centres. It is not uncommon for people of one State making purchases in other States to avoid or reduce sales tax liability. Apparently, purchases from lower tax States to those where rates are higher are beneficial so long as the cost of transporting goods is lower than the tax differential. Purchase of truck chassis in Daman (a Union Territory levying a low rate of 3 per cent) by the residents of a far off State of Jammu and Kashmir is a popular case in point.

Similarly, rate differentials may cause flight of capital and enterprise from high to low tax rate States thereby distorting natural selection of production centres based on geographical advantages, leading to unnecessary transportation of raw materials and finished goods and hence cost escalations. Such a misallocation of resources undermines economic efficiency and thereby retards developmental efforts.

4. Sales tax has another disadvantage in that it discourages horizontal integration and on the contrary encourages vertical integration in industries. Firms try to produce their own components in order to avoid sales tax. This tendency harms the growth of ancillary units which are mainly in the small-scale sector.

5. Different types of sales tax (multi-point, double-point, and single point) with varying procedures and rules in different States cause difficulties for the traders, particularly small ones, leading to harassment, corruption, and litigation.

7.10 Alternative Remedies

To deal with the foregoing weaknesses of the sales tax system, experts have put forward various suggestions.

7.10.1 Sales Tax as Central Levy: It is argued that through a constitutional amendment, the levy of sales tax can also be made a Central subject and thereafter a rationalised system of indirect taxation of domestic production and consumption can be administered by the Centre. This is a drastic suggestion which has not found favour with statesmen. The Taxation Enquiry Commission (TEC), 1953-54, was quite categorical in rejecting this suggestion. Emphasising the impracticability of centralisation of sales tax the Commission observed, "On account of its yield and flexibility, sales tax has come to occupy a large and indispensable place in the State financial systems. Centralisation of the tax must be ruled out. Difficulties which confront the tax administrations vary considerably in character and composition from State to State and taken together present a large and almost bewildering variety of problems." [15]

The views of the TEC appear to be still valid considering the present fiscal arrangements and political equations. Thus, a constitutional amendment to make sales tax a Central subject has to be ruled out.

7.10.2 Complete Substitution of Sales Tax by Excise Duty: It is suggested, particularly by the business community, that in place of sales tax corresponding enhancements should be made in Central excises the proceeds of which could be earmarked for distribution among the States. This will facilitate rationalisation of commodity taxation and also reduce the cost of collection apart from saving the business community from harassment from the differing sales tax practices of the various States.

Is a complete substitution of sales tax by excise duties possible? Unfortunately not. Like sales tax, excise duties cannot become universal in scope because of administrative reasons. For instance, the Centre has the legal power to impose excises on agricultural products but it has refrained from doing so. Similarly, small and tiny units of the industrial sector are left out because of administrative reasons.

However, what is small for excise duty may be large for the purpose of sales tax. The Indirect Taxation Enquiry Committee, 1977, estimated that nearly Rs. 500 crore of sales tax was being collected on goods not subject to excise duties such as agricultural products, articles of jewellery which for administrative or other reasons cannot be reached by excises. It concluded, "The consequence of a simple abolition of sales tax from the angle of resource mobilisation would be a substantial loss of revenue to compensate for which something like a 50 per cent increase in excise duties on the average would be necessary, given the present base of excise taxation." [16]

Since excise duties are of all-India nature, they cannot take into account regional variations in the levels of income and patterns of consumption. However, different rates of sales tax in individual States permit consideration of regional factors. Moreover, if sales tax is levied at the retail stage, the value base of the tax is large and even low rates of tax can yield sufficient revenues. The cumulative effect is also absent.

7.10.3 Partial Substitution of Sales Tax by Excise Duty: The approach towards substitution of sales tax by excise duties has to be selective. Some arrangements already exist in this regard in the form of additional duties of excise in lieu of sales tax on three important commodities namely textiles, tobacco, and sugar. The extension of this arrangement to certain other commodities as recommended by Tripathi Committee has already been discussed in section 7.6 of this chapter.

7.10.4 Minimum Rate Agreement among States: As already noted, some States have been indulging in a sort of `rate-war' to attract trade and industry to their respective regions. To avoid this unhealthy competition, the Chief Ministers agreed, at their conference in New Delhi on February 9-10, 1989, that all the States would adopt the minimum floor level rates as recommended by the Committee of Sales Tax Commissioners in its report of 1984 in respect of 29 identified items. The follow up action is yet to take place. Even at the regional level, the response is not encouraging. The Chief Secretaries of northern States (Punjab, Haryana, Himachal Pradesh, Rajasthan, Delhi, and Uttar Pradesh) had recommended in May 1994 that there should not only be a uniform rate of sales tax but the slabs of this tax be reduced in these States. The recommendation is still to be implemented. The lack of concern on the part of States to harmonise their sales tax systems is apparent.

7.10.5 Single-Point VAT: To deal with the cascading effects of a traditional turnover tax, some experts have suggested a single-point VAT at the Central level to replace both excise duties and sales taxes. Since sales tax is the most important source of tax revenue for the States, such a drastic suggestion, which will leave the States at the mercy of the Centre, is difficult to implement. Replacement of existing system of excises, sales taxation, and octroi by a comprehensive VAT would require amendment of the Constitution by a two-thirds majority in Parliament and its approval by more than half of the States. A comprehensive VAT at the national level has to be ruled out on economic as well as political considerations.

Switch over to VAT has to be an independent exercise by the Central Government and 25 State Governments. In this connection the Tax Reforms

Committee, 1991, observed, "As regards sales tax, the Committee is of the view that this tax could be converted into a form of State VAT within the manufacturing sector. There may be no need for levying sales tax at more than two rates since the distributional and other non-revenue objectives could be left to be performed by the Central taxes which apply uniformly throughout the country." [17] Even this dual VAT system is difficult to achieve because it is highly unlikely that the 25 States will move in tandem to ensure smooth transition to a uniform system of VAT in place of their differing practices of sales tax. Thus, the problem of co-ordination is not only between the Centre and the States but also among the States themselves.

The introduction and extension of MODVAT scheme at the Central level is a step in the right direction to reform excise taxation. Unfortunately, similar reforms have not been introduced at the level of States. The State Finance Ministers' Conference held in New Delhi on May 27, 1994 failed to arrive at a consensus on the replacement of indirect taxes at the State level by a value added tax. The matter was deferred indefinitely by appointing a ten-member Committee of State Finance Ministers to go into this and related questions.

7.10.6 Agreement of November 1999: At a conference of Chief Ministers and Finance Ministers of the States in New Delhi on November 16, 1999, States and Union Territories decided to put an end to all sales tax-based incentives to industry and enforce floor rates of sales tax with effect from January 1, 2000. They also decided to move over to the simple, transparent and efficient regime of Value Added Tax (VAT) with effect from April 1, 2001.

The agreement to impose a set of minimum rates (floor rates) of sales tax on all commodities will ensure sales tax uniformity throughout the country. Four general floor rates of zero per cent, 4 per cent, 8 per cent and 12 per cent and two special floor rates of 1 per cent and 20 per cent were agreed upon.

Essential commodities such as foodgrains, raw meat, eggs, milk and plain water will be subject to the zero rate. There will be a minimum sales tax rate of 4 per cent on commodities such as edible oils, vanaspati, processed vegetables, kerosene, bicycles, chemicals and fertilisers. Products like electricals, tyres and tubes, butter and ghee, blades and razors, drugs and medicines, cooking gas, tea and coffee, biscuits and computers will attract a floor rate of 8 per cent. Television sets, VCRs, air-conditioners, diesel, paints, telephone equipment and carpets will attract the highest floor rate of 12 per cent.

The 1 per cent special floor rate will apply to bullion, gold and silver while the 20 per cent special floor rate will cover petrol, liquor, rectified spirit and narcotics.

It was also decided at the Conference that a standing committee of State

Finance Ministers will be constituted to oversee the preparations for the switch over to VAT and to review the progress of the implementation of sales tax floor rates in the interim.

The decision to implement these sweeping tax reforms came about after the Union Finance Minister gave an assurance to make good any consequential revenue loss the States may suffer.

The prolonged tax war among the States had strained the finances of several States. The race among the States to lure industries by offering competitive concessions in sales tax is expected to come to an end. If implemented sincerely, these tax reforms at the level of States will go a long way in creating conducive climate for the growth of country's economy, industry and trade.

However, some fiscal experts feel that the floor rates of sales tax fixed are too high and hence unrealistic. Since the floor rates are already high, there is hardly any scope for individual States to determine effective rates above the floor level depending on expectations of growth of industry and trade in each state. Moreover, the high floor rates are contrary to the post-liberalisation policy of low tax rates to ensure better tax compliance. It is also being felt in some quarters that uniformity in tax rates is not necessarily a desirable objective to pursue. In many federations (e.g. USA), state governments compete with each other to attract industry and trade to their respective areas.

7.10.7 Empowered Committee of State Finance Ministers, 2001: At a Conference of Chief Ministers and Finance Ministers of various States held on July 5, 2001 in New Delhi, the report of the Empowered Committee of State Finance Ministers on VAT, headed by West Bengal Finance Minister Asim Kumar Dasgupta, was accepted and adopted for the introduction of VAT with effect from April 1, 2002. The VAT design recommended by the Committee had the following elements.

1. The VAT system will eliminate the cascading burden of taxation by setting off the tax paid on inputs against that on output.
2. It will reduce distortions in the economy caused by double taxation.
3. It will end market fragmentation with a uniform regime of taxation followed in all the States.
4. There will be one category of tax-exempted commodities for all the States.
5. There will be two VAT rates: a uniform 4 per cent for all States on goods of basic necessities and a uniform floor rate of 10 per cent for other commodities (except a few items such as bullion and liquar).
6. A uniform set of procedures for VAT assessment will also be followed by all the States, including the use of Permanent Account Number (PAN) as a common business identifier.

7. The States which do not implement 100 per cent uniform floor rates of sales tax by July-end 2001 should be penalised by discontinuing Central Government assistance.
8. The Centre has undertaken to make good any revenue loss to States on their switch over to VAT. A committee of State Finance Secretaries would evolve clear and measurable criteria for judging revenue loss, if any, due to the introduction of VAT. It will also recommend the manner and quantum of compensation.

As many as 12 States have agreed to implement VAT by April 1, 2002.

However, the road to the Indian common market seems to be dotted with hurdles. Many fear that VAT, as worked out by the Empowered Committee of the State Finance Ministers, would make the Indian market place chaotic and confusing. There are many issues which must be resolved to smoothen the transition to the modern and efficient system of VAT.

1. The uniform floor rate of 10 per cent does not ensure that States would not charge various higher rates on the same commodity. There should be a cap rate of tax.
2. It is not sure whether the classification of goods into the zero rate VAT and the 4 per cent VAT would be done on a scientific basis.
3. It is not clear what treatment would be given to inter-State trade. The biggest concern of industry and trade is the non-eligibility for set-off of CST paid on inputs sourced from across the State border.
4. The fate of exemptions/concessions being enjoyed by various industries under the sales tax system is uncertain when switch over to VAT takes place. By its very nature, VAT cannot be successfully implemented if there are too many exemptions and concessions.
5. A few States have not yet fully implemented even the uniform floor rates of sales tax.
6. From the Government side also, the promised amendment to the Central Sales Tax Act is still to be carried out. Moreover, it is not clear whether changes in CST would coincide with the transition to VAT or not. To reduce distortions, the business circles would like the CST (levied at 4 per cent) to be abolished in one go rather than phased out.

The benefits of VAT at the State level can be achieved fully only when all the States comply with the recommendations of the Empowered Committee. If all the States move towards a uniform VAT system, it would be an example of cooperative federalism. The introduction of VAT in place of the existing sales tax system would make the common market dream a reality.

7.10.8 Agreement of January 23, 2002: At the Conference of State Finance

Ministers held on January 23, 2002 a final decision was taken that all States and Union Territories would introduce VAT from April 2003. This position was reiterated by all States at the Conference of State Chief Ministers held on October 18, 2002. Empowered Committee of State Finance Ministers endorsed the suggestion that every State Legislation on VAT should have a minimum set of common features. Accordingly, a model VAT Bill was circulated to all the States. Introduction of VAT is expected to increase revenue buoyancy, as the coverage expands to value addition at all stages of production and distribution chain.

Again, at a meeting of the Finance Ministers of all States/Union Territories on January 17, 2003, States and Union Territories again reiterated their firm commitment to introduce VAT from April 1, 2003. It was decided that the VAT legislations of all States and UTs would have common provisions in respect of all important matters and that a simple VAT legislation with maximum convergence would be implemented. It was also agreed that along with the introduction of VAT, the origin based Central Sales Tax would be phased out. It was also agreed that the Additional Duties of Excise (Goods of Special Importance) Act would be suitably amended to empower States to levy sales tax/VAT on sugar, textiles and tobacco with a ceiling rate of 4 per cent. This would be done without affecting the existing levy of Additional Duties of Excise on these items by the Union Government

In view of the apprehensions expressed by a large number of States about possible revenue losses in the initial years of introduction of VAT, an assurance was given to the States that the Government of India would compensate the States to the extent of 100 per cent of revenue loss in the first year (2002-03), 75 per cent of the loss in the second year (2003-04) and 50 per cent of the loss in the third year (2005-06).

The Empowered Committee of State Finance Ministers agreed upon the following sequence of steps to ensure introduction of VAT in place of retail sales tax system in States.

1. Passing of VAT legislation and framing of rules and regulations.
2. Computerisation of dealers who will fall within the ambit of VAT.
3. Training of tax officials, traders and consumer associations.
4. Publicity for consumers.
5. Implementation of VAT, assigning VAT identification numbers to tax payers.
6. Implementing transitional measures for introduction of VAT.

7.10.9 Task Force on Indirect Taxes, 2002: The Task Force on Indirect Taxes (Chairman: Vijay Kelkar), unanimously acknowledged that VAT is a major reform in the indirect tax system of India. For a smooth and speedy implementation of VAT at the level of Centre and States, it made the following recommendations.

1. A publicity awareness programme should be started jointly by the Central and State Governments and the former should extend financial support for this, if required. Since State VAT is expected to be implemented from 1.4.2003 it is also necessary that the publicity awareness programme should be implemented at the earliest.
2. An attempt should be made towards uniformity of all State legislations, procedures and documentation relating to VAT.
3. The issue of compensation, if it arises, must be primarily tackled through mutually acceptable mechanism of additional resource mobilization through service tax and not through budgetary support.
4. With the introduction of VAT, all other local taxes be discontinued.
5. Whereas additional duty of excise may continue for textiles up to 2005, it may continue even thereafter for cigarettes which should not be subjected to VAT.
6. The VAT scheme should provide for grant of credit of duty by the importing State for the duty paid in the exporting State, in the course of inter-State movement of goods.

For the stability and continuity of VAT, the possibility of a VAT Council or a permanent suitable alternative, vested with adequate powers to take steps against discriminatory taxes and practices and eliminate barriers to free flow of trade and commerce across the country, should be explored

7.10.10 Agreement of June 2004: At a meeting of the State Finance Ministers with the Union Finance Minister on June 18, 2004, it was decided that all States will introduce a uniform VAT from April 1, 2005. The proposed VAT will replace the taxes levied by different States like sales tax and octroi. Coinciding with the introduction of VAT, the Central Government will bring down the Central Sales Tax (CST) rate from 4 per cent to 2 per cent. The CST will be phased out in 2006-07. It was also decided that traders with an annual turnover up to Rs. 5 lakh will be exempt from VAT. This decision was aimed at ending traders' opposition to VAT. It may be recalled that States have missed at least five deadlines for the introduction of VAT, mainly due to resistance from trading community.

7.10.11 Salient Features of the State-level VAT Design: VAT is essentially a federal or central tax, while in India it is aimed at replacing State as well as Central sales taxes. Its effective implementation depends almost entirely on the co-operation of the State Governments. In an ideal situation, VAT is supposed to be a tax to end all taxes. Many countries that have adopted VAT do not levy excise duty, entry tax or luxury tax. However, State Governments in India are demanding the right to retain and, in fact, widen the tax net by levying a range of taxes, including entry tax. This would defeat the basic purpose of the imposition of VAT, namely unifying and harmonizing the complex commodity tax structure in the country.

A VAT regime is theoretically meant for a unified market in which the VAT levied can always be set off against taxes already paid, irrespective of the state-wise location of the manufacturing or trading entities. In India, these inter-state adjustments are proving to be difficult to implement in view of the existing constitutional provisions regarding distribution of taxation powers between the Centre and the States. It needs, however, to be emphasised that the States must think in terms of economic development of the country as a whole and encourage the free flow of trade and commerce in the economy. A national approach is necessary to harmonise and rationalise the existing system of commodity taxation.

In view of the above constraints and also to provide some flexibility to the States, the Empowered Committee, through its deliberations over the years, finalised a design of VAT to be adopted by the States. The model design seeks to retain the essential features of VAT, while at the same time, providing a measure of flexibility to the States, to enable them to meet their local requirements. The main features of the VAT design finalised by the Empowered Committee are the following:

1. Rates of VAT on various commodities shall be uniform for all the States/UTs. There are 2 basic rates of 4 per cent and 12.5 per cent, besides an exempt category and a special rate of 1 per cent for a few selected items. The items of basic necessities have been put in the zero-rate bracket or the exempted schedule. Gold, silver and precious stones have been put in the 1 per cent schedule. There is also a category with 20 per cent floor rate of tax, but the commodities listed in this schedule are not eligible for input tax rebate/set off. This category covers items like motor spirit (petrol), diesel, aviation turbine fuel, and liquor.
2. Model VAT design makes provision for eliminating the multiplicity of taxes. In fact, all the State taxes on purchase or sale of goods (excluding entry tax in lieu of octroi) are required to be subsumed in VAT.
3. Provision has been made for allowing input tax credit, which is the basic feature of VAT. However, since the VAT being implemented is intra-State VAT only and does not cover inter-State sale transactions, input tax credit will not be available on inter-State purchases.
4. There are provisions to make the system more business-friendly. For instance, there is provision for self-assessment by the dealers. Similarly, there is

provision of a threshold limit for registration of dealers in terms of annual turnover of Rs. 5 lakh. Dealers with turnover lower than this threshold limit are not required to obtain registration under VAT and are exempt from payment of VAT. There is also provision for composition of tax liability up to annual turnover limit of Rs. 50 lakh.

5. Regarding the industrial incentives, the States have been allowed to continue with the existing incentives, without breaking the VAT chain. However, no fresh sales tax/VAT-based incentives are permitted.
6. Exports will be zero-rated, with credit given for all taxes on inputs/purchases related to such exports.

7.10.12 Progress of VAT Implementation: According to *Economic Survey,* 2006-07, "VAT has been introduced by 30 States/UTs so far. Tamil Nadu has implemented VAT from January 1, 2007. The union territory of Puducherry has communicated its decision to implement VAT from April 1, 2007. Uttar Pradesh has not yet taken any decision in this regard. Since Sales Tax/VAT is a State subject, the Central Government has played the role of a facilitator. A compensation formula has also been finalised in consultation with the States, for providing compensation, during 2005-06, 2006-07 and 2007-08, for any losses on account of introduction of VAT and compensation is being released according to this formula. Technical and financial support has also been provided to the States for VAT computerisation, publicity and awareness and other related aspects. [18]

Broadly speaking, the experience of implementing VAT has been quite encouraging. The new system has been received well by all the stakeholders, and the transition has been quite smooth with the Empowered Committee constantly reviewing the progress of implementation. The EC has advised the States to constantly interact with trade and industry to remove their apprehensions, if any, and to ensure that the benefits of VAT due to input tax credit and reduction in tax rates (wherever applicable) are passed on to the consumers. The EC is also persuading the remaining States/UTs to implement VAT at the earliest.

7.10.13 Towards National Goods and Services Tax (GST): The strategy of the Government in respect of indirect taxes is to continue the tariff reform process towards mean ASEAN levels of customs tariff, convergence towards CENVAT rate for excise duty, widening of service tax base and phased move towards a fully integrated goods and services tax by April 1, 2010. In his 2006-07 budget speech, the Union Finance Minister observed, "It is my sense that there is a large consensus that the country should move towards a national level Goods and Services Tax (GST) that should be shared between the Centre and the States. I propose that we set April 1, 2010 as the date for introducing GST. World over, goods and services attract the same rate of tax. That is the foundation of a GST.

People must get used to the idea of a GST." [19]

In pursuance of the above policy, the Union Cabinet decided on February 22, 2007 to reduce Central sales tax (CST) by one percentage point from April 1, 2007. By reducing CST by one percentage point every year, the Government intends to phase out CST completely by the year 2010-11 to enable it to implement the uniform goods and services tax regime. The move is designed for the success of value added tax to facilitate the process of developing a national common market. In other words, the objective is to ensure that the Centre and all the States have a uniform rate of tax on goods and services. It is clear that the CST, being an origin-based and non-rebatable tax, is inconsistent with the concept of VAT and needs to be phased out.

The Centre will compensate the States for the loss of revenue arising from the phasing out of CST.

Notes

1. John F. Due, *The Problems of Tax Administration in Latin America* (Baltimore: The John Hopkins Press, 1959), p. 417.

2. Walter Mahler, *Sales and Excise Taxation in India* (New Delhi: Orient Longman Ltd., 1970), p. 151.

3. Government of India, Ministry of Finance, *Report of the Taxation Enquiry Commission, 1953-54* (Chairman: John Matthai), Vol. III, p. 26.

4. Walter Mahler, *op. cit.*, p. 154.

5. *Report of the Taxation Enquiry Commission,* 1953-54, Vol. III, *op. cit.*, p. 30.

6. *Ibid.*, p. 519.

7. Under Article 258(1), the Union has the power to delegate to any State Government any of its executive functions (including the power to assess and collect sales tax on inter-State trade). Thus, the power to levy and collect sales tax on inter-State trade belongs to the Centre [Article 269(1)(g)] though it has delegated the power to collect it to the States.

8. Clause (3) of Article 286 was further amended by the Constitution (Forty-sixth Amendment) Act, 1982. In its present form it is as follows.

Any law of a State shall in so far as it imposes, or authorises the imposition of

(a) a tax on the sale or purchase of goods declared by Parliament by law to be of special importance in inter-State trade or commerce; or

(b) a tax on the sale or purchase of goods, being a tax of the nature referred to in sub-clause (b), sub-clause (c) or sub-clause (d) of clause (29-A) of Article 366, be subject to such restrictions and conditions in regard to the system of levy, rates and other incidents of the tax as Parliament may by law specify.

9. In 1956, when the Central Sales Tax Act was passed the rate was fixed at 1 per cent. Subsequently, it was raised to 2 per cent, 3 per cent, and 4 per cent in 1958, 1966, and 1975 respectively. It was reduced to 3 per cent and 2 per cent in 2007 and 2008 respectively.

10. Originally, the rate was fixed at 1 per cent in 1956. It was raised to 2 per cent, 3 per cent, and 4 per cent in 1963, 1966, and 1975 respectively.

11. It means the States are free to fix the rate of sales tax on the internal sales of non-declared goods but there is a ceiling rate of 4 per cent on the sale of such goods in inter-State trade. For

example, if the rate of sales tax on internal sale is 6 per cent, it will be 4 per cent for inter-State trade, being lower of the two.

12. In other words, the rate of CST is a minimum of 10 per cent. For example, if general sales tax is charged at the rate of 5 per cent on the sale of colour television in a State, the rate of CST on the same will be 10 per cent, being higher of the two rates. In 1956, the minimum rate was fixed at 7 per cent but was raised to 10 per cent by the Central Sales Tax (Amendment) Act, 1963.

13. Government of India, *Report of the Commission on Centre-State Relations* (Chairman: Justice R.S. Sarkaria), 1988, Part I, p. 293.

14. Government of India, Ministry of Finance, *Report of the Indirect Taxation Enquiry Committee* (Chairman: L.K. Jha), 1977, Part I, p. 50.

15. *Report of the Taxation Enquiry Commission,* 1953-54, Vol. III, *op. cit.*, p. 519.

16. *Report of the Indirect Taxation Enquiry Committee,* 1977, Part I, *op. cit.*, p. 49.

17. Government of India, Ministry of Finance, *Tax Reforms Committee - Final Report*, Part I (Chairman: Raja Chelliah), August 1992, p. 174.

18. Government of India, *Economic Survey,* 2006-07, p. 46.

19. Government of India, Ministry of Finance, *Budget Speech of the Finance Minister,* 2006-07, Part B, p. 26.

8

Taxation of Agricultural Income

When income tax was introduced in India in 1860, agricultural income was also subject to taxation. However, the Income Tax Act, 1886, defined agricultural income and exempted it from the purview of income tax law and this arrangement continued till the enactment of the Government of India Act, 1935. The Act of 1935, segregated agricultural and non-agricultural incomes and provided, for the first time, a separate provincial levy on agricultural incomes.

8.1 Constitutional Provisions

The Constitution retained the distinction between the two types of income and allocated the power to tax agricultural incomes to the States. [1] Entry 82 of List I (Union List) in the Seventh Schedule of the Constitution empowers the Parliament to levy 'taxes on income other than agricultural income.' The State Governments enjoy exclusive powers to make laws with respect to taxes on agricultural incomes vide entry 46 of List II (State List) in the Seventh Schedule. Although exempt from Central income tax, agricultural incomes are taken into account for the limited purpose of determining the rate of tax on non-agricultural incomes in certain cases from the assessment year 1974-75.

Presently, about half a dozen States levy agricultural income tax, in three of them it is confined to plantation crops, and in all cases the revenue is meagre. The share of this tax in the total revenue from States' taxes is negligible (Table 8.1). Thus, agricultural income tax, which could have been a dependable source of revenue for the States, has remained largely untapped so far. Moreover, land revenue which formed the mainstay of States' tax revenue during pre-Independence years and even in the early post-Independence period, has receded into insignificance over the years (Table 8.1).

8.2 Committee on Taxation of Agricultural Wealth and Income, 1972

The Taxation Enquiry Commission, 1953-54, had suggested the taxation of agricultural income by all States on equity considerations. A more comprehensive examination of the question of direct taxation of agriculture was undertaken by the Committee on Taxation of Agricultural Wealth and Income (Chairman: K.N. Raj). [2] Appointed in February 1972 by the Government of India, the Committee was required, under the terms of reference, to suggest methods by which direct taxation of agricultural wealth and income could be used more effectively for raising additional resources for development. It was further asked to recommend specifically ways and means by which taxation of agricultural wealth and income could be used to reduce economic disparities and promote more efficient utilisation of the available land and labour resources. The Committee submitted its report in October 1972.

Table 8.1: Trends in the Relative Shares of Land Revenue and Agricultural Income Tax in States' Own Taxes: Selected Years

(Rs. crore)

State taxes	1950-51	1960-61	1970-71	1980-81	1990-91	2000-01	2006-07#
A+B Revenue from States' own taxes	222 (100.0)	455 (100.0)	1,546 (100.0)	6,665 (100.0)	30,145 (100.0)	1,16,717 (100.0)	2,56,982 (100.0)
A. Direct taxes of which	55 (24.8)	110 (24.2)	140 (9.0)	271 (4.1)	1,230 (4.1)	3,457 (3.0)	6,117 (2.4)
1. Land revenue	49 (22.1)	97 (21.3)	113 (7.3)	145 (2.2)	607 (2.0)	1,377 (1.2)	3,332 (1.3)
2. Agricultural income tax	3 (1.3)	10 (2.2)	10 (0.6)	46 (0.7)	169 (0.6)	76 (0.0)	36 (0.0)
3. Other taxes*	3 (1.3)	3 (0.6)	17 (1.1)	80 (1.2)	454 (1.5)	2,004 (1.7)	2,749 (1.1)
B. Indirect taxes	167 (75.2)	345 (75.8)	1,406 (91.0)	6,394 (95.9)	28,915 (95.9)	1,13,260 (97.0)	2,50,865 (97.6)

#Budget estimates.
*Profession tax, surcharge on cash crops and urban immovable property tax.
Figures in parentheses indicate corresponding percentages of the total revenue from States' own taxes.

Sources: Reserve Bank of India, *Report on Currency and Finance,* Vol. II, (various years); and Government of India, Ministry of Finance, *Indian Public Finance Statistics*, 2006-2007, Tables 1.7 and 3.2.

The Committee disfavoured, on practical considerations, a full-scale coverage of agricultural incomes under the Central income tax. However, it suggested partial integration of agricultural incomes with non-agricultural incomes for the limited purpose of determining the rates of taxation. It also maintained that the additional revenue realised as a result of the partial integration of agricultural with non-agricultural income in the above manner, should go entirely to the State of origin of the agricultural income so aggregated. Consequently, from the assessment year 1974-75, Central income tax takes into account the income of an assessee from agriculture for the limited purpose of determining the rate of tax on non-agricultural incomes in certain cases.

Although averse to the idea of full integration of agricultural and non-agricultural incomes for income tax purposes, the Committee favoured the possibility, with certain cautions, of integrated taxation of agricultural and non-agricultural wealth. While the power to tax agricultural income belongs exclusively to the States, there is no constitutional impediment to an integrated taxation of agricultural and non-agricultural wealth by the Centre.

As its main recommendation, the Committee suggested the imposition of Agricultural Holding Tax (AHT) which in its view would secure for the States an additional revenue from well-off sections of agriculturists with much less harassment of the assessees than is likely if Central income tax is extended to the farm sector. The Committee accepted the view that the incidence of direct taxation should broadly be the same on comparable income and wealth groups irrespective of the sources and the forms in which wealth is held. In devising a system of direct taxation of agriculture, it is necessary to ensure progressivity, a principle that has not governed the land revenue. The Committee emphasised that for purposes of direct taxation, the family should be the basic unit of assessment so as to prevent large-scale avoidance.

For a rational system of direct taxation of agriculture, the Committee laid down the following criteria: 1. It should take account of the difference in productivity of land depending upon the particular crops grown in a region. 2. Its incidence should be uniform in different parts of the country. 3. It should reflect changes in productivity and prices over a period of time. 4. It should be possible to build into the tax an element of progression. As for differences in productivity of land, the Committee pinpointed the following factors: (a) soil-climatic differences, (b) conditions of water supply, and (c) crops grown.

Taking into account various factors which cause variations in the productivity of land, the Committee recommended a scheme of Agricultural Holding Tax (AHT) with the following salient features.

1. The country should be divided into a sufficiently large number of soil-climatically homogenous districts/tracts so that differences having any significant influence on productivity are taken into account.
2. For each such district/tract norms of output of different crops per hectare for each year should be worked out on the basis of estimates of yield for the previous 10 years and these should be valued at the relevant average harvest prices of the preceding three years.

3. From the value of the gross output of the crops arrived at in the above manner, allowance should be made for the paid out costs of cultivation (40 to 50 per cent of the value of gross output) and also for depreciation of assets.
4. The norms arrived at in the above manner would form the rateable value of a hectare of land growing different crops in different districts/ tracts.
5. To provide for the costs of development, the Committee suggested granting of development allowance to all agricultural holdings at the rate of 20 per cent of the rateable value subject to a maximum of Rs. 1,000.
6. To determine the actual tax liability under AHT, the Committee devised a simple formula to be applied to the rateable value of the holdings minus the development allowance. If the rateable value of a holding (minus the development allowance) is 'X' thousand rupees, the AHT should form X/2 per cent of this amount. For example, if the rateable value of a holding is Rs. 10,000, the AHT would be 9/2 or 4.5 per cent of Rs. 9,000 (i.e. Rs. 10,000 minus Rs. 1,000 deductible as development allowance) which is equal to Rs. 405.
7. As the incidence of AHT decreases progressively on small holdings, the Committee favoured the application of the formula to rateable value up to Rs. 600. For holdings of rateable value below Rs. 600, the AHT may be fixed at a flat rate of Re. 1 per holding.

Although the recommendations of the Committee were widely welcomed, it is unfortunate that the State Governments have generally remained lukewarm in taxing agriculture directly. Exemption of agricultural income from taxation deprives the States of a potential source of revenue. Emphasising the need for taxing agricultural sector, the Sixth Five Year Plan noted, "Direct taxes on agriculture at present constitute less than 1 per cent of the total agricultural income. Land revenue, which is the principal direct tax on agriculture, is generally a flat rate levy and, consequently, regressive in character. Fixation of minimum support and procurement prices for major agricultural crops and provision of various inputs such as fertilisers, irrigation, and electricity at subsidised or concessional rates have helped raise agricultural incomes particularly of large farmers. It is, therefore, necessary to consider measures for raising additional resources from the agricultural sector and introducing a measure of progressivity in agricultural taxation." [3]

The near absence of direct taxation of the agricultural sector is partly due to the preponderance of big landlords and other vested interests in State legislatures. It shows how the rural rich have effectively resisted additional tax burden upon themselves. The absence or inadequacy of tax on agricultural incomes is an example of the insufficient use of taxation powers allotted to the States.

Moreover, the exclusion of agricultural incomes from the income tax base provides opportunities for tax evasion by camouflaging taxable income and black money as gains from agriculture. It is not uncommon among the urban elite to own agricultural farms on the outskirts of metropolitan cities for the sole purpose of diverting their high non-agricultural incomes from a taxable zone to a tax haven. The unequal tax treatment of similar incomes, though from different sources, violates the principle of horizontal equity.

8.2.1 Views of the State Governments: The States, on their part, have highlighted serious problems in the assessment of agricultural incomes. These include shrinkage of the tax base due to the ceiling on holdings, widely dispersed potential assessees, fluctuations in production due to uncertain weather conditions, and lack of accounting practices in the agricultural sector. Although disinterested in levying tax on agricultural incomes, States have also expressed themselves against any move to transfer the tax to the Union List. More interestingly, the Centre too is not enthusiastic to adopt the tax as was made clear in the Long Term Fiscal Policy, "It is often stated that exclusion of agricultural income is a major shortcoming of the personal income tax base in India and constitutes an important explanation for the weak revenue-raising capacity of the personal income tax. Taxing agricultural income presents many conceptual and administrative problems. Land revenue and taxation of agricultural income are State subjects under the Constitution. The Centre has no intention of seeking any change in this position." [4] For proper assessment of agricultural incomes, some knowledge of local conditions is required and so the primary responsibility of administering agricultural income tax should preferably be left to the States. Therefore, the taxation of agricultural incomes continues to remain a doubly neglected child of the Indian tax system.

It is well-known that since Independence, agriculture has remained the focus of developmental efforts in terms of irrigation facilities, availability of better quality seeds, subsidised fertilisers and electricity, credit and marketing facilities, and support prices for the main crops. The success of green revolution in many parts of the country is reflected in the increased productivity per hectare of various crops, and in the total production of foodgrains.

It is also a known fact that the benefits of green revolution are unevenly distributed, creating an affluent elite group in rural areas. It is this class which must pay its due to the national exchequer, and revenue so raised may be earmarked for ameliorating the economic conditions of the downtrodden in villages. The States must exercise their constitutional power and tax the upper income agriculturists.

8.3 Tax Reforms Committee, 1991

The Tax Reforms Committee (Chairman: Raja Chelliah), 1991, recommended that agricultural income above Rs. 25,000 accruing to non-agriculturist assessees should be brought under the tax net. To quote, "the provisions for the taxation of agricultural income by the Central Government that we have recommended would not affect those agriculturists who (a) have agricultural income not exceeding Rs. 25,000 per year; or (b) have non-agricultural income not exceeding Rs. 28,000. This means that agriculturists who have only agricultural income or who have also non-agricultural income but have agricultural income not exceeding Rs. 25,000 will be left out. Thus, the tax will fall mainly on the larger non-agricultural assessees whose agricultural incomes exceed Rs. 25,000." [5] The Committee suggested that the tax proceeds attributable to the agricultural component of income should be distributed in their entirety among the States on the basis of origin.

In terms of the recommendations of the Committee, a person having agricultural income say of Rs. 26,000 and non-agricultural income of Rs. 36,000 (above the then existing exemption limit of Rs. 35,000) pays tax on both the incomes while another person having agricultural income of say Rs. 3 lakh (or even more) and non-agricultural income of Rs. 34,000 has no tax liability on any of his income. Such an arrangement will hardly stand the test of equity. True, the entire tax yield attributable to the agricultural component of income is to be distributed among the States on the basis of origin, there is the need for obtaining the consent of State Governments for making a Central provision for such a tax. It can be a lengthy and uncertain process.

8.4 Task Force on Direct Taxes, 2002

The Task Force on Direct Taxes (Chairman: Vijay Kelkar) suggested the taxation of agricultural income in its report presented to the Government. [6] It recommended a tax rental arrangement between the Centre and the States (under Article 252 of the Constitution) authorising the Centre to impose a tax on agricultural incomes, the proceeds of which will be assigned to the States. The main argument for the proposal is the shifting of non-agricultural income to agricultural income by some unscrupulous assessees.

8.4.1 Critical Comments: The proposal needs to be examined from the following three different, though related, angles: economic logic, administrative feasibility, and political expediency. The case for taxing agricultural income is weak on all the three counts.

From the economic viewpoint, agriculture in India, for most farmers, is not a business as is the case in the United States, Canada, Australia, New Zealand and some other developed Western countries. It is essentially subsistence farming for the large majority of Indian farmers. This is borne out by the niggardly land-man ratio (0.33 hectare) and the utterly small average size of farms (1.6 hectares). With land availability remaining the same, the two ratios are expected to fall further in view of the increasing population. There is hardly any surplus for the tax collector.

Also, agriculture is gradually losing its shine as the leading sector of the Indian economy. A quarter of a century ago, it contributed around 50 per cent to India's national income. Presently, the figure stands at 27 per cent. Hence, agriculture is a receding economic activity, at least in relative terms. Conversely, the services sector has emerged as the dominant field of activity, accounting for 47 per cent share in national income. Tax collectors would do well if they concentrate on sunrise rather than sunset sectors.

The Kelkar Committee has taken the view that tax exemption of agricultural income violates the principle of horizontal equity (equal treatment of equals). This view is based on the erroneous assumption that incomes from various sources are alike. In fact, the amount of toil and suffering associated with an earning differs from case to case. Thus, it would be imprudent to treat alike Rs. 1 lakh earned by a property dealer in one transaction and Rs. 1 lakh earned by a farmer through year-long exertion and uncertainty. Income tax laws of various countries recognise this fact and accordingly treat different sources of income differently for tax purposes (called the schedular system of taxation). For example, in the United States the law distinguishes between earned and unearned incomes to provide tax credit (rebate) to earned income. Even in India, the distinction between earned and unearned incomes, introduced in 1945, continued for a long time before it was abolished from April 1, 1968. The present law of income tax does recognise and tax different sources of income differently, though to a limited extent. Thus, long-term capital gains enjoy special concessions including inflation indexing and a flat rate tax of 20 per cent. Till 1990-91, the differentiation principle was followed in the case of company taxation when trading and investment companies were subject to a higher flat rate tax (50 per cent) than industrial and other companies (45 per cent).

It is true, as pointed out by the Kelkar Committee, that some dishonest assessees do report their non-agricultural income as agricultural income to evade taxation. However, this is by no means a general practice and it would be unwise to punish the Indian farming community at large for the misdeeds of a few tax dodgers. Moreover, if such cases of fraud come to the notice of assessing officers, the culprits can be proceeded against under the existing anti-evasion laws. Showing non-agricultural income as agricultural income is simply a case of wrong-reporting of income and should be dealt with in the same manner as non-reporting and under-reporting of income.

Still further, Government concessions to the agricultural sector (fertiliser subsidy, minimum support price) are under review for possible reduction/withdrawal in the near future. To burden the agricultural sector with additional taxation at this juncture would be a retrograde step.

Administratively, taxing agricultural income is nothing short of a nightmare for tax authorities. There are serious conceptual and administrative problems in the assessment of agricultural incomes. These include widely dispersed potential assessees, fluctuations in production due to uncertain weather conditions, and lack of accounting practices in the agricultural sector. Furthermore, for proper assessment of agricultural incomes, some knowledge of local conditions is required and in the absence of it, the Central Government staff would be hard-pressed to administer agricultural income tax.

Taxing agricultural income is also politically inexpedient. The Kelkar Committee is not the first to recommend taxation of agricultural income. As far back as 1972, the Committee on Taxation of Agricultural Wealth and Income (Chairman: K.N. Raj) had also suggested direct taxation of agricultural income. More recently, the Tax Reforms Committee, 1991 (Chairman: Raja Chelliah) also favoured partial integration of agricultural income with non-agricultural income. However, these recommendations were never implemented.

The tax rental arrangement recommended by the Kelkar Committee is presumably based on the experience of the existing tax rental arrangement pertaining to additional excise duties on textiles, tobacco and sugar in lieu of sales tax. This arrangement was made way back in 1957 when the political climate of the country was far different from what it is presently. During the first two decades of Independence (1947-67), the Congress party ruled, with some exceptions, both at the Centre and in the States. This political homogeneity facilitated taxation agreements between the two tiers of the Government including the agreement reached in 1957. Since 1967, the politics of confrontation pursued by different political parties ruling at the Centre and in the States has hindered the rationalisation and harmonisation of India's tax system. Non-implementation of the recommendations of the Expert Committee on Replacement of Sales Tax by Additional Excise Duty, 1983 (Chairman: Kamlapati Tripathi) is a case in point. This Committee had recommended the replacement of sales tax by additional excise duty on *vanaspati*, drugs and medicines, cement, paper and paper board, and petroleum products.

Taxation of agricultural income is a State subject under the Constitution. Given the existing political equations, it is highly unlikely that the States would agree to surrender this right to the Centre.

Notes

1. For a historical account of agricultural income tax in India, see Government of India, Ministry of Finance, *Report of the Taxation Enquiry Commission* (Chairman: John Matthai), 1953-54, Vol. III, Chapter 3.

2. Government of India, Ministry of Finance, R*eport of the Committee on Taxation of Agricultural Wealth and Income* (Chairman: K. N. Raj), 1972.

3. Government of India, Planning Commission, *Sixth Five Year Plan*, p. 77.

4. Government of India, *Long-Term Fiscal Policy*, December 1985, p. 35.

5. Government of India, Ministry of Finance, *Report of the Tax Reforms Committee* (Chairman: Raja Chelliah), Part I, 1992, p. 26.

6. Government of India, Ministry of Finance and Company Affairs, *Report of the Task Force on Direct Taxes* (Chairman: Vijay Kelkar), December 2002.

9

Sharing of Revenue from Certain Central Taxes: Arrangements Prior to the Recommendations of the Eleventh Finance Commission

---

This chapter explains the sharing of revenue from income tax and Union excise duties between the Centre and the States prior to the Constitution (Eightieth Amendment) Act, 2000.

The Constitution (Eightieth Amendment) Act, 2000 substituted a new Article for Article 270 under which States are now given a percentage share of all Central taxes and duties. This has already been explained in section 3.6.1 of Chapter 3 of this book. Prior to this arrangement, proceeds from certain individual taxes were shared with the States. Thus, income tax was levied and collected by the Centre but the proceeds were shared mandatorily with the States. Similarly, excise duties were levied and collected by the Centre but their proceeds were shared permissively with the States. The recommendations of the first ten Finance Commissions regarding sharing of income tax revenue and excise revenue between the Centre and the States are summarised below.

9.1 Sharing of Income Tax Revenue

By virtue of entry 82 of List I of the Seventh Schedule of the Constitution, the Central Government is empowered to levy 'taxes on income other than agricultural income'. Before the Eightieth Amendment of the Constitution, these were compulsorily shareable between the Centre and the States under Article 270(1) of the Constitution. However, the proceeds attributable to Union Territories, taxes payable in respect of Union emoluments, and corporation tax were kept out of the divisible pool in accordance with the provisions contained in clauses (2), (3) and (4) of Article 270. Similarly, surcharge levied for purposes of the Union under Article 271 was also excluded from the divisible pool. The Finance Commission was required to make recommendations on the following matters pertaining to income tax.

1. Determination of the percentage of net proceeds of income tax to be assigned to the States,
2. Formula for the allocation of States' share among the States, and
3. Determination of the net proceeds attributable to Union Territories.

9.1.1 Determination of the Share of States: The share of the States in the net proceeds of income tax increased gradually ever since the recommendations of the First Finance Commission which fixed it at 55 per cent. The Second, the Third, and the Fourth Finance Commissions enlarged the share to 60 per cent, 66.66 per cent, and 75 per cent respectively. The Third and the Fourth Finance Commissions recommended the increase in the States' share to make good the loss sustained by the States on account of non-inclusion of corporation tax in the divisible pool beginning 1959. The Fifth Finance Commission did not recommend any further increase in the States' share. The Sixth Finance Commission raised the States' share from 75 per cent to 80 per cent which was further increased to 85 per cent by the Seventh Finance Commission, making the Central Government virtually a collecting agency on behalf of the State Governments. The Eighth and the Ninth Finance Commissions retained it at 85 per cent. The Tenth Finance Commission reduced the share of States in the net proceeds of income tax from 85 per cent to 77.5 per cent. Table 9.1 summarises the recommendations of various Finance Commissions regarding the distribution of income tax revenue between the Centre and the States and the principles followed for the distribution of States' share among themselves.

Table 9.1: Recommendations of Various Finance Commissions Regarding Distribution of Income Tax Revenue between the Centre and the States

		Bases of distribution among the states (per cent)		
Finance Commission and period of award	States' share in income tax (per cent)	Population	Contribution	Other factors
First (1952-57)	55.0	80.0	20	--
Second (1957-62)	60.0	90.0	10	--
Third (1962-66)	66.0	80.0	20	--
Fourth (1966-69)	75.0	80.0	20	--
Fifth (1969-74)	75.0	90.0	10	--
Sixth (1974-79)	80.0	90.0	10	--
Seventh (1979-84)	85.0	90.0	10	--
Eighth (1984-89)	85.0	22.5	10	67.5
Ninth (1990-95)*	85.0	22.5	10	67.5
Tenth(1995-2000)	77.5	20.0	--	80.0

* A separate report was submitted for the year 1989-90.

Sources: *Reports of Finance Commissions.*

In reducing the share of the States in the net proceeds of income tax, the Tenth Finance Commission was guided by the following two considerations, " (i) that the authority that levies and administers the tax should have a significant and tangible interest in its yield and (ii) that any change in the share on this account should not materially affect the level of overall devolution to the States. In other words, any downward revision in the share of States in the net proceeds of income tax should be mirrored in a revenue equivalent increase in their share in the net proceeds of Union excise duties." [1] The Commission did recommend enlargement in the share of States in excise duties from 45 per cent to 47.5 per cent.

9.1.2 Distribution of the Share of States Inter Se: Prior to the recommendations of the Eighth Finance Commission, population was the dominant factor in the distribution scheme. The weightage given to the population factor varied between 80 per cent and 90 per cent and that for the *contribution factor* between 10 per cent and 20 per cent.

Although the Eighth and the Ninth Finance Commissions retained the share of States in the proceeds of income tax at 85 per cent, they changed the formula for the distribution of States' share *inter se* drastically. The Eighth Finance Commission recommended the following formula.

1. 10 per cent of the net proceeds of income tax to be distributed among the States on the basis of assessment of income tax.
2. 90 per cent of the net proceeds to be distributed among the States on the following criteria:

- 25 per cent on the basis of population in 1971,
- 25 per cent on the basis of inverse of per capita income of the State multiplied by 1971 population, and
- 50 per cent on the basis of distance of per capita income of the State from the highest per capita income State (i.e. Punjab) multiplied by the 1971 population of the concerned State.

The formula of the Ninth Finance Commission was as follows.

1. 10 per cent on the basis of contribution.
2. 45 per cent on the basis of distance of per capita income of a State from that of the State with the highest per capita income multiplied by the 1971 population.
3. 22.5 per cent on the basis of the population of the State in 1971.
4. 11.25 per cent on the basis of a composite index of backwardness compiled by the Commission.
5. 11.25 per cent on the basis of the inverse of per capita income multiplied by

the population of the State in 1971. [2]

The Tenth Finance Commission adopted the following indices for determining the *inter se* shares of the States in the shareable proceeds of income tax.

1. 20 per cent on the basis of population in 1971.
2. 60 per cent on the basis of distance of per capita income. [3]
3. 5 per cent on the basis of *area adjusted* formula. [4]
4. 5 per cent on the basis of index of infrastructure, and
5. 10 per cent on the basis of tax effort.

The prominent weight given to the *distance factor* by the Eighth, the Ninth, and the Tenth Finance Commissions tilted the devolution scheme in favour of backward States and therefore was generally welcomed.

9.1.3 Controversies over Distribution of Income Tax Revenue: Major controversies between the Centre and the States regarding distribution of revenue from income tax were the following.

A. Corporation Tax: By virtue of entry 85 of List I read with Article 270(4)(a), the receipts from corporation tax belong exclusively to the Central Government. Consequent upon the simplification in the scheme of company taxation in 1959, the income tax paid by companies was reclassified as corporation tax. As an offshoot of this definitional change, company taxation ceased to be mandatorily shareable with the States as per provision of Article 270.

Ever since, States had been pressing for the inclusion of corporation tax in the divisible pool, particularly in view of its buoyant revenue. In the face of explicit Constitutional provision precluding revenue from corporation tax being shareable with the States, the Finance Commissions had gradually increased the share of States in the truncated divisible pool. The Centre had opposed the inclusion of corporation tax in the divisible pool on the ground that the disadvantage to the States due to definitional change in 1959 had been made good by Finance Commissions by enhancing their share in income tax which went up to 85 per cent and remained there till the recommendations of the Tenth Finance Commission. Taking note of this situation, the Commission on Centre-State Relations, 1988, observed, "It is a fundamental principle of taxation that the taxing authority should have interest in its proceeds. In order to maintain this principle and giving a more meaningful choice to the Union among fiscal alternatives, it is necessary to enlarge the base of devolution to the States but with a lower percentage share in individual taxes. This can be done by bringing into the divisible pool a major Union tax but still keeping a sizeable revenue source for exclusive utilisation by the Union." [5]

Therefore, the Commission recommended that the net proceeds of corporation tax could be made permissibly shareable with the States through an appropriate amendment of the Constitution. Simultaneously, it made it clear that in the event of inclusion of corporation tax in the divisible pool, necessary adjustments will have to be made by suitably lowering shares of the States in income tax and Central excise duties. Some State Governments also argued on these lines. For example, the Government of Maharashtra suggested to the Ninth Finance Commission that the share of the States in income tax could be reduced to 75 per cent provided 20 per cent of the receipts from corporation tax were assigned to the States. The Ninth Finance Commission, however, refused to examine the question of corporation tax because it was not referred to it by the President.

B. Surcharge on Income Tax: The Constitution provides under Article 271 for the levy of a surcharge on income tax wholly for the purpose of the Centre. Surcharge was levied in 1951 and continued uninterrupted (*albeit* with different nomenclatures like special surcharge, additional surcharge etc.) when it was withdrawn in 1985 following the recommendations of the Eighth Finance Commission. However, surcharge on income tax was reintroduced in 1987 for drought purposes and the same was replaced by an employment surcharge in 1989. Surcharge was abolished by the Finance Act, 1994. It was reimposed subsequently.

In fact, surcharge on income tax has remained almost a regular source of revenue for the Centre much against the spirit of the Constitutional provision. States have all along pleaded before successive Finance Commissions for the inclusion of surcharge in the divisible pool. The Commission on Centre-State Relations, 1988, was firmly of the view that surcharge on income tax should not be levied by the Central Government except for a specified purpose and for a strictly limited period only. The Eighth and the Ninth Finance Commissions opined that a surcharge continued indefinitely could be regarded an additional income tax and, therefore, shareable with the States. The Tenth Finance Commission emphasised that the surcharge on income tax should not be levied except to meet emergent requirements for a limited period. Thus, although the explicit Constitutional provision favours the Centre, the levy of surcharge remains an irritant in Centre-State relations till date.

C. Miscellaneous Receipts: Another point of controversy pertained to the receipts from penalties and interest recoveries under the head miscellaneous receipts. The Eighth Finance Commission was of the view that such receipts should form part of the divisible pool of income tax. Unfortunately, the Centre did not accept this recommendation, maintaining that interest and penalties, though payable under the Income Tax Act, are distinct from income tax. The Ninth Finance Commission disagreed with this view of the Centre and cited several judgements of the Supreme Court to prove that there was no essential difference between tax and penalties related to it. The Tenth Finance Commission also opined that receipts on account of interest recoveries and penalties form part of the divisible pool and should be shared with the States. It recommended that this should be done with effect from April 1, 1995.

In most European countries fines and penalties associated with a tax are part of the receipts from that tax. According to OECD, "Receipts from fines and penalties paid for infringement of regulations identified as relating to a particular tax and interest on payments overdue in respect of a particular tax are recorded together with receipts from that tax." [6] The stand taken by the Central Government in this regard is untenable.

D. Cost of Collection: Apportionment of the cost of collection between income tax and corporation tax was another contentious issue between the Centre and the States. The cost of collection was deducted from the proceeds of income tax while working out the share of States. On the suggestion of Eighth Finance Commission, an expert committee was set up in 1985 which apportioned the cost of collection in the ratio of 1:7 between corporation tax and non-corporation income tax.

Following the observations made by the Ninth Finance Commission in its First Report, the Government of India constituted another expert Committee in 1989 to examine the allocation of the cost of collection between income tax and corporation tax. The Committee, which included representatives of the State Governments, made a detailed study in this regard and fixed the ratio at 1:6.5 which was accepted and used by the Tenth Finance Commission.

9.2 Sharing of Excise Revenue

Excise duties, levied by the Centre under entry 84 of List I in the Seventh Schedule of the Constitution, occupied a predominant place in the overall transfer of resources from the Centre to the States. These duties belonged to the category of taxes which may be divided between the Centre and the States (Article 272) and the subject-matter of this division fell within the purview of the Finance Commission [Article 280(3)(a)].

9.2.1 Nature of Revenue Sharing: The sharing of excise duties was permissive and therefore different from the compulsory assignment to the States of the whole proceeds of taxes under Article 269 and compulsory sharing of the proceeds of income tax under Article 270. Hence, the States did not enjoy a constitutional right to claim a share out of the revenues from Central excises. It was for the Parliament to decide whether the States should at all be given such a share and in taking this decision it may consider recommendations of the Finance Commission made in this regard. This permissive provision in the Constitution aimed at providing additional resources to the States in the event of necessity to augment transfers which could be effected under other provisions of the Constitution.

Successive Finance Commissions had taken the view that permissive sharing, contemplated under Article 272, was not only justified but even necessary in view of the growing financial needs of the States for developmental and other essential services. Therefore, ever since April 1, 1952, the States had been getting a share in the proceeds of Central excises. In fact, successive Finance Commissions had increasingly relied upon excise duties in their schemes of revenue transfers with the result that these duties found an important place in the revenue accruals of the State Governments.

9.2.2 Determination of the Share of States: Understandably, there was near unanimity among the States to press for a higher proportion of excise revenue for distribution among themselves. This was thought necessary to impart viability and to introduce elasticity to finances of the States. However, Finance Commissions paying due regard to requirements of the States on the one hand and needs of the Centre on the other evolved their own sharing schemes considering the overall transfer of resources from the Centre to the States.

The sharing of excise revenue between the Centre and the States started on a rather low profile with the award of the First Finance Commission which recommended distribution of 40 per cent of excise revenue from three commodities (tobacco, matches, and vegetable products) among the States in proportion to their population. In making this recommendation, the Commission was guided by its desire to widen the field of divisible taxes so that a balanced scheme of distribution could be evolved for the benefit of the States. The division of excise revenue, however, was restricted to the above three commodities because the Commission thought it inadvisable to divide too many excises to begin with, particularly in view of the relatively small yield from some of the items. As regards the selection of excises for division, the Commission preferred commodities (a) which were of common and widespread consumption, (b) which yielded a sizeable sum of revenue for distribution, and (c) which possessed reasonable stability of yield. The selected commodities, namely tobacco, matches, and vegetable products were found to be the most suitable for the purpose.

Following the award of the First Finance Commission, a number of States urged upon the Second Finance Commission to bring all excise duties under the distribution scheme. Such a sweeping suggestion did not find favour with that Commission which striking a note of compromise, preferred to widen the range by increasing the number of items to be shared from three to eight. These were: tobacco, matches, vegetable products, sugar, coffee, tea, paper, and vegetable non-essential oils. The Commission, however, decreased the share of States in distributable duties from 40 per cent to 25 per cent keeping in view the sum it proposed to transfer to the States from Central excises in its overall scheme of devolution. However, the reduction in the share was more than made good by the widening of the coverage of divisible duties and each State received a larger sum from this source than before.

States again pleaded before the Third Finance Commission for inclusion of all excisable commodities in the distributable pool. In support of this demand the States argued that the expanding coverage of Central excises and their increasing incidence had adversely affected the revenue potential of sales tax. Accepting this demand of the States in principle the Commission observed, "The viability of the States could best be secured by a larger devolution of the Union excise duties and this should be effected by providing for the participation of the States, by conventions, in the proceeds of all Union excises. It would give a great deal of psychological satisfaction to the States and dissipate any suspicion that the Union is pursuing a policy of excessive centralisation of resources." [7] However, the Commission considering its own scheme of transfers, recommended for distribution among the States 20 per cent of the excise revenue from commodities which each yielded in 1960-61 revenue of Rs. 50 lakh or more. The number of such commodities was 35.

In their representations to the Fourth Finance Commission, the States again argued for a share out of the proceeds of excise duties on all commodities including the commodities which might be brought under the excise net during the quinquennium relevant for the Commission's award. Accepting the States' view, the Commission recommended the sharing of the proceeds of all excise duties between the Centre and the States in the ratio of 80:20. The Fifth and the Sixth Finance Commissions merely carried forward the recommendations of the Fourth Finance Commission in this regard.

The Seventh Finance Commission drastically increased the share of States in excise duties from 20 per cent to 40 per cent, making them the most important shareable tax between the Centre and the States. In doing so, the Commission was guided by the objective of leaving as many of the less affluent States as possible with a surplus on revenue account. It preferred bulk of fiscal transfers by way of tax shares than grants-in-aid. The Eighth Finance Commission further enhanced the share of States in excise duties to 45 per cent, out of which 5 per cent was set aside for distribution among those States which continued to have deficits even after the devolution of taxes and loans as recommended by it. The Ninth Finance Commission retained the share of States at 45 per cent but used 5 per cent and 7.425 per cent from it for post-devolution deficits, in its First, and Second Reports respectively. In other words, the portion of the net proceeds of excise duties from which all States received a share was 40 per cent for the Eighth Finance Commission, it remained so in the one year (1989-90) report of the Ninth Finance Commission but it was reduced to 37.575 per cent in the Second Report of the same Commission for the period 1990-95.

The Tenth Finance Commission raised the share of States in the net proceeds of Union excise duties from 45 per cent to 47.5 per cent, keeping in view the decrease in the States' share of the net proceeds of income tax from 85 per cent to 77.5 per cent recommended by it. Out of 47.5 per cent, 7.5 per cent was kept apart for distribution among deficit States.

From the foregoing account of the sharing of excise revenue between the Centre and the States, it is clear that in the wake of recommendations of the successive Finance Commissions, the States had come to claim an increasingly larger proportion of excise revenue over the years. The underlying philosophy in this respect was to enlarge States' share in a buoyant source of Central tax revenue. This development, however, had taken place contrary to what the framers of the Constitution had envisaged. As already noted, the permissive sharing of excise proceeds was intended to supplement, in the event of necessity, transfer of resources under other provisions of the Constitution. However, the supplementary source had become by far the biggest source of revenue transfer. This development was partly attributed to significant structural changes in the Indian tax system since Independence. For example, the expansion in the range of commodities subject to excise duties and the increasing incidence of such duties had considerably reduced the scope for sales tax levied by the States and it was therefore desirable that the States had a substantial interest in the proceeds of Central excises.

9.2.3 Distribution of the Share of States Inter Se: The next task of the Finance Commission was to evolve principles for distribution of the States' share of excises as between different States. In this connection, it is interesting to note the observations of the Sixth Finance Commission, "While there was near unanimity among the States in demanding an increase in the share of Union excise duties, there were naturally wide divergences in their approach to the principles for determination of relative shares of the States in the divisible pool. Each State was inclined to put forward a formula that would favour it most." [8]

The First Finance Commission distributed the States' share of excise duties among the States on the basis of States' respective population. The Second Finance Commission also preferred distribution largely on the basis of population. The Third Finance Commission, while agreeing to population being the major factor, also took into account other factors like the relative financial weakness of the States, disparity in the levels of development, percentage of scheduled castes and tribes, and population of backward classes. However, it did not specify either the exact manner of distribution or the weightage assigned to different indices of economic backwardness.

The Fourth Finance Commission accepted population as a general measure of the needs of States and distributed 80 per cent of the States' share on the basis of population. The remaining 20 per cent was distributed on the basis of social and economic backwardness of the States which was assessed on the basis of the following factors.

1. Per capita gross value of agriculture production.
2. Per capita value added by manufacture.
3. Percentage of workers (as defined in the Census) to the total population.
4. Percentage of enrolment in classes I to V to the population in age group 6-11.
5. Population per hospital bed.
6. Percentage of rural population to total population.
7. Percentage of population of scheduled castes and tribes to total population.

However, the Commission did not indicate the exact manner in which the above mentioned factors were combined.

The Fifth Finance Commission distributed 80 per cent of the States' share of excise duties on the basis of population and the remaining 20 per cent on the basis of socio-economic backwardness. Two-thirds of the 20 per cent was distributed among States whose per capita income was below the average per capita income of all States in proportion to the shortfall of the States' per capita income from all States' average multiplied by population of the respective States. The remaining one-third of the 20 per cent was distributed according to an integrated index of backwardness on the basis of the following six criteria.

1. Population of the scheduled tribes.
2. Number of factory workers per lakh of population.
3. Net irrigated area per cultivator.
4. Length of railway and surfaced roads per 100 sq. km.
5. Ratio of the number of school going children as compared to those of school going age.
6. Number of hospital beds per 1,000 population.

The Sixth Finance Commission, after having considered the long list of indicators of backwardness suggested by the States concluded, "Even a cursory look at the list would show that most of the indicators put forward by the States refer either to characteristics that are themselves the causes of low per capita income or to characteristics that are direct or indirect consequences of low per capita income." [9] Therefore, it adopted per capita income as the sole criterion in assessing the relative economic position of the States. This approach of the Commission was partly the result of the difficulty it felt in assigning weightage among different indicators of economic backwardness. The Commission distributed 75 per cent of the States' share of excise duties on the basis of population and the remaining 25 per cent on the basis of economic backwardness. The distribution of weightage for backwardness was recommended in relation to the 'distance' of a State's per capita income from that of the State with the highest per capita income multiplied by the population of the State concerned in 1971. Thus, the Sixth Finance Commission rejected the approach of the Fifth Finance Commission which had classified the States into two categories, rich and poor: States with per capita income above the national average being regarded rich, and those below the average as poor. According to the Sixth Finance Commission, this approach of its predecessor had affected most adversely those States whose per capita income was just above the dividing line.

The Seventh Finance Commission evolved its own overall indicators of backwardness, viz. per capita income and the proportion of people below the poverty line, in preference to partial indicators like level of schooling, health services, population of scheduled castes and tribes, and road mileage as adopted by previous Commissions. It determined the shares of States in the divisible pool of excises by giving equal weights (i.e. 25 per cent each) to the following four factors.

1. Population.
2. Inverse of per capita State Domestic Product (SDP).
3. Percentage of the poor in each State. [10]
4. A revenue equalisation formula evolved by the Commission. [11]

Thus, the Seventh Finance Commission not only significantly enhanced the share of States in excise proceeds but also drastically changed the principles of allocation of excise revenue among the States.

The Eighth Finance Commission was guided by the following three overriding considerations while deciding the criteria for allocating shares of excise duty among the States.

1. That the formula should be progressive in the sense that it should allocate a larger share to those States which have relatively lower per capita incomes or which are otherwise backward and financially weak.
2. The formula should be simple.

3. Firm and reliable data should be available for applying the formula.

Based on these considerations, the Commission recommended the distribution of States' share (45 per cent) among the States in the following manner.

(a) 40 per cent on the following bases (or the same formula as recommended by it for the distribution of 90 per cent of the States' share in income tax),

- one-fourth (i.e. 25 per cent) on the basis of 1971 population,
- one-fourth (i.e. 25 per cent) on the basis of the inverse of per capita income of the State multiplied by 1971 population,
- the remaining 50 per cent on the basis of distance of per capita income of the State from that of the State with the highest per capita income (i.e. Punjab).

(b) The remaining 5 per cent was set aside for distribution among the States which had deficits after taking into account their shares from the devolution of all taxes and duties.

The Ninth Finance Commission retained the share of States in excise duties at 45 per cent and recommended its distribution among the States in the following manner.

(a) 37.575 per cent on the following bases:

1. 29.94 per cent on the basis of 1971 population.
2. 14.97 per cent on the basis of Income Adjusted Total Population.
3. 14.97 per cent on the basis of the index of backwardness.
4. 40.12 per cent on the basis of distance of per capita income of a State from that of the State having the highest per capita income (i.e. Punjab).

(b) The remaining 7.425 per cent was distributed among the States with deficits, after taking into account their shares from various taxes and duties. [12]

The Tenth Finance Commission recommended the distribution of States' share (47.5 per cent) among the States in the following manner.

(a) 40 per cent on the following bases (or the same formula as recommended by it for the distribution of States' share in income tax).

1. 20 per cent on the basis of population in 1971.
2. 60 per cent on the basis of distance of per capita income.
3. 5 per cent on the basis of *area adjusted* formula.
4. 5 per cent on the basis of index of infrastructure.
5. 10 per cent on the basis of tax effort.

(b) The remaining 7.5 per cent of the net proceeds of excise duties was distributed among the deficit States in accordance with the shares specified by the Commission.

Table 9.2 summarises the recommendations of successive Finance Commissions regarding the distribution of excise revenue between the Centre and the States and the bases for allocating the States' share *inter se.*

Table 9.2: Recommendations of Various Finance Commissions Regarding Distribution of Central Excise Revenue between the Centre and the States

		Bases of distribution among the states (per cent)		
Finance Commission and period of award	Coverage (number of commodities)	States' share in excise revenue (per cent)	Population	Other factors
First (1952-57)	3	40	100	--
Second (1957-62)	8	25	90	10
Third (1962-66)	35	20	Major factor	Weightage not stated
Fourth (1966-69)	All	20	80	20
Fifth (1969-74)	All	20	80	20
Sixth (1974-79)	All	20	75	25
Seventh (1979-84)	All	40	25	75
Eighth (1984-89)	All	45	25	75
Ninth (1990-95)*	All	45	29.94	70.06
Tenth(1995-2000)	All	47.5	20	80

* A separate report was submitted for the year 1989-90.
Sources: *Reports of Finance Commissions.*

9.2.4 Varying Emphasis on Criteria Adopted: The foregoing account of the principles adopted by Finance Commissions to distribute States' share of excise duties among the States brings out the following points.

1. The proposal for devising the distribution scheme on the basis of consumption of excisable goods did not find favour with the Finance Commissions. The argument of some of the States that consumption of excisable goods reflected the *contribution* that each State made to the total excise proceeds was rejected because the purpose of sharing excise duties was not to return to the States what was collected from them.
2. Distribution in proportion to sales tax collections, justified on the ground that the levy of excise duties limited the scope for mobilisation of resources by the States in the form of sales tax, was also disfavoured by the Finance Commissions. However, this argument of the States was taken care of in the overall sharing of excise revenue between the Centre and the States.

3. The Finance Commissions generally accepted population as a criterion for determining the share of each State in excise revenue. Population was assigned predominant weightage, ranging between 80 to 100 per cent, by the first six Finance Commissions. However, the Seventh, the Eighth, the Ninth, and the Tenth Finance Commissions gave more weightage to backwardness factor in their distribution schemes. Population as a criterion was supported on the ground that it represented the needs of the States and proceeds of excises should be so distributed among the States that each got according to its needs. It was further argued that in the case of some commodities, population was a rough index of total consumption and therefore the proposal for devising the distribution scheme on the basis of consumption of excisable goods was partly taken care of. The undue emphasis on population criterion as a measure of general needs of the States by earlier Finance Commissions was somewhat unjustified. In India, States differ widely in respect of per capita income, geographical area, nature of the terrain, and population distribution over the area. Thus, it is not always that the populous States are poor or that the less populous States are rich. Under these circumstances, population may be taken as one of the determinants of the needs of a State but it cannot be considered an adequate measure of that need.
4. Beginning with the Third Finance Commission, relative economic backwardness was also accepted as a legitimate criterion in the distribution scheme. For this purpose, different Finance Commissions evolved their own indicators for measuring relative economic backwardness. The richer States had often argued against the adoption of backwardness as a criterion on the ground that excise duties should be related exclusively to non-discriminatory criteria such as population or consumption and that any special help to the backward States should be rendered through the mechanism of grants-in-aid under Article 275 of the Constitution. This view was rejected by the Finance Commissions.
5. Adoption of the backwardness criterion, though laudable, was assigned relatively low weightage (20 to 25 per cent) by the Third, the Fourth, the Fifth, and the Sixth Finance Commissions and therefore did not serve the needs of the backward States adequately. Thus, there was not only a late realisation of the need to adopt backwardness criterion but the weightage assigned to it was also low. However, the Seventh, the Eighth, the Ninth, and the Tenth Finance Commissions gave predominant weightage to the backwardness factor though indices of backwardness were obtained rather haphazardly and to some extent arbitrarily.

9.2.5 Areas of Controversy: Distribution of excise revenue between the

Centre and the States was beset with controversies some of which were the following.

A. Special Duties of Excise: Special duties were in the form of surcharges on basic duties and were levied on certain goods for the first time in 1963 in the wake of Chinese aggression. These were earmarked exclusively for the Centre and were not shareable with the States. States had all along contended that proceeds of special excises should also be shared with them. While the Constitution specifically mentioned in Article 271 that surcharges on income taxes were exclusively for the use of the Centre, there was no such provision for surcharges on excise duties. Their sharing was disallowed only in the Finance Acts and could always be reviewed by the Parliament, particularly in the light of the recommendations of Finance Commissions in this regard.

The Fourth Finance Commission had taken the view that it was open to it to suggest that proceeds of special duties of excise should also be made shareable with the States. However, on practical considerations, it did not favour bringing the proceeds of special duties of excise within the sharing scheme. The Commission, however, suggested that the recourse to special excises by the Central Government should be an exception rather than the rule.

The Fifth Finance Commission found no justification to exclude special duties of excise from the divisible pool and recommended their inclusion in the scheme of sharing of excise revenue from 1972-73 onwards. As a consequence, special duties of excise got merged with basic duties from April 1, 1972.

In the meantime, the Central Government devised another method to augment excise revenue exclusively for its own purpose. It had introduced regulatory duties of excise in 1961 for the purpose of empowering the Executive to vary rates of duties on any item within certain limits.

This provision had remained dormant till 1970-71 in the sense that revenue from regulatory duties was either nil or negligible during all these years and therefore it did not attract the attention of either the States or the Finance Commissions. The situation, however, changed significantly when in the wake of large influx of refugees from Bangladesh and conflict with Pakistan, the Central Government imposed in 1971 regulatory duties of excise on such items as steel, iron and steel products, copper, zinc, and aluminium. Furthermore, the regulatory duties were replaced by auxiliary duties (i.e. special duties) under the Finance Act, 1973 and it was specifically laid down in the Act that the auxiliary duties were for the purposes of the Centre, meaning thereby that proceeds there from were not to be shared with the States.

The States resented this arrangement, apprehending that continuance of auxiliary duties as a separate entity may encourage the Centre to raise additional revenue increasingly through auxiliary duties rather than the shareable basic duties. Upholding the States' view, the Sixth Finance Commission recommended the merger of revenue from auxiliary duties in the divisible pool. Consequently, auxiliary duties of excise, wherever applicable, were merged with the basic duties under the Finance Act of 1977. To forestall any future ambiguity as regards division of revenue from special duties of excise between the Centre and the States, the Seventh Finance Commission categorically stated that revenue from excise duties, whether they were designated special or regulatory or by any other name, should also be included in the divisible pool. The Eighth and the Ninth Finance Commissions endorsed this view and recommended that the divisible pool should include all excise duties including special excise duties but excluding earmarked cesses and duties collected under the Additional Duties of Excise (Textiles and Textile Articles) Act, 1978.

B. Earmarked Cesses: States also insisted for the inclusion of earmarked cesses and the additional excise duties under the Act of 1978 in the divisible pool. These were cesses on commodities which were not subject to excise duty like iron ore, and coal. Then there were items which were subject to regular excise duties along with cesses like tea, sugar, and paper. Additional excise duties on textiles were also a kind of earmarked levy meant to finance controlled cloth and *Janata* cloth schemes. Like surcharge on income tax, cesses had also become permanent feature of excise taxation, and since they reduced the scope for regular excise duties, the States wanted their merger in the divisible pool. The Eighth and the Ninth Finance Commissions examined the question of the inclusion of cesses in the divisible pool but were content to observe that their number should be kept to the minimum.

The Tenth Finance Commission was more forthright in its views on this issue. It observed, "As regards the inclusion of revenues from the cesses in the divisible pool, it may be mentioned that a cess is levied on a specified commodity and is governed by a special Act of Parliament with the stipulation that it should be utilised for the development of the specific industry, the products of which bear the cess. The proceeds of such cesses cannot, therefore, be shared with the States." [13]

C. Administered Prices: Another contentious issue pertained to frequent hikes in administered prices by the Centre. States desired that the Centre should raise resources by increasing excise duties instead of administered prices so that they could share the resources so raised. The Eighth Finance Commission distinguished between hike in administered prices to meet the increase in cost of production and for raising revenue. If revenue raising was the objective, then excise duties should be preferred. Ninth Finance Commission endorsed this view.

Notes

1. *Report of the Tenth Finance Commission*, December 1994, pp. 21-22.

2. The use of 1971 census data was considered appropriate because some States fared better in implementing the family planning programme between 1971 and 1981. Adoption of the 1981 census figures would have been detrimental to the interest of the States which are promoting this desirable national objective.

3. According to the Tenth Finance Commission, "the respective 'distances' are multiplied by the population of the States, and the share of a State is obtained by dividing the product by the sum of such products for all the States. This procedure of multiplying an index by respective populations and deriving shares according to such products has been called scaling" (*Report of the Tenth Finance Commission*, 1994, p. 23).

4. Although the Tenth Finance Commission used area as a factor, it made certain adjustments at the upper and lower ends. Thus, it ensured that no State received a share higher than 10 per cent at the upper end and no State received a share less than 2 per cent at the lower end.

5. Government of India, *Report of the Commission on Centre-State Relations* (Chairman: Justice R.S. Sarkaria) Part I, 1988, p. 274.

6. Organisation for Economic Co-operation and Development, *Revenue Statistics of OECD Countries: 1965-85* (Paris, 1988), p. 38.

7. *Report of the Finance Commission, 1961,* p. 21.

8. *Report of the Finance Commission, 1973,* p. 15.

9. *Ibid.*, p. 16.

10. The Commission used the per capita State Domestic Product in a comparable series at State current prices by adopting the annual average for the triennial 1973-76. The poverty percentage in each State was taken as the proportion of people below an augmented poverty line in the State to the aggregate poor population in all the States. The augmented poverty line was the minimum per capita consumption expenditure level for 1970-71 on the well-known Dandekar-Rath criterion plus the State budget expenditure per capita on selected public services in that year.

11. For the revenue equalisation principle, the per capita revenue potential of each State with reference to the average per capita SDP for the triennial 1973-76 was computed. The per capita average of each State's own tax and non-tax revenue for 1975-76 and 1976-77 were regressed on the average per capita income of the States to derive the estimated values of per capita revenue of each State. The distance of the per capita revenue thus estimated for each State from the maximum estimated per capita revenue among all the States (i.e. Punjab) was multiplied by the estimated population of the State as on March 1, 1976. The percentage of the product of the distance of the per capita revenue so estimated from that of Punjab and the population for each State in the total of these products for all the States gave the share of each State in the component of the divisible pool based on revenue equalisation formula. The adoption of this formula was recognition of the fact that States which are less favourably placed with regard to their resource potential are helped to take steps for the betterment of the people living in those States.

12. To put it differently, the 45 per cent share of the States was distributed among the States on the following bases: (i) 25 per cent on the basis of 1971 population. (ii) 12.5 per cent on the basis of Income Adjusted Total Population. (iii) 12.5 per cent on the basis of the index of backwardness. (iv) 33.5 per cent on the basis of distance of per capita income of a State from that of the State having the highest per capita income (i.e. Punjab). (v) The remaining 16.5 per cent was distributed among the States with deficits, after taking into account their shares from various taxes and duties.

The weights given in the text were derived by multiplying the weights given above by a factor of (100/83.5).

13. *Report of the Tenth Finance Commission*, December 1994, p. 22.

10

Constitution (Eightieth Amendment) Act, 2000 and the Sharing of Revenue from All Central Taxes

Prior to Constitution (Eightieth Amendment) Act, 2000, income tax and Union excise duties were the only taxes shared with the States, apart from the grants given in lieu of passenger tax, and the collections from additional excise duty in lieu of sales tax sugar, tobacco and textiles. Taxes on income and Union excise duties were shared with States under Article 270 and 272 respectively. This amendment altered the pattern of sharing of Central taxes between the Centre and the States significantly. It substituted a new Article for Article 270 and omitted the old Article 272. The new Article 270 provides for the sharing of the net proceeds of all Union taxes and duties with the States.

Under Article 270 of the Constitution, the Finance Commission is required to recommend such percentage of the net proceeds of all Central taxes and duties (except Union surcharge, cess levied for specific purposes and the duties and taxes referred to in Articles 268 and 269) that may be assigned to the States within which that tax or duty is leviable. [1] It is further required to recommend the manner in which the States' share may be distributed among the States.

10.1 History of Constitution (Eightieth Amendment) Act, 2000

The Constitution (Eightieth Amendment) Act, 2000 was based on a recommendation of the Tenth Finance Commission (TFC) which had recommended an Alternative Scheme of Devolution (ASD) in its report submitted in November 1994. Under this scheme, proceeds of all Central taxes, except surcharges, would constitute a common shareable pool from which a share was to be devolved to the States. The TFC recommended 29 per cent of the proceeds to be devolved to the States under this Scheme. This percentage share included devolution on account of additional excise duties levied in lieu of sales tax as well as the grant-in-lieu of the tax on railway passenger fares.

In December 1996, the Government of India brought out a Discussion Paper on the Alternative Scheme of Devolution spelling out the pros and cons of the proposed scheme. On the basis of a consensus reached in the Third Meeting of the Inter-State Council held on July 17, 1997, the Government accepted the scheme with some modifications. A Constitution (Eighty-fifth Amendment) Bill,

1998 was introduced in the 12th Lok Sabha. The Bill was referred to the Standing Committee of Parliament on Finance. The Standing Committee gave its report to the Parliament in February 1999. However, the Bill lapsed with the dissolution of the Lok Sabha. A modified version of the Bill was introduced in the Lok Sabha as 'The Constitution (Eighty-ninth Amendment) Bill, 2000 on March 9, 2000. The Bill was passed by Parliament and received the assent of the President of India on June 9, 2000 as Constitution (Eightieth Amendment) Act 2000.

On the basis of a consensus arrived at the third meeting of the inter-State Council held on July 17, 1997, the Government decided to accept in principle the recommendations of the Tenth Finance Commission regarding the alternative scheme of sharing of taxes between the Centre and the States from a single divisible pool at a uniform rate of 29 per cent. However, instead of freezing this percentage share for 15 years with effect from April 1, 1996 as suggested by the TFC, it was left open to successive Finance Commissions to review it.

The Constitution amendment bill to give effect to this decision was introduced in the Lok Sabha on July 14, 1998. However, it could not be passed due to the dissolution of the Twelfth Lok Sabha.

On February 8, 2000, the Union Cabinet again approved in principle the proposal that would give States a share of 29 per cent of the *net* proceeds of all Central taxes. It is noteworthy that the TFC had envisaged sharing of *gross* proceeds of Central Taxes. The Bill will be introduced again in the Lok Sabha to implement the decision. Since the scheme will come into force with retrospective effect from April 1, 1996, the Centre will have to pay arrears (estimated at Rs. 10,000 crore) to the States.

In short, this amendment brought about the following main changes:

(a) All Central taxes and duties, except those referred in articles 268 and 269 respectively and surcharges and cesses, are to be shared between the Centre and the States.

(b) Only States in which these taxes and duties are leviable in that year are entitled to get a share in these taxes and duties;

(c) A percentage of 'net proceeds' of these taxes and duties as may be prescribed by the President by order after considering the recommendations of the Finance Commission is to be shared by States.

(d) The percentage of 'net proceeds' of these taxes and duties which is assigned to the States in any financial year shall not form part of the Consolidated Fund of India.

(e) The article 270(2) which referred to taxes on income prior to the amendment contained the following provision:

"Such percentage as may be prescribed, of the net proceeds in any financial year of any such tax, except in so far as those proceeds represent proceeds attributable to Union Territories or to taxes payable in respect of Union emoluments, shall not form part of the Consolidated Fund of India."

In the new article 270 which refers to all taxes the words 'net proceeds' attributable to Union Territories or to 'taxes payable in respect of Union emoluments' have been omitted.

The new article 270 provides as follows:

“270 (1) All taxes and duties referred to in the Union List, except the duties and taxes referred to in articles 268 and 269, respectively, surcharge on taxes and duties referred to in article 271 and any cess levied for specific purposes shall be levied and collected by the Government of India and shall be distributed between the Union and the States in the manner provided in clause (2).

(2) Such percentage, as may be prescribed, of the net proceeds of any such tax or duty in any financial year shall not form part of the Consolidated Fund of India, but shall be assigned to the States within which that tax or duty is leviable in that year, and shall be distributed among those States in such manner and from such time as may be prescribed in the manner provided in clause (3).

(3) In this article, "prescribed" means: -

(i) until a Finance Commission has been constituted, prescribed by the President by order, and

(ii) after a Finance Commission has been constituted, prescribed by the President by order after considering the recommendations of the Finance Commission.”

(f) The recommendation of the Tenth Finance Commission regarding sharing of 'gross proceeds' was also not accepted in the new Amendment Act and the words, "the share of net proceeds" was prescribed in order to maintain consistency between articles 270, 279 and 280.

Article 269 has been recast by the Amendment Act. The new article includes only taxes on sale and purchase of goods and taxes on the consignment of goods. All other taxes that were listed under article 269 prior to the amendment have been deleted from this article. It has also drastically changed Article 269 of the Constitution which earlier provided for levy and collection of some taxes by the Government of India but which were assigned to the States.

10.2 The Constitution (Eightieth Amendment) Act, 2000

BE it enacted by Parliament in the Fifty-first Year of the Republic of India as follows:-

1. This Act may be called the Constitution (Eightieth Amendment) Act, 2000.

2. In article 269 of the Constitution, for clauses (1) and (2), the following clauses shall be substituted, namely:-

'(1) Taxes on the sale or purchase of goods and taxes on the consignment of goods shall be levied and collected by the Government of India but shall be assigned and shall be deemed to have been assigned to the States on or after the 1st day of April, 1996 in the manner provided in clause (2).

Explanation – For the purposes of this clause, -

(a) the expression "taxes on the sale or purchase of goods" shall mean taxes on sale or purchase of goods other than newspapers, where such sale or purchase takes place in the course of inter-State trade or commerce;

(b) the expression "taxes on the consignment of goods" shall mean taxes on the consignment of goods (whether the consignment is to the person making it or to any other person), where such consignment takes place in the course of inter-State trade or Commerce.

(2) The net proceeds in any financial year of any such tax, except in so far as those proceeds represent proceeds attributable to Union territories, shall not form part of the Consolidated Fund of India, but shall be assigned to the States within which that tax is leviable in that year, and shall be distributed among those States in accordance with such principles of distribution as may be formulated by Parliament by law'.

3. For article 270 of the Constitution, the following article shall be substituted and shall be deemed to have been substituted with effect from the 1st day of April, 1996, namely:-

'270. (1) All taxes and duties referred to in the Union List, except the duties and taxes referred to in articles 268 and 269, respectively, surcharge on taxes and duties referred to in article 271 and any cess levied for specific purposes under any law made by parliament shall be levied and collected by the Government of India and shall be distributed between the Union and the States in the manner provided in clause (2).

(2) Such percentage, as may be prescribed, of the net proceeds of any such tax or duty in any financial year shall not form part of the Consolidated Fund of India, but shall be assigned to the States within which that tax or duty is leviable in that year, and shall be distributed among those States in such manner and fr0m such time as may be prescribed in the manner provided in clause (3).

(3) In this article, 'prescribed" means, –

(i) until a Finance Commission has been constituted, prescribed by the President by order, and

(ii) after a Finance Commission has been constituted, prescribed by the President by order after considering the recommendations of the Finance

Commission.'

4. (1) Article 272 of the Constitution shall be omitted.

(2) Notwithstanding anything contained in sub-section (1), where any sum equivalent to the whole or any part of the net proceeds of the Union duties of excise including additional duties of excise which are levied and collected by the Government of India and which has been distributed as grants-in-aid to the States after the 1st day of April, 1996, but before the commencement of this Act, such sum shall be deemed to have been distributed in accordance with the provisions of article 270, as if article 272 had been omitted with effect from the 1st day of April, 1996.

(3) Any sum equivalent to the whole or any part of the net proceeds of any other tax or duty that has been distributed as grants-in-aid to the States after the 1st day of April 1996 but before the commencement of this Act shall be deemed to have been distributed in accordance with the provisions of article 270.

10.3 Eleventh Finance Commission: New Tasks

10.3.1 Impact of Constitution (Eightieth Amendment) Act, 2000: At the time of finalisation of recommendations and preparation of the report of EFC, the Constitution (Eightieth Amendment) Act, 2000 was enacted by the Parliament which had a bearing on the work of the EFC. The amendments made in the Constitution necessitated changes in the terms of reference of the EFC. These were modified by the Presidential Order dated June 19, 2000. By this Order, para 7 of the terms of reference was deleted. This para required the EFC to suggest changes, if any, in the principles governing the devolution amongst the States of the net proceeds of the additional excise duties leviable under the Additional Duties of Excise (Goods of Special Importance) Act, 1957 in lieu of the sales tax formerly levied by the State Governments, and the grants to be made available to the States in lieu of the tax under the repealed Railway Passenger Fares Act, 1957. Thus, the Report submitted on July 7, 2000, addressed the original terms of reference (excluding paragraph 7). The Constitution (Eightieth Amendment) Act, 2000 provides for sharing of the net proceeds of all Union taxes and duties with the States.

10.3.2 Impact of Seventy-third and Seventy-fourth Amendments to the Constitution: Finance Commission is constituted under Article 280 of the Constitution. Clause (3) of Article 280 lays down the following mandatory terms of reference for it.

"(a) the distribution between the Union and the States of the net proceeds of taxes which are to be or may be divided between them ... and the allocation between the States of the respective shares of such proceeds;

(b) the principles which should govern the grants-in-aid of the revenues of the States out of the Consolidated Fund of India."

By the Seventy-third and Seventy-fourth amendments to the Constitution, two new sub-clauses (bb) and (c) were introduced in clause (3) of Article 280. These sub-clauses make it obligatory upon the Finance Commission to make recommendations as to "the measures needed to augment the Consolidated Fund of a State to supplement the resources of the panchayats/municipalities in the State on the basis of the recommendations made by the Finance Commission of the State".

Thus, as per the amended clause (3) of Article 280, the Eleventh Finance Commission was duty bound to assess the resources required to be transferred from the Consolidated Fund of India to the State Government for passing on to the municipalities. This assessment has to be based on the recommendations of State Finance Commissions (SFCs) which enjoys complete freedom in this regard.

Hitherto, there were two primary functions of a Finance Commission: (a) to evolve a scheme of transfer of financial resources from the Centre to the States so as to ensure financial equilibrium at the two levels of Government during the period of its award, and (b) to design formulae to allocate resources so transferred among the States. Transfer of resources from the Centre to the States was designed to correct vertical imbalances while the distribution of resources among the States aimed at correcting horizontal imbalances in the availability of resources.

Now that it had to consider the needs of local bodies also, the Finance Commission had to ensure vertical equity in the distribution of resources not only between the Centre and the Sates but also between the States and the local bodies. By making the Finance Commission responsible for ensuring equitable distribution of resources at three levels instead of two, the Constitutional amendments distracted it from its traditional primary task of ensuring vertical fiscal equity as between the Centre and the States, and horizontal fiscal equity as among the States.

It is also well-known that while the States are unanimous in demanding an increase in their share of the divisible pool of Central taxes, their approach to the principles for determination of relative shares of the States differs widely. In their memoranda to the Finance Commission, the States suggest a variety of conflicting criteria for the distribution of States' share inter se. Each State suggests a formula which it considers will benefit it and most, the richer States emphasising the 'collection factor' and the poorer States the backwardness factor.

The Finance Commission had to consider not only the memoranda of the State Governments but also the Reports of SFCs, which in turn are based on the financial assessments of hundreds of municipalities and thousands of panchayats, it will have to perform a Herculean task to do justice to the work assigned to it. Generally, a Finance Commission takes one and a half years to complete its work. Now with the added burden of supplementing the resources of panchayats/municipalities, it will need more time. The old debate that Finance Commission should be converted from a quinquennial to a permanent body like the Planning Commission assumes relevance in this context.

Through greater devolution a Finance Commission may augment the Consolidated Fund of a State but how does it ensure supplementing the resources of the panchayats/municipalities. The Eleventh Finance Commission will have to make arrangements to operationalise enhanced transfer of resources from the States to the local bodies. Recommendations of the Commission in this regard will determine the efficacy of the Seventy-third and Seventy-fourth amendments.

A State Finance Commission has the power to decide the amount of assistance which may be needed from the Centre to supplement the resources of the municipalities of a State. It is plausible that a State Government may slacken its efforts to tap the potential available at its own level or the municipal level to contain expenditure and/or raise resources and instead put the burden on the national exchequer. If this happens, the National Finance Commission would find itself in the cobwebs of conflicting and exaggerated claims of not only Central and State Governments but also of thousands of municipalities through the SFCs.

It may be recalled that since the recommendations of the State Finance Commissions were not available to the Tenth Finance Commission, the latter was in doubt whether it could recommend measures for augmenting State resources for the purpose of supplementing the resources of panchayats and municipalities. To resolve the dilemma, it decided to make ad hoc provision of specific grants to States.

The Eleventh Finance Commission, which was the first to deal with the provisions of the Seventy-third and Seventy-fourth amendments on a full-fledged basis, had an enormous responsibility of assessing the financial needs of local bodies and recommending the scale of assistance to be given to them.

10.3.3 Share of States: On the basis of the analysis and assessment of the budgetary requirements of the Centre and the States, the EFC fixed the share of States at 28 per cent of the net proceeds of shareable Central taxes/duties for distribution amongst all such States where the Central tax/duty is leviable for each of the five years starting from April 1, 2000. Consequently, the recommendations made for the sharing of income tax and Union excise duties in the Interim Report got modified. In addition, 1.5 per cent of the net proceeds of shareable Central taxes/duties in a year was recommended for distribution amongst such States which do not levy sales tax on sugar, tobacco and textiles during that year, thus totalling 28 + 1.5 = 29.5 per cent of the net proceeds of all Union taxes and duties. The distribution of this 1.5 per cent among the States is to be done in the same manner as the distribution of 28 per cent of the net proceeds. It was further recommended that if any State levies and collects sales tax on sugar, textile and tobacco, it will not be entitled to any share from this 1.5 per cent. **See also Chapter 25 of this book.**

10.4 Share of States Determined by Twelfth Finance Commission

The Twelfth Finance Commission (TFC) raised the share of States in shareable Central taxes from 29.5 per cent to 30.5 per cent. Total transfers to States recommended by the TFC amount to Rs. 7,55,752 crore over the five year period 2005-10. Of this, transfers by way of share in Central taxes and grants-in-aid amount to Rs. 6,13,112 crore and Rs. 1,42,640 crore, respectively.

The total transfers recommended by the TFC were higher by 73.8 per cent over those recommended by the Eleventh Finance Commission (EFC). Within the total transfers, while the share in Central taxes was higher by 62.9 per cent, grants-in-aid recommended by the TFC were higher by 143.5 per cent over those recommended by the EFC. **See also Chapter 26 of this book.**

Note

1. Presently, all taxes except the expenditure tax and service tax are leviable in every State of the country. Expenditure tax and service tax are not leviable only in the State of Jammu and Kashmir (*Report of the Eleventh Finance Commission*, p. 54).

11

Additional Duties of Excise in Lieu of Sales Tax

Following a voluntary agreement between the Centre and the States at a meeting of the National Development Council (NDC) held in December, 1956, it was decided to replace sales tax on textiles, tobacco, and sugar by additional duties of excise and to distribute revenues derived there from among the States. The agreement provided also that the share accruing to each State shall not in any case be less than the revenue realised from the levy of sales tax on these goods for the financial year 1956-57 in that State. The Council's decision was implemented through the Additional Duties of Excise (Goods of Special Importance) Act, 1957, the First Schedule of which prescribed the rates of additional duties of excise and the Second Schedule the scheme of distribution of the net proceeds among the States.

The Act does not debar States from the levy of sales tax on the specified commodities, but it does provide that if in any year any State levies and collects a tax on the sale or purchase of such commodities, no sum shall be paid to that State in that year by way of share out of the net proceeds of the additional duties of excise, unless the Central Government by special order decides otherwise. The commodities covered under the scheme (textiles, tobacco, and sugar) were declared goods of special importance in inter-State trade so that no State could find it worthwhile to opt out of the voluntary agreement not to impose sales tax on these goods. [1] The revenue derived from additional duties of excise, levied and collected by the Centre, is distributed among the States in accordance with the formula prescribed by the Finance Commission. The Fourth Finance Commission described it as a *tax rental arrangement.* [2]

11.1 Rationale of the Scheme

The scheme of additional duties of excise in lieu of sales tax has the following advantages.

1. It minimises tax evasion by levying the tax at first point and saving industry, trade, and consumers from administrative complexities involved in the collection and payment of sales tax.
2. It helps in maintaining uniformity in the prices of widely consumed goods throughout the country.

3. Such an arrangement contributes to the development of an integrated market by facilitating movement of goods across State borders.
4. Rationalisation of commodity taxation at the national level becomes easy.
5. Cost of collection is reduced.

11.2 Views of the State Governments

The scheme of additional duties of excise in lieu of sales tax has been in force since 1957. While the business community has demanded extension of this scheme to other commodities, the States have generally remained disinclined in this regard. The distrust between the Centre and the States regarding the operation of this scheme by the Central Government is an irritant in Centre-State relations. States have argued on the following lines.

1. Sales tax is the only elastic source of revenue available to them and in view of its regional applicability it is also the only effective instrument for shaping their economic policies.
2. Replacement of it by Central levy will encroach on their constitutional rights leading to erosion of their financial autonomy.
3. If taxes are levied and collected by a State itself then it is more conscious of its responsibilities towards the taxpayers. Subventions from the Centre may lead to reckless spending causing fiscal indiscipline.

As regards the working of the existing scheme, the dissatisfaction of State Governments is borne out of their belief that revenue potential of additional duties of excise has not been fully exploited by the Centre. Their complaint is that the growth of revenue from additional excise duties on textiles, sugar, and tobacco lags behind the growth in revenue from basic excise duties on the same commodities. The States complain that once sales tax on the three commodities was replaced by additional excise duties, the Centre did not feel the need for consultation with the States for reviewing the working of the scheme. They claim that the growth rate of their sales tax revenue is much higher than the growth rate of the yield from additional excise duties.

11.3 Decisions of the National Development Council

Following complaints from the States, the whole issue was reconsidered by the National Development Council in its meeting held on December 28, 1970. The Council decided to continue the scheme with the following conditions: (a) that the incidence of additional duties would be stepped up to 10.8 per cent of the value of clearances within a period of two or three years, (b) that a ratio of 2:1 between basic and additional excise duties would be achieved and maintained, (c) that specific duties would be converted into ad valorem duties except in regard to unmanufactured tobacco. It was also agreed that a Standing Review Committee consisting of representatives of the Central and State Governments with the Economic Adviser, Planning Commission, as convenor, would be set up and the same would meet at least once a year to review the working of the new arrangement and make such recommendations as may be necessary for its further improvement.

As a follow up action, specific duties were replaced by ad valorem rates and significant enhancements were made in additional excise duties in the Central budgets for the three consecutive years 1971-72 to 1973-74. The Standing Review Committee met for the first time in February 1981 and appointed a sub-committee which recommended that the incidence of 10.8 per cent should be achieved in three stages: 8.5 per cent by 1984-85; 9.75 per cent by 1987-88; and 10.8 per cent by 1989-90. The Ninth Finance Commission was informed by the Union Finance Ministry that the incidence achieved by the end of 1988-89 was 10.7 per cent. The Commission hoped that the committed level of 10.8 per cent would be actually achieved by the end of 1989-90. In a significant move, the Commission recommended that during its award period (1990-95), if in any year the incidence of additional excise duties falls short of the level of 10.8 per cent of the value of clearances, the shortfall should be made good by the Centre by providing an equivalent amount by way of grants-in-aid to be distributed among the States in the same manner as recommended for sharing the proceeds of additional excise duties. [3] As regards the ratio between basic excises and additional excises, the Centre fulfilled its obligations by achieving the stipulated 2:1 ratio by 1981-82.

11.4 Role of the Finance Commission

The Finance Commission comes in the picture for the purpose of determining the principles of distribution of the net proceeds of additional duties of excise among the States.

11.4.1 Guaranteed Amount: The first issue before the Finance Commission is to determine the yield in 1956-57 from sales tax on the commodities subject to additional excise duties for the purpose of guaranteeing to the States concerned the amount so determined. The Second Finance Commission, which was the first to deal with this problem, adopted elaborate procedures for working out estimates of yield (i.e. the guaranteed amount for the year 1956-57). These were primarily based on consumption estimates and figures of collection of sales tax obtained from each State for the years 1954-55 to 1956-57. The later Finance Commissions did not consider it feasible, in view of the lapse of time, to reassess the likely yield in 1956-57 of sales tax to redetermine the guaranteed amount and therefore accepted the Second Finance Commission's estimates with adjustments whenever necessary. [4]

11.4.2 Procedure for Guaranteed Amount: The second issue for consideration by the Finance Commission is whether the guaranteed amounts should first be set apart from the net proceeds and the balance then distributed among the States or to distribute the entire net proceeds on appropriate principles subject to the overriding proviso that no State should get less than the guaranteed amount. The Second, the Third, the Fourth, and the Fifth Finance Commissions preferred the first alternative thinking that unless the guaranteed amounts were first set apart and the balance alone distributed among the States, there was the risk of the share of some States falling below the guaranteed amount. However, the Sixth and the subsequent Finance Commissions did not feel the need to set apart the guaranteed amount as there was no risk of the share of any State falling short of the guaranteed amount. In adopting the second alternative, i.e. distributing the entire net proceeds on some appropriate principles, the Sixth and the Seventh Finance Commissions were guided by an underlying philosophy to help the weaker States. To the question whether the guaranteed amount should first be set apart, the Seventh Finance Commission remarked, "If that were done, there is no doubt that some States would receive, in the period covered by our Report, shares slightly larger than the shares they would receive if the guaranteed amounts were not so set apart. While it is true that under the NDC resolution earlier agreed to, a State is entitled to have a share which should not be less than the guaranteed amount, the agreement does not assure to any State any extra benefit what it would receive were the guaranteed amount first set apart." [5]

Thus, taking a technical view of the matter, the Seventh Finance Commission applied the principle of distribution to the entire net proceeds from additional excise duties. The Eighth Finance Commission endorsed this view and followed suit.

11.4.3 Basis of Distribution: The third issue relates to the determination of the basis for the distribution of additional excise duties among the States. The assurances of the guaranteed amounts in the original agreement were an indication of the logic that in the distribution of the net proceeds the principle of compensation was to be followed. In other words, each State should be enabled to get almost the same amount as it would have got had sales taxes on these commodities been in operation with the same order of incidence as the additional excise duties. This view, which has generally been accepted by the Finance Commissions, precludes other considerations like needs of a State, relative backwardness etc. which are relevant in relation to allocation of other Central taxes.

For proper implementation of the compensation principle, it is widely recognised that State-wise figures of consumption of commodities on which additional excise duties are levied accord the best reflection of the potential loss of revenue sustained by States' surrender of authority to levy sales tax on them. However, Finance Commissions have differed in adopting methods to assess relative levels of consumption of these commodities in different States. The divergence of opinion on this account has been mainly due to paucity of reliable data on State-wise consumption of these commodities. Thus, the Second Finance Commission recommended the distribution of additional excise duties on the basis of the then available consumption figures with population as a correctional factor. The Third Finance Commission distributed the collections in excess of the guaranteed amounts partly on the basis of the percentage increase in the collection of sales tax in each State since 1957-58 and partly on the basis of population. It did not, however, indicate the relative weightage given to these factors. The Fourth Finance Commission felt that figures of collection of all sales taxes in a State were a more direct indicator of the contribution made by each State to the divisible surplus than population. Abandoning the population factor altogether, it recommended the distribution of the balance over the total of guaranteed amounts on the basis of the proportion of sales tax revenue realised in each State to the total sales tax collections in all the States taken together. The Fifth Finance Commission reverted back to the Third Finance Commission's formula and recommended distribution of additional excise duties giving equal weightage to both sales tax collections and population.

The Sixth Finance Commission rejected sales tax collections outright as a possible indirect indicator of the level of consumption of textiles, sugar, and tobacco in different States. It observed, "sales tax is applicable to a wide range of commodities comprising luxuries, semi-luxuries, raw materials, intermediate goods and the like. Sales tax revenue derived from these commodities may be a measure of the tax effort of the State Government but it does not provide even an indirect clue to the levels of consumption of textiles, sugar, and tobacco on which additional excise duties are being levied in lieu of sales tax." [6]

Alternatively, the Sixth Finance Commission preferred data of State Domestic Product as indicator of the likely consumption of these commodities in view of the close relationship between income and consumption. However, with regard to coarser varieties of cloth, the Commission felt that the consumption was more likely to depend on population (the commodity being a necessity) than on State Domestic Product. With such considerations in mind, the Commission recommended the distribution of the entire net proceeds of additional duties of excise on the basis of population, State Domestic Product at State current prices, and production in the ratio of 70:20:10.

The Seventh Finance Commission examined in detail the available statistics of State-wise consumption of the commodities to which additional excise duties are applicable. In particular, it studied the suitability of household consumer expenditure data of the National Sample Survey (NSS) for adoption as a measure of the consumption of these articles in each State. However, in view of the various limitations of NSS data, [7] the Commission did not find it proper to use these data for estimating the consumption in each State of the articles subject to additional excise duties.

Departing from the approach of the earlier Finance Commissions, the Seventh Finance Commission adopted different formulae for distribution of additional excise duties on different commodities. In the case of sugar, it recommended the distribution of the net proceeds of additional duties among the States in proportion to the despatches of sugar to each of the States averaged for three years ending with 1976-77. Statistics of despatches of sugar to each State, obtained from the Department of Food of the Government of India, were taken as a fair approximation of consumption of sugar in each State. In the case of textiles and tobacco, the average per capita State Domestic Product of each State for the 3 years ending 1975-76 was multiplied by the population of the State according to 1971 census and the percentage shares of this product of each State in the corresponding all-States' total figure were worked out. It is pertinent to note that the Seventh Finance Commission made a specific suggestion to the Central Government regarding collection of suitable statistics for reliable estimates of consumption of these articles in each State for the benefit of future Finance Commissions.

The Eighth Finance Commission also could not obtain reliable estimates of consumption of these commodities. It, therefore, recommended the distribution of additional duties of excise on all the three commodities (sugar, textiles, and tobacco) by giving equal weightage to State Domestic Product and population.

The Ninth Finance Commission maintained that since sales tax itself is a tax on consumption therefore the shares of various States in additional duties of excise should correspond to their shares in the consumption of these commodities. It observed, "The fact that the proceeds of Additional Excise Duties are distributed only in pursuance of a tax rental arrangement between the Centre and the States (which has its origin in the National Development Council meeting in 1956) would clearly imply that this distribution cannot be treated as devolution or grant-in-aid in the sense that these terms are normally understood. The terms of reference would, therefore, not bind us to use the 1971 population for computing the States' share of Additional Excise Duties. But for the tax rental arrangement, the States would have been collecting sales tax on the current consumption of the relevant commodities. Since population is being used only as a proxy for consumption along with SDP, we consider it as only logical that any criterion which links the shares of the States nearest to the consumption of the relevant items in the individual States should be preferred." [8]

11.5 Expert Committee on Replacement of Sales Tax by Additional Excise Duty, 1983

As already noted, sales tax on textiles, tobacco, and sugar was replaced by additional duties of excise in 1957. The scheme of additional excise duties was proposed to be extended to some more commodities in 1980. At a conference of the Chief Ministers convened by the Centre on September 16-17 of that year, it was resolved to bring *vanaspati*, and life-saving drugs under additional excise duties in lieu of sales tax. It was also decided to constitute a committee of Chief Ministers to consider what other items could be added to the list for additional excise duties. However, the Non-Congress (I) States viz. Kerala, Tamil Nadu, Tripura, and West Bengal did not agree with the resolution passed at the Chief Ministers Conference.

The matter was further examined at another conference of Chief Ministers held in February 1981, which recommended the appointment of an expert committee by the Central Government to look into this matter. The expert committee under the Chairmanship of Mr. Kamlapati Tripathi submitted its report [9] in January 1983. It recommended the replacement of sales tax by additional excise duty on *vanaspati*, drugs and medicines, cement, paper and paper board, and petroleum products. The recommendations were considered in a conference of Chief Ministers held on November 2, 1983. However, the six Chief Ministers of the non-Congress (I) States, viz. Andhra Pradesh, Jammu and Kashmir, Karnataka, Tamil Nadu, Tripura, and West Bengal opposed the Centre's initiative to implement the recommendations. The recommendations of the Tripathi Committee were further discussed at a conference of Chief Ministers held in New Delhi on February 9-10, 1989. Unfortunately, no progress could be made in this regard and the matter is still hanging fire.

The opposition of non-Congress (I) States was based on the belief that implementation of the scheme would erode their revenue position. However, a close perusal of the recommendations of the Tripathi Committee suggests that it evolved elaborate formulae for protecting the financial interests of the States. In the case of three commodities, namely paper and paper board, *vanaspati*, and drugs and medicines, it suggested that the annual growth rate of the amount to be collected by way of additional excise duty in lieu of sales tax should be related to the future annual growth rate of sales tax revenue of all the States. For petroleum products and cement, which are substantially subject to administered prices, the Committee recommended and worked out linkages between the amount to be collected by way of additional excise duty from year to year and value of consumption on which normal sales tax would be leviable.

In spite of these safeguards, the apprehension of some States that their resource position would be adversely affected reflects their lack of confidence in the Centre in implementing the scheme sincerely. Thus, an important tax reform has become a casualty of the distrust between the Central and the State Governments. The scheme of additional excise duties in lieu of sales tax has merits of its own. In view of the safeguards provided by the Tripathi Committee and the Ninth Finance Commission, the scheme should not only be retained but extended to other commodities as well.

It is pertinent to mention here that during the first two decades of Independence (1947-67), the Congress party ruled, with some exceptions, both at the Centre and in the States. This political homogeneity facilitated taxation agreements between the two tiers of the Government, e.g. the agreement reached in 1957 regarding substitution of sales tax by excise duties on sugar, textiles, and tobacco. Since 1967, the politics of confrontation pursued by different political parties ruling at the Centre and in the States has hindered the process of rationalisation and harmonisation of commodity taxation. In fact, reform of commodity taxation is closely interwoven with the political process. Unfortunately, the political response to economic logic so far has neither been adequate nor helpful.

11.6 Present Position

The Eleventh Finance Commission fixed the share of States at 28 per cent of the net proceeds of shareable Central taxes/duties for each of the five years starting from April 1, 2000. In addition, 1.5 per cent of the net proceeds of shareable Central taxes/duties in a year was recommended for distribution amongst such States which do not levy sales tax on sugar, tobacco and textiles during that year, thus totalling 28 + 1.5 = 29.5 per cent of the net proceeds of all Union taxes and duties. The distribution of this 1.5 per cent among the States is to be done in the same manner as the distribution of 28 per cent of the net proceeds. It was further recommended that if any State levies and collects sales tax on sugar, textile and tobacco, it will not be entitled to any share from this 1.5 per cent.

The Twelfth Finance Commission fixed the share of States in the net proceeds of shareable Central taxes at 30.5 per cent, treating additional excise duties in lieu of sales tax as part of the general pool of Central taxes.

Notes

1. Internal as well as inter-State sales tax on goods of special importance is governed by the Central Sales Tax Act, 1956. The present rate of CST is 2 per cent.

2. India's federal system of government creates a dual polity based on divided governmental functions and taxation powers. Taxation laws of the Central Government extend to the whole of the country while those of State Governments are applicable within their respective jurisdictions. A tax belonging to the States may be imposed with a varying base and/or rate in different States. Even the procedures and rules for its collection may differ from State to State. The lack of uniformity in the imposition of State tax laws can cause difficulties for traders and consumers and thus hinder inter-State trade. To overcome these problems, arrangements could be made to transfer from the States, the legal right to levy the tax, to the Centre with the proviso that revenue collected will be assigned to the States. This is known as 'tax rental arrangement'.

3. *Second Report of the Ninth Finance Commission,* December 1989, p. 34.

4. For example, the Third Finance Commission had to make adjustments in view of the bifurcation of Bombay State into Maharashtra, and Gujarat.

5. *Report of the Seventh Finance Commission*, 1978, p. 59.

6. *Report of the Sixth Finance Commission*, 1973, p. 20.

7. For example, NSS data related to the year 1972-73 and was considered outdated for the Commission's period of award (1979-84). While NSS data covered only household expenditure, the Commission was interested in non-household consumption as well.

8. *Report of the Ninth Finance Commission,* 1989, p. 20.

9. Government of India, Ministry of Finance, *Report of the Expert Committee on Replacement of Sales Tax by Additional Excise Duty* (Chairman: Kamlapati Tripathi), January 1983.

12

Grant in Lieu of Railway Passenger Fares Tax

Prior to Constitution (Eightieth Amendment) Act, 2000, Article 269(1) included tax on railway passenger fare. Article 269(2) clarified that the proceeds were to be assigned to the States within which the tax was levied. The Finance Commission was required to formulate principles for distribution of the proceeds among the States.

12.1 History of Railway Passenger Fares Tax

A tax on railway fares was levied in 1957 as a percentage of the fares and was recovered as an addition to the fare. The rates of tax were as follows.

1.	Passengers travelling on season ticket	Nil
2.	Passengers travelling for distance up to 15 miles (inclusive)	Nil
3.	Passengers travelling for distances from 16 miles to 30 miles (inclusive)	5 per cent of fare
4.	Passengers travelling for distances from 31 miles to 500 miles (inclusive)	15 per cent of fare
5.	Passengers travelling for distances over 500 miles	10 per cent of fare
6.	Passengers travelling on mileage coupons	12.5 per cent of cost of coupons

The tax remained in force till the end of 1960-61.

In 1960, the Railway Board represented to the Railway Convention Committee that in order to enable the Railways to obviate the necessity of making up the shortfall in their surplus in the quinquennium 1961-66, and to avoid the continued financing of the Railway Development Fund through loans from General Revenues, it was necessary to allocate to the railways the entire proceeds of the passenger tax to be collected in the period 1961-66, which were estimated to be about Rs. 70 crore. The Board suggested that the tax should be merged with existing fares, so that the proceeds accrue to the Railways in the first instance in the ordinary way; and that the Railways may be required to make every year a special payment, for transfer to the States, equal to the average collection of passenger tax during the three years 1958-61.

Following the recommendation of the Railway Convention Committee (1960) of the Parliament, the tax was repealed and merged in the basic fares from April 1, 1961. It may be recalled that the Railway Board had pleaded before the

Committee that the tax had reduced the scope for raising passenger fares. Obviously, the States were unhappy on being deprived of a potentially elastic source of revenue. To compensate the States for the loss of revenue, the Government decided to pay annually a sum of Rs. 12.50 crore for distribution among the States during the five year period 1961-62 to 1965-66. This was on the consideration that the States, to whom the proceeds from this tax were payable, were likely to have included this source of income as part of their resources for purposes of the Third Five Year Plan.

12.2 Recommendations of Successive Finance Commissions

Consequent upon representations made by the States to the Fourth Finance Commission, the Railway Board suggested to the Railway Convention Committee, 1965, that the grant may be raised to Rs. 16.25 crore, keeping in view the rate of increase in traffic during the five years 1960-61 to 1964-65 and the expected increase in subsequent years. For this purpose it was suggested that the Railways should pay to the Government of India an amount equal to 1 per cent of the capital at charge on March 31, 1964, out of which Rs. 16.25 crore may be paid as grant to States in lieu of the repealed tax and the balance of about Rs. 1.50 crore may be utilised to assist the States to provide their share of the cost of Railway safety works. In pursuance of the recommendations of the Railway Convention Committee (1965), the amount of this grant was raised to Rs. 16.25 crore per annum from 1966-67.

In their memoranda submitted to the Fifth Finance Commission, the States urged that either the tax on railway fares be reintroduced at the same rates at which it was levied in 1957-58, or the quantum of the grant in lieu of the tax be increased and fixed as a percentage of the railway passenger earnings, such percentage being fixed on the basis of actual tax collections and passenger earnings in the years up to 1960-61 prior to the repeal of the tax. Estimates made by the Commission revealed that the amounts payable to the States in lieu of the tax would be higher than the fixed grants recommended by the Railway Convention Committees, and would be of the order of Rs. 25 crore at that time.

In the wake of Bangladesh crisis, the tax on railway passenger fares was revived in 1971 and later again repealed on March 31, 1973. With the consent of the States, the proceeds of the tax were transferred to the Centre to meet the expenditure on Bangladesh refugees. However, the grant of Rs. 16.25 crore continued to be paid uninterrupted and unchanged till it was raised to Rs. 23.12 crore by the Railway Convention Committee (1980) and it remained at that level during the period 1980-81 to 1983-84. The same Committee also suggested that future increase in the quantum of grant could be considered on the basis of the recommendations of the Eighth Finance Commission which drastically increased the amount of grant from Rs. 23.12 crore to Rs. 95 crore per annum during the period of its award (1984-89), though the terms of reference did not require it to make any such recommendation. The new amount of grant (Rs. 95 crore) was calculated on the basis of the total non-suburban passenger earnings in 1981-82 and the fact that the tax, when in operation, constituted roughly 10.7 per cent of the total fare structure. The Commission on Centre-State Relations, 1988, suggested a periodical review and suitable adjustments of such lump sum grant on the recommendations of the Finance Commission.

Going beyond its terms of reference, the Ninth Finance Commission also examined the question of the quantum of grant. Some States pleaded before it that the grant should be 10.7 per cent of the non-suburban railway passenger earnings in each of the years of its award (1990-95). After having examined the railway finances, the Commission concluded that calculation of the grant at 10.7 per cent would put too much burden on the railways, jeopardising its modernisation plans. According to the Railway Board, calculation of grant at 10.7 per cent would have meant a commitment of Rs. 232 crore in 1988-89. [1] Striking a note of balance, the Ninth Finance Commission fixed the grant at a lump sum amount of Rs. 150 crore per annum for each year of the period 1990-95.

The Tenth Finance Commission recommended Rs. 380 crore (being the said 10.7 per cent) as grant in lieu of railway passenger fare to be paid to the States annually during the period of its award (1995-2000).

The other task of the Finance Commission was to formulate principles for the distribution of this grant among the States. The Second Finance Commission, which was the first to deal with this question, adopted actual passenger travel on the railways within each State as the basis for which it considered route length as the proxy. This formula was endorsed and continued by the subsequent Finance Commissions up to the Sixth. It was the Seventh Finance Commission which changed the formula and distributed the grant in proportion to the non-suburban passenger earnings from traffic originating in each State. The Eighth, the Ninth, and the Tenth Finance Commissions followed suit.

12.3 Constitution (Eightieth Amendment) Act, 2000 and Changes in Article 269

It may be noted that pursuant to the enactment of the Constitution (Eightieth Amendment) Act, 2000, net proceeds of all Union taxes and duties have become shareable with the States. The Act also drastically changed Article 269 of the Constitution, which earlier provided for levy and collection of some taxes by the Government of India but which were assigned to the States. [2] The amendments made in the Constitution necessitated changes in the terms of reference of the Eleventh Finance Commission (EFC) which was in the process of finalising its report. These were modified by the Presidential Order dated June 19, 2000. By this Order, para 7 of the terms of reference was deleted. This para required the EFC to suggest changes, if any, in the principles governing the devolution amongst the States of the net proceeds of the additional excise duties and the grants to be made available to the States in lieu of the tax under the repealed Railway Passenger Fares Act, 1957.

Notes

1. *First Report of the Ninth Finance Commission*, 1988, p. 40.

2. Provisions of Article 269 prior to the Constitution (Eightieth Amendment) Act, 2000 were as follows.

Taxes Levied and Collected by the Union but Assigned to the States (Article 269): These were: (a) duties in respect of succession to property other than agricultural land, (b) estate duty in respect of property other than agricultural land, (c) terminal taxes on goods or passengers carried by railway, sea or air, (d) taxes on railway fares and freights, (e) taxes other than stamp duties on transactions in stock exchanges and future markets, (f) taxes on the sale or purchase of newspapers and on advertisements published therein, (g) taxes on the sale or purchase of goods other than newspapers, where such sale or purchase takes place in the course of inter-State trade or commerce, and (h) taxes on the consignment of goods (whether the consignment is to the person making it or to any other person), where such consignment takes place in the course of inter-State trade or commerce. These taxes corresponded to entries 87, 88, 89, 90, 92, 92A and 92B in the Union List.

Provisions of Article 269 after the Constitution (Eightieth Amendment) Act, 2000 are as follows.

Article 269 mentions taxes which shall be levied and collected by the Union but assigned completely to the States, in which they are leviable. These taxes are: (a) taxes on the sale or purchase of goods other than newspapers, where such sale or purchase takes place in the course of inter-State trade or commerce, and (b) taxes on the consignment of goods where such consignment takes place in the course of inter-State trade or commerce. These taxes correspond to entries 92A and 92B in the Union List in the Seventh Schedule of the Constitution. It is noteworthy that out of these two taxes only one is being levied at present, viz. inter-State sales tax (entry 92A).

13

Grants-in-aid of Revenues

The expression *grants-in-aid of the revenues* has not been defined in the Constitution of India. [1] Both the Government of India Act, 1935, and the Constitution contain provisions under which assistance may be given to the States by way of grants. Section 142 of the Government of India Act provided for the payment of such sums as might be prescribed by His Majesty in Council as grants-in-aid of the revenues of such Provinces as His Majesty might determine to be in need of assistance, while Section 150 gave the Centre or a Province power to make grants for any purpose. Article 275(1) of the Constitution, in its substantive part, is worded similarly to Section 142 of the Government of India Act, 1935, while Article 282, except for the substitution of *any public purpose* for *any purpose,* also follows the wording of Section 150 of the Government of India Act, 1935. Thus Article 282 permits the Union or a State to make grants for any public purpose notwithstanding that the purpose is not one with respect to which Parliament or the Legislature of a State, as the case may be, may make laws.

Thus, even after the transfer to the States of a share of divisible taxes, the resources of some of the States may remain inadequate to meet their needs. Therefore, the Constitution provides for grants-in-aid by the Centre to such States as are in need of assistance. Two types of grants are provided by the Centre to the States: the first under Article 275 which are routed through the Finance Commission, and the Second under Article 282 which have traditionally been determined by the Planning Commission.

13.1 Principles of Grants-in-aid of Revenues

Article 280 (3)(b) requires the Finance Commission to make recommendations as to the principles which should govern the grants-in-aid of the revenues of the States under Article 275(1). The First Finance Commission enunciated the following principles for giving grants to the States.

13.1.1 Budgetary Needs: As budgetary needs are an important criterion for determining the eligibility of a State for a grant-in-aid as well as for the assessment of the amount of the grant-in-aid, the budget has necessarily to be the starting point of an examination of fiscal need. In using the budget as a basis for this purpose, several adjustments are, however, necessary in the State budgets. These adjustments should, in the first place, reduce all budgets to a comparable basis. Adjustments are called for in respect of any abnormal or unusual and non-recurrent items of receipts or expenditure which may vitiate comparisons unless these are excluded. Besides such adjustments, which should be made for the purpose of arriving at what might be broadly termed a normal budget, certain other allowances mentioned below have also to be made.

13.1.2 Tax Effort: The extent of self-help of a State should determine the eligibility for, as well as the amount of, help from the Centre. This requires an assessment of the general scope for additional taxation in the States and of their tax effort. The point may be made that differences in relative taxation from State to State are of no relevance for the purpose of determining the degree of Central assistance to various States, as such assistance should be based primarily on the comparative poverty or affluence of the States, as judged by indices of their relative *per capita* incomes. This argument seems to miss the rationale of taking the relative tax effort of States into consideration.

A State which is prepared to raise the maximum amount of revenue through taxation is better entitled to Central assistance than a State which does not itself act sufficiently in the same direction. In respect of a State in the letter class, there is no guarantee that the benefit of external assistance will, in fact, accrue to the weaker sections of the community for whom it would be intended. Assistance to such a State may have the effect of postponing action by the State to increase its own taxation. Such assistance from outside may thus go to relieve those who are comparatively well off from the necessity of contributing more to State revenues rather than help to increase public expenditure for the benefit of the general mass of the people. It may be observed that it is only in clear cases of inadequate taxation that this should affect the quantum of assistance a State would otherwise be qualified to get.

13.1.3 Economy in Expenditure: An allowance should be made for possibilities of economy in expenditure. The principle of self-help also implies that a State should utilise its existing resources to good account before it makes a claim for assistance from the Centre. It should be emphasised that it is not the purpose of any system of grants-in-aid to diminish the responsibility of the State Governments to balance their own budgets. The method of extending financial assistance should be such as to avoid any suggestion that the Central Government have taken upon themselves the responsibility for helping the States to balance their budgets from year to year. If the amount of grants-in-aid were to be merely in proportion to the financial plight of a State, a direct premium might be placed on impecunious policies and a penalty imposed on financial prudence. On the other hand, if a State is eligible for a grant on other grounds, it should not be precluded from this benefit, merely because its budget is in order as a result of its sound financial management.

13.1.4 Standard of Social Services: An important purpose of grants-in-aid is to help in equalising standards of basic social services. The standards of social services in a State may be a criterion for grant-in-aid. Thus, of two States whose budgets, with the adjustments already indicated, point to the need for an equal amount of assistance, the one with a significantly lower level of social services should, in our view, qualify for a higher amount of assistance than the other with a relatively high level of such services. Alternatively, in marginal cases, a State with a high level of such services may become ineligible, while another State with a low level of services is eligible for a grant. Factors like thc area of a State in relation to its population, economic backwardness etc. would be reflected in the level of social services and the standard of development of a State, and would be taken into account accordingly under this principle.

13.1.5 Special Obligations: Grants-in-aid may be given to help a State to meet special burdens or obligations of national concern, though within the State sphere, if they involve an undue strain on its finances. Certain States may have special obligations or burdens likely to continue for a period of years, i.e. commitments arising out of abnormal conditions. These would justify assistance by way of grants-in-aid to the States concerned. The circumstances necessitating assistance may, for example, include the consequences of partition, such as the disruption of the institutional framework of a State, the strain on the economy and administration of a State, and its increased responsibility in respect of security.

13.1.6 Broad Purposes of National Importance: Independently of the budgetary criterion, grants may be given to further any beneficent service of primary importance in regard to which it is in the national interest to assist the less advanced States to go forward. It is, in our view, desirable to provide grants-in-aid for a broad purpose, selected with reference both to the importance of the service assisted and to the practicability of measuring, from time to time, the standard of the service on the basis of reliable indices.

13.2 Approach of Various Finance Commissions

Despite these guidelines, the Finance Commissions have distributed these grants, by and large, on the basis of budgetary needs of the States, i.e. to cover non-Plan gap on revenue account variously described as *budgetary gap*, *financial need*, *revenue gap*, *fiscal needs* etc.

The first eight Finance Commissions confined themselves to the non-Plan revenue accounts of the States. They determined the grants equal to deficit of each State so that the non-Plan revenue accounts of all the States were balanced or left with a surplus every year. This was called the *gap-filling approach* (or more appropriately *net gap filling approach*) meaning that the deficits on non-Plan revenue account which remained after tax devolution were covered through grants. The *gap-filling approach* adopted by successive Finance Commissions was to some extent attributable to the terms of reference issued to them. The main disadvantage of the *gap filling approach* was that it encouraged wasteful expenditure and discouraged revenue efforts on the part of State Governments.

The shortcomings of the *gap-filling approach* led the Centre to ask the Ninth Finance Commission to adopt a normative approach to make the States more revenue conscious. This Commission broke new grounds in at least two areas. As is well-known, this Commission assessed revenue receipts of the States normatively and also applied certain norms to assess expenditures. Therefore, it recommended grants to fill the *normative gaps* as opposed to traditional *budgetary needs*. Secondly, it dealt with the total revenue account (i.e. including Plan revenue account) and worked to eliminate deficits in the revenue account as a whole. [2]

Reverting back to the *gap-filling approach*, the Tenth Finance Commission recommended grants-in-aid equal to the amount of residual deficits, emerging after taking into account the transfers pertaining to taxes and duties, for each of the years during 1995-96 to 1999-2000. Hence, no State has a post-devolution deficit on the non-Plan revenue account in the terminal year. The total amount of grants on account of non-Plan revenue deficit for the period 1995-2000 was Rs. 7,582 crore.

It is noteworthy that while a State cannot be denied a part of a shared Central tax even if it has no demonstrated financial need, grants are given upon genuine financial needs of the States. It is possible that even before tax devolution from the Centre, some high-income States have a surplus in their non-Plan revenue account. The Seventh Finance Commission identified Punjab, Haryana, Gujarat, Tamil Nadu, and Karnataka as such States. Thus, grants-in-aid along with shared taxes serve as a levelling up force to promote regional balanced development. From this, it may also be inferred that States as a whole are not affected whether transfers are made by one means (shareable taxes) or another (grants). It is the total amount transferred which is important for them. However, the sources of transfer become important when it comes to individual States because the formulae applied for various transfers are different. It is not possible to adopt a single formula for all transfers in view of the differing nature of taxes, duties, and grants.

Notes

1. On this issue, the First Finance Commission observed, "It is possible to argue that the term *grants-in-aid of the revenues* should be construed as confining it to such grants as are intended for the augmentation of the revenues of the receiving State without any limitation as to how the money so made available should be spent. We consider that the problem has to be viewed in the larger perspective of securing an equitable allocation of resources among the units. We are, therefore, of the view that the scope of Article 275 or Article 280(3)(b) should not be limited solely to grants-in-aid which are completely unconditional grants directed to broad but well defined purposes could reasonably be considered as falling within their scope. In enunciating the principles which should govern grants-in-aid of the revenues of the States we accordingly propose to cover both general grants and grants for broad purposes." (*Report of the First Finance Commission*, 1952, p. 91.

2. In India, budgets of the Central and State Governments are divided into revenue budget and capital budget under provisions of Articles 112 and 202 of the Constitution respectively. After the commencement of the Five Year Plans, the revenue budgets of the Governments came to be sub-divided into Plan and non-Plan budgets, particularly on the expenditure side. Traditionally, Plan side is considered by the Planning Commission and the non-Plan side by the Finance Commission. However, implementation of Plan projects has led to new expenditures on non-Plan revenue account. Moreover, the Constitution in no way restricts the Finance Commission's jurisdiction to only non-Plan side of the budget. This constitutional position was confirmed when the Government in its terms of reference asked the Ninth Finance Commission that Plan and non-Plan sides of the revenue accounts should be considered together in assessing receipts and expenditures of the Centre and the States or to assess the total revenues and total revenue expenditures of the Central and State Governments without making a distinction between Plan and non-Plan. The consideration of the Plan component of the revenue budget by the Ninth Finance Commission was a major departure from the past practice and in a way also an encroachment on the territory of the Planning Commission. It marked a turning point in the controversy regarding the role and authority of the Finance Commission versus the Planning Commission or the scope of Article 275 versus Article 282. For details of the controversy regarding the scope of Article 275, see *Second Report of the Ninth Finance Commission*, 1989, p. 28.

14

State-Local Financial Relations in India

This chapter describes the functional responsibilities and sources of revenue of local bodies, explains the present constitutional arrangements relating to State-Local fiscal relations in India, and examines the role of various statutory bodies in this regard.

Rapid urbanisation has increased the functional responsibilities of municipalities in India. To meet the scale and challenge of urbanisation, municipal governments are always looking for additional funds from various sources. Since a significant part of national income originates in urban areas, efforts must be made to maintain and enhance urban productivity which, in turn, depends on the level and quality of urban infrastructure. The demand for urban infrastructure services has increased, and is likely to accelerate further, due to rising personal incomes, rapid growth of population, and general increase in economic activities. Inability of municipal governments to meet the rising demand would adversely affect growth prospects of the economy.

14.1 Functions of Local Bodies

Functional responsibilities of local bodies vary from country to country and within a country. Still some common patterns are discernible. Broadly speaking, the functions of a local body (e.g. a municipality) can be divided into the following three categories.

14.1.1 Essential Civic Functions: The main function of a municipality is to provide and maintain core (or essential) civic services. These include: refuse collection, street lighting, water supply, sewage disposal, fire protection, abattoirs, and primary health services. These are services for which decision-making rests with the municipalities.

14.1.2 Regulatory Functions: These functions pertain to regulation of industry, trade and construction activities. Municipalities issue licences, permits and levy fees of various kinds, and also impose fines for violation of rules and regulations. Charges for regulatory functions should be so fixed as to cover at least the cost of administration and surveillance. If these services are subsidised it would put strain on resources.

14.1.3 Agency Functions: These are functions (e.g. protection of environment) which are funded out of State revenues by specific transfers.

14.2 Financing of Local Bodies

In the public finance literature, the following general rules are mentioned as regards the financing of local bodies.

1. Where the benefits of a local public service are measurable and accrue to readily identifiable individuals/households within a jurisdiction, user charges are the most appropriate method of financing the service.
2. Local public services which are services to general public in the sense that identification of beneficiaries and measurement of benefits to individuals /households is difficult, should be financed by taxes on local residents. Such services include traffic control, street lighting, security, and general administration.
3. Services the benefits of which spill over to neighbouring jurisdictions should be financed by intergovernmental transfers. These services include health, education, anti-pollution measures, and other social welfare activities.
4. Long-term borrowings are the appropriate source to finance capital projects with long-term gains.

Higher level governments generally assign certain taxes to local bodies to augment their resources. Tax literature suggests the following principles regarding assignment of taxes to local bodies.

1. Municipal governments should be assigned those taxes that are leviable on bases which are 'immobile' or 'location-specific' and those whose burden cannot be exported outside the municipal jurisdiction. Property tax is a case in point.
2. Local tax base should be easily identifiable and its incidence transparent.
3. Tax yield should be stable, predictable, and buoyant.
4. Rate schedule of the tax should possess a reasonable degree of progressivity.
5. The tax should be easy to administer.

Based on the foregoing considerations, the following taxes are generally assigned to local bodies: (a) property tax, (b) entertainment tax, (c) tax on professions, (d) tax on advertisements and (e) Octroi/tolls.

14.3 Constitutional Provisions

Entry 5 of List II (State List) of the Seventh Schedule to the Constitution of India refers to local bodies as institutions created by State Governments. Furthermore, the Directive Principles of the Constitution (Article 40) requires the strengthening of the units of local self-government in the States, particularly *panchayati raj* Institutions. However, little was done in this regard during the first three decades of Independence. As a result, these institutions could not function effectively because of (a) inadequate devolution of functions and financial powers (b) failure to hold regular elections and prolonged supersession and (c) lack of participation from weaker sections of society. Consequently, local bodies in many States had become weak and ineffective as units of self-government in our democratic set up. It was only in 1991 that Bills were introduced in the Parliament to amend the Constitution for providing constitutional status to the *panchayats* and municipalities.

14.4 Decentralisation Initiative, 1992

The Seventy-third and Seventy-fourth Amendment Bills relating to *panchayats* and municipalities respectively were introduced in the Parliament in September 1991 to provide constitutional remedy for the inadequacies plaguing these bodies which were unable to perform effectively as vibrant democratic units of self-government. The Bills were referred to two joint bodies of Parliament and after necessary revision were reintroduced in July 1992, and passed by Parliament in December 1992. Both the Bills were ratified by the required number of States [Article 368(ii)] and the President gave his assent in April 1993. The Seventy-third Amendment Act relating to *panchayats* came into force from April 24, 1993. The Seventy-fourth Amendment Act relating to municipalities came into force from June 1, 1993. The changes made by the Seventy-third and Seventy-fourth Amendment Acts to the Constitution were of historical importance and are summarised in Table 14.1.

The passage of the Constitution (Seventy-third Amendment) Act, 1992 marked a watershed in the history of modern India. With this amendment, a uniform structure of *panchayats* emerged throughout the country.

Article 243 G read with Eleventh Schedule of the Constitution explicitly requires the States to devolve powers and authority on *panchayats* which may be necessary to enable them to function as institutions of self-government. The Eleventh Schedule of the Constitution is reproduced in Table 14.2.

Similarly, the passage of the Constitution (Seventy-fourth Amendment) Act, 1992 was a landmark in the history of municipal administration in India. Article 243W read with Twelfth Schedule of the Constitution provides the illustrative list for the devolution of functions to the municipalities. The Twelfth Schedule of the Constitution is reproduced in Table 14.3. Many States have amended their municipal laws to ensure conformity with the new constitutional provisions.

In short, *panchayats* and municipalities are now constitutional bodies forming third tier to the federal polity of India. India's decentralisation initiative in the form of Seventy-third and Seventy-fourth Amendments poses challenges and offers opportunities.

Table 14.1: Seventy-third and Seventy-fourth Constitutional Amendment Acts

Act	Date on which came into force	Amendments made
Constitution (Seventy-third Amendment) Act 1992	24. 4. 1993	A new Part IX relating to Panchayats was inserted. In clause (3) of Article 280, sub-clause (bb) was inserted which provides for measures to supplement the resources of the Panchayats. Eleventh Schedule added to the Constitution which provides an illustrative list for the devolution of functions to Panchayats.
Constitution (Seventy-fourth Amendment) Act, 1992	1. 6. 1993	A new Part IXA relating to Municipalities was inserted. In clause (3) of Article 280, sub-clause (c) was relettered as sub-clause (d) and before sub-clause (d) as so relettered, sub-clause (c) was inserted which provides for measures to supplement the resources of the Municipalities. Twelfth Schedule added to the Constitution which provides an illustrative list for the devolution of functions to Municipalities.

Source: Government of India, Ministry of Law, Justice and Company Affairs, *The Constitution of India (Supplement to the Third Edition)*, 1994.

14.5 Constitution (Seventy-fourth Amendment) Act, 1992

Through this amendment a new Part IX-A relating to municipalities was incorporated in the Constitution to provide for, *inter alia,* the constitution of three types of municipalities, viz. *Nagar Panchayat* for a transitional area, i.e. an area in transition from a rural to urban area [1]; Municipal Council for smaller urban area, and Municipal Corporation for larger urban area (Article 243 Q).

The Constitution (Seventy-fourth Amendment) Act, 1992 conferred constitutional status to the structure and mandate of municipalities so as to enable them to function as vibrant democratic and self-governing institutions at the grassroots level. The objectives of the Seventy-fourth Amendment included decentralisation of power and popular participation in the planning, management, and delivery of civic services. The salient features of the Seventy-fourth Amendment were the following.

Table 14.2: Eleventh Schedule of the Constitution (Article 243 G)

1.	Agriculture, including agricultural extension.
2.	Land improvement, implementation of land reforms, land consolidation and soil conservation.
3.	Minor irrigation, water management and watershed development.
4.	Animal husbandry, dairying and poultry.
5.	Fisheries.
6.	Social forestry and farm forestry.
7.	Minor forest produce.
8.	Small-scale industries, including food processing industries.
9.	Khadi, village and cottage industries.
10.	Rural housing.
11.	Drinking water
12.	Fuel and fodder.
13.	Roads, culverts, bridges, ferries, waterways and other means of communication.
14.	Rural electrification, including distribution of electricity.
15.	Non-conventional energy sources.
16.	Poverty alleviation programmes.
17.	Education, including primary and secondary schools.
18.	Technical training and vocational education.
19.	Adult and non-formal education.
20.	Libraries.
21.	Cultural activities.
22.	Markets and fairs.
23.	Health and sanitation, including hospitals, primary health centres and dispensaries.
24.	Family welfare.
25.	Women and child development.
26.	Social welfare, including welfare of the handicapped and mentally retarded.
27.	Welfare of the weaker sections, and in particular, of the Scheduled Castes and the Scheduled Tribes.
28.	Public distribution system.
29.	Maintenance of community assets.

Table 14.3: Twelfth Schedule of the Constitution (Article 243 W)

1.	Urban planning including town planning.
2.	Regulation of land-use and construction of buildings.
3.	Planning for economic and social development.
4.	Roads and bridges.
5.	Water supply for domestic, industrial and commercial purposes.
6.	Public health, sanitation conservancy and solid waste management.
7.	Fire services.
8.	Urban forestry, protection of the environment and promotion of ecological aspects.
9.	Safeguarding the interests of weaker sections of society, including the handicapped and mentally retarded.
10.	Slum improvement and upgradation.
11.	Urban poverty alleviation.
12.	Provision of urban amenities and facilities such as parks, gardens, play-grounds.
13.	Promotion of cultural, educational and aesthetic aspects.
14.	Burials and burial grounds; cremations, cremation grounds and electric crematoriums.
15.	Cattle ponds; prevention of cruelty to animals.
16.	Vital statistics including registration of births and deaths.
17.	Public amenities including street lighting, parking lots, bus stops and public conveniences.
18.	Regulation of slaughter houses and tanneries.

14.5.1 Salient Features:

1. It provides a framework for the assignment of appropriate governmental functions to municipalities through the Twelfth Schedule of the Constitution read with Article 243 W. The Twelfth Schedule defines the functional domain of municipalities. Many of the functions included in this Schedule have distributional and developmental attributes.

The Twelfth Schedule generally contains traditional functions of municipalities. However, some non-traditional functions are also discernible from the list. These are: (a) protection of the environment and promotion of ecological aspects, (b) safeguarding the interests of weaker sections of society including the handicapped and mentally retarded, (c) urban poverty alleviation, and (d) promotion of cultural and aesthetic aspects.

2. States are statutorily required to constitute a finance commission (Article 243-I and 243-Y), once in every five years, to recommend to their legislatures measures to improve municipal finances including (i) assignment of taxes, duties, tolls, and fees, (ii) sharing of state taxes, and (iii) provision of grants-in-aid.

3. The Finance Commission constituted by the Government of India is obligated to recommend measures to augment the Consolidated Fund of State Governments to supplement the resources of the municipalities on the basis of the recommendations made by the State Finance Commissions [Article 280(3)(c)].

4. It is mandatory to constitute in every State at the district level a District Planning Committee to consolidate and prepare development plan for the district as a whole (Article 243 ZD). Similarly, it is mandatory to constitute in every metropolitan area a Metropolitan Planning Committee to prepare a development plan for the metropolitan area as a whole (Article 243 ZE).

5. It mandates that a municipality if dissolved by a State Government, must be reconstituted within six months [Article 243 U(3)]. This is meant to ensure the continuity of civic affairs by 'elected' representatives of the people.

6. It ensures reservation of seats for women and other disadvantaged categories (Article 243 T).

The situation existing before and after the Seventy-fourth amendment is summarised in Table 14.4.

14.5.2 New Status of Municipalities: The Seventy-fourth amendment was made with the intention to make municipalities self-governing units. Are they so?

In the federal polity of India, local bodies are institutions created by the State Governments (entry 5 of List II of the Seventh Schedule). They enjoy only those powers and responsibilities which are assigned to them. Twelfth schedule of the Constitution lists the functions and responsibilities that may be transferred to municipalities. The permissive nature of Seventy-fourth Amendment is clear and the State Governments enjoy full discretion as regards the transfer of functions to municipalities.

No doubt, municipalities have acquired constitutional status after the said Amendment, they are completely dependent on respective State Governments in terms of self-governance.

14.5.3 Desirability and Feasibility of Uniformity in Municipal Functions: A careful reading of the Twelfth Schedule shows that many of the functions listed in it found place in the Municipal Acts of various States even before the enactment of the conformity legislations by them. Hence, the Twelfth Schedule has been generally accepted as a guiding list of municipal functions.

Should there be all-India uniformity in delegating functions and financial powers to local bodies? There is a weak case for all-India uniformity as regards functional domain of local bodies. State Governments and their local bodies have diverse economic and social conditions. It is by no means rational to expect uniformity in the functions and powers of the Greater Bombay Municipal Corporation and the municipality of a small township of a backward State. Similarly, it is debatable if local bodies should have uniform taxation powers.

Table 14.4: Status of Municipalities in India

Before the 74th Amendment	After the 74th Amendment
No all-India framework for devolution of functions	12th Schedule read with Article 243 W of the Constitution provides guidepoints for assignment of functions to municipalities.
High degree of arbitrariness in the system of fiscal transfers from the State Governments to municipalities. No periodic assessment of financial needs of municipalities	State Finance Commission (SFC) to be constituted statutorily in every State every Fifth year (Article 243-I and 243-Y) to review the financial position of municipalities and suggest measures to improve the same.
No role for the National Finance Commission as regards the finances of urban local bodies.	National Finance Commission is required to augment the Consolidated Fund of State Governments to supplement the resources of the municipalities on the basis of the recommendations made by the SFCs [Article 280(3)(c)].
Absence of constitutional bodies to prepare development plans for local areas.	Mandatory constitution of District Planning Committees (Article 243ZD) and Metropolitan Planning Committees (Article 243ZE) for consolidation and preparation of development plans.
Failure to hold regular elections and prolonged supersessions.	A municipality if dissolved by a State Government must be reconstituted within six months [Article 243 U(3)].
Lack of participation from weaker sections of society	Reservation of seats for women and other disadvantaged categories (Article 243 T).

Though it will be useful to prepare a reference list regarding functions (Eleventh and Twelfth Schedules), assigned taxes, shareable taxes, user charges, fees etc., all-India uniformity in these matters would be too much to expect.

Feasibility of all-India uniformity as regards the functional jurisdiction of municipalities is poor in view of the permissive nature of Seventy-fourth Amendment. It is highly unlikely that the 25 States of India would make uniform transfer of functions and financial powers to their respective municipalities. All-India uniformity in the functions of municipalities has to be ruled out in view of inter-State disparities.

Even at the level of a State, uniformity is not desirable in view of diverse city conditions and intra-State disparities. This fact has been recognised by the Constitution while providing for the constitution of three types of municipal bodies: Nagar Panchayats, Municipal Councils, and Municipal Corporations (Article 243 Q). However, it does not distinguish between the functional domains of the three types of municipal bodies. The determination of the functions of municipalities of different sizes is left to the wisdom of the State Governments.

However, there exists a case for uniformity of functions among similar municipalities in a State. If a State chooses to allocate dissimilar functions and powers to similar municipalities (say Municipal Councils), there can be genuine resentment among the municipalities discriminated against. It is here that objective criteria based on population size, geographical area, or constitutional categorisation (Article 243 Q) are needed to prevent misuse of political authority.

The Constitution should provide, at least, a list of minimum functions to be transferred to municipalities of various types by the State Governments.

14.5.4 Role of State Finance Commissions: The State Finance Commission is set up under Article 243-I read with Article 243-Y of the Constitution. It is required to review the financial position of the municipalities and make recommendations as to

(a) the principles which should govern –

i. the distribution between the State and the Municipalities of the net proceeds of taxes, duties, tolls and fees leviable by the State, which may be divided between them, and the allocations between the Municipalities of their respective shares of such proceeds.

ii. the determination of the taxes, duties, tolls and fees which may be assigned to, or appropriated by, the Municipalities.

iii. the grants-in-aid to Municipalities from the Consolidated Fund of the State.

(b) the measures needed to improve the financial position of the Municipalities.

(c) any other matter referred to the Finance Commission in the interest of sound finance of the Municipalities.

As required under the Constitution, all State Governments have set up Finance Commissions. These State Finance Commissions (SFCs) are expected to strengthen local bodies so that they may function as democratic units for the socio-economic development of urban and rural areas of our country.

The task of the First Finance Commission of a State was difficult and arduous in the absence of precedence and it was expected to make suo moto all such studies in areas which never existed before. Nevertheless, the work of the First Finance Commission was crucial because it paved the way for subsequent commissions. The following observations may be made in this regard.

1. The new Constitutional arrangement (Seventy-fourth Amendment) implies that the whole range of a State's tax revenue is open to sharing with municipalities. SFCs are expected to evolve principles of tax assignment, tax sharing, and grants to municipalities with a view to mitigate their weak financial position. They are also required to evolve criteria with regard to adequacy and objectivity of grants.
2. Sharing of State tax revenue with municipalities depends wholly on the discretion of State Government.
3. In determining devolution of funds, the SFCs would do well to keep in mind, *inter alia*, the following factors.

(a) Resource position of the State.
(b) Normative deficits of municipalities. Any system which underestimates the gap between revenue and expenditure should be discouraged.
(c) The degree of dependence of municipalities for funds on the State Government.
(d) Capacity of a municipality to utilise devolved resources.
(e) A State Finance Commission may consider introduction of a system of incentives and disincentives into the entire governmental grants on objective lines. Municipalities which are able to raise resources through levy of user charges and benefit taxes should be considered for incentive grants from the State Government.

A. Determination and Filling of Budgetary Gaps: A State Finance Commission has to determine the budgetary gaps of municipalities for the period of its award. Thereafter, it has to devise formulae for filling the gaps so determined.

Determination of the Budgetary Gaps: Two approaches may be followed for this purpose: (a) trend growth rate and (b) normative approach.

Under the first approach, average annual growth rate in a variable during a reference period (say 1994-95 through 2003-04) is worked out and the same is projected for a future period (say 2004-05 through 2008-2009). It is assumed that past behaviour of the variable will be repeated in future. Thus, 'actuals' or 'accounts' of revenue and expenditure of a government may be used to compute the average annual growth rate of the two aggregates over a stated period. Applying the computed average to a future period, one can work out estimated revenue, expenditure and budgetary gap for any future year.

Under the second method, revenue of a government is assessed normatively and certain norms are applied to assess expenditure. In other words, 'needs' and 'capacities' of different governments are assessed normatively and such normative assessments are used to meet budgetary gaps of the governments. More specifically, fiscal performance of a government is judged on the basis of *what ought to be* rather than *what it actually is*.

In the context of the work of a State Finance Commission, normative approach should apply to both the State Government and municipalities and that the assessment of revenue and expenditure should be done in a manner so as to maintain incentives for greater revenue efforts and economy in spending.

Filling the Gap: Once budgetary gaps of municipalities are determined, the next task of a State Finance Commission is to devise formulae for filling these gaps. For this purpose, it has to work out a judicious mix of tax devolution and grants.

It is noteworthy that the term 'gap-filling' in the context of State-municipal fiscal relations has a different connotation than at the national level.

At the national level, even after the transfer to the States of a share of divisible taxes, the resources of some of the States may remain inadequate to meet their needs. Thus, a Finance Commission determines the grants equal to deficit of each State so that the non-Plan revenue accounts of the States are balanced or left with a surplus every year. In other words, deficits of non-Plan revenue account which remain after tax devolution are covered through grants. This is called the gap-filling approach (or more appropriately net gap-filling approach).

It is possible that even before tax devolution from the Centre, some high-income States have surplus in their non-Plan revenue account. Thus, while a State cannot be denied a part of a shared Central tax even if it has no demonstrated financial need, grants are given upon genuine financial needs of the States.

However, the working of a State Finance Commission is different. Like the National Finance Commission, it is not bound by any constitutional restrictions regarding the type of taxes to be shared with municipalities. In fact, the whole field of State taxation is open to it for determining tax devolution. In other words, tax devolution and grants are to be used simultaneously to cover the budgetary gaps of municipalities. In this case, gap-filling means how to cover the projected budgetary gaps of municipalities through a judicious mix of tax devolution and grants with due regard to the underlying principles of the two methods to effect transfers from a higher to a lower level government.

14.6 Municipal Commercial Borrowings

Plan allocations of Central and State Governments are the chief source of financing capital projects of municipal governments. Other sources of finance include (a) internal resources of municipalities, (b) institutional resources (HUDCO etc.), and (c) multilateral agencies.

The scope for additional funds from Central and State Governments is limited in view of the pressing need to reduce fiscal deficit. Similarly, institutional finances at low cost are unlikely to be available in the wake of financial sector reforms. Under such circumstances, municipal authorities should be permitted access to the capital market to mobilise additional resources. Recent expansion and modernisation of capital market in India suggests that inflow of capital into equity and debt market is quite high if attractive rate of return is offered.

14.6.1 Rationale for Municipal Commercial Borrowings: It is both fair and efficient that projects with long-term benefits are financed through long-term borrowings. If long-term capital projects are financed out of current revenues and/or short-term borrowings, the future generations would enjoy free-riding. Since the benefits of a capital project are reaped over a long period of time, i.e. by more than one generation of tax payers, the financing of such projects should place the repayment burden on the present as well as future generations.

14.6.2 Limitations: Municipal access to capital market, though desirable, is hindered by a variety of factors which may be classified into two categories: (a) restrictions imposed by the higher level government, and (b) other constraints.

The Constitution of India imposes various types of restrictions on the borrowing powers of the State Governments which, in turn, impose restrictions on the borrowing powers of the municipalities under them. Since borrowings by the lower level government are guaranteed, in most cases, by the higher level government, the latter has a right to impose such restrictions. These restrictions apply to (a) type of debt, (b) amount of debt, (c) term of the debt, and (d) use of debt funds. Approval of the higher level government, which is often cumbersome, is needed before the debt is floated.

Thus, no municipal authority can borrow without an explicit sanction of its State Government. When the loan amount exceeds Rs. 25 lakh or the repayment period is over 30 years, local borrowings need Central approval under the provisions of the Local Authorities Loan Act, 1914 (a Central Legislation).

Among the 'other constraints', the more important are the following: Low credit worthiness of municipalities, their poor tract record as borrowers, and lack of trustworthy financial intermediaries.

Despite the foregoing hurdles, some municipalities in India have successfully tapped the bond market.

14.6.3 Factors Determining Success of Municipal Bonds: To attract a share of capital market for municipalities, the following conditions need to be satisfied.

1. Urban infrastructure projects should be commercially viable.
2. Municipal bonds are rated by some recognised credit rating institution. This will help build confidence of investors in the bond issue as well as help in its subsequent trading on the secondary market.
3. Such bonds should carry tax concessions.
4. Revenues accruing to the municipal entity are sufficiently elastic.
5. Security behind the debt taken by the municipal entity is sound.
6. Municipal entity makes provision for the creation of debt-servicing funds and the legal procedures for seeking recourse in the event of default.
7. Municipal entity is competent to pledge revenues for debt-servicing and extend collateral in terms of commercial property, plant and machinery and other assets.

14.7 Privatisation of Municipal Services

The scope for privatisation of some municipal services in order to reduce costs is a moot question.

Municipalities alone cannot handle huge infrastructural projects like water supply, sewage disposal, and urban transport. Involvement of central, state, and private sector is required to meet the scale of investment needed in these areas. Similarly, greater participation of private sector is desirable in the provision of civic services, particularly those the consumption of which can be attributed to individuals/households. There are many types of arrangement in respect of public-private partnership depending on situation. However, care should be taken not to dilute current social commitments while embarking on public-private partnership.

The historical and ideological resistance to private sector participation persists in most places. Consequently, few local bodies have tried out private sector participation in civic services on any significant scale. Wherever it has happened, the experiment has remained limited to disposal of solid wastes, and maintenance of parks.

The disenchantment with utility enterprises of municipalities is not conceptual but borne out of their inefficient and sometimes corrupt management. The merits of privatisation are seen in terms of improvement in efficiency and reduction in the budgetary burden of state-owned enterprises.

Though the need for private sector participation is widely felt, it is not openly expressed. Very rarely political parties have spoken publicly against the public sector. Contrarily, there is a stiff opposition by political parties to any move to undermine the importance of public sector. The strong unions of public sector enterprises come in handy for politicians to prevent the erosion of state and municipal activities.

14.8 Tenth Finance Commission on Local Bodies

The Tenth Finance Commission did not have any mandate, in its terms of reference, to make recommendations for the local bodies. However, the 73rd and 74th Constitutional amendments had become effective before the Commission had finalised its report and, therefore, it took the view that in terms of the sub-clauses (bb) and (c) of the article 280(3), it was obliged to make recommendations regarding measures needed to augment thc Consolidated Fund of the States for supplementation of the resources of the panchayats and the municipalities. The Commission analysed the scope of such duty cast on it and made the following observations:

1. The need for augmentation of the Consolidated Fund of the States should first be ascertained and only thereafter the measures for such augmentation be recommended.
2. Such measures need not necessarily involve transfer of resources from the Centre.
3. Once the SFCs complete their task, the Finance Commission becomes duly bound to assess and build into the expenditure stream of the States the funding requirements for supplementing the resources of the panchayats and the municipalities. Measures needed for augmentation of the Consolidated Funds of the States may be determined accordingly.
4. The responsibility for sharing and assigning taxes and providing grants to the local bodies rests with the States and does not stand transferred to the Centre.
5. The transfer of duties and functions listed in the Eleventh and Twelfth Schedules of the Constitution would also involve concomitant transfer of staff and resources. Transfers of duties and functions to the local bodies should, therefore, not entail any extra financial burden.

Since the recommendations of the State Finance Commissions were not available to the Tenth Finance Commission, the latter was in doubt whether it could recommend measures for augmenting State resources for the purpose of supplementing the resources of panchayats and municipalities. To resolve the dilemma, it decided to make ad hoc provision of specific grants to States in the following manner.

1. An ad hoc provision of Rs. 100 per capita of rural population in each State to be distributed amongst panchayats over and above their due by way of their share of the assigned taxes, duties, tolls, fees etc.

2. A provision of Rs. 1,000 crore for the five year period (1995-2000) covered by its recommendations for urban local bodies.

While making these provisions for grants to panchayats/municipalities, the Commission made it clear that this need not necessarily be a precedent for future Commissions.

14.9 Eleventh Finance Commission on Local Bodies

EFC was the first to be required by the President, in terms of the 73rd and 74th Amendments to the Constitution, to recommend the measures needed to augment the Consolidated Fund of a State to supplement the resources of the panchayats and municipalities in the State on the basis of the recommendations of the State Finance Commissions.

The EFC recommended grants totalling Rs. 10,000 crore for local bodies during 2000-2005, to be utilised mainly for maintenance of civic services. Of this, Rs. 1,600 crore per annum is for rural local bodies and Rs. 400 crore per annum is for urban local bodies. EFC recommended that the amounts of Rs. 1,600 crore and Rs. 400 crore provided for the panchayats and municipalities respectively, for each of the five years (2000-05) be distributed among the States on the following criteria and weights.

1. Population 40 per cent.
2. Index of decentralisation 20 per cent.
3. Distance from highest per capita income 20 per cent.
4. Revenue effort 10 per cent.
5. Geographical area 10 per cent.

The grants given to local bodies are primarily meant for maintenance of civil services including primary health and family welfare, education as well as other public utility services. Details regarding inter-State distribution are given in Chapter VIII of the Report of the Commission.

It is noteworthy that while a State cannot be denied a part of share in Central taxes even if it has no demonstrated financial need, grants are given upon genuine financial needs of the States. It is possible that even before tax devolution from the Centre, some high-income States have a surplus in their non-Plan revenue account. The Seventh Finance Commission identified Punjab, Haryana, Gujarat, Tamil Nadu, and Karnataka as such States. Thus, grants-in-aid along with share in taxes serve as a levelling up force to promote regional balanced development. From this, it may also be inferred that States as a whole are not affected whether transfers are made by one means (share in Central taxes) or another (grants). It is the total amount transferred which is important for them. However, the sources of transfer become important when it comes to individual States because the formulae applied for various transfers are different. It is not possible to adopt a single formula for all transfers in view of the differing nature of taxes and grants.

14.10 Twelfth Finance Commission on Local Bodies

The Commission made the following recommendations regarding local bodies.

A total grant of Rs. 20,000 crore for the panchayati raj institutions and Rs. 5,000 crore for the urban local bodies may be given to the states for the period 2005-10.

The PRIs should be encouraged to take over the assets relating to water supply and sanitation and utilize the grants for repairs/rejuvenation as also the O&M costs. The PRIs should, however, recover at least 50 percent of the recurring costs in the form of user charges.

Out of the grants allocated for the panchayats, priority should be given to expenditure on the O&M costs of water supply and sanitation. This will facilitate panchayats to take over the schemes and operate them.

At least 50 per cent of the grants provided to each state for the urban local bodies should be earmarked for the scheme of solid waste management through public-private partnership. The municipalities should concentrate on collection, segregation and transportation of solid waste. The cost of these activities, whether carried out in house or out sourced, could be met from the grants.

Besides expenditure on the O&M costs of water supply and sanitation in rural areas and on the schemes of solid waste management in urban areas, PRIs and ULBs should, out of the grants allocated, give high priority to expenditure on creation of data base and maintenance of accounts through the use of modern technology and management systems, wherever possible. Some of the modern methods like GIS (Geographic Information Systems) for mapping of properties in urban areas and computerization for switching over to a modern system of financial management would go a long way in creating strong local governments, fulfilling the spirit of the 73rd and 74th Constitutional amendments.

The states may assess the requirement of each local body on the basis of the principles stated by us and earmark funds accordingly out of the total allocation re-commended by us.

Grants have not been recommended separately for the normal and the excluded areas under the fifth and sixth schedule of the Constitution. The states having such areas may distribute the grants recommended by us to all local bodies, including those in the excluded areas, in a fair and just manner.

The central government should not impose any condition other than those prescribed by us, for release or utilization of these grants, which are largely in the nature of a correction of vertical imbalance between the centre and the states.

The normal practice of insisting on the utilization of amounts already released before further releases are considered, may continue and the grants may be released to a state only after it certifies that the previous releases have been passed on to the local bodies. The amounts due to the states in the first year of our award period i.e. 2005-06 may be released without such an insistence.

State governments should not take more than 15 days in transferring the grants to local bodies after these are released by the central government. The centre should take a serious view of any undue delay on the part of the state.

The central government should take note of our views on the issues, while formulating or revising various policy measures. In particular, action may be taken to raise the ceiling on profession tax.

The state should adopt the best practices to improve the resources of the panchayats.

The suggestions made by us in respect of state finance commissions should be acted upon with a view to strengthening the institution of SFCs, so that it may play an effective role in the system of fiscal transfers to the third tier of government.

Note

1. Here, 'a transitional area', 'a smaller urban area', or 'a larger urban area' means such area as the Governor may specify by public notification having regard to the population of the area, the density of the population, the revenue generated for local administration, the percentage of employment in non-agricultural activities and such other factors.

15

First Finance Commission

The First Finance Commission was constituted by an Order of the President dated November 22, 1951. It was charged with the duty of making recommendations to the President as to (a) the distribution between the Union and the States of the net proceeds of taxes which are to be, or may be divided between them under the provisions of the Constitution and the allocation between the States of the respective shares of such proceeds, (b) the principles which should govern the grants-in-aid of the revenues of the States out of the Consolidated Fund of India, (c) any other matter referred to the Commission by the President in the interest of sound finance.

Summary Statement	
Chairman	Mr. K.C. Neogy
Members	Shri V.P. Menon Justice R. Kaushalendra Rao Dr. B.K. Madan Shri M.V. Rangachari, Member-Secretary
Year and month of establishment	November 1951
Year and month of reporting	December 1952
Period of award	1952-53 to 1956-57
Main Recommendations	
• States' share in income tax fixed at (per cent): 55 • Bases of distribution of States' share in income tax inter se (per cent): Population: 80; Contribution: 20; Other factors: Nil • States' share in Union excise duties fixed at (per cent): 40 (from 3 commodities) • Bases of distribution of States' share in Union excise duties inter se (per cent): Population: 100; Other factors: Nil	

The task of the Commission was by no means a simple one. It had to grapple with problems created by the Partition of the country in 1947. In its own words, "The three years that followed the advent of Independence witnessed a transformation in the political, economic and financial background. The partition divided three Provinces while large areas comprised in the former Indian States were merged with Provinces or formed into new political units as Part B and Part C States. The developments during these years added appreciably to Central expenditure. After Independence, defence involved additional commitments. Besides, Independence gave a natural stimulus to expansion of social services and called for large additional outlays on nation-building activities, while the deficit position of the country in regard to food in an inflationary context rendered necessary the continuance of subsidies on foodgrains." [1]

15.1 Financial Assistance to States: Approach of the Commission

In drawing up the scheme of assistance to the States, the Commission kept three main considerations in view.

1. Additional transfer of resources from the Centre must be such as the Centre could bear without undue strain on its resources, taking into account its responsibility for such vital maters as the defence of the country and the stability of its economy.
2. Principles for the distribution of revenues between the States and the determination of grants-in-aid must be uniformly applied to all the States.
3. Scheme of distribution should attempt to lessen the inequalities between States.

During the course of discussions a number of State Governments drew the Commission's attention to the finances required for meting expenditure on capital schemes. As the Commission was primarily concerned with the distribution of revenues between the Centre and the States and the determination of grants-in-aid of the revenues of the States, which have to come from Central revenues, it made no recommendations in regard to grants for meeting the capital requirements of the States.

15.2 Distribution of Income Tax

15.2.1 Determination of the Share of States: The Commission considered it undesirable to concentrate on income tax as a balancing factor in the adjustment of resources between the Centre and the units. It believed that an increase in the States' share of this tax should not be used as a major factor in the devolution of further revenues to the States. On the other hand, the State Governments had put forward an almost unanimous demand for an increase in the States' share of income tax. On a consideration of all the circumstances, the Commission came to the conclusion that some increase in the share assignable to the States was justified although it could not be of the order suggested by the majority of State Governments. It accordingly recommended that the percentage of the net proceeds of income tax to be allocated to the States be raised from 50 per cent to 55 per cent.

15.2.2 Distribution of the Share of States Inter Se: Various bases were suggested for the distribution of income tax among the States, the more important of which were the following.

1. Collection of income-tax in the various States.
2. Amount of income-tax realised in respect of incomes, wherever earned, of individuals resident in the different States.
3. Collection of income-tax in the various States adjusted with reference to the origin of the income.
4. Relative population of each State.
5. Relative volume of industrial labour in each State.
6. Relative per capita income of the States.
7. Needs of the different States according to various criteria, e.g. area of sparseness of population, economic backwardness or the inverse relative per capital income of each State.

The first three factors primarily sought to relate the distribution to the respective contributions of the different States to the total proceeds, and were intended to provide the most adequate or convenient measure of such contribution. At the other end were factors like the area of a state in relation to its population, economic backwardness and inverse relative per capita income which were specialised measures of needs. Between these categories fell suggestions for the adoption of such factors as population, industrial labour etc. which were supposed to reflect both the needs and, to an extent, the contribution of the States.

As regards the factor of contribution, the Commission Observed, "The relevance of the factor of contribution in the distribution of a shared tax will be generally acknowledged. It is recognised, however, that collection is an inadequate index of contribution. Some consideration of the facts regarding collection will serve to bring this out clearly. Between them, the two States of Bombay and West Bengal account for nearly three-quarters of the collections of income tax in the country: of these collections again, about three-quarters are made within the cities of Bombay and Calcutta. It is clear that the collections of income-tax within the limits of these two cities which account for the greater part of the collections in the country, do not in the main arise on account of activities which are confined to those limits. Nor can the high collections be accounted for by economic activity which is restricted largely to the States of which they are the capitals. Indeed, though it is impossible to indicate in what degree income subjected to tax in these cities should be ascribed to other States, there is no doubt that a substantial part of the tax receipts in these big port cities in fact accrues in respect of incomes originating beyond the boundaries of the respective States. The high collections of income-tax in these all-India cities are due in a large measure to their being in a sense *entrepots* of the country's import and export trade and to the concentration within their confines of the head offices of companies and other concerns operating all over the country. A study of the information collected by us from some of the larger concerns indicates that the basis of income-creation are far more diversified and widely spread over the country than the facts of collection would seem to suggest.

Apart from the impracticability of establishing the precise contribution of different regions to a common tax, the doctrine of economic allegiance on which the principle of contribution is based is open to objection when applied to the sharing of the proceeds of a tax among the units of a federation. The bases of residence or origin – in so far as origin can be identified – may be conveniently used for providing relief from double taxation as between two sovereign states, but may not give proper results in the allocation of the proceeds of a Central tax like income-tax among the States of a country. The incomes which are earned in different States in India cannot be put in the same category as incomes earned in the different sovereign States. Unlike the incomes earned in the different units of a federation the incomes which are taxable by a sovereign state are not necessarily or directly conditioned by the policies pursued by other States. In a federation the policies of the federal government are mainly conceived in the national interest and these may confer unequal benefits and may impose unequal burdens on the different units. To illustrate the point, Central policies governing the regulation of company operations, the development of railways and ports, tariffs and subsidies, freight rates, food subsidies, control, regulation and location of industries and price control are conceived and operated in the broad national interest. These policies have a bearing on the pattern of development of large-scale enterprise in industry and trade which are important contributory sources of income-tax. Since the benefits which result in the growth of enterprise flow from policies pursued on the ground of national interest, there is every reason why national considerations should in a large measure influence the sharing of the proceeds to taxes on such enterprise.

Another argument in favour of giving collections some importance in the distribution of income-tax is based on the heavier responsibilities of States where large collections are made to look after the problems of law and order and welfare in respect of the concentration of industrial labour in those States. The very concentration of industries and business enterprises in those States, however, leads to increased receipts in the State sphere from such heads as stamps, sales taxes and entertainment duties which directly benefit the State finances.

Taking all the considerations into account, we believe that the basis of collections, either unadjusted or adjusted with reference to residence of tax-payers, will not secure by itself an equitable distribution among the various States. We think, besides, that even if it were practicable to ascertain precisely the contribution of the various units to the pool of income tax, distribution based solely on this criterion might not be satisfactory. It might not substantially conform to the relative responsibility of the various States to provide governmental services to the people. Whatever the theoretical validity of alternative indexes of contribution, a proper scheme of distribution should not overlook the broad purpose of the devolution of revenues to the States, which is to make larger funds available to them to meet their expanding responsibilities in respect of the welfare of their population." [2]

Therefore, the Commission relied on the following factors to distribute States' share of income tax among the States. (a) general measure of needs furnished by population and (b) contribution. It gave a moderate weightage in the scheme of distribution to the factor of contribution.

As regards the actual distribution of the States' share in each year, it considered it convenient, both to the States and to the Centre, if the shares were expressed as fixed percentages (as was the practice existing then) instead of its formula being left to be applied each year. The Commission accordingly proposed that the shares of each of the States should be expressed as a percentage of the total States' share. It applied the formula for distribution which it related to the actual figures of collections for the three years ending 1950-51, with suitable adjustments, and figures of population taken from the 1951 census. The percentage share of the net proceeds of income tax assigned to the States was recommended to be distributed among the States in the manner shown in Table 15.1.

15.3 Division of Union Excises

Tracing the history of excise duties the Commission noted, "Prior to the 1st April 1921 there were excise duties on intoxicating spirits and drugs, salt, cotton cloth and petroleum. The excise duty on salt, cotton cloth and petroleum was retained wholly by the Centre. The excise on intoxicating spirits and drugs was wholly provincial in some of the Provinces and a divided head in others. The Government of India Act, 1919, allocated the excise duty on intoxicating liquors and drugs wholly to the Provinces and left the other excise duties to the Centre. The duty on cotton cloth was subsequently removed but duties on matches, sugar, steel ingots and kerosene were levied from time to time. By 1937-38 the total revenue from these four excises and the excise on petrol amounted to Rs. 7.66

crore, against Rs. 2.71 crore realised from the excise duties on cotton cloth and petrol in 1921-22. With the outbreak of the war, the need to meet the rising cost of defence expenditure led to increases in the rates of duty on these commodities and to the levy of excise duties on other articles. A duty on pneumatic tyres and tubes was imposed in 1941-42 while in 1942-43 the first step was taken in the levy of an excise duty on tobacco, which has since developed into the most fruitful single source of excise tapped so far. An excise duty on "vegetable products" was levied in 1943-44 and duties on betelnuts, tea and coffee were imposed in the following year. An excise duty on cloth was imposed in 1947-48 while the duty on betelnut was withdrawn in 1948-49. At present twelve important commodities are subject to Union excises and the revenue from them in 1951-52 amounted to Rs. 84 crore.

Table 15.1: Percentage Shares of the States in the Net Proceeds of Income Tax Assigned to the States as Recommended by the First Finance Commission

State	Per cent
Assam	2.25
Bihar	9.75
Bombay	17.50
Hyderabad	4.50
Madhya Bharat	1.75
Madhya Pradesh	5.25
Madras	15.25
Mysore	2.25
Orissa	3.50
Patiala and East Punjab States Union	0.75
Punjab	3.25
Rajasthan	3.50
Saurashtra	1.00
Travancore-Cochin	2.50
Uttar Pradesh	15.75
West Bengal	11.25

Source: *Report of the First Finance Commission*, 1952, pp. 76-77.

The Taxation Enquiry Committee recommended that excise duties levied for revenue purposes, which in many cases may have to be regulated with reference to customs duties and where consumption of the commodities may also be difficult to trace, should be Central. During the discussions preceding the enactment of the Government of India Act, 1935, the question of utilising Union excises for making more resources available to the units was first considered by the Statutory Commission. The Commission proposed that a Provincial Fund should be established from the proceeds of certain new excises and possibly of the salt duty. The amount in the fund was to be automatically distributed to the Provinces on a per capita basis. The Percy Committee (1932) recommended that the Federal Legislature should be empowered to assign to the units the whole or any part of the proceeds of federal excises. This was endorsed by the Joint Committee of Parliament on Indian Constitutional Reforms and embodied in section 140(1) of the Government of India Act, 1935. The provision in this section was, however, not availed of for transferring a part of any Central excise to the Provinces.

The Expert Committee on the Financial Provisions of the Union Constitution recommended no change in the Constitutional position as embodied in the Government of India Act, 1935, but suggested that one-half of the net proceeds of the duty on tobacco should be assigned to the Provinces and distributed on the basis of estimated consumption. The Constitution made no specific provision for the sharing of any excise duty and left the matter to be regulated, as in the past, by an Act of the Union Parliament.

While Union excises were not shared between the Centre and the Provinces, there were arrangements for the sharing of some of the excises like those on matches, sugar, tobacco and vegetable products with some of the former Indian States before their integration. These sharing arrangements, the basis of which sometimes varied from State to State, lapsed with the financial integration of these States and no State is now in receipt of a share of any Central excise duty." [3]

15.3.1 Determination of the Share of States: The first issue before the Commission in this regard was whether the States should be given a share in all the Union excises or in only one or more selected excises. It considered it inadvisable, at any rate to begin with, to divide too many excises, particularly as the yield from some of them was relatively small, and that it was desirable to restrict the division to a few selected excises. The selected excises should be such as are levied on commodities which are of common and widespread consumption and which yield a sizeable sum of revenue for distribution. There should also be reasonable stability of yield and comparative immunity of the duties selected from fluctuations related to changes in the customs tariff. Taking all these factors into account, the Commission came to the conclusion that duties on tobacco (including cigarettes, cigars etc.), matches and vegetable products were the most suitable for distribution. It, therefore, recommend that 40 per cent of the net proceeds of these duties be allocated to the States.

15.3.2 Distribution of the Share of States Inter Se: The question of determining the mode of distribution still remained. The resources of the States required to be strengthened. At the same time, the scheme of distribution needed to be balanced and equitable as a whole. Considering all these factors, the Commission recommended the distribution of the excise duties on a per capita basis. In other words, States' share of the excise duties was distributed among them on the basis of population.

Some States suggested consumption as the basis of distribution. That basis was not considered by the Commission as, in its opinion, there were no reliable data regarding the consumption of each of the commodities in the various States. It, however, recommended that steps should be taken to collect and maintain statistics of the consumption of all major commodities that may be subject to Union excise from time to time, so that the data may be available to the Commissions in future. The manner of distribution of the share of the net proceeds of the three excises suggested by the Commission for allocation to the States (Table 15.2) represents the percentages of the population of the different States in accordance with the Census of 1951.

15.4 Grants-in-aid in Lieu of Export Duty on Jute

The Government of India Act, 1935, read with the Government of India (Distribution of Revenues) Order, 1936, provided for the distribution of 62.5 per cent of the net proceed of the export duty on jute and jute products among the jute-growing Provinces in proportion to the volume of jute grown therein.

Consequent upon the division of Bengal and Assam on the partition of the country in 1947, roughly 70 per cent of the jute growing area of undivided India got included in Pakistan, necessitating the reconsideration of the allocation of the duty made in the Government of India Act, 1935, particularly as the basis of distribution between the Provinces was the amount of jute grown in them. In the altered circumstances the Government of India decided that the share of the jute export duty allocable to the Provinces should be reduced from 62.5 per cent of the net proceeds to 20 per cent, the basis of allocation among the Provinces continuing to be the amount of jute grown in them. This reduction in the share of the jute export duty led to protests from certain jute-growing States. The difficulty created for the Government of West Bengal by the loss of revenue from this source was recognised by the Government of India which sanctioned ad hoc grants of Rs. 40 lakh in 1947-48 and Rs. 50 lakh in each of the years 1948-49 and

1949-50. The Expert Committee on the Financial Provisions of the Constitution of Independent India held that export duties were unsuitable for sharing with the Provinces and recommended that these should be entirely Central. They, however, proposed that the Provinces which were receiving a share of the export duty on jute and jute products should be compensated for the loss of this item of revenue. They suggested following grants for the four States: West Bengal (Rs. 100 lakh), Assam (Rs. 15 lakh), Bihar (Rs. 17 lakh) and Orissa (Rs. 3 lakh).

Table 15.2: Distribution of States' Share of Excise Duties on Tobacco, Matches and Vegetable Products among the States Recommended by the First Finance Commission

State	Per cent
Assam	2.61
Bihar	11.60
Bombay	10.37
Hyderabad	5.39
Madhya Bharat	2.29
Madhya Pradesh	6.13
Madras	16.44
Mysore	2.62
Orissa	4.22
Patiala and East Punjab States Union	1.00
Punjab	3.66
Rajasthan	4.41
Saurashtra	1.19
Travancore-Cochin	2.68
Uttar Pradesh	18.23
West Bengal	7.16

Source: *Report of the First Finance Commission*, 1952, p. 83.

The Constitution made no provision for the sharing of export duties. The principle of compensation, for a transitional period, to the four jute-growing States was incorporated in Article 273. The sums to be paid were not, however, specified but were left to be prescribed by the Order of the President. After a Finance Commission have been constituted, the President is required to make the Order after considering the recommendations of the Commission. In November 1949 the Government of India requested Shri C.D. Deshmukh to determine the grants-in-aid payable to the four States mentioned above. Shri Deshmukh held that the grants-in-aid payable to these States must necessarily be related to the sums actually received in the past by the States concerned, viewed as part of their revenue, and could not be related to any estimates of the net proceeds in future years of the export duty. He decided that, until the Finance Commission proposed any revision, the following annual grants-in-aid should be paid to these States: West Bengal (Rs. 105 lakh), Assam (Rs. 40 lakh), Bihar (Rs. 35 lakh and Orissa (Rs. 5 lakh). These grants-in-aid were paid in 1950-51 and 1951-52.

In their representations to the First Finance Commission, the Governments of affected States stated that the reduction of the provincial share of the jute export duty by the Government of India in 1947 without consulting the Provinces was unjustified. Considering the whole matter, the Commission recommended the following amounts as grants-in-aid payable annually to these States under Article 273 of the Constitution, with effect from 1952-53: West Bengal (Rs. 150 lakh), Bihar (Rs. 75 lakh), Assam (Rs. 75 lakh) and Orissa (Rs. 15 lakh).

15.5 Grants-in-aid of Revenues

The First Commission formulated certain principles which should regulate the assessment of fiscal needs and, in doing so, it defined also their scope. It considered that the budgetary needs of the States should first be estimated by a detailed examination of the forecasts of revenue and expenditure submitted and then these should be reduced to a comparable basis by the exclusion of abnormal, unusual and non-recurring items of expenditurc. Adjustments in this analysis should be made to take account of the extent of tax effort made by each State individually; and also the measure of economy it had effected in administration. This would help a broad judgement on the quantum of assistance that would be justified. That Commission, however, felt that this analysis should not, by itself, limit grants-in-aid, but that the level of social services reached in a State and any special disabilities arising out of its constitution should entitle it to a further moiety of assistance. It added that grants should also be made for broad purposes of national importance to bring up deficient States to an acceptable minimum level.

Taking a liberal meaning of the term *grants-in-aid of the revenues,* the Commission enunciated principles which should govern grants-in-aid of the revenues of the States to cover both general grants and grants for broad purposes. In the case of specific grants, the following factors were taken into account.

1. Deficiency of States' resources in relation to functions.

2. Concern of the Central Government in seeing that welfare services (e.g. education, health etc.) and developmental activities (e.g. roads) are maintained at a certain minimum standards throughout the country.
3. Interest of the Central Government in developing some activities which State Governments, left to themselves, might neglect (e.g. unemployment insurance, social security etc.).
4. Possibility of improving the quality of performance in the sphere of social services, owing to the superior technical advice available to the higher level of government.
5. Desirability of some co-ordination of standards which can be achieved thereby.

As regards the policy and the role of grants from a higher level of government to a lower level of government, the Commission opined, "The most important factors that appear to have influenced policy in the field of conditional grants are the increasing adaptation of these grants on the one hand to the ability or fiscal capacity of the units and on the other to their relative need for the specific services concerned. The former factor leads to the varying of the requirement to *match* the federal grant with a State contribution so as to reduce the State contribution in the case of financially weaker States. The principle of need is, of course, innate in the purpose of grant, and implies that States with a deficiency of the particular service which is assisted, e.g. education or roads, would receive a proportionately greater measure of assistance than those which are relatively better served.

As regards the relative role of unconditional and conditional grants in the scheme of financial assistance by the federal authority, there is no clear lead in the experience of other federations, there being no single system of universal applicability in regard to this sector of federal financial relations. It appears that each country has tried to find for itself the system or combination of systems which best fits the facts of its political, economic and administrative conditions.

We believe that both the methods of conditional and unconditional grants should have their part to play in the scheme of assistance by the Centre. Unconditional grants should reinforce the general resources of the State Governments, which they would be free to allocate among competing purposes according to their best judgement, subject to the usual administrative and parliamentary checks. Grants for broad purposes may be given to stimulate the expansion of particular categories of services rather than specified schemes under those categories." [4]

In line with its thinking, the Commission enunciated the following principles for giving grants to the States. Firstly, in determining the eligibility of a State for grants-in-aid, its budgetary needs would be an important criterion. In studying the budgetary needs of a State, receipts from shared Central taxes would be taken into account, adjustments would be made for unusual or non-recurring items of revenue and expenditure and due allowance would be made for failure to maximise tax effort or to economise expenditure. Secondly, grants-in-aid should help equalise the standards of basic social services in the various States. Thirdly, grants-in-aid may be given to promote any beneficent service of primary importance in regard to which it is in national interest to assist the less advanced States to get forward.

In assessing the needs of the States and formulating its recommendations in regard to the sums to be paid as grants-in-aid, it considered the budgetary position of the States and the probable amount which would accrue to them under its plan for the devolution of revenue from income tax and Union excises. It took into account the additional burdens arising out of the partition of the country which had been placed upon some of the States. The Commission also kept in view the need for assisting to some extent, the less developed States by the provision of special grants which would enable them to raise the standards of one of the important social services.

With the above philosophy in mind, the Commission came to the conclusion that Madras, Uttar Pradesh, Bihar, Madhya Pradesh, Hyderabad, Rajasthan, Madhya Bharat and the Patiala and East Punjab States Union (PEPSU) could not be considered as being in need of assistance. Bombay, West Bengal, Orissa and Saurashtra were categorised as marginal cases, while Punjab and Assam were considered in need of assistance. The Commission recommended following annual grants for various States: West Bengal (Rs. 80 lakh), Orissa (Rs. 75 lakh), Saurashtra (40 lakh), Punjab (Rs. 1.25 crore), Assam (Rs. 1 crore), Mysore (Rs. 40 lakh) and Travancore-Cochin (Rs. 45 lakh).

Some of the State Governments impressed upon the Commission, the need for taking large strides in the field of primary education. It, therefore, considered it in the national interest to allocate a part of such assistance as the Centre may be able to give to the advancement of such an important social service as primary education. Grants-in-aid of the revenues of these States for this purpose recommended by the Commission are set out in Table 15.3.

15.6 Permanent Secretariat for the Finance Commission

In a significant recommendation, which has not found favour with successive governments at the Centre, the Commission felt the need for a small permanent office to continuously monitor and record developments in the Central and State finances and other indicators which could be of use for the work of a finance commission. It observed, "Our experience as the first Commission has impressed us with the need for a small organisation being set up, preferably as part of the secretariat of the President, to make a continuous study of the finances of the State Governments so that whenever the Commission are constituted in the future, they will have sufficient material available to them at the very commencement of their enquiry. This organisation should work in close liaison with the Finance Ministry and should make a study of the budgets of the State Governments, the changes in their finances from time to time, the rates of taxes in operation, the effects of the further measures of taxation undertaken by them, the working of their commercial enterprises and their effect on the State finances and cognate matter.

Table 15.3: Grants-in-aid of the Revenues of the States for Primary Education Recommended by the First Finance Commission

(Rs. lakh)

State	1953-54	1954-55	1955-56	1956-57
Bihar	41	55	69	83
Madhya Pradesh	25	33	42	50
Hyderabad	20	27	33	40
Rajasthan	20	26	33	40
Orissa	16	22	27	32
Punjab	14	19	23	28
Madhya Bharat	9	12	15	18
Patiala and East Punjab States Union	5	6	8	9
Total	**150**	**200**	**250**	**300**

Source: *Report of the First Finance Commission*, 1952, p. 104.

A study should be made of the various reports on the administration of State Governments, the report of the proceedings of the State Legislatures and the reports of their Public Accounts and Estimates Committees, and points of interest affecting the State finances noted. The organisation should also obtain direct from the State Governments periodical information in regard to the progress of various social services such as education, medical and public health. Current data about the number of schools, the number of children attending schools, the number of hospitals and dispensaries, the number of beds provided, the number of patients treated and the dispersal of facilities, both medical and educational, in rural as distinct from urban areas, should be obtained periodically and tabulated.

Information should be collected regarding the progress of local self-government in each State, the resources raised by local bodies, their dependence on the State Government of their finance and the extent to which the local bodies provide services in the field of education, public health and other social services. Information about the facilities provided by non-government agencies in these fields should also be obtained. Data about the development and maintenance of communications should be obtained periodically from the State Governments. Annual returns may be prescribed so that there is a continuous flow of information for tabulation and study. The results of these studies should be embodied in periodical papers, copies of which should be made available to the Commission. We suggest that the question of setting up this organisation be taken up immediately and the details worked out in consultation with the appropriate-Ministries." [5]

Notes

1. *Report of the First Finance Commission*, 1952, p. 45.
2. *Ibid.,* pp. 73-75.
3. *Ibid.*, pp. 79-81.
4. *Ibid.*, pp.95-96.
5. *Ibid.*, p. 110.

16

Second Finance Commission

This Finance Commission, the second to be set up under Article 280 of the Constitution, was constituted by an Order of the President dated June 1, 1956.

Summary Statement	
Chairman	Mr. K. Santhanam
Members	Shri Ujjal Singh Shri L.S. Misra Shri M.V. Rangachari Dr. B.N. Ganguli
Year and month of establishment	June 1956
Year and month of reporting	September 1957
Period of award	1957-58 to 1961-62
Main Recommendations	
• States' share in income tax fixed at (per cent): 60 • Bases of distribution of States' share in income tax inter se (per cent): Population: 90; Contribution: 10; Other factors: Nil • States' share in Union excise duties fixed at (per cent): 25 (from 8 commodities) • Bases of distribution of States' share in Union excise duties inter se (per cent): Population: 90; Other factors: 10	

In addition to making recommendations as to the matters specified in sub-clauses (a) to (c) of clause (3) of article 280, the Commission was asked to make recommendations as to the following matters.

(a) Sums which may be prescribed under article 273 as grants-in-aid of the revenues of the States of Assam, Bihar, Orissa and West Bengal, in lieu of assignment of any share of the net proceeds in each year of export duty on jute and jute products to those States.

(b) States which are in need of assistance by way of grants-in-aid of the revenues of those States under article 275, and the sums to be paid to those States, having regard, among other considerations to (i) the requirements of the

Second Five Year Plan and (ii) the efforts made by those States to raise additional revenue from the sources available to them.

(c) Principles which should govern the distribution under article 269 of the net proceeds in any financial year of estate duty in respect of property other than agricultural land, levied by the Government of India in the States within which such duty is leviable.

(d) Modifications, if any, in the rates of interest and the terms of repayment of the loans made to the various States by the Government of India between the August 15, 1947 and March 31, 1956.

16.1 Distribution of Income Tax

As usual the States were unanimous in suggesting an increase in the percentage of the net proceeds assigned to them. As regards the principles of distribution of the States' share there was a wide divergence of opinion.

The Commission first dealt with the determination of the share of the net proceeds to be assigned to the States. In its opinion, income tax had ceased to be an expanding source of revenue it once was. In the changing pattern of Union taxation, income tax could not be a major factor in the devolution of further revenues to the States. However, the Commission felt that some increase in the States' share of this tax was justified in view of the unanimous desire of the States. After a careful review of the matter in all its aspects, it came to the conclusion that the percentage of the net proceeds assigned to the States should be raised from 55 to 60. Some States had suggested the inclusion of corporation tax, the tax on Union emoluments and the surcharge on income tax levied for Union purposes in the divisible pool. The Commission expressed its inability to consider these suggestions as they were against the provisions of the Constitution.

Turning to the problem of distribution of the share assigned to the States, the Commission noted that claims put forward by the States generally followed those put forward before the First Finance Commission. In its Report, the First Commission had exhaustively dealt with the validity of these claims. The Commission found itself in substantial agreement with the First Commission that such consideration as the proportion of the scheduled castes and tribes and backward classes in the population, the area of the State, its backwardness etc. were not relevant to a scheme for the distribution of a tax. It also agreed that there was no legal basis for the claim that the Union was in some way required to return to the States the income tax attributable to them after retaining its share.

It considered two principles, namely population and collection, on the basis of which the States' share was distributed. Population found the widest measure of support among the States while collection had been urged by the two industrially advanced States of Bombay and West Bengal. In all previous schemes of distribution, some weight had been given to collection but this had been reduced in favour of population. In the opinion of the Commission this had been a move in the right direction. Considering that income tax was paid by an infinitesimal portion of the population and that the bulk of the tax arose out of business incomes which was derived from the country as a whole, the principle of collection could no longer be considered an equitable basis of distribution. While there might be a case for weightage being given to collection in the restricted field of personal income tax, the Commission came to the conclusion that collection should bc completely abandoned in favour of population as the basis of distribution. However, it did not desire to cause a sudden break in the continuity and hence recommended that the distribution of the States' share should be 10 per cent on the basis of collection and 90 per cent on the basis of population.

In this, as in all other matters, where population had to be taken into account as a factor in the distribution of taxes, the Commission adopted the population figures of the 1951 census as the only practicable basis. As regards the actual manner of distribution of the States' share in each year, it agreed with the First Finance Commission that it would be convenient both to the States and to the Union if the shares were expressed as fixed percentages. It recommended that 60 per cent of the net proceeds in any financial year of taxes on income other than agricultural income, except in so far as those proceeds represented proceeds attributable to Union territories or to taxes payable in respect of Union emoluments, be assigned to the States and distributed among them in the manner shown in Table 16.1. It further recommended that 1 per cent of the net proceeds of the income tax be prescribed as the net proceeds attributable to Union territories.

16.2 Division of Union Excises

Prior to April 1, 1952, no duty of excise was shared between the Union and the States. The First Finance Commission broke new ground when it recommended that, with effect from 1952-53, 40 per cent of the net proceeds of the excise duties on matches, tobacco and vegetable products should be distributed among the States in proportion to their population. This recommendation was accepted by the Government and embodied in the Union Duties of Excuse (Distribution) Act, 1953. In the case of Jammu and Kashmir, after its financial integration with India from April 1, 1954, sums equivalent to 40 per cent of the net proceeds of these excise duties levied and collected by the Government of India in that State were paid to it, under an agreement entered into with that State, until April 1, 1957, when that State came within the scheme of distribution of the Second Finance Commission.

Table 16.1: Percentage Shares of the States in the Net Proceeds of Income Tax Assigned to the States as Recommended by the Second Finance Commission

State	Percentage
Andhra Pradesh	8.12
Assam	2.44
Bihar	9.94
Bombay	15.97
Kerala	3.64
Madhya Pradesh	6.72
Madras	8.40
Mysore	5.14
Orissa	3.73
Punjab	4.24
Rajasthan	4.09
Uttar Pradesh	16.36
West Bengal	10.08
Jammu and Kashmir	1.13

Source: *Report of the Second Finance Commission*, 1957, p. 41.

With taxes on income ceasing to be an expanding source of revenue, it was obvious that any further substantial devolution of revenues to the States by sharing of taxes had to come from Union excises. The coverage and yield of these duties had expanded considerably after Independence. The State Governments were asked for their suggestions in regard to the range of dutiable commodities which could be shared between the Union and the States, the proportion to be allocated to the States and the principles which should govern the distribution of the States' share.

All States asked for an increase in the number of commodities the duties on which should be shared. As regards the States' share of the divisible duties, Assam, Bihar, Bombay, Madras, Orissa, Punjab, Uttar Pradesh, West Bengal and Jammu and Kashmir suggested 50 per cent; Andhra Pradesh, Kerala and Madhya Pradesh, 60 per cent; and Mysore and Rajasthan, 70 per cent. Several suggestions were made about the principles of distribution of the shares allocated to the

States. Andhra Pradesh, Bihar, Kerala, Madhya Pradesh, Madras and Uttar Pradesh suggested population as the sole criterion; Bombay and West Bengal favoured consumption. Orissa proposed that 80 per cent should be distributed on the basis of population with a weightage for scheduled castes, scheduled tribes, backward classes and the rural population, and the balance on the basis of area. Assam suggested the distribution of 80 per cent on the basis of population, 10 per cent with reference to the backwardness of the area and 10 per cent on the basis of needs for developing the industries on the products of which Union excises are levied. Mysore recommended the distribution of 50 per cent on the basis of population and the rest on the basis of collection.

It was urged by a number of States that all excise duties should be shared. The Commission considered these suggestions and came to the conclusion that it is neither necessary nor expedient to make such a sweeping change. However, it felt the need to widen the range by increasing the number of duties to be shared. Accordingly, it decided to expand the existing list of three duties, viz. duties on matches, tobacco and vegetable products, by adding the duties on sugar, tea, coffee, paper and vegetable non-essential oils. As to the States' share of these duties, keeping in view the sum it proposed to transfer to the States from Union duties of excise in its overall scheme of devolution, it recommended that it should be 25 per cent. The reduction in the share allocated to the States out of the duties on tobacco, vegetable products and matches was more than made good by the widening of the range of divisible duties and each State received a larger sum from this source than previously.

As regards distribution of the States' share of the divisible excises, it noted that the First Finance Commission had suggested consumption of the taxed commodities as a suitable basis for distribution but, in the absence of any reliable data of consumption, it recommended population as indicating the nearest measure of consumption. The First Commission also suggested that arrangements should be made for the collection of statistics of consumption of the more important commodities subject to excise. Such statistics were still not available. Hence, the Second Commission also adopted population as the sole basis for distribution. However, it made a small correction in favour of the poorer by recommending that 90 per cent of the States' share of the divisible Union excise duties should be distributed on the basis of population, the balance of 10 per cent being used for adjustments.

In short, it recommended that (a) 25 per cent of the net proceeds in any financial year of the Union duties of excise on matches, tobacco (including manufactured tobacco), vegetable products, tea, coffee, sugar, paper and vegetable non-essential oils be paid to the States and (b) this amount be distributed among them in the following manner shown in Table 16.2.

Table 16.2: Distribution of States' Share of Excise Duties among the States Recommended by the Second Finance Commission

State	Percentage
Andhra Pradesh	9.38
Assam	3.46
Bihar	10.57
Bombay	12.17
Kerala	3.84
Madhya Pradesh	7.46
Madras	7.56
Mysore	6.52
Orissa	4.46
Punjab	4.59
Rajasthan	4.71
Uttar Pradesh	15.94
West Bengal	7.59
Jammu and Kashmir	1.75

Source: *Report of the Second Finance Commission*, 1957, p. 44.

16.3 Grants-in-aid in Lieu of Export Duty on Jute

Under the Government of India Act 1935, the net proceeds of the export duty on jute and jute products were shared with the Provinces of Assam, Bihar, Orissa and West Bengal. The Constitution did not provide for the sharing of any duty of customs between the Union and the States, but to enable these States to fill the gap in their revenues caused by the elimination of these receipts, provision was made in article 273 for the payment of grants-in-aid to them for a limited period in lieu of the assignment of any share of these duties. This period expired with the financial year 1959-60. These grants-in-aid were fixed sums, unrelated to the actual yield from the export duty; and although owing to the suspension of the duty and the ban on exports, the revenue had almost been wiped out during the early 1960s, these States continued to receive fixed grants-in-aid.

In their representations, the Governments of Bihar and West Bengal desired that the existing grants should be permanently secured to them as grants under article 275. The Government of Assam suggested that the amount of the grant should be recalculated with reference to the increase in the production of raw jute since 1949-50, as the First Finance Commission took into account the production in that year in arriving at the amounts of the grants-in-aid recommended by them. The Government of Orissa suggested that the total sum of Rs. 315 lakh, which the States were receiving, should be redistributed among them on the basis of the relative production of jute in these States during the year 1952-53 to 1955-56. They also suggested that the grants-in-aid should be continued after 1959-60 and if there was any constitutional difficulty in extending the period prescribed by article 273, corresponding amounts should be paid as grants-in-aid under article 275 separately and specifically on this account.

Second Finance Commission was asked to make recommendations as to the sums which should be prescribed as grants-in-aid for the three years 1957-58 to 1959-60. These grants-in-aid had no relation to the actual revenue of the Government of India from the export duty on jute and jute products. There was, therefore, no question of relating them in any way to the production of jute. It recommended sums under article 273 as follows: Assam (Rs. 75.00 lakh), Bihar (Rs. 72.31 lakh), Orissa (Rs. 15.00 lakh) and West Bengal (Rs. 152.69 lakh)

16.4 Grants-in-aid of Revenues

The grants-in-aid, which the Commission recommended were much larger than the grants-in-aid paid to the States in the past. This was mainly due to the fact that, in the past, the requirements of the States for development were not fully taken into account, while this Commission did so. It should, however, be understood that the sums recommended by the Commission, while justified in the context of the Second Five Year Plan, did not indicate permanent requirements of the States for their ordinary budgetary needs.

By the devolution of revenue which the Commission proposed, the States received a significant measure of assistance which enabled them to implement the Second Five Year Plan. In this connection, the Commission observed, "We wish to emphasise that they cannot depend wholly on this; they will still have to help themselves by raising at least the additional revenue expected of them towards the execution of the current plan, by securing all possible economies in administrative expenditure and by maximising their revenue through the tightening up of the machinery for collection and by the recovery of overdue arrears." [1] Table 16.3 records the amounts of grants-in-aid recommended by the Commission for various States.

As to the question whether these grants should be conditional or not, the Commission maintained, "Since our scheme of devolution involved substantial transfer of resources for implementing the revenue portion of the plan, which for most States is reflected in the grants-in-aid recommended for them, we considered whether we should make any part of the grants-in-aid conditional on such implementation. We would have liked to do so, if the assistance provided under our scheme had represented the major part of the expenditure. Under our scheme, the States will be receiving a little less than a third of the outlay and a little over a third will come by way of specific assistance from the Union under the plan; for the balance they will have to raise their own resources. We have, therefore, decided not to impose any condition on the grants-in-aid recommended by us." [2]

Table 16.3: Grants-in-aid Recommended by the Second Finance Commission for Various States

(Rs. crore)

State	1957-58	1958-59	1959-60	1960-61	1961-62	Total
Andhra Pradesh	4.00	4.00	4.00	4.00	4.00	20.00
Assam	3.75	3.75	3.75	4.50	4.50	20.25
Bihar	3.50	3.50	3.50	4.25	4.25	19.00
Kerala	1.75	1.75	1.75	1.75	1.75	8.75
Madhya Pradesh	3.00	3.00	3.00	3.00	3.00	15.00
Mysore	6.00	6.00	6.00	6.00	6.00	30.00
Orissa	3.25	3.25	3.25	3.50	3.50	16.75
Punjab	2.25	2.25	2.25	2.25	2.25	11.25
Rajasthan	2.50	2.50	2.50	2.50	2.50	12.50
West Bengal	3.25	3.25	3.25	4.75	4.75	19.25
Jammu and Kashmir	3.00	3.00	3.00	3.00	3.00	15.00
Total	**36.25**	**36.25**	**36.25**	**39.50**	**39.50**	**187.75**

Source: *Report of the Second Finance Commission*, 1957, p. 50.

16.5 Distribution of Estate Duty

Estate duty was first levied in India in 1953 and the total collections up to March 31, 1957 amounted to Rs. 4.75 crore. Pending Parliamentary legislation, the net proceeds had been provisionally distributed among the States in the same ratio as the States' share of the divisible pool of income tax.

A variety of suggestions were made by the States in regard to the principles of distribution. Estate duty being a tax on property, the basis of location would be the most appropriate principle of distribution. It is, however, not possible to apply this principle in the case of the part relating to movable property, which may be included in an estate, and in respect of it some general principle of distribution such as population is inescapable. Keeping these limitations in mind, the Second Finance Commission made the following recommendation.

1. Out of the net proceeds of the duty in any financial year, a sum equal to one per cent be retained by the Union as proceeds attributable to Union territories.
2. Balance be apportioned between immovable property and other property in the ratio of the gross value of all such properties brought into assessment in that year.
3. Sum thus apportioned to immovable property be distributed among the States in proportion to the gross value of the immovable property located in each State.
4. Sum apportioned to property other than immovable property be distributed among the States in proportion to their population.

On the basis of above principles, the percentage share of each State was worked out as shown in Table 16.4. This scheme of distribution took effect from the financial year 1957-58.

Table 16.4: Percentage Shares of States in Estate Duty Recommended by the Second Finance Commission.

State	Percentage
Andhra Pradesh	8.76
Assam	2.53
Bihar	10.86
Bombay	13.52
Kerala	3.79
Madhya Pradesh	7.30
Madras	8.40
Mysore	5.43
Orissa	4.10
Punjab	4.52
Rajasthan	4.47
Uttar Pradesh	17.71
West Bengal	7.37
Jammu and Kashmir	1.24

Source: *Report of the Second Finance Commission*, 1957, p. 52.

16.6 Union Loans to States

The Commission also considered the question of modification, if any, in the rates of interest and the terms of repayment of the loans made to the various States by the Government of India between August 15, 1947 and March 31, 1956. It observed, "On 15th August 1947, the total debt of the Provincial Governments to the Centre was only Rs. 43.97 crore. Between that date and 31st March 1951, the number of loans had risen by about 220 and the outstanding amount had gone up to Rs. 195.41 crore. During the period of the First Five Year Plan, namely from 1st April 1951 to 31st March 1956, the number of outstanding loans rose by about 2570, the total outstanding debt on the latter date being approximately Rs. 900 crore. These loans have been made for a variety of purposes, but largely to implement the Plan. The amounts of individual loans have ranged from small sums to crore of rupees. The rates of interest have varied from 1 to 5 per cent, some of the loans being free of interest. Except where a concessional rate has been given, the rates have generally been determined with reference to the redemption yield of Central loans with a remaining maturity approximating to the period for which the loans are given. A number of loans are due to be repaid in equated annual instalments, including both principal and interest. Others are repayable in periods ranging from 1 to 40 years." [3]

The need for consolidation and rationalisation of loans was felt because the large number of loans given and the wide variations in the rates of interest and the terms of repayment had introduced an avoidable complication in the financial relations between the Union and the States. However, it dealt separately with two types of loans which were not part of its scheme of consolidation, viz. loans given for the rehabilitation of displaced persons and interest-free loans.

16.6.1 Loans for Rehabilitation of Displaced Persons: As regards these loans, the Commission observed, "The terms on which loans have been given to the States for the rehabilitation of displaced persons have caused a great deal of discontent. These loans fall into two categories, namely those sanctioned before January 1, 1950 and those sanctioned subsequently. In regard to the former category, the States have to bear initially and on a provisional basis fifty per cent of the shortfall in the actual collections of principal and interest in any year, as compared with the amounts which are due to be recovered; the States are entitled to retain on the same provisional basis fifty per cent of the excess, if any, collected by them. These losses and gains are intended to be adjusted against the payments, which may be due from the State governments, when the final settlement takes place. In respect of loans granted after January 1, 1950, the Government of India have agreed to bear in full such losses on account of principal or accrued interest as may arise on account of default by the parties or individuals from whom they are due; but the State Governments have been asked, for the time being, to pay to the Union, in addition to the amounts collected from the displaced persons, ten per cent of the deficiency in collection, and have been allowed to retain ten per cent of the excess collection, if any.

All the States, to which these rehabilitation loans have been given, contended that the distinction between these two categories was unfair and untenable. They argued that these loans were not, in a real sense, for State purposes, that the policy in respect o these loans was laid down by the Union and that the State Governments administered them merely as agents of the Union. They, therefore, urged that they should not be put to any loss on this account and that their sole obligation with respect to these loans should be to pay to the Union whatever they were able to collect by way of interest and principal.

This request of the States is reasonable and we recommend that, with effect from April 1, 1957, the States should pay to the Union only the amounts of principal and interest they collect on account of these loans, including the arrears outstanding on that date. We do not apprehend that this will lead to any relaxation in the efforts of the State Governments to recover these loans; we are confident that they realise their responsibilities in this matter." [4]

16.6.2 Interest-free Loans: The Commission noted that about 335 loans of the total value of approximately Rs. 8 crore had been given free of interest. They were mostly for the construction of educational buildings, assistance to handloom and cottage industries, industrial and other housing etc. In many cases these loans had been passed on by the State Governments to local bodies, universities or other agencies on the same terms and the connected transactions could not be re-opened. It, therefore, did not recommend any modifications in the terms of repayment of these loans. The Commission expressed the view that the policy of giving loans interest-free or at concessional rate of interest was open to objection. First, such a concession conveyed wrong impression regarding the interest burden which had to be met. Secondly, concessions of this kind were not subject to Parliamentary control as no funds were voted to cover them. In the opinion of the Commission if a scheme had to be subsidised, the subsidy should be given directly and not through reduction in the interest burden and any assistance sought to be given through concessional rates of interest should take the form of a direct subsidy.

In short, the Commission recommended that outstanding balances on March 31, 1957 of all loans by the Government of India to State Governments made between August 15, 1947 and March 31, 1956, excluding the loans given for rehabilitation of displaced persons and interest-free loans, be consolidated, for each State, as follows.

1. Balances of all loans carrying interest at 3 per cent or more per annum and repayable on or after April 1, 1977, be consolidated into one single loan at 3 per cent per annum repayable on March 31, 1987.
2. Balances of all loans carrying interest at 3 per cent or more per annum and repayable on or before March 31, 1977, be consolidated into one single loans at 3 per cent per annum repayable on March 31, 1972.
3. Balances of all loans carrying interest at less than 3 per cent per annum and repayable on or after April 1, 1977, be consolidated into one single loans at 2.5 per cent per annum repayable on March 31, 1987.
4. Balances of all loans carrying interest at less than 3 per cent per annum and repayable on or before March 31, 1977, be consolidated into one single loan at 2.5 per cent per annum repayable on March 31, 1972.

16.7 Distribution of Additional Duties of Excise

It may be recalled that consequent upon a voluntary agreement between the Centre and the States at a meeting of the National Development Council (NDC) held in December, 1956, it was decided to replace sales tax on textiles, tobacco, and sugar by additional duties of excise and to distribute revenues derived there from among the States. The agreement provided also that the share accruing to each State shall not in any case be less than the revenue realised from the levy of sales tax on these goods for the financial year 1956-57 in that State. The Council's decision was implemented through the Additional Duties of Excise (Goods of Special Importance) Act, 1957, the First Schedule of which prescribed the rates of additional duties of excise and the Second Schedule the scheme of distribution of the net proceeds among the States.

The Finance Commission comes in the picture for the purpose of determining the principles of distribution of the net proceeds of additional duties of excise among the States. The first issue before the Finance Commission is to determine the yield in 1956-57 from sales tax on the commodities subject to additional excise duties for the purpose of guaranteeing to the States concerned the amount so determined.

The Second Finance Commission, which was the first to deal with this problem, adopted elaborate procedures for working out estimates of yield (i.e. the guaranteed amount for the year 1956-57). These were primarily based on consumption estimates and figures of collection of sales tax obtained from each State for the years 1954-55 to 1956-57. It also explored the possibility of working out the estimates from the consumption data as available from the Fourth Round of the National Sample Survey, the estimates prepared by the Textile Commissioner, the statistics of the clearance of off-take of sugar prepared by the

Sugar and Vanaspati Directorate and the statistics of consumption of tobacco contained in the report on the marketing of tobacco prepared by the Agricultural Marketing Directorate of Government of India. Taking all the relevant statistics into account, that Commission worked out its own estimates of the likely revenue. These were primarily based on consumption estimates but a corrective on the basis of population was also applied. It was the view of the Commission that the figures taken by it, which were a mixture of consumption-based yield and population, were the nearest possible approximation to the income of each State from sales taxes on the relevant commodities during the financial year 1956-57.

The Commission made recommendations as to the principles which should govern the distribution of the net proceeds among the States and the amounts which should be assured to them as the income derived from the levy of sales taxes on mill-made textiles, sugar and tobacco (including manufactured tobacco).

The recommendations of the Commission in this respect were as follows.

1. In respect of Union territories, 1 per cent of the net proceeds in any financial year of the additional duty of excise on each of the three commodities, namely mill-made textiles, sugar and tobacco (including manufactured tobacco) be retained by the Union.
2. A sum equal to 1.25 per cent of such net proceeds be paid to the State of Jammu and Kashmir.
3. Out of the balance of the net proceeds, i.e. after deduction of the sums mentioned in (1) and (2), the following sums (Table 16.5), being the *present income* of the States on account of sales taxes, by whatever name called, be paid to them.
4. The remainder, if any, of the net proceeds be distributed in the percentage ratios applicable to each commodity as set out in Table 16.6.

If, for the purposes of the guarantees and the distribution of the net proceeds, the additional duties were to be taken together, the Commission recommended that in lieu of the sums and percentages mentioned in Tables 16.5 and 16.6, the sums guaranteed and payable to, and the percentage shares of, the States be as mentioned in Table 16.7.

16.8 Distribution of Tax on Railway Passenger Fares

The Commission was of the opinion that for this tax the principle should be such as to secure for each State, as nearly as possible, the share of the net proceeds on account of the actual passenger travel on railways within its limits. It observed, "The ideal method would, perhaps, be to split up the tax collected on each ticket according to the mileage of the routes lying in each State. This, however, is impracticable. Collections of passenger fares within a State will not reflect correctly the actual passenger travel within its limits on account of inter-state traffic; distribution based on figures of such collections would also be unfair to the States through which traffic passes without originating or terminating in them. The net proceeds due to passenger travel in a State may, however, be determined with reasonable accuracy by allocating the passenger earnings among the States on the basis of the route mileage within each State, with due allowance for the wide variations in the density of traffic between the various railway zones and as between the various gauges in each zone. Hence, if the earnings of each zonal railway are allocated by route mileage located in each State separately for each gauge, this would give, as nearly as possible, an allocation of passenger travel in terms of passenger earnings. The distribution of the tax in the ratio of the earnings thus allocated will give to each State a share that will approximate closely to the actual passenger travel in it." [5]

Table 16.5: Distribution of Additional Excise Duties among the States on the Basis of *Present Income*

(Rs. lakh)

State	Mill-made textiles	Sugar	Tobacco
Andhra Pradesh	120	40	75
Assam	40	15	30
Bihar	80	30	20
Bombay	600	245	115
Kerala	38	20	37
Madhya Pradesh	83	40	32
Madras	168	60	57
Mysore	48	25	27
Orissa	50	20	15
Punjab	95	50	30
Rajasthan	50	25	15
Uttar-Pradesh	400	112	63
West Bengal	204	36	40
Total	**1976**	**718**	**556**

Source: *Report of the Second Finance Commission*, 1957, p. 62.

The Commission worked out the States' shares on the basis of the average of recent earnings and expressed these shares as fixed percentages applicable for five years from 1957-58. These are given in Table 16.8.

Table 16.6: Distribution of the Remainder, if any, of Additional Excise Duties among the States

Percentages

State	Mill-made textiles	Sugar	Tobacco
Andhra Pradesh	7.38	6.65	10.47
Assam	2.72	2.55	2.98
Bihar	11.19	8.20	8.90
Bombay	16.46	20.17	17.41
Kerala	3.10	3.03	3.43
Madhya Pradesh	6.97	7.67	7.10
Madras	7.26	7.43	9.53
Mysore	4.98	5.13	5.58
Orissa	3.32	2.87	3.21
Punjab	5.56	7.21	4.36
Rajasthan	4.36	4.81	3.59
Uttar-Pradesh	18.19	15.63	16.13
West Bengal	8.51	8.65	7.31

Source: *Report of the Second Finance Commission*, 1957, p. 63.

Table 16.7: Distribution of Additional Excise Duties among the States on the Basis of Sums Guaranteed

State	Sum to be guaranteed (Rs. lakh)	Percentage
Andhra Pradesh	235	7.81
Assam	85	2.73
Bihar	130	10.04
Bombay	960	17.52
Kerala	95	3.15
Madhya Pradesh	155	7.16
Madras	285	7.74
Mysore	100	5.13
Orissa	85	3.20
Punjab	175	5.71
Rajasthan	90	4.32
Uttar-Pradesh	575	17.18
West Bengal	280	8.31
Total	**3250**	100.00

Source: *Report of the Second Finance Commission*, 1957, p. 63.

Table 16.8: Percentage Shares of the States in the Earnings from Tax on Railway Fares Recommended by the Second Finance Commission

State	Percentage
Andhra Pradesh	8.86
Assam	2.71
Bihar	9.39
Bombay	16.28
Kerala	1.81
Madhya Pradesh	8.31
Madras	6.46
Mysore	4.45
Orissa	1.78
Punjab	8.11
Rajasthan	6.77
Uttar Pradesh	18.76
West Bengal	6.31

Source: *Report of the Second Finance Commission*, 1957, p. 65.

16.9 Miscellaneous

In its study of the expenditure of State Governments in recent years, the Commission was struck by the dislocation caused to the finances of many of them by unforeseen expenditure on natural calamities like famine, droughts and floods and it felt the need for making some regular provision to meet this type of expenditure. In its estimate of the committed expenditure of the States, it included a margin for enabling them to set apart annually from their revenue sizeable sums to be accumulated in a fund for meeting expenditure on natural calamities. Table 16.9 records the annual amounts, based roughly on the average annual expenditure over the last decade, allowed by the Commission for individual States.

The Commission also referred to the overlap of functions of the Planning and Finance Commissions and had urged that there was a real need for effectively co-ordinating the work of the two Commissions. It had also stressed the desirability of eliminating the necessity of making two separate assessments of the needs of the States. It lamented that the scope of the work of the Finance Commission in assessing the needs of the States had become restricted as a result of the setting up of the Planning Commission.

Table 16.9: Annual Amounts Recommended by the Second Finance Commission to Meet Expenditure on Natural Calamities

State	Amount (Rs. lakh)
Andhra Pradesh	75
Assam	25
Bihar	100
Bombay	40
Kerala	10
Madhya Pradesh	15
Madras	50
Mysore	30
Orissa	50
Punjab	40
Rajasthan	40
Uttar Pradesh	50
West Bengal	80
Jammu and Kashmir	10
Total	**615**

Source: *Report of the Second Finance Commission*, 1957, p. 66.

Notes

1. Report of the Second Finance Commission, 1957, pp. 47-48.
2. *Ibid.*, p. 50.
3. *Ibid.*, pp. 52-53.
4. *Ibid.*, pp. 53-54.
5. *Ibid.*, pp. 64-65.

17

Third Finance Commission

In addition to the matters on which, under the provisions of sub-clauses (a) and (b) of clause (3) of article 280 of the Constitution, the Commission was required to make recommendations, this Commission was also asked to make recommendations in regard to

(a) States which are in need of assistance by way of grants-in-aid of their revenues under article 275, and the sums to be paid to those States other than the sums specified in the provisos to clause (1) of that article, having regard, among other considerations, to (i) the requirements of the Third Five Year Plan, and (ii) the efforts to be made by those States to raise additional revenue from the sources available to them,

Summary Statement	
Chairman	Mr. A.K. Chanda
Members	Shri P. Govinda Menon Shri Dwijendra Nath Roy Professor M.V. Mathur Shri G.R. Kamat, Member-Secretary
Year and month of establishment	December 1960
Year and month of reporting	December 1961
Period of award	1962-63 to 1965-66
Main Recommendations	
• States' share in income tax fixed at (per cent): 66 • Bases of distribution of States' share in income tax inter se (per cent): Population: 80; Contribution: 20; Other factors: Nil • States' share in Union excise duties fixed at (per cent): 20 (from 35 commodities) • Bases of distribution of States' share in Union excise duties inter se (per cent): Population: Major factor; Other factors: Weightage not stated	

(b) changes, if any, to be made in the principles governing the distribution amongst the States under article 269 of the net proceeds in any financial year of estate duty in respect of property other than agricultural land,

(c) changes, if any, to be made in the principles governing the distribution among the States under article 269 of the net proceeds in any financial year of taxes on railway fares and

(d) changes, if any, to be made in the principles governing the distribution of the net proceeds in any financial year of the additional excise duties levied on each of the following commodities, namely (i) cotton fabrics, (ii) rayon or artificial silk fabrics, (iii) woollen fabrics, (iv) sugar and (v) tobacco, including manufactured tobacco, in replacement of the States sales taxes formerly levied by the State Governments: Provided that the share accruing to each State shall not be less than the revenue realised from the levy of sales tax in the financial year 1956-57 in that State.

The Commission was required to make recommendations for the four years commencing with 1962-63.

17.1 Determination of the Budgetary Needs of the States

The first task before the Commission was the determination of the budgetary needs of the States. This involved a detailed analysis of the forecasts of revenue and expenditure of each of the States as presented to it, its reconciliation with the forecasts settled with the Planning Commission and an examination of the trends of growth of revenue and expenditure on the basis of past actuals, also of additional demands subsequently placed before it. The Commission undertook this overall review independently but obtained full and complete explanations of the State Governments on points of doubt during its visits to the States.

In determining the budgetary gap of each State, the Commission adopted the following procedures.

1. It maintained the procedure adopted by the Second Finance Commission in regard to assistance towards unforeseen expenditure on natural calamities, such as famine, droughts and floods. It accordingly included in the expenditure estimates of the States the same provision for each year as was made by the Second Commission (Table 17.1).
2. It did not include in its assessment the probable loss to the States arising out of introduction or extension of prohibition, as no firm decision on this question was made available to it. However, it took full account of the impact of prohibition on the revenues of the States where this had already been introduced.
3. It excluded from the forecasts the provision for redemption of debt as it consider that there was no purpose in allowing this where the States were in revenue deficit. In the case of Maharashtra, however, which had a revenue surplus, the Commission allowed a provision for this purpose.

Table 17.1: Unforeseen Expenditure on Natural Calamities Included in the Expenditure Estimates of the States by the Third Finance Commission

State	(Rs. lakh)
Andhra Pradesh	75
Assam	25
Bihar	100
Gujarat	40
Jammu and Kashmir	10
Kerala	10
Madhya Pradesh	15
Madras	50
Maharashtra	40
Mysore	30
Orissa	50
Punjab	40
Rajasthan	40
Uttar Pradesh	50
West Bengal	80
Total	**655**

Source: *Report of the Third Finance Commission*, 1961, p. 11.

4. In computing the budgetary gaps of the States, the Commission took into consideration the liability arising out of the changed pattern of central assistance for post-stage II community development blocks etc., grants to Universities to meet the committed expenditure on development schemes sponsored by the University Grants Commission and the special requirements of the States as given in their supplementary memoranda and subsequent communications. These included revision of pay-scales in several States, re-organisation of police and district administration, introduction and extension of Panchayati Raj, continuance of subsidised sale of foodgrains, special relief measures etc.

The Commission adhered to the principle that the budgetary needs of the States, as assessed, should be met as far as possible by the devolution of taxes, and grants-in-aid should be made to provide residuary fiscal aid.

17.2 Distribution of Assigned Taxes

17.2.1 Estate Duty: Some of the States were content with the principles laid down by the Second Finance Commission for the distribution of revenue from estate duty. However, some others suggested a revision on the lines submitted for the consideration of the Second Commission. After discussion with the Third Commission, all the States agreed that the principles enunciated by the Second Commission might be left undisturbed. Therefore, the Third Commission recommended the continuance of these principles which were as under.

1. Out of the net proceeds of the duty in each financial year, a sum equal to 1 (one) per cent be retained by the Union as proceeds attributable to Union territories.
2. Balance be apportioned between immovable property and other property in the ratio of the gross value of all such properties brought into assessment in that year.
3. Sum thus apportioned to immovable property be distributed among the States in proportion to the gross value of the immovable property located in each State.
4. Sum apportioned to property other than immovable property be distributed among the States in proportion to their population.

The percentages laid down by the Second Commission, however, needed revision on the basis of 1961 census. Revised percentages are given in Table 17.2.

Table 17.2: Percentage Shares of States in Estate Duty Recommended by the Third Finance Commission.

State	**Percentage**
Andhra Pradesh	8.34
Assam	2.75
Bihar	10.78
Gujarat	4.78
Jammu and Kashmir	0.83
Kerala	3.92
Madhya Pradesh	7.51
Madras	7.80
Maharashtra	9.16
Mysore	5.46
Orissa	4.08
Punjab	4.71
Rajasthan	4.67
Uttar Pradesh	17.10
West Bengal	8.11

Source: *Report of the Third Finance Commission,* 1961, p. 14.

17.2.2 Grant in Lieu of Tax on Railway Passenger Fares: The Act imposing a tax on railway passenger fares was repealed by Act No. VIII of 1961 after the Commission had been constituted. The Union Government, however, decided to make to the States an ad hoc grant for the quinquennium 1961-66 of Rs. 12.5 crore per year representing the average of the actual collections during the two years 1958-59 and 1959-60. The terms of reference of the Commission were accordingly modified and it was asked to recommend instead the principles on which this ad hoc grant should be distributed. Meanwhile, the estimates of revenue and expenditure submitted to the Planning Commission by the States had taken account of the receipts from this levy. It was presumably on this score that the ad hoc grant had been provided. The Commission, therefore, considered that the distribution should be on the principle of compensation to place the States broadly on the same footing as before. It accordingly recommended that the distribution of the sum of Rs. 12.5 crore per year amongst the States be given in the following manner (Table 17.3).

Table 17.3: Distribution of the Grant in Lieu of Tax on Railway Passenger Fares among the States as Recommended by the Third Finance Commission

State	(Rs. lakh)
Andhra Pradesh	1.11
Assam	0.34
Bihar	1.17
Gujarat	0.68
Kerala	0.23
Madhya Pradesh	1.04
Madras	0.81
Maharashtra	1.35
Mysore	0.56
Orissa	0.22
Punjab	1.01
Rajasthan	0.85
Uttar Pradesh	2.34
West Bengal	0.79

Source: *Report of the Third Finance Commission,* 1961, p. 15.

17.3 Devolution of Union Taxes/Duties

17.3.1 Income Tax: All the States pointed out that, as a result of a change brought about in the Income Tax Act by the Finance Act of 1959, the income tax paid by companies was classified as corporation tax and was thus excluded from the pool of income tax hitherto available for distribution. This, they represented, had deprived them of an expanding source of revenue to which they had hitherto a constitutional entitlement. The States argued that the Commission should take into account at least such part of the corporation tax as was attributable to this yield, if not the entire tax. Suggestion had also been made that the surcharge on income tax levied under article 271, which had been in force for about the last 15 years, should be merged in the basic rates. It was urged that this would abate partly the impact of the loss sustained, as this would indirectly bring within the pool of distribution an excluded amount.

However, the Commission made it clear to the State Governments that the recommendations that it would make should necessarily be in accordance with the provisions of the Constitution and its terms of reference. While appreciating this position, all the States claimed that the percentage of the tax to be assigned to them should be substantially increased. On the considerations mentioned above, the Commission fixed the share of the States in the net proceeds of income tax at 66.66 per cent.

As to the question of distribution of the share assigned to the States, widely divergent views were expressed, ranging from distribution entirely on the basis of collection to distribution wholly on the basis of population. In between, there were suggestions that population should be weighed to take account of the proportion of scheduled castes and tribes and backward classes in the population, that the area of the State should be a relevant consideration and that its backwardness should not be ignored. There were also suggestions that distribution should be based on considerations of population as also collection in various proportions.

The Commission was in general agreement with the approach of previous Finance Commissions that the relevant considerations were population and collection. It did not find it feasible to introduce other factors in the distribution of this tax. In all previous schemes of distribution, there had been a blending of these two principles, but in different proportions. While the First Finance Commission recommended that distribution of the States' share should be on the basis of 20 per cent for collection and 80 per cent for population, the Second Commission reduced the element of collection to 10 per cent and expressed the view that in due course the factor of collection should be eliminated altogether and distribution be made entirely on the basis of population.

The Second Commission had recognised that there could be a case for weightage being given to collection in the restricted field of personal income tax.

The First Commission had also stated that there was all over the country a core of incomes which could be treated as of local origin. Hence, the Third Commission maintained, "In our view, while population should remain the main factor for the distribution of the net proceeds of income-tax amongst the States, the factor of contribution should receive adequate recognition. It has been urged before us by the industrial and urban States, in whose territory large amounts are collected by way of income-tax, that they should have an incentive and the wherewithal to maintain the environments which would preserve and promote industrial and trade activities. Since the Second Finance Commission made its recommendations, the taxes on income paid by companies have been excluded from the divisible pool. Bulk of this tax paid by companies would have accrued from income of all-India origin. With the exclusion of this element from the divisible pool, a higher percentage than before of the total yield of income-tax now represents tax derived from incomes of local origin. We consider, therefore, that a higher weightage should be given to the factor of contribution in the distribution of income-tax than that recommended by the Second Commission. We have also been impressed with the submission that the industrial States having larger collections have problems of their own. Large concentration of population, more particularly of industrial labour, creates problems of law and order and gives rise to an increased demand for the administrative and social services. Further, the unit cost of providing these services is larger in such areas than elsewhere, more particularly in the non-urbanised parts." [1]

Taking all these considerations into account, the Commission felt that it would be fair and equitable to restore the formula of the First Commission for the distribution of income tax, namely 80 per cent on the basis of population and 20 per cent on the basis of collection. As regards the actual manner of distribution of the States' share in each year, it agreed with the earlier Commissions that it would be convenient both to the States and to the Union if the Shares were expressed as fixed percentages. Hence, the Commission recommended that two-thirds, that is to say 66⅔ per cent of the net proceeds in any financial year of taxes on income other than agricultural income, except in so far as those proceeds represent proceeds attributable to Union territories or to taxes payable in respect of Union emoluments, be assigned to the States and distributed among them in the manner given in Table 17.4. It further recommended that 2.5 per cent of the net proceeds of the income tax be prescribed as the net proceeds attributable to Union territories.

17.3.2 Union Excise Duties: Article 272 of the Constitution empowers Parliament to provide by legislation the distribution to the States of the whole or a part of the net proceeds of the Union duties of excise on specified commodities, prescribing, at the same time, the principles on which the distribution should be made. This permissive provision was embodied in our Constitution to provide for additional financial assistance to the States, should the necessity arise to augment sums which could be made available under other provisions of the Constitution.

Table 17.4: Percentage Shares of the States in the Net Proceeds of Income Tax Assigned to the States as Recommended by the Third Finance Commission

State	Percentage
Andhra Pradcsh	7.71
Assam	2.44
Bihar	9.33
Gujarat	4.78
Jammu and Kashmir	0.70
Kerala	3.55
Madhya Pradesh	6.41
Madras	8.13
Maharashtra	13.41
Mysore	5.13
Orissa	3.44
Punjab	4.49
Rajasthan	3.97
Uttar Pradesh	14.42
West Bengal	12.09

Source: *Report of the Third Finance Commission,* 1961, p. 19.

Till April 1952, the proceeds of this duty were not brought into distribution and were retained wholly by the Union. The First Finance Commission broke new ground by recommending the sharing of the proceeds of duties on three commodities between the Union and the States. It was presumably influenced in this conclusion by the growing financial needs of the States in fulfilling a complementary role in the development of the national economy and the provision of a higher level of social services. The Second Commission expanded the list of duties to eight commodities as in their view the taxes on income were ceasing to be an expanding source of revenue and increasing dependence should be placed for purposes of devolution on the growing source of excise revenue. The impact of planning on the States also called for a larger measure of devolution which could be suitably provided by using the permissive provisions of article 272 more extensively.

On their part, the States again pleaded before the Third Finance Commission for inclusion of all excisable commodities in the distributable pool. In support of this demand the States argued that the expanding coverage of Central excises and their increasing incidence had adversely affected the revenue potential of sales tax. Accepting this demand of the States in principle the Commission observed, "We consider that the inadequacy of resources that has developed in the States is attributable mainly to the planning process and this inadequacy may become more pronounced with the completion of each successive Plan for some years to come. The viability of the States could best be secured by a larger devolution of the Union excise duties and this should be effected by providing for the participation of the States, by convention, in the proceeds of all Union excises. It would give a great deal of psychological satisfaction to the States and dissipate any suspicion that the Union is pursuing a policy of excessive centralisation of resources." [2]

However, the Commission considering its own scheme of transfers, recommended for distribution among the States 20 per cent of the excise revenue from commodities which each yielded in 1960-61 revenue of Rs. 50 lakh or more. The number of such commodities was 35, namely sugar, coffee, tea, tobacco, kerosene, refined diesel oils, diesel oil not otherwise specified, furnace oil, asphalt and bitumen, vegetable non-essential oils, vegetable products, pigments etc., soap, tyres and tubes, paper, rayon and synthetic fibres and yarn, cotton fabrics, silk fabrics, woollen fabrics, rayon or artificial silk fabrics, cement, pig iron, steel ingots, aluminium, tin plate and tin sheets, internal combustion engines, electric motors and parts thereof, electric batteries and parts thereof, electric lighting bulbs and fluorescent lighting bulbs, electric fans, motor vehicles, cycles, foot wear, cinematograph films exposed, and matches

As regards the distribution of the States' share of the divisible excises, the First Commission had suggested that consumption of taxed commodities could provide a suitable basis for distribution, but in the absence of reliable data, it adopted population as the basis. Confronted with the same situation of non-availability of reliable statistics, the Second Commission felt that population was the best basis of adopt, more particularly, as distribution on consumption, even if the relevant data were available, would benefit the more urbanised and the financially stronger States. The Third Commission was of the view that while population should continue to be the major factor of distribution, the relative financial weaknesses of the States, the disparity in the levels of development reached, the percentage of scheduled castes and tribes and backward classes in their population etc. should also be taken into account in determining the share to be allocated to each State individually. In other words, it felt that in this permissive participation, an attempt should be made to bring all the States, as far as possible, to a comparable level of financial balance. It, therefore, recommended the distribution of the States' share among the States in the manner given in Table 17.5.

Table 17.5: Distribution of States' Share of Excise Duties among the States Recommended by the Third Finance Commission

State	Percentage
Andhra Pradesh	8.23
Assam	4.73
Bihar	11.56
Gujarat	6.45
Jammu and Kashmir	2.02
Kerala	5.46
Madhya Pradesh	8.46
Madras	6.08
Maharashtra	5.73
Mysore	5.82
Orissa	7.07
Punjab	6.71
Rajasthan	5.93
Uttar Pradesh	10.68
West Bengal	5.07

Source: *Report of the Third Finance Commission,* 1961, p. 24.

17.4 Distribution of Additional Duties of Excise

It may be recalled that in May 1957, the Government of India, in consultation with State Governments, decided that an additional duty of excise should be levied on mill-made textiles, sugar and tobacco including manufactured tobacco, in replacement of sales tax levied by the State Governments, and that the net proceeds should be distributed among the States, subject to the then income derived by each State being assured to it. The Commission was required to make recommendations in regard to the changes, if any, to be made in the principles governing the distribution of the net proceeds in any financial year of the additional excise duties levied on cotton fabrics, rayon or artificial silk fabrics, woollen fabrics, sugar, tobacco including manufactured tobacco, provided that the share accruing to each State was not less than the revenue realised from the levy of sales tax in the financial year 1956-57 in that State.

The Second Finance Commission was the first to deal with this problem. It was required to recommend the principles which should govern the distribution of the net proceeds. It was required to determine also for each State the amount which should be assured to it as being the income derived to it from the levy of sales tax. As the additional duties replaced sales tax which was tax on consumption, it explored the possibility of adopting consumption as the basis of distribution. It prepared its own estimates of consumption of each of the three commodities on the basis of estimates prepared by the associated official agencies and the estimates furnished by the State Government and applied population as a corrective. It came to the conclusion that the estimates so compiled provided the best index for determining the incomes of the States individually from sales tax on these three commodities. Some of the States questioned the correctness of the amounts guaranteed in pursuance of the Second Commission's recommendations, but they were unable to any produce material more reliable than that submitted to that Commission.

Some of the States urged before the Third Commission that the guaranteed amounts should be revised to take account of increases in rates of sales tax effected by them after the amounts guaranteed had been determined. The Second Commission had rejected the suggestion that not only the revenues currently derived but prospective revenues should also be taken into account in determining the guaranteed amounts. The Third Commission was of the opinion that re-opening of these issues would only complicate a settled matter and create problems which were best avoided. It, therefore, adopted the amounts of guarantee prescribed by the Second Commission.

The recommendations of the Third Commission in regard to additional excise duties were as follows.

A sum equal to 1 per cent of the net proceeds of these additional duties of excise should be retained by the Union as being attributable to Union territories. Further, 1.25 per cent of the net proceeds paid to the State of Jammu and Kashmir be appropriately increased to 1.50 per cent a year. In respect of other States, the annual guaranteed amounts with the addition of additional excise duty on silk fabrics should be distributed in the manner shown in Table 17.6.

As regards the distribution of any balance of net collections remaining after meeting the guaranteed amounts, the Commission took the view that it would be equitable to distribute the excess collections partly on the basis of the percentage increase in the collection of sales tax in each State since the year 1957-58 when the additional excise duties were imposed and partly on the basis of population. It recommended that in addition to the amounts guaranteed, the States should participate in the distribution of collections in excess of amounts so provided in the following ratios (Table 17.7).

Table 17.6: Distribution of Additional Excise Duties among the States Recommended by the Third Finance Commission

State	**(Rs. Lakh)**
Andhra Pradesh	235.24
Assam	85.08
Bihar	130.16
Gujarat	323.45
Kerala	95.08
Madhya Pradesh	155.17
Madras	285.34
Maharashtra	637.77
Mysore	100.10
Orissa	85.10
Punjab	175.19
Rajasthan	90.10
Uttar Pradesh	575.81
West Bengal	280.41
Total	**3254.00**

Source: *Report of the Third Finance Commission,* 1961, p. 26.

17.5 Grants-in-aid of Revenues

Commenting on the principles enunciated by the First Finance Commission to distribute grants-in-aid of the revenues of the States, the Third Commission observed, "These principles are unexceptionable in themselves, but difficulties as appreciated by the First Commission arise in their application. The comparative determination of the tax efforts of the States cannot be in absolute terms. It has to be related to their tax potential, and this calls for a special study. Similarly, the assessment of the measure of economy effected or the degree of efficiency reached in a State's administration is a complicated exercise which, in any event, we could hardly undertake with the organisation and time at our disposal. Yet, without reliable and comparable information on these two essential ingredients of grants-in-aid, it is difficult to determine the quantum of assistance that would be necessary and justified. This and other considerations lead us to the suggestion that an independent Commission should be constituted to review, amongst other things, the financial relations which, in the new situation of planned development, should subsist between the Union and the States....In the enumeration of principles, the First Commission acknowledged that it was not sufficient to cover the amount of budgetary needs but also the fiscal needs arising out of development programmes undertaken. The Second Commission re-affirmed that fiscal needs should be considered in a comprehensive sense and that grants-in-aid should subserve the requirements of planned development. It added that the priorities and provisions in the Plan itself should determine the fiscal needs for development for the period of the Plan." [3]

Table 17.7: Distribution of the Remainder, if any, of Additional Excise Duties among the States

State	Percentage
Andhra Pradesh	7.75
Assam	2.50
Bihar	10.00
Gujarat	5.40
Kerala	4.25
Madhya Pradesh	7.00
Madras	9.00
Maharashtra	10.60
Mysore	5.25
Orissa	4.50
Punjab	5.25
Rajasthan	4.00
Uttar Pradesh	15.50
West Bengal	9.00

Source: *Report of the Third Finance Commission,* 1961, p. 27.

On the considerations placed before it, the Third Commission recommended that the total amount of grants-in-aid should be of an order which would enable the States, along with any surplus out of the devolution, to cover 75 per cent of the revenue component of their Plans. In determining the revenue component, it deducted in full the amount of additional tax to be raised by each State as incorporated in the Plan itself. In making this recommendation, it was influenced, amongst other things, by the fact that the Plan contains repetitive schemes of continuing character. The expenditure on these was unavoidable and was of the nature of committed expenditure.

The Commission had not intended to make any special-purpose grant, but during the course of discussions with the States, it was convinced that impetus should be given to the development of communications more extensively. There was the pressing need to open up backward areas, to break down barriers of isolation and stagnation, to develop social services and social sense, to mobilise economic resources, and above all, to bring about a feeling of oneness in the minds of the people of these regions with the rest of the community. It noted that due to financial stringency, the State Governments had made inadequate provision for the proper maintenance of existing roads and for new construction. It, therefore, felt that in the special circumstances an earmarked grant should be made for improvement of communications in the interests of national economy and national integration. It recommended a total sum of Rs. 36 crore for distribution for this purpose. Keeping in view the relative needs of the different States and the resources available to them, it recommend the special grant of Rs. 36 crore to be distributed as indicated in Table 17.8.

Table 17.8: Grants Recommended by the Third Finance Commission for Improvement of Communications

(Rs. lakh)

State	Per year	Total for four years, 1962-1966
Andhra Pradesh	50	200
Assam	75	300
Bihar	75	300
Gujarat	100	400
Jammu and Kashmir	50	200
Kerala	75	300
Madhya Pradesh	175	700
Mysore	50	200
Orissa	175	700
Rajasthan	75	300

Source: *Report of the Third Finance Commission,* 1961, p. 33.

In addition, it recommend the following grants-in-aid in each of the four years 1962-63 to 1965-66 to cover budgetary gaps where needed and 75 per cent of the revenue component of the Plan. The assistance towards the Plan made available in its scheme of devolution and grants-in-aid in each of these years are indicated separately in Table 17.9.

Table 17.9: Grants-in-aid and Assistance towards the Plan Recommended by the Third Finance Commission

(Rs. lakh)

State	Grant-in-aid	Assistance towards Plan included in devolution and grants-in-aid in col. 2
Andhra Pradesh	1,200	300
Assam	900	375
Bihar	800	800
Gujarat	950	525
Jammu & Kashmir	325	175
Kerala	850	300
Madhya Pradesh	625	500
Madras	800	500
Maharashtra	-	675
Mysore	775	150
Orissa	1,600	450
Punjab	275	275
Rajasthan	875	425
Uttar Pradesh	200	800
West Bengal	850	850

Source: *Report of the Third Finance Commission,* 1961, p. 33.

17.6 Finance Commission versus Planning Commission

The Third Finance Commission made some interesting remarks as regards the relative, and often overlapping, roles of the Finance Commission and the Planning Commission. It remarked, "The scope and magnitude, which the successive Five Year Plans will assume for the development of our national economy and the level of social services, could not be fully appreciated when the Constitution was drafted. It became necessary, therefore, from the very beginning, to operate on the permissive provision of participation in the excise duties, and the First Finance Commission made recommendations for division of the yield of excise duties on three commodities in addition to other provisions of devolution and grants-in-aid. The Second Commission considered it necessary to expand the list of eight commodities, along with some other adjustments.

A general weakness of Federal-State financial relations, more particularly in the field of devolution, is that federal assistance tends to be discretionary in character, not necessarily on principles of uniform application. To safeguard the position of the States, our Constitution provides, therefore, that the assessment of the needs of the States as well as the measure of assistance to be afforded and the form in which this should be given, are determined by an independent Commission to be constituted at intervals of not more than five years. But this role and function of the Finance Commission, as provided in the Constitution, can no longer be realised fully due to the emergence of the Planning Commission as an apparatus for national planning. Against this background, the role of the Finance Commission comes to be, at best, that of an agency to review the forecasts of revenue and expenditure submitted by the States and the acceptance of the revenue element of the Plan as indicated by the Planning Commission for determining the quantum of devolution and grants-in-aid to be made; and, at worst, its function is merely to undertake an arithmetical exercise of devolution, based on amounts of assistance for each State already settled by the Planning Commission, to be made under different heads on the basis of certain principles to be prescribed." [4]

It, therefore, favoured the enlargement of the functions of the Finance Commission to embrace total financial assistance to be given to the States, whether by way of loans or devolution of revenues, to enable them both to balance their normal budgets and to fulfil the prescribed, targets of the Plans. This would be in harmony with the spirit and even express provisions of the Constitution. This would also make the Commission's recommendations more realistic as they would take account of the inter-independence of capital and revenue expenditure in a planned programme. It went further to suggest that Planning Commission should be transformed into Finance Commission at the appropriate time.

Notes

1. *Report of the Third Finance Commission*, 1961, p. 18.
2. *Ibid.*, p. 21.
3. *Ibid.*, pp. 28-29.
4. *Ibid.*, pp. 34-35.

18

Fourth Finance Commission

The Commission was constituted by the President in his Order dated May 5, 1964. In addition to the matters on which, under the provisions of sub-clauses (a) and (b) of clause (3) of article 280 of the Constitution, the Commission was required to make recommendations, the Commission was also asked to make recommendations in regard to

Summary Statement	
Chairman	Mr. P.V. Rajamannar
Members	Shri Mohal Lal Gautam Shri D.G. Karve Professor Bhabatosh Datta Shri P.C. Mathew, Member-Secretary
Year and month of establishment	May 1964
Year and month of reporting	August 1965
Period of award	1966-67 to 1968-69
Main Recommendations	
• States' share in income tax fixed at (per cent): 75 • Bases of distribution of States' share in income tax inter se (per cent): Population: 80; Contribution: 20; Other factors: Nil • States' share in Union excise duties fixed at (per cent): 20 • Bases of distribution of States' share in Union excise duties inter se (per cent): Population: 80; Other factors: 20	

(a) States which are in need of assistance by way of grants-in-aid of their revenues under articles 275, and the sums to be paid to those States other than the sums specified in the provisos to clause (1) of that articles, having regard, among other considerations, to (i) the revenue resources of those States for the five years ending with the financial year 1970-71 on the basis of the levels of taxation likely to be reached in the financial year 1965-66, (ii) the requirements of those States to meet the committed expenditure on maintenance and upkeep of Plan schemes completed during the Third Plan, (iii) any further expenditure likely to devolve upon those States for the servicing of their debt, (iv) creation of a fund out of the excess, if any, over a limit to be specified by the Commission of the net proceeds of estate duty on property other than agricultural land accruing to a State in any financial year, for the repayment of the State's debt to the Central Government and (v) the scope for economy consistent with efficiency, which may be effected by the States in their administrative expenditure.

(b) Changes, if any, to be made in the principles governing the distribution amongst the States under article 269 of the net proceeds in any financial year of estate duty in respect of property other than agricultural land.

(c) Changes, if any, to be made in the principles governing the distribution amongst the States of the grant to be made available to the States in lieu of taxes on railway fares.

(d) Changes, if any, to be made in the principles governing the distribution of the net proceeds in any financial year of the additional excise duties levied on each of the following commodities, namely (i) cotton fabrics, (ii) silk fabrics, (iii) rayon of artificial silk fabrics, (iv) woollen fabrics, (v) sugar and (vi) tobacco (including manufactured tobacco) in replacement of the States' sales taxes formerly levied by the State Governments.

Provided that the share accruing to each State shall not be less than the revenue realized from the levy of the sales tax for the financial year 1956-57 in that State.

(e) Effect of the combined incidence of a State's sales tax and Union duties of excise on the production, consumption or export of commodities or products, the duties on which are shareable with the States, and the adjustments, if any, to be made in the State's share of Union excise duties if there is any increase in the State's sales tax on such commodities or products over a limit to be specified by the Commission.

The recommendations of the Commission covered the period of five years commencing from April 1, 1966.

18.1 Views of the Commission on Taxation Provisions in the Constitution

Commenting on the constitutional provisions pertaining to taxes, the Commission observed, "The principle behind all these provisions is that in regard to some of the major revenue-yielding taxes and also in the case of some other taxes, where a country-wide uniformity of rates is desirable, the best authority for legislating and in most cases also of collecting, is the Union Government. The requirements of the Centre as well as those of the component States could be met in the most equitable and efficient manner, by distributing the proceeds after these have been collected by the Central Government, rather than by dividing powers of tax collection between the Centre and the States as has been done in some federations – which would not only mean high costs of decentralized collection and large scope for evasion, but also varying rates of taxation in different areas and rigidity of distribution in the face of changing requirements. Under this system, the Union Government is the agency for raising certain revenues for the benefit of both the Central and the States and for distributing the proceeds between the Centre and the States and among the States themselves according to the principles and procedures set out in the Constitution.

This makes the problem of determining what part of the divisible revenues should go to the States and what should be the distribution among the States *inter se* very important. Whatever principles are laid down with regard to these two issues have, however, to be based upon the economic realities of the country and formulated within the framework of the provisions of the Constitution. It is not possible to derive much direct help from the experiences of other Federal Countries, though the course of evolution by which each federation has sought to adapt its system of financial relations to changing political and economic conditions is very instructive." [1]

18.2 Plan versus Non-Plan Expenditure

The distinction between Plan and Non-Plan expenditure arose with the launching of the First Five Year Plan on April 1, 1951. This distinction has proved an irritant for almost all the Finance Commissions. The Constitution of India does not provide for any such distinction. The successive Finance Commissions have often expressed their displeasure at this distinction. [2]

Many States urged upon the Fourth Commission to include expenditure on the Fourth Plan in the estimates for the coming five years. Some States supplied detailed expenditure forecasts on new projects and also on the likely revenue components of their Fourth Plan outlays. The Commission, however, felt it desirable to leave all such expenditure out of its consideration. This decision was based not on grounds of any Constitutional limitation of the powers of the Finance Commission but on practical considerations consequent on institutional arrangements relating to the Five Year Plans. In this connection the Commission remarked, "The Constitution does not make any distinction between plan and non-plan expenditure, and it is not unconstitutional for the Finance Commission to go into the whole question of the total revenue expenditure of the States. It has been pointed out to us that the reference to "Capital and recurring sums" in the first proviso to article 275(1) of the Constitution suggests that even capital expenditure need not necessarily be outside the scope of the Finance Commission. It is, however, necessary to note that the importance of planned economic development is so great and its implementation so essential that there should not be any division of responsibility in regard to any element of plan expenditure. The Planning Commission has been specially constituted for advising the Government of India and the State Governments in this regard. It would not be appropriate for the Finance Commission to take upon itself the task of dealing with the States' new plan expenditure.

The present Finance Commission has, therefore, confined itself to non-plan revenue expenditure vis-à-vis the revenue receipts anticipated in the coming five-year period on the basis of taxation levels in 1965-66. We have not, however, taken the view that the function of the Finance Commission is simply to recommend such devolution and grants-in-aid as would merely fill up the non-plan revenue deficit as reported by the States because such an approach will be extremely mechanical." [3]

18.3 Estate Duty

A number of suggestions were made to the Commission by the States in regard to the principles of distribution. The different suggestions were as under.

1. Distribution of estate duty wholly on the basis of population.
2. Distribution partly on the basis of collection and partly on the basis of location.
3. Distribution on the basis of population with weightage to Scheduled Castes and Scheduled Tribes.
4. Distribution on the basis of 80 per cent population and 20 per cent location.
5. Continuance of the existing scheme of distribution.

The Commission expressed agreement with the principles laid down by its predecessors and recommended the continuance of the following principles. It, however, raised the share of Union Territories to 2 per cent, taking into account population and the value of immovable property assessed in these territories in recent years.

1. Out of the net proceeds of the duty in each financial year, a sum equal to two per cent be retained by the Union as proceeds attributable to Union territories.
2. Balance be apportioned between immovable property and other property in the ratio of the gross value of all such properties brought into assessment in that year.
3. Sum thus apportioned to immovable property be distributed among the States in proportion to the gross value of the immovable property located in each State.
4. Sum apportioned to property other than immovable property be distributed among the States in proportion to their population.

On the basis of the 1961 Census figures, the percentages were worked out as given in Table 18.1.

Table 18.1: Percentage Shares of States in Estate Duty Recommended by the Fourth Finance Commission

States	Percentage
Andhra Pradesh	8.34
Assam	2.75
Bihar	10.76
Gujarat	4.78
Jammu & Kashmir	0.83
Kerala	3.92
Madhya Pradesh	7.50
Madras	7.80
Maharashtra	9.16
Mysore	5.46
Nagaland	0.09
Orissa	4.07
Punjab	4.70
Rajasthan	4.67
Uttar Pradesh	17.08
West Bengal	8.09
Total	**100.00**

Source: *Report of the Fourth Finance Commission*, 1965, p. 13.

18.4 Grant in Lieu of Tax on Railway Passenger Fares

It may be recalled that the tax on railway passenger fares was imposed under the Railway Passenger Fare Act, 1957 and the Second Finance Commission was, for the first time, asked to make recommendations as to the principles which should govern the distribution under Article 269 of the Constitution of the net proceeds in any financial year of the tax. The Second Commission decided that the proceeds of the tax should be distributed among the States in the ratio of passenger earnings which may be determined with reasonable accuracy by allocating passenger earnings among States on the basis of railway route mileage within each State with due allowance for variation in density of traffic between the various railway zones and as between the various gauges in each zone. Thus, the earnings from passenger traffic of each zonal railway (excluding earnings from suburban services) were allocated by route mileage located in each State separately for each gauge. The Second Commission recommended that the proceeds of the tax be distributed in the ratio of State-wise earnings so worked out and indicated each State's share as a fixed percentage applicable for five years from 1957-58.

Railway Passenger Fares Act, 1957 was repealed 1961 and the tax was merged in the basic fares. The Central Government, however, decided to make an *ad hoc* grant of Rs. 12.50 crore per annum to the States in lieu of the tax for a period of five years from 1961-62 to 1965-66. Third Finance Commission which was asked to recommend principles on which the *ad hoc* grant should be distributed, recommended that the distribution should be on the principle of compensation to place the States broadly on the same footing as before and accordingly worked out the distribution of the sum of Rs. 12.50 crore per year.

The Fourth Finance Commission agreed that the distribution of this grant should be on the basis of compensation and that the percentage share of each State in which the tax is leviable should be worked out on the principles enunciated by the Second Finance Commission. However, in its term of reference on the subject, the Fourth Commission was asked to make recommendations regarding changes, if any, to be made in the principles governing distribution among States of the grant to be made available to the States in lieu of taxes on railway passenger fares, but the actual amount of grant to be distributed was not indicated. Therefore, instead of recommending the sums payable to each State, it considered it desirable to express the States' shares in percentages. In determining the percentage share (Table 18.2), it used the latest available statistics of railway route length in each State under each gauge and the average annual earnings from passenger traffic (excluding earnings from suburban traffic) for three years ending 1964 for which actuals were available:

18.5 Income Tax

The Commission was asked to make recommendations in regard to the following three matters.

1. Percentage of the *net proceeds* of income tax to be assigned to the States.
2. Manner of distribution among the States of their share.
3. Percentage of the *net proceeds* which shall be deemed to represent proceeds attributable to Union territories.

Almost all the States urged upon the Commission for an increase in the share to be assigned to them. They pointed out that as a result of the change in the classification of the income tax paid by companies brought about by the Finance Act, 1959, the rate of growth of the divisible pool had been adversely affected. It was further argued that what the framers of the Constitution had intended to be a flexible and expanding source of revenue to the States had ceased to have the significance that was once contemplated. Some of the States reiterated the views placed by them before the previous Commissions that though the Government of India was competent to levy any surcharge, wholly for the purposes of the Union under article 271, such a levy in the very nature of things, was intended to be a temporary measure to serve a particular situation. It was, therefore, urged that during normal times there should be no need for any surcharge exclusively for the Union. However, if at all such a surcharge was levied, it should as a matter of course be merged with the basic rates after a period of three years.

Table 18.2: Percentage Share of Each State in Grant in Lieu of Tax on Railway Passenger Fares

States	Percentage Share
Andhra Pradesh	9.05
Assam	2.79
Bihar	9.99
Gujarat	7.11
Jammu & Kashmir	-
Kerala	1.85
Madhya Pradesh	9.85
Madras	5.81
Maharashtra	8.98
Mysore	3.98
Nagaland	0.01
Orissa	2.12
Punjab	7.43
Rajasthan	6.40
Uttar Pradesh	18.23
West Bengal	6.40
Total	**100.00**

Source: *Report of the Fourth Finance Commission*, 1965, p. 15.

As regards the percentage of the States' share, while some States did not suggest any change in the existing percentage, some others suggested that the entire net proceeds be assigned to the States. The suggestions by other States fell between these two views. Another view was that the permanent solution to the shrinkage in the divisible pool was suitably to amend the Constitution so as to provide for inclusion of the proceeds from corporation tax in the divisible pool, alternatively the Centre should make good to the States by way of grants the loss on account of non-inclusion of corporation tax in the divisible pool.

After considering the claims put forward by the States, the Fourth Commission expressed general agreement with the observation of the Third Finance Commission that in the case of a divisible tax in which there was obligatory participation between the Union and the States, a sound principle to observe would be that all participating Governments, more particularly the one responsible for levy and collection, should have a significant interest in the yield of that tax. Considering the various facts placed before it, the Commission took the view that some further increase in the States' share was justified. Accordingly it recommended that 75 per cent of the divisible pool of income tax should be allocated to the States for distribution among them.

As regards the principles of distribution of the States' share *inter se,* the views expressed by the States, as usual, were widely divergent. While some States wanted the share to be distributed entirely on the basis of population, another view was that the distribution should be solely on the basis of collection. The other suggestions made were that the distribution should be made taking into account the proper weightage to Scheduled Castes and Tribes, relative financial weakness and economic backwardness, inverse ratio of per capita income etc. The Commission had no hesitation in rejecting some of the factors put forward by the States like area, backwardness and financial weakness and proportion of Scheduled Castes and Tribes in the population as proper bases for a scheme of distribution of the proceeds of income tax among the States. There remained only two factors which, the Commission believed, were relevant, namely population and contribution. Taking these two factors of population and collection, there could be divergence of opinion as to the relative proportion to be assigned to these two factors. Eventually, it decided that the principle of distribution to individual States of their share in the divisible pool of income tax proceeds should be the same as recommended by the First Finance Commission and by the Third Finance Commission, i.e. 80 per cent on the basis of population and 20 per cent on the basis of collection.

As regards the actual manner of distribution of the States' share in each year, it felt it convenient both to the States and to the Union if the shares were expressed as fixed percentages. Taking, therefore, the average of the collections of the three years ending with 1963-64, and the population figures according to the 1961 Census, the percentage share of each State in the distributable amount were worked out as given in Table 18.3. It also prescribed 2.5 per cent of the net proceeds of the tax to represent proceeds attributable to Union territories.

Table 18.3: Percentage Shares of the States in the Net Proceeds of Income Tax Assigned to the States as Recommended by the Fourth Finance Commission

States	Percentage
Andhra Pradesh	7.37
Assam	2.44
Bihar	9.04
Gujarat	5.29
Jammu & Kashmir	0.73
Kerala	3.59
Madhya Pradesh	6.47
Madras	8.34
Maharashtra	14.28
Mysore	5.14
Nagaland	0.07
Orissa	3.40
Punjab	4.36
Rajasthan	3.97
Uttar Pradesh	14.60
West Bengal	10.91
Total	**100.00**

Source: *Report of the Fourth Finance Commission*, 1965, p. 20.

18.6 Union Excise Duties

The first issue before the Commission was whether the States should at all be given a share out of Union excises. It noted that under the Constitution the distribution of proceeds of Union excise duties between the Centre and the States was merely permissive and did not stand on the same footing as the compulsory assignment to the States of proceeds of taxes enumerated under Article 269 of the Constitution or compulsory distribution between the Centre and the States of the proceeds of income tax under Article 270 of the Constitution. Thus, the States did not have a constitutional right to claim a share out of the proceeds of Union excises. It was for the Parliament to decide if the States should at all be given a share. The factual position was that ever since 1952-53, the States had been getting a share out of Union excise proceeds. The first three Finance Commissions had taken the view that having regard to the growing requirements of funds by the States for developmental and other essential services, recourse to permissive sharing contemplated under article 272 of the Constitution was not only justified but even necessary. This view was endorsed by the Fourth Finance Commission also.

Having accepted that Union excises were to be shared with the States, the next question before the Commission was which of the excisable commodities should be selected for the distribution of proceeds and what percentage of the total proceeds on those commodities should be made over to the States?

The first two Finance Commissions confined the sharing scheme to a few selected items: the First Finance Commission to three, viz. tobacco, matches and vegetable products and the Second to eight, viz. tobacco, matches, vegetable products, sugar, tea, coffee, paper and vegetable non-essential oils. The Third Finance Commission's approach to the question of selection of items for sharing was different from that of the earlier Commissions. It accepted in principle the reasonableness of the demand of the States for participation in the proceeds of all Union excises. For purposes of distribution, however, it included only the commodities on which duties collected in 1960-61 amounted to Rs. 50 lakh or more. The number of such commodities was 35. The duty on motor spirit was excluded from the sharing scheme as that Commission had recommended a separate special purpose grant of corresponding amount for the development of communications. In their representations to the Fourth Commission, the States almost unanimously argued that whatever reservations the last Finance Commission's distribution scheme had should go and that they should be entitled to a share out of the proceeds of excise duties on all commodities, including the commodities which might be taken up for the levy in the coming quinquennium. Following were the arguments advanced by the States in favour of extending the sharing scheme to all commodities.

1. If a co-ordination between the excise policy of the Union Government and the sales tax policies pursued in the States is at all to be achieved, it would be necessary to put the States in a position in which they have and continue to have a substantial interest in the collection and levy of Union excises. One method of achieving this object would be to make Union excise duties on all commodities sharable with the States.
2. The larger the number of commodities brought within the divisible pool, the greater would be the evenness in the flow of resources to the States, as fluctuations in the yield on certain items would be neutralized by fluctuations in the yield of some other items. The States' requirements are growing and,

therefore an elastic source of revenue like a share in excises on all commodities would go to strengthen their position.

3. As the commodities covered by the Union excise duties are of country-wide consumption, there is no justification for selecting only a few of the commodities for sharing.
4. The system of sharing only selected commodities suffers from the defect that if, for one reason or another, the excuse duty on a shared commodity is reduced or abolished and substituted in part or whole by a levy on a related product not included in the sharable list, the States stand to lose. For example, the excise duty on steel ingots was one of the shareable items listed by the Third Finance Commission. For various reasons, the Union Government later substituted the duty on steel ingots by a levy on iron and steel products, but the States did not get any share out of the new levy although it was in replacement of a levy, proceeds of which were sharable.
5. In any economy where industry is getting diversified, new lines of production will emerge continuously and any formula for the sharing of excise duties should therefore cover such new products.

Convinced by the arguments given by the States, the Fourth Commission recommended that all existing Union excise duties as also those that might be levied in the coming five years should be shared between the Centre and the States.

On the question of the percentage of the proceeds of distributable excises, the Commission took the view that in determining the over-all share of the States, due regard had to be given to the requirements of the States on the one hand and the needs of the Union Government on the other. Having considered the issue in this light and keeping in mind the estimates of yield from the existing excise duties in the coming quinquennium as also the requirements of the States, it came to the conclusion that the States' share out of the distributable excises be fixed at 20 per cent of the net proceeds.

In regard to the principles for the distribution of the total of the States' share as among different States, there were divergent placed before it. After examining various viewpoints, it decided to take into account economic and social backwardness also as indicated by the following factors.

1. Per capita gross value of agricultural production.
2. Per capita value added by manufacture.
3. Percentage of workers (as defined in the Census) to the total population.
4. Percentage of enrolment in Classes I to V to the population.
5. Population per hospital bed.
6. Percentage of rural population to total population.

7. Percentage of the population of Scheduled Castes and Tribes to total population.

The Commission gave the factor of relative economic and social backwardness a weight equivalent to 20 per cent. For the other factor, namely population, it recommended a weight equivalent to 80 per cent. The percentage share of each State was worked out as shown in Table 18.4.

Table 18.4: Distribution of States' Share of Excise Duties among the States Recommended by the Fourth Finance Commission

States	Percentage
Andhra Pradesh	7.77
Assam	3.32
Bihar	10.03
Gujarat	4.80
Jammu & Kashmir	2.26
Kerala	4.16
Madhya Pradesh	7.40
Madras	7.18
Maharashtra	8.23
Mysore	5.41
Nagaland	2.21
Orissa	4.82
Punjab	4.86
Rajasthan	5.06
Uttar Pradesh	14.98
West Bengal	7.51
Total	**100.00**

Source: *Report of the Fourth Finance Commission*, 1965, p. 29.

18.7 Additional Duties of Excise in Lieu of Sales Tax

The Commission examined the issue whether out of the net proceeds of additional duties of excise, the total of the guaranteed amounts should first be set apart and then the balance be distributed in a certain manner, or the entire net proceeds should first be distributed in a particular manner and then the question of guaranteed amounts brought in. It felt that the latter procedure might create difficulties inasmuch as under certain circumstances it might happen that some States' share fell short of the guaranteed amount. It, therefore, took the view that the appropriate course would be the first and the more direct one, namely that of giving to each State the guaranteed amount first and then distributing the balance between different States on the basis of certain uniform principles.

As regard to the principles for the distribution of the balance of the net proceeds over the total of the guaranteed amounts, it may be recalled that the Third Finance Commission considered that it would be equitable to distribute the excess collections partly on the basis of the percentage increase in the collection of sales tax in each State since the year 1957-58 when the additional excise duties were imposed and partly on the basis of population. However, it did not indicate the relative weightage given to these factors. In the opinion of the Fourth Commission, figures for collections of all sales taxes in a State were a more direct indicator of the contribution made by each State to the divisible surplus than population. Therefore, it recommended that the distribution of the balance over the total of guaranteed amounts may be made on the basis of the proportion of sales tax revenue realised in each State to the total sales tax collections in all the States taken together. For the purpose of determining the proportion for each State, it utilised the data relating to actual collections of sales taxes over the year 1961-62 to 1963-64.

When the scheme of additional excise duties in lieu of sales tax was introduced in 1956-57, the State of Jammu and Kashmir did not have any sales tax and, therefore, the question of giving any guaranteed amount to that State did not arise. The Second Finance Commission had taken the view that since the incidence of the additional duties of excise would fall as much on the people of this State as on the people of other States, Jammu and Kashmir should be given a share out of the net proceeds. That Commission had fixed the share of Jammu and Kashmir at 1.25 per cent of the net proceeds. The Third Finance Commission increased it to 1.50 per cent. The Commission under review retained it at the level suggested by the Third Commission.

On the basis of the principles outlined above, the Commission recommended that in each of the years 1966-67 to 1970-71, the net proceeds of additional duties of excise on cotton fabrics, silk fabrics, rayon or artificial silk fabrics, woollen fabrics, sugar and tobacco including manufactured tobacco, be distributed among the States on the following basis.

1. A sum equal of 1.00 per cent of the net proceeds of these duties in any year be deemed as being attributable to Union territories and may, therefore, be retained by the Centre.
2. A sum equal to 1.50 per cent of the net proceeds in any year be paid to the State of Jammu and Kashmir.

3. A sum equal to 0.05 per cent of the net proceeds in any year be paid to the State of Nagaland as its share.
4. Out of the remaining 97.45 per cent of the net proceeds, the following sums representing the revenue realised in 1956-57 by each respective State on account of sales taxes on the six commodities be first paid annually to the following States (Table 18.5).

Table 18.5: Distribution of Additional Excise Duties among the States Recommended by the Fourth Finance Commission

States	(Rs. lakh)
Andhra Pradesh	235.24
Assam	85.08
Bihar	130.16
Gujarat	323.45
Kerala	95.08
Madhya Pradesh	155.17
Madras	285.34
Maharashtra	637.77
Mysore	100.10
Orissa	85.10
Punjab	175.19
Rajasthan	90.10
Uttar Pradesh	575.81
West Bengal	280.41
Total	**3254.00**

Source: *Report of the Fourth Finance Commission*, 1965, p. 35.

5. Difference between 97.45 per cent of the net proceeds in any year and the total guaranteed amount of Rs. 3,254 lakh would constitute the balance which might be distributed among 14 States, namely all States other than Jammu and Kashmir and Nagaland, as specified (Table 18.6).

18.8 Principles Governing Grants-in-aid of Revenues

The rules regarding grants-in-aid were considered by the First Finance Commission in detail and it recommended that budgetary needs of the States should be an important criterion for determining the assistance required by the

States. However, in arriving at these needs, appropriate allowances have to be made based on a number of considerations as listed below.

Table 18.6: Distribution of the Remainder, if any, of Additional Excise Duties among the States

States	Percentage
Andhra Pradesh	7.42
Assam	1.98
Bihar	6.17
Gujarat	7.43
Kerala	5.65
Madhya Pradesh	4.62
Madras	11.13
Maharashtra	19.87
Mysore	5.21
Orissa	2.58
Punjab	5.01
Rajasthan	3.17
Uttar Pradesh	7.83
West Bengal	11.93
Total	**100.00**

Source: *Report of the Fourth Finance Commission*, 1965, p. 36.

1. Budgets should be reduced to a standard form by eliminating non-repetitive items.
2. Due consideration should be given to the tax efforts by the State and the extent to which the State itself had made efforts to raise resources in relation to its tax potential.
3. Allowance should be made for the scope for economy in expenditure.
4. System of grants-in-aid should be designed to avoid large disparities in the standards of basic social services.
5. Grants-in-aid may be given to help individual States to meet their special burdens, if such burdens are of national concern and if they are likely to cause undue strain on the States' finances.
6. Grants-in-aid may be given for broad national purposes with a view to further any beneficent service of primary importance in regard to which it is in the national interest to assist the less advanced States to go forward.

These principles were considered unexceptionable by the Second Finance Commission. It, however, added that the eligibility of a State to grants-in-aid and the quantum of such aid should depend upon its fiscal need in a comprehensive sense. That Commission also felt that the gap between the ordinary revenue of a State and its normal revenue expenditure should, as far as possible, be met by sharing of taxes and that grants-on-aid should be the residuary form of assistance. Although it recognised that specific purpose grants might be given, no such grants were given by that Commission.

The Third Finance Commission also was in agreement with the general principles enunciated by the earlier Commissions. It, however, felt that the *fiscal needs* as assessed by the Commission should take into account not only non-plan expenditure but also plan expenditure. It also felt that it would be advisable to attach strict conditions of utilisation to any grants-in-aid given for activities meant to serve national purposes but that States should have freedom to reappropriate funds from one allocation to another in respect of grants meant generally to strengthen the State sector.

The Commission under review agreed with the principles formulated by its predecessors except to the extent that it did not recommend the inclusion of plan grants and special purpose grants in grants-in-aid. In applying these principles and working out the grants-in-aid admissible to States, its terms of reference required it to have due regard to certain special considerations which were not specifically mentioned in the terms of reference to the earlier Commissions. Among these considerations were the expenditure devolving on the States for servicing of their debt, the creation of a fund out of part of the proceeds of estate duty, and the scope for economy consistent with efficiency which might be effected by the States in their administrative expenditure.

The Second and Third Finance Commissions took into account in their assessment the likely expenditure on the cost of relief measures, necessitated by unforeseen natural calamities like famine, floods and droughts. The amounts so included were estimated by the Second Finance Commission roughly on the basis of the average annual expenditure incurred over a decade. The Commission under review reassessed the amounts likely to be required by each State for this item on the basis of the figures of gross expenditure for eight years ending with 1964-65. Where the reassessed figure was lower than the figure adopted by the Second and Third Finance Commissions, it retained the latter figure. The annual amounts included by it in its estimates of expenditure were the following (Table 18.7).

The Commission added in its estimates of expenditure the requirements of the States for payment of annual interest on loans outstanding at the end of the Third Plan period (public loans, Central loans and other loans) on the basis of annual outstanding amounts as at the end of each year (i.e. net of repayments) as reported by the State Governments and the Accountants-General. Interest liability on account of other non-plan loans likely to be raised during the Forth Plan period were also allowed in its estimates of expenditure, on the basis of information obtained from the State Governments. The interest liability during the Fourth Plan period on account of the above two classes of loans was as follows (Table 18.8).

Table 18.7: Annual Amounts Included in the Estimates of Expenditure of the States on Account of Unforeseen Natural Calamities

States	Annual estimated expenditure on relief from natural calamities (Rs. lakh)
Andhra Pradesh	75
Assam	40
Bihar	140
Gujarat	80
Jammu and Kashmir	28
Kerala	10
Madhya Pradesh	30
Madras	50
Maharashtra	60
Mysore	33
Orissa	123
Punjab	197
Rajasthan	93
Uttar Pradesh	75
West Bengal	535
Total	**1,569**

Source: *Report of the Fourth Finance Commission*, 1965, p. 50.

The Commission also included in its assessment of expenditure the requirements for payment of full interest on Fourth Plan loans that would be raised by the States during 1966-71. However, it did not allow for capitalisation of any portion of the interest. It used the date obtained from the Planning Commission for its estimates of borrowings by the individual States. The amounts estimated by it on this account for each State, for interest payments on the gross Fourth Plan loans were as follows (Table 18.9).

Table 18.8: Annual Amounts Included in the Estimates of Expenditure of the States on Account of Interest Liability

States	Amount (Rs. crore)
Andhra Pradesh	76.95
Assam	30.20
Bihar	86.08
Gujarat	50.81
Jammu and Kashmir	20.14
Kerala	40.48
Madhya Pradesh	73.53
Madras	79.13
Maharashtra	97.81
Mysore	58.66
Orissa	62.37
Punjab	75.53
Rajasthan	58.01
Uttar Pradesh	104.21
West Bengal	73.73
Total	**987.64**

Source: *Report of the Fourth Finance Commission*, 1965, p. 51.

The Commission expressed the opinion that the service and amortisation of the market borrowings of the State Governments must form part of the revenue liabilities of the State Governments. Accordingly, it included in its assessment expenditure on these items estimated on the basis of the existing practices adopted by the State Governments. The amounts included for the five years for the various States on account of sinking fund provision for public loans were as follows (Table 18.10).

Based on the foregoing considerations, the assessment of revenue receipts and non-plan revenue expenditure of different States for the five-year period 1966-67 to 1970-71 worked out to the following estimates of non-plan revenue gap (Table 18.11).

After meeting the revenue deficits estimated for the five year period, the amounts accruing to the following States as their shares of the various taxes and duties resulted in the surplus noted against each State for the five year period (Table 18.12). Hence, the Commission did not recommend any grants for them under Article 275 of the Constitution.

Table 18.9: Annual Amounts Included in the Estimates of Expenditure of the States on Account of Interest on Fourth Plan Loans

State	Amount (Rs. crore)
Andhra Pradesh	43.48
Assam	16.10
Bihar	41.31
Jammu and Kashmir	8.90
Gujarat	25.30
Kerala	22.00
Madhya Pradesh	37.97
Madras	41.61
Maharashtra	51.15
Mysore	29.92
Orissa	31.58
Punjab	29.99
Rajasthan	29.46
Uttar Pradesh	68.38
West Bengal	45.14
Total	**522.29**

Source: *Report of the Fourth Finance Commission*, 1965, p. 52.

Table 18.10: Annual Amounts Included in the Estimates of Expenditure of the States on Account of Sinking Fund Provision

State	Amount (Rs. crore)
Andhra Pradesh	4.94
Assam	11.19
Bihar	9.04
Gujarat	28.41
Jammu and Kashmir	-
Kerala	3.63
Madhya Pradesh	7.19
Madras	8.90
Maharashtra	46.85
Mysore	15.00

Contd...

Nagaland	-
Orissa	31.49
Punjab	12.15
Rajasthan	16.90
Uttar Pradesh	61.97
West Bengal	28.56
Total	**286.22**

Source: *Report of the Fourth Finance Commission*, 1965, p. 53.

Table 18.11: Estimates of Non-Plan Revenue Gap of Different States Made by the Fourth Finance Commission

State	**Non-Plan revenue gap during 1966-67 to 1970-71 (Rs. crore)**
Andhra Pradesh	202.73
Assam	144.96
Bihar	108.21
Gujarat	113.55
Jammu and Kashmir	66.10
Kerala	188.61
Madhya Pradesh	162.03
Madras	207.32
Maharashtra	44.72
Mysore	202.52
Nagaland	58.46
Orissa	231.85
Punjab	75.03
Rajasthan	130.41
Uttar Pradesh	306.75
West Bengal	183.44
Total	**2426.69**

Source: *Report of the Fourth Finance Commission*, 1965, p. 58.

The revenue deficits for the 5 year period were in excess of the amounts accruing to the following 10 States as their shares of the various taxes and duties by the sum shown against each (Table 18.13). The Commission recommended that annual grants equal to one-fifth of the sum be given to each of them under Article 275 of the Constitution.

Table 18.12: Estimates of Revenue Surplus of Different States Made by the Fourth Finance Commission

State	Surplus (Rs. Crore)
Bihar	89.04
Gujarat	8.00
Maharashtra	215.66
Punjab	29.83
Uttar Pradesh	17.02
West Bengal	13.97
Total	**373.73**

Source: *Report of the Fourth Finance Commission*, 1965, p. 59.

Table 18.13: Estimates of Revenue Deficit of Different States Made by the Fourth Finance Commission

State	Deficit (5 times annual grant) (Rs. crore)
Andhra Pradesh	36.10
Assam	82.60
Jammu and Kashmir	32.85
Kerala	104.10
Madhya Pradesh	13.50
Madras	34.20
Mysore	91.20
Nagaland	35.35
Orissa	145.90
Rajasthan	33.65
Total	**609.45**

Source: *Report of the Fourth Finance Commission*, 1965, p. 59.

Notes

1. *Report of the Fourth Finance Commission*, 1965, pp. 7-8.

2. The distinction between Plan and non-Plan expenditure evolved in India with the launching of Five Year Plans in 1951. When the provisions regarding the Centre-State financial relations were incorporated into the Constitution, it was not possible for any one to anticipate the importance and magnitude of successive Five Year Plans. There was no reference to Plan expenditure as such in the terms of reference of the First Finance Commission (appointed in November 1951) and that body did not find it necessary to draw a line of distinction between Plan and non-Plan expenditure. In fact, it emphasised the need for taking into account development

expenditure of various types in determining the transfer of resources from the Centre to the States. The Second Finance Commission (appointed in June 1956) was, however, specifically asked to take into account both the requirements of the Second Five Year Plan (1956-57 to 1960-61) and the efforts made by States to raise additional revenues. The dimensions of Plan expenditure, however, increased rapidly and it became the normal practice to make grants for plan expenditure under the discretionary provisions of Article 282 instead of making statutory grants under Article 275, on the basis of the pre-determined plan allocations as phased and modified by the annual plan discussions. The Third Finance Commission (appointed in December 1960) recommended grants under Article 275 to cover 75 per cent of the States' revenue expenditure on the Third Five Year Plan (1961-62 to 1965-66), but the Government of India did not accept this recommendation.

3. *Report of the Fourth Finance Commission*, 1965, p. 9.

19

Fifth Finance Commission

The Fifth Commission was constituted by an Order of the President dated February 29, 1968. It was asked to make recommendations as to the following matters.

(a) Distribution between the Union and the States of the net proceeds of taxes which are to be, or may be, divided between them under Chapter 1 of Part XII of the Constitution and the allocation between the States of the respective shares of such proceeds.

Summary Statement	
Chairman	Mr. Mahavir Tyagi
Members	Shri P.C. Bhattacharyya Shri M. Seshachalapathy Dr. D.T. Lakdawala Shri V.L. Gidwani
Year and month of establishment	February 1968
Year and month of reporting	July 1969
Period of award	1969-70 to 1973-74
Main Recommendations	
• States' share in income tax fixed at (per cent): 75 • Bases of distribution of States' share in income tax inter se (per cent): Population: 90; Contribution: 10; Other factors: Nil • States' share in Union excise duties fixed at (per cent): 20 • Bases of distribution of States' share in Union excise duties inter se (per cent): Population: 80; Other factors: 20	

(b) Principles which should govern the grants-in-aid of the revenues of the States out of the Consolidated Fund of India and the sums to be paid to the States which are in need to assistance by way of grants-in-aid of their revenues under article 275 for purposes other than those specified in the provisos to clause (1) of that article and other than the requirements of the Five Year Plan, having regard, among other considerations, to (i) the revenue resources of those States for the five years ending with the financial year 1973-74 on the basis of the levels of taxation likely to be reached at the end of the financial year 1968-69, (ii) the requirements on revenue account of those States to meet the expenditure on administration, interest charges in respect of their debt, maintenance and upkeep of Plan schemes completed by the end of 1968-69, transfer of funds to local bodies and aided institutions and other committed expenditure and (iii) the scope for better fiscal management as also for economy consistent with efficiency which may be effected by the States in their administrative, maintenance, developmental and other expenditure.

(c) Changes, if any, to be made in the principles governing the distribution amongst the States of the grant to be made available to the States in lieu of the repealed tax on railway passenger fares.

(d) Changes, if any, to be made in the principles governing the distribution amongst the States under article 269 of the net proceeds in any financial year of estate duty in respect of property other than agricultural land.

(e) Desirability or otherwise of maintaining the existing arrangements under the Additional Duties of Excise (Goods of Special Importance) Act, 1957, in regard to the levy of additional duties of excise on sugar, textiles and tobacco in lieu of the States' sales taxes thereon, with or without any modifications and the scope for extending such arrangements to other items or commodities;

(f) Irrespective of the recommendations made under item (e) above, the changes, if any, to be made in the principles governing the distribution of the net proceeds in any financial year of the additional excise duties leviable under the 1957 Act aforesaid on each of the following commodities, namely (i) cotton fabrics, (ii) silk fabrics, (iii) woollen fabrics, (iv) rayon or artificial silk fabrics, (v) sugar and (vi) tobacco including manufactured tobacco, in replacement of the States' sales taxes formerly levied by the State Governments. Provided that the share accruing to each State shall not be less than the revenue realised from the levy of the sales tax for the financial year 1956-57 in that State.

(g) Principles which should govern the distribution of the net proceeds of such additional items or commodities as may be recommended under item (e) above for levy of additional excise duties in lieu of the States' sales taxes thereon.

(h) Scope for raising revenue from the taxes and duties mentioned in article 269 of the Constitution but not levied at present.

(i) Scope for raising additional revenue by the various State Governments from the sources of revenue available to them.

(j) Problem of unauthorised overdrafts of certain States with the Reserve Bank and the procedure to be observed for avoiding such overdrafts.

19.1 Income Tax

The Commission made the following recommendations regarding income tax.

(a) In respect of distribution of the unadjusted balance of advance tax collections up to the year 1966-67: (i) out of the amount of such advance tax collections, as determined by the Comptroller and Auditor-General of India, a sum equal to 2.5 per cent thereof be deemed to be the portion which represent the proceeds attributable to Union territories, as constituted immediately prior to the Punjab Reorganisation Act, 1966, (ii) percentage of the amount of advance tax as determined by the Comptroller and Auditor-General of India except the portion attributable to Union territories, to be assigned to the States should be 75 per cent, (iii) distribution among the States *inter se* of the share assigned to the States should be made on the basis of the percentages recommended by the Fourth Finance Commission, with appropriate adjustments in regard to the share of reorganised Punjab and Haryana States and Union territories in accordance with the Punjab Reorganisation Act, 1966 and (iv) share of each State should be paid to the State Government in three equal annual instalments during the year from 1971-72 to 1973-74.

(b) In respect of distribution between the Union and the States of the net proceeds of income tax in the years 1967-68 and 1968-69, there should be no change in the distribution as prescribed in the Constitution (Distribution of Revenues) Order, 1965, in the event of the said net proceeds being certified by the Comptroller and Auditor-General of India on the revised basis.

(c) In respect of the distribution of net proceeds of income tax in the financial year from 1969-70 to 1973-74: (i) out of the net proceeds of taxes on income in each financial year, a sum equal to 2.6 per cent thereof be deemed to be the portion which represents the proceeds attributable to Union territories, (ii) percentage of the net proceeds of taxes on income, except the portion which represents proceeds attributable to Union territories, to be assigned to the States should be 75 per cent and (iii) distribution among the States *inter se* of the share assigned to the States in respect of each financial year should be made on the basis of the following percentages (Table 19.1).

19.2 Union Excise Duties

The Commission under review made the following recommendations in regard to the distribution of Union excise duties.

(a) During each of the years 1969-70 to 1971-72 a sum equivalent to 20 per cent of the net proceeds of Union duties of excise on all articles levied and collected in that year, excluding special excises, regulatory duties and duties and cesses levied under special Acts and earmarked for special purposes, should be paid out of the Consolidated Fund of India to the States.

Table 19.1: Percentage Shares of the States in the Net Proceeds of Income Tax Assigned to the States as Recommended by the Fifth Finance Commission

State	Percentage
Andhra Pradesh	8.01
Assam	2.67
Bihar	9.99
Gujarat	5.13
Haryana	1.73
Jammu and Kashmir	0.79
Kerala	3.83
Madhya Pradesh	7.09
Maharashtra	11.34
Mysore	5.40
Nagaland	0.08
Orissa	3.75
Punjab	2.55
Rajasthan	4.34
Tamil Nadu	8.18
Uttar Pradesh	16.01
West Bengal	9.11
Total	**100.00**

Source: *Report of the Fifth Finance Commission*, 1969, p. 30.

(b) During the years 1972-73 and 1973-74, a sum equivalent to 20 per cent of the net proceeds of Union duties of excise on all articles levied and collected in the respective year, including special excises, but excluding regulatory duties and duties and cesses levied under special Acts and earmarked for special purposes, should be paid out of the Consolidated Fund of India to the States.

(c) Distribution among the States of the sum payable to the States in respect of each financial year should be made on the basis of the following percentages (Table 19.2).

Table 19.2: Distribution of States' Share of Excise Duties among the States Recommended by the Fifth Finance Commission

State	Percentage
Andhra Pradesh	7.15
Assam	2.51
Bihar	13.81
Gujarat	4.17
Haryana	1.49
Jammu and Kashmir	1.12
Kerala	4.28
Madhya Pradesh	8.48
Maharashtra	7.93
Mysore	4.65
Nagaland	0.08
Orissa	4.72
Punjab	2.17
Rajasthan	5.28
Tamil Nadu	6.50
Uttar Pradesh	18.82
West Bengal	6.84
Total	**100.00**

Source: *Report of the Fifth Finance Commission*, 1969, p. 37.

19.3 Additional Duties of Excise in Lieu of Sales Tax

The Commission made the following observations in regard to additional duties of excise, "(a) It would not be desirable to maintain the existing arrangements in regard to the levy of additional duties of excise on textiles, sugar and tobacco, unless the Government of India, after discussing the matter further with the State Governments, can arrive at a general agreement for the continuance of the present scheme with suitable modifications; (b) While the arrangements are continued, the rates of duties may be made *ad valorem* as far as possible, and may be revised periodically so as to secure reasonable incidence having regard to the prevailing prices and the general level of sales taxes on similar items levied by the States; There is no scope at present for extending such arrangements to other items or commodities." [1]

It recommended the distribution of the net proceeds of the additional excise duties, during each financial year in which the existing arrangements continue, on the following basis.

1. A sum equal to 2.05 per cent of such net proceeds be retained by the Union as attributable to Union territories.
2. A sum equal to 0.83 per cent of such net proceeds be paid to the State of Jammu and Kashmir as its share.
3. A sum equal to 0.09 per cent of such net proceeds be paid to the State of Nagaland as its share.
4. Out of the remaining balance of 97.03 per cent of such net proceeds the sums specified (Table 19.3), representing the revenue realised in the financial year 1956-57 by each respective State from the levy of sales taxes on the commodities subject to additional excise duties, be paid as guaranteed amounts.

Table 19.3: Distribution of Additional Excise Duties among the States Recommended by the Fifth Finance Commission

State	Guaranteed amount (Rs. lakh)
Andhra Pradesh	235.24
Assam	85.08
Bihar	130.16
Gujarat	323.45
Haryana	65.49
Kerala	95.08
Madhya Pradesh	155.17
Maharashtra	637.77
Mysore	100.10
Orissa	85.10
Punjab	96.07
Rajasthan	90.10
Tamil Nadu	285.34
Uttar Pradesh	575.81
West Bengal	280.41

Source: *Report of the Fifth Finance Commission*, 1969, p. 45.

5. The balance be distributed among the States other than Jammu and Kashmir and Nagaland in accordance with their respective percentage shares of such balance as under (Table 19.4).

Table 19.4: Distribution of the Remainder, if any, of Additional Excise Duties among the States

State	Percentage distribution of excess amount
Andhra Pradesh	8.13
Assam	2.47
Bihar	8.40
Gujarat	6.33
Haryana	1.70
Kerala	4.84
Madhya Pradesh	6.34
Maharashtra	13.89
Mysore	6.00
Orissa	3.13
Punjab	2.98
Rajasthan	4.42
Tamil Nadu	9.63
Uttar Pradesh	12.99
West Bengal	8.75
Total	**100.00**

Source: *Report of the Fifth Finance Commission*, 1969, p. 46.

6. In case the existing arrangements are discontinued during the course of a financial year, the sums specified in clause (4) above, be reduced *pro rata* to the period for which the arrangements have continued.

19.4 Grants-in-aid of Revenues under Article 275 of the Constitution

After reviewing the recommendations of the earlier Commissions and taking into account its own scheme of devolution, the Commission recommended that the following States be paid the sums specified against each of them as grants-in-aid of their revenues in the respective years indicated (Table 19.5).

Table 19.5: Grants-in-aid of Revenues Recommended by the Fifth Finance Commission (Rs. crore)

State	Total in 5 years	1969-70	1970-71	1971-72	1972-73	1973-74
Andhra Pradesh	65.01	15.54	14.27	13.00	11.73	10.47
Assam	101.97	20.80	20.60	20.39	20.19	19.99
Jammu and Kashmir	73.68	16.81	15.77	14.74	13.70	12.66
Kerala	49.65	9.93	9.93	9.93	9.93	9.93
Mysore	17.99	6.48	5.04	3.60	2.16	0.71
Nagaland	77.95	17.40	16.49	15.59	14.69	13.78
Orissa	104.67	24.51	22.72	20.94	19.14	17.36
Rajasthan	51.49	12.36	11.33	10.30	9.27	8.23
Tamil Nadu	22.82	6.61	5.59	4.56	3.54	2.52
West Bengal	72.62	22.29	18.41	14.52	10.64	6.76
Total	**637.85**	**152.73**	**140.15**	**127.57**	**114.99**	**102.41**

Source: *Report of the Fifth Finance Commission*, 1969, p. 66.

19.5 Taxes and Duties under Article 269 of the Constitution

The Commission under study was required to make recommendations as to the scope for raising revenue from the taxes and duties mentioned in Article 269 of the Constitution but not being levied at that time. Article 269 mentioned the following taxes and duties.

(a) Duties in respect of succession to property other than agricultural land.
(b) Estate duty in respect of property other than agricultural land.
(c) Terminal taxes on goods or passengers carried by railway, sea or air.
(d) Taxes on railway fares and freights.
(e) Taxes other than stamp duties on transactions in stock-exchanges and futures markets.
(f) Taxes on the sale or purchase of newspapers and on advertisements published therein.
(g) Taxes on the sale or purchase of goods other than newspapers, where such sale or purchase takes place in the course of inter-State trade or commerce.

Of these taxes and duties, those mentioned in (b) and (g) were already being levied and they were therefore outside the purview of the matters referred to it. In regard to item (c), a terminal tax on passengers carried by railway from or to a place of pilgrimage etc. was being levied under the provisions of the Terminal

Tax on Railway Passengers Act, 1956. The Commission considered whether it could examine the scope for raising revenue from this source. Although such a tax on passengers carried by railway falling under item (c) of Article 269 (1) of the Constitutions was in force, the Act itself restricted the levy of the tax to places of a particular category, namely places of pilgrimage, or places where fairs, melas or exhibitions are held and the Government had no general power under the Act to levy terminal tax on passengers carried to other categories of towns.

In other words, the existing law did not cover most of the towns to or from which railway passengers were carried, and the field of taxation was limited to a part of the available field over which the tax could be levied. The Commission, therefore, took the view that it was required to consider this item also insofar as the levy of such tax in respect of other places was concerned, and to make recommendations regarding the scope for raising revenue therefrom.

19.5.1 Duties in Respect of Succession to Property other than Agricultural Land: Though succession duties and estate duty in respect of property other than agricultural land were both specified in Article 269, their incidence fell on the same object, namely property passing on the death of the owner to his successors. In the case of succession duties, the levy would be based on the parts of an estate devolving on each of the successors, while in the case of estate duty the levy was regulated by the value of the whole estate, though recovery of the duty was made from all the persons benefiting by the estate. Estate duty was already being levied and the Commission thought that there would be no particular advantage in levying succession duties also.

19.5.2 Terminal Taxes on Goods or Passengers Carried by Railway, Sea or Air

A. Terminal Tax on Goods Carried by Railway: Although terminal taxes on goods or octroi duties are being levied since long by a number of local bodies, a separate terminal tax on goods carried by rail has not been imposed so far by the Government of India. The Commission was of the opinion that a terminal tax levied on goods carried by railway would be administratively inconvenient, as it would involve collection of tax at different rates according to destinations, and separate accounting of receipts to be transferred to each State for different local areas therein. It would be far simple for municipal bodies to suitably modify their octroi or terminal tax rates, or preferably, impose some levy on the sale or consumption of the goods entering their territorial limits.

B. Terminal Tax on Passengers Carried by Railway: The Commission tried to estimate the likely revenue from a terminal tax on passengers carried by railway, on the basis of information furnished by the Railway Board about the numbers of passengers of each class other than suburban passengers in the year 1967-68, originating from cities having a population of more than one lakh according to the 1961 Census. It was stated by that Board that, over a period of time, the numbers of passengers originating from and those terminating at any place might be assumed to be not significantly different. On the assumption that the terminal tax would be levied on non-suburban passengers travelling over distance exceeding 50 kilometres at rates similar to those at which such tax was at that time levied on pilgrims, the revenue was estimated at Rs. 5 crore per annum. Having regard to the administrative difficulties and inconvenience involved in collection, and the need to levy a corresponding tax on passengers travelling by road, the Commission opined that it would not be worthwhile to levy this tax.

C. Terminal Tax on Goods and Passengers Carried by Sea: The Commission examined the scope for levy of a terminal tax on goods and passengers carried by sea on the basis of the facts available to it. The Ministry of Shipping and Transport pointed out that the coastal passenger traffic was mainly in the Konkan sector and there were persistent complaints that the fares were already high. There was overseas passenger traffic only on a few routes. A passenger welfare cess was already being levied at Rs. 1 per unberthed passenger and Rs. 2 per saloon or cabin passenger. The Commission estimated that even if a terminal tax was levied at Rs. 2 to Rs. 5 per deck passenger and Rs. 10 to Rs. 15 per saloon or cabin passenger, the yield was not likely to exceed half a crore of rupee. It therefore took the view that revenue of this order would not justify the imposition of such tax on this mode of transport only.

The Commission held the view that a terminal tax on goods carried by sea could be levied either on the goods exported from or imported into the country or on coastal traffic. Such imports and exports as well as coastal traffic were already subject to various charges at the ports. The volume of goods shipped or landed at such ports was dependent on many factors of location, communication etc. and was related to the trade and industry of the various regions in the hinterland served by the ports. In view of this larger impact of the shipping cargo traffic, the Commission considered that the levy of a terminal tax for the benefit of the ports only would not be justified, and no such tax need be levied in addition to the port charges and other fees already in force.

D. Terminal Tax on Goods and Passengers Carried by Air: The internal air traffic at that time was mainly with the Indian Airlines Corporation while the international traffic was carried by Air India and the international airlines operating in India. Ministry of Tourism and Civil Aviation of the Government of India, Air India and the Indian Airlines expressed the view that, having regard to the existing levies on the air industry, there was little scope to introduce any new tax, particularly in the context of the need to attract more foreign tourists and to promote civil airlines activity. It was further urged that any levy on passengers or cargo at airports ought to be related to the facilities provided for them at the airports. The facilities provided at that time were inadequate compared to many airports abroad.

As regards internal air traffic, it was stated that such levy would hamper full utilisation of the increased capacity expected as a result of introduction of large capacity jets in India. It would also discourage growth of cargo traffic by air. The levy, therefore, would not be in the interest of growth of civil aviation in the country. There was already a fee of Rs. 15 per head levied on passengers leaving India for destinations abroad by air from the four international airports in India. Further, such terminal tax was levied in very few other countries. While appreciating foregoing arguments, the Commission believed that a moderate terminal tax on passengers carried by air could not be ruled out on such grounds. It estimated that a terminal tax on passengers levied at Rs. 5 per passenger on internal flights and Rs. 25 per passenger on international flights would yield about Rs. 2.5 crore only. In view of the small yield and also the fact that it did not recommend levy of a similar tax on passengers using other modes of transport, the Commission thought that levy of such a tax would not be expedient. As regards the levy of a terminal tax on air cargo, it felt that such a measure would not be advisable when this mode of transport of goods was still not sufficiently developed.

19.5.3 Taxes on Railway Fares and Freights

A. Tax on Railway Fares: A tax on railway fares was levied in 1957 as a percentage of the fares and was recovered as an addition to the fare. The tax was in force till the end of 1960-61.

Following the recommendation of the Railway Convention Committee (1960) of the Parliament, the tax was repealed and merged in the basic fares from April 1, 1961. It may be recalled that the Railway Board had pleaded before the Committee that the tax had reduced the scope for raising passenger fares. Obviously, the States were unhappy on being deprived of a potentially elastic source of revenue. To compensate the States for the loss of revenue, the Government decided to pay annually a sum of Rs. 12.50 crore for distribution among the States during the five year period 1961-62 to 1965-66. This was on the consideration that the States, to whom the proceeds from this tax were payable, were likely to have included this source of income as part of their resources for purposes of the Third Five Year Plan.

Consequent upon representations made by the States to the Fourth Finance Commission, the Railway Board suggested to the Railway Convention Committee, 1965, that the grant may be raised to Rs. 16.25 crore, keeping in view the rate of increase in traffic during the five years 1960-61 to 1964-65 and the expected increase in subsequent years. For this purpose it was suggested that the Railways should pay to the Government of India an amount equal to 1 per cent of the capital at charge on March 31, 1964, out of which Rs. 16.25 crore may be paid as grant to States in lieu of the repealed tax and the balance of about Rs. 1.50 crore may be utilised to assist the States to provide their share of the cost of Railway safety works. In pursuance of the recommendations of the Railway Convention Committcc (1965), the amount of this grant was raised to Rs. 16.25 crore per annum from 1966-67.

In their memoranda submitted to the Commission under review, the States urged that either the tax on railway fares be reintroduced at the same rates at which it was levied in 1957-58, or the quantum of the grant in lieu of the tax be increased and fixed as a percentage of the railway passenger earnings, such percentage being fixed on the basis of actual tax collections and passenger earnings in the years up to 1960-61 prior to the repeal of the tax. Estimates made by the Commission revealed that the amounts payable to the States in lieu of the tax would be higher than the fixed grants recommended by the Railway Convention Committees, and would be of the order of Rs. 25 crore at that time.

The Commission discussed with representatives of the Railway Board the suggestions of the States that either the tax should be reintroduced or the quantum of the grant in lieu of the tax increased. The Board represented to the Commission that the cost of passenger services had increased considerably, and that whatever additional revenues could be obtained by increase in fares would have to be utilised by them towards meeting the increased cost of operation. Further, they stated that their experience was that whenever fares were increased, there had been a set back in the rate of growth of passenger traffic and they felt that the reintroduction of the tax would affect the railway finances adversely.

The Commission accepted the viewpoint of the Railway Board and maintained that there was no scope for the reimposition of the tax on railway passenger fares in the then prevailing circumstances. As regards the States' suggestion for increase in the quantum of the grant as an alternative of the reimposition of the tax, the Commission hoped that the Railway Convention Committee would take into account the views of the States in this regard.

B. Tax on Railway Freights [2]: It was urged before the Commission by the Railway Board that the railways freight structure had been so framed as to assist industrial and agricultural development of the country. For example, coal was being carried at a rate which did not cover even the cost of carriage. Other instances of low-rated commodities were ores, manures and fodder. Such liberal treatment was allowed by the railways because the materials were used for industry, and if rates were increased up to the level justified by the cost of transport, there would be general increase in prices which would impede economic development.

The Commission was of the view that the freight structure should be consistent with the requirements of economic development of the country as a whole and it should conform to the objectives of the economic policies of Government. Having regard to the position of railway finances at that time, the levy of a tax on railway freights was not considered desirable by the commission. Such a tax would increase costs of transport which was not desirable in the interest of general economic policy, and it would also necessitate a corresponding tax on road freights.

19.5.4 Taxes other than Stamp Duties on Transactions in Stock Exchanges and Future Markets

A. Tax on Transactions in Stock Exchanges: In this regard the Commission noted, "There are two types of transactions in securities on stock exchanges – those for spot or hand delivery and the others for clearance. The transactions for the purpose of investments are made for spot or hand delivery, while the transactions for clearance are of a speculative nature. Apart from the brokerage, the purchases or sales of securities in stock exchanges are at present subject to certain levies. The Government of India levy stamp duty on the actual transfer of shares and debentures under entry 92 of the Union List in the Seventh Schedule. Some State Governments levy a stamp duty under entry 63 of the State List on instruments relating to purchase and sale transactions, in shares, debentures and other securities. Item (e) of Article 269 relates to taxes other than stamp duty which may be levied on transactions in stock exchanges and futures markets. The levy of such tax on transactions in stock exchanges under Article 269 would be in addition to the stamp duty levied by State Government on the instruments relating to the transactions." [3]

After examining the views State Governments and the various stock exchange associations, the Commission disfavoured the introduction of a separate tax on such transactions. It opined, "Since the stamp duties are already being levied by some State Governments on clearance lists and contract notes relating to transactions in stock exchanges and there is already in existence machinery for collection of such stamp duties, we feel that further scope, if any, for revenue from these transactions could be better exploited by an increase in the rate of such stamp duties, and it is not desirable to introduce a separate tax under Article 269 of such transactions." [4]

B. Tax on Transactions in Future Markets: Ruling out the possibility of tax on transactions in future markets, the Commission observed, "The forward contracts in the country are regulated by the Forward Contracts (Regulation) Act, 1952. This Act is primarily concerned with the regulation of forward contracts other than non-transferable specific delivery contracts in notified commodities other than securities. It also provides for the regulation of non-transferable specific delivery contracts if considered necessary by Government. At present futures trading under recognised or registered associations is permitted under the Act in cotton seed, linseed, castor seed, coconut oil, turmeric, pepper, jute goods, kapas and kardi seed. The rate of a tax on transactions in future markets has necessarily to be very moderate as in the case of transactions in stock exchanges. It is estimated by the Forward Markets Commission that a tax of 25 paise for every Rs. 10,000 value of transactions would yield revenue of about Rs. 16 lakh only. In view of such small yield, we consider that it would not be worthwhile to impose the tax, and that such levy could be justified more as regulatory measure rather than on revenue considerations." [5]

19.5.5 Taxes on the Sale or Purchase of Newspapers and on Advertisements Published Therein: Taxation Enquiry Commission (Chairman: John Matthai), 1953-54, had examined the question and felt that a sales tax on newspapers would entail a degree of hardship disproportionate to the revenue, particularly on newspapers with smaller circulation, to which category belonged most of the newspapers published in regional languages. They were of the opinion that such sales tax or a tax on advertisements in newspapers would not at that stage be worthwhile, having regard to the fairly widespread opposition.

In their representation to the Commission under review, many States expressed themselves in favour of a levy on sale or purchase of newspapers. Others felt that the newspaper reading habit had not yet spread sufficiently and any tax on sale of newspapers would retard improvement in this regard. As regards the tax on advertisements published in newspapers, some States were of the view that such tax would affect the revenues of small newspapers. A number of States were, however, in favour of this levy and had pointed out that the burden of the tax would fall on the advertisers and not on publishers. The advertisers being mostly companies and business concerns, the addition of the tax would not make any material difference to them. Advertisement agents also obtained large commissions and part of the incidence of the tax could be absorbed by them. The Ministry of Information and Broadcasting, Government of India, had stated that newspaper readership in the country was low and confined primarily to large cities and towns. A vast majority of the people was unable to subscribe to newspapers. Therefore, any taxation on the sale of newspapers was likely to hit their existing low sales and circulation and restrict the dissemination of news. As regards levy of a tax on advertisements appearing in newspapers, it was pointed out that this would adversely affect the starting of new newspapers, so necessary in a democracy, and might also cause difficulties to existing newspapers with tight budgets, particularly those with small and medium circulation.

Considering all the viewpoints, the Commission took the stand that as the incidence of a tax on the sale of newspapers would be passed on to the reader, it was likely to affect adversely newspaper readership. In many States text books and other reading matter were exempted from sales tax. If a tax was levied on the sale of newspapers, smaller newspapers would have to be exempted. It was estimated that even at the rate of 10 per cent on newspapers with a circulation of more than 15,000, the likely revenue from such tax would not exceed Rs. 3.5 crore. Taking into account the paltry revenue potential of the tax and the adverse effect on newspaper readership, the Commission formed the opinion that there was not much scope for raising revenue from a tax on the sale or purchase of newspapers.

Regarding tax on advertisements published in newspapers, the Commission could not obtain data relating to the total revenue accruing from advertisements to publishers of newspapers. However, it was convinced that advertisement revenue formed an important source of the income of newspapers, which in some cases might be as much as 50 to 75 per cent of the total income. While the burden of such a tax would mainly fall on the advertisers and advertising agents and not on the publishers, it was possible that the tax might adversely affect the finances of smaller newspapers. It, therefore, thought is necessary to exempt small newspapers and periodicals from such tax, if at all it was levied. Moreover, a part of the burden of the tax might indirectly fall on the Government of India and State Governments. Still, it considered this tax a reasonable source from which additional revenues assignable to States could conveniently be raised. It noted that taxes on parallel forms of publicity media like film slides, hoardings etc. were already being levied. A tax levied at suitable rates, with higher rates on some advertisement like those inserted by companies, large business houses, cinema exhibitors etc. might not be an undue burden if provision was made for exemption of small newspapers. In the absence of requisite data, it could not arrive at a reliable estimate of the likely revenue. However, it opined that there was scope for the levy of this tax and suggested that the Government of India might examine the question of its levy, rate structure, exemptions to be given, and other relevant matters.

Notes

1. *Report of the Fifth Finance Commission*, 1969, pp. 44-45.

2. The difference between a tax on railway freights and the terminal tax on goods carried by railways is that the former is leviable on the freight chargeable for carriage of goods irrespective of the place of origin or destination, while the latter is leviable at fixed amounts with reference to specified places. The levy of a terminal tax has the effect of raising prices of commodities in some places only; but the levy of a tax on freights results in a general increase in the prices of commodities transported according to the distances covered. It increases the differences in prices prevailing in different regions due to increase in the cost of transport. Besides, such a tax has a cumulative effect in many cases as it is leviable on raw materials as well as on goods manufactured therefrom.

3. *Report of the Fifth Finance Commission*, 1969, p. 75.

4. *Ibid.*, p. 76.

5. *Ibid.*, pp. 76-77.

20

Sixth Finance Commission

The Commission was constituted by the President in his Order dated June 28, 1972 to make recommendations as to the following matters.

(a) Distribution between the Union and States of the net proceeds of taxes which are to be, or may be divided between them under Chapter I of Part XII of the Constitution and the allocation between the States of the respective shares of such proceeds.

Summary Statement	
Chairman	Mr. K. Brahmananda Reddy
Members	Justice Syed Sadat Abul Masud Dr. B.S. Minhas Dr. I.S. Gulati Shri G. Ramachandran, Member-Secretary
Year and month of establishment	June 1972
Year and month of reporting	October 1973
Period of award	1974-75 to 1978-79
Main Recommendations	
• States' share in income tax fixed at (per cent): 80 • Bases of distribution of States' share in income tax inter se (per cent): Population: 90; Contribution: 10; Other factors: Nil • States' share in Union excise duties fixed at (per cent): 20 • Bases of distribution of States' share in Union excise duties inter se (per cent): Population: 75; Other factors: 25	

(b) Principles which should govern the grants-in-aid of the revenues of the States out of the Consolidated Fund of India and the sums to be paid to the States which are in need of assistance by way of grants-in-aid of their revenues under article 275 of the Constitution for purposes other than those specified in the provisos to clause (1) of that article having regard, among other considerations, to (i) the existing practice in regard to determination and distribution of Central assistance for financing State Plans, (ii) the revenue resources of those States for the five-years ending with the financial year 1978-79 on the basis of the levels of taxation likely to be reached at the end of the financial year 1973-74, (iii) the requirements on revenue account of those States to meet the expenditure on administration taking also into account such provision for emoluments of Government employees, teachers and local body employees as obtaining on a specified date as the Commission deem it proper in the light of the States' capacity and needs, interest charges in respect of their debt, transfer of funds to local bodies and aided institutions and other committed expenditure, (iv) adequate maintenance and upkeep of capital assets and maintenance of Plan schemes completed by the end of 1973-74, the norms, if any, on the basis of which specified amounts are allowed for the maintenance of different categories of capital assets being indicated by the Commission, (v) the requirements of States which are backward in standards of general administration for upgrading the administration with a view to bringing it to the levels obtaining in the more advanced States over a period of ten years and (vi) the scope for better fiscal management and economy consistent with efficiency which may be effected by the States in their administrative, maintenance, developmental and other expenditure.

(c) Changes, if any, to be made in the principles governing the distribution amongst the States of the grant to be made available to the States in lieu of tax under the repealed Railway Passenger Fares Tax Act, 1957.

(d) Changes, if any, to be made in the principles governing the distribution amongst the States under article 269 of the Constitution of the net proceeds of any financial year of estate-duty in respect of property other than agricultural land.

(e) Changes, if any, to be made in the principles governing the distribution of the net proceeds in any financial year of the additional excise duties leviable under the Additional Duties of Excise (Goods of Special Importance) Act, 1957 on each of the following commodities; namely (i) cotton fabrics, (ii) woollen fabrics, (iii) rayon or artificial silk fabrics, (iv) sugar and (v) tobacco including manufactured tobacco, in replacement of the States' sales taxes formerly levied by the State Governments. Provided that the share accruing to each State shall not be less than the revenue realised from the levy of sales tax for the financial year 1956-57 in that State.

(f) Principles governing the distribution among the States of the grant to be made available to the States on account of wealth tax on agricultural property.

20.1 Income Tax

It may be recalled that the First Finance Commission had fixed the assignment of the net proceeds of income tax to the States at 55 per cent which was enlarged progressively by the succeeding Commissions and placed at 75 per cent by the Fourth Finance Commission. The Fifth Finance Commission retained the States' share of the net proceeds of income tax at 75 per cent, despite the request of many State Governments for further enhancement. The Commission refrained from recommending upward revision of States' shares, among other things, on the ground that for the period covered by their award, the proceeds of the income tax distributable among the States would for the first time be inclusive of advance tax collections and that this change would have the effect of augmenting the divisible pool.

Almost all the States again pleaded before the Commission under study for a significant increase in the divisible pool of income tax. In justification of a further increase in the States' share of income tax, the States put forward two main arguments: (a) The continuance, almost on a permanent basis, of Union surcharge and its recent enhancement has in effect enlarged the Centre's share of the net proceeds of the income tax at the expense of the States. (b) While in terms of the provisions of Article 271 of the Constitution, the Centre is entitled to levy a surcharge exclusively for purposes of the Union, the levy of such a surcharge should be only a transitory phenomenon. The continuance of surcharge as a permanent element of the income tax rate structure was against the spirit, if not the letter, of the provisions of the Constitution.

State Governments also contended that the exclusion of income tax paid by Companies from the divisible pool since 1959-60 had deprived them of a source of revenue that was bound to be far more elastic than income tax. Almost all the State Governments had gone a step further and argued that the Commission should recommend that corporation tax should also be brought within the divisible pool through an amendment of the Constitution.

Considering the explicit provisions of the Constitution, the Commission did not recommend the inclusion of the surcharge on income tax for Union purposes and the corporation tax in the divisible pool. However, having regard to the near unanimity in the views expressed by the State Governments, it suggested that the question of bringing corporation tax within the divisible pool be brought up for examination before the National Development Council.

Turning to the States' share of the net proceeds of income tax, it agreed with the earlier Commissions that the Centre which was responsible for the levy and collection of the income tax should continue to have a significant interest in it. It, therefore, recommended that the States' share of the net proceeds of income tax be raised from 75 to 80 per cent during the period covered by its award.

As regards the manner of distribution among the States of the percentage of the net proceeds of income tax assigned to them, the views of the States were understandably divergent. While some of the relatively advanced States pressed for a higher weightage for the factor of contribution, the other States urged that the net proceeds of income tax should be distributed wholly on the basis of population. Some of the States also suggested weightage for other factors such as area, proportion of Scheduled Castes and Scheduled Tribes population.

All the earlier Finance Commissions had recognised population and contribution to be the only two relevant factors in the distribution of the proceeds of income tax among the States, though they had differed on the relative weightage to be accorded to these two factors. None of them had taken into account other considerations such as economic backwardness, area and proportion of Scheduled Castes and Scheduled Tribes population. The Commission under review also endorsed this approach of its predecessors both because there were advantages in India's complex federal system in maintaining a reasonable measure of stability in the principles of distribution of shareable taxes and also because the country was seeking to mitigate the economic disabilities of some of the States through weightage for relative economic backwardness in the distribution of Union excise duties and through grants-in-aid for upgradation of standards of administrative and social services.

Having given careful consideration to the relative weightage to be accorded to population and contribution, the Commission noted that in view of the increasing integration of India's national economy and the influence of Central policies on the location and development of industrial and tertiary sectors, it was difficult to assign the factor of contribution any higher weightage than at that time in the distribution of income tax. Also such enhanced weightage would further aggravate regional imbalances. At the same time, particularly after the exclusion of income tax paid by the companies from the divisible pool, it could not be denied that a small, but not clearly identifiable, percentage of personal incomes should be deemed to have purely local origin. In respect of income tax ascribable to such local incomes at least, the States could lay a claim based on contribution. Bearing all these considerations in mind, the Commission decided that 10 per cent of the net proceeds of income tax should be distributed on the basis of contribution.

Yet another issue which cropped up for consideration in this context was how precisely the factor of contribution should be measured. The Fifth Finance Commission considered assessment as a more reliable index than collection of the contribution of the different States. The reasons adduced by it were as follows: (a) Collections did not make due allowance for incomes originating outside the State. (b) Large amounts of deduction of tax at source on dividends, interest payments and in other cases gave undue benefit to States having metropolitan and industrial centres, in so far as such deductions relate to assesses residing in other States. On the other hand, any refunds made to such assesses would reduce still further the figures of collection of the States where they reside. (c) Figures of collection might include large over-payments or under-payments which were adjusted only on assessment.

The Commission under review felt that above considerations were still valid and hence in determining the States' share of the net proceeds of income tax it took assessment as the measure of contribution. Accordingly, it recommended that during the period covered by its award, namely 1974-75 to 1978-79, 90 per cent of the States' share of the divisible pool of income tax should be distributed among them on the basis of population according to 1971 census and the remaining 10 per cent on the basis of figures of assessment after allowing for reductions on account of appellate orders, revisions, refunds and rectification. All the previous Commissions had prescribed the respective shares of States worked out on the principles enunciated by them in terms of fixed percentages. For the sake of administrative convenience, the Commission under review continued this practice.

It further recommended that 1.79 per cent of the net proceeds of income tax might be taken to be the portion of such proceeds attributable to Union Territories. In short, it made the following recommendations in respect of the distribution of the net proceeds of income tax in each of the financial years from 1974-75 to 1978-79.

1. Out of the net proceeds of taxes on income in each financial year, a sum equal to 1.79 per cent thereof be deemed to represent the proceeds attributable to Union Territories.
2. 80 per cent of the net proceeds of taxes on income, except the portion representing the proceeds attributable to Union Territories, be assigned to the States.
3. Distribution among the States *inter se* of the share assigned to the States in respect of each financial year should be on the basis of the following percentages (Table 20.1).

20.2 Union Excise Duties

Sharing of Union excise duties with the States started on a rather modest scale with the award of the First Finance Commission which recommended sharing in respect of only three of the major commodities then subject to excise duties.

Table 20.1: Percentage Shares of the States in the Net Proceeds of Income Tax Assigned to the States as Recommended by the Sixth Finance Commission

State	Percentage
Andhra Pradesh	7.76
Assam	2.54
Bihar	9.61
Gujarat	5.55
Haryana	1.77
Himachal Pradesh	0.60
Jammu & Kashmir	0.81
Karnataka	5.33
Kerala	3.92
Madhya Pradesh	7.30
Maharashtra	11.05
Manipur	0.18
Meghalaya	0.18
Nagaland	0.09
Orissa	3.73
Punjab	2.75
Rajasthan	4.50
Tamil Nadu	7.94
Tripura	0.27
Uttar Pradesh	15.23
West Bengal	8.89
Total	**100.00**

Source: *Report of the Sixth Finance Commission*, 1973, p. 13.

Consequent upon the recommendations of successive Finance Commissions, the share of the States in Union excise duties had progressively enlarged. By the time the Fifth Finance Commission was set up, the States were already sharing the proceeds of all Union excise duties excepting only special excise duties, regulatory duties of excise and cesses on commodities. The Fifth Finance Commission saw no justification for the exclusion of special duties of excise from the divisible pool and recommended that they should also be brought within the scheme of sharing from 1972-73 onwards. The regulatory duties, however, still remained outside the shareable pool. It should, however, be noted that the yield from regulatory duties was nil in 1970-71. No credit was also taken under this head in the budget estimates for 1971-72.

However, in the new situation created by large influx of refugees from Bangladesh and hostilities with Pakistan, Government of India invoked the powers available to it under section 12 of the Finance Act of 1971 to levy regulatory duties of excise on certain products such as steel, iron and steel products, copper, zinc, aluminium and unmanufactured tobacco. The yield from these regulatory duties amounted to Rs. 22.88 crore in 1971-72 and was placed at Rs. 80.37 crore in 1972-73. The levy of regulatory duties of excise was replaced under the Finance Act of 1973 by auxiliary duties on excisable goods. The Finance Act specifically laid down that these auxiliary duties had been levied for purposes of the Union and that the proceeds therefrom were not to be distributed among the States.

The States argued before the Commission under study that auxiliary duties were indistinguishable from basic duties of excise. They also apprehended that continuance of auxiliary duties as a separate entity might encourage the Centre to raise additional revenues increasingly through enhancement of rates and coverage of auxiliary duties of excise rather than of basic duties. The Commission recognised that under certain special circumstances the Centre might have to resort to levy of excise duties in a form not shareable with the States. However, it felt that levy of excise duties on a non-shareable basis should be confined to short periods of two or three years at the most to meet the large demands on national exchequer that might unexpectedly arise. It, therefore, recommended that revenue from auxiliary duties should be brought within the divisible pool from 1976-77 onwards. This would enable the Centre to meet its pressing needs in the immediate future and at the same time allay the apprehensions of the States that auxiliary duties of excise might be resorted to on a large scale in order to deprive them of their legitimate share in the growth of revenues from Union excise duties.

Almost all the States pressed for augmentation of their share in the divisible pool of Union excise duties. Striking a balance between the plea of the States for a substantial increase in the divisible pool and the needs of the Centre, the Commission recommended that the States' share of all basic duties of excise should be retained at 20 per cent during the period covered by its award. 20 per cent of the net proceeds of auxiliary duties of excise were also made shareable from 1976-77 onwards. Revenues from cesses on excisable commodities, levied under special enactments and reserved for special purposes, continued to remain excluded from the divisible pool.

While there was near unanimity among the States in demanding an increase in the share of Union excise duties, there were naturally wide divergences in their approach to the principles of determination of the relative share of the States in the divisible pool. Each State was inclined to put forward a formula that would favour it most. Some of the States contended before the Commission that per capita income by itself would not be a wholly dependable index of the relative economic position of the States. They urged that the Commission should take into account some other indicators relating to certain specific areas of economic or social significance. The more important indicators of backwardness suggested by the States were as follows.

1. Percentage of rural population to total population of each State.
2. Percentage of scheduled castes population.
3. Percentage of literacy.
4. Enrolment in primary classes I to V as percentage of population in age group 6-11.
5. Number of workers registered in factories per lakh of population.
6. Number of registered factories in terms of area.
7. Value added per capita by manufacture.
8. Number of hospitals in terms of area or per lakh of population.
9. Per capita gross value of agricultural production.
10. Net irrigated area per cultivator.
11. Percentage of villages with public water supply.
12. Landless agricultural labour in each State.
13. Installed capacity for generation of electricity.
14. Number of villages electrified.
15. Percentage of villages electrified.
16. Per capital consumption of energy.
17. Motor vehicles per lakh of population.
18. Length of railways and roads in terms of area.
19. Area of each State.
20. Per capita availability of calories or proteins in different States.
21. Percentage of population below 'poverty line' in each State.
22. Extent of unemployment in each State.

According to the Commission, "This long list, of course, is not exhaustive. Each State was understandably anxious to put forward such indicators as would reflect its own interests more fully." [1] After considering the conflicting claims of the States, the Commission recommended that while the weightage for backwardness should be raised from 20 per cent to 25 per cent, the *inter se* distribution of this portion of Union excise duties should be in relation to the *distance* of a State's per capita income from that of the State with the highest per capita income multiplied by the population of the State concerned according to 1971 census. The balance of 75 per cent of the States' share of the divisible pool of Union excise duties should be distributed on the basis of population of the States according to 1971 census. It worked out the relative shares of the States in terms of percentages according to the principles enunciated above.

In short, its recommendations pertaining to Union excise duties were as follows.

1. During each of the years 1974-75 and 1975-76, a sum equivalent to 20 per cent of the net proceeds of Union duties of excise on all articles levied and collected in that year, excluding auxiliary duties of excise and cesses levied under special Acts and earmarked for special purposes, should be paid out of the Consolidated Fund of India to the States.
2. During the years 1976-77, 1977-78 and 1978-79, a sum equivalent to 20 per cent of the net proceeds of Union duties of excise on all articles levied and collected in the respective year, including auxiliary duties of excise, but excluding cesses levied under special Acts and earmarked for special purposes, should be paid out of the Consolidated Fund of India to the States.
3. Distribution among the States of the sum payable to the States in respect of each financial year should be made on the basis of the percentages prescribed (Table 20.2).

20.3 Additional Duties of Excise

Commenting on the working of the scheme of additional excise duties in lieu of sales tax, the Commission remarked, "The scheme of levy of additional excise duties in lieu of sales tax has now been in force for over 15 years. All available evidence indicates that the continuance of the scheme is welcomed by trade and industry who have in fact frequently pleaded for its extension to other commodities. But till quite recently, most of the State Governments would seem to have had reservations about the utility of the existing system. Dissatisfaction of the State Governments with the inadequate exploitation of the revenue potential of the additional excise duties on these commodities by the Union Government led the Government of India to request the last Finance Commission to investigate and report on the desirability or otherwise of continuing the scheme of levy of additional excise duties in replacement of sales tax. Later in the wake of the recommendations of the Fifth Finance Commission the whole question was considered by a representative group of Central and State Government officials. In the light of the proposals made by the group, the National Development Council at its meeting held on 28-12-1970 agreed to the continuance of the present arrangements subject to certain conditions. The main condition stipulated by the National Development Council for the continuance of the scheme was that the incidence of the additional excise duties should be stepped up to 10.8 per cent of the value of the clearances within a period of two or three years. These recommendations were accepted by the Government of India and have since been implemented through successive Finance Acts." [2]

Table 20.2: Distribution of States' Share of Excise Duties among the States Recommended by the Sixth Finance Commission

State	Percentage
Andhra Pradesh	8.16
Assam	2.71
Bihar	11.47
Gujarat	4.57
Haryana	1.53
Himachal Pradesh	0.63
Jammu & Kashmir	0.90
Karnataka	5.45
Kerala	3.86
Madhya Pradesh	8.15
Maharashtra	8.58
Manipur	0.21
Meghalaya	0.19
Nagaland	0.11
Orissa	4.06
Punjab	1.87
Rajasthan	5.00
Tamil Nadu	7.43
Tripura	0.30
Uttar Pradesh	17.03
West Bengal	7.79
Total	**100.00**

Source: *Report of the Sixth Finance Commission*, 1973, p. 17.

The first issue before the Commission to consider was whether it was possible or necessary to re-determine the yield in 1956-57 from sales tax on the commodities subject to additional excise duties for purposes of guaranteeing to the States concerned the amounts so determined. The Third, Fourth and Fifth

Finance Commissions accepted the estimates worked out by the Second Finance Commission and did not consider it feasible in view of the lapse of time to reassess the likely yield in 1956-57 of sales tax on the commodities on which additional excise duties had been imposed. In view of the further lapse of time, the Commission found it impossible to frame any fresh estimates of the likely yield of sales tax in 1956-57 on these commodities and on that basis re-determine the guaranteed amounts. It, therefore, adopted the estimates worked out by the Second Finance Commission subject to the subsequent adjustments made by the Third Finance Commission in view of the bifurcation of Bombay State into Maharashtra and Gujarat and by the Fifth Finance Commission in view of the formation of the new States of Punjab and Haryana. The Commission under study had to make a similar apportionment of the sum guaranteed to Assam between Assam and Meghalaya.

The next question that arose for consideration was whether the guaranteed amounts should first be set apart from the net proceeds and the balance then distributed among the States on suitable principles or whether the entire net proceeds should be distributed on whatever principles were considered appropriate subject to the overriding proviso that no State should get in any year less than the guaranteed amount as its share. The earlier Commissions had preferred the first alternative. They presumably felt that unless the guaranteed amounts were first set apart and the balance alone distributed among the States, there was the risk of the share of some of the States falling short of the guaranteed among. However, this Commission was convinced that there was absolutely no risk of the share of any State not coming up to the guaranteed amount. It, therefore, felt that there was no need to set apart the guaranteed amounts and distribute the balance alone among States. The initial reservation of guaranteed amounts conferred an unintended advantage on certain States and introduced an avoidable element of distortion in the scheme of distribution of additional excise duties.

Regarding the basis of distribution of additional excise duties among the States, the view had gained general acceptance among the Finance Commissions that every State should be enabled to get the equivalent of what it would have secured if it had not surrendered its power to levy sales tax on these commodities. The Finance Commissions had recognised the principle of compensation to be the only valid principle in the distribution of the additional excise duties. Other considerations such as preferential treatment for backward States, valid in relation to allocation of other Central taxes, were totally irrelevant to any scheme of distribution of additional excise duties. Their levy by the Centre was in pursuance of what was equivalent to a tax rental agreement. Similarly, State-wise figures of consumption of the commodities on which additional excise duties were levied would afford by far the best indication of the potential loss of revenue sustained by their surrender of authority to levy sales tax on them. Having regard to all other considerations, the Commission felt that by far the most equitable basis for distribution of additional excise duties would be to allocate the proceeds of additional excise duties on the basis of population, State Domestic Product at State current prices and production in the ratio of 70:20:10. It worked out the relative percentage share of each State on this basis. Accordingly, it recommended that the net proceeds of the additional excise duties during each financial year be distributed on the following basis.

1. A sum equal to 1.41 per cent of such net proceeds be retained by the Union as attributable to Union Territories.
2. The balance of 98.59 per cent of such net proceeds be distributed among the States in accordance with their respective percentage shares of such balance as given in Table 20.3.

20.4 Grant in Lieu of Tax on Railway Passenger Fares

In this connection the Commission observed, "The existing principles of distribution, which are substantially the same as those formulated by the Second Finance Commission, have stood the test of time. In the continuing absence of statistics on passenger earnings in each State on account of actual travel within its limits, the allocation of passenger earnings from non-suburban services from each gauge for each railway zone separately among the States according to route length lying within each State would be the most equitable basis for distribution of the grant. We have accordingly worked out the percentage shares of different States on the basis of statistics of gauge-wise route length of railways in each State and the actual passenger earnings from non-suburban traffic for each zonal railway for the four years ending 1971-72." [3] The percentages worked out by the Commission are set forth in Table 20.4.

20.5 Estate Duty

Estate duty on property other than agricultural land was one of the taxes visualised under Article 269 of the Constitution to be levied and collected by Government of India; but the net proceeds (except in so far as the proceeds represent proceeds attributable to Union Territories) had to be assigned to the States and distributed amongst them in accordance with the principles formulated by Parliament by law. The then existing scheme of distribution of this tax was as follows.

Table 20.3: Distribution of Additional Excise Duties among the States Recommended by the Sixth Finance Commission

State	Percentage of distribution
AndhraPradesh	8.39
Assam	2.47
Bihar	9.36
Gujarat	5.91
Haryana	1.94
Himachal Pradesh	0.59
Jammu & Kashmir	0.73
Karnataka	5.62
Kerala	3.58
Madhya Pradesh	6.98
Maharashtra	11.65
Manipur	0.17
Meghalaya	0.17
Nagaland	0.08
Orissa	3.59
Punjab	2.68
Rajasthan	4.17
Tamil Nadu	7.27
Tripura	0.25
Uttar Pradesh	16.10
West Bengal	8.30
Total	**100.00**

Source: *Report of the Sixth Finance Commission*, 1973, p. 21.

1. Out of the net proceeds of the estate duty in each financial year, a sum equal of three per cent thereof was retained by the Union as being the proceeds attributable to Union Territories.
2. The balance of net proceeds was distributed among the States in accordance with the following principles: (a) such balance be first apportioned between immovable property and other property in the ratio of the gross value of all such properties brought into assessment in that year, (b) The sum thus apportioned to immovable property be distributed among the States in proportion to the gross value of the immovable property located in each State and brought into assessment in that year and (c) the sum apportioned to

property other than immovable property be distributed among the States in proportion to the population of each State.

Table 20.4: Percentage Share of Each State in Grant in Lieu of Tax on Railway Passenger Fares

State	Percentage share
Andhra Pradesh	8.01
Assam	2.70
Bihar	10.58
Gujarat	7.47
Haryana	2.57
Himachal Pradesh	0.17
Jammu & Kashmir	0.02
Karnataka	3.47
Kerala	1.61
Madhya Pradesh	9.89
Maharashtra	8.87
Manipur	-
Meghalaya	-
Nagaland	0.01
Orissa	2.24
Punjab	5.06
Rajasthan	6.59
Tamil Nadu	5.14
Tripura	0.02
Uttar Pradesh	19.85
West Bengal	5.73
Total	**100.00**

Source: *Report of the Sixth Finance Commission*, 1973, p. 23.

The Commission under study elicited the views of the State Governments on the principles that might be laid down for the distribution of the net proceeds of estate duty. Most of them were in favour of continuance of the then existing principles. Suggestions made by some other States sought a change in the scheme of distribution. These were the following.

1. Distribution of 50 per cent on the basis of population and the remaining 50 per cent on the basis of accepted indicators of backwardness.

2. Distribution of duty notionally attributable to immovable property on the basis of location, duty attributable to other property being distributed on the basis of collections in each of the States.
3. Some weightage for scheduled castes and scheduled tribes in the population of the State.
4. Distribution of 75 per cent on the basis of population and the remaining 25 per cent in the inverse ratio of per capita income, the latter being distributed only among those States which are below the national average.
5. Distribution of the entire proceeds on the basis of collection.

After considering the various suggestions of the States, the Commission was convinced that the principles of distribution enunciated by the Second Finance Commission and endorsed by all the subsequent Commissions did not call for any change. It, therefore, held that no change was necessary in the then existing principles governing the distribution of the net proceeds of the duty among the States. Accordingly, it recommended as follows.

1. Out of the net proceeds of the estate duty in each financial year, a sum equal to 2.5 per cent thereof be retained by the Union as being the proceeds attributable to Union Territories.
2. The balance of net proceeds be distributed among the States in accordance with the following principles: (a) such balance be first apportioned between immovable property and other property in the ratio of the gross value of all such properties brought into assessment in that year, (b) the sum thus apportioned to immovable property be distributed among the States in proportion to the gross value of the immovable property located in each State and brought into assessment in that year and (c) the sum apportioned to property other than immovable property be distributed among the States in proportion to the population of each State (Table 20.5).

20.6 Grant on Account of Wealth Tax on Agricultural Property

Though the Wealth Tax Act had been enacted as early as 1957, agricultural property was exempt from the levy of wealth tax up to and inclusive of the assessment year 1969-70. The Finance Act of 1969 amended the Wealth Tax Act so as to extend the levy of wealth tax to agricultural property (except such property situated in Jammu & Kashmir), subject to certain exemptions, with effect from the assessment year 1970-71. The decision to subject agricultural property to wealth tax was taken by Government with a view to bring about equality of treatment as between persons having investments in non-agricultural property and those having investments in agricultural property.

Table 20.5: Percentage Shares of States in Estate Duty Recommended by the Sixth Finance Commission

State	Percentage share
Andhra Pradesh	8.04
Assam	2.70
Bihar	10.41
Gujarat	4.93
Haryana	1.86
Himachal Pradesh	0.64
Jammu & Kashmir	0.85
Karnataka	5.41
Kerala	3.94
Madhya Pradesh	7.70
Maharashtra	9.31
Manipur	0.20
Meghalaya	0.19
Nagaland	0.10
Orissa	4.05
Punjab	2.50
Rajasthan	4.76
Tamil Nadu	7.61
Tripura	0.29
Uttar Pradesh	16.32
West Bengal	8.19
Total	**100.00**

Source: *Report of the Sixth Finance Commission*, 1973, p. 26.

Wealth tax was not one of those taxes or duties which, under the provisions of the Constitution, were to be shared with the States either on an obligatory or permissive basis. It was also not a tax levied and collected by the Centre and assigned in their entirely to the States, as for example, was the case with estate duty on property other than agricultural land. However, when in 1969, agricultural land held by individuals and Hindu undivided families was made liable to wealth tax, subject to certain limits, the Central Government decided *suo moto* that the net proceeds of wealth tax on agricultural land would be passed on to the States as grants-in-aid.

The Commission obtained the views of the State Governments on the principles to be evolved for the distribution amongst them of the grant-in-aid to be made available to them on account of wealth tax on agricultural property. Divergent views of the States on this matter were the following.

1. Distribution on the basis of location of property.
2. Distribution on the basis of population.
3. Distribution on the basis of collection.
4. Distribution on the same basis as for income tax.
5. Distribution partly on the basis of population and partly on the basis of backwardness.
6. Distribution in proportion of the rural population living below the subsistence level to the total of such population of all States taken together.
7. Distribution in such a manner as to make available more funds to agriculturally less developed States in comparison to those which are highly developed.

Wealth tax on agricultural property was comparable in its incidence to estate duty in so far as the latter relates to immovable property. The location of property in each case was clearly identifiable and provided therefore a reliable basis for distribution of the proceeds of the tax among the States. The Commission, therefore, recommended that the grant on account of wealth tax on agricultural property should be distributed among the States in proportion to the value of agricultural property situated in the State and brought into assessment. It was presumed that the grant payable to the States would be equivalent to the net collections of wealth tax on agricultural property less collections attributable to Union Territories.

20.7 Financing of Relief Expenditure

In this connection the Commission noted, "In a predominantly agrarian economy like ours, the failure of crops over large tracts resulting from deficiency of failure of rainfall necessitates State intervention on a large scale for provision of alternative opportunities for employment, supply of foodgrains and other essentials at fair prices and initiation of protective and preventive works against recurrence of similar calamities in the future. The State has to step in when other natural calamities such as floods, cyclones and earthquakes cause extensive damage to crops and property. Even prior to Independence, it was one of the main tasks of the administrative machinery to tackle emergencies of this nature and consequently, rules and instructions for the guidance of field staff in administering programmes of relief came to be codified. Famine Codes are available in many of the States and some of them have been updated. These codes, despite many deficiencies, assured a reasonable measure of uniformity among the States in their approach to problems of relief. However, the practice, envisaged in these Codes, of keeping ready a list of works to be taken up for execution as relief programmes appears to have fallen into disuse in many States. The result is that in an emergency, relief works are in many cases taken up on an ad hoc basis with inadequate attention to their long term utility." [4]

After examining various alternatives for providing finance for relief expenditure to the States, the Commission determined the provisions needed by the States for gratuitous and other relief on the basis of average of expenditure under "64-Famine Relief" over the period from 1956-57 to 1971-72 inclusive. The provisions recommended by it for different States are given in Table 20.6.

Table 20.6: Amounts of Relief Expenditure for Different States Recommended by the Sixth Finance Commission

State	Annual provisions (Rs. crore)
Andhra Pradesh	4.31
Assam	1.25
Bihar	4.61
Gujarat	4.55
Haryana	1.24
Himachal Pradesh	0.03
Jammu & Kashmir	0.35
Karnataka	1.91
Kerala	0.30
Madhya Pradesh	3.41
Maharashtra	4.17
Manipur	0.04
Meghalaya	0.04
Nagaland	0.02
Orissa	3.58
Punjab	0.33
Rajasthan	10.19
Tamil Nadu	1.52
Tripura	0.07
Uttar Pradesh	2.18
West Bengal	6.61
Total	**50.71**

Source: *Report of the Sixth Finance Commission*, 1973, p. 66.

20.8 Grants-in-aid of Revenues

Making a departure from the approach of the earlier Finance Commissions, this Commission initiated process of enabling the States that were backward in standards of general administration to come up to a certain national minimum. For this purpose, it identified certain administrative and social services as to be of crucial importance and proposed that the State whose expenditure in per capita terms was below the all-States average should be enabled to come up to such an average by the last year of its award. Among these services, it considered primary education, medical and public health and welfare of Scheduled Castes, Scheduled Tribes and other backward classes to be of critical importance for the well being of the people and particularly the weaker sections. It, therefore, thought it essential to devise suitable special safeguards against diversion of the funds so provided for improvement of these services to other purposes.

It may be recalled that the special grants-in-aid provided by the First Finance Commission for promoting primary education in backward States and the grants provided by the Third Finance Commission for improvement of communications in certain States were not utilised for the purposes for which they were intended. In the light of the experience, it emphasised the need for effective and purposeful monitoring of the special grants earmarked for administrative upgradation. To this end, it made an important suggestion. The concerned administrative Ministry at the Centre and the Planning Commission should, as part of their scrutiny of the Annual Plans of the States, take special care to verify whether the funds provided by it for primary education, medical and public health and welfare of Scheduled Castes, Scheduled Tribes and other backward classes had been utilised on these services. The Commission suggested that only such expenditure on these services, as was in excess of the provisions indicated by it under these heads, should alone be treated as Plan expenditure qualifying for Central assistance.

Apart from the statutory grants made under the substantive provision of Article 275(1) of the Constitution, States were also receiving from the Centre non-Plan grants for other purposes, the more important being the following.

1. Relief and rehabilitation of displaced persons.
2. Relief and other measures necessitated by hostilities.
3. Construction and maintenance of border roads.
4. Labour and employment.
5. Development of border areas.
6. Assistance to Jammu and Kashmir for transport of rice and wheat.
7. Incentive bonus for higher procurement of foodgrains.
8. Modernisation of police force.
9. Education.

10. Social welfare.
11. Central Road Fund.

It gave careful consideration to the question of the treatment to be accorded to these grants and the corresponding or relatable expenditure met from revenue in the forecasts furnished by the State Governments. In respect of Central assistance for schemes which were not uniformly applicable to all States, such as payments of bonus for procurement of foodgrains, development of border areas and construction of roads from Central Road Fund, it omitted both revenue receipts on account of Government of India's grants to the State Governments and the related expenditure in the State forecasts.

20.9 Rescheduling of Central Loans

The Commission made an assessment of the non-Plan capital gap of the States on uniform and comparable basis for the five years ending with 1978-79. In the light of this assessment, it made a general review of the States' debt position with particular reference to the Central loans advanced to them and likely to be outstanding as at the end of 1973-74 and recommended changes in the existing terms of repayment having regard to all relevant factors including the overall non-Plan gaps of the States, their relative position, the purposes for which the loans had been utilised and the requirements of the Centre. Its proposals for consolidation of outstanding Central loans and revision of their terms of repayment were estimated to ensure relief in the amount falling due for repayment by the States to the Centre over the period 1974-75 to 1978-79. Amounts of estimated relief in repayment of Central Loans are given in Table 20.7.

Table 20.7: Estimated Relief in Repayment of Loans to Central Government Recommended by the Sixth Finance Commission

State	Estimated Relief in Repayment of Loans to Central Government (Rs. crore)
AndhraPradesh	191.20
Assam	162.49
Bihar	133.35
Gujarat	36.25
Haryana	33.14
Himachal Pradesh	34.57
Jammu & Kashmir	133.43

Contd...

Karnataka	127.04
Kerala	109.77
Madhya Pradesh	87.16
Maharashtra	66.58
Manipur	15.23
Meghalaya	7.64
Nagaland	5.84
Orissa	157.32
Punjab	15.18
Rajasthan	258.14
Tamil Nadu	87.05
Tripura	14.35
Uttar Pradesh	150.77
West Bengal	143.12
Total	**1,969.62**

Source: *Report of the Sixth Finance Commission*, 1973, p. 110.

Notes

1. *Report of the Sixth Finance Commission*, 1973, p. 16.
2. *Ibid.,* p. 18.
3. Ibid., p. 23.
4. Ibid., p.63.

21

Seventh Finance Commission

The Commission was constituted by an Order dated June 23, 1977 of the Vice-President acting as President. It was asked to make recommendations as to the following matters.

Summary Statement	
Chairman	Justice J.M. Shelat
Members	Dr. Raj Krishna Dr. C.H. Hanumantha Rao Shri H.N. Ray Shri V.B. Eswaran, Member-Secretary
Year and month of establishment	June 1977
Year and month of reporting	October 1978
Period of award	1979-80 to 1983-84
Main Recommendations	
• States' share in income tax fixed at (per cent): 85 • Bases of distribution of States' share in income tax inter se (per cent): Population: 90; Contribution: 10; Other factors: Nil • States' share in Union excise duties fixed at (per cent): 40 • Bases of distribution of States' share in Union excise duties inter se (per cent): Population: 25; Other factors: 75	

1. Distribution between the Union and the States of the net proceeds of taxes which are to be, or may be, divided between them and the allocation between the States of the respective shares of such proceeds.
2. Principles which should govern the grants-in-aid of the revenues of the States out of the Consolidated Fund of India and the sums to be paid to the States which are in need of assistance by way of grants-in-aid of their revenues under article 275 of the Constitution for purposes other than those specified in the provisos of clause (1) of that article.

In making its recommendations, the Commission was asked to have regard to the following considerations.

1. Resources of the Central Government and the demands thereon on account of

the expenditure on civil administration, defence and border security, debt servicing and other committed expenditure or liabilities.

2. Existing practice in regard to determination and distribution of Central assistance for financing State Plans.
3. Revenue resources of those States for the five years ending with the financial year 1983-84 on the basis of the levels of taxation likely to be reached at the end of the financial year 1978-79 and the targets set for additional resource mobilisation for the Plan.
4. Requirements on revenue account of those States to meet the expenditure on administration and other non-Plan commitments or liabilities, keeping however in view national policies and priorities. In assessing such requirements, the Commission shall take into account (a) such provision for emoluments of Government employees, teachers and local body employees as obtaining on a specified date as the Commission deem it proper and with reference to appropriate objective criteria rather than in terms of actual increases that may have been given effect to and (b) commitments in regard to interest charges on their debt, transfer of funds to local bodies and aided institutions.
5. Adequate maintenance and upkeep of capital assets and maintenance of Plan schemes completed by the end of 1978-79, the norms, if any, on the basis of which specified amounts are allowed for the maintenance of different categories of capital assets and the manner in which such maintenance expenditure could be monitored being indicated by the Commission.
6. Requirements of States which are backward in general administration for upgradation of standards in non-developmental sectors and services with a view to bringing them to the levels obtaining in the more advanced States over the period covered by the Report of the Commission; the manner in which such expenditure could be monitored, being also indicated by the Commission.
7. Scope for better fiscal management and economy in expenditure consistent with efficiency.
8. Need for ensuring reasonable returns on investments in irrigation and power projects, transport undertakings, industrial and commercial enterprises and the like.

The Commission was further required to suggest changes, if any, to be made in the principles governing the distribution among the States of the following.

1. Net proceeds in any financial year of estate duty in respect of property other than agricultural land.
2. Net proceeds in any financial year of the additional excise duties leviable

under the Additional Duties of Excise (Goods of Special Importance) Act, 1957, in replacement of the sales tax levied formerly by the State Governments on each of the following commodities, namely (i) cotton fabrics, (ii) woollen fabrics, (iii) rayon or artificial silk fabrics, (iv) sugar and (v) tobacco including manufactured tobacco. Provided that the share accruing to each State shall not be less than the revenue realised from the levy of sales tax for the financial year 1956-57 in that State.

3. Grant to be made available to the States in lieu of the tax under the repealed Railway Passenger Fares Tax Act, 1957.
4. Grant to be made available to the States on account of wealth-tax on agricultural property.

In making its recommendations on the various matters aforesaid, the Commission was asked to adopt population figures of 1971 in all cases where population was regarded as a factor for determination of devolution of taxes and duties and grants-in-aid.

21.1 Financing of Relief Expenditure

In the light of review of the existing policy and arrangements in regard to the financing of relief expenditure and after considering the expenditure incurred by the State Governments in providing gratuitous relief and on repair and restoration works of public properties after natural disasters, the Commission recommended the following annual provisions on account of natural calamities for different States (Table 21.1).

The Commission was of the view that the then existing policy and arrangements of Central assistance to States for relief expenditure needed modifications. It observed, "For drought relief expenditure in excess of the margin we have provided, the State Government should make a contribution from its Plan for providing relief employment. The extent to which the State Government should contribute from its Plan in this manner should be assessed by a Central Team after consultation with the State Government and approved by the Central Government. This contribution should not exceed about 5 per cent of the Annual Plan outlay. This Plan contribution of the State Government should be treated as an addition to the Plan outlay in that year and covered by advance Plan assistance as in the present scheme. The adjustment of the advance Plan assistance against a ceiling of the Central assistance for the Plan of the State should be effected within five years following the end of the drought. If the expenditure requirement, as assessed by the Central Teams and the High Level Committee cannot be adequately met in a particular case after the State Plan contribution is taken into account, the extra expenditure should be taken an indication of the special severity of the calamity which would justify the Central Government assisting the State to the full extent of the extra expenditure, half as grant and half as loan. In regard to the expenditure on relief and repairs and restoration of public works following floods, cyclones and other calamities of this nature, Central assistance should be made available as non-Plan grant, not adjustable against the Plan of the State or against Central assistance for the State Plan, to the extent of 75 per cent of the total expenditure in excess of the margins. Where a calamity is of rare severity, it may be necessary for the Central Government to extend assistance to the States concerned even the scheme/s we have suggested." [1]

Table 21.1: Amounts of Relief Expenditure for Different States Recommended by the seventh Finance Commission

State	**(Rs. lakh)**
Andhra Pradesh	858
Assam	346
Bihar	1,308
Gujarat	956
Haryana	147
Himachal Pradesh	51
Jammu & Kashmir	130
Karnataka	200
Kerala	159
Madhya Pradesh	183
Maharashtra	457
Manipur	8
Meghalaya	7
Nagaland	14
Orissa	871
Punjab	268
Rajasthan	774
Sikkim	1
Tamil Nadu	859
Tripura	18
Uttar Pradesh	1,080
West Bengal	1,360
Total	**10,055**

Source: *Report of the Seventh Finance Commission*, 1978, pp. 47-48.

21.2 Estate Duty

The duty was levied under the Estate Duty Act, 1953. [2] The Second Finance Commission examined for the first time the principles which should govern the distribution of the net proceeds of the duty among the States. That Commission held that the most appropriate principle of distribution would be the location of the property assessed to duty. That Commission also observed that it would not be possible to apply the principle of location in the case of duty attributable to movable property, in respect of which that Commission considered some general principle such as population. The latter Finance Commissions generally endorsed the principles recommended by the Second Finance Commission. Each of the Commissions had also specified the percentage of the net proceeds of the estate duty in a financial year to be retained by the Central Government as being the proceeds attributable to the Union Territories.

The principles laid down by the Sixth Finance Commission were the following.

(i) Out of the net proceeds of the estate duty during each financial year, a sum equal to 2.5 per cent thereof be retained by the Union as being the proceeds attributable to Union Territories.

(ii) The balance of net proceeds be distributed among the States in accordance with the following principles: (a) Such balance be first apportioned between immovable property and other property in the ratio of the gross value of all such properties brought into assessment in that year, (b) The sum thus apportioned to immovable property be distributed among the States in proportion to the gross value of the immovable property located in each State and brought into assessment in that year and (c) The sum apportioned to property other than immovable property be distributed among the States in proportion to the population of each State.

In their memoranda to the Commission under study, most of the States suggested continuance of the above-mentioned principles of distribution. The Commission was in agreement with the views of the earlier Commissions that in the distribution of the proceeds of estate duty, which was one of the taxes and duties leviable under Article 269, each State should get, as near as may be, a share equivalent to what it would have obtained if it had the power to levy and collect the duty. It would also be incorrect, the Commission held, to determine the shares of the States in proportion to the collections of the duty in each State, since collections may take place in a State on account of duty assessed on properties situated in other States. The Commission accordingly recommended that the net proceeds of estate duty in respect of property other than agricultural land brought to assessment in each of the years from 1979-80 to1983-84, should be distributed among the States in proportion to the gross value of the immovable property as also property other than immovable property taken together located in each State, excepting in regard to property located abroad.

The Commission did not deem it necessary to determine the portion of the net proceeds of estate duty attributable to the Union territories, for the period of its award. This portion for each year, it recommended, should be determined in the same manner and on the same principles as for the determination of the shares of each State, taking the Union Territories as one unit for the purpose.

21.3 Additional Duties of Excise

It may be recalled that the additional duties of excise were levied by the Central Government in pursuance of a unanimous agreement recorded by the National Development Council (NDC) in December 1956. That agreement was that sales taxes levied in the States on mill-made textiles, tobacco including manufactured tobacco and sugar should be replaced by a surcharge on the Central excise duties on these articles and that the income derived therefrom should be distributed among the States on the basis of consumption. It also provided that the distribution among the States should assure to them the income derived by them at that time from their respective sales taxes. NDC had also agreed that the sharing and distribution among the States should be referred to the Finance Commission. The aforesaid arrangement was in the nature of tax rental as noted by the earlier Commissions. Though the States had the constitutional right to levy sales tax on any of these articles, but by virtue of Sections 14 and 15 of the Central Sales Tax Act, which had declared these articles to be goods of special importance in inter-State trade and commerce, the rate of the tax could not exceed 4 per cent.

The predecessors of the Commission under review, which recommended the principles for distribution of the net proceeds of additional excise duties among the States, found that the most appropriate basis of distribution would be that of consumption of the articles in each State, since such a basis ensured to the States shares more or less equivalent to what they would have obtained if they had continued to levy and collect sales taxes. The Commissions had, however, faced the difficulty arising from lack of reliable statistics of consumption of these articles in each State. Each of them had therefore devised formulae which it considered would most closely approximate to the basic principle.

The amounts which each State had derived from sales taxes on the articles in the year 1956-57 had generally been referred to by the earlier Commissions as the guaranteed amount. Such guaranteed amount was first estimated by the Second Commission. The later Commissions accepted the Second Commission's estimations. Except the Sixth Commission the other Commissions had first set apart and distributed the guaranteed amount from the net proceeds of each year covered by their reports. The balance of the net proceeds was then recommended to be shared among the States in accordance with the formulae which, as mentioned above, each Commission evolved.

This Commission made the following recommendations in this regard.

1. "There is no need to set apart any guaranteed amounts to the States out of the net proceeds of additional duties of excise as in our view there is no risk of the share of any States falling short of the revenue realised in the financial year 1956-57 in a State from the levy of the Sales tax on the commodities subject to additional duties of excise in lieu of sales tax.
2. Sikkim should have a share in the net proceeds of these duties except the duties on textiles on which the State levies sales tax;
3. A sum equal to 3.271 per cent of the net proceeds of the additional duties of excise on sugar in each of the years from 1979-80 to 1983-84 should be retained by the Central Government as attributable to the Union territories and the balance of 96.729 per cent of the net proceeds should be distributed among the States in the percentages shown in the following table (Table 21.2).
4. A sum equal to 2.192 per cent of the net proceeds of additional duties of excise on textiles and on tobacco in each of the year from 1979-80 to 1983-84 be retained by the Central Government as attributable to the Union territories.
5. The balance of 97.808 per cent of such net proceeds of the additional duties of excise on textiles and tobacco be distributed among the States in the percentages shown in the following table (Table 21.3)." [3]

21.4 Grant in Lieu of Tax on Railway Passenger Fares

The Commission recommended that the grant to be made available to the States in each of the five years commencing from 1979-80, in lieu of tax under the repealed Railway Passenger Fares Tax Act 1957 be distributed among the States as given in Table 21.4.

21.5 Grant on Account of Wealth Tax on Agricultural Property [4]

The Commission noted the complexities involved in calculating the element attributable to agricultural property out of the total wealth tax collections, following the amendment in the law with effect from 1975-76 by which the exemption for agricultural property became linked with the exemption for other assets. Based on the information provided by the Ministry of Finance, Government of India, the Commission concluded that the revenue on account of wealth tax on agricultural property would be very small and shares therein would make no material difference to the States. [5]

It, therefore, recommended that the share of each State in the grant in each of the years from 1979-80 to 1983-84 would be an amount equivalent to the net collection in that State in each year. Considering the very small amounts involved, and also the fact that it was not possible to estimate what the shares of the States would be in each year in the future, it decided to ignore the shares out of this grant from its computations of the revenue receipts of the States in the period covered by its report.

Table 21.2: Distribution of Additional Duties of Excise on Sugar among the States Recommended by the Seventh Finance Commission

State	Percentage
Andhra Pradesh	5.245
Assam	2.408
Bihar	5.933
Gujarat	8.742
Haryana	2.656
Himachal Pradesh	0.860
Jammu & Kashmir	0.831
Karnataka	4.901
Kerala	3.783
Madhya Pradesh	6.019
Maharashtra	17.082
Manipur	0.143
Meghalaya	0.029
Nagaland	0.115
Orissa	2.178
Punjab	6.220
Rajasthan	4.729
Sikkim	0.057
Tamil Nadu	6.449
Tripura	0.172
Uttar Pradesh	13.184
West Bengal	8.254

Source: *Report of the Seventh Finance Commission*, 1978, p. 62.

Table 21.3: Distribution of Additional Duties of Excise on Textiles and Tobacco among the States Recommended by the Seventh Finance Commission

State	Textiles	Tobacco
Andhra Pradesh	8.020	8.018
Assam	2.298	2.297
Bihar	7.221	7.219
Gujarat	6.015	6.013
Haryana	2.790	2.789
Himachal Pradesh	0.734	0.734
Jammu & Kashmir	0.744	0.744
Karnataka	6.083	6.081
Kerala	4.020	4.019
Madhya Pradesh	6.422	6.419
Maharashtra	13.510	13.506
Manipur	0.185	0.185
Meghalaya	0.171	0.171
Nagaland	0.084	0.084
Orissa	3.457	3.456
Punjab	4.270	4.268
Rajasthan	4.366	4.365
Sikkim	-	0.034
Tamil Nadu	7.710	7.707
Tripura	0.257	0.256
Uttar Pradesh	12.549	12.544
West Bengal	9.094	9.091

Source: *Report of the Seventh Finance Commission*, 1978, p. 63.

21.6 Sharing of Income Tax

In respect of distribution of the net proceeds of income tax in each of the years 1979-80 to 1983-84, the Commission recommended as follows.

1. Out of the net proceeds in each financial year, a sum equal to 2.19 per cent thereof be deemed to represent the proceeds attributable to Union territories.
2. 85 per cent of the net proceeds, except the portion representing the proceeds attributable to Union territories, be assigned to the States.
3. Distribution among the States inter se of the share assigned to the States in respect of each financial year should be on the basis of the following

percentages (Table 21.5).

Table 21.4: Percentage Share of Each State in Grant in Lieu of Tax on Railway Passenger Fares

State	Percentage
Andhra Pradesh	6.99
Assam	2.46
Bihar	9.50
Gujarat	5.28
Haryana	1.97
Himachal Pradesh	0.13
Jammu & Kashmir	0.74
Karnataka	3.21
Kerala	2.61
Madhya Pradesh	5.84
Maharashtra	15.87
Manipur	-
Meghalaya	-
Nagaland	0.26
Orissa	1.73
Punjab	3.81
Rajasthan	5.48
Sikkim	-
Tamil Nadu	6.85
Tripura	0.04
Uttar Pradesh	18.58
West Bengal	8.65

Source: *Report of the Seventh Finance Commission*, 1978, p. 69.

21.7 Sharing of Union Excise Duties

Turning to the principles of distribution of the shares of the States in the net proceeds of excise duties, the Commission observed, "It is now well established that the distribution of the net proceeds of excise duties among the States is used by the Finance Commissions to make their contribution to the reduction of imbalances among the States. We have already referred to the growing concern in the country over the widening economic disparities between the States. It is true that the reasons are not only to be found in the financial strength or weakness of the States, but also in cultural and institutional factors which could facilitate or retard economic growth. Some of these important factors are susceptible to being changed by Government action if there is a will to do so. Notwithstanding such considerations, there is no doubt that financial strength would be a decisive influence in favour of growth. It is axiomatic that the potential for mobilising financial resources is not the same in States which have different levels of development and domestic product. This also means that the people in the poorer States do not have the same opportunities for advancement and the same access to public services as those in the advanced States." [6]

Table 21.5: Percentage Shares of the States in the Net Proceeds of Income Tax Assigned to the States as Recommended by the Seventh Finance Commission

State	Percentage with Sikkim	Percentage without Sikkim
Andhra Pradesh	8.021	8.023
Assam	2.521	2.522
Bihar	9.536	9.540
Gujarat	5.957	5.959
Haryana	1.819	1.819
Himachal Pradesh	0.595	0.595
Jammu & Kashmir	0.818	0.818
Karnataka	5.440	5.442
Kerala	3.948	3.950
Madhya Pradesh	7.354	7.356
Maharashtra	10.949	10.953
Manipur	1.188	0.188
Meghalaya	0.178	0.178
Nagaland	0.085	0.085
Orissa	3.738	3.739
Punjab	2.713	2.714
Rajasthan	4.362	4.364
Sikkim	0.035	-
Tamil Nadu	8.048	8.050
Tripura	0.258	0.258
Uttar Pradesh	15.422	15.429
West Bengal	8.015	8.018
All States	**100.000**	**100.000**

Source: *Report of the Seventh Finance Commission*, 1978, p. 83.

It may be recalled that the earlier Finance Commissions had distributed some part of the proceeds of excise duties on the basis of relative backwardness of States. Each Commission had evolved its own method of assessing States' relative backwardness. Since the proportion of the net proceeds of excise duties distributed on this principle was not large, the contribution which the past Commissions made towards reduction of inter-State imbalance was modest. The Commission under review was inclined to do more in this direction. It proposed to do so by a combination of different measures. According to it, population, as a determinant of the shares of States in divisible taxes, was merely a scale factor. Therefore, appropriate factors other than this factor had to be built into the scheme of distribution of the proceeds of excise to realise the basic objective of our scheme of fiscal transfer.

Regarding the indicators of levels of development of States, it thought that it would be desirable to adopt the overall indicators of backwardness such as per capita income and the proportion of people below the poverty line, instead of partial indicators such as the level of schooling, health services, road mileage etc. Partial indicators, in its opinion, reflected very much the particular pattern of allocation of resources by different States. It was possible that a State which had the necessary resource potential neglected certain sectors whereas even a less developed State lacking in resources might show more than average performance in respect of certain services. Moreover,, construction of an overall index of backwardness or level of development on the basis of individual or partial indicators was beset with the problem of relative weights to be assigned to these indicators. Any set of such weights decided on the basis of factor analysis was bound to be arbitrary.

In view of the above and other considerations, the Commission decided that the shares of the States in the divisible pool of excise should be determined giving equal weight to the population factor, the inverse of the per capita State Domestic Product, the percentage of the poor in each State measures by a method evolved by one of its members, namely Professor Raj Krishna, and a formula of revenue equalisation which was worked out by the Commission. Each of these principles were given equal weight of 25 per cent to determine the shares of the States in the divisible pool. The Commission came to the conclusion that by adopting such multiple criteria for the distribution of the pool of excise revenue among States, instead of on the basis of any single criterion of backwardness, it would be reducing the chance of the formula becoming either unduly favourable to certain States or working harshly against some others.

The Commission used the per capita State Domestic Product in comparable series of State current prices which had been worked out for it by the Central

Statistical Organisation. The Commission adopted the annual average for the triennial 1973-76. The poverty percentage in each State was the proportion of people below an augmented poverty line in the State to the aggregate poor population in all the States. The augmented poverty line was the minimum per capita consumption expenditure level for 1970-71 on the well-known Dandekar-Rath criterion plus the State budget expenditure per capita in the year on selected public services directed towards the welfare and security of the citizens.

The revenue equalisation principle adopted by the Commission was recognition of the fact that the States which were less favourably placed in regard to their resource potential should be specially helped in order to place them in a position where they could also take steps more readily for the betterment of the people living in those States. The Commission computed the per capita revenue potential of each State with reference to the average per capita SDP for the triennium 1973-76. The per capita average of each State's own tax and non-tax revenue for 1975-76 and 1976-77 were regressed on the average per capita income, excluding the five atypical States of Manipur, Meghalaya, Nagaland, Sikkim and Tripura. It, thus, derived the estimated values of per capita revenue of each State. The distance of the per capita revenue thus estimated for each State from the maximum estimated per capita revenue among all the States (i.e. Punjab) was multiplied by the estimated population of the State as on March 1, 1976. For the atypical States, their own average per capita revenue for the years 1975-76 and 1976-77 was adopted. The percentage of the product of the distance of the per capita revenue so estimated from that of Punjab and the population for each State in the total of these products for all the States gave the share of each State in the 25 per cent component of the divisible pool of excise.

The Commission worked out the relative shares of all the States in terms of percentages in accordance with the principles it adopted. At that time Union duties of excise were not leviable in Sikkim and therefore it was not entitled to a share in the net proceeds of these duties. The Commission, however, provided for a share for Sikkim in case the duties become leviable in it within the period covered by its award. The Commission worked out, on the same principles as for the other States, the percentage shares for Sikkim as well as the other States. These were to become operative if and when Union duties of excise were levied in Sikkim.

In short, the Commission made the following recommendations regarding the sharing of Union excise duties during each of the years 1979-80 to 1983-84.

1. The entire net proceeds of the Union excise duty on generation of electricity should be paid out of the Consolidated Fund of India to each State in an amount equal to the collection in or attributable to that State.

2. Out of the balance of the net proceeds of the Union excise duties levied and collected on all other articles excluding cesses levied under special Acts and earmarked for special purposes, 40 per cent should be paid out of the Consolidated Fund of India to the States and distributed among the States on the basis of the following percentages (Table 21.6).

Table 21.6: Distribution of States' Share of Excise Duties among the States Recommended by the Seventh Finance Commission

(Percentages)

State	Excluding Sikkim	Including Sikkim
Andhra Pradesh	7.698	7.691
Assam	2.793	2.793
Bihar	13.025	13.021
Gujarat	4.103	4.101
Haryana	1.177	1.177
Himachal Pradesh	0.521	0.521
Jammu & Kashmir	0.839	0.839
Karnataka	4.877	4.876
Kerala	4.036	4.035
Madhya Pradesh	8.727	8.725
Maharashtra	6.633	6.632
Manipur	0.218	0.218
Meghalaya	0.200	0.200
Nagaland	0.097	0.097
Orissa	4.682	4.682
Punjab	1.226	1.226
Rajasthan	4.813	4.813
Sikkim	-	0.028
Tamil Nadu	7.641	7.637
Tripura	0.373	0.373
Uttar Pradesh	18.293	18.290
West Bengal	8.028	8.025

Source: *Report of the Seventh Finance Commission*, 1978, p. 88.

21.8 Upgradation of Standards of Administration

For an assessment of the existing standards and of the gaps between the backward and the more advanced States, the Commission under study decided to confine itself to the sectors and services which were the more important elements in the basic administrative infrastructure of government. The following services and sectors were focussed upon by the Commission.

1. Administration of taxes.
2. Treasury and Accounts administration.
3. Judicial administration.
4. General administration, consisting of revenue, district as well as tribal administration, and the Secretariat services.
5. Police.
6. Jails.

For the upgradation of judicial administration in the various States during 1979-80 to 1983-84, the total provisions made by the Commission added up to Rs. 2,399.45 lakh, as shown in Table 21.7.

Table 21.7: Provisions for Upgradation of Judicial Administration in Various States Recommended by the Seventh Finance Commission

State	Revenue (Rs. lakh)	Capital (Rs. Lakh)
Andhra Pradesh	54.77	29.20
Assam	108.96	60.10
Bihar	373.43	208.30
Himachal Pradesh	5.02	2.80
Jammu & Kashmir	5.02	2.80
Kerala	8.56	4.10
Madhya Pradesh	22.88	12.95
Manipur	17.57	9.80
Nagaland	-	70.00
Orissa	68.64	35.25
Rajasthan	136.41	73.05
Tamil Nadu	10.04	5.60
Tripura	42.51	21.35
Uttar Pradesh	374.58	217.20
West Bengal	262.26	156.30
Total	**1,490.65**	**908.80**

Source: *Report of the Seventh Finance Commission*, 1978, pp. 96-97.

21.9 Non-Plan Capital Gap of States

The Commission made an assessment of the non-plan capital gap of the States on a uniform and comparable basis for the five years ending with 1983-84.

In the light of the non-Plan capital gaps of the States as assessed by it, the Commission reviewed the debt position of the States with particular reference to the Central loans advanced to them and likely to be outstanding as at the end of 1978-79. Taking into consideration the overall non-Plan gap of the States, their relative position and the purposes for which the loans were utilised and the requirements of the Centre, it recommended the following measures for dealing with the non-Plan capital gap of the States.

1. "The existing terms of repayment of Central loans advanced to Orissa for Hirakund Project Stage I and to all States for rehabilitation of displaced persons, repatriates etc. and outstanding at the end of 1978-79, may remain undisturbed;
2. Short-term loans, if any, by the Central Government to the States that may remain outstanding at the end of 1978-79 may be recovered according to the existing terms applicable to such loans;
3. Central loans advanced to State Governments by way of share out of net collections of small savings, and outstanding at the end of 1978-79, may be converted into loans in perpetuity, in respect of which the States need make no repayment of principal from 1979-80 but should continue to pay interest at the existing rate;
4. The balance of the Central loans outstandings against the State Governments at the end of 1978-79 may be consolidated, in respect of each State, into one loan as on 1st April, 1979;
5. A portion of the Central loans so consolidated may be written off;
6. A further portion of the loans so consolidated may be converted into 30-year loan, recoverable in equal annual instalments commencing from 1979-80, together with interest at the rate of 4.75 per cent per annum;
7. The balance of the Central loans so consolidated may be converted into 15-year loan recoverable in equal annual instalments commencing from 1979-80, together with interest at the rate of 5 per cent per annum; and
8. While making financial assistance available to the States from 1979-80, whether for Plan or for non-Plan purposes, the Government of India and the Planning Commission should determine the loan and the grant components with due regard to the end-use of the assistance and, having so determined the loan component, prescribe the terms of repayment thereof consistently with the terms that we have recommended in relation to the loans that may be outstanding against the States at the end of 1978-79." [7]

Notes

1. *Report of the Seventh Finance Commission*, 1978, p. 126-27.

2. *The duty was abolished with effect from March 16, 1985.*

3. *Report of the Seventh Finance Commission*, 1978, p. 121-1222.

4. It may be recalled that wealth tax on agricultural property was introduced with effect from the assessment year 1970-71 by amending Section 2(e) of the Wealth Tax Act, 1957. The amendment was a part of the measures in the Finance Act of 1969. Prior to this amendment, assets defined for the purposes of the wealth tax did not include agricultural property. The effect of the amendment of the Wealth Tax Act in 1969 was that agricultural property stood included in the properties taxable under the Act. This amendment was not applicable to the State of Jammu and Kashmir.

Wealth tax was not one of the taxes and duties which, under the provision of the Constitution, were to be shared with the States either on an obligatory or permissive basis. Nor was it a tax levied or collected by the Centre and assigned to the States. However, when agricultural property was made liable to wealth tax as aforesaid, the Central Government decided on its own that the net proceeds of the tax on agricultural land would be passed on to the States as grants-in-aid.

5. For the year 1975-76, the revenue from wealth tax on agricultural property was Rs. 0.91 crore.

6. *Report of the Seventh Finance Commission*, 1978, p. 85.

7. *Ibid.*, pp. 127-28.

22

Eighth Finance Commission

This Finance Commission, the eighth since the commencement of the Constitution, was constituted by the President by his Order dated the June 20, 1982. The Commission was asked to make recommendations as to the following matters.

Summary Statement	
Chairman	Mr. Y.B. Chavan
Members	Justice Sabyasachi Mukherje Dr. C.H. Hanumantha Rao Shri G.C. Baveja, Secretary Shri. A.R. Shirali
Year and month of establishment	June 1982
Year and month of reporting	April 1984
Period of award	1984-85 to 1988-89
Main Recommendations	
• States' share in income tax fixed at (per cent): 85 • Bases of distribution of States' share in income tax inter se (per cent): Population: 22.5; Contribution: 10; Other factors: 67.5 • States' share in Union excise duties fixed at (per cent): 45 • Bases of distribution of States' share in Union excise duties inter se (per cent): Population: 25; Other factors: 75	

1. Distribution between the Union and the States of the net proceeds of taxes which are to be, or may be, divided between them and allocation between the States of the respective shares of such proceeds.
2. Principles which should govern the grants-in-aid of the revenues of the States out of the Consolidated Fund of India and the sums to be paid to the States which are in need of assistance by way of grants-in-aid of their revenues under article 275 of the Constitution for purposes other than those specified in the provisos to clause (1) of that article.

In making its recommendations, the Commission was required to have regard to the following considerations.

1. Resources of the Central Government and the demands thereon on account of the expenditure on civil administration, defence and border security, debt servicing and other committed expenditure or liabilities.
2. Existing practice in regard to determination and distribution of Central assistance for financing State Plans.
3. Revenue resources of those States for the five years ending with the financial year 1988-89 on the basis of the levels of taxation likely to be reached at the end of the financial year 1983-84 and the targets set for additional resource mobilisation for the Plan.
4. Requirements on revenue account of those States to meet the expenditure on administration and other non-Plan commitments or liabilities, keeping however in view national policies and priorities. In assessing such requirements, the Commission shall take into account (a) such provision for emoluments and terminal benefits of Government employees, teachers and employees of local bodies as obtaining on a specified date as the Commission deems it proper and with reference to appropriate objective criteria rather than in terms of actual increases that may have been given effect to and (b) commitments in regard to interest charges on their debt, transfer of funds to local bodies and aided institutions.
5. Adequate maintenance and upkeep of capital assets and maintenance of Plan schemes completed by the end of 1983-84, the norms, if any, on the basis of which specified amounts are allowed for the maintenance of different categories of capital assets and the manner in which such maintenance expenditure could be monitored, being indicated by the Commission.
6. Requirements of States for upgradation of standards in non-developmental sectors and services particularly of States which are backward in general administration with a view to bringing them to the levels obtaining or likely to obtain in the more advanced States, the manner in which such expenditure could be monitored, being also indicated by the Commission.
7. Scope for better fiscal management and economy in expenditure consistent with efficiency.
8. Need for ensuring reasonable returns on investments in irrigation and power projects, transport undertakings, industrial and commercial enterprises and the like.

The Commission was also asked to suggest changes, if any, to be made in the principles governing the distribution among the States of the following.

1. Net proceeds in any financial year of estate duty in respect of property other than agricultural land.

2. Net proceeds in any financial year of the additional excise duties leviable under the Additional Duties of Excise (Goods of Special Importance) Act, 1957 in replacement of the sales tax levied formerly by the State Governments on each of the following commodities, namely (i) cotton fabrics, (ii) woollen fabrics, (iii) rayon or artificial silk fabrics, (iv) sugar and (v) tobacco including manufactured tobacco. Provided that the share accruing to each State shall not be less than the revenue realised from the levy of sales tax for the financial year 1956-57 in that State.
3. Grant to be made available to the States in lieu of the tax under the repealed Railway Passenger Fares Tax Act, 1957.
4. Grant to be made available to the States on account of wealth tax on agricultural property.

In making its recommendations on the various matters aforesaid, the Commission was required to adopt the population figures of 1971 in all cases where population was regarded as a factor for determination of devolution of taxes and duties and grants-in-aid.

22.1 Approach of the Commission on Financial Transfers

In the context of its duty of recommending the division of shareable taxes between the Centre and the States, and the making of grants-in-aid to the States in need of assistance, the Commission observed, "The crux of the problem is that the resources are limited, and the needs of the States are enormous. It is to their credit that they are impatient to achieve further development as fast as possible. The degrees of development vary. Some States are relatively more advanced while others are lagging behind. Naturally, this leads to many competing claims, and the Finance Commission is compelled to adopt some approach in fixing priorities. At the same time, it has to have regard to the needs of the Centre which has many responsibilities. The overriding consideration which has guided this Commission, is the national interest taken as a whole. Ultimately, the solutions we have chosen have been judged on this touchstone.

We have carefully considered the memoranda sent to us by the States, and the points made by the Chief Ministers and their colleagues during our discussions with them. They are unanimous in their demand for a larger share in the total Central revenues. There are divergent views as to how this should be done. The common thread, in all that they urged, was the desire for accelerated economic development, and the need for proper maintenance of assets already created. The extent of the share demanded by the States from the Centre's revenue varies from 40 per cent to 75 per cent.

In this connection, the demands on the Centre's resources, also, need to be remembered. The expenditure on defence, subsidies on food and fertilizers, and interest payments is, in the present circumstances, inescapable. These items alone absorb nearly half the Centre's revenues. Out of what remains with the Centre, about 37 per cent is at present being transferred to the States, largely on the recommendations of the Finance Commission and the Planning Commission.

While we have the greatest sympathy for the needs of the States, the parameters within which we have to function are, thus, obvious. Within the scope which was available to us, we have tried to do our best." [1]

22.2 Reassessment of the Revenue and Expenditure Forecasts

In order to assess the revenue resources of States on a comparable and uniform basis, State Governments were requested to send their forecasts of revenue receipts and revenue expenditure in the proformae prescribed by the Commission. The forecasts of revenue receipts were required to be based on the levels of taxation likely to prevail at the end of 1983-84. The forecasts of expenditure were similarly to be based on the normal level of standing charges on non-Plan account as at the end of 1983-84 i.e. after excluding all provisions for any fresh expenditure during the forecast period.

The Commission engaged the services of National Institute of Public Finance and Policy (NIPFP), New Delhi to help it in the matter of forecasting of receipts and expenditure of the State Governments. The NIPFP submitted reports on the following subjects which pertained to the State forecasts: (a) Revenue and Expenditure Projections: Evaluation and Methodology. (b) Relative Taxable Capacity and Tax Effort of Indian States. Similarly, the Commission requested the Ministry of Finance, Government of India to send to it forecasts of the Central Government's receipts and expenditure on revenue account and capital account for the five years ending with the financial year 1988-89. The inputs received from various quarters were carefully examined and reassessed by the Commission.

22.3 Sharing of Income Tax Revenue

It recommended that the States' share in the net proceeds of income tax be maintained at 85 per cent of the divisible pool during each of the years covered by its recommendations, i.e. 1984-85 to 1988-89.

Turning to the inter se allocations of income tax among the various States, the Commission noted that all the earlier seven Commissions had given weight to only two factors, namely *population* and *contribution*. While the First, Third and Fourth Finance Commissions gave 80 per cent weightage to population, the

Second, Fifth, Sixth and Seventh Finance Commissions gave it a weightage of 90 per cent. Collection as a measure of contribution was given a weightage of 10 per cent by the Second and the Fifth Finance Commissions and 20 per cent by the First, Third and the Fourth Finance Commissions. The Sixth and the Seventh Finance Commissions gave 10 per cent weightage to *assessment*, in preference to *collection* as a measure of the States' contribution.

As regards the criteria to be adopted for making the allocation, the Commission was in favour of more progressive criteria for allocating income tax than was the case with previous Commissions. In order to achieve this result, it suggested that 90 per cent of the States' share of income tax remaining after distributing 10 per cent on the basis of contribution, should be allocated amongst the States on the very same principles as those it applied for allocating the predominant part of their share of excise duties. In other words, the balance of 90 per cent of the States' share of income tax, which remained after distributing 10 per cent on the basis of contribution, was allocated among the States by giving a weightage of 25 per cent to population, 25 per cent to the inverse of per capita income multiplied by population, and 50 per cent to the distance of per capita income. On the basis of these recommendations, the composite percentage shares of each State were determined.

As income tax had not yet been extended to Sikkim, the Commission worked out the State-wise composite shares in income tax amongst the States including Sikkim as well as without Sikkim on the consideration that in case income tax was extended to that State, the basis of its distribution amongst the States might not pose any problem.

In short, the Commission recommended the following steps for the distribution of the net proceeds of income tax in each of the years 1984-85 to 1988-89.

1. Out of the net proceeds in each financial year, a sum equal to 1.792 per cent thereof be deemed to represent the proceeds attributable to Union territories.
2. 85 per cent of net income tax proceeds, except the portion representing the proceeds attributable to Union territories and Union emoluments, be assigned to the States.
3. Distribution amongst the States inter se of the share assigned to the States in respect of each financial year should be on the basis of the percentages shown in the Table 22.1.

22.4 Sharing of Union Excise Duties

The Commission was of the opinion that the transfer of resources to the States should leave as many of them as possible with surpluses on revenue account so that they were able to implementation Five Year Plans. At the same time, it had also to keep in view the amount of surplus with the Centre as reassessed by it. Taking into account these considerations, it came to the conclusion that the share of the States in the net proceeds of excise duties, other than the duty on electricity, should be increased from 40 per cent fixed by the Seventh Finance Commission to 45 per cent. It further recommended that this be distributed amongst the States on the following basis.

Table 22.1: Percentage Shares of the States in the Net Proceeds of Income Tax Assigned to the States as Recommended by the Eighth Finance Commission

State	Percentage with Sikkim	Percentage without Sikkim
Andhra Pradesh	8.187	8.190
Assam	2.789	2.789
Bihar	12.080	12.085
Gujarat	4.409	4.410
Haryana	1.074	1.074
Himachal Pradesh	0.555	0.555
Jammu & Kashmir	0.838	0.838
Karnataka	4.979	4.981
Kerala	3.760	3.761
Madhya Pradesh	8.378	8.382
Maharashtra	8.392	8.396
Manipur	0.220	0.220
Meghalaya	0.184	0.184
Nagaland	0.088	0.088
Orissa	4.202	4.203
Punjab	1.744	1.744
Rajasthan	4.545	4.547
Sikkim	0.035	-
Tamil Nadu	7.565	7.567
Tripura	0.269	0.269
Uttar Pradesh	17.907	17.914
West Bengal	7.800	7.803
Total	**100.000**	**100.000**

Source: *Report of the Eighth Finance Commission*, 1984, p. 45.

(a) 40 per cent of the net proceeds of shareable excise duties excluding that on electricity, be distributed during each year of the forecast period among all States in the following manner:

(i) ¼th of this amount (i.e. 25 per cent) should be distributed among the States on the basis of the 1971 population.

(ii) Another ¼th (i.e. 25 per cent) should be distributed to States on the basis of inverse of per capita income.

(iii) The remaining 50 per cent should be distributed on the basis of the distance of per capita income.

(b) The remaining 5 per cent of the net proceeds of excise duties excluding that on electricity, be set aside and distributed to those States which have deficits after taking into account their shares from the devolution of all taxes and duties, including their shares of excise duties, under clause (a) above and grants in lieu of the repealed tax on railway passenger fares, but excluding their shares of estates duty and grants on account of wealth tax on agricultural property. This distribution should be based on the proportion of the deficit of each State to the total of the deficits of all States as estimated by us, worked out separately for each year of the forecast.

The percentage share of each State in 40 per cent of the net proceeds of shareable excise duties excluding that on electricity were worked out as shown in Table 22.2.

Table 22.2: Distribution of States' Share of Excise Duties among the States as Recommended by the Eighth Finance Commission

State	Percentage share in 40 per cent of the net proceeds of excise duties for the years 1984-85 to 1988-89
Andhra Pradesh	8.587
Assam	2.977
Bihar	13.202
Gujarat	3.506
Haryana	1.017
Himachal Pradesh	0.589
Jammu & Kashmir	0.856
Karnataka	5.077
Kerala	3.800

Contd...

Madhya Pradesh	8.852
Maharashtra	6.216
Manipur	0.233
Meghalaya	0.194
Nagaland	0.096
Orissa	4.592
Punjab	1.317
Rajasthan	4.695
Sikkim	0.039
Tamil Nadu	7.317
Tripura	0.292
Uttar Pradesh	19.097
West Bengal	7.449
Total	**100.000**

Source: *Report of the Eighth Finance Commission*, 1984, p. 54.

The percentage share of the deficit States in the 5 per cent of the net proceeds of the shareable excise duties excluding that on electricity were also worked out by the Commission for each of the 5 years commencing from April 1, 1984 and these percentages are shown in Table 22.3.

Table 22.3: Distribution of the Shares of Deficit States in 5 per cent of Excise Duties as Recommended by the Eighth Finance Commission

State	**1984-85**	**1985-86**	**1986-87**	**1987-88**	**1988-89**
Assam	12.728	12.578	12.713	13.418	12.023
Himachal Pradesh	10.340	11.528	12.914	14.098	16.475
J&K	15.475	16.661	17.818	18.560	20.254
Manipur	6.969	7.742	8.722	9.545	11.217
Meghalaya	5.575	6.180	6.944	7.570	8.863
Nagaland	8.837	9.944	11.240	12.371	14.482
Orissa	9.214	8.154	5.457	3.109	0.598
Rajasthan	1.940	-	-	-	-
Sikkim	1.659	1.836	2.051	2.232	2.593
Tripura	8.200	9.104	10.207	11.162	12.956
West Bengal	19.081	16.273	11.934	7.935	0.539
Total	**100.000**	**100.000**	**100.000**	**100.000**	**100.000**

Source: *Report of the Eighth Finance Commission*, 1984, p. 54.

22.5 Additional Duties of Excise

Having considered all pros and cons, the Commission recommended the distribution of the net proceeds of the additional excise duties on textiles, sugar and tobacco on the following basis.

1. A sum equal to 2.391 per cent of such net proceeds be retained by the Central Governments as attributable to the Union territories.
2. The balance should be distributed amongst the States in accordance with the percentages mentioned (Table 22.4).

Table 22.4: Distribution of Additional Duties of Excise among the States as Recommended by the Eighth Finance Commission

State	Percentage
Andhra Pradesh	7.504
Assam	2.566
Bihar	8.627
Gujarat	5.941
Haryana	2.488
Himachal Pradesh	0.663
Jammu & Kashmir	0.853
Karnataka	5.561
Kerala	3.963
Madhya Pradesh	6.942
Maharashtra	11.461
Manipur	0.178
Meghalaya	0.183
Nagaland	0.098
Orissa	3.653
Punjab	3.675
Rajasthan	4.827
Sikkim	0.039
Tamil Nadu	7.549
Tripura	0.287
Uttar Pradesh	14.318
West Bengal	8.624
Total	**100.000**

Source: *Report of the Eighth Finance Commission*, 1984, p. 128.

22.6 Estate Duty in Respect of Property other than Agricultural Land

Recommendations of the Commission in this regard were as follows.

1. Net proceeds of estate duty in respect of property other than agricultural land attributable to Union territories should be determined in the same manner and on the same principles as for the determination of the shares of each State, taking the Union territories as one unit for the purpose.
2. Balance of the net proceeds of estate duty in each year should be distributed among the States, in proportion to the gross value of the immovable property and property other than immovable property taken together, located in each State and brought into assessment. The location of property other than immovable property should be determined in accordance with the rules framed under the Estate Duty Act, 1953. As for property located abroad, it should be deemed to be located in the State where it is brought to assessment.
3. Sikkim would also be entitled to a share in the net proceeds of this duty, calculated in the same manner as for the other States, as from the date the duty becomes leviable in that State in the period covered by the award of the Commission.

22.7 Grant in Lieu of Tax on Railway Passenger Fares

The Commission increased the annual quantum of the grant in lieu of a tax on railway passenger fares to Rs. 95 crore in each of the year 1984-85 to 1988-89. The percentage share of each State was worked out for the purpose of distribution of this grant (Table 22.5).

22.8 Grant on Account of Wealth Tax on Agricultural Property

The Commission recommended that the share of each State in the grant on account of wealth tax on agricultural property should be an amount equivalent to the net collection in that State in that year.

22.9 Financing of Relief Expenditure

After examining in detail the various arrangements made by the earlier Commissions, the Commission under review observed as under.

1. "The existing arrangements are basically sound and should continue subject to the following modifications:

(a) The amounts of margin money per year be fixed for each State as mentioned (Table 22.6).

(b) The State Governments should provide 50 per cent of the margin money mentioned above under the Head of Account '289 – Relief on Account of Natural Calamities'.

Table 22.5: Percentage Share of Each State in Grant in Lieu of Tax on Railway Passenger Fares

State	Percentage
Andhra Pradesh	7.68
Assam	2.03
Bihar	9.51
Gujarat	6.67
Haryana	1.84
Himachal Pradesh	0.14
Jammu & Kashmir	0.95
Karnataka	3.43
Kerala	3.18
Madhya Pradesh	5.85
Maharashtra	15.70
Manipur	0.02
Meghalaya	0.05
Nagaland	0.16
Orissa	1.58
Punjab	3.88
Rajasthan	4.87
Sikkim	0.01
Tamil Nadu	6.61
Tripura	0.04
Uttar Pradesh	17.85
West Bengal	7.95
Total	**100.00**

Source: *Report of the Eighth Finance Commission*, 1984, p. 128.

(c) The Centre should contribute the balance of 50 per cent of the margin money in every year as a grant-in-aid. On the occurrence of a natural calamity, a State will be entitled to draw on the Centre's contribution after it has exhausted its own share of the margin money. Provisions not released to the States will be carried forward to the next year.

(d) Expenditure on relief of distress caused by fire should also be treated on the same footing as a natural calamity of the category of floods.

(e) The cost norms adopted for items such as repairs/reconstruction of damaged houses etc. for which assistance is provided may be reviewed by the Centre.

(f) In respect of damages caused to public works by cyclones, floods etc., if the Centre is satisfied about the extent of expenditure required to be met, the Central assistance should extend, subject to the contributions of the State Government, to the whole of the expenditure on repairs and restoration of public works regardless of whether such expenditure can be incurred in the financial year in which the calamity occurs or it will have to be spread over the next and subsequent financial years.

2. Subject to the above modifications, for drought relief expenditure in excess of the margin we have provided, the State Government should make a contribution from its plan for providing relief employment. The extent to which the State Government should contribute from its Plan in this manner should be assessed by a Central Team after consultation with the State Government and approved by the Central Government. This contribution should not exceed 5 per cent of the Annual Plan outlay. This Plan contribution of the State Government should be treated as an addition to the Plan outlay in that year and covered by Advance Plan assistance. The adjustment of the Advance Plan assistance against the ceiling of the Central assistance for the Plan of the State should be effected within five years following the end of the drought. If the expenditure requirement, as assessed by the Central Team and the High Level Committee cannot be adequately met in a particular case after the State Plan contribution is taken into account, the extra expenditure should be taken as an indication of the special severity of the calamity which would justify the Central Government assisting the State to the full extent of the extra expenditure, half as grant and half as loan. In regard to the expenditure on relief and repairs and restoration of public works following floods, cyclones and other calamities of this nature, Central assistance should be made available as non-Plan grant, not adjustable against the Plan of the State or against Central assistance for the State Plan, to the extent of 75 per cent of the total expenditure in excess of the margins. Where a calamity is of rare severity it may be necessary for the Central Government to extend assistance to the States concerned even beyond the schemes we have suggested." [2]

22.10 Upgradation of Standards of Administration

The Commission estimated that the proposals for upgradation received from all States would require a total outlay of Rs. 19,424 crore. The proposals covered the whole gamut of administration. Given the limitation of resources, the Commission found it difficult to provide for all the upgradation needs for which it had received requests. It, therefore, selected the following sectors for upgradation.

Table 22.6: Amounts of Margin Money Per Year Fixed by the Eighth Finance Commission

State	Amount of margin money (Rs. crore)
Andhra Pradesh	24.50
Assam	7.25
Bihar	33.75
Gujarat	28.75
Haryana	4.50
Himachal Pradesh	1.75
Jammu & Kashmir	1.50
Karnataka	6.00
Kerala	5.00
Madhya Pradesh	4.75
Maharashtra	7.25
Manipur	0.25
Meghalaya	0.25
Nagaland	0.25
Orissa	26.25
Punjab	6.00
Rajasthan	16.75
Sikkim	0.25
Tamil Nadu	8.75
Tripura	0.75
Uttar Pradesh	32.50
West Bengal	23.75
Total	**240.75**

Source: *Report of the Eighth Finance Commission*, 1984, p. 73.

1. Police.
2. Education.
3. Jail administration.
4. Tribal administration.
5. Health.

6. Judicial administration.
7. District and revenue administration.
8. Training.
9. Treasury and accounts administration.

To cover the requirements of upgradation and special problems of the States, during the five years commencing from April 1, 1984, the Commission recommended the amounts of grant as shown in Table 22.7.

Table 22.7: Grants for Upgradation of Administration and Special Problems of the States during the Period 1984-85 to 1988-89 as Recommended by the Eighth Finance Commission

(Rs. crore)

State	For upgradation	For special problems	Total
Andhra Pradesh	80.49	-	80.49
Assam	58.35	5.00	63.35
Bihar	130.27	-	130.27
Himachal Pradesh	15.76	0.50	16.26
Jammu & Kashmir	46.07	2.48	48.55
Kerala	16.81	-	16.81
Madhya Pradesh	147.69	10.00	157.69
Manipur	20.30	2.00	22.30
Meghalaya	18.20	1.00	19.20
Nagaland	10.81	-	10.81
Orissa	74.84	-	74.84
Punjab	-	20.00	20.00
Rajasthan	43.48	10.00	53.48
Sikkim	3.14	1.00	4.14
Tripura	13.79	0.80	14.59
Uttar Pradesh	108.18	-	108.18
West Bengal	126.37	-	126.37
Total	**914.55**	**52.78**	**967.33**

Source: *Report of the Eighth Finance Commission*, 1984, p. 127.

22.11 Grants-in-aid of Revenues

Under the substantive part of clause (1) of Article 275 of the Constitution, the Commission recommended for various States grants to cover the deficits on revenue account in the respective years as indicated in Table 22.8.

Table 22.8: Grants-in-aid of Revenues of the States as Recommended by the Eighth Finance Commission

(Rs. crore)

State	Total 1984-89	1984-85	1985-86	1986-87	1987-88	1988-89
Assam	274.33	78.58	66.92	55.08	47.37	26.38
Himachal Pradesh	223.04	57.65	53.91	47.35	40.76	23.37
Jammu & Kashmir	329.18	89.22	81.14	68.79	57.34	32.69
Manipur	146.95	38.14	35.51	31.25	26.87	15.18
Meghalaya	119.15	30.92	28.96	25.30	21.75	12.42
Nagaland	190.52	48.76	45.96	40.65	35.19	19.96
Orissa	207.60	67.55	54.94	37.78	27.42	19.91
Rajasthan	42.63	34.25	8.38	-	-	-
Sikkim	36.16	9.38	8.71	7.66	6.59	3.82
Tripura	187.05	47.83	44.71	39.57	34.41	20.53
West Bengal	443.61	142.11	113.31	82.59	63.00	42.60
Total	2200.22	644.39	542.25	436.02	360.70	216.86

Source: *Report of the Eighth Finance Commission*, 1984, p. 126.

22.12 Non-Plan Capital Gap of the States

For purposes of debt relief, non-Plan capital gap was computed by the Commission after excluding repayments of overdraft loans and small savings loans. The Commission did not recommend any relief in respect of overdraft loans given to States in 1982-83 and 1983-84. Similarly, no relief was recommended in respect of repayment of small savings loans, except that in 1984-85, no repayment was to be made. Loans for relief and rehabilitation of displaced persons were recommended to be written off. The estimated relief to States in the 5 year period 1984-85 to 1988-89, including write off of repayments of Rs. 405.20 crore, is given in Table 22.9.

Further, the Commission suggested 4.75 per cent rate of interest on pre-1979 loans recommended for consolidation by it. For loans sanctioned after April 1, 1979 and outstanding on March 31, 1984 and which were recommended for consolidation by the Commission, rates of interest as shown in Table 22.10 were recommended, depending on period of repayment as rescheduled.

Table 22.9: Debt Relief to States as Recommended by the Eighth Finance Commission

State	(Rs. crore)
Andhra Pradesh	204.64
Assam	205.50
Bihar	330.98
Gujarat	17.80
Haryana	31.79
Himachal Pradesh	16.52
Jammu & Kashmir	212.72
Karnataka	48.45
Kerala	53.80
Madhya Pradesh	143.65
Maharashtra	27.83
Manipur	11.18
Meghalaya	6.39
Nagaland	7.81
Orissa	195.62
Punjab	38.71
Rajasthan	239.41
Sikkim	3.07
Tamil Nadu	28.19
Tripura	2.57
Uttar Pradesh	337.92
West Bengal	120.84
Total	**2285.39**

Source: *Report of the Eighth Finance Commission*, 1984, p. 130.

Table 22.10: Rates of Interest Recommended by the Eighth Finance Commission on Loans Rescheduled for Repayment

Rescheduled for 15 years	6.00 per cent
Rescheduled for 20 years	6.25 per cent
Rescheduled for 25 years	6.50 per cent
Rescheduled for 30 years	6.75 per cent

Source: *Report of the Eighth Finance Commission*, 1984, p. 130.

22.13 Taxes and Duties Mentioned in Articles 268 and 269 of the Constitution

As regards duties under Article 268, the Commission was of the opinion that some scope for raising the rates of stamp duties existed only in respect of bills of lading excluding those in respect of inland navigation, letters of credit and policies of general insurance including marine insurance. However, there was no scope for enhancing revenues from excise duties on medicinal and toilet preparations.

Regarding taxes and duties mentioned in Article 269 but not being levied at that time, the Commission held that there was scope for levying tax on railway passenger fares but no such tax should be levied so long as the then existing arrangement by which the Centre gave grants to the States in lieu of such a tax, continued to exist. There was scope for raising revenues by levying a tax on advertisements published in newspapers and journals.

22.14 General Observations

The Commission reiterated the suggestion made by the First Finance Commission that there should be a permanent secretariat which should continue to function during the interregnum between one Commission and the next. Such a secretariat should be headed by a senior officer and function as a Division in the Ministry of Finance during the period intervening between two Finance Commissions. The Division which the Commission proposed should have the following functions.

1. To watch the implementation of the recommendations of the Finance Commission.
2. To watch closely and analyse the trends in the non-Plan receipts and expenditure of the State Governments and identify the reasons for variation between actuals and estimates made by the Finance Commission.
3. To monitor and evaluate the utilization of upgradation grants.
4. To preserve the records of the previous Commissions, and take such necessary action to obtain further information as might be of use to the future Commissions.
5. To continuously collect and keep up-to-date information on all aspects of State finances, including the financial working of the State enterprises.
6. To conduct studies and publish papers and data having a bearing on States' finances.

Notes

1. *Report of the Eighth Finance Commission*, 1984, p. 7.
2. *Ibid.*, pp. 129-30.

23

Ninth Finance Commission

This Finance Commission, the ninth to be set up under Article 280 of the Constitution, was constituted by an Order of the President dated June 17, 1987. The Commission was asked to make recommendations as to the following matters.

Summary Statement	
Chairman	Mr. N.K.P. Salve
Members	Shri V.P. Menon Justice R. Kaushalendra Rao Dr. B.K. Madan Shri M.V. Rangachari, Member-Secretary
Year and month of establishment	June 1987
Year and month of reporting	December 1989
Period of award	1990-91 to 1994-95
Main Recommendations	
• (A separate report was submitted in July 1988 for the year 1989-90) • States' share in income tax fixed at (per cent): 85 • Bases of distribution of States' share in income tax inter se (per cent): Population: 22.5; Contribution: 10; Other factors: 67.5 • States' share in Union excise duties fixed at (per cent): 45 • Bases of distribution of States' share in Union excise duties inter se (per cent): Population: 29.94; Other factors: 70.06	

(a) the distribution between the Union and the States of the net proceeds of taxes which are to be, or may be, divided between them and the allocation between the States of the respective shares of such proceeds;

(b) the principles which should govern the grants-in-aid of the revenues of the States out of the Consolidated Fund of India and the sums to be paid to the States which are in need of assistance by way of grants-in-aid of their revenues under article 275 of the Constitution for purposes other than those specified in the provisos to clause (1) of that article.

In making its recommendations, the Commission was required to (i) adopt a normative approach in assessing the receipts and expenditures on the revenue account of the States and the Centre and, in doing so, keep in view the special problems of each State, if any, and the special requirement of the Centre such as defence, security, debt servicing and other committed expenditure or liabilities, (ii) have due regard to the need for providing adequate incentives for better resource mobilisation and financial discipline as well as closer linking of expenditure and revenue-raising decisions, (iii) take into account the need for speed, efficiency and effectiveness of Government functioning and of delivery systems for Government programmes and (iv) keep in view the objective of not only balancing the receipts and expenditure on revenue account of both the States and the Centre, but also generating surpluses for capital investment.

The Commission was also asked to suggest changes, if any, to be made in the principles governing the distribution among the States of (a) the net proceeds in any financial year of the additional duties of excise leviable under the Additional Duties of Excise (Goods of Special Importance) Act, 1957 and (b) the grants to be made available to the States in lieu of the tax under the repealed Railway Passenger Fares Tax, 1957.

In making its recommendations on the various matters aforesaid, the Commission was asked to adopt the population figures of 1971 in all cases where population was regarded as a factor for determination of devolution of taxes and duties and grants-in-aid. Furthermore, the Commission was required to make two reports, the first report covering a period of one year commencing on April 1, 1989 and the second report covering a period of five years commencing on April 1, 1990.

23.1 Normative Approach

With a view to making the recommendations of the Finance Commissions co-terminus with the Five Year Plans, the Ninth Finance Commission was asked to make two reports, the first covering one year period (1989-90), and the second covering five years period (1990-91 to 1994-95).

The terms of reference of the Ninth Finance Commission were wider as compared to previous Commissions. For example, one term of reference provided that the Commission might examine the feasibility of the merger of additional duties of excise in lieu of sales tax with basic duties of excise.

The Commission was asked to adopt a normative approach in assessing receipts and expenditures on revenue account of both the Centre and the States. The normative approach was considered essential to ensure fiscal discipline and adequate efforts to augment revenues.

The Commission presented its first report for the year 1989-90 to the

President on July 29, 1988. The second report for the five year period 1990-91 to 1994-95 was submitted in December 1989. The report of the Commission was not unanimous as one of its members Justice A.S. Qureshi disagreed with certain recommendations. His note of dissent formed part of the report.

The Ninth Finance Commission made a basic departure from the practice of previous Finance Commissions by adopting the normative approach. Under this approach, the *needs* and *capacities* of different governments were assessed normatively and such normative assessments were used as the basis for determining the volume and pattern of federal transfers. In other words, the fiscal performance of the governments was judged on the basis of *what ought to be* rather than on the basis of *what it actually is*. To put it differently, the Commission rejected the base year figure on the receipts as well as the expenditure side as the *right* figures. The Commission emphasised that the normative approach would be applied to both the Centre and the States and that the assessment of revenues and expenditures would be done in a manner so as to maintain incentives for greater revenue efforts and economy in spending.

On the revenue side, estimates were derived separately for tax and non-tax revenues. In the words of the Commission, "In respect of taxes, a modified representative tax system approach has been applied in order to determine what a particular State would be able to raise by way of tax revenue had it exploited its tax bases to an average extent. Such 'tax capacity' figures have been derived for a base year and are then projected to the year 1989-90. As regards non-tax revenues, while actuals have been used in the case of fees and user charges, in the case of dividends and interest to be received by the government, normative rates of return have been used. As in the case of revenues, in regard to a substantial part of non-Plan revenue expenditures, the average behaviour has been taken as the norm." [1] However, considering the request of some State Governments, the application of normative norms by the Commission was moderated and spread over a period of years. Moreover, the Special Category States were kept out of the normative approach and actuals were used to project receipts and expenditure.

The normative approach applied by the Commission generated considerable controversy among fiscal experts. The soundness of the normative approach was questioned by no less a person than Justice Qureshi, a member of the Commission. In his note of dissent appended to the report of the Commission, he observed: "Although the normative approach is in itself a very beneficial thing, there is a practical difficulty in its application. Normative standards can be applied to States easily and effectively, but they cannot be applied to the Centre with the same rigour. It is difficult to set normative standards to certain items, such as, defence expenditure, debts etc. It would, therefore, always be the grouse of the States that the normative approach is applied only to the States and not to the Centre. I have an objection to the results arrived at by adopting the normative approach in assessing the receipts and expenditures on the revenue account of the States and the Centre. It is on the ground that they have been worked out on the basis of econometric models relying on proxies, dummies, variables etc. in the absence of accurate or reliable data. Moreover, certain considerations have been built in to arrive at the desired results. I am really doubtful about the efficacy of such a mechanical approach towards normative assessment of receipts and expenditures of States, in such a vast country with widely varying social and economic conditions and historical background." [2]

23.2 Alternative Terms of Reference

The guidelines issued by the Central Government to the Ninth Finance Commission, such as to follow the normative approach in assessing the revenue and expenditure of the Central and State Governments and keep in view the special requirements like defence, security, debt servicing and other committed expenditures or liabilities of the Centre, were resented by some State Governments. On January 30, 1988, a group of Chief Ministers met the Prime Minister to present alternative terms of reference for the already set up Ninth Finance Commission. Almost simultaneously the Government released a summary of the report of the Sarkaria Commission on Centre-State relations.

The alternative terms of reference for the Ninth Finance Commission were jointly submitted to the Prime Minister on behalf of the seven non-Congress (I) Chief Ministers who unanimously framed them at their meeting in Bangalore on January 11, 1988. The seven non-Congress (I) States (West Bengal, Haryana, Karnataka, Andhra Pradesh, Kerala, Tripura and Assam) believed that the terms of reference of the Ninth Finance Commission were one-sided in favour of the Centre and the reference in them of normative approach was vague and devoid of operational content. The Chief Ministers demanded the holding of a tripartite meeting between the Ninth Finance Commission, the Centre and the State Governments to evolve the normative approach on the receipts and expenditure.

The alternative terms of reference, *inter alia*, stipulated (i) inclusion of the corporation tax in the divisible pool, (ii) review of the working of the scheme of additional excise duties in lieu of sales tax including the feasibility of reverting to the pre-1957 arrangement, (iii) discontinuation of the grants in lieu of tax on railway passenger fare and the simultaneous reintroduction of tax on railway passenger fare. The Chief Ministers reiterated their demand for the early constitution of the Inter-State Council as envisaged in the Constitution. They also pleaded that the meetings of the National Development Council should be convened more frequently, at least twice a year.

23.3 First Report (for the year 1989-90)

In making its recommendations for the year 1989-90, the Commission was guided by two basic considerations: (a) the Centre and the State Governments should be given adequate time to adjust to the normative approach and its implications and (b) the financial assumptions on which the Seventh Five Year Plan was based, should not be disturbed drastically.

23.3.1 Sharing of Income Tax: Recommendations of the Commission in this regard for the year 1989-90 were as follows.

1. Out of the net proceeds, a sum equal to 1.044 per cent thereof be deemed to represent the proceeds attributable to Union Territories.
2. Share of net income tax proceeds, except the portion representing the proceeds attributable to Union Territories and Union emoluments, to be assigned to the States be 85 per cent.
3. Distribution amongst the States *inter se* of the share assigned to the States in respect of the financial year 1989-90 be on the basis of percentages shown in Table 23.1.

Table 23.1: Percentage Shares of the States in the Net Proceeds of Income Tax Assigned to the States as Recommended by the Ninth Finance Commission for the Year 1989-90

State	Percentage with Sikkim	Percentage without Sikkim
Andhra Pradesh	7.344	7.346
Arunachal Pradesh	0.066	0.066
Assam	2.507	2.507
Bihar	12.314	12.318
Goa	0.090	0.091
Gujarat	4.232	4.233
Haryana	1.048	1.049
Himachal Pradesh	0.505	0.505
Jammu & Kashmir	0.682	0.682
Karnataka	4.937	4.938
Kerala	3.553	3.554
Madhya Pradesh	8.000	8.003
Maharashtra	10.110	10.112

Contd...

Manipur	0.181	0.181
Meghalaya	0.183	0.183
Mizoram	0.059	0.059
Nagaland	0.064	0.064
Orissa	4.054	4.055
Punjab	1.522	1.522
Rajasthan	4.773	4.775
Sikkim	0.028	-
Tamil Nadu	7.614	7.616
Tripura	0.269	0.269
Uttar Pradesh	18.326	18.331
West Bengal	7.539	7.541
Total	**100.000**	**100.000**

Source: *First Report of the Ninth Finance Commission*, July 1988, p. 30.

23.3.2 Sharing of Union Excise Duties: The Commission made the following recommendations in this regard.

1. It continued the then existing arrangement under which 45 per cent of the net proceeds of shareable excise duties were distributed among States for the year 1989-90.
2. 40 per cent of the net proceeds of shareable excise duties be distributed amongst all the States on the basis of percentages shown (Table 23.2).
4. The remaining 5 per cent of the net proceeds of shareable excise duties be distributed amongst the deficit States on the basis of the percentages shown (Table 23.3).

23.3.3 Additional Duties of Excise in Lieu of Sales Tax: The Commission recommended that the net proceeds of the additional duties of excise on textiles, sugar and tobacco be determined on the following basis.

1. A sum equal to 2.023 per cent of such net proceeds be retained by the Central Government as attributable to the Union Territories.
2. The balance should be distributed amongst the States in accordance with the percentages indicated (Table 23.4).

The Commission also desired that the Standing Review Committee appointed by National Development Council to review the working of the tax rental arrangement might submit a report to it by the end of October 1988, regarding the misgivings of the States on numerous exemptions granted from duties of additional excise and the expansion of the coverage of these duties.

Table 23.2: Distribution of States' Share of Excise Duties among the States as Recommended by the Ninth Finance Commission for the Year 1989-90

State	Percentage share in 40 per cent of the net proceeds of excise duties for the year 1989-90
Andhra Pradesh	7.858
Arunachal Pradesh	0.070
Assam	2.707
Bihar	13.573
Goa	0.074
Gujarat	3.109
Haryana	1.077
Himachal Pradesh	0.549
Jammu and Kashmir	0.713
Karnataka	5.092
Kerala	3.707
Madhya Pradesh	8.726
Maharashtra	5.635
Manipur	0.197
Meghalaya	0.199
Mizoram	0.065
Nagaland	0.070
Orissa	4.454
Punjab	1.310
Rajasthan	5.097
Sikkim	0.032
Tamil Nadu	7.785
Tripura	0.295
Uttar Pradesh	19.877
West Bengal	7.729
Total	**100.000**

Source: *First Report of the Ninth Finance Commission*, July 1988, p. 34.

23.3.4 Grant in Lieu of Tax on Railway Passenger Fares: In keeping with the spirit of the Constitutional provisions applicable to the repealed tax on railway passenger fares, the Commission did not consider it possible to allot a share of the grant in lieu thereof to a State wherein there was no railway line nor any out agency and in which no railway ticket was purchased. Similarly, taking into account the financial difficulties of the railways and its unique role in the economic life of the nation from which all the States benefit, the Commission retained the quantum of grant at the then existing level of Rs. 95 crore. The distribution of this grant among the States as recommended by the commission is shown in Table 23.5.

Table 23.3: Distribution of the Shares of Deficit States in 5 per cent of Excise Duties as Recommended by the Ninth Finance Commission for the Year 1989-90

State	Percentage
Arunachal Pradesh	7.158
Assam	14.233
Goa	1.695
Himanchal Pradesh	10.031
Jammu and Kashmir	19.499
Manipur	6.787
Meghalaya	4.837
Mizoram	8.199
Nagaland	8.108
Orissa	5.806
Rajasthan	3.946
Sikkim	1.408
Tripura	8.293
	100.000

Source: *First Report of the Ninth Finance Commission*, July 1988, p. 34.

23.3.5 Financing of Relief Expenditure: Provision of relief of victims of natural calamities is one of the basic responsibilities of State Governments in India and requirements in this regard have been taken into account by the Finance Commissions. The scheme of financing of relief expenditure as recommended by Eight Finance Commission was continued by the Commission under review. The Commission fixed the amounts of margin money for each State as indicated in Table 23.6. The State Governments should provide 50 per cent of the margin money and the remaining 50 per cent of the margin money should be provided by the Centre as grant-in-aid under the substantive part of Clause (1) of Article 275 of the Constitution.

Table 23.4: Distribution of Additional Duties of Excise among the States as Recommended by the Ninth Finance Commission for the Year 1989-90

State	Percentage
Andhra Pradesh	7.933
Arunachal Pradesh	0.100
Assam	2.711
Bihar	8.519
Goa	0.230
Gujarat	6.094
Haryana	2.358
Himachal Pradesh	0.652
Jammu and Kashmir	0.916
Karnataka	5.581
Kerala	3.834
Madhya Pradesh	7.070
Maharashtra	11.763
Manipur	0.192
Meghalaya	0.179
Mizoram	0.061
Nagaland	0.127
Orissa	3.680
Punjab	3.478
Rajasthan	4.636
Sikkim	0.048
Tamil Nadu	7.120
Tripura	0.279
Uttar Pradesh	14.109
West Bengal	8.330
Total	**100.000**

Source: *First Report of the Ninth Finance Commission*, July 1988, p. 37.

23.3.6 Special Problems of Debt Relief: Since some of the States had suffered enormously on account of unprecedented drought and other calamities, the Commission recommended the following debt relief measures for them.

1. "Moratorium on the interest payments and the repayment of principal due in 1989-90 should be granted in respect of the Central loans given to the States in 1986-87 and 1987-88 by way of additional Plan assistance towards

approved relief expenditure over and above 5 per cent of the annual Plan outlay on account of unprecedented drought during those years.

Table 23.5: Percentage Share of Each State in Grant in Lieu of Tax on Railway Passenger Fares for the Year 1989-90

State	**Percentage**
Andhra Pradesh	7.574
Arunachal Pradesh	0.006
Assam	1.472
Bihar	8.215
Goa	0.131
Gujarat	5.772
Haryana	1.600
Himachal Pradesh	0.101
Jammu and Kashmir	0.522
Karnataka	3.282
Kerala	3.602
Madhya Pradesh	5.936
Maharashtra	22.767
Manipur	0.015
Meghalaya	0.037
Mizoram	-
Nagaland	0.152
Orissa	1.552
Punjab	3.081
Rajasthan	4.772
Sikkim	0.008
Tamil Nadu	6.924
Tripura	0.038
Uttar Pradesh	15.174
West Bengal	7.267
Total	**100.000**

Source: *First Report of the Ninth Finance Commission*, July 1988, p. 40.

2. Moratorium on the interest payment and repayment of principal due in 1989-90 in respect of special loans given to Punjab during 1984-89 should be continued during 1989-90 also.

3. The loans already advanced and those proposed to be advanced to Madhya Pradesh in connection with the Bhopal Gas Tragedy should be converted into interest-free loans to be set off against the compensation as and when received from the Union Carbide Limited. There should also be moratorium on the repayment of the principal as well as interest falling due in 1989-90 in respect of those loans.

Table 23.6: Amounts of Margin Money Fixed by the Ninth Finance Commission

State	Amount of Margin Money (Rs. crore)
Andhra Pradesh	43.25
Arunachal Pradesh	0.25
Assam	13.00
Bihar	33.75
Goa	0.25
Gujarat	28.75
Haryana	5.75
Himachal Pradesh	3.25
Jammu and Kashmir	2.75
Karnataka	6.00
Kerala	9.00
Madhya Pradesh	6.00
Maharashtra	13.00
Manipur	0.50
Meghalaya	0.50
Mizoram	0.50
Nagaland	0.25
Orissa	46.25
Punjab	10.75
Rajasthan	16.75
Sikkim	0.50
Tamil Nadu	15.50
Tripura	1.50
Uttar Pradesh	57.25
West Bengal	23.75
Total	**339.00**

Source: *First Report of the Ninth Finance Commission*, July 1988, p. 41.

4. The Government of India should take the final view on the action plan involving an outlay of Rs. 371.29 crore submitted by the Government of Madhya Pradesh to finance relief activities including medical, economic, social and environmental rehabilitation in connection with the Bhopal gas leak tragedy. Union Government's decision on items and the scale of expenditure should be made available to the Commission by September, 1988." [3]

23.3.7 Grants-in-aid of Revenues: Recommendations of the Commission in this regard were as follows.

1. To cover the deficits on non-Plan revenue account, grants-in-aid under the substantive part of clause (1) of Article 275 of the Constitution were recommended as shown in Table 23.7.

Table 23.7: Grants-in-aid of Revenues of the States as Recommended by the Ninth Finance Commission for the Year 1989-90

State	**Amount (Rs. Crore)**
Arunachal Pradesh	70.44
Assam	140.05
Goa	16.68
Himachal Pradesh	98.72
Jammu and Kashmir	191.89
Manipur	66.79
Meghalaya	47.61
Mizoram	80.67
Nagaland	79.78
Orissa	57.14
Rajasthan	38.82
Sikkim	13.86
Tripura	81.61
Total	984.06

Source: *First Report of the Ninth Finance Commission*, July 1988, p. 50.

2. For meeting the requirements of the revenue component of the State Plan, grants-in-aid were recommended as shown in Table 23.8.
3. Grants-in-aid to cover the requirements of upgradation and special problems recommended by the Commission are shown in Table 23.9.

Table 23.8: Grants-in-aid Recommended by the Ninth Finance Commission for Meeting the Revenue Component of the State Plans for the Year 1989-90

State	Amount (Rs. crore)
Andhra Pradesh	116.10
Arunachal Pradesh	118.50
Assam	151.86
Bihar	165.48
Goa	28.84
Gujarat	48.12
Haryana	13.86
Himachal Pradesh	133.27
Jammu and Kashmir	148.85
Karnataka	63.38
Kerala	57.68
Madhya Pradesh	115.84
Maharashtra	92.53
Manipur	128.25
Meghalaya	111.19
Mizoram	79.94
Nagaland	106.97
Orissa	70.62
Punjab	10.72
Rajasthan	89.78
Sikkim	58.83
Tamil Nadu	96.51
Tripura	154.46
Uttar Pradesh	234.06
West Bengal	79.88
Total	**2475.52**

Source: *First Report of the Ninth Finance Commission*, July 1988, p. 51.

4. Grants-in-aid recommended by the Commission to meet the margin money requirements of States are shown in Table 23.10.

Table 23.9: Grants-in-aid Recommended by the Ninth Finance Commission for Upgradation and Special Problems

State	For upgradation	For special problems	Total
Andhra Pradesh	10.75	20.44	31.19
Arunachal Pradesh	2.55	12.78	15.33
Assam	11.97	-	11.97
Bihar	24.01	41.07	65.08
Goa	2.55	3.00	5.55
Haryana	-	24.88	24.88
Himachal Pradesh	3.43	10.20	13.63
Jammu & Kashmir	11.35	33.98	45.33
Karnataka	-	12.64	12.64
Kerala	2.11	-	2.11
Madhya Pradesh	19.61	22.17	41.78
Maharashtra	-	50.00	50.00
Manipur	5.78	0.80	6.58
Meghalaya	4.21	-	4.21
Mizoram	2.55	14.50	17.05
Nagaland	3.37	14.50	17.87
Orissa	18.22	10.58	28.80
Punjab	-	89.01	89.01
Rajasthan	6.06	23.37	29.43
Sikkim	0.50	2.70	3.20
Tamil Nadu	-	25.00	25.00
Tripura	2.74	0.32	3.06
Uttar Pradesh	18.44	69.61	88.05
West Bengal	21.47	70.00	91.47
Total	**171.67**	**551.55**	**723.22**

Source: *First Report of the Ninth Finance Commission*, July 1988, p. 58.

23.4 Second Report (for the years 1990-91 to 1994-95)

The Commission made recommendations regarding the distribution between the Union and the States of the net proceeds of income tax and Union excise duties and the allocation among the States of their respective shares of such proceeds. It also made recommendations on two additional issues: (a) the principles on which the shares of the net proceeds of additional duties of excise in lieu of sales tax should be distributed among the States and their *inter se* shares therefrom and (b) the principles which should govern the distribution among the States of grants to be made available to them in lieu of the repealed Railway Passenger Fares Tax Act, 1957, and a few related issues.

Table 23.10: Grants-in-aid Recommended by the Ninth Finance Commission for Meeting the Margin Money Requirements of the States

State	Amount (Rs. Crore)
Andhra Pradesh	21.625
Arunachal Pradesh	0.125
Assam	6.500
Bihar	16.875
Goa	0.125
Gujarat	14.375
Haryana	2.875
Himachal Pradesh	1.625
Jammu and Kashmir	1.375
Karnataka	3.000
Kerala	4.500
Madhya Pradesh	3.000
Maharashtra	6.500
Manipur	0.250
Meghalaya	0.250
Mizoram	0.250
Nagaland	0.125
Orissa	23.125
Punjab	5.375
Rajasthan	8.375
Sikkim	0.250
Tamil Nadu	7.750
Tripura	0.750
Uttar Pradesh	28.625
West Bengal	11.875
Total	**169.500**

Source: *First Report of the Ninth Finance Commission*, July 1988, p. 58.

23.4.1 Sharing of Income Tax: With the enactment of the Finance Act,

1989, the extension of the Income Tax Act, 1961, to Sikkim from the assessment year 1990-91 onwards was formalised. Therefore, the State-wise shares of income tax that the Commission prescribed included the share of Sikkim also.

The Commission was required to prescribe the shares of the Union Territories in the divisible pool of income tax under Article 270(3) of the Constitution. All the Union Territories were treated notionally together as one unit for the purpose of its scheme of devolution and it prescribed the share of Union Territories at 1.437 per cent.

It may be recalled that in its first report, the Commission had retained the States' share at 85 per cent of the divisible pool. Almost all State Governments had asked for the enlargement of the States' share beyond the level of 85 per cent. However, the Commission did not consider it necessary to increase the States' share beyond 85 per cent.

As regards the criteria to be adopted for the distribution of income tax among the States, the Commission had assigned a weight of 10 per cent to *contribution* factor in its first report which was retained in the second report. After considering other factors, the Commission finally recommend that the shareable proceeds of income tax be distributed among the States in the following manner.

1. 10 per cent on the basis of *contribution* as measured by the assessment of income tax for the years 1985-86 to 1987-88.
2. 45 per cent on the basis of *distance* of the per capita income of a State from that of the State with the highest per capita income multiplied by the 1971 population of the State concerned.
3. 22.5 per cent on the basis of the population of the State in 1971.
4. 11.25 per cent on the basis of composite index of backwardness compiled by the Commission.
5. 11.25 per cent on the basis of the inverse of per capita income multiplied by the population of the State in 1971.

To sum up, the Commission made the following recommendations as regards the sharing of income tax between the Centre and the States and the States' share amongst the States for the period 1990-91 to 1994-95.

1. Out of the net distributable proceeds of income tax, a sum equal to 1.437 per cent be deemed to represent the proceeds attributable to Union Territories.
2. Share of net income tax proceeds assigned to the States be 85 per cent.
3. Distribution among the States of the share assigned to each of them in each financial year should be on the basis of the percentages shown (Table 23.11).

23.4.2 Distribution of Additional Excise Duties in Lieu of Sales Tax: The Commission had expressed the view in its first report that since the additional duties of excise were levied in lieu of sales tax which itself was a tax on consumption, the shares of various States should correspond to their shares in the consumption of these commodities (textiles, sugar and tobacco).

Table 23.11: Percentage Shares of the States in the Net Proceeds of Income Tax Assigned to the States as Recommended by the Ninth Finance Commission for the Period 1990-91 to 1994-95

State	Percentage share
Andhra Pradesh	8.208
Arunachal Pradesh	0.073
Assam	2.631
Bihar	12.418
Goa	0.110
Gujarat	4.550
Haryana	1.244
Himachal Pradesh	0.595
Jammu and Kashmir	0.695
Karnataka	4.928
Kerala	3.729
Madhya Pradesh	8.185
Maharashtra	8.191
Manipur	0.171
Meghalaya	0.208
Mizoram	0.073
Nagaland	0.096
Orissa	4.326
Punjab	1.706
Rajasthan	4.836
Sikkim	0.030
Tamil Nadu	7.931
Tripura	0.303
Uttar Pradesh	16.787
West Bengal	7.976
Total	**100.000**

Source: *Second Report of the Ninth Finance Commission*, December 1989, p. 19.

In the absence of reliable data of State-wise consumption of these commodities, it had to rely on proxies, namely SDP and population of the respective States. It assigned equal weights to SDP and population in determining the shares of the individual States in the net proceeds of additional duties of excise. The share of the Union Territories was fixed at 1.903 per cent. The balance should be distributed among the States in each year in accordance with the percentage shares prescribed by the Commission (Table 23.12).

Table 23.12: Distribution of Additional Duties of Excise among the States as Recommended by the Ninth Finance Commission for the Period 1990-91 to 1994-95

State	Percentage Share
Andhra Pradesh	7.680
Arunachal Pradesh	0.107
Assam	2.743
Bihar	8.317
Goa	0.228
Gujarat	5.905
Haryana	2.317
Himachal Pradesh	0.621
Jammu and Kashmir	0.929
Karnataka	5.865
Kerala	3.723
Madhya Pradesh	7.164
Maharashtra	11.886
Manipur	0.213
Meghalaya	0.190
Mizoram	0.068
Nagaland	0.120
Orissa	3.486
Punjab	3.533
Rajasthan	4.689
Sikkim	0.052
Tamil Nadu	7.064
Tripura	0.278
Uttar Pradesh	14.657
West Bengal	8.165
Total	**100.000**

Source: *Second Report of the Ninth Finance Commission*, December 1989, p. 20.

23.4.3 Grant in Lieu of Tax on Railway Passenger Fares: This tax was first imposed in 1957 and was repealed in 1961. In fact, the tax was merged with the basic fare and the grant was introduced only to compensate the States for the consequential loss of revenue. The tax was revived in 1971 and again repealed in 1973. The Seventh Commission adopted the formula of distribution of the grant in proportion to the non-suburban passenger earnings from traffic originating in each State. The Eight Commission endorsed this practice. That Commission found it only logical that the taxable event being the payment of fare, the States should get the grant on the basis of the fare, paid within their boundaries. The route or the length of the journey was not material. The Commission under study agreed with the logic adopted by the Seventh and the Eighth Commissions. However, it recommended an increase in the size of the grant from the then existing level of Rs. 95 crore to Rs. 150 crore annually for the period 1990-91 to 1994-95. Shares of the States in each year were prescribed as shown in Table 23.13.

Table 23.13: Percentage Share of Each State in Grant in Lieu of Tax on Railway Passenger Fares for the Period 1990-91 to 1994-95

State	Percentage Share
Andhra Pradesh	7.484
Arunachal Pradesh	0.008
Assam	1.509
Bihar	8.266
Goa	0.133
Gujarat	5.717
Haryana	1.637
Himachal Pradesh	0.098
Jammu and Kashmir	0.520
Karnataka	3.271
Kerala	3.562
Madhya Pradesh	6.061
Maharashtra	22.634
Manipur	0.013
Meghalaya	0.040
Mizoram	-
Nagaland	0.165

Contd...

Orissa	1.614
Punjab	3.110
Rajasthan	4.579
Sikkim	0.004
Tamil Nadu	6.893
Tripura	0.042
Uttar Pradesh	15.437
West Bengal	7.203
Total	**100.000**

Source: *Second Report of the Ninth Finance Commission*, December 1989, p. 21.

23.4.4 Union Excise Duties: In its first report, the Commission had recommended that 40 per cent of the net proceeds of excise duties should be distributed among all the States to take care of the revenue needs of the States in general. Another 5 per cent was earmarked to help the deficit States so that their non-Plan revenue deficits could be reduced. Making a departure from this approach, it recommended distribution of the entire amount of 45 per cent as consolidated amount without dividing it into two components of 40 per cent and 5 per cent. The Commission also revised the formula of devolution adopted in its first report. Accordingly, it recommended that the distribution among the States during 1990-91 to 1994-95 of 45 per cent of the net proceeds of Union excise duties be done in the following manner:

1. 25 per cent on the basis of 1971 population.
2. 12.5 per cent on the basis of Income Adjusted Total Population (IATP). [4]
3. 12.5 per cent on the basis of the index of backwardness.
4. 33.5 per cent on the basis of *distance* of per capita income (New Series) of a State during the triennium 1982-83 to 1984-85 from that of the State having the highest per capita income, i.e. Punjab, multiplied by its 1971 population.
5. The remaining 16.5 per cent be distributed among the States with deficits, after taking into account their shares from the income tax, excise duties, additional excise duties in lieu of sales tax•and the grant in lieu of the repealed tax on railway passenger fares. Distribution should take place on the basis of the proportion of deficit of each State to the total of all States' deficits worked out by the Commission.

The percentage share of each State as worked out by the Commission for each of the year during 1990-91 to 1994-95 is given in Table 23.14.

Table 23.14: Distribution of States' Share of Excise Duties among the States as Recommended by the Ninth Finance Commission for the Period 1990-91 to 1994-95

State	Percentage Share
Andhra Pradesh	7.170
Arunachal Pradesh	0.897
Assam	3.810
Bihar	11.028
Goa	0.523
Gujarat	3.183
Haryana	1.099
Himachal Pradesh	1.943
Jammu and Kashmir	3.548
Karnataka	4.104
Kerala	3.087
Madhya Pradesh	7.224
Maharashtra	5.185
Manipur	1.174
Meghalaya	0.891
Mizoram	1.109
Nagaland	1.348
Orissa	5.358
Punjab	1.362
Rajasthan	5.524
Sikkim	0.260
Tamil Nadu	6.379
Tripura	1.556
Uttar Pradesh	15.638
West Bengal	6.600
Total	**100.000**

Source: *Second Report of the Ninth Finance Commission*, December 1989, p. 22.

23.4.5 Financing of Relief Expenditure: The Commission made the following significant recommendations as regards the system of financing of relief expenditure.

1. "The existing arrangements for financing relief expenditure should be replaced by a new one under which the States will have much greater

autonomy and accountability.

2. A Calamity Relief Fund should be constituted for each State with the amount in each year as indicated (Table 23.15).
3. Government of India shall contribute to the Calamity Relief Fund of each State to the extent of 75 per cent in the form of non-Plan grant. The balance 25 per cent shall be contributed by each State out of its own resources. The contribution to the Fund will be made by Governments in quarterly instalments.
4. The Relief Fund would have existence outside the general revenues of the State and will be deposited in a nationalised bank.
5. A State-level Committee headed by the Chief Secretary of the State and consisting of officials connected with the relief work and other experts shall be constituted by the State Government to administer the Calamity Relief Fund. The Committee will decide all matters connected with the financing of the relief expenditure, including variations in the norms of assistance.
6. The yearly accretion to the Fund together with the interest accruing thereon would be used to meet all expenditure on calamities. No further Central assistance would be made available for the purpose. However, if in a particular year the money required is more than the balance available in the Fund, the State may draw 25 per cent of the Centre's contribution due to it in the following year in advance. (The Central Government may, at its discretion, allow higher percentage of advance also).
7. The balance left in the Fund unspent at the end of fifth year (i.e. 1994-95) will be available for being used as a Plan resource.
8. All calamities such as drought, flood, cyclone and fire which qualified for relief assistance in the past will continue to be covered in the present scheme. The distinction between drought and other calamities like flood, cyclone etc. will be dispensed with.
9. The Centre should constitute an Export Group to monitor relief work done in States utilising the Calamity Relief Fund and also to give such advice as it deems appropriate to the State agencies involved in relief work.
10. The Centre should contribute 75 per cent of the relief expenditure (over and above its contribution to the Calamity Relief Fund) of Rs. 163 crore on relief and rehabilitation of gas victims in Bhopal, during 1990-95 by way of non-Plan grant. The balance 25 per cent will be borne by the Government of Madhya Pradesh." [5]

23.4.6 Grants-in-aid of Revenues: To cover the net five-year (1990-91 to 1994-95) deficits on non-Plan revenue account and part of the deficits on plan revenue account, the Commission recommended grants-in-aid of the revenues of various States (Table 23.16) under the substantive part of Clause (1) of Article 275 of the Constitution

Table 23.15: Calamity Relief Fund Recommended by the Ninth Finance Commission for Each State with Amount in Each Year

State	Amount (Rs. crore)
Andhra Pradesh	86
Arunachal Pradesh	2
Assam	30
Bihar	35
Goa	1
Gujarat	85
Haryana	17
Himachal Pradesh	18
Jammu and Kashmir	12
Karnataka	27
Kerala	31
Madhya Pradesh	37
Maharashtra	44
Manipur	1
Meghalaya	2
Mizoram	1
Nagaland	1
Orissa	47
Punjab	28
Rajasthan	124
Sikkim	3
Tamil Nadu	39
Tripura	3
Uttar Pradesh	90
West Bengal	40
Total	**804**

Source: *Second Report of the Ninth Finance Commission*, December 1989, p. 44.

Grants-in-aid to the States in each of the five years commencing from April 1, 1990 were also recommended by the Commission as Centre's contribution towards Calamity Relief Fund suggested by it (Table 23.17).

Table 23.16: Grants-in-aid of Revenues of the States as Recommended by the Ninth Finance Commission

State	1990-95	1990-91	1991-92	1992-93	1993-94	1994-95
Andhra Pradesh	341.25	46.07	54.60	66.54	78.49	95.55
Arunachal Pradesh	302.79	57.65	59.45	60.76	61.48	63.45
Assam	874.23	205.61	179.68	172.87	161.42	154.65
Bihar	1374.27	185.53	219.88	267.98	316.08	384.80
Goa	166.58	33.66	33.31	33.06	32.88	33.67
Himachal Pradesh	523.09	113.75	109.67	104.50	98.32	96.85
Jammu & Kashmir	1096.42	210.99	213.60	224.35	220.87	226.61
Kerala	412.54	55.69	66.01	80.45	94.88	115.51
Madhya Pradesh	1047.81	141.45	167.65	204.32	241.00	293.39
Manipur	371.65	74.92	74.90	74.40	73.32	74.11
Meghalaya	256.18	58.88	50.32	51.27	48.54	47.17
Mizoram	379.79	74.75	76.22	76.16	76.43	76.23
Nagaland	458.67	92.26	92.48	93.88	90.54	89.51
Orissa	1082.98	146.20	173.28	211.18	249.09	303.23
Punjab	53.91	7.28	8.63	10.51	12.40	15.09
Rajasthan	1446.79	195.32	231.49	282.12	332.76	405.10
Sikkim	84.68	17.59	17.37	17.03	16.50	16.19
Tamil Nadu	43.79	5.91	7.01	8.54	10.07	12.26
Tripura	466.01	101.19	101.27	96.52	87.25	79.78
Uttar Pradesh	3235.10	436.74	517.62	630.84	744.07	905.83
West Bengal	998.65	134.82	159.78	194.74	229.69	279.62
Total	**15017.18**	**2396.26**	**2614.22**	**2962.02**	**3276.08**	**3768.60**

Source: *Second Report of the Ninth Finance Commission*, December 1989, p. 45.

Table 23.17: Grants-in-aid Recommended by the Ninth Finance Commission as Centre's Contribution towards Calamity Relief Fund

State	Amount of Grant (Rs. crore)
Andhra Pradesh	64.50
Arunachal Pradesh	1.50
Assam	22.50
Bihar	26.25
Goa	0.75
Gujarat	63.75
Haryana	12.75
Himachal Pradesh	13.50
Jammu and Kashmir	9.00
Karnataka	20.25
Kerala	23.25
Madhya Pradesh	27.75
Maharashtra	33.00
Manipur	0.75
Meghalaya	1.50
Mizoram	0.75
Nagaland	0.75
Orissa	35.25
Punjab	21.00
Rajasthan	93.00
Sikkim	2.25
Tamil Nadu	29.25
Tripura	2.25
Uttar Pradesh	67.50
West Bengal	30.00
Total	**603.00**

Source: *Second Report of the Ninth Finance Commission*, December 1989, p. 45.

The Commission recommended an amount of Rs. 122.25 crore for Madhya Pradesh by way of grants-in-aid of revenue in five equal instalments commencing from April 1, 1990, towards the expenditure on rehabilitation and relief of victims of Bhopal Gas Leak Tragedy.

23.4.7 Debt Relief: After detailed examination of the debt position of the States, the Commission made the following recommendations in this regard.

1. "The formula of 70:30 for the apportionment of the Plan assistance in the case of non-Special Category States may be continued. But the loan component so worked out may be contributed from two sources – an amount equal to the grant portion may come in the form of Central loan and the balance may be made available by way of additional market borrowings.
2. The Reserve Bank of India may work out a formula for amortisation of States' market borrowings.
3. From 1990-91, the direct Central loans for State Plans should have a maturity period of 20 years with 50 per cent of the loans enjoying grace period of 5 years.
4. There should be no change in the terms and conditions relating to the Central loans against the small savings collections.
5. The entire external assistance received for externally-aided projects should, in all cases, be passed on to the States implementing those projects. No part of funds received exclusively for such projects should be withheld by the Centre.
6. The loan and grant portion of the World Bank assistance to be passed on to States should also be in the ratio of 70:30 as in the case of general Plan assistance. However, while the loan portion should carry the same rate of interest as applicable to other Plan loans, the repayment period should be the same as applicable to the assistance received from the Bank.
7. The entire amount of IDA assistance shall be passed on to the States as loans carrying a rate of interest of 6 per cent per annum and repayment period of 30 years including a grace period of 5 years.
8. The States with unduly low share in assistance for externally aided projects should be allocated a larger share of the 10 per cent of the Plan assistance reserved for 'Special problems' under the modified Gadgil formula.
9. The Central loans obtained on Plan account by each of the three newly constituted States of Arunachal Pradesh, Goa and Mizoram, up to 1986-87 as Union Territories (as outstanding on 31st March 1990), in excess of what it would have received during that period by way of loan on the basis of the 90:10 or 30:70 formula applicable to States, should be written off.
10. The loans given to States on account of drought during 1986-89 as outstanding on 31st March, 1989 shall be written of.
11. The loans of Rs. 91.62 crore given to Madhya Pradesh during 1984-89 in connection with the Bhopal Gas Leak Tragedy shall be written off and repayment or payment on account thereof made already by the State Government by way of principal and interest shall be adjusted against other payments due from the State Government.

12. A moratorium of 2 years (1990-92) on repayment of principal and payment of interest should be granted in respect of the special loans given to Punjab during 1984-89. Meanwhile, the Central Government should work out a suitable package of relief measures for the State.
13. The State Plan loans advanced to States during the 5 years 1984-89 and outstanding as on 31st March 1990 should be consolidated and rescheduled to 15 years in the case of all the States. During the first 5 years 1990-95, repayments should be less than due on existing basis to the extent of 10 per cent in the case of Andhra Pradesh, Karnataka, Madhya Pradesh, Maharashtra, Orissa, Tamil Nadu, Goa and Special Category States, 7.5 per cent in the case of Gujarat, Rajasthan and Uttar Pradesh and 5 per cent in the case of Bihar, Haryana, Kerala, Punjab and West Bengal." [6]

Notes

1. *Second Report of the Ninth Finance Commission*, December 1989, p. 4.
2. *Ibid.*, p. 54.
3. *First Report of the Ninth Finance Commission*, July 1988, p. 57.
4. For calculating IATP, the 1971 population of the States was to be weighted with the inverse of the average per capita income as per the New Series for the triennium 1982-83 to 1984-85. The share of a State was to be determined by the percentage of the Income Adjusted Total Population of that State to the aggregate of the income adjusted total population of all States.
5. *Second Report of the Ninth Finance Commission*, December 1989, p. 44.
6. Ibid., pp. 45-46.

24

Tenth Finance Commission

This Finance Commission, tenth since the commencement of the Constitution, was constituted by the Order of the President dated June 15, 1992. The Commission was asked to make recommendations relating to the following matters.

Summary Statement	
Chairman	Mr. K.C. Pant
Members	Dr. Debi Prosad Pal Shri B.P.R. Vithal Dr. C. Rangarajan Shri M.C. Gupta
Year and month of establishment	June 1992
Year and month of reporting	November 1994
Period of award	1995-96 to 1999-2000
Main Recommendations	
• States' share in income tax fixed at (per cent): 77.5 • Bases of distribution of States' share in income tax inter se (per cent): Population: 20; Contribution: Nil; Other factors: 80 • States' share in Union excise duties fixed at (per cent): 47.5 • Bases of distribution of States' share in Union excise duties inter se (per cent): Population: 20; Other factors: 80	

(a) Distribution between the Union and the States of the net proceeds of taxes which are to be, or may be divided between them and the allocation between the States of the respective shares of such proceeds.

(b) Principles which should govern the grants-in-aid of the revenues of the States out of the Consolidated Fund of India and the sums to be paid to the States which are in need of assistance by way of grants-in-aid of their revenues under article 275 of the Constitution for purposes other than those specified in the provisos to clause (1) of that article.

In making its recommendations, the Commission was required to have regard to following considerations.

1. The objective of not only balancing the receipts and expenditure on revenue account of both the States and the Central Government, but also generating surplus for capital investment and reducing fiscal deficit.
2. The resources of the Central Government and the demands thereon, in particular, on account of expenditure on civil administration, defence and border security, debt-servicing and other committed expenditure or liabilities.
3. The maintenance and upkeep of capital assets and maintenance expenditure on plan schemes to be completed by March 31, 1995 and the norms on the basis of which specified amounts are recommended for the maintenance of the capital assets and the manner of monitoring such expenditure.
4. The requirements of States for modernization of administration, e.g. computerization of land records and providing faster channels of communication up to and above district level, and for upgrading the standards in non-developmental sectors and services, and the manner in which such expenditure can be monitored.
5. The revenue resources of the States for the five years commencing on April 1, 1995, on the basis of the levels of taxation likely to be reached in 1993-94, targets set for additional resource mobilization for the Plan and the potential for raising additional taxes.
6. The requirements of the States for meeting the Non-Plan revenue expenditure also keeping in view the potential for raising additional taxes.
7. The tax efforts made by the States.
8. The need for ensuring reasonable returns on investment by the States in irrigation projects, power projects, state transport undertakings, departmental commercial undertakings, public sector enterprises etc.
9. The scope for better fiscal management consistent with efficiency and economy in expenditure.

The Commission was also asked to suggest changes, if any, in the principles governing the distribution of (a) the net proceeds in any financial year of the additional excise duties leviable under the Additional Duties of Excise (Goods of Special Importance) Act, 1957, in replacement of the sales tax levied formerly by the State Governments and (b) the grants to be made available to the States in lieu of the tax under the repealed Railway Passenger Fares Act, 1957.

Furthermore, in making its recommendations on the various maters aforesaid, the Commission was required to adopt the population figures of 1971 in all cases where population was regarded as a factor for determination of devolution of taxes and duties and grants-in-aid.

24.1 Alternative Formula of Devolution

It is noteworthy that the Government dropped the *normative approach* (which was in the guidelines of the Ninth Finance Commission) from the terms of reference of the Commission under study. It was replaced by the *gap-filling approach*.

The Commission recommended an alternative scheme of devolution, i.e. a system of vertical resource sharing under which Central taxes were to be pooled and a proportion thereof devolved to the States. It recommended a share of 26 per cent for States in the gross receipts of Central taxes. It further recommended that the tax rental arrangement (i.e. additional duties of excise in lieu of sales tax) should be terminated, and additional excise duties merged with basic excise duties. If this was done, a further share of 3 per cent in the gross tax receipts of the Centre should accrue to the States. This share (26 + 3 = 29 per cent), based on the amounts currently accruing to the States, should be suitably provided for in the Constitution and reviewed once in 15 years. The Commission recommended that the alternative scheme of resource sharing suggested by it may be brought into force with effect from April 1, 1996 after necessary amendments to the Constitution.

The Commission claimed the following benefits of the alternative scheme of devolution suggested by it: "(a) With a given share being allotted to the States in the aggregate revenues from Central taxes, States will be able to share the aggregate buoyancy of Central taxes. (b) The Central Government can pursue tax reforms without the need to consider whether a tax is shareable with the States or not. (c) The impact of fluctuations in Central tax revenues would be felt alike by the Central and State Governments. (d) should the taxes mentioned in article 268 and/or 269 form part of this arrangement, there will be a greater likelihood of their being tapped." [1]

However, this scheme of Commission overlooked the standard principles of tax assignment and tax sharing in a federal polity. Moreover, it was not clear whether the contemplated 29 per cent of the States' share would be distributed *inter se* on the basis of one formula or a separate formula would be followed as hitherto for the distribution of additional duties of excise in lieu of sales tax. The basis for the distribution of additional excise duties among the States had traditionally been different. In his 1997-98 budget speech the Finance Minister announced the acceptance of the Tenth Finance Commission's alternative formula for devolution of resources from the Centre to the States.

24.2 Sharing of Income tax

The Commission recommended that the share attributable to the Union

Territories in the net distributable proceeds of income tax for each of the financial years during 1995-96 to 1999-2000 should be 0.927 per cent.

Regarding the share of the States in the net proceeds of income tax, it may be recalled that the States' share out of the net proceeds of income tax was fixed at 55 per cent by the First Finance Commission. The succeeding three Commissions enlarged the share progressively to 60 per cent, 66.66 per cent and 75 per cent. While recommending the increase in the States' share, the Third and Fourth Commissions took due note of the representation of the States about the need for making good in some measure the loss sustained by them on account of the non-inclusion of corporation tax in the divisible pool consequent upon the reclassification brought about in the Income Tax Act in 1959.

The Fifth Commission did not recommend any further increase in the States share, on the ground that the divisible pool of income tax would for the first time also include advance tax collections. Arrears pertaining to the advance tax collections were distributed among the States in three instalments during the period covered by the recommendations of that Commission. The Sixth Commission raised the States' share from 75 to 80 per cent taking into consideration various factors including the fact that the arrears referred to above were no longer available. The share of the States was further increased to 85 per cent by the Seventh Commission keeping in view the States grievance in regard to the levy of surcharge by the Centre as a normal tax revenue measure. The Eight and the Ninth Commissions maintained it at 85 per cent.

Having considered this matter at length, the Commission came to the conclusion that the following two considerations should guide its recommendations in this regard: (a) that the authority that levies and administers the tax should have a significant and tangible interest in its yield and (b) that any change in the share on this account should not materially affect the level of overall devolution to the States. In other words, any downward revision in the share of States in the net proceeds of income tax should be mirrored in a revenue equivalent increase in their share in the net proceeds of Union excise duties. Accordingly, it recommended that the share of States in the net proceeds of income tax be fixed at 77.5 per cent. Simultaneously, it recommended a suitable increase in the share of the States in Union excise duties.

24.3 Sharing of Union Excise Duties

To recapitulate, the sharing of Union excise duties started with the First Finance Commission itself, although the beginning was modest. It was restricted to 40 per cent of just three commodities, viz. tobacco, matches and vegetable products. After that the sharing of the net proceeds of Union excise duties became a regular feature, with successive Finance Commissions devolving larger amounts to the States, through either upward revisions of the coverage of the shareable items, or by increasing the magnitude of the States' share. The Second Commission extended the list of shareable commodities to eight but reduced the States' share to 25 per cent. The Third Commission reduced the States' share to 20 per cent but enlarged the list of shareable items to 35, the yield from each of which was Rs. 50 lakh or more per year.

Beginning with the Fourth Finance Commission, the coverage of items for States' share had been almost total, but the States' share was limited to 20 per cent. The Seventh Finance Commission doubled the States' share to 40 per cent on the ground that if the States had sufficient resources with them their dependence on the Centre would be reduced. The Eight Finance Commission raised this share to 45 per cent, but the increment of 5 per cent was used for meeting the assessed post-devolution deficits of the States. The Ninth Finance Commission maintained the overall share at 45 per cent, but used 5 per cent and 7.425 per cent from it for deficit-based devolution, in its First and Second Reports, respectively. In other words, the portion of the net proceeds of Union excise duties from which all States received a share was 40 per cent for the Eight Finance Commission. It remained so in the one year (1989-90) report of the Ninth Commission, but it was reduced to 37.575 per cent in its second report pertaining to the period 1990-91 to 1994-95.

Taking into account the views of the Central and the State Governments in the matter, and having recommended a decrease in the States' share in the net proceeds of income tax, the Commission under review recommended that the share of States in the net proceeds of Union excise duties be raised to 47.5 per cent.

24.4 Distribution of Divisible Amounts

The Commission based its criteria for determining the *inter se* shares of the States in the shareable proceeds of income tax on the following indices.

1. 20 per cent on the basis of population of 1971.
2. 60 per cent on the basis of distance of per capita income.
3. 5 per cent on the basis of *area adjusted*.
4. 5 per cent on the basis of index of infrastructure.
5. 10 per cent on the basis of tax efforts.

Thus, it recommended as follows for each financial year in the period 1995-96 to 1999-2000.

(a) Out of the net distributable proceeds of income tax, a sum equal to 0.927 per cent be deemed to represent the proceeds attributable to Union Territories.

(b) The share of the net proceeds of income tax assigned to the States be 77.5 per cent.

(c) The distribution among States of the share assigned to them in each financial year be on the basis of the percentages shown (Table 24.1).

Table 24.1: Percentage Shares of the States in the Net Proceeds of Income Tax Assigned to the States as Recommended by the Tenth Finance Commission

State	Per cent
Andhra Pradesh	8.465
Arunachal Pradesh	0.170
Assam	2.784
Bihar	12.861
Goa	0.180
Gujarat	4.046
Haryana	1.238
Himachal Pradesh	0.704
Jammu & Kashmir	1.097
Karnataka	5.339
Kerala	3.875
Madhya Pradesh	8.290
Maharashtra	6.126
Manipur	0.282
Meghalaya	0.283
Mizoram	0.149
Nagaland	0.181
Orissa	4.495
Punjab	1.461
Rajasthan	5.551
Sikkim	0.126
Tamil Nadu	6.637
Tripura	0.378
Uttar Pradesh	17.811
West Bengal	7.471
Total	**100.000**

Source: *Report of the Tenth Finance Commission*, 1994, p. 25.

The Commission used the same set of criteria (i.e. as for income tax) for distribution of 40 per cent of the net proceeds of Union excise duties. Accordingly it recommended that 40 per cent of the net proceeds of Union excise duties during each financial year in the period 1995-96 to 1999-2000, should be distributed as per the share indicated (Table 24.2).

Table 24.2: Distribution of States' Share of Excise Duties among the States as Recommended by the Tenth Finance Commission

State	**Per cent**
Andhra Pradesh	8.465
Arunachal Pradesh	0.170
Assam	2.784
Bihar	12.861
Goa	0.180
Gujarat	4.046
Haryana	1.238
Himachal Pradesh	0.704
Jammu & Kashmir	1.097
Karnataka	5.339
Kerala	3.875
Madhya Pradesh	8.290
Maharashtra	6.126
Manipur	0.282
Meghalaya	0.283
Mizoram	0.149
Nagaland	0.181
Orissa	4.495
Punjab	1.461
Rajasthan	5.551
Sikkim	0.126
Tamil Nadu	6.637
Tripura	0.378
Uttar Pradesh	17.811
West Bengal	7.471
Total	**100.000**

Source: *Report of the Tenth Finance Commission*, 1994, p. 25.

It further recommended that the remaining 7.5 per cent of the net proceeds of Union excise duties be distributed among the States in accordance with the shares specified by it for each financial year in the period 1995-96 to 1999-2000 (Table 24.3).

Table 24.3: Distribution of the Remaining 7.5 Per Cent of the Net Proceeds of Excise Duties among the States as Recommended by the Tenth Finance Commission

(per cent)

State	1995-96	1996-97	1997-98	1998-99	1999-00
Andhra Pradesh	12.069	7.988	0.000	0.000	0.000
Arunachal Pradesh	3.410	4.300	5.871	6.224	6.667
Assam	8.543	9.836	11.849	10.748	9.290
Bihar	6.434	2.965	0.000	0.000	0.000
Goa	0.973	1.058	1.161	0.917	0.604
Himachal Pradesh	8.816	10.744	14.057	14.230	14.338
Jammu & Kashmir	13.366	16.491	21.985	22.741	23.700
Manipur	3.930	4.891	6.602	6.917	7.348
Meghalaya	3.590	4.403	5.815	5.994	6.130
Mizoram	3.676	4.628	6.278	6.784	7.074
Nagaland	5.818	7.417	10.247	11.072	12.025
Orissa	4.815	5.248	4.934	2.773	0.680
Rajasthan	0.835	0.000	0.000	0.000	0.000
Sikkim	1.199	1.473	1.938	1.982	2.055
Tripura	5.465	6.807	9.263	9.618	10.089
Uttar Pradesh	17.061	11.751	0.000	0.000	0.000
Total	100.00	100.00	100.00	100.00	100.00

Source: *Report of the Tenth Finance Commission*, 1994, p. 25.

24.5 Distribution of Additional Duties of Excise

In this regard the Commission observed, "In evolving our approach for the distribution of the States' shares, we have kept in view the basis adopted by the earlier Commissions, the views of the State Governments and the availability of reliable data for the proxies which would represent a fair approximation to the consumption of the three articles. The commodities on which additional excise duties are levied are articles of mass consumption and accordingly, in our view, population should have a substantial weight in the formula. We also agree with the views of the earlier Commissions that the level of State income has a significant bearing on the consumption of sugar, textiles and tobacco and should be a factor in distribution.

Since sales tax is a levy on consumption, some of the past Commissions have accepted proportion of sales tax revenues as capturing the consumption levels of the three commodities. Some of the States are of the same view. The other point of view is that since sales tax is levied on a host of commodities ranging from luxuries to raw materials, the proceeds of this tax do not represent the consumption levels of these three alone. Nevertheless, there is a relationship between consumption, as represented by sales tax, and consumption of these commodities. Accordingly, we feel some weight can be given to sales tax." [2]

Hence, the Commission worked out the shares of the States by assigning a weight of 50 per cent to population according to the 1991 census, 40 per cent to the average of state domestic product for the three latest years 1987-88 to 1989-90 for which the requisite data was available and 10 per cent to the average collection of State sales tax (excluding inter-State sales tax) for the three years 1990-91 to 1992-93, these being the latest three years for which final accounts were available. It agreed with the view of the Ninth Finance Commission that distribution of additional excise duty was not in the nature of devolution for which the population figures of 1971 census should be used as per its terms of reference. Hence, it used the latest census figures of 1991. As regards the share of the Union territories, the Commission agreed that their share be determined on the same basis as that of all the States. Accordingly, it fixed the share of Union territories at 2.203 per cent to be retained by the Central Government. The balance was distributed among the States as shown in Table 24.4.

24.6 Grants in Lieu of Tax on Railway Passenger Fares

The Commission agreed with the views expressed by most States that of the Eight Finance Commission that the grants should be equal to 10.7 per cent of the non-suburban railway passenger earnings. State-wise figures of non-suburban passenger earnings were made available to the Commission by the Ministry of Railways for the Year 1992-93. The total non-suburban passenger earnings for that year were Rs. 3540.82 crore. Hence, the Commission recommended that 10.7 per cent of this i.e. Rs. 380.00 crore be paid to the States annually during the period covered by its award.

Turning to the principles of distribution, the Commission was in agreement with the Seventh, Eight and Ninth Commissions which recommended distribution of the grant in proportion to the non-suburban passenger earnings from traffic originating in each State. The taxable event being the payment of fare, a State should get a grant in relation to the fare paid within its boundary. Considerations like route length etc. were immaterial in the opinion of the Commission. It also considered the views of States which did not have railway lines. In view of the clear position laid down in Article 269(1)(d) and Article 269(2)d of the Constitution, the Commission expressed its inability to accept the contention that such States ought to be compensated on the ground that the people of such States purchase tickets from stations falling within the boundaries of other States.

Table 24.4: Distribution of Additional Duties of Excise among the States as Recommended by the Tenth Finance Commission

State	**Per cent**
Andhra Pradesh	7.820
Arunachal Pradesh	0.104
Assam	2.483
Bihar	7.944
Goa	0.232
Gujarat	5.995
Haryana	2.366
Himachal Pradesh	0.595
Jammu & Kashmir	0.856
Karnataka	5.744
Kerala	3.740
Madhya Pradesh	7.236
Maharashtra	12.027
Manipur	0.197
Meghalaya	0.188
Mizoram	0.079
Nagaland	0.137
Orissa	3.345
Punjab	3.422
Rajasthan	4.873
Sikkim	0.053
Tamil Nadu	7.669
Tripura	0.286
Uttar Pradesh	14.573
West Bengal	8.036
Total	**100.000**

Source: *Report of the Tenth Finance Commission*, 1994, p. 28.

In short, the Commission made the following recommendations in the matter.

1. The quantum of the grant in lieu of the railway passenger fares tax for 1995-96 to 1999-2000 should be Rs. 380 crore annually.
2. Share of the States be allocated in the same proportion as the average of the non-suburban passenger earnings in each State during the years 1988-89 to 1992-93 bears to the average of the aggregate non-suburban earnings in all States in those years. On this basis the shares of the States were calculated as shown in Table 24.5.

24.7 Upgradation Grants

The Commission recommended a total sum of Rs. 2,608.50 crore as grants for upgradation and special problems for the period 1995-96 to 1999-2000.

24.8 Financing of Relief Expenditure

The amount worked out for this purpose for all the States for the period of the Commission's award was Rs. 6304.27 crore. Out of this, the Centre was required to contribute Rs. 4728.19 crore (75 per cent) and the States Rs. 1576.08 crore (25 per cent). The Commission recommended the continuation of the current scheme of the Calamity Relief Fund with modifications suggested by it.

In addition to the Calamity Relief Funds for States, the Commission proposed a National Fund for Calamity Relief to which the Centre and the States would contribute and which would be managed by a National Calamity Relief Committee on which both the Centre and the States would be represented. The size of the National Fund for Calamity Relief would be Rs. 700 crore, to be built up over the period 1995-96 to 1999-2000, with an initial corpus of Rs. 200 crore to which the Centre would contributed Rs. 150 crore and the States Rs. 50 crore in the proportion of 75:25. In addition, for each of the five years from 1995-96 to 1999-2000 the contributions of the Centre and the States would be Rs. 75 crore and Rs. 25 crore respectively. The contribution by both the Centre and the States would be made annually in the beginning of the financial year. Contribution of States *inter se* would be in the same proportion as their estimated total tax receipts after devolution.

24.9 Grants for Local Bodies

Breaking new grounds, the Commission observed and made recommendations in this regard as follows: "An estimate of financial needs for operation and maintenance of core municipal services in urban India made by the National Institute of Urban Affairs indicates that the estimated gap in 1995 worked out to Rs. 5,987 crore. It is expected to go up to Rs. 12,980 crore in the year 2000. While the accuracy of these estimates and the measures that the state and urban local bodies can adopt to bridge the gap are matters to be discussed and studied by the State Finance Commissions, we are of the view that a provision of Rs. 1,000 crore for the five year period covered by our recommendation will go a long way in enabling the urban local bodies to meet their primary obligations. The inter-State distribution of this sum is based on the inter-State ratio of the slum population derived from the urban population figures as per 1971 Census.

Table 24.5: Percentage Share of Each State in Grant in Lieu of Tax on Railway Passenger Fares

State	**Per cent**
Andhra Pradesh	8.345
Arunachal Pradesh	0.005
Assam	1.368
Bihar	9.326
Goa	0.194
Gujarat	6.901
Haryana	1.917
Himachal Pradesh	0.108
Jammu & Kashmir	0.728
Karnataka	3.388
Kerala	3.495
Madhya Pradesh	6.882
Maharashtra	17.548
Manipur	0.018
Meghalaya	0.034
Mizoram	0.001
Nagaland	0.145
Orissa	1.715
Punjab	3.280
Rajasthan	4.445
Sikkim	0.010
Tamil Nadu	6.458
Tripura	0.039
Uttar Pradesh	15.568
West Bengal	8.082
Total	**100.000**

Source: *Report of the Tenth Finance Commission*, 1994, p. 30.

While we have made these provisions for grant to panchayats/municipalities for the discharge of their enhanced responsibilities, this need not necessarily be a precedent for future Commissions. In any case after the report of the State Finance Commissions become available, the need for measures required for augmentation would have to be determined in terms of Article 280(3) of the Constitution. For the present, grants recommended by us should be made known to the State Finance Commissions. Further, these amounts should be an additionality over and above the amounts flowing to the local bodies from State. They should draw up suitable schemes with detailed guidelines for utilisation of the grant. The local bodies should be required to provide suitable matching contributions by raising resources. The grant is not intended for expenditure on salaries and wages. The total provision should be made available to the States in four equal instalments commencing from 1996-97, as the rural and urban local bodies are not likely to be fully functional prior to that." [3]

24.10 Grants-in-aid of Revenues [4]

After taking into account the transfers pertaining to taxes and duties, some States still emerged with residual deficits. Hence, the Commission recommended grants-in-aid to be given to the States, under the substantive portion of Article 275(1), equal to the amount of these deficits as estimated for each of the years during 1995-96 to 1999-2000. These amounts are shown in Table 24.6.

24.11 Debt Relief

The Commission recommended a scheme for debt relief in two parts.

1. A scheme for general debt relief for all States linked to fiscal performance.
2. Specific relief for States with high fiscal stress, special category States and States with debt problems warranting special attention.

In addition it recommended a scheme for encouraging retirement of debt from the proceeds of disinvestment of equity holdings of State Governments. It recommended specific relief for all special category States, and three other States, viz. Orissa, Bihar and Uttar Pradesh, which were characterised by high fiscal stress. For these States the Commission recommended writing-off of 5 per cent of repayment due with respect to fresh Central loans given during 1989-90 to 1994-95 and outstanding on March 31, 1995. Furthermore, it recommend the waiver of one-third of the repayment of principal falling due during 1995-96 to 1999-2000 on special term loans to Punjab in view of the special circumstances when these term loans were advanced and the need for the State to re-invigorate its development efforts.

Table 24.6: Grants-in-aid of Revenues of the States as Recommended by the Tenth Finance Commission

(Rs. crore)

State	1995-96	1996-97	1997-98	1998-99	1999-00	Total
Andhra Pradesh	483.47	202.98	0.00	0.00	0.00	686.45
Arunachal Pradesh	136.60	109.26	45.63	16.11	0.00	307.60
Assam	342.20	249.94	92.08	27.81	0.00	712.03
Bihar	257.72	75.34	0.00	0.00	0.00	333.06
Goa	38.98	26.88	9.03	2.37	0.00	77.26
Himachal Pradesh	353.11	273.00	109.25	36.82	0.00	772.18
Jammu & Kashmir	535.39	419.05	170.85	58.84	0.00	1184.13
Manipur	157.43	124.28	51.31	17.90	0.00	350.92
Meghalaya	143.83	111.89	45.19	15.51	0.00	316.42
Mizoram	147.25	117.60	48.79	17.55	0.00	331.19
Nagaland	233.04	188.46	79.63	28.65	0.00	529.78
Orissa	192.87	133.35	38.34	7.18	0.00	371.74
Rajasthan	33.45	0.00	0.00	0.00	0.00	33.45
Sikkim	48.05	37.45	15.06	5.13	0.00	105.69
Tripura	218.92	172.98	71.99	24.89	0.00	488.78
Uttar Pradesh	683.40	298.60	0.00	0.00	0.00	982.00
Total	**4005.71**	**2541.06**	**777.15**	**258.76**	**0.00**	**7582.68**

Source: *Report of the Tenth Finance Commission*, 1994, p. 51.

24.12 National Security

The terms of reference of the Commission under study required that in making its recommendations, it should have regard, among other factors, to the resources of the Central Government and the demands thereon, in particular, on account of expenditure on civil administration, defence and border security etc. Earlier Commissions were also required to take into account the demands of defence while assessing the resources of the Central Government.

The Commission, therefore, carried out a detailed study of the requirements of defence expenditure so as to accord it a proper weight while assessing the resources of the Centre. The in-house study on defence expenditure was, for reasons of confidentiality, forwarded separately to the Ministry of Defence with the expectation that the Ministry would take full advantage of the findings.

However, the Commission highlighted some of the broad conclusions of its findings which are quoted below.

1. "A large part of the allocations for defence are pre-empted by manpower costs and related expenditure. Since 1986-87, these have grown at an average rate of 13.4 per cent per annum. As against this the total defence budget during the last five years has grown annually only at an average of 11.9 per cent. It is important to protect the availability of funds for the purchase of hardware, particularly spares and equipment.
2. The expenditure on defence pensions has risen from Rs. 479.88 crore in 1984-85 to Rs. 2,706 crore in 1994-95. There is an urgent need to contain the rising bill on pensions.
3. Linked with the reduction in expenditure on pensions is also the consideration of reducing the age profile of combatant troops.
4. There is a need to examine the possibilities of optimal utilisation of available resources by prioritising defence expenditure. A pattern of inter-service allocation of resources best suited to obtain a balanced force structure, the need for adequate funding for spares replenishment and for training purposes, a cost-effective mix of weapon system, the balance between new acquisitions and upgradation of the existing hardware and facilities, more economical alternatives to current structures and capabilities etc. are some of the factors which need to be evaluated in the context of a comprehensive assessment of threats and security requirements of the country.
5. Since the defence and para-military forces have been quite often utilised on the maintenance of law and order duties in States, a revised balance should be evolved between the roles of local police, on the one hand, and that of the defence and para military forces on the other. If a holistic view of the internal and external security scenario is taken, it would suggest that the local law and order problems are best left to be dealt with by a strengthened local police force, suitably supplemented by the State's own armed police. It would reduce the strain placed on the resources of the para-military and defence forces.
6. Common recruitment and training of para-military forces engaged on the borders and combatant troops serving in the army would facilitate soldiers moving over to the para-military formations after an initial period of, say, seven years service. A certain percentage of vacancies in various government organisations in the States and at the Centre are already reserved for ex-servicemen. Full use should be made of these quotas to facilitate the absorption of servicemen. The defence ministry and the armed forces, who have a large number of non-combatant posts, should take a lead in this matter.

This would not only enable the army to maintain a youthful profile of its combatant troops but also reduce its pensionary commitments in future.

7. The present budgetary system for defence is not conducive either to yielding relevant management information regarding the cost of a job service done or utilisation of resources. A less opaque and feasible two para-budgetary scheme, involving inputs and outputs (mission/function) should be adopted." [5]

Notes

1. *Report of the Tenth Finance Commission*, 1994, p. 59.
2. Ibid., p. 28.
3. Ibid., p. 48.
4. Grants-in-aid of revenues are meant for covering assessed deficits on non-plan revenue account of the States, are calculated after considering transfers to the States on account of (a) devolution of income tax and Union excise duties, (b) share in additional excise duties and (c) share in grants in lieu of tax on railway passenger fares.
5. *Report of the Tenth Finance Commission*, 1994, p. 62.

25

Eleventh Finance Commission

Eleventh Finance Commission was constituted by an order of the President dated July 3, 1998. The Commission was asked to make recommendations as to the following matters.

Summary Statement	
Chairman	Mr. A.M. Khusro
Members	Shri N.C. Jain Shri J.C. Jetly Dr. Amaresh Bagchi Shri T.N. Srivastava
Year and month of establishment	July 1998
Year and month of reporting	July 2000
Period of award	2000-01 to 2004-05
Main Recommendations	
• States' share in net proceeds of all Central taxes fixed at 28 per cent. • 1.5 per cent of the net proceeds of all Central taxes recommended for distribution amongst such States which do not levy sales tax on sugar, tobacco and textiles. • Total share of States in the net proceeds of all Union taxes: 28+1.5=29.5 • Bases of distribution of States' share inter se (per cent): Population: 10; Income (distance method): 62.5; Area: 7.5; Index of infrastructure: 7.5; Tax effort: 5.0; Fiscal discipline: 7.5	

1. Distribution between the Union and the States of the net proceeds of taxes which are to be, or may be, divided between them and the allocation between the States of the respective shares of such proceeds.
2. Principles which should govern the grants-in-aid of the revenues of the States out of the Consolidated Fund of India and the sums to be paid to the States which are in need of assistance by way of grants-in-aid of their revenues under Article 275 of the Constitution for purposes other than those specified in the provisos to clause (1) of that article.
3. Measures needed to augment the Consolidated Fund of a State to supplement

the resources of the Panchayats in the State on the basis of the recommendations made by the Finance Commission of the State.

4. Measures needed to augment the Consolidated Fund of a State to supplement the resources of the Municipalities in the State on the basis of the recommendations made by the Finance Commission of the State.

The Commission was further required to review the state of the finances of the Union and the States and suggest ways and means by which the governments, collectively and severally, might bring about a restructuring of the public finances so as to restore budgetary balance and maintain macro economic stability. In making its recommendations, the Commission was asked to have regard to following considerations.

1. Resources of the Central Government and the demands thereon, in particular, on account of expenditure on civil administration, defence and border security, debt-servicing and other committed expenditure or liabilities.
2. Revenue resources of the States for the five years commencing on 1st April, 2000, on the basis of the levels of taxation possible to be reached in 1998-99, targets set for additional resource mobilisation for the Plan and the potential for raising additional taxes.
3. Requirement of the States for meeting the Plan and non-Plan revenue expenditure; keeping in view the need for generating surplus for capital investment and reducing fiscal deficit.
4. Maintenance and upkeep of capital assets and maintenance expenditure of plan schemes to be completed by 31st March, 2000 and the norms on the basis of which specified amounts are recommended for the maintenance of the capital assets and the manner of monitoring such expenditure.
5. Requirements of States for upgradation of standards in non-developmental and social sectors and services particularly of States which are backward in general administration with a view to modernise and rationalise the administrative set up in the interest of speed, efficiency and sound fiscal management.
6. Need for ensuring reasonable returns on investment by the States in irrigation projects, power projects, state transport undertakings, departmental commercial undertakings, public sector enterprises, etc.
7. Such provisions for emoluments and terminal benefits of Government employees including teachers and other employees of aided institutions as obtaining on a specified date as the Commission deems it proper and with reference to appropriate objective criteria rather than in terms of actual increases that may have been given effect to.
8. Scope for better fiscal management consistent with efficiency and economy

in expenditure including the incentives that need to be provided for better realisation of tax and non-tax revenue.

In the case of local bodies (a) the commission was asked to take into account the recommendations of the State Finance Commissions and (b) where the State Finance Commissions had not been constituted the Commission would make its own assessment about the manner and extent of augmentation of Consolidated Fund of the State to supplement the resources of the Panchayats and Municipalities in the State.

It was asked to give recommendations on specified aspects of Centre-State fiscal relations during the five years period commencing from April 1, 2000. The Commission submitted its Report on July 7, 2000. [1]

Recommendations of the EFC relating to (a) devolution of taxes and duties to the States, (b) grants-in-aid under Article 275 of the Constitution, (c) financing of relief expenditure and (d) debt relief to the States are summarised below:

25.1 Devolution of Central Taxes/Duties to the States

Article 280(3) of the Constitution requires the Finance Commission to make recommendations as to the distribution of the net proceeds of shareable taxes between Union and the States, and the allocation between the States of their shares in such proceeds. Formulation of principles that should guide the assignment of share to the States and the determination of individual share of each State constitutes a central task of the Commission.

The Constitution (Eightieth Amendment) Act, 2000 altered the pattern of sharing of Central taxes between the Centre and the States in a fundamental way. Prior to this amendment, taxes on income other than agriculture income and Union duties of excise were shared with States under Articles 270 and 272 respectively. The Eightieth Amendment Act substituted a new Article for Article 270 and omitted the old Article 272. The new Article 270 provided as follows: "All taxes and duties referred to in the Union List, except the duties and taxes referred to in Articles 268 and 269, respectively, surcharge on taxes and duties referred to in Article 271 and any cess levied for specific purposes under any law made by Parliament shall be levied and collected by the Government of India and shall be distributed between the Union and the States."

25.1.1 Share of States: Under Article 280 (3)(a), the Commission was required to determine, first, the aggregate share of the States in all Union taxes and duties. This task required a comprehensive view of (a) expenditure needs of the Centre, (b) aggregate resources of the Centre, (c) aggregate requirements of States on revenue account and (d) resources of the States from their own sources.

On the basis of the analysis and assessment of the budgetary requirements of the Centre and the States, the Commission fixed the share of States at 28 per cent of the net proceeds of shareable Central taxes/duties for distribution amongst all such States where the Central tax/duty was leviable for each of the five years starting from April 1, 2000. Consequently, the recommendations made for the sharing of income tax and Union excise duties in its Interim Report got modified. In addition, 1.5 per cent of the net proceeds of shareable Central taxes/duties in a year was recommended for distribution amongst such States which did not levy sales tax on sugar, tobacco and textiles during that year, [2] thus totalling 28 + 1.5 = 29.5 per cent of the net proceeds of all Union taxes and duties. The distribution of this 1.5 per cent among the States was to be done in the same manner as the distribution of 28 per cent of the net proceeds. It was further recommended that if any State levies and collects sales tax on sugar, textile and tobacco, it would not be entitled to any share from this 1.5 per cent.

As regards States' views on the new scheme of devolution, the Commission observed, "In their memoranda, States are in unison in asking for the changeover to the alternative scheme of devolution and for giving up the present system of tax sharing of revenues from specified taxes, viz. income tax and Union excise duties. Many have, however, asked for a higher share in the pool of Central taxes as compared to the 29 per cent share that was recommended by the Tenth Finance Commission." [3]

25.1.2 Distribution of the Share of States Inter Se: While States were almost unanimous in demanding an increase in the share of Union taxes, there were naturally wide divergences in their approach to the principles for determination of relative shares of the States in the divisible pool. Each State suggested a formula which it considered would benefit it the most, the richer States emphasising the *collection factor* and the poorer States the *backwardness factor*. The various criteria, often conflicting, suggested by the States to the Commission, included population, consumption, collection of revenue, economic backwardness, relative financial weakness, sales tax collections, and percentage of scheduled castes and scheduled tribes. Not surprisingly, relatively industrialised States like Gujarat, and Maharashtra argued in favour of collection factor because bulk of the tax revenue originated there. Poorer States like Uttar Pradesh, Orissa, and Bihar wanted significant weightage for backwardness criterion while Madhya Pradesh and Rajasthan preferred high weightage for geographical area. It has rightly been said that fiscal federalism in India is a tug-of-war not only between the Centre and the States but also among the States themselves.

After examining claims and counter-claims of the States, the Commission recommended percentage share of each State (in the share of all States) and indicated the criteria adopted in arriving at those percentage shares.

The Commission asserted that the basic emphasis in its approach was to evolve a suitable structure of incentives in all mechanism of fiscal transfers. It may be recalled that the Tenth Finance Commission had made a beginning in this direction by utilising an index of tax effort made by the States. Carrying forward the scheme of incentives, the Commission under review observed, "we feel that given the present fiscal situation of the States and the need for restructuring, as also the reference in our TOR for better fiscal management, further incentives need to be provided for fiscal discipline, and that this may be integrated in the principles of devolution. Accordingly, we are suggesting the use of an index of fiscal discipline." [4] Keeping all these requirements in mind, the Commission suggested six criteria with relative weights for determining the *inter se* shares of the States (Table 25.1). There were three main considerations before the Commission in the selection of criteria: (a) resource deficiency of States, (b) higher cost of providing services and (c) fiscal discipline.

Table 25.1: Criteria and Relative Weights for Determining Inter Se Shares of States

S. No.	Criteria	Relative weight (per cent)
1.	Population	10.0
2.	Income (distance method)	62.5
3.	Area	7.5
4.	Index of infrastructure	7.5
5.	Tax effort	5.0
6.	Fiscal discipline	7.5

Note: State-wise data on these criteria are given in Annexures VI.2 to VI.7 of the Report of the Commission.

Source: *Report of the Eleventh Finance Commission*, June 2000, p. 58.

Based on the criteria and their relative weights as given in Table 23.1, the percentage shares of different States in the net proceeds of all shareable Union taxes and duties (except the expenditure tax and service tax) [5] were worked out in each of the financial years from 2000-01 to 2004-05. These percentage shares are shown in Table 25.2.

Expenditure tax and service tax were not at that time leviable in the State of Jammu and Kashmir. Share in the net proceeds of these taxes was, therefore, not assignable to this State. The Commission recommended the share of each of the remaining 24 States in the net proceeds of expenditure tax and service tax as indicated in Table 25.3. The Commission clarified that if in any year, these taxes become leviable in the State of Jammu and Kashmir, the share of each State including that of Jammu and Kashmir would be in accordance with the percentages given in Table 25.2.

Table 25.2: Inter se Shares of States in the Net Proceeds of All Shareable Union Taxes and Duties

State	**Share (per cent)**
Andhra Pradesh	7.701
Arunachal Pradesh	0.244
Assam	3.285
Bihar	14.597
Goa	0.206
Gujarat	2.821
Haryana	0.944
Himachal Pradesh	0.683
Jammu & Kashmir	1.290
Karnataka	4.930
Kerala	3.057
Madhya Pradesh	8.838
Maharashtra	4.632
Manipur	0.366
Meghalaya	0.342
Mizoram	0.198
Nagaland	0.220
Orissa	5.056
Punjab	1.147
Rajasthan	5.473
Sikkim	0.184
Tamil Nadu	5.385
Tripura	0.487
Uttar Pradesh	19.798
West Bengal	8.116
All States	100.000

Source: *Report of the Eleventh Finance Commission*, June 2000, p. 59.

Furthermore, the Commission made it clear that if in any year during 2000-2001 to 2004-05, a tax under Union was not leviable in a State, the share of that

State in that tax should be put to zero and the entire proceeds should be distributed among the remaining States by proportionately adjusting their share.

Table 25.3: Share of States, other than Jammu and Kashmir, in the Expenditure Tax and Service Tax

State	Share (per cent)
Andhra Pradesh	7.802
Arunachal Pradesh	0.247
Assam	3.328
Bihar	14.788
Goa	0.209
Gujarat	2.858
Haryana	0.956
Himachal Pradesh	0.692
Jammu & Kashmir	0.000
Karnataka	4.994
Kerala	3.097
Madhya Pradesh	8.954
Maharashtra	4.693
Manipur	0.371
Meghalaya	0.346
Mizoram	0.201
Nagaland	0.223
Orissa	5.122
Punjab	1.162
Rajasthan	5.544
Sikkim	0.186
Tamil Nadu	5.455
Tripura	0.493
Uttar Pradesh	20.057
West Bengal	8.222
Total All States	100.000

Source: *Report of the Eleventh Finance Commission*, June 2000, p. 60.

The percentage share of each State in the 29.5 per cent of the net proceeds of shareable Central taxes varied as per the fixed formula suggested by the Commission. The Commission distributed weights on the basis of six criteria:

population, distance, area, index of infrastructure, tax effort and fiscal discipline. 72.5 per cent of the weights were accounted for by population and distance factors. It may be recalled that the Tenth Finance Commission used only the first five criteria. The criterion of fiscal discipline was used by the Commission under review for the first time. At the same time, the weightage given to each of these criteria was also altered. For instance, the weightage given to poverty or income was increased from 60 per cent in the devolution formula used by the Tenth Commission to 62 per cent. Weights for area and index of infrastructure development were increased as compared to those assigned five years ago by its predecessor, the Tenth Commission. Weightage for tax effort was halved. In other words, the Commission under study opted for large weights for distributive factors like *distance* but small weights for fiscal efficiency parameters. Understandably, under its dispensation, poorer States got a bigger share of Central taxes while richer States with better infrastructure, administrative and fiscal apparatus got less as compared to Tenth Commission's formula. The biggest losers were Gujarat, Maharashtra, Haryana, Andhra Pradesh, Punjab and Tamil Nadu. This happened because the Commission altered the weights given to different criteria in the devolution formula used to determine the *inter se* distribution. Successive Finance Commission have directed Central transfers more and more to weaker States so that they may come out of the slow growth trap. However, the weaker states have continued to be weak.

The recommendations of the Commission were severely criticised by the Chief Ministers of relatively developed States, particularly Andhra Pradesh and Maharashtra. It was argued that by reducing the percentage share of these States, the Commission had penalised the States which had performed well, introduced reforms and contributed to national development.

25.2 Grants-in-aid of Revenues of States

Even after the transfer to the States of a share of divisible taxes, the resources of some of the States may remain inadequate to meet their needs. Therefore, the Constitution provides for grants-in-aid by the Centre to such States as are in need of assistance. Two types of grants are provided by the Centre to the States: the first under Article 275 which are routed through the Finance Commission, and the second under Article 282 which have traditionally been determined by the Planning Commission.

Grants-in-aid of revenues recommended by the Commission under study were as follows.

25.2.1 Grants-in-aid to Cover Non-Plan Gap on Revenue Account: The Commission recommended grants-in-aid to be given under Article 275(1) equal to the amount of deficits assessed for each year during the period 2000-01 to 2004-05. Grants-in-aid amounting to Rs. 35,359 crore were recommended to such States, The amount of the grant for each State, having non-Plan deficits is indicated in Table 25.4.

Table 25.4: Grants-in-aid to Cover Non-Plan Gap on Revenue Account as Recommended by the Eleventh Finance Commission

(Rs. lakh)

State	2000-01	2001-02	2002-03	2003-04	2004-05	Total
Arunachal Pradesh	24463	24674	24612	24196	24857	122802
Assam	11068	-	-	-	-	11068
Himachal Pradesh	104947	100218	94653	83923	71185	454926
Jammu & Kashmir	211166	224087	223939	229064	232863	1121119
Manipur	35468	35503	35198	34460	33865	174494
Meghalaya	33813	33042	32623	30090	27670	157238
Mizoram	32278	32958	33482	35105	33807	167630
Nagaland	64432	67396	72015	73404	76377	353624
Orissa	35849	3643	27868	-	-	67360
Punjab	28421	-	-	-	-	28421
Rajasthan	95526	28942	-	-	-	124468
Sikkim	16970	17073	16983	16644	16388	84058
Tripura	49329	49302	49532	47605	45648	241416
Uttar Pradesh	102674	-	-	-	-	102674
West Bengal	168972	103451	52186	-	-	324609
Total	**1015376**	**720289**	**663091**	**574491**	**562660**	**3535907**

Source: *Report of the Eleventh Finance Commission*, June 2000, p. 97.

25.2.2 Grants-in-aid for Upgradation of Standards of Administration and Special Problems of States: The Commission recommended grants totalling to Rs. 4,972 crore towards upgradation of standards of administration and special problems of States for the period 2000-01 to 2004-05. In this connection the Commission observed, "The power to sanction individual schemes as well as to determine the unit costs in respect of projects to be taken up under the upgradation and special problem grants should vest with the State Level Empowered Committee (SLEC). There is no need for any case to be sent to the

Government of India for sanction of a project. Once a project has been sanctioned by the SLEC, a copy of the same indicating the time schedule for various stages of the project and for requirement of funds should be submitted to the Government of India, who should release the funds according to the time schedule indicated in the project. The unutilised grants for a particular year may be carried forward to the next year. However, the grants that remain unutilised as on March 31, 2005 shall lapse.

The States should show greater commitment for timely and qualitative implementation of the project undertaken through the upgradation and special problem grants. The physical and financial monitoring of the projects should be done by the SLEC. The States should send quarterly report to the Ministry of Finance of the Government of India, to facilitate release of grants." [6]

25.2.3 Grants to States for Financing Local Bodies: The Commission under study was the first to be required by the President, in terms of the 73rd and 74th Amendments to the Constitution, to recommend the measures needed to augment the Consolidated Fund of a State to supplement the resources of the panchayats and municipalities in the State on the basis of the recommendations of the State Finance Commissions.

The Commission recommended grants totalling Rs. 10,000 crore for local bodies during 2000-01 to 2004-2005, to be utilised mainly for maintenance of civic services. Of this, Rs. 1,600 crore per annum was for rural local bodies and Rs. 400 crore per annum was for urban local bodies. The Commission recommended that the amounts of Rs. 1,600 crore and Rs. 400 crore provided for the panchayats and municipalities respectively, for each of the five years (2000-01 to 2004-05) be distributed among the States on the following criteria and weights:

1. Population 40 per cent.
2. Index of decentralisation 20 per cent.
3. Distance from highest per capita income 20 per cent.
4. Revenue effort 10 per cent.
5. Geographical area 10 per cent.

The grants given to local bodies were primarily meant for maintenance of civil services including primary health and family welfare, education as well as other public utility services.

The Commission made many recommendations to strengthen and streamline the functioning of local bodies (i.e. panchayats and municipalities). These were as follows.

1. "Article 243I should be amended to enable the States to set up the State Finance Commissions (SFC) at the expiration of every fifth year or earlier,

akin to the provision that already exists under Article 280 for constituting the Finance Commission. The synchronisation of availability of the SFC reports may also be ensured through either a Central Legislation or an appropriate provision in the Constitution.

2. SFC reports may contain specific chapters so as to make them more useful to the Finance Commission.
3. State Governments should take their decision on the recommendations of the SFC, especially in regard to matters relating to resource transfer, and place the ATRs (Action Taken Reports) on the floor of the State Legislature within six months. Amendments to the laws, if necessary, should be made to ensure this at the earliest.
4. The words *on the basis of the recommendations made by the Finance Commission of the State*, appearing in sub-clauses (bb) & (c) of Article 280(3) of the Constitution, may be deleted.
5. State should, by legislation, ensure that the chairperson and members of the SFCs may be drawn from amongst experts in specific disciplines such as economics, law, public administration and public finance.
6. Taxes on land/farm income may be levied in suitable form to strengthen the resource base of the local bodies. The amounts so collected may be passed on to these bodies for improving and strengthening the civic services. Local bodies may also be involved in collection of these taxes.
7. Cess on land based taxes and other State taxes/duties may be levied and devolved to the local bodies for augmenting specific civic services.
8. States should levy profession tax with a view to supplementing the resources of local bodies, or they should empower the local bodies to levy it. The rates should be suitably revised from time to time.
9. Property tax/house tax has not been exploited to its full potential. The relevant tax legislation should be suitably modified to delink this tax from the rent control laws. Where a property has been let out, the property tax should be made recoverable from the occupier.
10. Abolition of octroi should invariably be accompanied with its replacement by a suitable tax that is buoyant and can be collected by the local bodies.
11. The rate structure of user charges levied by the local bodies should be revised regularly to keep pace with inflation and to recover at least, as far as possible, the full operations and maintenance cost. Local bodies should have the power to fix the rates of taxes and user charges.
12. The grants recommended for local bodies in this report should be given to those local bodies which have the primary responsibility for maintenance of civic services. The grant should be untied, but should not be used for payment

of salaries and wages.

13. States should review the existing accounting heads under which funds are being transferred to the local bodies. For each major head/sub-major head, six minor heads should be created - three for the panchayati raj institutions and another three for the urban local bodies. This may be done in consultation with Comptroller and Auditor General of India (C&AG) and the Controller General of Accounts, to ensure uniformity among the States.
14. The C&AG should be entrusted with the responsibility of exercising control and supervision over the maintenance of accounts and their audit for all the tiers/levels of panchayats and urban local bodies.
15. The Director, Local Fund Audit, or any other agency made responsible for the audit of accounts of the local bodies, should work under the technical and administrative supervision of the C&AG. In no case, should the Director for Panchayats or for Urban Local Bodies be entrusted with this work. The prescribed authority entrusted with the audit and accounts of the local bodies should not have any functional responsibility in regard to these bodies, so as to ensure his independence and accountability.
16. The C&AG should prescribe the format for the preparation of budgets and for keeping of accounts by the local bodies, which should be amenable to computerisation.
17. Local bodies, which do not have trained accounts staff, may contract out the upkeep of accounts to outside agencies/persons. The C&AG may lay down the qualification and experience required for this purpose. The Director, Local Fund Audit, or his equivalent authority, may do the registration of such agencies/persons.
18. Audit of accounts of the local bodies may be entrusted to the C&AG, who may get it done through his own staff, or by engaging outside agencies on payment of remuneration fixed by him. An amount of half per cent of the total expenditure incurred by the local bodies should be placed with the C&AG for this purpose.
19. The report of the C&AG, relating to audit of accounts of the panchayats and the municipalities, should be placed before a committee of the State Legislature constituted on the same lines as the Public Accounts Committee.
20. An amount of Rs. 4,000 per panchayat per annum, on an average, should be adequate to meet the expenditure on maintenance of accounts on contract basis, if the staff/facilities are not available within the panchayat. The amount may be paid from the grants that are recommended for the rural local bodies. Any additional fund required for this purpose should be met from the grants given to the States for the panchayats. Where a panchayat has got staff

available for upkeep of accounts, these funds need not be so earmarked. If any municipality does not have a regular staff for this purpose, the grants provided to it may also be so earmarked.

21. A database on the finances of the panchayats and municipalities should be developed at the district, State and Central Government levels and be easily accessible by computerising it and linking it thorough V-SAT. The Director, Local Fund Audit, or the authority prescribed for conducting the audit of accounts of the local bodies, may be made responsible for this task. The Chief Secretary of the State may do the State level coordination and monitoring. The C&AG should be involved at all stages.
22. A total grant of Rs. 1,600 crore for the panchayats and Rs. 400 crore for the municipalities is recommended to be given to States for each of the five years starting from the financial year 2000-01. The amounts indicated for maintenance of accounts, audit of accounts and for the development of database, would be the first charge on these grants and would be released by the concerned Ministries of the Government of India, after the arrangements suggested become operational. Shares in respect of the scheduled, tribal and other excluded areas should be made available to the respective States only after the relevant legislative measures are taken extending the provisions of the 73rd and 74th amendments to such areas.
23. *Inter-se* share of States in the grants provided for the panchayats and the municipalities is based on the rural/urban population of the States (40 per cent), index of decentralisation (20 per cent), distance from the highest per capita income (20 per cent), revenue effort of the local bodies (10 per cent) and geographical area (10 per cent).
24. While all the States barring Arunachal Pradesh have either enacted a new Panchayat/Municipal Act or have amended the existing legislation in conformity with the 73rd and 74th amendments, the schemes relating to the subjects included in the Eleventh and Twelfth Schedules have not yet been transferred to these bodies in most of the States as contemplated in Articles 243G and 243W. Transfer of functions and schemes to the local bodies should be specifically provided by legislation.
25. The roles of the three tiers of the panchayats have generally not been delineated in the State legislations and the matter has usually been left to be decided by way of executive instructions. Legislative arrangements should be made to clearly indicate the role that these bodies have to play in the system of governance in the rural areas of a district.
26. The two Union Ministries—the Ministry of Rural Development and the

Ministry of Urban Development—have to ensure that the local bodies function as institutions of self-government and all impediments to the realisation of this ideal are removed. These Ministries should take the initiative for transferring the schemes related to their subjects included in the Eleventh and Twelfth Schedules, to the local bodies.

27. The three-tier panchayati raj system is very rigid arrangement. States may be provided flexibility to decide whether a two-tier system would operate with greater efficiency and economy or a three-tier structure would be essential.
28. For extending the provisions of the 74th amendment to the Fifth Schedule areas, Parliament is yet to enact the enabling legislation. This may be speeded up.
29. The Legislatures in the States of Meghalaya, Mizoram and Nagaland should take suitable action for extending the provisions of the 73rd amendment to the non-Sixth Schedule areas. Alternatively, the existing village level institutions in these areas may be recognised as panchayats for the purposes of the 73rd amendment, by appropriate legislative changes.
30. Suitable enabling provisions in the Constitution may be introduced so that the hill areas in the State of Manipur and in the district of Darjeeling in West Bengal could get the benefit of the 73rd amendment.
31. Administrative reorganisation of panchayats is necessary to ensure their development as viable institutions of self-government.
32. The District Planning Committees and the Metropolitan Planning Committees should be constituted and made functional.
33. All Government properties of the Centre as well as the States, should be subject to the levy of user changes. It should be regulated by suitable legislation." [7]

25.3 Financing of Calamity Relief Expenditure

The Commission recommended the continuance of the then existing scheme of Calamity Relief Funds in States with an aggregate size of Rs. 11,008 crore during 2000-01 to 2004-05. This included the Centre's share of Rs. 8,256 crore and the States' share of Rs. 2,752 crore, worked out in the ratio of 75:25. In this connection the Commission made the following recommendations.

1. "The existing scheme of providing for contribution of 25 per cent by the States and 75 per cent by the Centre to the Calamity Relief Fund (CRF), may be continued.
2. The amount of CRF for 2000-05 has been worked out at Rs. 11,007.59 crore. This includes the Centre's share of Rs. 8,255.69 crore and the States' share of Rs. 2,751.90 crore.

3. Only the natural calamities of cyclone, drought, earthquake, fire, flood and hailstorm should be eligible for relief expenditure from CRF. The CRF should not be used for providing relief to the people affected by man-made and other disasters and the concerned units from which a man-made disaster emanated, should be made to pay for it.
4. The CRF should be kept separately outside the Public Account of the State and invested in a manner approved by the Central Government. Where, however, for some reasons, it is not possible to invest it in the manner approved by the Central Government, it should be kept in Public Account, on which the State Government should pay interest at a rate not less than the market rate as indicated by the Reserve Bank of India.
5. The State Government should incur expenditure from the CRF only on items included in the approved list. A committee of experts, having representatives from the States too, may be set up to review the list from time to time.
6. Regarding the amounts to be incurred from the CRF on the approved items of expenditure, the arrangements recommended by the TFC (Tenth Finance Commission) may be continued. In case any State Government exceeds the amounts prescribed, the excess expenditure should be borne from the normal budget of the State Government and not from the CRF.
7. There is a need for devising medium as well as long term strategies in every part of the country to reduce the frequency of occurrences of the natural calamities and their impact on the area and population. The Planning Commission, in consultation with the concerned State Governments and Ministries of the Government of India, may identify works of capital nature to prevent the recurrence of specific calamities. These works may be financed under the plan.
8. The expenditure on restoration of damaged capital works should ordinarily be met from the normal budgetary heads, except when it is to be incurred as part of providing immediate relief such as restoration on drinking water sources, provision of shelters, or restoration of communication links for facilitating relief operations. The expenditure from CRF should be incurred only for providing immediate relief to the affected population, and should be of short duration.
9. The National Fund for Calamity Relief (NFCR) may be discontinued in its present form.
10. A National Centre for Calamity Management (NCCM) should be established under the Ministry of Agriculture. This centre should be empowered to make recommendations regarding eligibility of a State for assistance from the Central Government.

11. Any assistance provided by the Centre to the States for calamity relief should be financed by the levy of a special surcharge on the Central taxes for a limited period. Collections from such surcharge should be kept in a separate fund to be known as National Calamity Contingency Fund (NCCF) created in the Public Account of the Government of India. The Government of India should contribute an initial core amount of Rs. 500 crore to this fund, to be replenished by the levy of the special surcharge as and when any drawals are made from it. In order to ensure that there is no delay in the flow of funds to the States for administration of relief, a legislation enabling the Central Government to levy such surcharge may be enacted.
12. The NCCM should also undertake studies on recurrence of various types of natural calamities, keep in readiness an inventory of materials needed for providing relief, locate the places/centres where these could be kept readily available, provide training to the State cadres identified for deployment for calamity relief duties, besides documentation and evaluation of calamity related matters.
13. The crop insurance scheme should be strengthened, but as a supplementary measure to what is done by the government for providing relief at the time of natural calamity.
14. Every major State needs to have trained manpower to cope with various types of natural calamities. A core multi-disciplinary group of about 200 to 300 persons should be created and trained suitably in each State for being deployed in any place in the country for calamity relief operations. An honorarium, as may be determined by the Government of India from time to time, may be paid to each such person as an incentive to participate in this scheme. The expenditure on their training should be met from the CRF.
15. Every State should be required to prepare and send to the Central Government an annual report on the calamities for which the State had incurred the relief expenditure. Based on the State-specific reports and the evaluation reports of the NCCM, the Ministry of Agriculture should prepare an annual report by the 31st December every year. The report should be released to the public." [8]

25.3.1 National Calamity Contingency Fund: The Commission recommended that the Central assistance to the States in national calamities should be financed by levy of a special surcharge on Central taxes for a limited period. It opined that a surcharge instils a feeling of national participation for a national cause. Collection from such surcharge should be kept in a separate fund, to be known as National Calamity Contingency Fund (NCCF), created in the Public Account of the Government of India.

25.4 Debt Relief to States

The Commission proposed the continuance of the then existing debt relief scheme, linked to improvement in the ratio of revenue receipts of a State to its total revenue expenditure, with enhanced incentive. In specific terms, its recommendations on this matter were the following.

1. "The scheme of general debt relief linked to fiscal performance, introduced by the TFC, may be continued with certain modifications.
2. Expenditure incurred on security by the State of Jammu & Kashmir prior to 1991 may be assessed by the Ministry of Home Affairs (MHA) and the Ministry of Finance (MoF) in consultation with the State Government and a debt relief to the extent of such expenditure may be provided to the State. In regard to Punjab, a moratorium on the instalments of debt and interest relating to the special term loan only, due to payment, may be given during the period 2000-05. The expenditure incurred on security may be worked out by the MHA in consultation with the State Government of Punjab and the MoF and, to the extent the State is entitled for reimbursement on account of security related expenditure, the relief on debt may be given to the State after the period of moratorium is over and after adjustment of any waiver earlier given.
3. Treating the borrowings of the States relating to small saving, as loans in perpetuity is neither desirable nor viable.
4. Limits on the guarantees given by the Centre and States may be fixed by suitable legislation and should form part of the overall limits to borrowing under Articles 292 and 293 respectively. This limit also should include borrowings from Public Account and other sources.
5. There is a need for setting up of a sinking fund in each State for the amortisation of debt." [9]

The Commission was criticised for its restrictive recommendations on the States' borrowings and for providing inadequate debt relief.

25.5 Ceiling on Total Revenue Account Transfers

While working out the total quantum of share in Central taxes/duties and grants-in-aid to States, the Commission considered the trends in total transfers from the Centre to the States on revenue account. It recommended that tax devolution and Plan/Non-Plan grants from the Centre to the States should not exceed 37.5 per cent of total Centre's revenues (both tax and non-tax). The rationale of the ceiling was explained by the Commission as follows, "in deciding the level of revenue transfers, all transfers have to be taken in their totality and their components like tax devolution, grants-in-aid and grants in other forms like Plan grants, should be decided in the light of the overall ceiling. Accordingly, after working out the likely profile of the revenue and expenditure of the Centre for the five years 2000-05, we have set a notional limit on the overall revenue transfers, taking into account the legitimate needs of the Centre to meet its revenue expenditure liabilities. In setting this ceiling, we have taken note of the level of transfers that have taken place as a proportion of Centre's revenues in recent years and postulated a proportion of 37.5 per cent in order that there is no disruption in government finances at the two levels. This will serve to raise the volume of resource flow to the States over what has been prevailing of late but not beyond what can be accommodated within the Centre's resource profile, and the contemplated deficit levels." [10]

While accepting this ceiling on total revenue account transfers from thc Centre to the States, the Government clarified that the acceptance of this recommendation did not imply the establishment of a principle of mandatory sharing of a fixed percentage of Centre's revenue receipts with the States.

The sharing of the proceeds from almost all Central taxes (global sharing) was welcomed universally. The earlier arrangement of sharing some of the taxes (itemised sharing) was criticised on the ground that Central Government paid more attention to the administration of non-shareable taxes and was lax in making the shareable taxes buoyant. In the new scheme, no tax, as such, is shareable. A percentage of the total tax proceeds of the Centre is assigned to the States. The total amount assigned has no identifiable parts to it. With the new scheme of tax devolution (effective April 1, 1996), the Central Government can pursue its tax reforms without the need to consider whether a tax is shareable with the States or not.

See also section 10.3 of Chapter 10 of this book.

Notes

1. Apart from its main report, the EFC also submitted an *interim report* on January 15, 2000 for making provisional arrangements for the year 2000-2001. It had recommended the share of States in income tax and Union excise duties for the year 2000-2001 at 80 per cent and 52 per cent respectively.

Again, at the stage of finalisation of its Report, an additional term of reference was added by the Presidential Order dated April 28, 2000 as follows:

"In particular the Commission shall draw a monitorable fiscal reforms programme aimed at reduction of revenue deficit of the States and recommend the manner in which the grants to States to cover the assessed deficit in their non-plan revenue account may be linked to progress in implementing the programme."

Formulation of a fiscal monitorable reforms programme required another round of consultations with the States and the Union Ministry of Finance. Therefore, although the main report was submitted on July 7, 2000, the report on the term of reference notified in the Order dated April 28, 2000 was submitted to the President on August 30, 2000. This *supplementary report* evolved a weightage formula for fiscal discipline in the devolution package for States from the Central taxes.

Following the recommendations of the EFC, the Central Government earmarked Rs. 10,607 crore as Incentive Fund for 5 years to encourage the States to implement monitorable fiscal reforms. To begin with an amount of Rs. 4,243 crore was provided for the Fund for the year 2001-2002 in the budget for the same year.

2. As a result of the Eightieth Amendment of the Constitution, the net proceeds of the additional excise duties levied under the Additional Excise Duties (Goods of Special Importance) Act, 1957, cannot be passed on to the States as Article 272 of the Constitution has been deleted. Additional excise duties are now part of the tax revenue of the Central Government and are shareable with the States. In view of these changes, there is a need to review the earlier arrangement. Pending that, the EFC recommended that 1.5 per cent of all shareable Union taxes and duties be allocated to the States separately.

3. *Report of the Eleventh Finance Commission*, June 2000, p. 54.

4. *Ibid.*, p. 58.

5. Expenditure tax and service tax are not presently leviable in the State of Jammu & Kashmir. Hence, share in the net proceeds of these taxes was not assignable to this State. The share of each of the remaining States in the net proceeds of expenditure tax and service tax was worked out separately.

6. *Report of the Eleventh Finance Commission*, op. cit, p. 114.

7. *Ibid.*, pp. 114-116.

8. *Ibid.*, p. 116.

9. Ibid., pp. 116-117.

10. *Ibid.*, p. 15.

26

Twelfth Finance Commission

Twelfth Finance Commission was constituted by an order of the President dated November 1, 2002. The Commission was asked to make recommendations as to the following matters.

Summary Statement	
Chairman	Dr. C. Rangarajan
Members	Shri Som Pal (Part-Time) Shri T.R. Prasad Professor D.K. Srivastava
Year and month of establishment	November 2002
Year and month of reporting	December 2004
Period of award	2005-06 to 2009-10
Main Recommendations	
• States' share in net proceeds of all Central taxes fixed at 30.5 per cent. • Additional excise duties in lieu of sales tax treated as a part of the general pool of central taxes. • Bases of distribution of States' share inter se (per cent): Population: 25; Income distance: 50; Area: 10; Tax effort: 7.5; Fiscal discipline: 7.5.	

1. Distribution between the Union and the States of the net proceeds of taxes which are to be, or may be, divided between them and the allocation between the States of the respective shares of such proceeds.
2. Principles which should govern the grants-in-aid of the revenues of the States out of the Consolidated Fund of India and the sums to be paid to the States which are in need of assistance by way of grants-in-aid of their revenues under article 275 of the Constitution for purposes other than those specified in the provisions to clause (1) of that article.
3. Measures needed to augment the Consolidated Fund of a State to supplement the resources of the panchayats and municipalities in the State on the basis of the recommendations made by the Finance Commission of the State.

The Commission was required to review the state of the finances of the Union and the States and suggest a plan by which the governments, collectively and severally, may bring about a restructuring of the public finances restoring budgetary balance, achieving macro-economic stability and debt reduction along with equitable growth.

In making its recommendations, the Commission was asked to have regard to the following considerations.

1. Resources of the Central Government for five years commencing on April 1, 2005, on the basis of levels of taxation and non-tax revenues likely to be reached at the end of 2003- 04.
2. Demands on the resources of the Central Government, in particular, on account of expenditure on civil administration, defence, internal and border security, debt-servicing and other committed expenditure and liabilities.
3. Resources of the State Governments, for the five years commencing on April 1, 2005, on the basis of levels of taxation and non-tax revenues likely to be reached at the end of 2003-04.
4. Objective of not only balancing the receipts and expenditure on revenue account of all the States and the Centre, but also generating surpluses for capital investment and reducing fiscal deficit.
5. Taxation efforts of the Central Government and each State Government as against targets, if any, and the potential for additional resource mobilisation in order to improve the tax-Gross Domestic Product (GDP) and tax-Gross State Domestic Product (GSDP) ratio, as the case may be.
6. Expenditure on the non-salary component of maintenance and upkeep of capital assets and the non-wage related maintenance expenditure on plan schemes to be completed by March 31, 2005 and the norms on the basis of which specific amounts are recommended for the maintenance of the capital assets and the manner of monitoring such expenditure.
7. Need for ensuring the commercial viability of irrigation projects, power projects, departmental undertakings, public sector enterprises etc. in the States through various means including adjustment of user charges and relinquishing of non-priority enterprises through privatisation or disinvestment.

In making its recommendations on various matters, the Commission was required to take the base of population figures as of 1971, in all such cases where population was a factor for determination of devolution of taxes and duties and grants-in-aid. Furthermore, the Commission was also asked to suggest corrective measures for debt sustainability and to review the Fiscal Reform Facility introduced by the Central Government.

The Commission submitted its report on November 30, 2004 covering the period 2005-06 to 2009-10. The recommendations of the Commission included a plan for restructuring of public finances of the Centre and the States through improvement in revenue mobilisation and bringing down debt levels, and through enactment of fiscal responsibility legislation by States. The Commission recommended debt relief to States linked to fiscal reforms, doing away with the present system of Central assistance to State plans in the form of grants and loans and transfer of external assistance to States on the same terms and conditions as attached to such assistance by external funding agencies.

26.1 Sharing of Union Tax Revenues

It may be recalled that prior to the enactment of the Constitution (Eightieth Amendment) Act, 2000, the sharing of the Union tax revenues with the states was in accordance with the provisions of Articles 270 and 272, as these stood then. While Article 270 provided for the compulsory sharing of the net proceeds of the income tax (excluding corporation tax), Article 272 permitted for sharing of the net proceeds of Union duties of excise (excluding duties of excise on medicinal and toilet preparations), if Parliament by law so provided. Consequently, the principles adopted for revenue sharing differed between the two taxes significantly.

The eightieth amendment of the Constitution altered the pattern of sharing of Union taxes in a fundamental way. Under this amendment, Article 272 was dropped and Article 270 was substantially changed. The new Article 270 provided for sharing of all the taxes and duties referred to in the Union list, except the taxes and duties referred to in Articles 268 and 269 respectively, surcharges on taxes and duties referred to in Article 271 and any cess levied for specific purposes. The basis for this change was the alternative scheme of devolution recommended by the Tenth Finance Commission. There was considerable merit in the change, as it gave greater freedom and flexibility to the Centre in pursuing the tax reforms in an integrated manner and enabled the States to share the aggregate buoyancy of central taxes. The Eleventh Finance Commission was the first to take these changes into account, while recommending the share of the states in the divisible pool.

Another Constitutional amendment that was of relevance to Centre-State fiscal relations was the eighty-eighth amendment, enacted in January 2004 through the Constitution (Eighty-eighth Amendment) Act, 2003. This was relating to service tax. This amendment provided for a specific entry in the Constitution to authorise levy of service tax. The Central Government had been imposing and collecting this tax as a residual item under Entry 97 in the Union List and the net proceeds thereof were distributed between the Centre and the States as per Article 270 of the Constitution on the recommendations of the

Finance Commission.

The Tenth Finance Commission in its alternative scheme of tax devolution suggested that instead of sharing of individual taxes, the States should have a share in the total net proceeds of all central taxes excluding surcharges and cesses. The Commission recommended that the share of States in the gross receipts of central taxes should be 26 per cent, and until the tax rental arrangement was terminated, a further share of 3 per cent in the gross tax receipts of the centre be given to the States as compensation for the additional excise duties *in lieu* of sale tax.

26.1.1 Vertical Sharing: The Eleventh Finance Commission recommended that the share of the States be fixed at 28 per cent of the net proceeds of all taxes and duties. It further noted that as a consequence of the amendment, which *inter alia* deleted Article 272, additional excise duties levied under the Additional Excise Duties (Goods of Special Importance) Act, 1957, had become part of the revenue receipts of the Central Government and were shareable with the States. It was felt that there was a need for a review of the earlier arrangement and pending such a review, the Commission recommended that 1.5 per cent of all shareable Union taxes and duties be allocated to the States separately and its *inter se* distribution among the States may be done in the same manner as the distribution of 28 per cent of the net proceeds. This brought the total tax devolution recommended by the Eleventh Finance Commission to 29.5 per cent of the net proceeds of all shareable Central taxes and duties.

Many States had asked the Commission under review for increase in the share of States in the shareable pool from 29.5 per cent to 33 per cent. Some States suggested a figure of 50 per cent. After considering various aspects of the issue, the Commission recommended that the share of the states in the net proceeds of shareable Central taxes be raised from 29.5 per cent to 30.5 per cent. For this purpose, additional excise duties *in lieu* of sales tax on textiles, tobacco and sugar were treated as part of the general pool of Central taxes. Further, the indicative amount of overall transfers to States in Central gross revenue receipts, which was fixed at 37.5 per cent by the Eleventh Finance Commission, was fixed at 38 per cent.

26.1.2 Horizontal Sharing: As regards the determination of the *inter se* shares of the states, the basic purpose of the finance commission transfers in the past has been to (a) to correct the differentials in revenue capacity and cost disability factors inherent in the economies of states and (b) to foster fiscal efficiency among the states. The criteria used in the past for these objectives can be grouped as under.

1. Factors reflecting needs, such as population and income measured either as

distance from the highest income or as inverse.

2. Cost disability indicators such as area and infrastructure distance.
3. Fiscal efficiency indicators such as tax effort and fiscal discipline.

As per the formula used by the Eleventh Finance Commission, the share of each State in tax devolution was determined by the following criteria and relative weights:

1. Population (10 per cent).
2. Income distance (62.5 per cent).
3. Area (7.5 per cent).
4. Index of infrastructure (7.5 per cent).
5. Tax effort (5 per cent)
6. Fiscal discipline (7.5 per cent).

The Commission under study examined each of these criteria and the weights assigned and suggested changes, where necessary. Criteria and the weights, thus assigned for inter se determination of shares of states by the Commission are shown in Table 26.1.

Table 26.1: Criteria and Weights Assigned for Inter Se Determination of Shares of States

Criteria	Weight (per cent)
Population	25.0
Income distance	50.0
Area	10.0
Tax effort	7.5
Fiscal discipline	7.5

Source: *Report of the Twelfth Finance Commission*, November 2004, p. 133.

The Commission tried to evolve a formula which could balance equity with fiscal efficiency. Table 26.2 records the shares of the States recommended by the Commission in the net proceeds of all the shareable Union taxes (excluding service tax, as it was not leviable in Jammu and Kashmir) in each of the five financial years during the period 2005-06 to 2009-10.

Since service tax was not leviable in the state of Jammu and Kashmir, and its proceeds were, therefore, not assignable to this state, the Commission worked out the share of each of the remaining 27 states in the net proceeds of service tax (Table 26.3). It further recommended that if in any year, this tax became leviable in the state of Jammu and Kashmir, the share of each state including that of

Jammu and Kashmir would be in accordance with the percentages given in Table 24.2.

Table 26.2: Inter se Shares of States in the Net Proceeds of All Shareable Union Taxes and Duties

State	Share (per cent)
Andhra Pradesh	7.356
Arunachal Pradesh	0.288
Assam	3.235
Bihar	11.028
Chhattisgarh	2.654
Goa	0.259
Gujarat	3.569
Haryana	1.075
Himachal Pradesh	0.522
Jammu & Kashmir	1.297
Jharkhand	3.361
Karnataka	4.459
Kerala	2.665
Madhya Pradesh	6.711
Maharashtra	4.997
Manipur	0.362
Meghalaya	0.371
Mizoram	0.239
Nagaland	0.263
Orissa	5.161
Punjab	1.299
Rajasthan	5.609
Sikkim	0.227
Tamil Nadu	5.305
Tripura	0.428
Uttar Pradesh	19.264
Uttranchal	0.939
West Bengal	7.057
All States	**100.00**

Source: *Report of the Twelfth Finance Commission*, November 2004, p. 133.

Similarly, if in any year during the period 2005-06 to 2009-10, a tax under Union was not leviable in a state, the share of that state in that tax should be put to zero and the entire proceeds should be distributed among the remaining states by proportionately adjusting their share.

Table 26.3: Shares of the States in the Net Proceeds of Service Tax

State	Share excluding Jammu and Kashmir (per cent)
Andhra Pradesh	7.453
Arunachal Pradesh	0.292
Assam	3.277
Bihar	11.173
Chhattisgarh	2.689
Goa	0.262
Gujarat	3.616
Haryana	1.089
Himachal Pradesh	0.529
Jharkhand	3.405
Karnataka	4.518
Kerala	2.700
Madhya Pradesh	6.799
Maharashtra	5.063
Manipur	0.367
Meghalaya	0.376
Mizoram	0.242
Nagaland	0.266
Orissa	5.229
Punjab	1.316
Rajasthan	5.683
Sikkim	0.230
Tamil Nadu	5.374
Tripura	0.433
Uttar Pradesh	19.517
Uttranchal	0.952
West Bengal	7.150
All States	**100.00**

Source: *Report of the Twelfth Finance Commission*, November 2004, p. 133.

In short, the recommendations of the Commission regarding sharing of Union tax revenue were as follows.

1. The share of States in the net proceeds of shareable Central taxes was fixed at 30.5 per cent, treating additional excise duties in lieu of sales tax as part of the general pool of Central taxes. Share of States to come down to 29.5 per cent, when States are allowed to levy sales tax on sugar, textiles and tobacco.
2. In case of any legislation enacted in respect of service tax, after the notification of the eighty-eighth amendment to the Constitution, revenue accruing to a State should not be less than the share that would accrue to it, had the entire service tax proceeds been part of the shareable pool.
3. The indicative amount of overall transfers to States was fixed at 38 per cent of the Centre's gross revenue receipts.

Thus, the Commission, raised the share of States in shareable Central taxes from 29.5 per cent to 30.5 per cent. Total transfers to States recommended by the Commission amount to Rs. 7,55,752 crore over the five year period 2005-06 to 2009-10. Of this, transfers by way of share in Central taxes and grants-in-aid amount to Rs. 6,13,112 crore and Rs. 1,42,640 crore, respectively. The total transfers recommended by the Commission were higher by 73.8 per cent over those recommended by the Eleventh Finance Commission. Within the total transfers, while the share in Central taxes was higher by 62.9 per cent, grants-in-aid recommended by the Commission were higher by 143.5 per cent over those recommended by the Eleventh Finance Commission.

26.2 Local Bodies

The recommendations of the Commission to strengthen and streamline the working of panchayats and municipalities were as under.

1. "A total grant of Rs. 20,000 crore for the panchayati raj institutions and Rs. 5,000 crore for the urban local bodies may be given to the states for the period 2005-10.
2. The PRIs should be encouraged to take over the assets relating to water supply and sanitation and utilize the grants for repairs/rejuvenation as also the O&M costs. The PRIs should, however, recover at least 50 percent of the recurring costs in the form of user charges.
3. At least 50 per cent of the grants provided to each state for the urban local bodies should be earmarked for the scheme of solid waste management through public-private partnership. The municipalities should concentrate on collection, segregation and transportation of solid waste. The cost of these activities, whether carried out in house or out sourced, could be met from the grants. Besides expenditure on the O&M costs of water supply and sanitation

in rural areas and on the schemes of solid waste management in urban areas, PRIs and ULBs should, out of the grants allocated, give high priority to expenditure on creation of data base and maintenance of accounts through the use of modern technology and management systems, wherever possible. Some of the modern methods like GIS (Geographic Information Systems) for mapping of properties in urban areas and computerization for switching over to a modern system of financial management would go a long way in creating strong local governments, fulfilling the spirit of the 73rd and 74th Constitutional amendments.

4. The states may assess the requirement of each local body on the basis of the principles stated by us and earmark funds accordingly out of the total allocation recommended by us. Grants have not been recommended separately for the normal and the excluded areas under the fifth and sixth schedule of the Constitution. The states having such areas may distribute the grants recommended by us to all local bodies, including those in the excluded areas, in a fair and just manner.
5. The central government should not impose any condition other than those prescribed by us, for release or utilization of these grants, which are largely in the nature of a correction of vertical imbalance between the centre and the states.
6. The normal practice of insisting on the utilisation of amounts already released before further releases are considered, may continue and the grants may be released to a state only after it certifies that the previous releases have been passed on to the local bodies. The amounts due to the states in the first year of our award period i.e. 2005-06 may be released without such an insistence.
7. State governments should not take more than 15 days in transferring the grants to local bodies after these are released by the central government. The centre should take a serious view of any undue delay on the part of the state.
8. The central government should take note of our views on the issues, while formulating or revising various policy measures. In particular, action may be taken to raise the ceiling on profession tax.
9. The state should adopt the best practices to improve the resources of the panchayats.
10. The suggestions made by us in respect of state finance commissions should be acted upon with a view to strengthening the institution of SFCs, so that it may play an effective role in the system of fiscal transfers to the third tier of government." [1]

26.3 Calamity Relief

The Commission recommended as follows.

- "The scheme of CRF be continued in its present form with contributions from the centre and the states in the ratio of 75:25.
- The size of the CRF for our award period is worked out at Rs. 21,333.33 crore.
- The scheme of NCCF may continue in its present form with core corpus of Rs.500 crore. The outgo from the fund may continue to be replenished by way of collection of National Calamity Contingent Duty and levy of special surcharges.
- The definition of natural calamity, as applicable at present, may be expanded to cover landslides, avalanches, cloud burst and pest attacks.
- The centre may continue to make allocation of foodgrains to the needy states as a relief measure, but a transparent policy in this regard is required to be put in place.
- A committee consisting of scientists, flood control specialists and other experts be set up to study and map the hazards to which several states are subject to.
- The provision for disaster preparedness and mitigation needs to be built into the state plans, and not as a part of calamity relief." [2]

26.4 Grants-in-aid to States

The Commission disfavoured the then existing system of imposing a 70:30 ratio between loans and grants for extending plan assistance to non-special category states (10:90 in the case of special category states). Instead, it recommended that the centre should confine itself to extending plan grants to the states, and leave it to the states to decide how much they wish to borrow and from whom.

It recommended a total non-plan revenue deficit grant of Rs. 56,855.87 crore during the award period for 15 States. Eight States were recommended for grants amounting to Rs. 10,171.65 crore over the award period for the education sector, with a minimum of Rs. 20 crore in a year for any eligible state. Seven States were recommended for grants amounting to Rs. 5,887.08 crore over the award period for the health sector, with a minimum of Rs.10 crore a year for any eligible State. The grants for the education and health sectors were an additionality, over and above the normal expenditure to be incurred by the States in these sectors.

A grant of Rs. 15,000 crore over the award period was recommended for maintenance of roads and bridges. This amount was in addition to the normal expenditure which the States would be incurring on maintenance of roads and bridges. This amount was to be provided in equal instalments over the last four years (i.e. 2006-07 to 2009-10) of the award period, so that the States got a year for making preparations to absorb these funds. An amount of Rs. 5,000 crore was recommended as grants for maintenance of public buildings.

A grant of Rs. 1,000 crore spread over the award period was recommended for maintenance of forests. This was an additionality over and above what the States would be spending through their forest departments. A grant of Rs. 625 crore spread over the award period was recommended for heritage conservation. This grant was to be used for preservation and protection of historical monuments, archaeological sites, public libraries, museums and archives, and also for improving the tourist infrastructure to facilitate visits to these sites. An amount of Rs. 7,100 crore was recommended as grant for state specific needs.

26.5 Debt Relief and Corrective Measures

The Commission made the following recommendations in this regard.

1. "Each state must enact a fiscal responsibility legislation prescribing specific annual targets with a view to eliminating the revenue deficit by 2008-09 and reducing fiscal deficits based on a path for reduction of borrowings and guarantees. Enacting the fiscal responsibility legislation on the lines indicated will be a necessary pre-condition for availing of debt relief.
2. Debt relief may not be linked with performance in human development or investment climate.
3. The central loans to states contracted till 31.3.04 and outstanding on 31.3.05 (amounting to Rs. 1,28,795 crore) may be consolidated and rescheduled for a fresh term of 20 years (resulting in repayment in 20 equal instalments), and an interest rate of 7.5 per cent be charged on them. This will be subject to the state enacting the fiscal responsibility legislation and will take effect prospectively from the year in which such legislation is enacted.
4. A debt write-off scheme linked to the reduction of revenue deficit of states may be introduced. Under the scheme, the repayments due from 2005-06 to 2009-10 on central loans contracted up to 31.3.04 and recommended to be consolidated will be eligible for write off. The quantum of write off of repayment will be linked to the absolute amount by which the revenue deficit is reduced in each successive year during the award period. The reduction in the revenue deficit must be cumulatively higher than the cumulative reduction attributable to the interest relief recommended by us. Also, the fiscal deficit of the state must be contained at least to the level of 2004-05. In effect, if the revenue deficit is brought down to zero, the entire repayments during the

period will be written off. The enactment of the fiscal responsibility legislation would be a necessary pre-condition for availing the debt relief under this scheme also with the benefit accruing prospectively.

5. The central government should not act as an intermediary for future lending and allow the states to approach the market directly. If some fiscally weak states are unable to raise funds from the market, the centre could borrow for the purpose of on lending to such states, but the interest rates should remain aligned to the marginal cost of borrowing for the centre.
6. External assistance may be transferred to states on the same terms and conditions as attached to such assistance by external funding agencies, thereby making government of India a financial intermediary without any gain or loss. The external assistance passed through to states should be managed through a separate fund in the public account.
7. The moratorium on repayments and interest payments on the outstanding special term loan amounting to Rs. 3,772 crore as on 31.03.2000 given to Punjab may continue for another two years i.e. up to 2006-07, by which time the central government must finalize the quantum of debt relief to be allowed in terms of the recommendations of the EFC.
8. In respect of relief and rehabilitation loans given to Gujarat from ADB and World Bank through the central government, the central government may, if the government of Gujarat so desires, alter the terms and conditions of these loans, so that these are available to Gujarat on the same terms on which the external agencies have extended these loans.
9. All states should set up sinking funds for amortization of all loans including loans from banks, liabilities on account of NSSF etc. The fund should be maintained outside the consolidated fund of the states and the public account and should not be used for any other purpose, except for redemption of loans.
10. States should set up guarantee redemption funds through earmarked guarantee fees. This should be preceded by risk weighting of guarantees. The quantum of contribution to the fund should be decided accordingly." [3]

26.6 Restructuring Public Finances

The Commission made the following recommendations in this regard.

1. Centre and States should improve the combined tax-GDP ratio to 17.6 per cent by 2009-10.
2. Combined debt-GDP ratio, with external debt measured at historical exchange rates, should be brought down to 75 per cent by 2009-10.
3. Fiscal deficit to GDP targets for the Centre and States should be fixed at 3 per cent.

4. Revenue deficit of the Centre and States should be brought down to zero by 2008-09.
5. Interest payments relative to revenue receipts should be brought down to 28 per cent and 15 per cent in the case of the Centre and States respectively.
6. States to follow a recruitment policy in a manner so that the total salary bill, relative to revenue expenditure, net of interest payments, does not exceed 35 per cent.
7. Each State should enact a fiscal responsibility legislation providing for elimination of revenue deficit by 2008-09 and reducing fiscal deficit to 3 per cent of State Domestic Product.
8. The system of on-lending should be brought to an end over time. The long-term goal should be to bring down debt-GDP ratio to 28 per cent each for the Centre and the States.

26.7 Permanent Secretariat for the Finance Commission

It has become almost a ritual for finance commissions to suggest to the Central Government the need for a permanent secretariat in the Ministry of Finance for the work related to the finance commission on a continuing basis. Successive finance commissions have argued that such an arrangement is necessary for effective functioning of the finance commission and for proper implementation of the recommendations made by it. Unfortunately, the recommendations of the finance commission in regard to creation of a permanent secretariat have not been taken seriously.

It is noteworthy that finance commissions are set up as temporary bodies every five years or so for a specific duration and are wound up as soon as they submit their recommendations. The temporary character of finance commissions necessitates that each time a finance commission is constituted, all administrative and infrastructural arrangements such as hiring of office building, appointment of personnel, procurement of equipment etc. are made afresh. It also necessitates that each commission collects data and information afresh due to which considerable time lapses before the commission can start functioning in an effective manner.

Although the finance commission division (FCD) in the Ministry of Finance provides support to the new finance commission in the form of continuity of data, it falls short of the expectations of the commission. For example, the Eleventh Finance Commission complained that the sole job of the FCD had been to monitor the expenditure and release of upgradation grants to the states and that it had not devoted itself to building a database on central/state finances. It had only been keeping the records left over by previous finance commissions, without proper referencing. The Commission recommended that there should be a permanent secretariat with core research staff placed under an officer of the level of an additional secretary to Government of India and that this would facilitate coordination with the Ministries/Departments of the Government of India as also with the State Governments at appropriate levels. This would also ensure an up-to-date building of data base on centre-state finances and documentation, which could be used by the commission when it is constituted.

The Commission under study also lamented that FCD remained a small cell in the Ministry of Finance and did not appear to be capable of providing the necessary assistance to it. Moreover, FCD is accountable only to the Ministry of Finance. Bulk of problems faced by successive finance commissions can be overcome by providing for a permanent secretariat for the purpose of doing the preliminary work both in terms of collecting data and organising research. [4] The Commission, therefore, recommended that the finance commission division should be converted into a full fledged department serving as the permanent secretariat for finance commission. Legally and constitutionally, there is no infirmity in putting such an arrangement in place.

In spite of successive finance commissions stressing the importance and need for constant upgradation of data and organising studies relevant to the working of the future commissions, not much attention seems to have been paid by the Ministry of Finance to this need.

Notes

1. *Report of the Twelfth Finance Commission*, November 2004, pp. 260-63.
2. Ibid., p. 263.
3. Ibid., p. 265-66.
4. It is noteworthy in this connection that the terms of reference of the finance commission were initially confined to its role under the Constitution viz., the distribution between the Union and the States of the net proceeds of taxes and the grants-in-aid to the revenues of the states. However, over the period since the commencement of the Constitution, more and more items have been added to the terms of reference of finance commissions. The most notable among these are the additional terms arising from the 73rd and 74th amendments of the Constitution as a result of which finance commissions are required to make recommendations on the measures needed to augment the consolidated fund of the states to supplement the resources of panchayats and municipalities. Even the other issues referred to the commission at the discretion of the President have become more numerous and complex. For example, Eleventh Finance Commission and the Twelfth Finance Commission were required to make recommendations on the restructuring of the finances of the Union and the State Governments. Similarly, most commissions were required to address issues relating to the debt position of the states and the financing of calamity relief. The Twelfth Finance Commission was also required to review the Fiscal Reform Facility introduced by the central government on the basis of the recommendations of the Eleventh Finance Commission and suggest measures for effective achievement of its objectives. The expanding

scope of the terms of reference and the need to have a mechanism to monitor implementation of the recommendation of the finance commission, place enormous demands on the preparatory and continuing work of the commission that was not envisaged by the framers of the Constitution.

27

Issues in Centre-State Financial Relations

Since the commencement of the Constitution in 1950, various problems and conflicts have arisen in Centre-State financial relations in India. Such problems are endemic of all federal governments in the world.

27.1 Centralisation of Revenues and Certain State Functions

States have often complained that there is a perceptible trend of centralisation of resources, in addition to centralisation of certain State functions.

27.1.1 Centralisation of Revenues: Constitutional provisions regarding taxation and borrowing powers of the Centre and the States, place the former in a commanding position. Not only the major sources of tax revenue belong to the Centre, its borrowing powers are also unlimited. Moreover, the Central Government enjoys the exclusive right to print currency. (For Statistical evidence, see section 3.4 of chapter 3 of this book).

It may be recalled that as a result of a change brought about in the Income Tax Act by the Finance Act of 1959, the income tax paid by companies was classified as corporation tax and was thus excluded from the pool of income tax hitherto available for distribution with the States. At that time the States had pointed out to the Third Finance Commission that the change had deprived them of an expanding source of revenue to which they had hitherto a constitutional entitlement. Though the amendment was made to simplify levy and collection, the indirect effect was a diminution in the amount available for distribution with the States.

Similarly, the tax on railway passenger fares was repealed and merged in the basic fares from April 1, 1961. The States were unhappy on being deprived of a potentially elastic source of revenue to which they were legally entitled in terms of Article 269 of the Constitution. To compensate the States for the loss of revenue, the Government decided to pay annually a sum of Rs. 12.50 crore for distribution among the States during the five year period 1961-62 to 1965-66. In any case, it was only a discretionary grant in lieu of a legal right extinguished. (For more details, see chapter 12 of this book).

Such unilateral financial decisions by the Centre did not go well with the States. It is important and even disturbing to note that the States are becoming dependent on Central assistance on an ever increasing scale. This arises partly out of the impact of committed expenditure of the completed plan projects and partly for other reasons. This increasing dependence is diluting the accountability of the State Cabinets to their Legislatures. Moreover, it is coming in the way of the development of a greater sense of responsibility in their administration.

27.1.2 Centralisation of Certain State Functions: Although the division of taxation powers between the Centre and the States is clear-cut, it is not so in the case of economic activities. A number of economic functions fall in the Concurrent List and those which belong to State List are subject, in many cases, to the provisions of the Union List. As these situations are described below, it will be noticed that they are partly the result of the original scheme of the Constitution and partly attributable to the amendments of the Constitution after it became operative in 1950. Although each such amendment had a logic of its own, they can be said to have encroached upon States' sphere of legislation if considered collectively (Table 27.1).

Agriculture as such figures in the State List (Entry 14) but certain aspects of agriculture fall in the Concurrent List/Union List. Thus, fisheries belong to the State List (Entry 21) but fishing and fisheries beyond territorial waters belong to the Union List (Entry 57). The enlargement of Entry 33 in the Concurrent List through the Constitution (Third Amendment) Act, 1954 made agriculture virtually a concurrent subject. It reads as follows: "Trade and Commerce in, and the production, supply and distribution of: (a) the products of any industry where the control of such industry by the Union is declared by Parliament by law to be expedient in the public interest, and imported goods of the same kind as such products; (b) foodstuffs, including edible oilseeds and oils; (c) cattle fodder, including oilcakes and other concentrates; (d) raw cotton, whether ginned or unginned and cotton seeds; and (e) raw jute." Thus, trade, commerce, production, supply and distribution of foodstuffs including edible oils and oil seeds are covered by the Concurrent List.

Similarly, animal husbandry and veterinary training are State subjects (Entry 15) but prevention of cruelty to animals is a concurrent subject (Entry 17). Forestry and protection of wild animals and birds originally belonged to the State List (Entries 18 and 20). However, they were transferred to the Concurrent List (Entries 17A and 17B) through the Constitution (Forty-second Amendment) Act, 1976.

Also included in the Concurrent List are other economic activities such as economic and social planning, population control and family planning, commercial and industrial monopolies, trade unions, social security, and price control (Entries 20, 20A, 21, 22, 23 and 34 respectively).

Table 27.1: Constitutional Amendments Affecting Division of Financial/Economic Powers between the Centre and the States

Name of the Act	Date of Commencement	Nature of the Amendment
Constitution (Third Amendment) Act, 1954	22.2.1955	Entry 33 of Concurrent List of the Seventh Schedule was enlarged by transferring the contents of Article 369. Parliament was enabled to have concurrent jurisdiction to legislate on trade, commerce, production, supply, and distribution of foodstuffs, raw cotton, raw jute etc.
Constitution (Sixth Amendment) Act, 1956	11. 9. 1956	Articles 269 and 286, and Entry 54 of State list of the Seventh Schedule amended. Entry 92A inserted in the Union List of the same schedule. Parliament was empowered to impose sales tax on inter-State trade.
Constitution (Seventh Amendment) Act, 1956	1. 11. 1956	Entry 24 of State List of the Seventh Schedule pertaining to industries was made subject to entries 7 and 52 of the Union List of the same schedule. Entry 7 relates to industries considered necessary for defence while entry 52 covers industries the control of which is considered expedient in public interest. Before the amendment entry 24 was subject only to the provisions of entry 52.
Constitution (Forty Second Amendment) Act, 1976	Different provisions came into force on different dates commencing from 3.1.1977	Forests, and protection of wild animals and birds originally belonging to State List were transferred to Concurrent List. Population control and family planning were inserted in the Concurrent List as entry 20A. States power to levy tax on advertisements broadcast by radio or television was precluded in entry 55 of State List in addition to the already existing exception in that entry of tax on 'advertisements published in newspapers'.
Constitution (Forty Sixth Amendment) Act, 1982	2. 2. 1998	Parliament was empowered to levy taxes on the consignment of goods in inter-State trade. Entry 92B was inserted in the Union List of the 7th Schedule for the purpose and simultaneously sub-clause 269(1)(h) was inserted in Article 269.

Sources: Compiled from (1) Government of India, Ministry of Law, Justice and Company Affairs, *The Constitution of India*; (2) *Report of the Commission on Centre-State Relations*, Part I, 1988, pp. 93-96; and (3) Durga Das Basu, *Introduction to the Constitution of India* (New Delhi: Prentice Hall of India Pvt. Ltd., 1987), pp. 403-12.

Water and power development is another important area of State activity subject to the Central control. Water supplies, irrigation and canals, drainage and embankments, water storage and water power belong to the State List (Entry 17) but these are subject to the provisions of Union List (Entry 56) which deals with the regulation and development of inter-State rivers and river valleys. Since electricity belongs to Concurrent List (Entry 38), the Centre's concurrent jurisdiction on water power is automatic.

Regulation of mines and mineral development belongs to State List (Entry 23) subject to certain provisions of the Union List. Thus, mineral resources necessary for the production of atomic energy (List 1, Entry 6) belong to the Centre and so also oil fields and mineral oil resources, petroleum and petroleum products, and other dangerously inflammable liquids and substances (Entry 53). Similarly, Central Government is empowered to regulate mines and mineral development to the extent to which it is in public interest to do so (Entry 54). Moreover, the regulation of labour and safety in mines and oil fields is also a Central subject (Entry 55).

In the field of transport, roads, bridges, ferries, and other means of communication (not specified in List I), municipal tramways, ropeways, inland waterways and traffic thereon and vehicles other than mechanically propelled vehicles belong to the State List (Entry 13). However, this is subject to certain provisions in the Union List and the Concurrent List. Thus, national highways, and national waterways (List I, Entries 23 and 24 respectively) belong to the Central Government. Similarly, the Centre has concurrent jurisdiction over ports other than major ports, and shipping and navigation on inland waterways (List III, Entries 31 and 32 respectively). It may be noted that Centre enjoys exclusive powers in major areas of transport and communications. The following fields are included in the Union List: Railways, maritime shipping and navigation, major ports, airways, and posts and telegraphs (entries 22, 25, 27, 29 and 31 respectively).

The all important sphere of industries falls within the purview of Sate List (Entry 24) but through the Constitution (Seventh Amendment) Act, 1956, this field was made subject to Entries 7 and 52 of the Union List. Before this amendment entry 24 of State List was subject only to the provisions of Entry 52 of Union List. Entry 7 covers industries considered necessary for the purpose of defence or for the prosecution of war. Entry 52 covers industries the control of which by the Centre is considered expedient in public interest. Besides this, the Centre also enjoys concurrent jurisdiction (List III, Entry 33) in many matters related to industries. The main legislation used by the Centre to exercise its right under entry 52 is the Industrial (Development and Regulation) Act, 1951, the first schedule of which includes industries brought under the Central control in public interest. Almost all important industries in the country are included in this schedule. Added to this control is the Central ownership of a vast public sector comprising industrial, financial and commercial enterprises.

In view of the foregoing account, it cannot be gainsaid that Centre's inroads into State subjects have caused stresses and strains in the relations between the two-tiers of the Government.

27.2 Inter-regional Inequalities and Transfers

Federalism is not only a unifying but also a levelling up force. Considerable economic inequalities exist among different States of India and their reduction is an argument in favour of centralisation of resources.

Depending upon the availability of data, a number of indicators can be used to describe inter-State economic disparities in a federation. The most representative of these indicators is the per capita income in different States. Wide disparities exist in the per capita income of various States in India (Table 27.2). Various policy instruments have been used to mitigate inter-State economic disparities, including the transfer of resources from the Centre to the States, particularly to financially weaker States.

Regional imbalances may be natural due to unequal distribution of natural resources and/or man-made in the sense of neglect of some regions and preference for others for investment and infrastructural facilities. Since different provinces are not equally endowed with resources, they have dissimilar industrial bases. As a result, the well-endowed provinces have a higher per capita income and hence a sound revenue base for their governments than the less-endowed provinces.

In India, apart from uneven distribution of geographical advantages, historical factors have also contributed to regional inequities. The British rulers developed only those regions which possessed facilities for manufacturing and trading activities. Thus, in the pre-1947 period almost all industrial and commercial activities remained confined to major cities, viz. Bombay (in Maharashtra), Calcutta (in West Bengal), and Madras (in Tamil Nadu).

Uneven development during British rule left many States of the country much backward as compared to certain other States. To ensure that benefits of development planning flow to all parts of the country, regional balanced development has all along been accepted as an important objective of economic planning. No doubt, priority has been given in the plans to the development of notified backward areas.

Table 27.2: Per Capita Net State Domestic Product (SDP) of Different States at Factor Cost, 2004-2005 (At Current Prices) (New Series, Base: 1993-94)

Descending order (Rs.)

Sl. No.	State/UT	Per Capita Net SDP
1.	Chandigarh	67,370
2.	Goa	58,184
3.	Pondicherry	56,034
4.	Delhi	53,976
5.	Haryana	32,712
6.	Maharashtra	32,170
7.	Punjab	30,701
8.	Gujarat	28,355
9.	Himachal Pradesh	27,485
10.	Kerala	27,048
11.	Tamil Nadu	25,965
12.	Sikkim	24,115
13.	Karnataka	23,945
14.	Andhra Pradesh	23,153
15.	West Bengal	22,497
16.	Arunachal Pradesh	19,724
17.	Uttrakhand	19,652
18.	Meghalaya	19,572
19.	Rajasthan	16,212
20.	Jammu & Kashmir	16,190
21.	Chhattisgarh	15.073
22.	Manipur	14,901
23.	Madhya Pradesh	14,069
24.	Assam	13,633
25.	Orissa	13,601
26.	Jharkhand	13,013
27.	Uttar Pradesh	11,477
28.	Bihar	5,772
All India Per Capita Net National Product		**23,241**

Source: Reserve Bank of India, *Handbook of Statistics on the Indian Economy,* 2006-2007, Table 8 (excerpted).

Ever since the launching of the First Five Year Plan in 1951, regional balanced development of the country has remained an important objective of the planning process. In fact, the urgency of reducing regional inequalities has increased with every plan.

Successive plans have stressed the need to develop backward regions of the country. In promoting regional balanced development, public sector enterprises were located in most backward areas of the country. It has helped these areas in terms of development of infrastructure, employment opportunities, and growth of ancillary industries to a limited extent.

True, there has been a significant improvement in the living conditions of the people after Independence. In some States of the country, life expectancy, infant mortality, literacy, and availability of basic services such as drinking water and domestic electricity have reached satisfactory levels. However, there are considerable disparities across States, between the urban and the rural areas, between males and females, and between those who work in organised sector and those who are in the unorganised sector. These disparities are reflected in the levels of poverty in different States (Table 27.3) and growth rates recorded by different States in recent Five Year Plans (Table 27.4). Economic reforms process since the early 1990s has left in its trail a variety of inequalities which have caused socio-politico tensions. Some States (Karnataka, Andhra Pradesh, Maharashtra) have surged ahead while others are lagging behind.

It may be recalled that New Agricultural Strategy (popularly called Green Revolution) of the mid-1960s also promoted inter-regional and inter-personal inequalities. The bulk of increase in output remained concentrated in a few regions, particularly Punjab, Haryana and Western Uttar Pradesh while many backward States remained unaffected by the new agricultural techniques.

The Indian Central Plans have traditionally focused on setting only national targets. However, recent experience suggests that the performance of different States varies considerably, and cognisance has to be taken of this issue. For example, although the economy as a whole has accelerated, the growth rates of different States have diverged and some of the poorest States have actually seen a deceleration in growth. It is important to recognise that the sharp increase in the growth rate and significant improvement in the social indicators will be possible only if there is a corresponding improvement in the performance of the relatively laggard States.

In order to emphasise the importance of ensuring a balanced development for all States, the Tenth Five Year Plan (2002-07) included a State-wise break-up of the broad developmental targets, including targets for growth rates and social development, which are consistent with the national targets (Table 27.5). These State-specific targets took into account the needs, potentialities and constraints present in each State and the scope for improvement in their performance, given these constraints. It needs to be emphasised that these State-wise targets were not meant to be a substitute for or to over-ride the process of State Plan formulation. They were more in the nature of indicative guidelines for facilitating planning in the States.

Table 27.3: Poverty Projections for Different States: 2006-07

Sl. No.	State/UT	Rural		Urban		Combined	
		% of poor	No. of poor (lakh)	% of poor	No. of poor (lakh)	% of poor	No. of poor (lakh)
1.	Andhra Pradesh	4.58	26.97	18.99	41.75	8.49	68.72
2.	Arunachal Pradesh	37.89	3.54	4.48	0.14	29.33	3.68
3.	Assam	37.89	95.36	4.48	1.78	33.33	97.14
4.	Bihar	44.81	482.16	32.69	54.74	43.18	536.91
5.	Goa	2.00	0.13	2.00	0.16	2.00	0.29
6.	Gujarat	2.00	6.88	2.00	4.38	2.00	11.25
7.	Haryana	2.00	3.30	2.00	1.51	2.00	4.81
8.	Himachal Pradesh	2.00	1.18	2.00	0.14	2.00	1.32
9.	Jammu & Kashmir	N.A	N.A	N.A	N.A	N.A	N.A
10.	Karnataka	7.77	28.66	8.00	16.34	7.85	45.00
11.	Kerala	1.63	4.03	9.34	8.01	3.61	12.04
12.	Madhya Pradesh	28.73	192.07	31.77	74.46	29.52	266.54
13.	Maharashtra	16.95	101.61	15.20	72.68	16.18	174.30
14.	Manipur	37.89	8.10	4.48	0.27	30.52	8.37
15.	Meghalaya	37.89	7.99	4.48	0.24	31.14	8.23
16.	Mizoram	37.89	1.88	4.48	0.23	20.76	2.12
17.	Nagaland	37.89	8.01	4.48	0.21	31.86	8.22
18.	Orissa	41.72	139.12	37.46	23.57	41.04	162.69
19.	Punjab	2.00	3.40	2.00	1.95	2.00	5.35
20.	Rajasthan	11.09	54.41	15.42	23.44	12.11	77.86
21.	Sikkim	37.89	2.08	4.48	0.03	33.78	2.12
22.	Tamil Nadu	3.68	12.46	9.64	31.61	6.61	44.07
23.	Tripura	37.89	10.70	4.48	0.28	31.88	10.98
24.	Uttar Pradesh	24.25	373.16	26.17	111.25	24.67	484.41
25.	West Bengal	21.98	137.53	8.98	22.21	18.30	159.73
26.	A&N Island	3.68	0.10	9.64	0.14	5.82	0.24
27.	Chandigarh	2.00	0.02	2.00	0.19	2.00	0.21
28.	Dadra & Nagar Haveli	2.00	0.04	2.00	0.02	2.00	0.06
29.	Daman & Diu	2.00	0.03	2.00	0.01	2.00	0.04
30.	Delhi	2.00	0.19	2.00	3.18	2.00	3.38
31.	Lakshadweep	1.63	0.01	9.34	0.02	4.59	0.03
32.	Pondicherry	3.68	0.13	9.64	0.70	7.72	0.83
	All India	21.07	1705.26	15.06	495.67	19.34	2200.94

Source: Government of India, Planning Commission, *Tenth Five Year Plan* (2002-07), Volume I, p. 45.

Table 27.4: Growth Rates in State Domestic Product in Different Plans

Sl. No.	State/UT	Eighth Plan	Ninth Plan	Tenth Plan
1.	Andhra Pradesh	5.4	4.6	6.8
2.	Arunachal Pradesh	5.1	4.4	8.0
3.	Assam	2.8	2.1	6.2
4.	Bihar	2.2	4.0	6.2
5.	Goa	8.9	5.5	9.2
6.	Gujarat	12.4	4.0	10.2
7.	Haryana	5.2	4.1	7.9
8.	Himachal Pradesh	6.5	5.9	8.9
9.	Jammu & Kashmir	5.0	5.2	6.3
10.	Karnataka	6.2	7.2	10.1
11.	Kerala	6.5	5.7	6.5
12.	Madhya Pradesh	6.3	4.0	7.0
13.	Maharashtra	8.9	4.7	7.4
14.	Manipur	4.6	6.4	6.5
15.	Meghalaya	3.8	6.2	6.3
16.	Mizoram	---	---	5.3
17.	Nagaland	8.9	2.6	5.6
18.	Orissa	2.1	5.1	6.2
19.	Punjab	4.7	4.4	6.4
20.	Rajasthan	7.5	3.5	8.3
21.	Sikkim	5.3	8.3	7.9
22.	Tamil Nadu	7.0	6.3	8.0
23.	Tripura	6.6	7.4	7.3
24.	Uttar Pradesh	4.9	4.0	7.6
25.	West Bengal	6.3	6.9	8.8
26.	A&N Islands	10.3	3.7	6.6
27.	Chandigarh	---	9.5	10.6
28.	Delhi	4.3	9.4	10.6
29.	Pondicherry	7.7	12.5	10.7
30.	Chhattisgarh	---	---	6.1
31.	Jharkhand	---	---	6.9
32.	Uttranchal	---	---	6.8

Source: Government of India, Planning Commission, *Tenth Five Year Plan* (2002-07), Volume I, p. 41.

It is an unfortunate fact that many States have de-emphasised the planning process and have allowed their planning systems to degenerate.

Table 27.5: State-Wise Growth Target for the Tenth Five Year Plan

Sl. No.	States/UT	State-Wise Growth Target			GSDP Growth
		Agriculture	Industry	Services	
1.	A&N Island	1.00	10.41	7.97	6.6
2.	Andhra Pradesh	3.05	8.01	8.39	6.8
3.	Arunachal Pradesh	4.00	8.90	10.50	8.0
4.	Assam	3.82	5.00	9.00	6.2
5.	Bihar	3.75	6.00	8.00	6.2
6.	Chandigarh	-2.00	10.41	10.96	10.6
7.	Chhattisgarh	3.00	7.50	7.00	6.1
8.	Delhi	-12.21	6.90	12.01	10.6
9.	Goa	-0.90	6.25	12.36	9.2
10.	Gujarat	4.03	12.23	10.44	10.2
11.	Haryana	4.07	9.56	10.33	7.9
12.	Himachal Pradesh	4.55	12.49	8.26	8.9
13.	Jammu & Kashmir	4.20	5.21	8.00	6.3
14.	Jharkhand	3.00	7.44	8.00	6.9
15.	Karnataka	4.99	11.34	12.51	10.1
16.	Kerala	3.05	5.89	8.17	6.5
17.	Madhya Pradesh	4.00	7.75	9.00	7.0
18.	Maharashtra	3.56	8.22	8.09	7.4
19.	Manipur	3.59	8.33	7.39	6.5
20.	Meghalaya	4.00	6.87	7.05	6.3
21.	Mizoram	2.00	4.16	6.84	5.3
22.	Nagaland	4.00	7.29	5.78	5.6
23.	Orissa	4.07	4.88	8.73	6.2
24.	Pondicherry	1.10	13.01	9.19	10.7
25.	Punjab	4.07	8.06	8.00	6.4
26.	Rajasthan	4.50	10.06	9.63	8.3
27.	Sikkim	5.00	5.21	10.36	7.9
28.	Tamil Nadu	3.54	7.37	9.77	8.0
29.	Tripura	3.90	9.37	8.43	7.3
30.	Uttranchal	3.50	7.00	8.70	6.8
31.	Uttar Pradesh	4.67	11.05	7.92	7.6
32.	West Bengal	5.09	9.15	10.76	8.8
	All India	4.0	8.9	9.4	8.0

Source: Government of India, Planning Commission, *Tenth Five Year Plan* (2002-07), Volume I, p.42.

As a result, many State Plans are not based on any rigorous and analytically meaningful appraisal of resources and capabilities or of the strategies that can be used to accelerate the development process.

The presentation of State-wise targets in the national Plan will serve as a catalyst to reinvigorate planning at the State level. There are two dimensions to this. First, the very recognition of the diversities that exist in the country should lead to a similar recognition at the sub-State level. Different districts within a State are at different levels of development and have different capabilities. A State Plan will, therefore, have to recognise these differences, and ensure that the State-wise targets set in the State Plan are consistent with what is planned at the district level. This will require careful consideration of the sectoral pattern of growth and its regional dispersion within the State. It will also focus attention on the nature of reforms that will have to be implemented at the State level to achieve the growth targets set for the States. Secondly, a statement of the comparative position of the various States in different dimensions of development is in itself an important method for encouraging introspection, leading hopefully to effective benchmarking for future progress. Much has been said about the value of experience-sharing and best practice adoption, but these are contingent upon recognition of the possibilities that exist.

Expressing concern at regional inequalities, the Approach Paper on Eleventh Five Year Plan (2007-2012) released by the Government in November 2006 noted, "Regional divides are another challenge for the 11th Plan. Balanced regional development has been an important objective in our planning and various instruments including fiscal incentives, industrial policies and directly targeted programmes have been deployed in the past to achieve it. Some policies, such as industrial licensing, are no longer relevant in today's economic environment since investment cannot be directed to particular locations. In a competitive world, investment must be allowed to flow to locations perceived to have an attractive investment climate and better infrastructural facilities. While this has definitely generated efficiency, there is, at the same time, evidence of increasing regional divides. Growth performances across states have been varied; the performance of poorer states with poorer infrastructure has been lagging.

While income growth performance has diverged, there is welcome evidence of some convergence in education and health indicators across the states. The gap between the well and poor performing states has somewhat narrowed and the health and education outcomes in the poorer states have registered improvement. Regardless, a much larger effort is needed in this area. Sarva Shiksha Abhiyan and National Rural Health Mission have already put the institutional architecture in place. The states will be supported to improve their governance for delivering these services effectively.

These improvements in social infrastructure must be complemented by improvements in physical and economic infrastructure, which make for a pro-investment environment. This is the surest way of ensuring an improvement in growth performance of poorer states. The emphasis on infrastructure in the 11th Plan will help to achieve a more balanced regional development. However, the Centre's efforts to improve infrastructure need to be complemented by parallel efforts by the states. The role of the state governments is especially important in the power sector where operational responsibility lies entirely in their hands." [1]

27.3 Public Borrowings and Indebtedness of States

Public debt is a method by which governments obtain money. Public debts are incurred through public loans. A loan may be either voluntary or compulsory. A government may raise loans either internally or externally. Clearly, external loans are voluntary in nature. Public loans may be for short, medium or long period. Short-term loans are also known as *floating debt.* Long term loans are also called *funded debt.* Debt requirements of a government may be classified on the basis of purpose also. A government may resort to borrowings for productive or unproductive purposes.

Public borrowings involve problems of debt management which is clearly related to monetary policy. The payment of interest on and the repayment of principal of public debt (debt servicing) form part of public expenditure. Public debts, unlike taxes, leave behind liabilities for future generations.

Long-term borrowings by a government are justified when the benefits of a capital project undertaken by it are likely to be reaped over a long period of time, i.e. by more than one generation of taxpayers. The financing of such projects should place the repayment burden on the present as well as future generations. If long-term capital projects are financed out of current revenues and/or short-term borrowings, the future generations would enjoy free riding. Thus, it is both fair and efficient that projects with long-term benefits are financed through long-term borrowings.

Access to long-term borrowings by a lower level government though desirable is hindered by a variety of factors. Generally, central government imposes restrictions on the borrowing powers of the state governments which, in turn, impose restrictions on the borrowing powers of the local bodies under them. Since borrowings by the lower level government are guaranteed, in most case, by the higher level government, the latter has a right to impose such restrictions. These restrictions apply to (a) the type of debt, (b) amount of debt, (c) term of the debt, (d) rate of debt, and (e) use of debt funds. Approval of the higher level government, often cumbersome, is needed before the debt is floated.

Moreover, capital markets in underdeveloped countries are not fully developed. As in the developed West, bond markets cannot be successfully introduced in the absence of institutional set up in place. Besides, the track record of state/local governments as borrowers is rather poor. Till they establish their credit worthiness, and financial intermediaries come of age, borrowings by lower level governments in underdeveloped countries are not likely to dominate their finances.

27.3.1 Instruments of Government Borrowings: The Government of India borrows heavily both internally and externally. Internal borrowings of the Government are chiefly meant to meet budgetary deficit. External borrowings are meant to meet deficit in the balance of payments.

The main sources of internal borrowings are: individuals, commercial banks, financial institutions and the Reserve Bank of India. Borrowings from the RBI are through ways and means advances (WMA).

Another important instrument of Government borrowing is the Statutory Liquidity Ratio (SLR). Under this system, commercial banks and other financial institutions are required to invest prescribed proportions of their assets/liabilities in Government securities. Government also raises loans from the general public through regular floatation of securities and bonds like Kisan Vikas Patras and various other small saving schemes.

The major sources of external borrowings are the international agencies like the IMF and the World Bank, foreign governments, and foreign private sources. Short-term borrowings from abroad are mainly used to meet balance of payments requirements. Long-term foreign borrowings are needed to finance development projects under the Five Year Plans.

27.3.2 Constitutional Provisions Pertaining to Public Borrowings: Under Article 292 the executive power of the Centre extends to borrowing, either within or outside India, upon the security of the Consolidated Fund of India, within such limits, if any, as may from time to time be fixed by Parliament. However, the borrowing power of a State (Article 293) is subject to a number of restrictions: (i) it cannot borrow outside India; (ii) it can borrow within the territory of India subject to the following conditions (a) limitations as may be imposed by the State Legislature, (b) consent of the Union Government to raise fresh loan if the Union has guaranteed an outstanding loan of the State, (c) consent of the Union to raise fresh loan if a Union loan to the State remains outstanding. Since all the States are in debt to the Centre, they have to obtain Centre's permission for raising loans. These restrictions are meant to avoid uncontrolled borrowings by the States and thus to prevent the possibility of any State becoming defaulter or insolvent.

There is a feeling in some quarters that the Constitution has unduly restricted the borrowing powers of the States. The Commission on Centre-State Relations, 1988 had suggested that a distinction should be made between short-term loans (under one year) and medium and long-term loans. It recommended that the Centre should give its consent freely to States for borrowing from banks and other financial institutions for periods less than one year under clause (4) of Article 293.

The suggestion that a thorough examination of the States indebtedness should be undertaken by a National Debt Commission as *one-shot operation* did not find favour with the Commission which believed that in the fast changing situation, the results from such an operation will soon be outdated. The problem of States indebtedness is serious and remedial measures are called for in this regard. Any delay in this matter would only compound the difficulties of the States, particularly highly indebted States.

27.3.3 Indebtedness of States: The mounting debt and debt-servicing liabilities of the States have attracted considerable attention in recent years. The non-Plan revenue gap of the States is looked after by the Finance Commission while the Planning Commission takes care of the Plan gap, both on revenue and capital accounts. Thus, the deficit in non-Plan capital account of the States which mainly concerns repayment of Central loans has remained neglected.

Another reason for the high and growing indebtedness of the States is the composition of Central assistance for Plans given under the Gadgil Formula. The existing pattern of assistance has a loan-grant ratio of 70:30. The States are generally unhappy with this arrangement made way back in 1969. The large loan component of Plan assistance has proved very burdensome for the States over the years. [2] In the context of grant-loan components of Plan assistance, it is important to bear in mind that Centre itself raises a significant part of its total resources through borrowings.

The problem of States indebtedness is not new though it has aggravated in recent years. Debt-related relief to the States may be provided in various forms, viz. write-offs, rescheduling of the loans with a view to shifting the timing of repayments, consolidation of past loans on common terms, and reduction of interest rate.

The Second Finance commission was asked to examine this problem and make suitable recommendations to reduce States debt burden. The Commission recommended, *inter alia*, the postponement of repayments but it did not help to tackle the problem on a long-term basis. The matter was again referred to the Fourth Finance Commission which expressed its inability to make a thorough investigation of the problem and suggest lasting solutions in a short period of time at its disposal.

At the time of appointment of the Fifth Finance Commission, the problem of States unauthorised overdrafts had become quite serious. The Central Government asked this Commission to examine the issue and suggest measures to discourage the States from resorting to unauthorised overdrafts. The Commission came down severely on the States and recommended that the Central Government should repay the amount of States unauthorised overdrafts to the Reserve Bank of India by adjusting that amount against the grants payable to the concerned States. The Commission further recommended that even after such repayments through grant adjustment, if the States continue to over borrow unauthorisedly from the Reserve Bank of India, the Central Government should invoke constitutional provisions to assume administrative responsibility on account of the financial breakdown of the concerned States. The Government accepted the first recommendation in principle and rejected the second one.

The matter again came up in the terms of reference of the Sixth Finance Commission. It was asked to estimate the non-Plan capital gaps in the States budget and recommend the extent of revision of terms of repayment of outstanding Central loans to the States so as to reduce such gaps. The Commission recommended moratorium on the repayment of certain Central loans and writing off a few old loans of small amount. The Eighth and the Ninth Finance Commissions recommended debt reliefs of Rs. 2,285 crore (for the period 1984-89) and Rs. 494 crore (for the period 1990-95) respectively.

The Tenth Finance Commission noted the following disturbing features of the debt profile of States and its management, "(i) diversion of borrowed funds for meeting revenue expenditure, (ii) use of loans in unproductive enterprises, or enterprises which are potentially productive but are beset by poor performance, and currently yielding low or even negative returns, (iii) non-provision for depreciation or amortisation funds in respect of government owned assets, leading to repayments out of fresh borrowing." [3]

The Commission considered debt relief measures keeping in view the following objectives, "(i) that the quantum of relief is limited; (ii) that priority is given to States under severe fiscal strain; and (iii) that incentives are given for better fiscal management." [4] Its scheme for debt relief had two parts, "(i) a scheme for general debt relief for all States linked to fiscal performance, and (ii) specific relief for States with high fiscal stress, special category States, and States with debt problems warranting special attention." [5] The Commission estimated the quantum of relief on account of special debt relief schemes at Rs. 701 crore. The quantum of relief with respect to the incentive scheme suggested by it could not be estimated as it depended on the future performance of the States.

In its Report submitted to the Government in November 2004, the Twelfth Finance Commission made the following points concerning debt restructuring:

- "In 2002-03, the central government brought out a debt-swap scheme to facilitate the state governments to swap their high cost debt owed to government of India with additional market borrowings and a part of current small saving transfers...The central government has used the receipts under the debt-swap scheme to repay its liabilities to the National Small Savings Fund (NSSF). This has the effect of bringing down centre's overall debt as well as its effective interest rate.
- The central government should phase out its intermediation in borrowing by the states. Where necessary, this should be managed through a public account. However, there is a need to determine borrowing limits for each state taking into account borrowing from all sources including small savings and states public accounts and reserve funds. The prescribed borrowing limit on states' aggregate fiscal deficit in our restructuring plan is 3 per cent. In their case also, revenue deficits should be brought to zero by 2008-09. Once stabilized, these deficit rules should be taken to apply over the medium term with some changes to take into account the cyclical pattern.
- Our suggested debt restructuring programme for the states will have two components: a consolidation of all state debt to the centre outstanding at the end of 2004-05 at an interest rate of 7.5 per cent to be repaid in 20 years, and a debt relief scheme linked to achievement in reducing revenue deficits. We are proposing that as a precondition for availing the benefit of the scheme, all states should enact a fiscal responsibility legislation, that provides for eliminating revenue deficit in the respective states no later than 2008-09, incorporates annual targets for reduction of fiscal and revenue deficits, and presents to the respective legislatures a consolidated growth and fiscal strategy statement along with their budgets. As the states are increasingly exposed to the markets for borrowing, their fiscal positions would be increasingly assessed by the markets. They may be forced to pay higher than average interest rates to cover additional risk if the public finances are not evaluated to be robust by the assessment of the market. We are relying therefore on two mechanisms for fiscal correction: self evaluation under the Fiscal Responsibility Act and exposure to market. These in our view may prove to be effective instruments of fiscal discipline without compromising the autonomy of the states." [6]

27.4 Taxation of Services

Service sector is very wide in its range. It includes, *inter alia*, health care, education, social security, leasing, entertainment, credit rating agencies, telecommunications, transport, publicity and advertising, insurance, banking, legal and financial services.

From equity point of view, services should be taxed in the same way as goods. Taxation of goods and exclusion of services distorts the relative prices of goods vis-à-vis services, encouraging artificially the demand for services. In the process, the allocation of resources is also distorted. If tax is imposed on goods and not on services, a relatively high rate of tax would be required on goods to generate a given amount of revenue. If tax is imposed both on goods and services, a moderate tax rate can yield the given revenue. Administratively, taxation of both goods and services is desirable because it would reduce disputes pertaining to distinction between goods and services.

Like goods, services can also be classified into two broad categories: essential services (e.g. health and education) and luxury services (e.g. entertainment and tourism). The rationale for exemption/lenient tax treatment of essential services is the same as for essential goods. Similarly, luxury services should be taxed at a high rate like luxury goods.

The Indian tax system has traditionally relied on commodity taxation for generating revenue for the Central and State Governments. The two major commodity taxes of the Central Government are excise duties and customs duties while at the level of the States, sales tax is the main commodity tax, accounting for about two-thirds of States' own tax revenue.

The extension of excise duties to more and more commodities of the industrial/manufacturing sector has reached a saturation point. However, the service sector remained outside the tax net till 1994. This pattern of tax structure development in India was contrary to the experience of most other countries where taxation of commodities and services grew hand in hand.

In view of the need for additional resources and rising contribution of service sector to GDP, a modest effort was made in the 1994-95 budget when a 5 per cent tax was imposed on telephone and non-life insurance services and services of stock brokers with effect from July 1, 1994. The coverage of service tax was extended to more and more services in the successive budgets. Table 27.6 records the growth in revenue from service tax in India.

27.4.1 Constitutional Provisions: A scrutiny of List II (State List) in the Seventh Schedule of the Constitution of India shows that State Governments are empowered to tax entertainment and professional services (entries 16 and 18 of List II). The Central Government had no specific powers to tax services when it introduced service tax on select services in 1994. It was done under its residual powers of taxation vide entry 97 of List I (Union List in the Seventh Schedule). The collection of service tax was entrusted to the excise department.

Table 27.6: Growth of Service Tax in India

(Rs. crore)

Year	Number of services	Number of assesses	Tax rate (per cent)	Revenue (Rs. crore)
1994-95	3	3,943	5	407
1995-96	3	4,866	5	862
1996-97	6	13,982	5	1,059
1997-98	15	45,991	5	1,586
1998-99	26	1,07,479	5	1,957
1999-00	26	1,15,495	5	2,128
2000-01	26	1,22,326	5	2,613
2001-02	41	1,87,577	5	3,302
2002-03	52	2,32,048	5	4,122
2003-04	60	4,03,856	8	7,891
2004-05	75	7,40,267	10	14,200
2005-06	84	8,05,591	10	23,055
2006-07	99	---	12	38,169*
2007-08	104	---	12	50,200#

* Revised estimates; # Budget estimates.

Sources: Government of India, *Economic Survey*, 2006-07, p. 29, Table 2.4; Government of India, Budget Papers, *Budget at a Glance,* 2007-2008.

However, the Constitution (Eighty-eighth Amendment) Act, 2003 put service tax in the Union List by inserting entry 92C in that List. Furthermore, service tax was put under Article 268A of the Constitution which specifies that the principles of collection and appropriation of taxes on services will be determined by Parliament. In other words, revenue from service tax is outside the purview of the Finance Commission. **See also section 3.3.4 of chapter 3 of this book.**

27.5 Constitution (Forty-sixth Amendment) Act, 1982 and the Consignment Tax (see section 7.7 of chapter 7 of this book).

27.6 Financial Autonomy for States

Although the proponents are vague in defining greater financial autonomy for the States, it should, *inter alia*, include transfer of additional taxation heads from the Centre to the States. If such a transfer is to take place, the main beneficiaries would be the richer States who have adequate bases to collect tax revenues. What will a poor State like Orissa or Bihar do with more taxation powers in view of the already low standard of living of their people? The solution lies more in the speedy development of the backward States which will increase tax collections automatically with existing taxation powers.

Another question is whether the States have adequately used the taxation powers already available to them? Taxation of agricultural incomes is a State subject but unfortunately this source has not been tapped by the States. Presently, about half a dozen States levy agricultural income tax, in three of them it is confined to plantation crops, and in all the cases the revenue is meagre. The share of this tax in the total revenue from States' own taxes has remained negligible, just around 1 per cent. Similarly, land revenue which was the principal direct tax of the States at the time of Independence has been given up partially or fully by most of the States.

Moreover, any weakening of the financial strength of the Central Government will adversely affect the economic viability of weaker States and Special Category States. The backward States have often argued for a financially strong Centre to ensure their own speedy development. After all, Centre's duties are not confined to defence and external affairs only but extend also to correct regional imbalances.

Is there a need to make changes in the existing arrangements relating to division of taxation powers between the Centre and the States? In this connection, the Commission on Centre-State Relations, 1988, observed, "Generally, the States have stated that there is no need to make any changes in the division of the areas of taxation envisaged in the Constitution. In fact, one State has pointed out that any transfer of taxation fields now with the Union to the States would make the rich States richer and the poor States poorer. The Union Ministry of Finance also holds that the present system has a sound rational basis and may not require any alteration." [7] A pragmatic approach based on national outlook is required to remove irritants in Centre-State financial relations.

27.7 Towards Co-operative Federalism

According to the Ninth Five Year Plan (1997-2002), "The essence of a co-operative federalism is that the Centre and the State Governments should be guided by the broader national concerns of using the available resources for the benefit of the people. Co-operative federalism encourages the Government at different levels to take advantage of a large national market, diverse and rich natural resources and the potential of human capabilities in all parts of the country and from all sections of the society for building a prosperous nation. Co-operative federalism makes it possible to raise all the available resources by the Government at different levels in a co-ordinated way and channel them for use for the common good of the people. This requires a harmonious relationship and co-operative spirit between the Centre and the States and among the States themselves. While a healthy competition among the States for evolving efficient and socially desirable policies and programmes is welcome, any competition which nullifies each other's advantages in development and erodes the resource base of the States should be avoided. Co-operative federalism is intended to ensure a minimum bundle of basic services and a nationally acceptable level of living for all the people of the country." [8]

Notes

1. *An Approach to the Eleventh Five Year Plan*, November 2006, op. cit., p. 87.

2. Article 293(2) empowers the Union Government to make loans to the States and it has been doing so ever since the commencement of the Constitution. These loans are largely given for implementing Five year Plans.

3. *Report of the Tenth Finance Commission*, December 1994, p. 55.

4. *Ibid.*, p. 56.

5. *Ibid.*, p. 57.

6. *Report of the Twelfth Finance Commission*, November 2004, pp. 83-84.

7. Government of India, *Report of the Commission on Centre-State Relations* (Chairman: Justice R.S. Sarkaria), 1988, Part I, p. 255.

8. Government of India, Planning Commission, *Ninth Five Year Plan* (1997-2002), Vol. I, p. 241.

Appendices

Appendix 1

Pre-Independence History of Income Tax in India

Income Tax Act, 1860

Consequent upon the financial difficulties created by the events of 1857, income tax was introduced in India for the first time by the British in the year 1860. [1] However, the imposition of income tax remained irregular till the year 1886 when a systematic legislation was enacted for its operation on a permanent basis. Since then the form of income tax has undergone a series of changes to meet the changing requirements of Government finances and economic policy.

The Act of 1860 was passed only for five years and therefore it lapsed in 1865. It was replaced in 1867 by a licence tax on professions and trades and the latter was converted into a certificate tax in the following year. The certificate tax was replaced in 1869 by a general income tax which after remaining in force for four years was abolished in 1873. In 1876, the Government imposed a licence tax on traders to create a famine fund to deal with the famine of 1876-78. This licence tax on traders remained in operation till 1886 when it was merged in the Income Tax Act of that year. Noting the haphazard nature of enactments, the Indian Taxation Enquiry Committee, 1924-25, remarked, "...the whole period (1860-1886) was one of continuous trial and error with different schemes of direct taxation, no less than 24 Acts being passed in 26 years." [2]

Income Tax Act, 1886

The Act of 1886 levied a tax on the income of residents as well as non-residents in India. The Act defined agricultural income and exempted it from tax liability in view of the already existing land revenue, a kind of direct tax. (In the 1860 legislation, agricultural income was also subject to taxation). The absolute exclusion of agricultural income from the purview of income tax law continued till the Government of India Act, 1935 made it a provincial (State) subject. This provision was retained in the Constitution of independent India.

The Act of 1886 exempted life insurance premiums paid by an assessee on policies on his own life or on that of his wife, a provision that has continued till now. Under another provision of the Act, a Hindu undivided family was treated as a distinct taxable entity, a position maintained by all subsequent Income Tax Acts.

The assessment and collection procedures of income tax in the early days of its operation were simple and somewhat arbitrary. As the Taxation Enquiry Commission, 1953-54 noted, "The Income Tax Act of 1886 laid an obligation only on companies to file every year statements of their net income and it was entirely within the discretion of the Collector to devise means for finding out other persons likely to have taxable income and to adopt the appropriate method of determining their income ... the procedure for assessment was summary, and the Collector could intimate the amount of income and tax determined by him to the assessee either through a list published in his office or through an individual notice." [3] In 1886-87, the total income assessed was Rs. 33 crore and the net collection from income tax was Rs. 1.37 crore. The Act of 1886 remained in force for 32 years, i.e. until 1918 and during this period a number of amendments were made in it including the introduction of the principle of graduation in income tax in 1916 and of super tax in 1917.

Income Tax Act, 1918

The Act of 1918 brought under charge also receipts of casual or non-recurring nature pertaining to business or profession. This was contrary to the generally accepted meaning of income that it should, *inter alia*, be received with some degree of regularity. The Act granted exemption to contributions to provident funds governed by the Provident Funds Act.

Although income tax in India has been a charge on net income since inception, it was in the Act of 1918 that specific provisions were inserted for the first time pertaining to business deductions for the purpose of computing net income. Prior to that, deductions were granted on the basis of executive orders. For example, there was no specific provision for depreciation allowance in the Act of 1886 but the Act of 1918 inserted in the statute itself the provision for depreciation allowance on the straight-line method.

The Act of 1918 remained in force for a short period and was replaced by a new Act (Act XI of 1922) in view of the reforms introduced by the Government of India Act, 1919.

Income Tax Act, 1922

The Act of 1922 provided for the first time the set off of loss from one source against income from other sources in the same year. An amendment of the Act in 1939 permitted carry forward of unabsorbed business losses for a period of six years with the restriction that carried forward loss could be set off only against the profits of the same business. Pursuant to a recommendation of the Income Tax Investigation Commission (1948), the income tax law was appropriately amended in 1953 to provide for the set off of speculative losses, even during the same year, only against speculative gains.

Under the Act of 1886, the paying officers had the obligation to deduct tax at source from the salaries of Government servants and employees of local bodies. However, the Act of 1922 extended to all employers the responsibility to deduct tax at source on salaries. Prior to 1922, there was no separate department for income tax administration. The assessment and collection of income tax was done by the land revenue officers as a subsidiary duty. It was only in 1922 that a separate Central Department was created to deal with income tax administration.

Recommendations of the Indian Taxation Enquiry Committee, 1924-25

The Government of India appointed this Committee under the chairmanship of Sir Charles Todhunter to examine in detail the entire field of taxation in India. Chapter IX of its report contained recommendations pertaining to income tax. The Committee rejected the idea of differentiation between earned and unearned income for income tax purpose.

A major recommendation of the Committee pertained to the distribution of income tax revenue between the Centre and the Provinces. Prior to 1919, income tax was a 'divided head' of revenue. However, the Montague-Chelmsford Reforms resulted in a complete separation of Central and Provincial finances, and income tax became a part of the Central revenues. The Todhunter Committee opined that in the event of any division of taxes between the Centre and the Provinces, the choice of income tax as the main balancing factor was inevitable. The Government of India Act, 1935, did assign to the Provinces a part of the net proceeds of income tax levied by the Centre.

Income Tax Enquiry Committee, 1935-36

This Committee was appointed by the Government of India "to make an investigation of the Indian income tax system in all its aspects and to report upon both the incidence of the tax and the efficiency of its administration". Many amendments based on its recommendations became law in 1939. According to one such amendment, i.e. Income Tax (Amendment) Act, 1939, the then prevailing step rates system of income tax was changed to a slab rates system in 1939. (Under the step system of rates, all persons in a particular income bracket bear the same effective rate on every rupee of their income. Under a slab system of rates, tax on each slab of income is calculated separately and then added up). Under another amendment, closely-held companies were required to distribute 60 per cent of their net of tax profits as dividend. Similarly, another amendment provided also for the taxation of profits of the business of mutual life insurance which had remained exempt from tax prior to 1939.

In 1939, as a result of the recommendations of the Committee, the entire income of a resident, whether accruing in (British) India or outside, became chargeable to tax. The remittance basis, therefore, faded into the background except for its applicability to persons 'resident but not ordinarily resident' and to a small portion of the foreign income of 'resident and ordinarily resident' persons in some instances. The liability of non-residents to tax on income deemed to accrue or arise in India through business connection was amplified to cover income arising through certain other activities also. At the same time, resident, non-resident and not ordinarily resident persons were, for the first time, defined in the law.

The entire income of local authorities was being treated as exempt even from 1886, and the Income Tax Acts of 1918 and 1922 placed the exemption on a statutory footing. Pursuant to a recommendation of this Committee, the scope of the exemption was restricted by the Income Tax (Amendment) Act of 1939. The income arising to a local authority from business became liable to tax, except where the business consisted of the supply of a service or commodity within its own jurisdictional area.

Excess Profit Tax

Another notable development in the evolution of income tax was the imposition of excess profit tax in 1940. It was levied on profits earned by businesses and professions between September 1, 1939 and March 31, 1946. A 'standard profit' was calculated for each accounting year falling within the above years. Standard profit was approximately equated with the profits earned in normal times, i.e. in the pre-War years. Companies started before 1936 had the following five options to choose from for determining standard profit: profits during 1935-36 or 1936-37 or average of the profits during 1935-36 and 1936-37 or 1936-37 and 1937-38 or 1937-38 and 1938-39. In the case of companies started after 1936, the 'capital standard' was used. Thus, a statutory 8 per cent of the capital invested was considered the standard rate of profit. Excess profit tax was levied at the rate of 50 per cent on the excess over the standard profits earned between September 1, 1939 and March 31, 1941. For the period between April 1, 1941 and March 31, 1946, the rate of excess profit tax was 66.66 per cent.

During the pre-Independence period, revenue-raising was the main purpose of income tax system. There were hardly any concessions/exemptions for savings, investments, industrial growth, and other desirable socio-economic objectives. Incentives for such activities started building up in the system soon after Independence. Thus, a provision introduced in 1949 exempted from tax new industrial undertakings for the first five years of their manufacturing operations.

Shortly after Independence, the Government appointed the Income Tax Investigation Commission (1947) under the chairmanship of Srinivasa Varadachariar to (a) investigate and report on all matters relating to taxation of income, with particular reference to preventing evasion and avoidance, and (b) to investigate specific cases referred to the Commission by the Government. The Commission submitted its report in 1948 and recommended several changes in the law to plug loopholes in the income tax system. For example, it recommended that the law should be amended so as to allow speculative losses to be set off only against speculative gains. A number of Commission's recommendations were incorporated in the law by the Income Tax (Amendment) Act, 1953.

Notes

1. For historical details of income tax in India, see 1. Government of India, *Report of the Indian Taxation Enquiry Committee* (President: Sir Charles Todhunter), 1924-25, chapter 9, pp. 189-91; 2. Government of India, *Income Tax Investigation Commission* (Chairman: Sir Srinivasa Varadachariar), 1947, pp. 1-4; 3. Government of India, Ministry of Finance, *Report of the Taxation Enquiry Commission* (Chairman: John Matthai), 1953-54, Vol. II, chapter 1.
2. *Report of the Indian Taxation Enquiry Committee*, 1924-25, *op. cit.* Vol. 1, para 259.
3. *Report of the Taxation Enquiry Commission,* 1953-54, op. cit., Vol. II, chapter 1, p. 16.

Appendix 2

Pre-Independence History of Excise Duties in India

In India, the history of excise taxation in its modern form can be traced back to the year 1894 when excise duty at the rate of 5 per cent was imposed on yarn above twenty counts. Since then, the Indian excise system, which represents the single largest source of tax revenue for the government, has undergone various changes.

Prior to Independence in 1947, excise taxation in India was selective in terms of commodity coverage and modest from revenue angle. Excise duties were not important as a source of revenue due to the narrow production base of the Indian economy. The relative share of Central excises in total tax revenue of the Government was 4.7 per cent and 4.4 per cent in 1920-21 and 1925-26 respectively. The policy of *discriminating protection* followed from the mid-1920s did give some impetus to domestic industry and the share of excise revenue increased to 8.8 per cent in 1931-32. At the start of the Second World War, the contribution of excise revenue was 10.7 per cent (Table A2.1).

Table A2.1: Pre-Independence Trends in the Relative Share of Excise Duties in Total Tax Revenue of the Central Government: Selected Years

(Rs. crore)

Year	Total tax revenue	Central excise revenue	Col. 3 as per cent of Col. 2
1	2	3	4
1920-21	60.85	2.85	4.7
1925-26	72.86	3.21	4.4
1931-32	75.62	6.19	8.2
1938-39	81.37	8.72	10.7

Source: Government of India, Ministry of Finance, *Report of the Taxation Enquiry Commission* 1953-54, Vol. II, p. 258, Table 3 (excerpted).

The selected commodities on which excise duties were imposed included cotton textiles, salt, motor spirit, and kerosene. A commodity-wise history of excise taxation is as follows:

Cotton Textiles

Cotton textile mills were first built in India in the 1850s. By 1896 their number had risen to 167 and by 1923 to 323. Following pressure from Britain, an excise duty of 5 per cent, corresponding to the duty imposed on imported goods, was imposed in 1894 on Indian yarn above twenty counts. It was in the nature of a countervailing duty on domestic yarn and hence on cloth which competed with imported goods from Lancashire. In 1896, excise duty on yarn was changed to duty on cloth at a reduced rate of 3.5 per cent. Simultaneously, import duty was reduced to the same level as the excise duty. The policy of equal duties on imported and domestically produced goods continued till 1917. It was from this year that the period of differential duties started with the raising of the import duty on cloth to 7.5 per cent. It was further raised to 11 per cent in 1921. The domestic producers thus enjoyed protection to the extent of 7.5 per cent on cloth. The Indian Fiscal Commission, 1921-22 examined in detail the question of protection to domestic industries and recommended that the Tariff Board should consider the rate of import duty necessary for the protection of the domestic industry. When duty is imposed on local production, the import duty should be enhanced by a like amount. Following its recommendations, the Government adopted what came to be called the policy of 'discriminating protection' under which tariff protection was granted to selected industries against foreign competition. The industries which benefited from the policy of discriminating protection included, *inter alia*, iron and steel, cement, textiles, sugar, paper, matches, and jute.

Salt: Excise on salt was another important source of revenue for the Government during pre-Independence days. The commodity was preferred for taxation because of its inelastic demand and also because it is used in small quantity by all strata of society. Even a low rate of duty on this essential commodity yields some revenue for the exchequer without anybody feeling the pinch. However, the duty was opposed on the ground that it falls on an absolute necessity of life. Since salt is necessary for human existence, duty on it is in the nature of a poll tax. Even the poorest of the poor are made to contribute to state exchequer.

The Indian Taxation Enquiry Committee, 1924-25, examined in detail the pros and cons of salt duty. It opined, "It may be concluded that, if it is desirable to impose any tax on the mass of the community at all, there is much to be said for the continuance of the salt tax. The present rate of duty is appropriate and causes no serious hardship." [1] Excise duty on salt remained a major source of revenue till Independence. Abolition of salt duty was chosen by Mahatma Gandhi to spearhead his non-co-operation movement against the British rulers. The duty on salt was abolished with the achievement of Independence in 1947.

Petroleum Products

Excise duty at the rate of 6 *annas* (Rs. 0.37) per Imperial Gallon (4.55 litres) was imposed on motor spirit in 1917. The purpose of this levy was to restrict consumption of petrol to conserve supplies for war needs. Kerosene was another petroleum item placed on the tariff list in 1922. The rate of duty was one *anna* (Rs. 0.06) per Imperial Gallon. The duty on motor spirit was mainly a tax on transport while the burden of kerosene duty fell chiefly on almost all classes of the population. For the next 34 years (i.e. until 1956) there was no addition to the list of petroleum products subject to excise tariff. It may be mentioned here that before Independence, the Indian oil industry was characterised by small-scale, localised operations under foreign firms. The Assam Oil Company (a subsidiary of Burmah Oil Company) produced about half a million tonnes of crude oil in Assam. A small refinery of the company at Digboi processed this crude. With the Digboi refinery producing about 7 per cent of the total consumption of petroleum products in India, the remainder was imported and marketed by various foreign oil companies operating in India, the chief among them being Burmah Oil, and Stanvac.

Tobacco

Taxation of tobacco and tobacco products in India was suggested, for the first time, by the Indian Taxation Enquiry Committee, 1924-25. It observed, "The absence of any internal taxation on tobacco is a feature which distinguishes the fiscal system of India from that of almost every other civilised country in the world. The considerations which have led in other countries to the selection of tobacco as one of the principal subjects for consumption taxation apply with equal force to India. It is a typical instance of a conventional luxury whose use goes down to the poorest classes, and it is an article the consumption of which can be varied greatly both in quality and quantity according to the means of the consumer." [2] Following the recommendations of the Committee, the taxation of tobacco was examined on various occasions, but the administrative difficulties involved in implementing such a levy prevented its imposition. Moreover, taxation of tobacco was a State subject before the enactment of the Government of India Act, 1935. After this enactment, the power to impose tobacco excise was vested in the Central Government.

Excise on unmanufactured tobacco was levied for the first time with effect from April 1, 1943 with a view to mobilising additional resources to meet the requirements of the Second World War. The levy was imposed under the Tobacco (Excise Duty) Act, 1943 which was subsequently merged with the consolidated Central Excises and Salt Act, 1944. The revenue realised from tobacco in the first year of the excise, viz. 1943-44 was Rs. 9.65 crore.

The rates of duty levied on unmanufactured tobacco in 1943 were designed on a progressive scale depending upon the intended use of the commodity. In addition to this, a graduated duty on the basis of value slabs was imposed on the higher grades of the manufactured cigars and cheroots. The tobacco tariff was extended in 1948 when an excise duty was imposed on cigarettes on the same pattern as the tariff for cigars and cheroots, namely value slabs for fixation of rates. Duty on unmanufactured tobacco brought the excise machinery into contact with a large number of growers and licensees and thus led to tariff complexities and administrative difficulties.

Other Products

Excise duty on silver was imposed in 1930. To quote, "It was in 1934 that the first step in the rationalisation of excise levies was made and their coverage extended. Excise duties were imposed mainly as a revenue measure on sugar, matches, steel ingots and mechanical lighters. Sugar and matches production had made rapid strides under heavy protection in the years following the First World War and the stage had been reached when they could be taxed." [3] Duties were imposed on tyres in 1941 and on vegetable products and tobacco in 1943, mainly to meet the exigencies of war finances. The year 1944 saw excise duties being imposed on coffee, tea, and betel nut. Cigarettes came within the excise net in 1948. Prior to 1944, excise duties were levied under separate enactments for different goods. For example, tobacco levies were imposed under the Tobacco (Excise Duty) Act, 1943. About 16 such separate laws were in force till 1944. However, in that year the various enactments were consolidated into the Central Excises and Salt Act and the Central Excise Rules, 1944.

According to Lakdawala and Nambiar, "In the early stages of its evolution, the Indian excise system has had a basic purpose and philosophy behind its development. The main objective was either to restrict internal consumption of such commodities whose supply was scarce or to make good the loss of revenue resulting from the shrinkage of revenue from protective customs duties on imports of parallel commodities. The initial imposition of duties on items such as motor spirit and kerosene belonged to the first category while the subsequent levies on items such as tyres, textiles and cigarettes belonged to the second category." [4]

Rules of Excise Taxation

This brief description of pre-Independence developments in the excise system may be concluded by quoting the five golden rules of excise taxation enunciated by the Indian Fiscal Commission, 1921-22, which with necessary modifications, seem to be relevant to this day.

"1. Excise duties should ordinarily be confined to industries which are concentrated in large factories or small areas.

2. They may properly be imposed for the purpose of checking the consumption of injurious articles and especially on luxuries coming under this category.

3. Otherwise they should be imposed for revenue purpose only.

4. While permissible on commodities of general consumption, they should not press too heavily on poorer classes.

5. When an industry requires protection, any further necessary taxation on its products may, if the other conditions are fulfilled, take the form of excise duty *plus* an additional import duty. The latter should fully countervail the former and may be pitched at a higher price." [5]

Notes

1. Government of India, *Report of the Indian Taxation Enquiry Committee* (President: Sir Charles Todhunter), 1924-25, Vol. I, para 168.

2. *Ibid.*, para 155.

3. Government of India, Ministry of Finance, *Report of the Central Excise Reorganisation Committee* (Chairman: A.K. Chanda), 1963, p. 4.

4. D. T. Lakdawala and K.V. Nambiar, *Commodity Taxation in India* (Ahmedabad: Sardar Patel Institute of Economic and Social Research), 1972, p. 41.

5. Government of India, *Report of the Indian Fiscal Commission* (Chairman: Ibrahim Rahimatoola), 1921-22, p. 87.

Appendix 3

Indian Taxation Enquiry Committee, 1924-25

The Indian Taxation Enquiry Committee was appointed by the Government of India on May 26, 1924. Its terms of reference were as follows:

- To examine the manner in which the burden of taxation is distributed at present between the different classes of the population.
- To consider whether the whole scheme of taxation—Central, Provincial and Local—is equitable and in accordance with economic principles, and, if not, in what respects it is defective.
- To report on the suitability of alternative sources of taxation.

Composition of the Committee

Charles Todhunter	President
Bijay Chand Mahtab	Member
Percy Thompson	Member
Jogendra Singh	Member
R.P. Paranjpye	Member
L.K. Hyder	Member
B. Rama Rau	Secretary

Chapter IX of the report of the Committee contained recommendations pertaining to income tax. It may be recalled that income tax was introduced in India for the first time by the British in the year 1860. However, the imposition of income tax remained irregular till the year 1886 when a systematic legislation was enacted for its operation on a permanent basis. The Act of 1860 was passed only for five years and therefore it lapsed in 1865. It was replaced in 1867 by a licence tax on professions and trades and the latter was converted into a certificate tax in the following year. The certificate tax was replaced in 1869 by a general income tax which after remaining in force for four years was abolished in 1873. In 1876, the Government imposed a licence tax on traders to create a famine fund to deal with the famine of 1876-78. This licence tax on traders remained in operation till 1886 when it was merged in the Income Tax Act of that year. Noting the haphazard nature of enactments, the Indian Taxation Enquiry Committee, 1924-25, remarked, "...the whole period (1860-1886) was one of continuous trial and error with different schemes of direct taxation, no less than 24 Acts being passed in 26 years." [p. 259 of the Report]

A major recommendation of the Committee pertained to the distribution of income tax revenue between the Centre and the Provinces. Prior to 1919, income tax was a 'divided head' of revenue. However, the Montague-Chelmsford Reforms resulted in a complete separation of Central and Provincial finances, and income tax became a part of the Central revenues. The Committee opined that in the event of any division of taxes between the Centre and the Provinces, the choice of income tax as the main balancing factor was inevitable. The Government of India Act, 1935, did assign to the Provinces a part of the net proceeds of income tax levied by the Centre.

The Committee examined, for the first time, the desirability of differentiation between earned and unearned incomes for the purpose of income tax. The Committee, however, rejected the idea, maintaining that it was premature in the context of the Indian conditions. It was in 1945 that a distinction between earned and unearned incomes was introduced when assessees were allowed to exclude from their earned incomes a fixed proportion subject to a maximum limit.

The Committee examined in detail the pros and cons of salt duty. It opined, "It may be concluded that, if it is desirable to impose any tax on the mass of the community at all, there is much to be said for the continuance of the salt tax. The present rate of duty is appropriate and causes no serious hardship." [p. 168 of the Report] Excise duty on salt remained a major source of revenue till Independence. Abolition of salt duty was chosen by Mahatma Gandhi to spearhead his non-co-operation movement against the British rulers. The duty on salt was abolished with the achievement of Independence in 1947.

Export duties formed an important part of the customs tariff soon after the events of 1857. They were gradually abolished and between 1880 and 1916, rice was the only item subject to export duty. The financial difficulties created by the First World War led to their revival. Jute and tea were brought under the export duty net in 1916 and hides and skins in 1919. Justifying the export duty on rice, the Committee observed, "Though rice is not a monopoly of India, the export duty has been in operation for many years without any bad effects. Its justification lies in special circumstances. The only countries which export appreciable quantities of rice are India, Siam (now Thailand), and Indo-China. The Indian share of the trade varies between one-third and one-half. As each of these countries levies an export duty, the Indian duty does not handicap the producer and its remission would in fact put an equivalent amount of money into the hands of the producers and the middlemen." [p. 157 of the Report] Export duty on tea was justified on similar grounds because India's principal competitor

Ceylon (now Sri Lanka) also imposed export duty on tea.

An adverse consequence of the high rates of customs duty during and after the First World War was the encouragement to smuggling. The Committee examined the smuggling problem at length and observed, "...while the present high tariff offers great temptations to the smuggler, there is a lack of cohesion in the preventive arrangements, which certainly offer many facilities for his operations. It is not desirable to recite instances of the way in which advantage has been taken of these facilities, but it may be said that, though there is no evidence that any considerable percentage of the customs revenue is lost through smuggling, it is clear that there is a loss amounting at least to several lakhs a year." [p. 152 of the Report]

Edited Extracts from the Report

Scope of the Problem

The sources of the revenue of a State have been classified by modern writers on the following lines (a) State domains and tributes, (b) Fines and penalties, (c) Business undertakings and monopolies, (d) Fees, (e) Taxes.

In order to determine which items of revenue fall within the scope of their enquiry, the Committee have adopted the following definition of taxation as a working basis: "Taxes are compulsory contributions made by the members of a community to the governing body of the same towards the common expenditure, without any guarantee of a definite measured service in return".

The Committee do not consider revenues from State domains, from fisheries and mines or forests. The land revenue has some of the characteristics of a rent as well as of a tax, but they have been specifically instructed to enquire into its incidence and they therefore include it.

Fines and penalties are of two kinds:

- those imposed in connection with regulation of revenue, which the Committee treat as taxes;
- those imposed primarily for purposes of restraint, which they do not.

There is no agreement among economists as to the classification of revenue from State undertakings. In determining the element of taxation in the net profits from railways, posts and telegraphs and opium, profits on coinage, irrigation receipts, and receipts from enterprises of local authorities, the Committee have been largely guided by practical considerations.

As regards fees, where the utilisation of services is rendered compulsory by legislation, there is an element of taxation, but the element of payment for services still prevails. When the fees exceed the value of the services, there is true taxation.

Capitation and Apportioned Taxes

Poll taxes are open to the obvious objection that they are regressive in character; they are far more common than is generally supposed in Europe, in America, in the British Empire and in Eastern countries, but they have ceased to be important sources of revenue in the more advanced States.

The principal taxes of this nature that now survive in India are confined to Burma.

- The *thathameda* of Upper Burma is theoretically not a poll tax, but in many parts operates as one.
- The capitation tax of Lower Burma, being a poll tax at a flat rate, operates will less discrimination than the *thathameda,* and has never lost the stigma which attached to it when it was imposed by the Burmese Kings as a tax on conquered races.

The grant of the option to local bodies under the Burma Rural Self-government Act of 1921 of converting these taxes into a circumstances and property tax is an appropriate way of providing for their extinction. The Committee recommend that the process of conversion should be expedited.

The proposed tax on sea passengers, which seems likely to operate as a tax on transport and to impose a check on the flow of labour from province to province, is regarded as a development in the wrong direction.

The endeavours made to replace the arrangements under which the villagers tax themselves for watch and ward have led to confusion and inequality.

The *chowkidari* and other taxes still levied in certain provinces for this purpose are theoretically unobjectionable, but are complained of in practice. The conversion of these also into sources of local taxation, subject to proper control, is recommended as a desirable development.

Land Revenue

Revenue from Agricultural Land: From a survey of the systems of land taxation in other countries it would appear that the tendencies of modern development are as follows:

- The flat rate of tax on annual or capital value is kept comparatively low.
- Incomes from and property in land are treated for purposes of income-tax and death duties on exactly the same footing as other incomes and property.
- Where an increasing share has been taken of the return from land, it has

generally been taken for local purposes.

The Indian systems are the result of a gradual process of evolution from indigenous practices and they have been moulded into their present shape by British officers quite independently of one another to suit local circumstances in different provinces.

Except in British Baluchistan, the land revenue has ceased to represent a portion of the gross produce. In the United Provinces, the Punjab and the Central Provinces the Government demand is theoretically based on economic rent, but actually takes many other factors into consideration. In the case of Madras and Burma the assessment is theoretically based on the net produce, while in Bombay the rate of assessment is arrived at empirically with reference to general economic considerations, and in practice is based rather on the actual rents paid than on any theoretical calculations of the net produce.

The Committee are divided in opinion as to whether or not the land revenue should be regarded as a tax on the individual who pays it, but they are agreed that, since it forms a deduction from the national dividend, it should be taken into consideration in dealing with the question of the incidence of taxation on the country-as a whole.

Application of the canons of taxation to the land revenue.

Certainty: This canon is satisfied.

Convenience: Convenience has in some respects been sacrificed to certainty.

The inelasticity of the systems drives a number of people to the money-lender during bad seasons.

The system of making settlements that last for a generation may necessitate a change in the standard of living when the period comes to a close.

When the process of settlement continues for years and involves meticulous enquiry by a large staff, the inconvenience and expense to the ryots concerned is very considerable.

Economy: The application of this canon cannot be decided on considerations relating to the land revenue alone. If the assessment and collection of the land revenue were the only mater in issue, it would be practicable to devise a scheme under which the president revenue could be collected at a much smaller cost. The justification of the high cost of the settlement and collectorate establishments must be looked for in directions that are outside the scope of the Committee's terms of reference.

Ability: Land revenue is essentially a tax on things and not o n persons and as such it is not a tax to which the doctrine of progression can be applied. The Committee therefore confine their attention to the question of the burden of the land revenue on the land, in other words, the proportion which the Government demand bears to the economic rental or net profits in the different provinces. Even in this respect they are unable to discover any acceptable basis of comparison and are forced to the conclusion that the uncertainty as to both the basis of the assessment and the rate is one of the chief respects in which the systems are open to criticism.

The results flowing from the fact that land revenue viewed as a scheme of taxation is not only not progressive, but actually tends in the opposite direction, are aggravated by the conspicuous absence of provision for an income-tax on agricultural incomes or a death duty, which serve in the more advanced European countries and Japan to introduce an element of progression into the taxation of the land.

Of the alternatives suggested, the proposals for the redemption of the land revenue either in the part or in whole, or for the substitution for it of a tax on produce are impracticable for reasons given. The adoption of a tax on capital value on Australian lines is less so, but would involve changes of a more radical nature than is necessary.

the essentials of a new scheme of temporary settlements are that it should be definite as regards both the basis and the pitch of assessment; that it should be as simple and cheap as possible; that it should so far as possible ease or steady the burden on the smallest cultivator; and finally that it should, in common with the rest of the system of taxation, involve some element of progression in the case of the large owners.

The Committee recommend that these essentials should be secured by providing that for the future the basis of the settlement should be annual value, i.e., the gross produce less cost of production, including the value of the labour actually expended by the farmer and his family on the holding, and the return for enterprise. The functions of the settlement officer should be limited to the ascertainment of this value on a uniform basis. A uniform rate fixed for a whole province should then be applied to these valuations as they were made on districts falling in for resettlement.

In the case of controlled rents, where the rent is fixed by the settlement officer or is limited by law or by custom having the force of law, such rent should be taken to be the annual value.

Where the practice of levying *nazaranas* exists, their annual equivalent spread over the term of the lease should be added to the rent for the purpose of determining the annual value.

The rate of assessment should be standardised a comparatively low figure not exceeding 25 per cent of the annual value.

The reduction in the share borne by the land revenue to the total taxation should be accompanied by an increase in the local rate, the maximum for the ordinary rates being fixed at about 25 per cent of the sum taken as land revenue.

It is not possible, in the case of a tax in rem to relieve the poorest cultivator by an exemption. The relief of his difficulties is to be found in a better system of rural economy generally.

The obvious ways of introducing an element of progression in the case of the large holder are through an income-tax on agricultural incomes, or through something in the nature of a succession duty, or both.

Revenue from Non-agricultural Land: Where land outside the limits of towns or villages which is assessed to land revenue on the basis of its crop value is diverted from use for cultivation, it should be liable to re-assessment on the basis of its annual value for other purposes.

House sites in villages should continue free of assessment, but all future grants should be made subject to the levy of ground-rend, if and when the village becomes a town.

In the case of town lands that have been permitted to be occupied free of provincial taxation or at a nominal rent, it is impracticable at present to impose anything in the shape of a provincial tax.

In the case of town lands that pay agricultural assessment, there is no reason why the assessment should not be based on annual value, provided due notice is given.

In the case of lands still under Government control, the procedure laid down in the orders relating to ground-rents is satisfactory.

The practice of making over to municipalities a substantial fraction of the receipts from town lands should be generally adopted, but the management of the lands should be left in the hands of the revenue authorities.

As regards the taxation of unearned increment-

- It is both impracticable and unfair to impose a tax on increments in land values that have already accrued.
- It is not impracticable to tax future increments, especially in large towns which can afford to employ highly paid competent staffs, if an account is maintained of improvements effected after a fixed date with a view to deduction of their value on the occasion on which the duty is levied.

Charge for Water

Wherever possible the charge for water should be separated from the charge on the land.

The minimum charge, except in the case of protective works, should be the cost of supplying the water, that is to say, the cost of maintenance of the irrigation work plus interest on capital cost, and the normal charge should be a moderate share of the value of the water to the cultivator.

The rates, which should be fixed with regard to prices, area irrigated, crop raised and other considerations should be as few as possible, and they should be examined periodically with a view to increase or decrease.

Where the demand is not constant and the ryots agree to pay for water, whether they require it or not, a reduced payment for a term of years may be accepted.

Where a guarantee of supply is newly given, a reasonable share of the addition made to the capital or annual value of the land by such guarantee may be taken.

Taxes on Consumption: Customs

Import Duties: Recent revisions of the tariff have had far-reaching effects. Some of the duties that are not protective in intention are protective in operation. Other duties are exercising a restrictive effect on trade. So far as conclusions can be drawn from the figures of incidence, they tend to indicate a certain amount of shifting of the burden from the richer classes to the general population.

A higher rate of duty can safely be imposed on wine, beer and spirits.

A reduction of the duty on the conventional necessities of life, such as sugar, and on the raw materials of industry and means of production is desirable.

The Committee endorse the opinion of Dr. Gregory that the customs tariff should be the object of periodical survey, and recommend that an expert enquiry be undertaken forthwith.

When the Sea Customs Act comes up for revision, section 30 should be amended so as to make the charge on invoice price plus cost of freight the normal procedure and the charge on a price which includes the wholesaler's profit the exceptional one.

Conditions in India offer many facilities for smuggling operations. The Committee recommend that a skilled preventive officer should be deputed to compare and co-ordinate the arrangements in the different provinces, not only at the main ports, but also at minor ports, along the coasts and on the land frontiers.

An ideal arrangement would be the institution of a customs zollverein, but this is not practical politics at present.

Export Duties: The Committee accept in general the recommendations of the Indian Fiscal Commission, that export duties should be levied on articles of which India has a complete or a partial monopoly, that the rates in any case should be low and that an export duty should not be utilised for the purpose of protecting an industry.

They do not recommend any increase in the rate of duty on jute or any alteration in the rate of duty on rice.

The duty on tea may continue for the present, but it should be removed or reduced if and when the conditions of the trade indicate that it is having a prejudicial effect.

The majority of the Committee agree with the Fiscal Commission in considering that the duty on hides is wrong in principle and dangerous in its effects, and advise its early abolition. The duty on skins may however be retained, but the matter should be examined by the Tariff Board at a suitable opportunity.

The imposition of an export duty on lac is recommended.

As regards oil-seeds and manures a majority of the Committee recommend that an export duty should be levied and that a part of the export duty should be applied towards educating the cultivator to make an increased use of artificial manures.

Taxes on Consumption: Excises for Purposes of Revenue

Salt: The duty on salt falls on a necessary of life and to the extent that salt is essential for physical existence it is in the nature of a pool tax.

The present rate o duty is appropriate and causes no serious hardship; changes in the rate should not be made except in cases of grave emergency.

The system of monopoly supply in Northern India and at Kharaghora results in the issue of salt of a good quality at a reasonable price.

The Committee do not recommend any radical change in the systems of supply in Bombay and Madras, but think it desirable that steps should be taken to secure more control over stocks and prices and to assimilate the arrangements in the two provinces, especially in the matter of guarding and accounts.

The obstacles to the supply of Indian salt to Bengal should be removed, and India should be made self-supporting in the mater of salt supply, if this end can be secured by the grant of a strictly temporary advantage to the local manufacturer by means of a rebate of duty or of a differential duty on imports. An enquiry should be made into this aspect of the question by the Tariff Board.

The rules regulating the issue of duty-free salt for use in industries are satisfactory. The rules in force in Bombay regarding issues for use in agriculture should be made general.

The present concession as regards duty-free issues for the purpose of fish-curing should be continued so long as it does not involve any cost to the Imperial Government in excess of the actual duty remitted. The concession should, however, be extended to all provinces.

Cotton Piece-goods: If for revenue purposes a general excise is considered necessary, an excise duty on locally-manufactured cotton goods, coupled with an adequate customs duty on imported goods, need not necessarily be condemned so long as the burden on the consumer is not too great.

The Government of India are, however, pledged to remove the present tax as soon as financial considerations permit. The Committee therefore class it among the taxes to be abolished.

Petroleum: There is no urgent case for the reduction of the duty on petrol. Should remission of taxation become possible, the Committee would give preference to the tax on kerosene, which falls on all classes of the population.

Matches: The statistics available to the Committee do not indicate that the time for the introduction of an excise duty on matches has yet arrived; but the matter will require examination by an expert body sooner or later.

Aerated Waters: An excise duty on aerated waters, to be levied by means of a tax on cylinders of carbonic acid gas issued for this purpose, is a comparatively unobjectionable way of raising revenue.

Patent Medicines: An excise duty on patent medicines, accompanied by the application of a similar duty to imported patent medicines, is a suitable form of taxation.

Tobacco: Tobacco is universally recognised as a suitable object for taxation.

Of the plans suggested, a Government monopoly in India would be too vast an undertaking to be considered.

An acreage duty presents considerable administrative difficulties and would probably excite resentment, and it is consequently not recommended.

A local excise on al production would be impracticable, but the increases in the tariff make one desirable in the case of cigarettes and pipe tobacco made in factories.

The experience of Indian States and Foreign territories in India disprove the idea that very little revenue is to be derived from a system of licensing.

The Committee recommend and excise duty on locally-made cigarettes and pipe tobacco, accompanied by an indirect excise through a system of licensing in the case of country tobacco.

Taxes on Consumption: Restrictive Excises

In the case of country spirit, a system of supply through a managed monopoly should be extended wherever possible, and the rate of duty should be raised in Bihar and Orissa and Assam. Where it is proposed to depart from the auction system of disposal of licenses, the sliding scale system is recommended as satisfactory, if supported by a sufficiently large and efficient preventive staff.

In the case of foreign liquors, a definite increase in the tariff rate is recommended in lieu of vend fees being imposed in the shape of additions to the tariff rate. The tariff rate should also be levied on 'foreign' liquors made in India, and arrangements should be made to credit all the duty on foreign liquor, whether country-made or imported, to the Imperial head.

In the case of country fermented liquors, the tree-tax system should be extended wherever possible, but only under rigid and systematic control; and experiments should be expedited in the direction of bringing the brewing of country beers under control.

In the case of hemp drugs, a system of contract supply or managed monopoly should be introduced where it does not exist, and enquiries should be made as to the proportion of the intoxicating principle in the *bhang* consumed and as to the practicability of making up the *ganja* in a more uniform and consistent form.

In the case of opium, the cultivation should be restricted, the stock should be reduced, the duty made uniform, the auction system abandoned and experiments made in making up the drug into pills of a fixed size.

The necessity for employing a special force to deal with inter-provincial smuggling is emphasised.

Action already taken in the direction of prohibition has involved a very large loss of revenue and increase in crime.

The consistent pursuit of a policy of real prohibition would involve the exploitation of every alternative source of possible revenue.

Taxes on Incomes

General: In the assessment of incomes the loss sustained in any one year should be allowed to be set off against the profits in the next subsequent year, subject to the condition that any assessee who claims to have made a loss must prove the fact by producing his accounts as soon as possible after the close of the year in which the loss is made.

The effect of section 42 (1) of the Income-tax Act is to impose a much wider charge on the non-resident than is desirable. The law and practice should be brought into conformity with those adopted in England.

The law in respect of refunds to non-residents should also be similar to that prevailing in England at present.

The high limit of exemption and the almost universal practice of marriage make allowances for dependents unnecessary.

A differentiation between earned and unearned income is not recommended in the present circumstances of India, but the case would be different if at any time incomes derived from agriculture were made liable to the tax.

The limit for super-tax should at the same time be reduced to Rs. 30,000 and a new rate of super-tax of 6 pies on the first Rs. 20,000 or part thereof in excess of that sum introduced. In the case of the joint Hindu family the limit of exemption might be reduced to Rs. 60,000, the anna rate being applied to the first Rs. 40,000 of excess.

The super-tax on companies should be converted into a corporation profits tax, the exemption of the first Rs. 50,000 should be removed, and holding companies should not be assessed to this tax on profits which represent dividends of subsidiary companies.

The necessary steps should be taken to secure an appeal to the Privy Council on points of law in respect of which conflicting decisions have been given.

While secrecy in respect of income-tax matters is desirable, exceptions might be made (a) by permitting income-tax officers to draw up lists of persons who are liable to local taxes which are based on income and (b) by publishing in the annual reports the names of persons penalised for income-tax offences.

The most suitable method of preventing evasion by the formation of private companies and the with-holding of dividends is to give the income-tax authorities power to treat such companies as if they were firms.

In order to prevent evasion through the formation of bogus firms,

- the incomes of married couples living together should be taxed at the rates applicable to their aggregate incomes;
- the income-tax officer should be given power in particular cases to require the partners in an unregistered firm to furnish particulars of the partnership, and to compute the liability of the partners on the same basis as if the partnership had been registered;
- particulars of the registration of any firm should be recorded by the income-tax officers and should be open to inspection; and
- it is desirable to provide for the imposition of a heavy penalty in cases where loss of duty has arisen through failure to distribute the profits in accordance with the terms of a partnership.

Income-tax on Agricultural Incomes

There is no historical or theo0retical justification for the continued exemption from the income-tax of incomes derived from agriculture. There are, however, administrative and political objections to the removal of the exemption at the present time.

There is ample justification for the proposal that incomes from agriculture should be taken into account for the purpose of determining the rate at which the tax on the other income of the same person should be assessed, if it should prove administratively feasible and practically worth while.

The planter or other manufacturer who derives his income partly from cultivation and partly from manufacturing the produce so derived is fortunate in securing the benefit of the exemption.

The money-lender who is a landlord only in name ought in equity to pay the tax, but it does not seem administratively practicable to impose it.

Taxes on Transactions

The existing entertainment taxes are appropriate and may be levied elsewhere. The power to levy the tax and the administration of it should be retained in the hands of the Local Governments, a share of the proceeds being made over to the local bodies concerned.

Betting is recognised in many countries as a suitable object for taxation, and the form of the taxes levied in India is not objectionable.

Municipal bodies should be given discretionary power to levy taxes on advertisements.

A tax on railway tickets of the higher classes, which has been advocated by some witnesses, is not recommended.

Duties under the Stamp Act: The Indian Stamp Law fulfils its purpose satisfactorily and no drastic changes are recommended.

The duty on documents of indebtedness such as bonds and mortgage deeds should be reduced as soon as circumstances permit.

The distinction drawn between documents by which possession is given and that by which it is nothing should be removed.

The rate charged on reconveyances should be reduced to 2 annas per Rs. 100 of the mortgage debt and the existing maximum of Rs. 10 should be removed.

In the case of deeds of cancellation, the duty should be that payable on the instrument sought to be cancelled, subject to a maximum of Rs. 5.

The duty on deeds of transfer should have regard to the value of the rights actually transferred.

The duty on deeds of adoption should be reduced to Rs. 5 where the property involved is of a value not exceeding Rs. 2,000. A reduction may also be made in the case of deeds of authority to adopt.

The duty on a settlement should be enhanced to the equivalent of the duty on a deed of gift.

When a deed of release operates to convey property, it should be charged at the rate appropriate to a conveyance.

In the case of deeds of partition land should be valued for purposes of duty at its actual value and not at a multiple of the assessment.

The present fixed duties on instruments of partnership might be abolished and a duty at 4 annas per Rs. 100 substituted.

In the case of companies an *ad valorem* stamp duty on the nominal share capital at the rate of 8 annas per Rs. 100 might be levied and the duty on the articles of association and memorandum of association might be reduced to Rs.10.

It is recommended that the distinction for purposes of duty between documents that are attested and those that are not should be done away with.

Also that it should not be optional to the parties to fix values for purposes of duty other than the true values.

Stock and Produce Transactions: The issue of a contract note should be compulsory, both where a broker acts in that capacity and where he sells stock on his own account.

It is hoped that it may be possible, with the aid of the stock exchange authorities, to put a stop to the loss of revenue arising from the use of blank transfers.

In the absence of such action, the duty on contract notes should be raised to 4 annas for every Rs. 10,000, subject to a maximum of Rs. 40.

In the case of the produce exchanges the taxation of future is not only practically impossible, but on other grounds it would be undesirable to recognise these gambling transactions and to attempt to secure a revenue from them. It may be possible hereafter to secure a revenue from contract notes on the lines indicated in the case of the stock Exchanges.

Penalties: For the existing maximum penalty on unstamped or insufficiently stamped documents there should be substituted a penalty of twice the deficient duty *plus* a sum of Rs. 5.

The limitation of the period within which a document can be voluntarily produced for rectification of the stamp duty should be removed.

The disability of inadmissibility in evidence should be limited to the case of bills of exchange and promissory notes.

From the point of view of the administration of the stamp law uniform legislation and unified rates of stamp duty are desirable.

Fees: Fees for the registration of vehicles should not be more than sufficient to cover the expenses of examining and registering the vehicles and testing the drivers.

The fees for possession of firearms might be increased in the case of weapons licensed for purposes of sport and display and in that of numerous weapons possessed by the same person.

A cautious experiment might be made in selected local areas in the imposition of a fee for the registration of marriages, provided it is made clear that the purpose of the registration is merely to afford superior probative value of the fact of marriage.

The fees charged for the registration of companies might be reduced, if a stamp duty on the nominal share capital is levied as recommended by the Committee.

Recent increases in the fees for the registration of documents do not represent an increase in the element of taxation. It is permissible to increase these fees up to the point where they correspond to the probable value of the benefit derived.

The fees for mutation of names in the revenue registers might with advantage be made more uniform. *Ad valorem* fees would not be appropriate in this case.

Court-fees: The pitching of the scale of the court-fees so as to produce a revenue just sufficient to cover all the costs of the administration of civil justice is an ideal to be aimed at, but financial, considerations may justify the State in charging something more, provided that the fees charged do not cause substantial hardship to any class.

A record should be maintained on uniform lines in each province to determine what is the amount of fees actually levied in the course of litigation, what is the actual cost of the courts and how the one compares with the other.

The copyist and process services should just pay for themselves.

The system under which the fees are fixed on a graduated and regressive scale with reference to the value of the subject matter litigated is suitable, but effect might be given to the principle of measuring court-fees by the cost of the service rendered to the extent of taking the fee in two instalments, the first being payable at the institution of the suit and the second on or immediately after the settlement of issues.

The Court Fees Act and the schedules thereto need through revision by an expert committee.

Section 7 should be recast and a schedule prepared similar to that in the Indian Limitation Act of suits and appeals which commonly arise in civil courts with a method of valuation prescribed for each.

Provision should be made for recovery of deficient fees in decided suits.

A series of instances is given of cases in which the fees are inadequate.

In the matter of court-fees uniformity is desirable, not only as regards general principles, procedure and methods of realisation, but also as regards rates.

In particular it is desirable that steps should be taken to render the fees on the Original Sides of the Chartered High Courts so far as possible uniform with one another and not less than those in courts in the mufassal.

The fees payable on applications to revenue and other officers should be examined and abolished except possibly in the case of those on applications which involve enquiries of a judicial nature.

Fees paid in cash to officers of Government should also be subjected to scrutiny.

An audit of receipts is recommended in the case both of stamp duties and of court-fees.

Probate Duties: A succession duty is impracticable in India, but a duty on the lines of the English Estate Duty, which may initially take the form of a transfer or mutation duty on death, is more practicable.

This involves representation of the deceased, which is desirable on other grounds.

The existing law provides for it in certain cases, but is limited to particular communities.

The taxation that it involves is very inequitable in its incidence.

The Committee recommend its modification extension to all communities, and discuss the means effecting this.

They do not find the law of the joint Hindu family an insuperable obstacle.

The legislation dealing with the question should be undertaken by the Central Legislature.

Local Taxation

A comparison with conditions in other countries indicates that the difficulties in local administration in India, and especially the unwillingness of the people to submit to taxation, is mainly due to the large jurisdictions of the local bodies.

Taxes on Trade: The octroi and the terminal tax in the form in which they are levied in India offend against all the canons of taxation.

It is a function inherent in the Imperial Government to protect inter-provincial traffic from obstruction by taxes imposed by subordinate authorities, and it is regretted that the Government of India have to so large an extent abandoned their control of a matter that is of paramount importance to the trade of the country.

Four possible means of replacing these taxes are discussed, viz:

- a rate on land and houses,
- a profession tax,
- market dues and taxation of private markets,
- a tax on retail sales.

If it is not possible to adopt any of these alternatives, general principles to govern the levy of octroi and terminal taxes in future are indicated.

Tolls: Where a terminal tax is levied and the rates are raised beyond a certain level, terminal tolls on the roads are necessary to prevent evasion.

General municipal tolls are justified when they form part of a scheme for the taxation of vehicles.

Ferry charges are apt to develop into a pure tax on transit.

Toll on district roads are undoubtedly an impediment to through traffic. It is desirable to abolish them, at least in the case of motor vehicles, and to replace them by a provincial tax on the vehicle. In case this is done, the import duty should be reduced.

Taxes on Property: The rates of property tax in India are very low and there is considerable scope for increase in the assessment of town property.

Another outstanding feature of the property tax in India is the inefficiency f the machinery of collection and assessment. The remedy for this state of affairs lies in provincial control.

In view of the recommendation for the standardisation of the land revenue at a comparatively low rate, it is suggested that the maximum limit on the rate of cess on agricultural land be altogether removed, or at least be raised to 6¼ per cent of the annual value.

In the case of works executed by local authorities for the benefit primarily of specific areas, it is recommended that the local authority concerned should be in a position to recover the whole or a portion of the cost in the shape of an annual cess imposed for a limited period on land in those areas.

Taxes on Persons: The assessment of the tax on circumstances and property has given rise to widespread complaints of unfair incidence, while the levy of the profession tax has been found to be administratively difficult. It is recommended that the assessment and collection of these taxes in rural areas should be entrusted to the general administrative staff of the districts.

The tax on pilgrims is theoretically objectionable, but the rate is so low that it involves little hardship or addition to the expenditure which the pilgrimage normally involves.

A light terminal tax on passengers may be appropriate in the case of a large city, but the tax of Rs. 2 levied in Rangoon on passengers departing by sea is difficult to justify.

General: The general rate of local taxation in India is very low. This is partly due t the fact that the taxation of land, which should be the main basis of local taxation, has in a great measure in India been reserved for the State, and partly to the fact that the jurisdictions of local bodies are so large as to remove them from effective touch with the tax-payers.

It is recommended that, from the point of view of taxation at any rate, the development of the future should be in the direct of restoring the influence of the village panchayati and limiting the functions of the bodies at present operating.

Local Taxation of Railways: Where it is proposed to include a railway colony within the area of a municipality, it is recommended that provision should be made for the railway authorities to be heard by the Local Government before any order is issued approving the inclusion.

In the case of an existing colony within a municipality where the railway company derives some benefit from a municipal service or services, for which a specific tax is imposed, but not the full benefit which the levy of the tax implies, it is suggested that a reasonable basis of agreement between the company and the municipality would be the remission of a proportion of the tax paid by the colony, to be fixed on principles indicated.

The assessment of railway property to the general municipal rates should be based on the principle that the service rendered to a railway can best be gauged by the extent and value of property used for the reception and despatch of goods and passengers. The method of assessment of such property followed in Bombay is recommended for general adoption.

The exemption from the cess on land enjoyed by the State and guaranteed railways under the Bengal Cess Act should be extended throughout India, if there are any railways that do not enjoy it.

There is no sufficient justification for the exemption of railways from the *chowkidari tax.*

Local Taxation of Mines: There is no necessary anomaly in the fact that the general taxes on mines are based on annual value and net profits and the special taxes sometimes on raisings and sometimes on despatches.

But an arrangement under which the same rate of taxation is applied to the annual net profits of a mining enterprise as to the annual value of agricultural land must make for differential taxation.

Distribution of the Burden

An estimate of the proportion borne by average taxation to average income has a very limited value.

It was not possible within the time of the Committee's appointment to secure new date on these or any other lines, nor is the existing material sufficient to enable an estimate to be framed of the economic condition of the various classes of the people.

The Committee are therefore thrown back on such general considerations relating to typical classes of the population as a prudent Finance Minister would examine in framing or revising a scheme of taxation.

Urban Labourer: The burden on this class has increased during recent years. It will, to some extent, be reduced by the abolition of the cotton excise duty. It is not desirable to reduce the salt duty or the excises on intoxicants, and a decrease in the customs duties and in the municipal taxes on consumption is indicated as the more satisfactory course.

Landless Agricultural Labourer: The burden on this class is very low, and it would be benefited by the abolition of the excise duty on cotton goods and by a reduction in customs duty on goods consumed by all classes.

Small Landholder: The difficulties of this class are not primarily the result of taxation. In order to afford it relief it has been suggested that the land revenue should be standardised at a flat rate not exceeding 25 per cent of the annual value.

Peasant Proprietor: The burden of this class is comparatively light. The only recommendations made that are likely to affect it are the extension of the probate duties and the raising of the rate of local cesses.

Large Landholder: Except in individual cases, the burden of this class is comparatively light. The possible means of increasing its contribution are by the imposition of an income-tax on agricultural incomes or the extension of the probate duty.

Village Trader: This class escapes certain taxes intended to affect it and should be brought within the scope of further taxation by a more general extension and a more efficient administration of taxes of the nature of the circumstances and property tax and the profession tax.

Small Trader in Towns: The contribution of this class is more than that of the previous one owing to municipal taxation, which may well be raised.

Larger Trader: This class escapes with a comparatively light burden, but would be affected by the extension of the probate duties, the steepening of the graduation of the income-tax and the increase in local taxation.

Big Merchants: Though this class bears a large portion of the tax revenue, its burden is not as heavy as that of similar classes in other countries. It would be increased by the extension of the probate duties, by the increase in the super-tax and by the abolition of the exemption limit in the case of companies.

Lower Grade Professional Classes: This class has suffered under recent developments, but its tax burden is comparatively small.

Higher Grade Professional Classes: The position of this class is similar to that of the largest merchants.

Order of Precedence

A change almost amounting to a revolution has already taken place in the proportions borne by the different taxes to the total revenue. The tendencies that have brought this about have been generally in the right directions.

As regards the tendencies that are now is operation,

- a policy of real prohibition would involve a loss of revenue exceeding the return from any new proposal which can be put forward,
- the pledge given in relation to the cotton excise involves provision for its replacement,
- it is impossible to forecast the further effects of the policy of discriminating protection or of high customs duties for revenue purposes,
- an increase in the import duties on imported liquors is desirable or special grounds.

The Committee do not include local taxation in their recommendations regarding the order in which taxes may be remitted or imposed.

Subject to these considerations, the following is the order of priority suggested in the case of the remission of taxation:

- Reduction in the customs duties on conventional necessities, especially on sugar, with a view to affording relief to the poorest classes.
- The removal of the export duty on hides. In the case of non-judicial stamps, a revision of the scheme in the direction of reduction, especially in relation to documents such as bonds and agreements.
- In the case of non-judicial stamps, a revision of the schedule in the direction of reduction, especially in relation to documents such as bonds and agreements.
- Standardisation of the land revenue, which was ultimately result in a further reduction of the proportion borne by the land revenue to the total taxation.
- Reduction of court-fees, especially by the collection of the court-fees on suits in two instalments and by the cessation of the practice of making a profit out of the fee for copying and for service of processes.

The following order of priority has been suggested in the matter of substitutes for taxes removed or reduced, including the cotton excise and the loss under restrictive excises:

- Proper collection of duties on stock exchange transactions.
- Conversion of the super-tax on companies into a corporation profits tax and the abolition of the exemption limit.
- Regarding of the income-tax and introduction of a super-tax on incomes from Rs. 30,000 to Rs. 50,000.
- Enhancement in the rate of duty on country-made 'foreign' liquors up to the tariff rate and an increase n the excise duty on country spirits in Bihar and Orissa and Assam.

- Increase in the license fees for firearms.
- Taxation of patent medicines.
- A general extension of probate duties.
- Extension of the tax on entertainments and betting.
- Imposition of taxation on tobacco through means of an excise on local manufactures or an increase in the import duty on unmanufactured tobacco, coupled with a system of licensing of sales of country tobacco.
- Export duties on lac, oil-seeds, bones and other manures.
- An excise duty on aerated waters.
- The imposition of income-tax on agricultural incomes is put in the last place for reasons which are explained.

Division of the Proceeds

Imperial and Provincial: There is no ideal system of division of sources of taxation between Imperial and State Governments.

A system of separation of sources is the best if a scheme can be discovered which gives to each Government a revenue adequate to its needs and at the same time effects a fair division between them.

Where this is not possible, a system of division of the proceeds of taxes is better than a system of subsidies.

Certain taxes are essentially imperial, namely import duties; revenue excises; and revenue derived from the export of opium.

The revenue from non-judicial stamps is much more appropriate to the Imperial than to the Provincial head. It is desirable that the duty on country-made 'foreign' liquors should be levied at the tariff rate and be credited to the same head as the import duty. The increasing restrictions that are being imposed upon excise opium suggest that it is desirable that this item of revenue also should be credited to the Imperial Government, which undertakes responsibility for the restrictions.

Certain taxes are essentially Provincial, namely, land revenue and receipts from irrigation; taxes on transactions other than those levied under the Stamp Act; fees, including court-fees; and revenue from the licensing of sale of tobacco.

The following taxes afford possible balancing factors: income-tax, export duties, restrictive excises other than on opium, and probate duties.

The absence of an income-tax on agricultural incomes and the large proportion of the total revenue that is derived from the land make a division of the income-tax unavoidable if the division is to be fair to industrial and agricultural provinces alike.

If equilibrium can be secured by this means alone, it is undesirable to use the other balancing factors; in other words, the export duties should be entirely Imperial and the restrictive excises, other than that on opium, and the probate duty entirely Provincial.

The Committee's proposals therefore reduce themselves to the transfer of non-judicial stamps and the excise duty on country-made 'foreign' liquors, and possibly the revenue now derived from excise opium, to the Imperial Government, and the establishment of equilibrium by the transfer to the provinces of a share of the income-tax.

The most satisfactory means of determining such a share is to make over the proceeds of a basic rate on personal incomes, graduated proportionately to the general rate, to which should be added a small proportion of the receipts from the corporation profits tax.

It is not within the Committee' functions to suggest a detailed revision of the settlement between the Government of India and the Provinces, and they therefore leave the application of the principles suggested by them to some other body.

While Devolution Rule 15 appears to have failed of its object, it does not appear practicable to revise it except as part of the general revision.

Provincial and Local: The Committee have recommended an increase in the resources of local bodies:

- by conversion of the *thathameda,* the capitation tax and the chowkidari into sources of local revenue;
- by standardising the land revenue so as to give greater scope for local taxation of land, and by the imposition of special assessments;
- by transfer to local bodies of a share of the collections of Local Governments from ground-rents in towns and by increasing the rates on non-agricultural land;
- by giving municipalities the power to tax advertisement;
- by extending the imposition of taxes on entertainments and betting and giving local bodies a substantial share of the proceeds;
- by extending and improving the administration of the taxes on circumstances and property and the profession tax;
- by reducing the import duty on motor cars and enabling Local Governments to levy a Provincial tax for distribution in lieu of toll;
- by grant of power to levy a fee for the registration of marriages in selected areas.

When all these allotments are made, the resources of local authorities will still require to be supplemented by subsidies.

The manner in which these should be distributed is an administrative question, but the following principles are recommended:

- Subsidies should ordinarily be restricted to services which are of national importance.
- They should be granted on a system which will enable the Provincial Government effectively to enforce efficiency.
- They should be granted on some uniform and easily comprehensible plan so worked out in advance that the local body can arrange its programme of expenditure in good time and provide for a due adjustment between that, its expected receipts and its scheme of taxation.

Machinery of Taxation

The effect of past developments has been:

- that the Collector has been relieved in a great measure of the function of assessment, while remaining responsible for collection and remittance;
- that the increase of specialisation and the separation of Imperial from Provincial functions have led to multiplication of departments; and
- that, in the case of local bodies, there has been a transfer to elected representatives of functions which are not rightly theirs.

The Committee's recommendations are as follows:

Imperial Taxes: The pivot of the tax administration in the case of these taxes should be the Central Board of Revenue, directing separate but co-ordinated staffs to deal with the income-tax, customs and salt.

Provincial Taxes: In the case of Provincial taxes, there is no similar central head, but the Collector should be the district head of the staffs responsible for land revenue, excise, registration, taxes on transactions and fees.

Local Bodies: The pivot of the administration in the case of local bodies should be the executive officer, who might be a lent officer of the district staff, and who would be in touch, in the administration of the taxes, with certain Provincial and Imperial officers.

The Collector should act as a liaison officer between the Imperial and Provincial and between the Provincial and Local departments, and he or one of his assistants should also be the appellate authority in all cases of appeals against assessments to local taxes, except where provision is made for appeal to a court.

Appendix 4

Committee on Sales Tax, 1964

The Committee on Sales Tax was constituted by the Government of India on June 7, 1963 to study the question of incidence of sales tax on commodities exported from India and to suggest measures for the grant of appropriate relief in the interests of export trade.

The terms of reference of the Committee were as follows:

1) To study the incidence of State and Central sales taxes on commodities entering the export trade of India and to indicate the quantum of relief to be provided in respect of each commodity;
2) To make recommendations in regard to the manner in which such relief is to be provided whether by way of exemptions, rebates or set-offs, and the procedure to be followed in connection therewith by each of the State Governments and the Central Government and for different export commodities;
3) To review the existing provisions in the sales tax laws in different States with particular reference to the provisions relating to the grant of relief in respect of export commodities and make recommendations for such amplification or modification thereof as may be considered necessary; and
4) To suggest such supplementary or ancillary measures as may be necessary in order to remove or mitigate the burden of States and Central sales taxes on exportable commodities in the interests of the development of India's export trade.

Composition of the Committee

R. G. Saraiya	Chairman
V.M. Bhide	Member
Anna R. George	Member
V.L. Gidweani	Member
I.P. Gupta	Member
M.N. Heble	Member
C.A. Ramakrishan	Member
K.K. Ray	Member
C. Thomas	Member
R.M. Honavar	Member-Secretary

Edited Extracts from the Report

Sales Tax System in the States

We have considered it convenient to begin our study by examining first the nature of the various taxes on sales and purchases prevalent in the country. According to the Constitutions of India, the power to levy taxes on the sale or purchase of goods, other than newspapers, has been vested in the States provided such sales and purchases do not take place in course of inter-State trade or commerce. In the case of the latter, the power of levy tax vests with the Union Government. As a result of this distribution of power sales of goods in all States are governed by two sets of laws. On thc one hand there is a Local Sales Tax Law which is applicable to the local dealings and on the other there is Central Sales Tax Act, 1956, which applies to sales in course of inter-State trade.

The powers of the State Governments to levy sales tax are further restricted under provisions of Article 286 of the Constitution. According to this Article levy of any sales tax on sales or purchases "in course of import of goods into and export of goods from the territory of India" is not permissible. The Constitution, however, does not define what constitutes the sale or purchase "in the course of export". The Parliament has been given the power to define "sales in the course of export: for this purpose. Section 5(1) of the Central Sales Tax Act, 1956, accordingly, gives the definition of sales and purchases in the course of export as follows:

"A sale or purchase of goods shall be deemed to take place in the course of export of goods out of the territory of India only if the sale or purchase either occasions such export or is effected by a transfer of documents of title to the goods after the goods have crossed the customs frontiers of India."

Three principles appear to emerge from the analysis of this section, namely: (a) a sale is in the course of export if it occasions the export of the commodity (b) a sale is in the course of export if it is effected by transfer of documents of title to the goods after the goods have crossed the customs frontiers of India and (c) sales not falling under (a) or (b) are not sales in the course of export.

It is clear from this definition that when a manufacturer or a dealer exports the commodity, the sale is not liable to be taxed but where he sells it to another who in turn export it, the first sale attracts the provision of the sales tax but the second does not. Thus a substantial part of the goods exported by the Exporting Houses are subject to the incidence of sales tax when they are purchased by them or at earlier stages unless the State authorities specifically exempt any such earlier transactions. When such purchases are made in the course of inter-State trade, these transactions would be liable to Central Sales Tax unless similarly exempted.

Central sales tax is levied under the provisions of the Central Sales Tax Act, 1956. This tax is confined to sales in the course of inter-State trade. A sale or purchase of goods takes place "in the course of inter-State trade" if the sale or purchase occasions the movement of goods from one State to another or is effected by the transfer of documents of title to the goods during their movement from one State to the other. The Central Sales Tax Act has declared certain goods such as coal, cotton, cotton yarn, hides and skins, iron and steel, jute, oil seeds, cotton fabrics, silk fabrics, rayon or art silk fabrics, woollen fabrics, sugar and tobacco as goods of special importance in inter-State trade or commerce. On the sales of such "declared" goods the rate of Central sales tax cannot exceed 2 per cent. On other goods when the sales are to persons other than the dealers registered under the Central Sales Tax Act or to Governments, Central and State, the rate is 10 per cent except that wherever the rate of tax under the local law is higher than 10 per cent on any goods the said higher rate apply to the inter-State sale. When sales are made to dealers registered under the Central Sales Tax Act and to Government against appropriate certificates in the prescribed forms, the rate is 2 per cent. These rates are subject to a general exception that if a commodity is subject to tax in a State at a rate lower than 2 per cent or is exempt from tax, the inter-State sale of that commodity from that State would be subjected to tax at that lower rate or would be exempt from tax, as the case may be, whether such a sale is made to a registered dealer or not.

Central Sales Tax is complementary to the sales tax levied by the State and administration of the law is entrusted to the Sales Tax Authorities of the States who generally exercise the same powers for the purpose of levy, collection and enforcement of the payment of Central Sales Tax as are available to them under the Local Sales Tax Act. The Proceeds from the Central, Sales Tax become a part of the Consolidated Fund of the State where the sale takes place. In addition to the general provisions, the States are empowered under a section of the Central Act to grant exemption or reduction in the rates of tax in inter-State sales of goods or classes of goods if it is considered expedient in the public interest to do so. Such a power is not available with the Central Government under the present Act.

The State sales taxes are either selective or general. Sales of certain specific commodities like motor spirit, foreign liquor, etc., are taxed in some States under separate laws. The remaining goods in general are governed by the generally of sales tax of each State under which certain specific goods may be totally exempted while in the case of other goods the rates may be different for different goods. The major part of the sales tax structure of the States consists of multi-point, single-point or two-point taxes or a combination of these.

Broadly speaking, while multi-point sales tax is levied in Andhra Pradesh, Bihar, Kerala, Madras, Mysore, and UP, the States of Assam, Jammu & Kashmir, Madhya Pradesh, Orissa, Punjab, Rajasthan and West Bengal impose a single-point tax. Except Madhya Pradesh and Rajasthan, the States belonging to the second group levy tax on the last sale. Maharashtra and Gujarat have a two-point sales tax on the sales of certain commodities and an others single-point tax is levied. There is, however, no clear-cut demarcation among the three systems and in every State, where levying a single-point, a two-point or a multi-point tax, higher sales tax at a suitable stage is levied on certain luxury goods, known as specified goods. Besides, in all States sales tax on "declared goods" is levied at any one stage which may vary from State to State and from commodity to commodity in the same State. Multi-point tax has been combined with single-point tax in some of the multi-point States. There are several other variations also from the general pattern.

Sales tax rates vary from State to State and often from commodity to commodity within the same State. The system of taxation is also not uniform in all the States. The basis of levy is different, the minimum taxable turnover limit is not uniform and there is diversity in the coverage and in the schedule of exempted goods. Among the single-point States the general rate of sales tax varies. It has been fixed at 4 per cent in Assam, Madya Pradesh and Rajasthan and 5 per cent in Orissa and West Bengal and 6 per cent in Punjab. The minimum rate is ½ per cent and the maximum rate generally 10 per cent. In regard to foreign liquor the rate is higher still: in seven States it is more than 20 per cent.

In the States where, a multi-cum-single-point tax system is prevalent i.e. in Andhra Pradesh, Bihar, Kerala, Madras, Mysore, and U.P. the general rate of multi-point tax is 2 per cent except in the case of Bihar where it is ½ per cent. In some States like Madras, and Mysore a special rate of 1 per cent is imposed on the sale of foodgrains whereas in Andhra Pradesh a higher rate of 3 per cent is levied on the articles of food and drinks sold in hotels, restaurants, etc. In UP, unlike other States, there are many special rates between ¼ per cent and 3 per cent depending upon the nature of commodities. The minimum rate of single-point tax in multi-cum-single-point States fluctuates between ½ per cent and 3 per cent.

In all States the liability to pay tax arises only when the taxable turnover is more than the minimum fixed for that purpose. This minimum also varies from State to State. In the majority of the cases it is about Rs. 10,000 per annum though in some cases it is as low as Rs. 5,000. Again, although most of these tax systems contain a list of articles which are exempted from the tax their number varies from State to State. From the tax laws prevalent in different States it would seem that Kerala has the smallest number of exemptions while Madras has the largest. Both are, incidentally, multi-point systems. In most of the States the exemptions are confined to essential goods, raw materials, goods sold to certain institutions like schools, hospitals, charitable organisations, etc., goods produced by cottage or village industries, etc.

A brief description of the sales tax system in different States is given below:

Andhra Pradesh: Sales tax in Andhra Pradesh is levied under the Andhra Pradesh General Sales Tax Act, 1957. This provides for a basic multi-point levy at the rate of 2 per cent at every point of sale except in respect of certain goods, specified in three schedules appended to the Act. The tax on the scheduled goods is levied at a single-point only ranging from ½ per cent to 10 per cent. The taxable turnover in goods other than declared goods is also subject to an additional tax at ¼ per cent in respect of the dealers whose total turnover for the years is Rs. 3 lakh or more. The Andhra Pradesh system does not provide for any concession or remission of tax on sales of raw materials, etc. to a manufacturer or on sales of finished prod' cs to exporter who purchases such products for export out of India.

Assam: The Assam Sales Tax Act, 1947, prescribed a single-point levy in the State at the last point of sale. The general rate of tax is 4 per cent. There are certain goods which are taxable at the rate of 10 per cent while the rate of tax on declared goods is 20 per cent. A few items have been transferred to be taxed at the same rate but at the first point of sale under a separate law called the Assam Finance (Sales Tax) Act, 1956. None of these Acts provides for any concession from sales tax on sales to exporters. Sales of goods including raw materials to a manufacturer registered under the Act are exempt from tax if the goods purchased are used in the manufacturer of taxable goods.

Bihar: The Bihar Sales Tax Act, 1959 provides for the levy of tax on multi-point-cum-single-point basis. The rate of general sales tax is ½ per cent at every point of sale and in addition a tax of 4 per cent is levied at the last point when the goods leave the sector of registered dealers. Declared goods and certain specified goods are taxed only once inside the State at the rate of 2 per cent and 10 per cent respectively. The Act provides that the sale to a registered dealer who purchases goods including raw materials for use directly in the processing manufacture of goods for sale would be taxed at the concessional rate of 1 per cent. The Act also provides that the turnover of a dealer relating to sale of goods to a registered dealer who purchases for the purpose of exports of such goods out of India would not be subjected to the special sales tax of 4 per cent. No cession is allowed by the State Government under the Central Sales Tax Act on inter-State sales preceding the export transaction.

Gujarat and Maharashtra: The Bombay Sales Tax Act, 1959 as adopted by the State of Gujarat and Maharashtra after the bifurcation of former State of Bombay is in operation in these two States. Separate amendments to the original Act have been made in Gujarat and Maharashtra which have made for slight difference in the systems prevailing in the two States. The basic structure which is still common provides for a schedule of tax-free goods, the levy of tax at the single-point at the first stage of sale by the producer or importer in the State on a bulk of items imported in the State or producer or importer in the State on a bulk of items imported in the State or produced in medium or large-scale industries. On a few commodities thee is a single-point tax at the penultimate stage of sales by the wholesaler or semi-wholesaler to the retailer. On a few scheduled terms and on all residuary items there is a two-point tax which is levied at the stage of the first sale and then at the stage of the penultimate sale. In addition, in respect of these items the retailer pays a retail turnover tax at the rate of ½ per cent.

In both the States there is provision for registration of the dealers. There is also provision for authorisation of dealers engaged in exports. Sales to such authorised for authorisation of dealers engaged in exports. Sales to such authorised dealers are exempt from the tax on the certificate that the goods purchased against such certificates are exported outside the States within a period of nine months, either by themselves or by another dealer to whom they may have sold them.

There are certain concessions in tax available to manufacturers on their purchase of goods required in the manufacture of goods for sale. In Maharashtra, manufacturers who have obtained a recognition certificate are entitled to purchase their requirements for use in the manufacture of taxable goods at concessional rate of 1 per cent on all articles taxed at the higher rate. In Gujarat, manufacturers holding the recognition certificate can buy all such goods liable to tax at rates in excess of 2 per cent, free of tax. However, in respect of purchases of machinery and spare parts and goods taxable at the rate of 2 per cent or less no concession is available in these two States under the Central Sales Tax in respect of inter-State sales made to exporters in other States.

Jammu & Kashmir: The Jammu and Kashmir General Sales Tax Act 1962, imposes a tax on 54 items named in the State Government's notification at rates ranging from 1 per cent to 10 per cent. No concession from the sales tax is allowed by the State Government on sales of raw materials to manufacturers or on sales of finished products to exporters who export such products out of India.

Kerala: The Kerala General States Tax act, 1963 imposes a liability to pay tax on a multi-point basis on all sales of goods at the rate of 3 per cent. Declare goods and certain other items are taxed at rates ranging from 1 per cent to 10 per cent at the first point of sale or at the last point of purchase in the State. There are three items namely liquor, motor spirit other than petrol and petrol on which the rat of tax is at 50 per cent, 20 per cent and 15 per cent, respectively. Sales of certain goods, mentioned in the Act, to manufacturer in the State are taxable at a concessional rate of 1 per cent if such goods are used as component parts of the goods manufactured for sale. No concession from the tax is allowed in the State on transactions preceding the actual export.

Madhya Pradesh: The Madhya Pradesh General Sales Tax Act, 1958 provides for the levy on a single-point basis at 4 per cent on the first point of sale. Declared goods and a few other goods are taxed at the last point of sale. The rate of tax ranges from 1 per cent to 10 per cent. Tax on raw materials sold to a manufacturer for use in the manufacture of major export commodities is levied at the rate of 1 per cent. The State Government grants a refund of local sales tax and exemption from Central sales tax on local/inter-State sale immediately preceding actual export transaction of the following goods:

- Minerals
- Shellac
- Vegetable oils
- Hides and skins
- Oil cakes and
- Carpets

Madras: Sales tax in Madras is governed under the provisions of Madras General Sales Tax Act, 1959. The Act provides for the levy of tax on the purchase of a number of goods and on the sale of others. The rate of tax is generally 2 per cent multi-point but declared goods and certain specified articles are taxed on a single-point basis at rates ranging from 1 per cent to 10 per cent. No cessions from tax are generally allowed by the State Government on raw materials used in the manufacture of finished products but there is a provision under which in respect of the sale of goods mentioned in the first schedule of the act by a dealer to another for use by the latter as a component part of any other goods mentioned in that Schedule which he intends to manufacture inside the State for sale, the tax liability is reduced to 1 per cent. This concession is available only for the article which along with the others goes to make up the finished product and is not available for raw materials as such. In the Madras system, there is no concession on the sale to or purchase by exporters of goods exported by them out of India.

Mysore: Mysore has a multi-point system of sales tax governed by the provision of the Mysore Sales Tax Act, 1957. The rate of tax is 2 per cent on all sales of goods. A few goods are subject to purchase tax also, while certain goods are taxed at a single point only at rates ranging from ½ per cent in the case of bullion to 10 per cent in the case of certain specified goods. No concession of sales tax or purchase tax is allowed on raw materials used in manufacture of finished products or on goods purchased by exporters for export out of India.

Orissa: The Orissa Sales Tax Act, 1947, provides for the levy of tax on the last point of sales. The general rate of tax is 5 per cent. Certain specified goods are taxed at the rate of 10 per cent while in respect of certain others, the rate is only 1 per cent. No concession is allowed in the State on the sale of raw materials to manufacturers or on sales of finished products to the exporters who export such goods out of India.

Punjab: The Punjab General Sales Tax Act, 1948, provides for levy of tax on the lat point of sale. The general rate of tax is 6 per cent. In addition, a surcharge of 1 percent is levied on a temporary basis for a specific purpose under the Punjab Temporary Taxation Act, 1962. Certain specified goods are taxed at the rate of 10 per cent whereas the rate of tax on declared goods is 2 per cent. A lower rate has also been fixed in respect of certain goods. Sales to a manufacturer (registered under the Act) of such goods as are specified in the registration certificate and are required for use in the manufacture in the Stat of Punjab of any goods for sale, are allowed tax free. The State Government also allows exemption from local sales tax on sales of goods to a registered dealer who purchases them for the purpose of export out of India. No concession is allowed under the Central Sales Tax Act on inter-State sale preceding the actual export transaction.

Rajasthan: Sales tax is levied under the Rajasthan Sales Tax Act, 1956, on a single point basis generally at the first point of sale. Certain goods are taxed on the last point also when they leave the registered sector. The general rate of tax is 4 per cent whereas certain goods are taxed at lower rates also. Sales of raw materials (including fuel and lubricants) to manufacturers under the Act are taxable at the concessional rate of 1 per cent. The State Government also allows exemption from local and Central sales tax on the transaction immediately preceding the export of the following goods:

- Oilseeds
- Raw wool
- Cotton and
- Mica

Uttar Pradesh: The scheme of taxation under UP Sales Tax Act, 1948, is essentially multipoint, the general of tad being 2 per cent. However, certain goods specified by the State Government are taxed on a single point basis either at the point of the last or the first sale or purchase at different rates not exceeding 10 per cent. The State Government does not allow any concession on sales of raw materials to manufacturers, but it allows full rebate of local sales tax and complete exemption from Central Sales Tax on the transaction immediately preceding export of the following goods:

- Tea
- Jute goods
- Mica
- Mineral ores (metallic)
- Spices
- Vegetable oil
- Raw wool
- Hides and skins (raw and tanned leather)
- Raw cotton
- Walnuts
- Sandalwood oil
- Carpets and rugs
- Silk and silk manufactures
- Sports goods
- Sewing machines and accessories
- Bicycles and accessories
- Diesel engines
- Oil pressure lamps, and
- Electric fans

West Bengal: The Bengal Finance (Sales Tax) Act, 1941 provides for levy of tax the lat point of sale in the State. The general rate of tax is 5 per cent. Certain goods are taxable at lower rates (minimum rate being 1 per cent except for gold of not less than 90 per cent fineness for which the rate is ½ per cent) while luxury goods are taxed at the rate of 10 per cent. Some of the goods which have been taken out of the purview of the above Act are taxed under the West Bengal Sales Tax Act, at the first point of sale in the hands of importers and manufacturers. All sales of goods (including raw materials) to manufacturer who is a registered dealer under the Act and who purchases such goods for use in the manufacture of goods for the sale whether, locally, outside the State or outside India, are exempt from tax. The scheme of levy in the State being such, sales of finished products to an exporter, who is registered under 1941 Act, are also exempt an do not suffer local sales tax. However, no concession is allowed under the Central Sales Tax on inter-State transactions preceding the actual export sale.

Union Territories: The only Territory that needs consideration is Delhi – in others there is either no sales tax or no significant export. Delhi has adopted the West Bengal Sales Tax system as provided in the Bengal Finance (Sales Tax) Act, 1941.

Problem of Sales Tax in Relation to Exports

1. The rates of sales tax in the State vary generally between 2 per cent and 10 per cent on most commodities and the Central sales tax on commodities normally exported out of India is generally limited to 2 per cent. Although we will go into greater details regarding the incidence of sales tax later, it would appear that the burden is not likely to be higher than the percentages mentioned above. Where sales tax is levied on a multi-point, basis and where there are a number of transactions, both intra-State and inter-State, before a commodity is exported. It is likely that the cumulative burden would be higher. It is necessary to examine why a tax burden of this order affects out competitive ability in international trade.
2. Trade in international markets is exposed to world market forces. Competition is so fierce that even advanced countries try to protect their agriculture and industry by means of assistance to exports including relief from internal taxes. Prices of export goods constitute the most important factor influencing help to secure and maintain a proper place in the world market. Competition is so intense that price margins in trade between various countries tend to disappear. A transaction in the international trade is ultimately won by the country which offers the goods on the most competitive terms as regards price for the required quality, delivery, etc. Even with regard to commodities, prices of which fluctuate widely during the same year, the main determining factor is price at which the commodities are offered at the place of delivery desired by the importer at the point of time he enters the market. For instance, in a commodity like raw cotton or oilseeds or spices, prices of which may fluctuate during a season by as much as 15 to 25 per cent, what matters to the importer is the price at the particular point to time that he chooses to enter the market and the place at which he wants his goods delivered. A margin of as little as a quarter to half peer cent may make all the difference, other terms as regards quality, delivery, etc., being equal, in determining the award of a contract.

3. Under the Constitution, sales tax has become a major source of revenue to the State Governments, and it is being levied on a wide range of commodities. While, within the country, the tax is passed on to the consumer though a rise in internal prices, it cannot be so passed on to the buyer in the export market, because of the competitiveness of world trade. Therefore, any incidence of sales tax, howsoever small it may appear by itself in the total price, acts as a built in handicap when facing the rigours of world competition in the free-for-all international market. This applied equally to other items of incidental expenses such as freight, insurance, internal transportation to the port, warehousing charges, interest, etc. The incidence of any particular items in the price may, by itself, appear small or insignificant, but along with that of others, it becomes a strong deterrent to exports. It is, therefore, necessary, if we have to develop exports, to eliminate the burden of taxes like sales tax along with other taxes like excise duties, export duties and octroi duties. All other incidental expenses like transport cost, cost of storage, credit, etc. should also be kept as low as possible.
4. While some assistance is given to the exports in the way of import entitlements, etc., the need for removing the incidence of internal taxes from the goods that are exported cannot be questioned. Removal of avoidable taxes and the reduction of internal costs and charges are better ways of increasing the competitive position of our products than reliance on incentives.
5. An advantageous location or modern machinery or better management may give a differential advantage to one produce or manufacturer over others in the same country and enable him to export a part of his production in spite of some of the handicaps mentioned above. This does not reduce the force of the argument that the burden of tax on exports and other costs, should be reduced in this country at this juncture, because our export drive requires the participation of all reasonably efficient manufactures. This can happen only when they all become more competitive through the elimination or reduction of some of the burdens imposed on them at present.
6. It is possible that we may be in a position to export a certain commodity or article of manufacture to one country with what may appear to be a competitive margin, but not to another country where we are priced out. Since our development programme requires us to increase our exports as much as possible we cannot afford to be content with the limited markets which are available to us at present. Our aim should be to widen the field as much as possible, and this can be done only if our prices become more competitive over a larger area.
7. Lastly, there are some commodities where India happens to be a near-

monopoly supplier or one of the major suppliers. It is possible to argue that in such cases, no such relief should be given, because we are in a position to dictate to the world market. Prices for such commodities can be maintained at desired levels up to a point. But in this age of technical advance, there may be no lasting monopolies. Substitutes can be and are being found. Nothing stimulates the search for such substitutes so much as the attempt to hold prices at high level. A number of instances of the development of substitutes as a reaction to the high and unstable prices of the natural commodities can be cited; for example, the substitution of paper bags for jute sacks, synthetic rubber for natural rubber, plastics for shellac, polyurethane foam for short-staple cotton. There is urgent need, therefore, to cut down all the incidental fiscal handicaps, in order to promote exports.

8. In considering the question of removing the burden of sales tax on exports, two questions arise as to (i) the extent of relief to be given, and (ii) the manner in which such relief should be given. Since it has been argued above that the burden of all internal taxes should be eliminated, the obvious answer to the first question is that relief to the extent of the entire burden should be given. The difficulty arises in ascertaining the burden of tax borne by the exported goods in regard to sales tax. There are different systems of taxation prevalent in different States; in addition, there is the burden of the Central Sales Tax on sales in the course of inter-State trade which may culminate in exports; in some cases there may be a combined burden of local taxes and the Central Sales Tax. The problem of calculating the burden in respect of manufactured products where raw materials and other goods required in the manufacture of goods have been purchased from different sources in different States is even more complicated.
9. With regard to the second question that is posed in the previous paragraph, two ways of granting such relief would be: (1) initial exemption from payment of sales tax on purchases resulting in exports, and (2) the refund of sales tax which is provided to have been borne on goods which are actually exported. If the first method is adopted, ways will have to be devised to see that such exemptions are not claimed on goods sold later on in the internal market. If the second alternative is adopted, the refund will have to prompt enough to be reflected in the prices of exported goods.
10. An important problem which arises with regard to the grant of such relief is as to who should bear the burden of this relief. Should the burden be borne exclusively by the Centre or exclusively by the States which are equally interested in exports, or shared by both?
11. We would like to add that the idea of exempting the exports from the burden

of sales tax is nothing peculiar to this country. In fact, from this point of view, Indian exporters have been at a serious disadvantage all these years compared to their competitors in foreign markets. Turn-over taxes like other indirect taxes such as excise and import duties are levies meant primarily to fall on production/consumption within a country and, by their very concept, are not intended to fall on goods exported out of a country. In accordance with this approach, the tax systems of most of the countries levying turn-over taxes on one kind or the other contain provisions for relieving the exports of the burden of such taxes through exemption of refund or by a combination of both these methods.

Relief from Sales Tax

1. The Committee, by one of its terms of reference, is required to study the incidence of State and Central Sales Taxes on commodities entering into the export trade of India and to indicate the quantum of relief to be provided in respect of each commodity. We have given considerable attention to this question. We also sought the assistance of the various Trade Bodies which submitted memoranda to us and the trade and other representatives who met us, to indicate to us the incidence of sales tax on the commodities with which they were concerned. For reasons stated hereafter, we have not found it practicable to calculate the incidence of sales tax on each commodity entering into the export trade of India. Having regard to the difficulty of calculating the incidence, we have attempted alternative solutions which would afford substantial relief to the export trade without involving the necessity of such complicated calculations.
2. The problem of the incidence of sales tax on commodities entering the export trade of India is two-fold: There is the problem of the Sales Taxes borne on the goods which actually figure in the export either as raw-materials or as semi-manufactured goods or as manufactured goods; on the other hand, there is the further problem of incidence of sales tax paid on the purchase of raw materials, fuel, lubricants, machinery and other goods used in the manufacture of finished or semi-finished goods which are eventually exported. With regard to both these aspects, there are certain basic difficulties which arise from the fact that there are different Sales Tax laws in operation in different States in addition to the Central Sales Tax Act which is in operation throughout India. The systems of taxation followed by the different States in their different laws also vary. These systems vary from the single point, which again is levied either at the first stage of sale or at the last stage, the multiple point, the two point and to various combinations of these. Thus,

while the incidence can be readily ascertained where the tax is leviable at one stage, it would be difficult to assess it precisely in a multi-point system wherein the goods may have passed through several stages before export, particularly when the number of such stages varies from consignment to consignment. Under some State laws, as in West Bengal, all transactions which take place through a chain of registered dealers resulting in the final export are free from the system broadly in operation in Maharashtra and Gujarat, two sales prior to the sale in the actual course of export are exempted from levy of tax, namely, the sales preceding the actual export sale and the sale immediately prior to it. Elsewhere in some States, such as Uttar Pradesh, Punjab, Rajasthan and Madhya Pradesh, provision has been made for grant of rebates or exemptions in respect of sales of specified goods on transaction preceding the one resulting in export of those goods.

3. Apart from the different systems of taxation in operation in different States, the goods exempted from sales tax differ from State to State and the rates of tax leviable on sales of different goods also vary. For instance, oil-cakes are exempt from tax in Maharashtra, Gujarat and West Bengal, while they are subject to sales tax levy in Madras. Similarly, raw cotton is exempt from tax in West Bengal while it is subject to tax in Maharashtra, Gujarat and Madras. Such instances could be multiplied. The rates of tax on the same commodities also vary from State to State. Such variation is accounted for by general economic considerations such as the state of industrial development, alternative sources of revenues, importance of a particular commodity in the internal trade of that State etc. For instance in some States hydrogenated oil or vanaspati is subjected to a high rate of tax because it is considered that the consumers of vanaspati in these States have the capacity to bear a higher burden.

4. Similarly, with regard to the Central Sales Tax, even though the law administered throughout India is a common law framed by Parliament, the rates of tax leviable differ from State to State on inter-State sales originating in the different States subject to the prescribed maxima. For instance, in regard to declared goods, the prescribed maximum rate is 2 per cent, while in regard to most of the other goods the prescribed maximum is 10 per cent. But where the rate of tax under the local law in the State in which the sale originates is either lower than 2 per cent on all goods or higher than 10 per cent on goods other than declared goods, the rate of Central Sales Tax is the lower rate of tax in the former case and the higher rate of tax in the case of the latter. If the sale of any goods is unconditionally exempt under the local law, an inter-State sale originating in the same State is similarly exempt. Besides,

sales of goods other than declared goods, on which the ordinary rate of tax is 2 per cent or more would attract tax at eh rate of 2 per cent only, if made to registered dealers who furnish declaration in Form C prescribed under the Central Sale Tax Act.

5. Besides, it is possible that goods which have figured in an inter-State sale prior to a sale in the course if export may have themselves been the subject matter of several local seals in the State in which the inter-State sale originated. In such cases, the price would include an incidence of the local tax also. Where the local system prevalent is the multi-point system, the incidence of the local tax would have had cumulative effect.
6. The aforesaid difficulties increase and get more pronounced when calculating the incidence of the tax element in the costs structure of manufactured or processed goods which enter into the export trade. Since the manufacture of commodities may be spread over a large number of units, big and small, devoted to a single commodity or a diverse set of commodities, the consumption of raw materials and components by the different manufacturing units would be anything but uniform. The rate of utilization of raw materials would differ from unit to unit depending on the technical know how, the nature of process used, the type and age of machinery, the combination of goods produced, the managerial efficiency etc. A factory producing a large range of commodities may be able to utilize some of the waste material more fruitfully and thereby spread out the incidence of the taxes paid on the raw material. The burden of sales tax on the volume of production would thus vary from unit to unit. Even the Economists' fiction of a 'Representative Firm' for any particular industry may not be available to fall back upon because the search for such a representative firm for each of the numerous industries whose products enter into the export trade may well turn out to be fruitless.
7. Besides, even the same manufacturing unit may purchase its raw materials and other goods required in the manufacture of goods and for packing materials from different sources at different points of time. If at a particular moment, the market within the State is favourable, the purchases of a commodity may be intra-State. Where such purchases can be made free of sales tax under the local system, as in West Bengal, or at concessional rates as under the Bombay system, the incidence may be small. Where the purchases are required to bear tax and that too under a multiple point system, the incidence may be fairly heavy. At another point of time, it may not at all be profitable for the manufacturer to make purchases within the State; or for that matter, the requisite supplies of the particular goods may not be forthcoming

in that State. For instance, a manufacturer of oil or oil products in Maharashtra would only be able to buy a certain quantity of oil-seeds within the State which is deficit in the production of oil-seeds within the State which is deficit in the production of oil-seeds compared to its requirements for production. In such cases, the producer has to seek other sources for supply. The goods would then bear the incidence of the Central Sales Tax which is visible, in addition to an invisible incidence on account of earlier transactions in the same goods in the other State.

8. Among the Associations which replied to our Questionnaire and their representatives whom we interviewed, only a very few ventured to make calculations of the incidence of tax entering into the cost of manufactured articles with which they were most directly concerned. Even they took care to caution us against the imperfections of their calculations. The Mudaliar Committee also recommended an *ad hoc* relief of sales tax of 2 per cent on all exports without detailed reasons in support of calculations obviously because of the various tangles of the vexed question, which have been debated for nearly a decade, regarding the calculation of incidence of sales tax.
9. Our Committee has considered carefully the recommendation for an *ad hoc* rate of relief made by the Mudaliar Committee. Having regard to the differences in sales tax rates in different States in the context of different systems of sales tax prevalent therein, we feel that an *ad hoc* rate may have the effect of an unintended subsidy in certain States like West Bengal where no sales tax is at all levied on transactions which pass through a claim of registered dealers resulting in export, while at the same time being less than adequate to meet the incidence of the tax elsewhere where it is borne at much higher rates. The Committee would not however rule out the suggestion of an *ad hoc* rate of relief altogether. It would consider this suggestion only to meet that part of the incidence in respect of which it is difficult to make other arrangement for compensation and where such part of the incidence is by its nature somewhat incalculable and imponderable.
10. For the purpose of relief from the incidence of sales tax, the following aspects require consideration:

- Incidence of local sales tax borne within the State on sales prior to the sale in the course of export.
- Incidence of Central Sales Tax on sales prior to the sale in the course of export.
- Incidence of local sales tax entering into the cost of production of manufactured or processed goods which enter into the export trade.

- Incidence of Central Sales Tax entering into the cost of production of manufactured or processed goods which enter into the export trade, and
- Other invisible incidence.

Each of these aspects will be dealt with seriatim.

11. With regard to the incidence of local sales tax, many trade bodies in their memoranda and their representatives in their meetings with us have commended the system prevalent in the State of Maharashtra and Gujarat where by exemption from sales tax is available on two sales prior to the sale occasioning the export of goods. Under this system a registered dealer whose annual turn-over of export from the State exceeds Rs. 30,000, can obtain an authorisation. A dealer who has obtained such authorisation is enabled to purchase goods for the purpose of export without attracting incidence of tax on his purchase or on the vendor's sale to him on his giving a certificate in a prescribed form that he will export the goods so purchased either himself or through another authorised dealer to whom he may sell the goods, within a period of 9 months. In both the States, in addition to the exemption thus available the law also makes provision for a dealer who has purchased the goods without issue of such certificate and his incurred the incidence of tax at the time of this purchase to claim "set-off" of the tax borne on his purchase if he subsequently exports the goods within a period of 9 months from the date of his purchase. The amount of set-off is admissible as a refund if there is no tax liability against which the amount can be adjusted as a set-off. It goes without saying that no concession of this type is required in a State like West Bengal where sales resulting in export have taken place through a chain of registered dealers and as such are already not taxed. The Committee generally recommends that the Bombay system may be adopted by all other States if they find that certain administrative problems arising there from can be surmounted without difficulty. The administrative difficulties may be of a larger order in a non-maritime State which is not able, through the agency of its own Administration, to check the accounts etc., of the final exporter. Particularly, when the exporter has obtained goods from several States and such goods when put together lose their identity, there might be difficulty in identifying that the goods actually exported out of such goods were the very goods on which exemption was obtained from a particular non-maritime State. It is true that such difficulties would not altogether disappear under any alternative system. But if a system of rebate or set off, as is now obtaining in respect of commodities exported from Uttar Pradesh, is preferred on account of greater administrative, convenience such arrangement would also serve the

purpose. The Committee, however, would stress the necessity of giving relief in respect of the incidence of tax on at least two sales prior to the sale in the course of export either by way of exemption or set-off or by grant of rebate of tax leviable on such sales.

12. At this state, it would be worthwhile to answer a question which might well be raised, namely, why is it that the Committee recommends relief in respect of tax on two sales prior to the sale in the course of export. The actual sale in the course of export is already exempted from any sales tax. Under Article 286(1) of the Constitution no law of a State may impose or authorise the imposition of a tax on the sale or purchase of goods where such sale or purchase takes place in the course of the export of the goods out of the territory of India.

13. Under the complex conditions of modern economy, manufacture and export are two distinct activities requiring separate and specialised types of skill and resources. It may not be practicable or even desirable for every manufacturer to devote his energies and resources for seeking and developing export markets. While some of the larger manufacturers may have the organisation and resources to develop exports, the majority of them would have to rely on Export Houses for marketing their goods in foreign countries. An established exporter with his technical knowledge and resources may be able to achieve much better results if these tasks are left to him. Obviously, therefore, there can be no question of the necessity of giving relief from sales tax at least in respect of one sale prior to the exporter's sale. The necessity for exempting the second sale preceding the sale in the course of export arises from the manner of working of the export trade itself. The export trade depends to a large extent on incalculable international factors and vicissitudes. An exporter A may have purchased certain goods for export to a country Z. At the relevant time, as a result of political turmoil in country Z or for other reasons, he may find that the market which he is looking forward to in country Z is not available. At that very moment, another exporter B may be in a position to sell similar goods to country Y. In such circumstances, unless exporter B, who can readily obtain goods from exporter A and divert them to his requirements, is enabled to do so without incurring the incidence of tax etc., he may find such diversion so unremunerative as to make him lose the market in country Y for that trade. The Bombay system, where under concession is available in respect of two sales prior to the sale in the course of export, has stood the test of time. The concession under that system is so framed that the assessing authorities look to the first certifying dealer only for the actual proof of export even when he has sold the goods to another authorised dealer

who may later export them. We therefore, consider that there should be no administrative difficulties experienced by the States in exempting from sales tax the two sales immediately preceding the sale in the course of export. If, however, any State Administration can conveniently extend the concessions to earlier sales also, he has already been done in West Bengal, such measures could also be helpful in promoting exports.

14. With regard to the second aspect, namely, relief from the incidence of Central Sales Tax, the Committee has carefully examined whether it would be possible to recommend the extension of the Bombay system for grant of exemptions. There are certain administrative difficulties in the way of adopting such a system for Central Sales Tax. The exporters by and large, have their principal offices in the maritime States. They are answerable to the assessing authorities of the maritime States in respect of any purchases made by them in the course of inter-State in respect of any purchases made by them in the course of inter-State trade and commerce. The actual loss of revenue, in case they make purchases free of tax, would have to be borne not by their home State but by the State in which they make such purchases. It is impracticable to ask the exporters to submit themselves to assessment and examination by each such State where in they may have made their purchases. The States standing to lose the revenue may, on the other hand, be unwilling to give a concession regarding the use of which their own authorities are unable to obtain verification directly, and understandably so. They may, therefore, prefer an alternative system of granting rebates or refunds to the selling dealers of their own State on certain conditions such as (1) that the goods are actually exported outside the country within a specified period, (2) that the assessee furnishes proof of such export and (3) that the assessee furnishes proof that if he has charged sales tax to the exporter, the same has been refunded. Such a system is already in operation in Uttar Pradesh. Under this system a dealer is required to make an application in a prescribed form to his assessing authorities claiming a rebate. The application has to be accompanied by declaration in a prescribed form, duly verified by the Customs authorities, in proof of the goods actually having been exported. On verification, either refund is allowed to the dealer or he is allowed to make an adjustment against the tax due form him. After careful consideration of the pros and cons of both the systems, the Committee recommends that the system of rebate may be adopted with the following modifications namely, that the selling dealer of the State of origin may be allowed to set-off of tax in respect of his sales to exporters from his tax liability under his periodical returns without being called upon to pay the tax on the one hand and

separately claim refund or rebate on the other. The dealer making such adjustment in his return may be called upon to furnish satisfactory proof as regards the actual export of the goods sold to the exporter within a reasonable period. On his failure to produce such proof, he may be held liable to pay sales tax which would otherwise have been levied with such penalty as may be prescribed. If the scheme of rebate is thus modified the Committee feels that the exporters would he enabled to obtain their goods in the course of inter-State trade and commerce without incurring the incidence of Central Sales Tax.

15. There is undoubtedly some scope for evasion of taxes under either system. In order that the scope for evasion may be minimised and the concession either of exemption or of rebate is not misused and is only availed of by *bona fide* exporters, the Committee recommends that the Central Government should maintain under a appropriate statutory regulations a list of Registered Exporters enlisting there only *bona fide* exporters whose annual turnover of exports is not less than Rupees one lakh. The concessions regarding exemption or rebate would be allowed only to such Registered Exporters and provisions should be made in the regulations for removing from the list any exporter who is found to indulge in malpractices resulting in the abuse of concessions given. There is no objection, however, to any exporter being allowed refund of taxes actually paid by him on satisfactory proof of such payment and of the exports made by him being furnished to the Sales Tax Administration of the originating State through his vendor in that State. Section 8(5) of the Central Sales Tax Act has at present an enabling provision for the State Governments to grant exemptions of or reductions in tax on the sale of any goods or any class of goods subject to certain conditions. The Central Sales Tax Act should be suitably modified to enable the State Governments to grant rebates or set-offs of tax in addition to outright exemption of tax or reduction in tax in appropriate cases.

16. With regard to the incidence of local sales tax borne by a manufacturer manufacturing goods for export, on the purchases made by him in his own home State for use in the manufacture of goods, the Committee considers that there should be no practical difficulty in the way of the manufacturer showing from his accounts the total amount of such tax borne on his purchases by him during a particular year. The manufacturer would also have ready date regarding the total value of goods produced by him as also the total value of that portion of his production which has been exported either directly by him or through other exporters. If these data are furnished by the manufacturer to the assessing authorities of his home State, on the basis of these data it should

be possible for that State to grant a refund or rebate bearing the same proportion of the total tax paid by the manufacturer on purchases of raw materials, components etc., as the quantity of goods exported from his production bears t the total quantity of this production during the same year. Where the proportionate quantities cannot be readily ascertained or where the manufacturer so prefers, the proportion may be struck on the basis of the value of goods exported to the total value of goods produced.

17. The problem of the incidence of Central Tax on raw materials components and packing material, etc. used by a manufacturer is much more difficult. The manufacturer may have made his purchases from several different States at different times. It would be difficult for his home State to ascertain the proportionate rebate in respect of Central Sales Tax paid by the manufacturers to the various states from which he has made his purchases. After devoting considerable thought to this subject, the Committee feels that there are far too many administrative difficulties in devising a readily workable system for the apportionment of such rebate to different States.

18. There is also an allied problem of certain imponderable or incalculable elements of sales tax which may have entered into the cost of production of manufactured goods. Where raw materials and other goods have been purchased from another State in addition to the incidence of Central Sales Tax they may also have borne the incidence of local sales tax. Where the local system is a multipoint system such incidence may have been borne at more than one stage. Besides, it has been represented by trade associations and witness on their behalf that sales tax enters indirectly in several ways in a manufacturer's cost. For instance, when a truck is purchased, in addition to the direct sales tax payable by the truck, the price paid for the truck includes incidence of sales tax paid by the manufacturer of trucks on tyres, batteries, etc. Sales tax charged on petrol and other fuel oils used in transport vehicles also contributes to the cost of production. To the extent that such tax is reflected in the tariff of goods vehicles plying on road the incidence is reflected in a higher transport cost. Thus, the incidence of sales tax in respect of purchases of raw material etc. may be covered only partially by the system of rebate which has been recommended in paragraph 16.

19. On careful consideration, the Committed feels that in order to make our exports competitive in the foreign markets, it is necessary to give some relief in the price in respect of the imponderable elements referred to in the preceding paragraph and the incidence of Central Sales Tax borne on purchase of raw materials, components and other goods used in the manufacturer of goods. The Committee recommends that an *ad hoc* relief

calculated at 1 per cent of the f.o.b. value in the case of manufactured and processed goods and ½ per cent in the case of other goods may be granted to the actual exporter in respect of the goods exported by him in each year, by the Central Government.

20. Our recommendation for grant of relief on exports to the extent that such relief is to be granted by the States Tax Administrations of the different States is bound to have important financial repercussions on the State Administrations. Under our federal structure, the field for levying taxes open to the States under the Constitution is limited Sale Tax is the only major elastic source of revenue now left to the State Administrations. In some States, like Kerala, a substantial portion of the sales tax revenue itself is derived from important items of export like fish, cashew nuts, coir and tea. It may not be reasonable to expect such administrations to bear significant loss in their sales tax revenue, in the light of their ever increasing commitments for development, unless suitable compensation is paid to them by the Centre. No State making its contribution to the Export Drive by grant of the concessions, we have recommended, should be called upon to suffer in its capacity to carry out its Development plants. We, therefore, recommend that adequate compensation should be given by the Centre to States where our recommendations lead to loss of revenue which is not insignificant. The loss to be made good should be calculated on the basis of present rates to tax and only in respect of commodity which are being taxed at present so that there is no inducement to the States to raise the rates or widen the list of taxed commodities are being taxed at present so that there is no inducement to the States to raise the rates or widen the list of taxed commodities only in order to quality for a larger amount of compensation. This is not to say that the States should be barred from levying a higher rate of tax in future on the internal trade in such goods but the amount of compensation in respect of loss of revenue on export sales should be related to the present rates of tax only. To the extent that there is an increase in the volume of exports, the compensation should be suitably raised on the basis of the present rates.

Allied Problems

1. We have given our recommendations regarding relief from sales tax in respect both of goods exported as well as raw materials and components used in their manufacture. We feel that this scheme, if adopted, would cover the generality of goods and afford sufficient relief to the exporter. In the course of our investigation, however, we were confronted with some specific problems concerning the incidence of sales tax on export commodities, some

of which would not be covered by the recommendations contained in the previous chapter. These problems will now be considered.

2. There are a few commodities such as mica and shellac, which are produced mainly for export. Over 80 per cent of the total production of these is exported. It has been suggested that such goods require special treatment. If the formula we have suggested is applied to such commodities, the complicated administrative processes required for the levy and collection of the sales tax initially and the grant of refund, set-off or rebate thereafter, may not be worthwhile considering the small net revenue which would be derived by the State Governments from the internal sale of these commodities. We, therefore, recommend that in case of goods where eighty per cent or more of the indigenous production is exported, and the loss of revenue would not be significant, the States should exempt them from the payment of sales tax altogether.
3. Another problem that was raised was concerning exports on consignment basis. Earlier, we have dealt with the need to give relief from sales tax in respect of two sales prior to the sale in the course of export. The recommendation would not, however, in itself, help the sales resulting in exports on consignment basis. At present there is a sizeable export trade on consignment basis in items such as jewellery, precious stones and handicrafts. With increasing participation by our country in international fairs and opening of Trade Centres abroad, there is considerable scope for expansion of exports of a wider range of goods like engineering goods etc. on such basis. In order the exports on consignment basis, which subsequently result in sales in the foreign countries, should receive every encouragement, we recommend that relief from sales tax on the lines that we have recommended for two sales prior to the sale in the course of export, should be available also *mutatis mutandis* in the case of two sales prior to the export on consignment basis. It would be enough, if, for the grant of above relief, a stipulation is made that the exports made on consignment basis result in actual sales abroad within a period o two years from the date of export. In the case of articles like jewellery and precious stones, where under Customs regulations such exports on consignment basis can be re-imported within a period of three years without inviting import duties, the stipulation may be that the foreign sale is effected within the corresponding period of three years.
4. Exports to Nepal create a problem, in that the goods, though meant for export, have sometimes to be taken delivery of at point in India before they finally cross the border. It goes without question that sales in the course of export to Nepal are exempted from sales tax under the provision of Article 286 of the

Constitution. Due to the fact that delivery is required to be given at specified border points within our country, such sales become liable to tax. Some States have made provision whereby such sales are exempted from Central sales tax when satisfactory proof is furnished that delivery at a border point in another State has been followed by subsequent transhipment to Nepal. It has been, however, brought to our notice that some States have been advised that under the Central Sales Tax Act, as it now stands, they are not competent to grant exemption in respect of sales to Nepal where delivery is offered at a border point in another State. This view is apparently not shared by the Central Government. The question is one of legal interpretation. Since there is no dispute on the necessity of granting exemption in the case of such sales, where the goods are finally transhipped to Nepal, though delivery may be at a border point in another State, such amendment as is considered necessary may be made in the Central Sales Tax Act, in order that the legal position may be completely free from doubt.

5. Another complaint which we receive was that in some States the concession available in respect of a sale which later results in a sale in the course of export, is limited to those cases where the export movement starts from the very State and is made by the office or branch of the dealer in that State. If the dealer has another office at a port in another State and consigns the goods to that office which later makes the export, the concession is not available. In law, both the offices i.e. the head office and the branch would be the same legal person, and a branch transfer does not involve a sale. But if the contrary view is taken by a Tax Administration, the arrived parties would be put to considerable expense of time and money in litigation to obtain redress. To avoid such hardships, we recommend that all the concessions in this behalf should be available alike whether the export is made by a firm from its office or branch in the originating State or from some other office or branch in another State.

Conclusion

1. The representatives of the various Associations of trade and industry that submitted memoranda to us as also the person who came for oral evidence made a number of other suggestions which in their opinion would give relief to exporters in so far as sales tax was concerned. We have not been able to accept all these suggestions but we think it is necessary for us to mention some of the more important suggestions made and to explain why it had not been possible for us to accept these suggestions. At the same time we are making a few more recommendations with a view to meeting some of the

problems.

2. A suggestion was made that goods entering into the export trade should be completely exempted from sales tax even in respect of internal trade in such goods. A further suggestion was that the definition of sales in the course of export, contained in Section 5(1) of the Central Sales Tax Act, should be made more comprehensive. The trade interests generally felt that the definition adopted in our country was much narrower than the interpretation put on this phrase by the Supreme Court of the United States. We have carefully considered whether a widening of the definition is necessary. We understand that the suggestion has not been favoured by the Law Commission. If our recommendation that relief should be available for at least two sales prior to the sale in the course of export were to be accepted, it was generally admitted that, for all practical purposes, there would be no need for such widening of the definition.
3. A suggestion which was repeatedly pressed before us by almost all the organisations of trade and industry was that, to the extent that excise duty can administratively replace sales tax effectively, the sales tax should be abolished and replaced by additional excise duty, as has already been done in the case of cotton textiles, tobacco and sugar. It goes without saying that if a large number of sales tax laws, diverse in diverse in their structures and in their rates, operating in different parts of the country are replaced by a single uniform system of duty administered by only one authority, the trade and industry would be saved a great deal of inconvenience and hardship. The problem is, however, not susceptible of a simple solution. The demand has been considered time and again by both the Union Ministry of Finance and the various State Governments. With the existing distribution of the sphere of taxation as between the Union and the States, sales tax is now the chief elastic source of revenue to the State Governments. The State Governments, therefore, are understandably reluctant to agree to give up their right to levy Sales Tax on any commodities. It appears that their experience of the substitution of sales tax by additional excise duty in respect of the three items of cotton textiles, tobacco and sugar, has not been uniformly happy. The receipts from additional excise by several States under this head have not kept pace with the general growth of their sales tax revenue in the corresponding period. No satisfactory formula has also so far been evolved under which the distribution of receipts of this nature would be acceptable equally to the more populous States with a backward economy and those where the per capita consumption of such goods is much larger. While noting the strength of feeling on this subject on the part of the trade and industrial circles generally,

we consider that having regard to all the aforesaid factors, it would not be a practical proposition to extend to other commodities in the present context, the scheme of replacing sales tax by additional excise duty.

4. Some of the witnesses suggested to us that while they recognise the need for the State having the power to tax sales and purchases, there should be uniformity in the law and procedure relating to sales tax. While we agree that uniformity in the principles, policies, legislations and practices of sales tax would considerably reduce the impediments to the free flow of inter-state trade and commerce, we have not been convinced that uniformity for its own sake would necessarily encourage exports. Beside, we realise that each State has adopted a particular system of taxation in view of its special needs. The economic conditions differ from State to State, as also their need for revenue. In some States, therefore, a single-point sales tax has been considered desirable while in others the multi-point tax system had to be adopted. We have, therefore, not recommended any uniformity for its own sake.
5. We, however, consider that there should be an arrangement under which the Sales Tax Commissioners of different States should periodically meet and exchange views in order to minimise the practical difficulties in regard to the administration of sales tax, felt both by the administration and the commercial community. At present there is considerable difference in the definitions of such terms as 'dealer', 'sale price', 'turnover' etc., in the sales tax laws of different States. This leads to much difficulty for the trade particularly when it involves inter-state transactions. The procedure for filling returns and payments of taxes, for assessment, for appeals and revision etc., and the rules regarding maintenance of accounts vary considerably from State to State. The proposed meetings of Sales Tax Commissioners may help to bring about some uniformity in the rules and procedures without affecting the fundamental principles of the sales tax laws in any ways.
6. The members of our Committee, some of whom are associated with the Sales Tax Administration in different States, have derived substantial benefit from discussions not only amongst themselves but also with trade and industrial interests in different parts of the country. Such discussions have helped them to understand the working of the laws in different States as also to appreciate the hardships and difficulties experienced by trade and industry in such working. We consider, therefore, that periodic exchange of views across the table between representatives of trade and industry on the one side and representatives of the Tax Administration of all the different States on the other, would go a long way in simplifying procedure and facilitating the collection of tax and at the same time reducing the hardships and

inconvenience caused to the trading and industrial community in such processes. In some States there are Sales Tax Advisory Committees functioning at State and District levels. But obviously these Committees can deal with only local problems. What we have in mind are problems of all-India interest. For this purpose, we suggest that from time to time such matters may be discussed at an all-India Conference including representatives of the Sales Tax Administrations of various States on the one hand and prominent non-officials and representatives of trade and industry on the other.

7. Before concluding, we would like to add that our recommendations have been formulated as mutually related parts of a consistent scheme and should be considered together in their entirety. These recommendations require action both by the Central Government and the State Governments. They also require whole-hearted cooperation from the exporting interests so as to enable them to secure the benefits to the export trade which would result from the acceptance of our recommendations. We trust that our recommendations taken as a whole will be of some significant value in helping to develop the export trade of India.

Appendix 5

Committee on Taxation of Agricultural Income and Wealth, 1972

The Committee on Taxation of Agricultural Income and Wealth, 1972 was appointed by the Government of India on February 24, 1972. The Committee had the following terms of reference:

(a) To examine the present system of direct taxation of agricultural wealth and income (including capital gains) and suggest methods by which such taxation can be used more effectively for raising additional resources for development and for helping to achieve the objective of self-reliance;

(b) To recommend specifically ways and means by which taxation of agricultural wealth and income can be used to reduce economic disparities and promote more efficient utilisation of the available resources of land and labour;

(c) To examine in detail, and make recommendations on, the necessary changes in the system of assessment, collection and distribution of these taxes such that the resources available to the States from such taxation can be maximised, without detriment to the rights and legitimate interests of any State;

(d) To suggest the consequential changes if any, in the system of taxation of wealth and income in general; and

(e) To indicate and make suggestions, if any, on any related matters.

Composition of the Committee

K.N. Raj	Chairman
V.M. Dandekar	Member
G.S. Kalkat	Member
Anwar Karim	Member
Dharm Narain	Member
M.B. Palekar	Member
A. Vaidyanathan	Member
B.P.R. Vithal	Member-Secretary

The Committee disfavoured, on practical considerations, a full-scale coverage of agricultural incomes under the Central income tax. However, it suggested partial integration of agricultural incomes with non-agricultural incomes for the limited purpose of determining the rates of taxation. It also maintained that the additional revenue realised as a result of the partial integration of agricultural with non-agricultural income in the above manner, should go entirely to the State of origin of the agricultural income so aggregated. Consequently, from the assessment year 1974-75, Central income tax takes into account the income of an assessee from agriculture for the limited purpose of determining the rate of tax on non-agricultural incomes in certain cases.

Although averse to the idea of full integration of agricultural and non-agricultural incomes for income tax purposes, the Committee favoured the possibility, with certain cautions, of integrated taxation of agricultural and non-agricultural wealth. While the power to tax agricultural income belongs exclusively to the States, there is no constitutional impediment to an integrated taxation of agricultural and non-agricultural wealth by the Centre.

As its main recommendation, the Committee suggested the imposition of Agricultural Holding Tax (AHT) which in its view would secure for the States an additional revenue from well-off sections of agriculturists with much less harassment of the assessees than is likely if Central income tax is extended to the farm sector. The Committee accepted the view that the incidence of direct taxation should broadly be the same on comparable income and wealth groups irrespective of the sources and the forms in which wealth is held. In devising a system of direct taxation of agriculture, it is necessary to ensure progressivity, a principle that has not governed the land revenue. The Committee emphasised that for purposes of direct taxation, the family should be the basic unit of assessment so as to prevent large-scale avoidance.

For a rational system of direct taxation of agriculture, the Committee laid down the following criteria: 1. It should take account of the difference in productivity of land depending upon the particular crops grown in a region. 2. Its incidence should be uniform in different parts of the country. 3. It should reflect changes in productivity and prices over a period of time. 4. It should be possible to build into the tax an element of progression. As for differences in productivity of land, the Committee pinpointed the following factors: (a) soil-climatic differences, (b) conditions of water supply, and (c) crops grown.

Taking into account various factors which cause variations in the productivity of land, the Committee recommended a scheme of Agricultural Holding Tax (AHT) with the following salient features.

1. The country should be divided into a sufficiently large number of soil-climatically homogenous districts/tracts so that differences having any

significant influence on productivity are taken into account.

2. For each such district/tract norms of output of different crops per hectare for each year should be worked out on the basis of estimates of yield for the previous 10 years and these should be valued at the relevant average harvest prices of the preceding three years.
3. From the value of the gross output of the crops arrived at in the above manner, allowance should be made for the paid out costs of cultivation (40 to 50 per cent of the value of gross output) and also for depreciation of assets.
4. The norms arrived at in the above manner would form the rateable value of a hectare of land growing different crops in different districts/ tracts.
5. To provide for the costs of development, the Committee suggested granting of development allowance to all agricultural holdings at the rate of 20 per cent of the rateable value subject to a maximum of Rs. 1,000.
6. To determine the actual tax liability under AHT, the Committee devised a simple formula to be applied to the rateable value of the holdings minus the development allowance. If the rateable value of a holding (minus the development allowance) is 'X' thousand rupees, the AHT should form X/2 per cent of this amount. For example, if the rateable value of a holding is Rs. 10,000, the AHT would be 9/2 or 4.5 per cent of Rs. 9,000 (i.e. Rs. 10,000 minus Rs. 1,000 deductible as development allowance) which is equal to Rs. 405.
7. As the incidence of AHT decreases progressively on small holdings, the Committee favoured the application of the formula to rateable value up to Rs. 600. For holdings of rateable value below Rs. 600, the AHT may be fixed at a flat rate of Re. 1 per holding.

Although the recommendations of the Committee were widely welcomed, it is unfortunate that the State Governments have generally remained lukewarm in taxing agriculture directly. Exemption of agricultural income from taxation deprives the States of a potential source of revenue.

Edited Extracts from the Report

Basic Considerations

The richest one-tenth of the households in the country account for about 25 per cent of the total private consumption, over 40 per cent of the total household incomes, and not less than two-thirds of privately-owned wealth. The major share of the additional resources has to come from this stratum.

Indirect taxes have an important role in the fiscal system. It would also be possible to achieve a degree of Progression through indirect taxation by levying it on commodities and services consumed by the richer sections of the population. Nevertheless, commodity taxation has serious limitations as an instrument of resource mobilization, since it is more easily shifted and very often leads to unintended cost escalations. For equitable distribution of the burden it is essential to use direct taxation to the maximum extent possible for resource mobilisation.

The incidence of direct taxation should be broadly the same on comparable income and wealth groups irrespective of the sources of income and the forms in which wealth is held. This does not necessarily mean that the forms of direct taxation adopted for application to different categories of income and wealth should be identical.

Direct taxes on agriculture levied by the States (viz., land revenue, cesses and surcharges based on land revenue, crop cesses and agricultural income-tax) account for barely 1 per cent of the Net Domestic Product from agriculture, and the proportion varies widely from State to State; it is about 0.24 per cent in Orissa and Punjab and 1.34 per cent in Rajasthan.

In devising a system of direct taxation of agriculture, it is necessary to ensure that the relatively better-off sections pay proportionately more out of their income and wealth so that there is a reasonable degree of progression in the tax. The principle of progression has not governed the land revenue – the largest element of direct taxation of agriculture. Since there is no perceptible progression in the incidence of surcharges on land revenue and since other taxes levied on agriculture are relatively light, income-earners belonging to the higher strata pay less than those in comparable strata deriving their income from non-agricultural sources.

The proposed ceilings on land holdings have greatly reduced the scope for progressive taxation in agriculture. Even so, there will be incomes earned from agriculture large enough to come within the purview of progressive tax. The size of operational ceilings would not necessarily be limited by the proposed ceilings. Further, with technological improvement, productivity of land is likely to increase in future.

For purpose of direct taxation the family – consisting of husband, wife and minor children – should be the basic unit of assessment. This is required also for preventing large-scale avoidance. If direct taxation is to become a major instrument of resource mobilization on an equitable basis, it is also necessary to close the loopholes offered by the various exemptions and deductions.

With a ceiling on land holdings, a growing percentage of the agricultural population particularly in the higher strata is likely to turn increasingly to non-agricultural sources of income. There has to be, therefore, a mechanism to ensure that incomes whether derived from agricultural of non-agricultural activities are taken into account for progressive direct taxation.

In looking for a suitable system of direct taxation of agriculture the facts of a federal polity and of the distribution of functions and powers between the form of Govt. Centre and the federating States have to be borne in mind.

Alternative Approaches to Direct Taxation of Agriculture

One alternative which is readily available for the direct taxation of agriculture is integrated taxation of agricultural and non-agricultural wealth. There is no constitutional impediment to the levy of such a tax by the Centre. If the coverage of the tax is widened by adopting the family as the basic unit or by reducing the basic exemption limit or by cutting down the exemptions wealth-tax can be a useful instrument of direct taxation. But if the exemption limit is lowered several difficulties will arise including problems of identifying potential assesses, the taxable assets and valuation of assets etc. In the conditions of Indian agriculture this will inevitably give rise to considerable harassment and possibly lead to savings being increasingly held in forms that are more easily concealed such as gold and currency hoards. Hence caution has to be exercised in the use of wealth-tax as the principal instrument of resource mobilisation from the agricultural population.

An alternative recommended by many is a completely integrated system of taxation of agricultural and non-agricultural incomes. This would require a major constitutional amendment to empower the Centre to levy tad on agricultural incomes. Such a course of action is not favoured by the States. Besides, since proper assessment of agricultural incomes requires a degree of knowledge of local conditions, in any practical system of taxation of agricultural incomes the primary responsibility for the levy and collection of the tax will have to be with the States. Apart from these considerations, taxation of agriculturist according to actual incomes assessed from year to year poses various problems. The computation of actual income from farming with any degree of precision is extremely difficult. Few among the farmers maintain detailed accounts. Hence the risk of harassment by tax officials and equally the opportunities for understating incomes are likely to be considerable if the tax is based on the 'actual income' concept.

An alternative often suggested is a progressive surcharge on the existing land revenue. But there is no uniformity in the principles and procedures followed in land revenue assessments in different States and in different areas within the same State. The existing land revenue therefore does not offer a satisfactory basis for a system of progressive surcharge.

A rational system of direct taxation of agriculture

- should take account of the differences in productivity of land depending upon the particular crops grown in a region;
- its incidence should be uniform in different parts of the country, and
- it should reflect changes in productivity and prices over a period of time. Moreover, it should be possible to build into the tax an element of progression.

Agricultural Holdings Tax

The major factors underlying differences in the productivity of land are

- soil-climatic differences;
- conditions of water supply; and
- crops grown.

An Agricultural Holdings Tax (AHT) needs to be devised to adequately take account of the factors making for such variations in the productivity of land.

The salient features of the proposed scheme of AHT are as under:

(a) The country should be divided into a sufficiently large number of soil-climatically homogeneous districts/tracts so that differences having any significant influence on productivity are taken into account;

(b) For each such district/tract norms of output of different crops per hectare for each year should be worked out on the basis of estimates of yield for the previous 10 years; these should be valued at the relevant average harvest prices of the preceding three years. The State Governments should notify the markets and post-harvest marketing periods relating to each crop in each district/tract and arrange to collect, record and publish the relevant prices on a regular basis;

(c) The norms so derived would provide the norms of the value of output per hectare of different crops of different districts/tracts;

(d) From the value of the gross output of the crops arrived at as above allowance should be made for the paid out costs of cultivation other than expenses of irrigation and also for depreciation of assets (other than livestock) along the lines indicated.

(e) The norms arrived at in the above manner would form the rateable value of hectare of land growing different crops in different district/tracts.

(f) If in a given year, the average output of a crop in a district is less than half the average output of earlier 10 years, the rateable value of land under such a crop should be taken at zero. Relief may be allowed for crop failures in part or parts of a district/tract after enquiry by an appropriate authority.

(g) Go simplify the computation crops under a district tract may be suitably grouped under a few crop-groups.

(h) For each district/tract there will be a schedule of rateable value of land per hectare under different crops/crop-groups. The schedule would be revised every year taking into account, the crop yields of the preceding 10 years, the harvest prices of the preceding 3 years and any revision that may be made from time to time in the scale of deduction to be made on account of the costs of cultivation of different crops. The Schedule of rateable value of lands under different crops in each district/tract should be prepared on this basis every year and included in the legislation of the year in question. The construction of the schedule for each district/tract in a State will be primarily the responsibility of the State Government concerned.

(i) The rateable value of an assessable land *holding* will be computed from the rateable values of land under the crops actually grown (harvested) on it during the year of assessment after deducting the expenses of irrigation in the manner indicated.

To provide for the costs of development, a development allowance should be given to all agricultural holdings at the rate of 20 per cent of the rateable value subject to a maximum of Rs. 1000.

The actual tax liability under the Agriculture Holdings Tax would be arrived at by applying a simple formula to the rateable value of the holdings minus the development allowance; if the rateable value of holding (minus the development allowance) is 'X' thousand rupees the AHT should form X/Z of a holding is Rs. 1,000 the AHT would be 9.02 or 4.5 per cent of Rs. 9,000 (*i.e.* Rs. 1,000 minus Rs. 1,000 deductible as development allowance), which is equal to Rs. 405.

As the incidence of the AHT decreases progressively on small holdings, the formula should be applied to rateable values up to Rs. 600. For holdings of rateable value below Rs. 600 AHT may be fixed at a flat rate of Re. 1 per holding.

Tax on agricultural holdings should be levied on operational holdings and on a family basis (family consisting of husband, wife and minor children). Adoption of the operational holding as the basis for the AHT will discourage illegal or concealed leases and thus help protect the rights of the tenants.

The implementation of the AHT may be made in two phases. In the first phase the present land revenue should be replaced by AHT on all operational holdings with rateable value of Rs. 5,000 or more. Suitable steps would need to be taken in the first phase for identification of all operational holdings likely to have rateable value of Rs. 5,000 and for aggregation of holdings of all family members. Holdings lying in different States should be treated as separate holdings and assessed as such. In the second phase the system may be extended to operational holdings of rateable value below 5,000 according to the convenience of each State Government.

To facilitate the determination of rateable values of holdings a system of crop inspection and recording of crop acreages should be evolved. Recording of crop acreages on assessable holdings must be done expeditiously so that the rateable value is ascertained well within the year of assessment. Reasonable opportunity should be given to each land holder to represent his case if in his opinion the crop acreage shown on his land holdings are incorrect. A regular procedure will have to be laid down for the purpose. It would be convenient if a separate 'Agricultural Holding Book' is issued to each assessable land holder in which are entered details relating to members of the family, details of operational holdings, changes in the area covered by the holding from time to time and crops grown in different seasons each year. The rateable value of the holding, the AHT assessment and the recovery of instalments as also all loan transactions related to the land holdings should be entered in this book. The book should be permanently with the land holder.

The assessment year should be uniformly from 1st July to 30th June. Every year on the basis of the recorded crop groups the rateable value of each holding should be worked out, the AHT computed at the prescribed rates and a notice of demand presented to each assessee before 30th June of the assessment year. The recovery of the tax may be made in suitable instalments in the following year.

The AHT should replace land revenue for all operational holdings of rateable value of Rs. 5,000 and more. Extension of the AHT to holdings of smaller rateable value may be made at the discretion of State Governments in the following phases:

(i) All operational holdings with rateable value of Rs. 2,500 and above may be covered;

(ii) On the remaining holdings a census of land utilisation and recording of crop acreage may be done once in 5 years. Their rateable value may be ascertained on this basis, the AHT assessed and kept fixed for the next 5 years. All agricultural holdings with the rateable value of less than Rs. 600 may be required to pay AHT at a flat rate of Re. 1 per holdings.

Where an operational holding stands in the name of a trust, the holding should be notionally apportioned among the beneficiaries in the proportion in which the income of the trust is enjoyed by them and the respective shares aggregated with the holdings of the families to which the beneficiaries belong. Where the share of the beneficiaries is indeterminate, the agricultural holdings of the trust should be assessed to AHT at a minimum rate of 20 per cent of the rateable value. There should be no concessional treatment for charitable or religious trusts.

In the case of cooperatives, in so far as a part or the whole of the operational agricultural holding of a cooperative society consists of lands identifiable as legally belonging to individual members such lands should be treated as part of the agricultural holdings of the family to which these members belong. Where such lands are not so identifiable they may be deemed to be operated by the members in equal parts and each such part treated as a component of the agricultural holdings of the respective members.

Holdings of agricultural companies may be assessed for AHT on the same basis as family holdings subject to a minimum of 20 per cent of the rateable value of their operational holdings. As regards holdings of plantation companies, the present system of agricultural income taxation on plantation companies may continue. However, to the extent the area operated by them is used for growing non-plantation crops, these companies should be subjected to AHT like any other agricultural company.

After the notice of demand is served an opportunity should be given to the tax-payer to challenge the correctness of the computation of the tax-liability.

While framing the scheme of the AHT the requirement that a tax statute like any other statute must respect the principle of equality enshrined in the Constitution has been kept in view.

To ensure uniform and objective application of the AHT all over the country there should be a standing All-India Committee on Agricultural Holdings Tax. This Committee should be appointed by the Planning Commission and it should consist of three members:

- A non-official economist;
- An official with experience of Revenue Administration at the State level; and
- A technical officer who is or has been a Director of Agriculture in a State.

The Committee should undertake every year a *post facto* review of the operation of the AHT in all the States and consult the State Government where significant departures are found from the desired uniformity and objectivity in the application of the AHT. The Committee should submit an Annual Review to the Planning Commission and the Review should be placed before the National Development Council.

On the basis of available data the Agricultural Holdings Tax may be expected to yield about Rs. 200 crore per annum, if applied to all holdings with rateable value of Rs. 5,000 and above. If this tax replaces land revenue and related surcharges and cesses, the net additional revenue that may be collected from this tax would be around Rs. 150 crore. If extended to all holdings of rateable value of Rs. 2,500 or more, the additional resources may be around Rs. 200 crore.

Partially Integrated Taxation of Non-agricultural Income with Income Derived from Agriculture

There should be some arrangement to ensure that the tax burden on assesses with similar incomes does not differ sharply merely because of the fact that part of it is derived from agriculture. This can be achieved without bringing agricultural incomes under the charge of Central income-tax if such incomes are taken into account in determining the rate of tax applicable to non-agricultural incomes. This would also help check evasion through the device of camouflaging taxable income as gains from agriculture.

A suitable provision should therefore be made in the Income-tax Act, 1961 whereby both agricultural and non-agricultural components of a tax-payer's income are aggregated and the tax on the non-agricultural portion is levied as if the latter were placed in the top slabs of the aggregate income. Integration of agricultural and non-agricultural incomes should take effect only if an assessee has taxable income exceeding the minimum exemption limit laid down for the levy of the Central income-tax. In determining the rate of tax on non-agricultural income, the agriculture income and non-agricultural income should be combined in the following manner and order:

- the initial exemption allowed out of non-agricultural income (Rs. 5000 at present),
- agricultural income and
- the balance of non-agricultural income.

Since the proposal does not envisage levy of any tax on agricultural income by the Centre it would not require any constitutional amendment.

The suggestion to achieve partial integration by allowing the States to levy tax on agricultural income at the rates appropriate to the total income comprising both agricultural and non-agricultural income is not practicable.

In computing net income from agriculture for the purpose of partial integration, all items of expenditure allowed under the Income-tax Act in the computation of income from business or profession, including depreciation of machinery and tools used in agriculture, should deducted from gross receipts. To avoid harassment to assesses, however, rules should be framed by the Central government in consultation with the State Government and the proposed All-India Committee on Agricultural Holdings Tax prescribing the maximum scale of expenses allowable under the major heads in computation of agricultural income in different districts/tracts.

The liability on account of the proposed Agricultural Holdings Tax should not be allowed as deductible expenditure while computing agricultural income.

Losses incurred in agriculture should be allowed to be set-off only against gains from agriculture.

Administrative arrangements should be made for certification of the extent of the aggregate agricultural holding of assesses, the nature of crops frown and the rateable value of the holdings by an appropriate revenue authority designated by the State Governments in each district.

Thc additional revenue realised as a result of the partial integration of agricultural with non-agricultural income in the above manner should go entirely to the State of origin of the agricultural income so aggregated.

Integrated Taxation of Agricultural Property through Wealth-tax and of Capital Gains on Agricultural Assets through Income-tax

The AHT should be supplemented with a tax on agricultural property and a tax on capital gains arising out of transactions in such property.

It is now well settled that Parliament can legislate for the levy of tax on net wealth including the value of agricultural land. At present, however, the wealth-tax in general has a member of limitations due to numerous exemptions allowed. Many of the exemptions now allowed are regressive in effect if it is considered necessary to stimulate saving or to promote saving in particular forms, the financial institutions concerned may be enabled to offer higher rates of return to all investors.

Wealth-tax should be levied on a family basis. The basic exemption limit may be raised to Rs. 1.5 lakh and all other exemptions done away with as far as possible. If the exemption limit is so fixed few families in agriculture would be required to pay any wealth-tax on their own agricultural holdings, unless they have substantial assets in other forms as well. With the removal of all exemptions other than that provided by the basic exemption limit, there would be a case for lowering the rates of tax in order that assesses on the margin of the exempted limit are not too heavily burdened.

Value of shares in companies and cooperatives should be included in full in the taxable wealth of the share holders and their market worth determined rigorously. No concession should be given to religious and charitable trusts in the matter of wealth-tax.

Valuation of farm land for wealth-tax purposes should, generally, be made through the method of income-capitalization. A simple and adequate method would be to take 4 to 6 times the rateable value of a holding averaged over a period of years. Guidelines may be issued to the assessing officers regarding factors to be kept in view while taking a decision about the figure of the multiplier to be adopted for income-capitalization.

The definition of capital asset should be so widened as to permit taxation of capital gains from transfer of all agricultural lands irrespective of their location. Gains from transaction in assets held for not more than a year should be treated as ordinary income and taxed accordingly. To mitigate the inequity involved in the taxation of capital gains derived from sale of assets held for more than a year at progressive rates a method of prorating the long-term capital gains over a number of years, without reopening any back year's assessment may be followed. Treatment of losses on long-term capital assets might continue as at present. The exemption of long-term capital gains from tax currently allowed (when a non-corporate assessee's income does not exceed Rs. 10,000 or when the gains are less than Rs. 5,000) should go once the prorating method is adopted.

As capital gains are not taxable until an asset is sold, other alternatives have to be looked for in order to recoup a part of the cost of development projects within a reasonable period.

The additional revenue likely to be realised if the tax on agricultural wealth and on capital gains on agricultural assets is operated on an integrated basis on the lines suggested would be around Rs. 100–150 crore.

Related Matters

As has been suggested for the AHT the basic unit of assessment for income-tax and wealth-tax also should be the family consisting of the husband, wife and minor children being the unit of income-receipt, of consumption and all related decision making. However, when the family is made the tax unit a deduction may be allowed from salary income at the rate of 10 per cent of the joint income of the spouses when both are employed outside the household (and 20 per cent of the income of a surviving spouse with minor children to maintain), subject to a maximum of Rs. 2,000.

With the adoption of the family as the basic tax unit, the recognition of the Hindu Undivided Family as a tax entity should be withdrawn.

Income from livestock-breeding and poultry and dairy farming, which is now exempt from taxation should be subjected to income-tax.

Irrigation water should be viewed as an input and should be priced to cover the cost of providing it. Under-pricing of inputs like water is, undesirable except in the initials stages. The betterment levy is unsuitable as an instrument for recovering capital cost of projects. In the case of certain kind of public investment, such as those involved in urban development, the capital costs may be recouped by setting up a Land Commission and vesting it with power to "acquire, manage and pricing of inputs like water is, undesirable except in the initial dispose of Land. The Land Commissions can play useful role in framing and securing the financial support for development programmes.

Appendix 6

Committee on Replacement of Sales Tax on Vanaspati, Drugs and Medicines, Cement, Paper and Paper Board and Petroleum Products by Additional Excise Duty, 1983

The Committee on Replacement of Sales Tax by Additional Excise Duty was constituted by the Government of India on December 21, 1981. It had the following terms of reference:

1) to study the financial implications of the proposal of inclusion in the list of declared goods and for levy of additional excise duty in lieu of sales tad on vanaspati, drugs and medicines, cement, paper and paper board and petroleum products and the manner in which the financial interests of the States can be safeguarded;
2) to suggest necessary changes in the relevant Central and State tax laws to give effect to the Committee's recommendations; and
3) to make recommendations regarding any other related matter.

Composition of the Committee

Mohan Lal Sukhadia	Chairman
P.H. Prasad	Member
N.V. Krishnan	Member

Shri Mohanlal Sukhadia assumed charge as the Chairman on the 9th January, 1982. However, after his sad demise on the February 2, 1982, Shri Kamlapati Tripathi was appointed as the Chairman of the Committee by the Government of India by its Resolution dated March 1, 1982.

The Committee submitted its report in January 1983. It recommended the replacement of sales tax by additional excise duty on vanaspati, drugs and medicines, cement, paper and paper board, and petroleum products. The recommendations were considered in a conference of Chief Ministers held on November 2, 1983. However, the six Chief Ministers of the non-Congress (I) States, viz. Andhra Pradesh, Jammu and Kashmir, Karnataka, Tamil Nadu, Tripura, and West Bengal opposed the Centre's initiative to implement the recommendations. The recommendations of the Tripathi Committee were further discussed at a conference of Chief Ministers held in New Delhi on February 9-10,

1989. Unfortunately, no progress could be made in this regard and the matter is still hanging fire.

The opposition of non-Congress (I) States was based on the belief that implementation of the scheme would erode their revenue position. However, a close perusal of the recommendations of the Tripathi Committee suggests that it evolved elaborate formulae for protecting the financial interests of the States. In the case of three commodities, namely paper and paper board, vanaspati, and drugs and medicines, it suggested that the annual growth rate of the amount to be collected by way of additional excise duty in lieu of sales tax should be related to the future annual growth rate of sales tax revenue of all the States. For petroleum products and cement, which are substantially subject to administered prices, the Committee recommended and worked out linkages between the amount to be collected by way of additional excise duty from year to year and value of consumption on which normal sales tax would be leviable.

In spite of these safeguards, the apprehension of some States that their resource position would be adversely affected reflects their lack of confidence in the Centre in implementing the scheme sincerely. Thus, an important tax reform has become a casualty of the distrust between the Central and the State Governments. The scheme of additional excise duties in lieu of sales tax has merits of its own. In view of the safeguards provided by the Tripathi Committee and the Ninth Finance Commission, the scheme should not only be retained but extended to other commodities as well.

Edited Extracts from the Report

During discussions, many States have urged that the Committee should go into the basic merits of the scheme and should not confine itself to the exercise of evolving a formula for protecting the financial interests of the States. We are of the view that instead of going into the proposal, *ab initio,* we should concentrate on the specific task assigned which is to assess the financial implications of the proposal and to evolve a scheme which could protect the States reasonable financial interests. In doing so, we have tried our best to keep in view the different important aspects forcefully brought out by the States and to shape the details of our recommendations in a manner which would minimise possible adverse effects and difficulties.

Approach to the Terms of Reference

The first part of the terms of reference requires us to study the financial implications of the proposed scheme. We have examined the scope and coverage of the expression "financial implications". Looking into the background of the proposal to extend the scheme, we have come to the conclusion that the first part of our assignment is substantially to assets the implications of the scheme on the financial resources of the Central and the State Government.

The second part of the terms of reference requires us to study the manner in which the financial interests of the States can be safeguarded in the proposed scheme. After examining the question from various angles we have come to the view that any study regarding safeguards can only aim at protecting the reasonable financial interests of the States both collectively and individually.

Having come to the above view, we have proceeded in our task as follows:

(i) first to compute the realisation of sales tax collections on the five commodities during the base year which we have taken as 1981-82;

(ii) then to arrive at a formula which will take into account, to the extent feasible, the relevant factors which influence the growth of sales tax from these commodities and ensure reasonable growth in the States' receipts on this account even after the extension of the scheme of additional excise duty; and

(iii)finally to evolve a scheme in which the States and the Centre can participate in a constant review of the implementation of the proposed scheme so that the States do not have the kind of grievance f\that they have expressed regarding the earlier scheme of additional excise duty on sugar, tobacco and textiles.

Safeguards for Protecting the Financial Interests of the States

As regards the question of ensuring reasonable growth in the States' receipts, we have divided the question into two parts as mentioned below:

(i) evolve a formula for the determination of the amount to be collected from year to year by way of additional excise duty in lieu of sales tax on the five commodities; and

(ii) determination of a formula for the distribution of the proceeds of additional excise duty among the States.

In dealing with the formula for the determination of the amount of additional excise duty to be collected from year to year, we do not propose to go into the issue of fixation of the exact rates of additional excise duty that are to be levied in order to collect the amount. The fixation of the rates of additional excise duty would be part of the Union budgetary exercise and cannot be predetermined as part of our recommendations.

It would be difficult to evolve a scheme by which an *ad valorem* levy is possible on all the five commodities.

If the States are to be convinced that their interests will be really protected, then to the maximum extent possible, any formula for fixing the amount to be collected as additional excise duty should have a built-in device evidently and perceptibly ensuring reasonable growth in the devolution of the additional excise duty proceeds after the replacement of sales tax on the five commodities.

The growth rate of devolution of the additional excise duty should take into account the future performance of the States.

Out of the five commodities, some are subject to statutory or informal price control or covered by administered prices scheme. The amount of additional excise duty to be collected from commodities covered by administered prices has to be determined from time to time by means of formula which will establish a linkage between such amounts and the value of the commodity under the administered prices scheme as obtaining from time to time. Therefore, in designing the formula for growth, a rational approach would appear to be to segregate the commodities into two groups: (i) those commodities which are subject to more or less free market conditions; and (ii) those which are not.

Among the commodities which are subject to more or less free market conditions are including paper and paper board, vanaspati and drugs and medicines, For these three commodities we suggest that the annual rate of growth of the amount to be collected by way of additional excise duty in lieu of sales tax should be related to the future annual growth rate of sales tax revenue of all the States.

So far as the above three commodities are concerned, the amount of additional excise duty to be collected each year on the three commodities should be fixed after loading the expected rate of growth of sales tax for that year by seventeen per cent.

For calculating the amount of additional excise duty to be collected in the first year of the implementation, the estimated general sales tax growth rate of all commodities should be loaded by seven per cent. Based on that figure that sales tax revenue of the three commodities as determined for the base year 1981-82 should be projected to arrive at the amounts of additional excise duty to be collected in the first year of implementation.

So far as petroleum products and cement are concerned, these commodities are, substantially, subject to administered prices. It would not, therefore, be proper to peg down the rate of growth on these commodities based on the expected revenue growth of sales tax for the future or on the basis of past trend of growth. The linkage has to be established between the amount to be collected from year to year and the value of consumption on which normal sales tax would be leviable. We have, therefore, estimated the percentage linkage between the present sales tax revenue collection on the two commodities with their existing value of consumption. We recommend that the quantum of additional excise duty to be collected in a particular year should be calculated using the percentage linkage so arrived at after estimating the value of consumption of the two commodities for that year. The amount so determined should be collected by the Centre by levying appropriate rate of additional excise duty as it may deem fit.

In respect of petroleum products the following bulk products account for nearly 91 per cent of sales tax revenue:

- motor spirit,
- high speed diesel oil,
- kerosene,
- aviation turbine fuel,
- L.D.O.,
- furnace oil,
- bitumen,
- naphtha and
- liquefied petroleum gas.

We have worked out ratios of incidence of sales tax collection on each of the above nine products in relation to the value of consumption based on their ex-marketing insulation/ex-refinery prices. We have furnished two ratios of incidence: (i) exclusive of sales tax, and (ii) inclusive of sales tax.

In the first year of operation when sales tax on petroleum products will be replaced, the value of likely consumption (inclusive of the value of likely imported products) of the above nine products should be estimated and then quantum of additional excise duty to be collected for each of those products should be calculated on the basis of the ratio given excluding sales tax. For the subsequent years the amount of additional excise duty to be collected should be on the basis of the ratio inclusive of sales tax.

To cover the gap of 9 per cent of the sales tax revenue which is being collected on other petroleum products, we recommend that apart from the quantum of compensation calculated in the above method on the nine products, additional compensation to the extent of ten per cent of the total compensation arrived at in respect of nine products should also be collected. This additional 10 per cent should be realised by way of additional excise duty on petroleum products other than the nine products.

In respect of cement also we have worked out the ratio of incidence of sales tax collection on cement with respect of its value of consumption based on the F.O.R. prices. We have worked out the ratios (i) exclusive of sales tax and (ii) inclusive of sales tax.

In the first year of replacement of sales tax on cement, the amount to be collected by way of additional excise duty should be estimated by suing the ratio exclusive of sales tax. For the subsequent years the amount of additional excise duty will be worked out on the basis of the ratio inclusive of sales tax.

At the time of fixing budget estimates of the Centre the ratios worked out by us in respect of petroleum products and cement will be applied to the estimated values of consumption and the amount to be collected as additional excise duty would be determined. On that basis suitable rates of additional excise would be fixed. If in the course of any year changes take place in the unit value of consumption, this calculation will have to be repeated and suitable rates refixed.

As regards distribution of the additional excise duty collected on each commodity among the States, we propose to keep undisturbed the existing system of the ratios of distribution among States being fixed on the basis of the recommendation of the Finance Commissions from time to time. As it is not practicable to do so for the initial period of five years, we suggest ratios for that period. In doing so we rely on tangible and irrefutable evidence of the immediate past, namely, the expected sales tax collection on each of these five commodities. We, therefore, recommend that the distribution of net proceeds of additional excise duty, after deducting Union Territories' share, should be made in the ratio of the averages of the sales tax revenue of each State separately for the three years 1979-80 to 1981-82.

Additional Safeguards and the Scheme for Review

The formula for arriving at the amounts of additional excise duty to be collected have been evolved against the background of the reality of the collection of sales tax for each of the five commodities in the immediate past. We, therefore, feel that the question of inability of the taxing agency to collect the amount should not normally arise in our scheme.

In respect of petroleum products and cement, our formula which is a percentage to the value of consumption does not cover the aspect regarding the potential for increase in the rates of taxation as part of the additional resources mobilisation efforts of the State Governments for financing plans. This can be achieved by a system of review suggested by us.

A review Committee should be appointed before the end of the second year of the implementation of the scheme and their recommendations should be made available by the middle of the third year. This Committee should look into the trend of growth in production and consumption and other relevant factors and come to a conclusion whether a percentage linkage we have suggested in respect of petroleum products and cement should be increased in order to give the States additional amounts on the lines of what they would have got by raising rates of sales tax. Percentages to value of consumption we have suggested may consequently go up from fourth year onwards and revised percentages will be in force for a period of 5 years after which the second review Committee's suggestions will come into force.

We recommend that the review Committee may also look into a revision of the amount to be collected a s additional excise duty from the three commodities, namely, paper and paper board, vanaspati and drugs and medicines with a view to, if necessary, increasing it above the level obtaining in fourth year of implementation on the basis of our formula.

In regard to the above three commodities we have used the machinery of annual plan resources discussions to project the growth rate of sales tax from year to year. This has some limitations, which also we propose to cover.

We recommend that, as far as possible, re sources discussions should make a realistic assessment of sales tax projections and should also take into account not only the additional resources mobilisation yield from measures implemented during this period but also the likely additional resources mobilisation next year.

The estimates of additional excise duty to be collected in a year in respect of five commodities may go wrong compared to actuals. Secondly even if estimates do not substantially go wrong, there might be marginal shortfalls when actuals are available. Thirdly there could be occasions when for policy considerations the Government of India may either reduce taxation on a particular commodity to give full exemption. We recommend that all these types of shortfalls or even occasional excess collections should be tackled in a continuing settlement of accounts between the Centre and the States. Where ever even at the time of doing budgetary exercise the Government of India anticipate some shortfall in receipts of additional excise duty from the level that have to be achieved applying our formula, there should be a specific separate budget provision in the next year's budget to play for the corresponding amounts as grants to the State Governments under Article 282 of the Constitution. In respect of the other two types of shortfalls adjustment should be made in a block of years to see that the States do not suffer on this account. For this purpose we recommend a period of 3 years as a block during which such adjustments should be done and if there is still any shortfall, it should be ensured that whatever amounts are due to the State Governments applying our formula are really made available to them by means of grants under Article 282.

We recommend that the Government of India should ensure that during the period before the first review and subsequently between the period of succeeding reviews the ratio between the total amount of excise duty and additional excise duty in the base year should not be disturbed to the disadvantage of the State Governments. Wherever it is not possible to adjust this through adjustments in the rates of additional excise duty, Government of India should provide for necessary separate budget provision to make such payments. In doing this recourse to the normal mechanism of adjustment in taxation rates should be adopted as far as possible. Recourse to the mechanism of separate budget provision to pay grants under this scheme should be kept to the absolute minimum.

We would recommend that the implementation of the scheme for the extension of additional excise duty on the five commodities, if it is decided on should start with 1984-85.

Our system is one in which, consistent with the concept of tax rental arrangement, there is a clear commitment on the part of the tax collecting agency, namely, the Centre to collect amounts which are as close as reasonably possible to what all the Stats together would have collected as sales tax. While this principle is adopted and uniform rate of tax is levied, there could arise a situation wherein some States' incidence of additional excise duty on consumers is higher than what would have been the incidence had the old rate of sales tax continued. Such States may raise a point that this aspect should be taken into consideration while determining the ratios of distribution. This is a valid point though it would be simplistic to assume that lower rates of tax necessarily result in corresponding lower receipts. As we have explained in the foregoing chapter, any normal scheme of devolution will be an exercise of projecting the experience of the immediate past to the immediate future. Our ratio of distribution for the initial five year period has been fixed on the experience of the immediate past. On the experience of the coming five year period the Ninth Finance Commission would appropriately modify these ratios keeping in view the above important aspect also.

The Review Committee under this scheme should consist of one Chief Minister each from the four regions for which even now there are regional Sales Tax Committees. There should be a Minister representing the Union Ministry of Petroleum, Industry and Chemicals. Either a Minister of State or a Deputy Minister of Union Finance Ministry should also be a member. This Committee will be nominated by the Government of India who will also nominate one of the Chief Ministers as Chairman. The Committee will be supported by an official machinery which, unlike the Committee itself, will be a permanent unit.

The official machinery we recommend is one which would go on collecting detailed data about the production and consumption and related matters relevant to the scheme. It should be a compact unit consisting of experts from the side of taxation, State financial administration, Central Statistical Organisation and wherever necessary the Departments responsible for the normal administration of matters relating to the five commodities. Such a unit will be located in the Finance Ministry and the head of that unit should be an officer not below the rank of Additional Secretary to the Government of India. That officer will also function as the Secretary of the Review Committees of Chief Ministers constituted from time to time. This Unit will also supply relevant data to future Finance Commission, in the context of the revision of the ratios of distribution.

Changes in the Relevant Central and State Laws

So far as the necessary changes in the relevant section of State tax laws to give effect to the Committee's recommendations are concerned, the scheme we have suggested can without difficulty be dovetailed into the existing scheme of additional excise duty on sugar, tobacco and textiles by carrying parallel exercises as were done in the existing scheme. This would basically involve appropriate amendments of the Central Sales Tax Act, 1956 and the Additional Excise Duties (Goods of Special Importance) Act 1957.

As regards additional excise duty on drugs and medicines are concerned, we have recommended that this amount may be collected by the Centre as additional excise duties on drugs and medicines which are not covered under the Medicinal & Toilet Preparations Act (i.e. which are liable to duty under the Central Excises & Salt Act, 1944). However, this would result in a situation whereby the drugs and medicines covered by M&TP Act would become cheaper to the extent that sales tax on the scheme would stand abolished whereas the drugs not covered by the M&TP Act would become costlier as they will have to bear the entire burden of the additional excise duty in lieu of sales tax. To remedy the situation we would suggest a suitable reduction in the rates of basic excise duty on drugs and medicine leviable under the Central Excises & Salt Act, 1944 and an appropriate increase in the rates of excise duty on medicinal preparations covered under the M&TP Act.

As regards the imported goods belonging to the five commodities are concerned, we recommend that the Centre may levy countervailing duty equivalent to the additional excise duty on the imported goods and find means of giving that amount to the States. This would necessitate the Centre levying countervailing duty equal to the additional excise duty on imported goods, accounting it separately from the other countervailing duties and then giving the amount to the States. The best way of giving this amount, in our opinion, would be by way of appropriate Constitutional amendment making countervailing duty also shareable with the States especially if the scheme of additional excise duty is to be extended to further commodities in the long run. For the immediate future it may suffice if the Centre gives the amount of countervailing duty equal to the additional excise duty to the States as grants-in-aid under Article 282 of the Constitution.

The legal position regarding consignment tax is yet to crystallise. In case consignment tax is for plugging the avoidance/evasion of sales tax, the States can come up with the plea that the sales tax as estimated by the Committee does not take into account the extra element of tax which they would have raised by plugging the evasion/avoidance of sales tax when the consignment tax comes into force. This aspect can be considered by the Review Committee while reworking the formula for fixing the amount of additional excise duty to be collected. If, on the other hand, consignment tax is going to be levied as additional source of tax revenue, the States may be free to levy such consignment tax.

It may so happen that because of the difference in interpretation, a product subject to additional excise duty may be claimed by the Central Excise Department, which will administer the Additional Duties of Excise Act, to be covered under that Act while the States may claim that it is not so covered under that Act and hence covered by the Sales Tax Act of the States. We recommend that in order to resolve such disputes, where the Sales Tax authority find that a State has any objection to the scope and interpretation of the Additional Duties of Excise Act, that authority can take it up with the Central Excise Department and the issue can be discussed in the forum of Tariff Conferences held by the Central Excise Department in which representatives of the Sales Tax Department of the concerned State should also be invited to participate.

Impact of the Scheme on Consumer Prices

We have generally speaking, limited the study to the financial implications of the scheme so far as it relates to the Centre/State financial resources. However, as the contentions of the States regarding the effect of the scheme on the consumer prices do have some force, we have tried to analyse this aspect.

On account of the scheme to extend additional excise duty there could be an impact on the consumer prices due to the shift to the point of levy of tax from one at the down stream channel of the trade to an earlier stage. Secondly, there would be an effect on the prices due to the fixation of the rate of additional excise duty at a uniform rate to the entire country.

The manufacturer pays the additional excise duty at the time of the clearances of the goods from his factory unlike in the case of sales tax where he is able to realise the tax from the customers before he pays the tax to the Government. This entails additional financial outlay and additional interest charges to finance this outlay. The amount of increase in consumer's price due to this additional interest charges will not be a significant order.

The price increase could also be by way of increase in the quantum of mark up by the trade. However, it practice, we find that in a large part of the trade especially relating to petroleum products and cement where administrative prices are ruling, the dealer's commission are fixed on the basis of quantity sold rather than on the prices at which the trade purchases them from the manufacturers. Therefore, we feel that the effect of any increase in prices based on and *ad valorem* trade mark should not be substantial.

In the process of fixing of the rates of additional excise duty at uniform rate for the entire country, it is likely that in certain States the incidence of additional excise duty might be higher than the prevailing incidence of sales tax, resulting in higher prices for consumers. This cannot be avoided altogether while implementing a scheme for achieving uniformity in the rates of tax and consequent uniformity of prices to the consumer.

We have, however, considered whether we could suggest some measures to reduce any adverse impact of prices or to stagger it over a period of time. The price increase resulting from the interest charges on the additional financial outlay required at the state of payment of additional excise duty is not likely to be substantial. Regarding profit mark up on a percentage basis in a large part of the trade involved in the scheme that is not the practice. Further, no particular consumer may directly experience the result of any price increase on account of additional outlay and trade mark up as the price difference really experienced by the consumers will depend substantially on the differences from State to State in the rates of sales tax now in force. However, when one takes the total value paid by all consumers together in the country on these commodities, one could take into account an increase in the total amount so paid by all the consumers together. We have examined whether it is possible to devise a way to meet this largely theoretical objection. Major part of the additional excise revenue from the five commodities will be collected from the duty on petroleum products which are mostly under administered prices. The capital that goes into the manufacture and marketing of petroleum products also substantially come with the control of the Government or Government controlled agencies like banks. It should therefore be possible for the Government to arrange to the deployment of funds, the service cost of these funds and the prices in such a manner that no additional liability is passed on to the consumers on account of the introduction of additional excise duty. In respect of commodities other than petroleum products the amount involved by way of additional interest is negligible and, therefore, similar arrangement does not seem to be necessary. However, in respect of commodities where formal or informal prices control is in force, it may be possible for the Government to influence the trade and avert or minimise any impact on prices. Wherever this also is not possible, Centre may consider adjusting different rates in such a manner that there is no serious upward impact on prices.

In the case of rise in price as a consequence of near uniform rates under additional excise duty as against the widely varying rates from State of State, it may be desirable to locate areas where the consequent price variation, particularly those upwards, are too steep and would have some kind of cascading effect on other areas of economic activity. We feel that such an effort should be attempted especially in the pricing of petroleum products. Once the quantum of total revenue is known and additional excise duty rates are fixed accordingly, it should be possible for the Governmental agencies controlling the price structure of petroleum products to work out a pricing pattern whereby the steep rise in prices in some States is staggered over a period of time by correspondingly staggering the steep fall in the price of those commodities in those States where the sales tax rates are now on the high side.

In any case, a pricing system as mentioned above should be attempted in respect of States normally known as special category States and Union Territories like Andaman & Nicobar Islands, Mizoram, etc. keeping in view their relative backwardness and the distances involved in transporting goods even if such a system is not attempted in all States where the price variation is likely to be considerable.

Appendix 7

White Paper on State-Level Value Added Tax, 2005

A White Paper on State-Level Value Added Tax was prepared by the Empowered Committee of State Finance Ministers (Convenor: Asim Kumar Dasgupta), constituted by the Ministry of Finance, Government of India. The White Paper was prepared on the basis of a Resolution adopted in the Conference of the Chief Ministers on November 16, 1999.

Text of the White Paper

This White Paper is a result of collective efforts of all the States in formulating the basic design of the State-level Value Added Tax (VAT) through repeated and candid discussions in the Empowered Committee of State Finance Ministers.

The State-level VAT, as elaborated in this White Paper, has certain distinct advantages over the existing sales tax structure. The VAT will not only provide full set-off for input tax as well as tax on previous purchases, but it will also abolish the burden of several of the existing taxes, such as turnover tax, surcharge on sales tax, additional surcharge, special additional tax, etc. In addition, Central Sales Tax is also going to be phased out. As a result, the overall tax burden will be rationalised, and prices, in general, will fall. Moreover, VAT will replace the existing system of inspection by a system of built-in self-assessment by traders and manufacturers. The tax structure will become simple and more transparent. This will significantly improve tax compliance and will also help increase revenue growth.

While this State-level VAT has all these advantages, it is a State subject derived from Entry 54 of the State List, for which the States are sovereign in taking decisions. On these decisions on VAT, the States, through discussion in the Empowered Committee, have found it in their interests, to avoid unhealthy competition and have certain features of VAT to be common for all the States. These features will constitute the basic design of VAT. At the same time, the States will have freedom for appropriate variations consistent with this basic design. This White Paper is a collective attempt of the States to strike a balance between this needed commonality and the desired federal flexibility in the VAT structure.

The White Paper also strikes a balance between what is possible in the VAT design to begin with and what can be improved upon in subsequent years as we gather more experience.

The White Paper further mentions how after working out a consensus on this VAT design, nearly all the States either have finalised their VAT Bills by now and are in the process of obtaining Presidential Assent, or will reach that stage very soon. Even for one major State where there are some ground-level problems, a positive interaction with the Empowered Committee has recently opened up the possibility of resolving most of these problems.

These efforts of the States towards formulation of VAT design and its implementation have received full cooperation of the Finance Ministry, Government of India. At the same time, the Finance Ministry has never imposed their views on us. We, therefore, remain thankful to the former Union Finance Ministers—Dr. Manmohan Singh, Shri Yashwant Sinha and Shri Jaswant Singh. We are specially grateful to Shri P. Chidambaram, the present Union Finance Minister, for his active support over the last eight months, when he not only helped formulate the modality of Central financial support to the States for possible loss of revenue in the transitional years of implementation of VAT, but also took time off his busy schedule to participate with us in the campaign for VAT in the States.

It has always been fruitful to have interaction with Dr. Parthasarathi Shome, Adviser to the Union Finance Minister, for his insightful observations on the analytical structure of VAT as well as his reference to vast experience in the implementation of VAT. The Secretary, Revenue, Additional Secretary, Revenue and all the concerned officials of the Revenue Department of the Finance Ministry have helped us by participating in the discussions whenever we requested them, and also by assisting in various procedural matters. Interaction with Dr. Govinda Rao, the Chairman of Technical Experts Committee on VAT and other members of the Committee has also been useful. We take this opportunity to thank all of them.

Discussions with the representatives of trade organizations and chambers of commerce and industry at the national level as well as in the States have been relevant in assessing the ground level difficulties. Together with them, we are determined to overcome these difficulties in implementing VAT in the States. We remain thankful to them, and our mutual interaction will take place regularly.

Finally, this White Paper could be written only on the basis of lively support of the Finance Ministers of the States, and with constant help from the Finance Secretaries and the Commissioners of Commercial Taxes of the States. The Commissioners of Commercial Taxes have often burnt their midnight oil, and their contribution should be particularly recorded. Shri Ramesh Chandra, Member-Secretary of the Empowered Committee had to carry on the difficult administrative task in the functioning of the Empowered Committee. We appreciate the efforts of Shri Chandra and the staff of the Empowered Committee.

Even after all these efforts, there may be some unavoidable shortcomings in this White Paper, which we will try to overcome as we learn more from the actual experience of implementation of VAT. With this background and the attitude, this White Paper is an expression of the genuine commitment of the States to the implementation of VAT from April 1, 2005, which we are all looking forward to.

Justification of VAT and Background

In the existing sales tax structure, there are problems of double taxation of commodities and multiplicity of taxes, resulting in a cascading tax burden. For instance, in the existing structure, before a commodity is produced, inputs are first taxed, and then after the commodity is produced with input tax load, output is taxed again. This causes an unfair double taxation with cascading effects. In the VAT, a set-off is given for input tax as well as tax paid on previous purchases. In the prevailing sales tax structure, there is in several States also a multiplicity of taxes, such as turnover tax, surcharge on sales tax, additional surcharge, etc. With introduction of VAT, these other taxes will be abolished. In addition, Central sales tax is also going to be phased out. As a result, overall tax burden will be rationalised, and prices in general will also fall. Moreover, VAT will replace the existing system of inspection by a system of built-in self-assessment by the dealers and auditing. The tax structure will become simple and more transparent. That will improve tax compliance and also augment revenue growth. Thus, to repeat, with the introduction of VAT, benefits will be as follows:

- a set-off will be given for input tax as well as tax paid on previous purchases,
- other taxes, such as turnover tax, surcharge, additional surcharge, etc. will be abolished,
- overall tax burden will be rationalised,
- prices will in general fall,
- there will be self-assessment by dealers,
- transparency will increase, and
- there will be higher revenue growth

The VAT will therefore help common people, traders, industrialists and also the Government. It is indeed a move towards more efficiency, equal competition and fairness in the taxation system.

For these beneficial effects, a full-fledged VAT was initiated first in Brazil in mid 1960's, then in European countries in 1970's and subsequently introduced in about 130 countries, including several federal countries. In Asia, it has been introduced by a large number of countries from China to Sri Lanka. Even in India, there has been a VAT system introduced by the Government of India for about last ten years in respect of Central excise duties. At the State-level, the VAT system as decided by the State Governments, would now be introduced in terms of Entry 54 of the State List of the Constitution.

The first preliminary discussion on State-level VAT took place in a meeting of Chief Ministers convened by Dr. Manmohan Singh, the then Union Finance Minister in 1995. In this meeting, the basic issues on VAT were discussed in general terms and this was followed up by periodic interactions of State Finance Ministers. Thereafter, in a significant meeting of all Chief Ministers, convened on November 16, 1999 by Shri Yashwant Sinha, the then Union Finance Minister, three important decisions were taken. First, before the introduction of State-level VAT, the unhealthy sales tax rate "war" among the States would have to end and sales tax rates would need to be harmonised by implementing uniform floor rates of sales tax for different categories of commodities with effect from January 1, 2000. Second, in the interest again of harmonisation of incidence of sales tax, the sales-tax-related industrial incentive schemes would also have to be discontinued with effect from January 1, 2000. Third, on the basis of achievement of the first two objectives, steps would be taken by the States for introduction of State-level VAT after adequate preparation. For implementing these decisions, an Empowered Committee of State Finance Ministers was set-up.

Thereafter, this Empowered Committee has met regularly, attended by the State Finance Ministers, and also by the Finance Secretaries and the Commissioners of Commercial Taxes of the State Governments as well as senior officials of the Revenue Department of the Ministry of Finance, Government of India. Through repeated discussions and collective efforts in the Empowered Committee, it was possible within a period of about a year and a half to achieve nearly 98 per cent success in the first two objectives on harmonisation of sales tax structure through implementation of uniform floor rates of sales tax and discontinuation of sales-tax- related incentive schemes. As a part of regular monitoring, whenever any deviation is reported from the uniform floor rates of sales tax, or from decision on incentives, the Empowered Committee takes up the matter with the concerned State and also the Government of India for necessary rectification.

After reaching this stage, steps were initiated for systematic preparation for the introduction of State-level VAT. In order again to avoid any unhealthy competition among the States which may lead to distortions in manufacturing and trade, attempts have been made from the very beginning to harmonise the VAT design in the States, keeping also in view the distinctive features of each State and the need for federal flexibility. This has been done by the States collectively agreeing, through repeated discussions in the Empowered Committee, to certain common points of convergence regarding VAT, and allowing at the same time certain flexibility for the local characteristics of the States.

Along with these measures at ensuring convergence on the basic issues on VAT, steps have also been taken for necessary training, computerisation and interaction with trade and industry, particularly at the State levels. This interaction with trade and industry is being specially emphasised.

It may be noted that while such preparation was going on, the Chief Ministers of all the States in an important meeting on State-level VAT convened by the Prime Minister on October 18, 2002, when Shri Jaswant Singh, the then Union Finance Minister was present, clearly stated their intention of introducing VAT from April 1, 2003. About 29 States and Union Territories had expeditiously sent their Bills to the Ministry of Finance, Government of India for prior vetting. The Union Ministry of Finance had considered these Bills of States and Union Territories, and sent their comments/suggestions to the States and Union Territories in line with the decisions of the Empowered Committee of the State Finance Ministers for incorporating the same in VAT Bills to be placed in the State legislatures and subsequent transmission to the Government of India for Presidential Assent. At this stage, there were certain developments which delayed the introduction of VAT.

Despite these developments, most of the States remained positively interested in implementation of VAT. Madhya Pradesh VAT Bill had already been accorded Presidential Assent in November 2002. One State, namely, Haryana, has already introduced VAT on its own with good results on revenue growth. It is important to note that in the meeting of Empowered Committee on June 18, 2004 when Shri P. Chidambaram, the Union Finance Minister, was invited and was kindly present, all the States, excepting one, once again categorically renewed their commitment to the introduction of VAT from April 1, 2005. Even for this particular State with certain problems, a positive interaction has recently been organised with that State to resolve certain genuine ground-level problems. Now nearly all the States have either finalised their VAT Bills and are in the process of obtaining Presidential Assent, or will reach that stage very soon.

Design of State-Level VAT

As already mentioned, the design of State-level VAT has been worked out by the Empowered Committee through several rounds of discussion and striking a federal balance between the common points of convergence regarding VAT and flexibility for the local characteristics of the States. Since the State-level VAT is centred around the basic concept of "set-off" for the tax paid earlier, the needed common points of convergence also relate to this concept of set-off/input tax credit, its coverage and related issues as elaborated below.

Concept of VAT and Set-off/Input Tax Credit

The essence of VAT is in providing set-off for the tax paid earlier, and this is given effect through the concept of input tax credit/rebate. This input tax credit in relation to any period means setting off the amount of input tax by a registered dealer against the amount of his output tax. The Value Added Tax (VAT) is based on the value addition to the goods, and the related VAT liability of the dealer is calculated by deducting input tax credit from tax collected on sales during the payment period (say, a month).

If, for example, input worth Rs. 1,00,000 is purchased and sales are worth Rs. 2,00,000 in a month, and input tax rate and output tax rate are 4 per cent and 10 per cent respectively, then input tax credit/set-off and calculation of VAT will be as shown below:

a. Input purchased within the month : Rs. 1,00,000
b. Output sold in the month : Rs. 2,00,000
c. Input tax paid : Rs. 4,000
d. Output tax payable : Rs. 20,000
e. VAT payable during the month : Rs. 16,000
f. after set-off/input tax credit
   [(d) – (c)]

Coverage of Set-Off / Input Tax Credit

This input tax credit will be given for both manufacturers and traders for purchase of inputs/supplies meant for both sale within the State as well as to other States, irrespective of when these will be utilised/sold. This also reduces immediate tax liability.

Even for stock transfer/consignment sale of goods out of the State, input tax paid in excess of 4 per cent will be eligible for tax credit.

Carrying Over of Tax Credit

If the tax credit exceeds the tax payable on sales in a month, the excess credit will be carried over to the end of next financial year. If there is any excess unadjusted input tax credit at the end of second year, then the same will be eligible for refund.

Input tax credit on capital goods will also be available for traders and manufacturers. Tax credit on capital goods may be adjusted over a maximum of 36 equal monthly instalments. The States may at their option reduce this number of instalments.

There will be a negative list for capital goods (on the basis of principles already decided by the Empowered Committee) not eligible for input tax credit.

Treatment of Exports

For all exports made out of the country, tax paid within the State will be refunded in full, and this refund will be made within three months. Units located in SEZ and EOU will be granted either exemption from payment of input tax or refund of the input tax paid within three months.

Inputs Procured from Other States

Tax paid on inputs procured from other States through inter-State sale and stock transfer will not be eligible for credit. However, a decision has been taken for duly phasing out of inter-State sales tax or Central sales tax. As a preparation for that, a comprehensive inter-State tax information exchange system is also being set up.

Treatment of Opening Stock

All tax-paid goods purchased on or after April 1, 2004 and still in stock as on April 1, 2005 will be eligible to receive input tax credit, subject to submission of requisite documents. Resellers holding tax-paid goods on April 1, 2005 will also be eligible. VAT will be levied on the goods when sold on and after April 1, 2005 and input tax credit will be given for the sales tax already paid in the previous year. This tax credit will be available over a period of 6 months after an interval of 3 months needed for verification.

Compulsory Issue of Tax Invoice, Cash Memo or Bill

This entire design of VAT with input tax credit is crucially based on documentation of tax invoice, cash memo or bill. Every registered dealer, having turnover of sales above an amount specified, shall issue to the purchaser serially numbered tax invoice with the prescribed particulars. This tax invoice will be signed and dated by the dealer or his regular employee, showing the required particulars. The dealer shall keep a counterfoil or duplicate of such tax invoice duly signed and dated. Failure to comply with the above will attract penalty.

Registration, Small Dealers and Composition Scheme

Registration of dealers with gross annual turnover above Rs. 5 lakh will be compulsory. There will be provision for voluntary registration. All existing dealers will be automatically registered under the VAT Act. A new dealer will be allowed 30 days time from the date of liability to get registered.

Small dealers with gross annual turnover not exceeding Rs. 5 lakh will not be liable to pay VAT. States will have flexibility to fix threshold limit within Rs. 5 lakh.

Small dealers with annual gross turnover not exceeding Rs. 50 lakh who are otherwise liable to pay VAT, shall however have the option for a composition scheme with payment of tax at a small percentage of gross turnover. The dealers opting for this composition scheme will not be entitled to input tax credit.

Tax Payer's Identification Number (TIN)

The Tax Payer's Identification Number will consist of 11 digit numerals throughout the country. First two characters will represent the State Code as used by the Union Ministry of Home Affairs. The set-up of the next nine characters may, however, be different in different States.

Return

Under VAT, simplified form of returns will be notified. Returns are to be filed monthly/quarterly as specified in the State Acts/Rules, and will be accompanied with payment challans. Every return furnished by dealers will be scrutinized expeditiously within prescribed time limit from the date of filing the return. If any technical mistake is detected on scrutiny, the dealer will be required to pay the deficit appropriately.

Procedure of Self-Assessment of VAT Liability

The basic simplification in VAT is that VAT liability will be self-assessed by the dealers themselves in terms of submission of returns upon setting off the tax credit. Return forms as well as other procedures will be simple in all States. There will no longer be compulsory assessment at the end of each year as is existing now. If no specific notice is issued proposing departmental audit of the books of accounts of the dealer within the time limit specified in the Act, the dealer will be deemed to have been self-assessed on the basis of returns submitted by him.

Because of the importance of the concept of self-assessment in VAT, provision for "self-assessment" will be stated in the VAT Bills of the States.

Audit

Correctness of self-assessment will be checked through a system of Departmental Audit. A certain percentage of the dealers will be taken up for audit every year on a scientific basis. If, however, evasion is detected on audit, the concerned dealer may be taken up for audit for previous periods. This Audit Wing will remain delinked from tax collection wing to remove any bias. The audit team will conduct its work in a time bound manner and audit will be completed within six months. The audit report will be transparently sent to the dealer also.

Simultaneously, a cross-checking, computerised system is being worked out on the basis of coordination between the tax authorities of the State Governments and the authorities of Central Excise and Income Tax to compare constantly the tax returns and set-off documents of VAT system of the States and those of Central Excise and Income Tax. This comprehensive cross-checking system will help reduce tax evasion and also lead to significant growth of tax revenue. At the same time, by protecting transparently the interests of tax-complying dealers against the unfair practices of tax-evaders, the system will also bring in more equal competition in the sphere of trade and industry.

Declaration Form

There will be no need for any provision for concessional sale under the VAT Act since the provision for setoff makes the input zero-rated. Hence, there will be no need for declaration form, which will be a further relief for dealers.

Incentives

Under the VAT system, the existing incentive schemes may be continued in the manner deemed appropriate by the States after ensuring that VAT chain is not affected.

Other Taxes

As mentioned earlier, all other existing taxes such as turnover tax, surcharge, additional surcharge and Special Additional Tax (SAT) would be abolished. There will not be any reference to these taxes in the VAT Bills. The States that have already introduced entry tax and intend to continue with this tax should make it vatable. If not made vatable, entry tax will need to be abolished. However, this will not apply to entry tax that may be levied in lieu of octroi.

Penal Provisions

Penal provisions in the VAT Bills should not be more stringent than in the existing Sales Tax Act.

Coverage of Goods under VAT

In general, all the goods, including declared goods will be covered under VAT and will get the benefit of input tax credit.

The only few goods which will be outside VAT will be liquor, lottery tickets, petrol, diesel, aviation turbine fuel and other motor spirit since their prices are not fully market determined. These will continue to be taxed under the Sales Tax Act or any other State Act or even by making special provisions in the VAT Act itself, and with uniform floor rates decided by the Empowered Committee.

VAT Rates and Classification of Commodities

Under the VAT system covering about 550 goods, there will be only two basic VAT rates of 4% and 12.5%, plus a specific category of tax-exempted goods and a special VAT rate of 1% only for gold and silver ornaments, etc. Thus the multiplicity of rates in the existing structure will be done away with under the VAT system.

Under exempted category, there will be about 46 commodities comprising of natural and unprocessed products in unorganized sector, items which are legally barred from taxation and items which have social implications. Included in this exempted category is a set of maximum of 10 commodities flexibly chosen by individual States from a list of goods (finalised by the Empowered Committee) which are of local social importance for the individual States without having any inter-state implication. The rest of the commodities in the list will be common for all the States. Under 4% VAT rate category, there will be the largest number of goods (about 270), common for all the States, comprising of items of basic necessities such as medicines and drugs, all agricultural and industrial inputs, capital goods and declared goods. The schedule of commodities will be attached to the VAT Bill of every State. The remaining commodities, common for all the States, will fall under the general VAT rate of 12.5%.

In terms of decision of the Empowered Committee, VAT on AED items relating to sugar, textile and tobacco, because of initial organisational difficulties, will not be imposed for one year after the introduction of VAT, and till then the existing arrangement will continue. The position will be reviewed after one year.

Effects of the VAT System

This design of the State-level VAT has been carefully worked out by the

Empowered Committee after repeated interactions with the States and others concerned and striking a balance between the needed convergence and federal flexibility as well as ground-level reality. If now all the components of the VAT design are taken together, then it will be seen that the total effect of this VAT system will be to rationalise the tax burden and bring down, in general, the price level. This will also stop unhealthy tax-rate "war" and trade diversion among the States, which had adversely affected interests of all the States in the past. Moreover, this VAT design will also significantly bring in simplicity and transparency in the tax structure, thereby improving tax-compliance and eventually also the revenue growth, as mentioned in the beginning.

Steps Taken by the States

It is now of significance to note that most of the States, after collective interaction in the Empowered Committee, have either already modified or agreed to modify their VAT Bills by incorporating these common points of convergence including flexibility as mentioned in the VAT design above, and are also taking other preparatory steps towards introduction of VAT from April 1, 2005.

As a part of the preparatory steps, the States have started the process of preparing the draft of VAT Rules, including Books of Accounts to be maintained. The objective will be to keep these as simple as possible so that it becomes easy for a small trader to comply with the requirements.

Moreover, the States have initiated, and in many cases also completed, steps for computerisation up to the levels of assessing officers and also at the check posts. This process will continue since this is extremely important for document-based verification and integration with Taxation Information Exchange System as well as with information of the Central excise and income tax systems as indicated earlier.

It may be mentioned here that appropriate Central funds for VAT-related computerisation in the North-Eastern States are also being released by the Government of India.

Related Issues

While the States have thus taken several steps towards introduction of VAT, certain supporting decisions were critically needed at the national level for more effective implementation of VAT from April 1, 2005.

It needs to be carefully noted that although introduction of VAT may, after a few years, lead to revenue growth, there may be a loss of revenue in some States in the initial years of transition. It is with this in view that the Government of India had agreed to compensate for 100 per cent of the loss in the first year, 75 per cent of the loss in the second year and 50 per cent of the loss in the third year of introduction of VAT, and the loss would be computed on the basis of an agreed formula. This position has not only been reaffirmed by the Union Finance Minister in his Budget Speech of 2004-05, but a concrete formula for this compensation has also now been worked out after interaction between the Union Finance Minister and the Empowered Committee.

As mentioned earlier, there is also a need, after introduction of VAT, for phasing out of Central Sales Tax (CST). However, the States are now collecting nearly Rs. 15 thousand crore every year from CST. There is accordingly a need of compensation from the Government of India for this loss of revenue as CST is phased out. Moreover, while CST is phased out, there is also a critical need for putting in place a regulatory frame-work in terms of Taxation Information Exchange System to give a comprehensive picture of inter-State trade of all commodities. As already mentioned, this process of setting up of Taxation Information Exchange System has already been started by the Empowered Committee, and is expected to be completed within one year. The position regarding CST will be reviewed by the Empowered Committee during 2005-06, and suitable decision on the phasing out of CST will be taken.

It is also essential to bring imports into the VAT chain. Because of the set-off, this will not result in any tax cascading effect, but will only improve tax compliance. A proposal for VAT on imports, including the collection mechanism with adequate safeguards for the protection of interest of land-locked States, is being discussed with the Government of India.

Similarly, discussion between the Empowered Committee and the Government of India is going on for an early decision on the question of collection and appropriation of service tax by the Centre and the States.

If decisions on VAT on imports and service tax are taken expeditiously at the national level, then these two important spheres of taxation can be integrated, along with the AED items as mentioned earlier, into the VAT system of the States from the second year of introduction of VAT.

It may be noted that this VAT design has been worked out carefully by the Empowered Committee to strike a balance not only between the common points of convergence and federal flexibility, but also a balance between what can be done to begin with and what should be incorporated subsequently for further perfection of the VAT system.

For successful implementation of State-level VAT, close interaction with trade and industry is specially important. The Empowered Committee has therefore also set up a Consultative Committee with one representative from each of the national level trade organisations and national level chambers of commerce and industry. This Committee has already started interacting with the Empowered Committee. This process of interaction will continue regularly to discuss issues and sort out problems of implementation of VAT. Such Consultative Committees will also be set up at the level of each State, and interaction with the State Government will take place in a similarly regular manner.

In course of discussion with representatives of trade and industry, reference has often been made to the earlier VAT Bills of some of the States. It should be clearly noted, as already mentioned before, that all the States have agreed to amend their earlier VAT Bills so as to conform broadly to the common design as elaborated in this White Paper. This process of amendment has also already started. The point of reference on VAT should therefore be this design of VAT as explained in this White Paper. It should also be mentioned that there are some important points on the ground-level implementation of VAT which have been raised by the representatives of trade and industry. Many of the points will be taken care of in the VAT rules of the States, with changes where necessary.

Finally, a comprehensive campaign on State-level will be launched to communicate in simple and transparent manner the benefit of VAT for common people, traders, industrialists and also the State Governments. This campaign will then be launched first at the national level on the basis of necessary coordination between the States and the Centre. This will then be simultaneously followed up at the level of every State and also in districts of the States. This campaign will be based on written materials as well as publicity through all media. The purpose of this campaign will be a two-way interaction between the Government and the trade and industry as well as the common people.

There is now only looking forward to the introduction of State-level VAT by all the States and Union Territories from April 1, 2005. We seek cooperation of all sections of people in the country.

Appendix 8

Thirteenth Finance Commission

The Thirteenth Finance Commission was constituted in pursuance of the provisions of Article 280 of the Constitution of India by the President under the Chairmanship of Dr. Vijay L. Kelkar vide a Notification dated November 13, 2007. The Commission shall make recommendations covering a period of five years commencing on the April 1, 2010.

Chairman	Dr. Vijay L. Kelkar
Members	Shri B.K. Chaturvedi (Part Time) Dr. Indira Rajaraman Dr. Abusaleh Shariff Professor Atul Sarma Shri Sumit Bose (Secretary)
Year and month of establishment	November 2007
Year and month of reporting	October 2009 (Expected)
Period of award	2010-11 to 2014-15

Terms of Reference of the Commission

1. The Commission shall make recommendations as to the following matters, namely:

- the distribution between the Union and the States of the net proceeds of taxes which are to be, or may be, divided between them under Chapter I Part XII of the Constitution and the allocation between the States of the respective shares of such proceeds;
- the principles which should govern the grants-in-aid of the revenues of the States out of the Consolidated Fund of India and the sums to be paid to the States which are in need of assistance by way of grants-in-aid of their revenues under article 275 of the Constitution for purposes other than those specified in the provisos to clause (1) of that article; and
- the measures needed to augment the Consolidated Fund of a State to supplement the resources of the Panchayats and Municipalities in the State on the basis of the recommendations made by the Finance Commission of the State.

2. The Commission shall review the state of the finances of the Union and the States, keeping in view, in particular, the operation of the States' Debt Consolidation and Relief Facility 2005-2010 introduced by the Central Government on the basis of the recommendations of the Twelfth Finance Commission, and suggest measures for maintaining a stable and sustainable fiscal environment consistent with equitable growth.

3. In making its recommendations, the Commission shall have regard, among other considerations, to

- the resources of the Central Government, for five years commencing on 1st April 2010, on the basis of levels of taxation and non-tax revenues likely to be reached at the end of 2008-09;
- the demands on the resources of the Central Government, in particular, on account of the projected Gross Budgetary Support to the Central and State Plan, expenditure on civil administration, defence, internal and border security, debt-servicing and other committed expenditure and liabilities;
- the resources of the State Governments, for the five years commencing on 1st April 2010, on the basis of levels of taxation and non-tax revenues likely to be reached at the end of 2008-09;
- the objective of not only balancing the receipts and expenditure on revenue account of all the States and the Union, but also generating surpluses for capital investment;
- the taxation efforts of the Central Government and each State Government and the potential for additional resource mobilisation to improve the tax-Gross Domestic Product ratio in the case of the Union and tax-Gross State Domestic Product ratio in the case of the States;
- the impact of the proposed implementation of Goods and Services Tax with effect from 1st April, 2010, including its impact on the country's foreign trade;
- the need to improve the quality of public expenditure to obtain better outputs and outcomes;
- the need to manage ecology, environment and climate change consistent with sustainable development;
- the expenditure on the non-salary component of maintenance and upkeep of capital assets and the non-wage related maintenance expenditure on plan schemes to be completed by 31st March, 2010 and the norms on the basis of which specific amounts are recommended for the maintenance of the capital assets and the manner of monitoring such expenditure;
- the need for ensuring the commercial viability of irrigation projects, power

projects, departmental undertakings and public sector enterprises through various means, including levy of user charges and adoption of measures to promote efficiency.

4. In making its recommendations on various matters, the Commission shall take the base of population figures as of 1971, in all such cases where population is a factor for determination of devolution of taxes and duties and grants-in-aid.

5. The Commission may review the present arrangements as regards financing of Disaster Management with reference to the National Calamity Contingency Fund and the Calamity Relief Fund and the funds envisaged in the Disaster Management Act, 2005(53 of 2005), and make appropriate recommendations thereon.

6. The Commission shall indicate the basis on which it has arrived at its findings and make available the estimates of receipts and expenditure of the Union and each of the States.

7. The Commission shall make its report available by the 31st day of October, 2009, covering the period of five years commencing on the 1st day of April, 2010.

Glossary of Fiscal Terms

Glossary of Fiscal Terms

—A—

Ability-to-Pay Principle of Taxation: It states that if a given amount of revenue is needed to finance public services, then each taxpayer should contribute in line with his ability-to-pay taxes. Those who possess more economic power (income and wealth) should contribute more to public exchequer and vice versa. The duty to pay taxes is seen as a collective responsibility rather than a personal one. The ability-to-pay principle views tax policy issues in isolation to incidence of public expenditure. This principle is regarded by many as the most equitable and just method of taxation. It is emphasised primarily for its redistributive role.

Accrued Income: It is the income earned during a particular accounting period but not actually received during that period.

Accumulated Depreciation: It is the total depreciation expense accrued from the date of purchase of an asset to the present.

Additional Resource Mobilisation (ARM): It means resources raised through additional efforts such as raising the rates of existing taxes and/or levying new taxes.

Administered Prices: These are prices set consciously by a government rather than being determined by the free play of market forces. Prices of petroleum products in India are a case in point.

Administrative Costs: These are costs incurred by public authorities in administering a tax. These costs (also called expense ratio) include wages of tax officials and expenditure on stores and supplies for running tax administration.

***Ad Valorem* Duty:** An *ad valorem* duty is imposed as a fixed percentage of the price of the product taxed.

Advance Tax Payment: It is a system under which assessees are required to pay tax in advance on incomes which they expect to earn during the current financial year. Advance tax, payable in instalments during the financial year itself, is adjusted against the tax liability determined after proper assessment. Under

Section 208 of the Indian Income Tax Act, 1961, it is obligatory to pay advance tax in every case where the advance tax payable is Rs. 5,000 or more.

Allowances: These are amounts the deductibility of which is statutorily allowed from the tax base, e.g. investment allowance. They have the effect of reducing the tax base.

Amortisation: In finance, it means the gradual repayment of a debt by means of a sinking fund. Thus, amortisation of debt means gradual reduction of a debt through periodic payments. In another context amortisation of an asset (machinery) refers to depreciation in its value over time.

Annuity: It is a fixed sum of money paid to an annuitant yearly, usually for the remaining part of his life. It is a form of pension which provides a regular annual income. An annuity may be purchased by making a lump sum cash payment.

Anti-dumping Tariff: It is imposed to discourage dumping. The tariff rate is usually the difference between the normal selling price and the dumping price. Dumping means the sale of a product in a foreign market at a price much below that at which it is being sold in the domestic market.

Assessee: An assessee is a person by whom a tax is payable under some tax law. It includes every person in respect of whom any proceeding has been taken up for the assessment of his income, wealth, etc. It also includes a person who is assessable in respect of income of another person.

Asset: Ownership of any physical property or right that has money value is called asset. Land, buildings, machinery and other forms of physical property are called *tangible assets*. Goodwill, patents, trademarks, copyrights and other non-material benefits are called *intangible assets*. Similarly, cash in hand, marketable securities, inventories and other assets which can be readily converted into money are called *current assets* while plant, equipment and time deposits are *fixed assets* because they are not readily convertible into money.

Assignment of Tax: Assignment of a tax means transfer of taxation power from a higher level to a lower level government. Taxation power includes the following: right to levy the tax, collect the tax, and appropriate the proceeds from the tax.

Average Tax Rate: It is derived by expressing tax amount as a percentage of taxable income. It is also called effective tax rate.

—B—

Balanced Budget: It is a situation in which current revenue of the government is exactly equal to its current expenditure.

Basic Personal Exemption: Income tax laws of almost all countries conventionally grant exemption of a given portion of income which does not reflect taxpaying capacity of a person. There are two considerations for this exemption. 1. Tax bite into income, barely sufficient for a minimum standard of living, is immoral. 2. It is administratively difficult to deal with low income earners.

Benefit Principle of Taxation: According to this traditional approach, an equitable tax system is one under which tax payments are based on the amount of benefits received from government services. In other words, the cost of government services should be apportioned among individuals according to the relative benefits they enjoy. Clearly, implementation of the benefit principle presupposes determination of the incidence of public expenditure before deciding distribution of tax burden. Thus, it encompasses issues of both tax and expenditure policies.

Best Judgement Assessment: It is an assessment made by a tax officer against a person who is in default of furnishing information as regards his income, wealth etc. Thus, where an assessee fails to file a return or submit documents called for or comply with the terms of a notice, the assessing officer may assess total income, wealth etc. according to the best of his judgement. This he can do after giving the assessee an opportunity of being heard.

Betterment Levy: It is a tax on unearned increment in connection with town improvement (betterment) schemes. Execution of a development scheme by public authorities generally leads to increase in the annual and capital value of land and buildings under the scope of the scheme. Such appreciation is not the result of any individual efforts, but materialises from the corporate activity of the community as a whole. Betterment levy on unearned increment in land values is justified on the ground that it provides additional resources to the government to liquidate partially or fully the capital cost of the development scheme.

Betting Tax: It is levied on horse races. The tax is levied on stakeholder who may be either a race club or a bookmaker. The law governing betting tax is generally regulatory in nature. The main objective is to discourage poorer sections of the population from gambling on horse races.

Bond: A bond is a promise to pay a stated sum of money as interest each year and to repay the face value of bond at some future redemption date. Some bonds, called *perpetuities*, pay a fixed sum of interest each year forever but never repay the principal, i.e. they have no redemption date.

Bonded Warehouse: It is a warehouse licensed and bonded by the government to insure against loss of customs duty. Goods subject to customs duty may be stored there without paying duty. Such goods are said to be under bond. These storage facilities are operated under the lock and key of a country's customs authorities and the owners of these facilities are bonded to ensure that they will satisfy all customs duty obligations. The importer will have to pay the existing duty on the goods if they enter the domestic market.

Bracket Creep: It is a situation when a person's income, rising at the same rate as price level, faces higher rates of taxation.

Budget: It is a financial plan listing expenditure and income expected during some given future period, usually one year. A budget may be prepared by an individual, a family, a company, or a government.

Budget Deficit: It is a situation signifying shortfall of current revenue of the government below its current expenditure.

Budget Incidence: It relates to the combined effects of an equal increase in tax and public expenditure on the distribution of income. It is also called net incidence and is obtained by summing, algebraically, both the tax incidence (negative) and expenditure incidence (positive) for each of the subgroups of the population.

Buffer Stock: It refers to the stock of a commodity (say wheat) kept to meet fluctuations in its demand and/or supply so as to keep its price under check. It is thus a residual between supply and demand. When demand is less than supply it stores the residual and when demand is greater than supply it supplies the residual.

—C—

Canons of Taxation: These are principles or maxims used in the designing or evaluation of a tax or a tax system. Given the level of taxation in a country, fiscal experts can design a tax system which best promotes the objectives of economic policy with due regard to social justice. Adam Smith (1723-1790), the famous 18th century British economist, was the first to set forth such maxims in his book *Wealth of Nations* published in 1776. He laid down the following four general guidelines for designing an ideal system of taxation: equity, certainty, convenience and economy.

Capital: It refers to all those man-made machines and appliances which are used for further production of goods and services rather than being consumed for their own sake.

Capital Allowances: These are deductions from business income for depreciation of assets used in business. These are allowed because fixed assets (like plant and machinery) are gradually used up in the production process. If their wear and tear is not taken into account, the taxable income will be overstated. Annual capital allowances traditionally take the form of a fixed percentage of the cost of an asset.

Capital Expenditure: In the context of taxation of income, the distinction between capital expenditure and revenue expenditure is important because only revenue expenditure is allowed to be deducted while computing income. Capital expenditure is deductible to the extent of depreciation allowance permitted.

Capital Gains Tax: It is a tax on the increase in capital value of an asset.

Capital Levy: It is a one-time tax on existing wealth. It is different from annual tax on wealth. Such a drastic fiscal measure is resorted to during or after a war or some other national emergency. The purpose of capital levy is to reduce the size of national debt and relieve the inflationary pressure associated with it.

Capital Loss: It is a decrease in the value of an asset. In terms of the net accretion principle, capital losses are set off against capital gains and net capital losses are treated as a reduction in income (economic power) of an individual.

Capital Receipts: Those receipts of an organisation which create liability or reduce assets are called capital receipts. Thus, money obtained by way of loan, from the sale of fixed assets, issue of shares and debentures are capital receipts. They are generally of a non-recurring nature. Capital receipts are exempt from income tax unless they are expressly taxable whereas revenue receipts are taxable unless they are expressly exempt from tax.

Cascading Effect: This concept is associated with a traditional turnover tax which is levied on transaction of goods and services at all levels of production and distribution. For example, excise duty may be levied on raw materials, components, semi-finished and finished goods. This system of taxation increases the price of a commodity much more than the tax collected, resulting in *cascading*. The price of a finished product reflects the taxes imposed on inputs used.

Casual Income: Refers to income which is non-recurring in nature. It is produced by chance, accident or fortune. It is neither calculated nor settled nor is there any likelihood of its coming at a certain time. In some countries, casual income up to a certain level is exempt from income tax. For example, under Section 10(3) of the Indian Income Tax Act, 1961, casual income is exempt from tax up to Rs. 5,000.

Cess: A levy, usually on plantation crops (tobacco, jute), to raise funds for research and improvement schemes related to those crops (e.g. high-yielding variety of seeds). A cess is different from a tax in that the proceeds of the former are used for the benefit of industry on which it is levied.

Compensatory Duty: It is a tariff levied on the import of a commodity to match some other tax which a country has imposed on local production of the same commodity. It is levied so that domestic producers are not put to any disadvantage.

Compliance Costs of a Tax: Compliance costs refer to costs incurred by taxpayers or third parties in complying with a tax, over and above the tax payment made to public authorities.

Compounded Levy: Levying of excise duty on the production of small-scale sector is a major problem of tax administration. The procedures adopted for collection of excise from large-scale units are often found expensive and time-consuming when applied to small firms. Under compounded levy, a lump sum payment is made on the basis of some installations, e.g. the number of looms in a textile unit. Once the compounded levy is paid, the producer becomes free from all excise formalities except to maintain a record of looms in operation.

Consignment Tax: It is a levy on inter-state transfer of goods. A consignment is a despatch or a stock-transfer from a company to its branch located in a different state. Since no sale is involved, it is called in-house transaction by a company. Sometimes, unscrupulous parties evade payment of inter-state sales tax by showing virtual sales as consignments from one state to another. By this method, the payment of inter-state sales tax is avoided. This problem was faced by the tax authorities in India. Hence, through a Constitutional amendment the Central Government was empowered to levy taxes on the consignment of goods (whether the consignment is to the person making it or to any other person), where such consignment takes place in the course of inter-state trade or commerce.

Corporate Income Tax: It is levied on the earnings of corporations. A corporation (or a company) is regarded as a separate entity for purposes of income tax. Total income of a corporation is arrived at with reference to its profits shown in its profit and loss account.

Cost-Yield Ratio: It is the cost of collection expressed as a proportion of tax revenue. A lower cost-yield ratio is considered indicative of the efficiency of tax administration. Unusually high cost-yield ratio is a drag on public exchequer. Thus, cost-yield ratios may be used to evaluate administration of competing taxes.

Countervailing Duty: It is a duty in addition to the normal import duty levied on goods imported into a country. The rate of countervailing duty is generally equal to the excise duty imposed on like items produced domestically. The argument is that normal import duty represents the desirable degree of protection to internally produced goods which are not subject to excise duty. When excise duty is levied or the rate of an existing one is increased, a corresponding enhancement in import duty is required to preserve the accepted degree of protection.

Crowding-out: The term is descriptive of any group/section being pushed out of a market. In the context of financial market, the demand for credit by the government and other public sector institutions may be so strong and inflexible that credit requirements of households and companies are crowded-out.

Customs Duty: It is a tax on the import and export of goods levied by a national government and payable to it when the goods cross the customs boundaries of the nation. Hence, it is also called border tax.

—D—

Debt Trap: It is a situation in which a government is unable to repay its past loans without fresh borrowings

Deductions: Deductions mean all amounts which are eligible for subtraction from gross receipts of a business. Strictly speaking, a deduction relates to an actual outlay e.g. expenditure on travelling. Tax laws must clearly specify as to which sums are allowed as deductions from gross receipts in order to determine the amount on which a given set of rates is to be applied.

Deficit Financing: When all types of government receipts fall short of its stipulated total expenditure, then the only alternative left with it is to print more currency. The net effect of deficit financing is to increase money supply in the economy. When money supply increases, it puts pressure on the supply of goods and services. Since supply cannot be increased so easily, prices have a tendency to rise. Price rise is accompanied by its own adverse effects because the burden of price rise falls inequitably on different classes. Deficit financing is a kind of inflation tax which drives the people into involuntary savings.

Deflation: It refers to decrease in the general price level in an economy.

Devaluation: As part of a government's commercial policy, it refers to deliberate reduction in the value of domestic currency in relation to foreign currencies. Devaluation makes domestically produced goods cheaper for the foreigners and foreign goods expensive for the locals. Hence, imports are reduced and exports are promoted to improve the trade balance. For successful devaluation, it is necessary that demand for imports as well as exports is relatively elastic.

Direct Tax: It is a tax the ultimate burden of which falls on the person on whom it is levied. In other words, it is a tax that cannot be shifted from the original payer to someone else. It is contrasted with indirect tax which can readily be shifted to ultimate consumers of the commodity or service taxed.

Discriminating Duty: An import duty levied at a level different from comparable import duties so as to encourage (or discourage) imports of a particular commodity or imports from a particular country.

Dumping: It is a practice of selling goods in a foreign country at a price below their domestic selling price, after allowing for differences due to transportation expenses, tariffs, and other cost justifications. Many governments view the activity as an unfair competitive practice and frequently expose those engaged in dumping to the imposition of an antidumping duty. This generally unfavourable view of the practice stems from the monopoly precondition which underlies it. Economic theory specifies that in order for a producer to discriminate in the pricing of identical goods between markets (or classes of consumers) some element of monopoly power must be present; otherwise, the producer is merely a price-taker forced to adopt the uniform competitive price determined in the overall marketplace.

Duty Drawback: It refers to repayment of import duty, partially or fully, to exporters of commodities in the manufacture of which imported materials and components are used. Duty drawback scheme is a device to encourage exports. Most often, the scheme is used for imported raw materials or semi-finished goods (like raw diamonds) that are incorporated into a finished product (cut and polished diamonds) and then re-exported. Complications arise when exported goods use raw materials and components some of which are imported and some produced domestically. The drawback in such cases means refund of an amount which represents the import duty paid on the imported materials used in the exported goods.

Duty-free Shop: A shop at airports, on ships etc. from where outgoing passengers may buy goods which are free of commodity taxes because the purchases are meant for exports. Similarly, incoming passengers may purchase certain goods from duty-free shop at a cheaper price than usual because they do not have to pay duty that is usually paid when goods are brought into a country.

—E—

Earmarking of Taxes: Earmarking is a fiscal practice under which revenues from one or more sources are pooled into a separate independent fund which is used to finance certain pre-determined public services.

Earned and Unearned Income: Earned income (or employment or labour income) is derived from actual work or services performed and includes wages, salaries and income from professions. Unearned income (or capital or property income) is derived from investment, rent etc.

Entertainment Tax: It is levied on the price charged for admission to various places of entertainment such as a cinema, circus, theatre, exhibition, variety show, cabaret, night-club and casino.

Estate Duty: It is a levy on the value of the entire estate left behind by a decedent before its division among the inheritors. It is contrasted with an inheritance tax which is based on the share of the estate received by each beneficiary. Estate duty (or death duty) is simpler and more productive than inheritance tax because the former avoids the difficult task of determining the value of the share of each inheritor. Estate duty is usually levied at a progressive rate to reduce economic disparities.

Excise Duty: It is a tax on goods produced or manufactured within a country. It is collected from the producers of excisable goods.

Exemptions: Exemptions (or exclusions) are those items which are explicitly and statutorily freed from the scope of a tax and therefore remain untaxed. They may be termed as non-taxable gross receipts. Several considerations weigh on a government to declare a host of receipts exempt, either fully or up to specified limits, from the scope of taxation.

Expenditure Tax: It is a tax on personal expenditure.

Export Subsidies: These are provisions of financial assistance to exporters for encouraging them to export and for making their exports cheaper and competitive in the foreign market.

—F—

Fee: Fee is charged by public authorities for providing certain services such as registration of marriages, births and deaths. Generally, the fee is charged equal to the cost of a service.

Financial Year: It is the year of account for financial purposes, often not coinciding with the calendar year. For example, in India the financial year (or fiscal year) runs from April 1 to March 31 of the following year. In USA, the fiscal year runs from July 1 to June 30.

Fine: A fine is a compulsory payment without any *quid pro quo* to curb certain offence. It is different from a tax because the objective is not to get revenue for the government.

Fiscal Capacity: It refers to the ability of an individual to pay taxes or the ability of a government to raise revenues.

Fiscal Drag: In a period of inflation, the value of money decreases. Therefore, the value of exemptions, deductions, and allowances allowed in the computation of income and tax liability becomes less in real terms. The brackets of taxable income chargeable at progressive rates also shrink in real terms. Taxpayers are pushed into higher income bands (and therefore higher rates) because of increasing money income which in real terms may remain the same. The higher rate of income tax may lead to reduction in real income owing to this fiscal drag.

Fiscal Federalism: A federal set up creates a multiple polity based on divided functions and powers among central, state and local governments. Fiscal federalism deals with financial arrangements and their working in a federal polity.

Fiscal Marksmanship: It refers to the degree of accuracy of budgetary forecasts. Extensive estimates of revenue and expenditure are set forth in the budget of a government for the ensuing financial year. The *actuals* or *accounts* of the revenue and expenditure become available after the expiry of the financial year under consideration. Perfectly accurate estimates of revenue, and expenditure are never possible and therefore some divergence is always there between the *budget estimates* and the *actuals*. The degree of deviation between the two indicates the skill and competence of budget-makers. Excessive deviation reveals the poor fiscal predictability (or marksmanship) of the experts.

Fiscal Monopolies: These are non-financial public enterprises exercising monopoly in the production and/or distribution of such commodities as tobacco, alcoholic beverages, and salt. Using the monopoly power, revenues are raised for the government which may otherwise be gathered through taxes if such commodities are produced/distributed by private units.

Fiscal Policy: It refers to the use of a government's taxation and expenditure policies to influence the level of economic activities at the macroeconomic level.

Flat Rate: Fixed rate of tax regardless of the amount of income.

Free Port: Free port or a free trade zone allows goods to be temporarily imported and held within the port area without paying duty, provided they are re-exported later. The goods may be stored, processed, and/or repackaged in this area, and then either imported in the normal way by paying customs duty or re-exported without paying tariff. Thus, Singapore is a free port and Kandla is a free trade zone.

Free Rider: A free rider is a person who receives benefits of a government service without paying for it.

Future Trading: It refers to commodity or currency trading done on contract for future delivery. The purpose is to insure against risks of price changes, exchange rate changes etc. or to make a profit by speculating on the price trends.

—G—

Gift Tax: It is imposed on the aggregate value of gifts made by a person (donor) during the year. A gift is defined as a transfer by one person to another of any existing movable or immovable property made voluntarily and without consideration in money or money's worth. In other words, before a transfer of property becomes liable to gift tax, the following conditions must be satisfied: (a) the transfer must be voluntary, (b) the transfer must be of existing property and (c) the transfer must be without consideration in money or money's worth.

Gilt-edged Securities: These are government securities free of risk of default.

Grants: Grants are unilateral transfers from one level of government to another (usually lower) level of government. They have the advantage of being targeted towards fiscally disadvantaged state/municipal governments to reduce horizontal fiscal imbalances. They can also be made conditional regarding their utilisation.

—H—

Highway-user Tax: It is a tax levied on the users of highways. The revenue is generally reserved for the construction and maintenance of highways. In USA, highway-user taxes are imposed by both the Federal and the State Governments. They are in the form of a fixed amount per gallon of gasoline sold, and licence fee for motor vehicles.

Horizontal Equity: It is a tax equity criterion advocating similar tax treatment of persons in similar economic circumstances.

—I—

Impact of Tax: It refers to the point at which the burden of a tax falls initially.

Imports: Imports are defined as goods taken into one country from another country in the conduct of foreign trade, with the first country being the importer and the second the exporter.

Imputed Income: Imputed income arises when a taxpayer is himself the producer and the consumer of a given commodity or service. Although no market transaction is involved yet the taxpayer enjoys a certain amount of consumption.

Incidence of Taxation: It refers to the final resting place of tax burden as against the impact which means the first place where a tax is imposed. The incidence of a tax is on the person who ultimately pays it, i.e. who cannot shift it any further.

Income Tax: It is a tax levied on the annual income of various taxable entities, mainly individuals and companies. The taxable income is determined after taking into account certain exemptions and deductions. No tax at all is paid on a basic income that is exempt. Rate schedule of the tax is generally progressive. The larger the taxable income, the higher the tax rate. Higher rates apply not to the total income but to increments of income. The progressive nature of income tax is based on the ability-to-pay principle of taxation.

Indirect Tax: It is a tax which can be shifted from the original payer to the ultimate consumer of the commodity or service taxed. Import duties, excise levies, and sales taxes are generally regarded as indirect taxes. Thus, an excise duty on cigarettes levied on producers is usually passed on to the consumers in the form of higher prices.

Inflation Tax: There are several ways through which resources can be acquired by the government for public use. One such method is deficit financing, i.e. printing more currency. Through deficit financing, it can purchase a part of goods and services available in the economy. Since such a policy usually leads to price rise, it is called *inflation tax*. The effects of such a policy are very disorderly in the sense that the burden of inflation falls inequitably on different classes.

Inheritance Tax: It is a levy on persons who receive property upon the death of a benefactor. It is different from estate duty which is based on the value of the entire estate left behind by a decedent and before it is divided among the heirs. A tax on each inheritance to which the estate gives rise is known as inheritance tax or succession duty.

Inter-corporate Dividends: These are dividends received by a company from another company. Income tax laws generally treat a parent (or a holding) company and its subsidiary company as separate legal entities and therefore tax them separately. Thus, if a holding company receives dividends from its subsidiary, the former has to pay tax on such dividends. Taxation of inter-corporate earnings is designed to prevent concentration of economic power in the hands of corporate giants. However, this provision is said to give rise to treble taxation of such dividends, first in the hands of the earning company, then in the hands of the receiving company, and finally in the hands of individual shareholders. Tax laws often provide certain concessions to facilitate inter-corporate investment.

Inter-governmental Transfers: Transfers (tax sharing and grants) are used to correct vertical imbalances, i.e. mismatch of revenue and expenditure responsibilities of different levels of a government. However, before such transfers are effected, it should be ensured that taxes, duties and levies assigned to a government are being optimally tapped. Thus, tax effort, if not a pre-condition, should at least form part of the formula for transfers. The need for transfers arises because the own revenues of a lower level government (through tax assignments and non-tax sources) are insufficient to meet the expenditure required for providing services allotted to it.

—J—

Joint Assessment: It refers to aggregation of the incomes of husband and wife for joint assessment by tax authorities.

Joint Occupancy of Tax Fields: It relates to concurrent taxation powers enjoyed by different tiers of government in a federal polity. Concurrent taxation powers are a characteristic feature of fiscal federalism in USA, Canada, and Australia. In India, the Central and the State Governments have no concurrent powers of taxation.

—L—

Levy: It is synonymous with tax.

Local Taxation: The term refers to taxes levied at the lower level of government in a federal polity such as municipalities, city corporations, district boards and other local bodies. These local bodies provide certain public services like basic health and education, construction and maintenance of local roads, sanitation, street lighting and parks. Taxes usually levied by local bodies are property tax, octroi, tax on professions and registration and licensing charges.

Lump Sum Tax: It refers to taxation of income, net wealth etc. expressed as a certain fixed sum rather than calculated under the ordinary tax law. This method is used for administrative convenience where facts are difficult to establish. In a lump sum tax, an individual cannot take action to alter his tax liability.

—M—

Marginal Tax Rate: It is the rate of tax, under a progressive rate schedule, applicable to the top slice or bracket of an assessee's income, net wealth or some other taxable item.

Minimum Alternative Tax (MAT): Income tax laws throughout the world generally provide for a number of tax concessions. A clever profit-making company may arrange its affairs in such a manner that the cumulative effect of all tax concessions is to reduce its income declared in the tax return to zero. MAT is a device to keep a zero tax company within the tax net.

Motor Vehicle Tax: It is a tax on vehicles suitable for use on roads. It is levied for granting registration, permit, driving licence etc., and is based on the type of vehicle (truck, bus, car, or scooter). It also means a tax paid periodically for the use of roads. Hence, it is also called road tax.

—N—

Nominal Rate of Tax: Rate of tax approved by the legislature is termed as nominal (or statutory) rate. It can be misleading when one takes into account exclusions, deductions, allowances, tax credits and tax evasion. These erosions in the tax base considerably reduce the average tax rate below the statutory one.

—O—

Octroi: It is a tax on the entry of goods into a local area from other areas for the purpose of consumption or sale. Though an important source of revenue for local bodies, it obstructs the free movement of vehicles carrying goods across the country.

—P—

Pay-As-You-Earn (PAYE): A system of collecting income tax from employees recommended by J.M. Keynes and introduced in Britain in 1944.

Perquisite: It means any casual emolument or benefit attached to an office or position in addition to salary or wages. It does not cover mere reimbursement of necessary disbursements. Perquisites may be provided in cash or in kind.

Poll Tax: Poll tax (also called head tax or capitation tax) is a direct tax of a fixed amount which is levied on individuals irrespective of income, wealth or any other such criterion. Since the amount of a poll tax is fixed, there are no problems of computation. The tax is apparently regressive because it takes a larger percentage of the income of the poor than of the rich.

Preferential Duty: It is an import duty levied at a relatively low level so as to favour imports of a particular commodity or imports from a particular country.

Presumptive Tax: Presumptive tax relates to the use of appropriate indicators of income, wealth etc. instead of the actual records of these tax bases. In the case of income tax, a presumptive tax is imposed on the basis of an estimated taxable income. Presumptive income is exogenously determined. The base for presumptive income tax is fixed and does not depend on the behaviour of individual entrepreneurs. In fact, a presumptive income tax works like a lump sum tax and therefore does not impose marginal tax burden on actual income. The chief advantage of presumptive taxation is its simplicity, both for tax collectors and taxpayers.

Professional Tax: It is a kind of registration fee for practising a profession. In India, State Governments are empowered to levy a tax on professions. However, according to Article 276 of the Constitution, the total amount payable in respect of any one person to the State by way of such tax is not to exceed Rs. 2,500 per annum.

Progressive Tax: A tax schedule is said to be progressive if the ratio of tax to income increases as one moves up the income scale.

Proportional Tax: A tax schedule is said to be proportional if the ratio of tax to income remains constant as one moves up the income scale.

—Q—

Quick Succession Relief: It means a reduction in estate duty if it is paid twice within a few years on the same estate due to a second death. An estate which has been subjected to duty may change hands quickly on account of successive deaths and again become liable to payment of duty. In such cases, estate duty puts undue burden on families suffering deaths at short intervals. This problem is mitigated by providing quick succession relief in the law.

—R—

Refund of Tax: Refund means to pay back. Where the amount of tax paid by a person in respect of any assessment year exceeds the amount of tax properly assessable for that year, he is entitled to a refund of such excess tax paid.

Regressive Tax: A tax schedule is said to be regressive if the ratio of tax to income declines as one moves up the income scale.

Revenue Deficit: It refers to the excess of revenue expenditure over revenue receipts.

Revenue Expenditure: It relates to the normal running of an organisation. Broadly speaking, all those expenditures of an organisation which do not result in the creation of physical or financial assets are treated as revenue expenditures.

Revenue Receipts: Moneys obtained in the normal course of business are called revenue receipts, e.g. sale proceeds, interest on deposits, and dividends on investment. Revenue receipts are normally of recurring nature and are not meant for any specific purpose.

Revenue Sharing: It is a term used in the context of fiscal federalism whereby a higher level of government imposes and collects certain taxes but shares, permissively or mandatorily, the proceeds with lower level governments.

—S—

Sales Tax: It is normally an *ad valorem* levy imposed on the seller with reference to the transaction of sale. Sales tax is generally regressive in nature because being paid by all consumers, it takes a larger proportion of small incomes than of larger ones. On the basis of the stage of collection, sales tax is classified into (a) multi-point sales tax and (b) single-point sales tax.

Securities: The term securities includes shares, bonds, debentures etc. of any body corporate or government. Securities which appear on the official stock exchange list and which may be bought and sold on the stock exchange are called listed securities.

Specific Duty: A specific or volumetric duty represents a fixed amount of tax on a unit of the physical quantity of the product. Customs duties, excise levies and sales taxes on commodities may take specific or *ad valorem* form.

Split Rate System: Under this system, profits distributed as dividends are taxed at a lower rate than retained earnings (i.e. undistributed profits).

Stamp Duty: It is a tax on documents dealing with such matters as transfer of property, shares, debentures and insurance policies. If unstamped, these documents become invalid. Stamp duty (or transfer tax) is generally collected through the sale of revenue stamps which must be affixed or imprinted on the document in question. Stamp duties are often under the jurisdiction of state and local governments.

Standard Deduction: It is common in the income tax laws of countries to allow deduction of expenditures from gross salary income incurred by taxpayers for employment purposes. If the deduction is allowed only on production or proof of having incurred such expenditure, the procedure will obviously be cumbersome for salaried persons. To simplify rules, many countries allow a standard deduction, from aggregate amount of salary, for all types of expenditure incurred towards employment.

Subsidy: A subsidy is a grant of money from an outside third party to either the buyer or the seller of a commodity. Subsidies allow a buyer to procure a commodity /service at a lower price than would otherwise have been necessary. The effect of a subsidy is opposite of the effect of a tax. A business firm will not stay in operation unless revenue is sufficient enough to cover cost plus some return on investment. If revenue from buyers is insufficient, a subsidy from an outside agency may keep the firm in operation.

Sumptuary Tax: It is a kind of excise on goods generally thought to have socially harmful effects. The best examples of such goods are alcoholic beverages and cigarettes. High taxes on these luxury items are imposed with a view to discourage their consumption and also on the ground that those who buy them can afford to pay additional tax.

Surcharge: It is an additional tax calculated on the normal tax liability. In other words, surcharge is assessed on the usual amount of tax due.

—T—

Tariff: It is a tax imposed by authorities on imports with various motives including cut in imports, protection to domestic industries or to earn revenue. Tariff imposed on imported goods according to their value is called *ad valorem* tariff.

Tax: A tax is a compulsory payment made to general government without any direct *quid pro quo*. General government includes central, state and local governments. Tax payments are compulsory and the benefits provided by government to taxpayers are neither direct nor proportional to such payments. Every tax is made up of two elements: a base, i.e. the object to be taxed, and a rate structure indicating how the base is to be taxed.

Tax Amnesty: It refers to an opportunity offered by a government to tax evaders to declare their past concealment of income, wealth etc., without fear of being prosecuted. Tax amnesty (or impunity) is granted only for the past in order to secure better compliance and higher tax yield in the present and future. A tax amnesty brings concealed money in the open, broadens the base of investment and hence accelerates economic development.

Tax Avoidance: It means preventing or reducing one's tax liability through manipulations within the framework of existing tax legislation. Tax avoidance, as against tax evasion, is legally permissible and hence a legitimate aim of taxpayers.

Tax Credit: Tax credit (or tax rebate) is a legal provision permitting taxpayers to deduct specified sums from their tax liability. A tax credit differs from a deduction because the former is subtracted after the total tax liability has been calculated whereas the latter is subtracted from the income subject to tax.

Apparently, a tax credit of a given amount is more valuable to a taxpayer than a deduction of the same amount. For example, a taxpayer who is in the 40 per cent bracket of individual income tax reduces his total burden by Rs. 1,000 if he is allowed a tax credit of Rs. 1,000. However, his tax burden is reduced by Rs. 400 if he is given a deduction of Rs. 1,000.

Tax Evasion: It is an illegal attempt to reduce tax payable through deliberate under-reporting/non-reporting taxable incomes or concealing one's true *state of affairs* from tax authorities. Tax evasion is a criminal offence and if detected is punishable by financial penalties or even by imprisonment or both.

Tax-free Zone: It is an area within the territory of a country in which customs duties and other indirect taxes are not applied. The area is used for export industries based on imported raw materials.

Tax-GDP Ratio: Level of taxation in a country is traditionally judged in terms of the ratio which taxes bear to some measure of national income. This ratio is called tax-GDP ratio and the change in it is determined by variations in both the numerator (total tax revenue) and the denominator (national income).

Tax Haven: It refers to any country or locality which levies very low taxes, or none at all, on foreigners.

Tax Holiday: It is a tax incentive targeted at new firms, and is not available to existing units. Under a tax holiday scheme, new enterprises are allowed a period of time free from the burden of income tax, subject to certain conditions.

Tax Incentives: These are provisions in tax laws which encourage individuals and corporations to undertake activities desired by the government.

Tax Lien: It refers to a government claim on property for which taxes have not been paid when due. In extreme cases, the property may revert to the government.

Toll: A toll (or octroi) is collected on goods that move into or through a local territory.

—U—

Units of Assessment: It means persons or taxable entities chargeable to tax under a tax law. For example, under the Indian Income Tax Act, 1961, there are seven units of assessment: 1. An individual, 2. A Hindu Undivided Family (HUF), 3. A company, 4. A Firm, 5. An association of persons or a body of individuals whether incorporated or not, 6. A local authority and 7. Every artificial juridical person, not falling within any of the preceding categories.

User Charge: It is a fee or charge for use of a government-supplied service, generally transportation service. It is applied so that those who benefit from public transport services repay the cost to the government. User charges are usually in the form of tolls, licence fees and fuel taxes and fall on highway and waterway traffic.

—V—

Value Added Tax (VAT): Value added tax is levied on the sellers of goods and services based on value added by their respective units. The base of VAT is determined by value added at a particular stage of production or distribution.

—W—

Ways and Means Advances: These are short-term loans (also called floating debt) made by the central bank of a country to the government of that country. The purpose of ways and means advances is to accommodate temporary mismatch in the receipts and payments of the government.

Wealth Tax: Wealth represents the command a person has over economic resources at any point of time. Tax base for purposes of wealth tax is normally the taxpayer's net wealth i.e. total assets less liabilities. The base is generally modified by exemptions and deductions.

Withholding Tax: It is a system of collecting income tax whereby money is periodically deducted by the employers, financial institutions, and others from wages of employees, returns on securities, and other payments. Thus, intermediaries (or third parties) do the job on behalf of the government as regards assessment of the taxable base and the collection of tax thereon.

—Z—

Zero-tax Company: Income tax laws usually provide for a host of deductions and incentives to promote socio-economic objectives of state policy. It is likely that a profit-making company may arrange its affairs in such a way that the cumulative effect of all deductions is to reduce its income declared in the tax return to zero. To deal with such situations, some countries have introduced minimum alternative tax.

Time-series Public Finance Data on India

Table 1: Combined Tax Revenue, Breakdown between Direct and Indirect Taxes with Percentage Shares, and Tax-GDP Ratios: 1950-51 to 2006-07

(Rs. crore)

Year	Combined tax revenue* (3+4)	Direct taxes	Indirect taxes	Col. 3 as % of Col. 2	Col. 4 as % of Col. 2	Col. 2 as % of GDP	Col. 3 as % of GDP	Col. 4 as % of GDP
1	2	3	4	5	6	7	8	9
1950-51	627	231	396	36.8	63.2	6.31	2.33	3.99
1951-52	739	244	495	33.0	67.0	6.99	2.31	4.68
1952-53	678	252	426	37.2	62.8	6.54	2.43	4.11
1953-54	672	242	430	36.0	64.0	5.96	2.15	3.81
1954-55	720	240	480	33.3	66.7	6.74	2.25	4.50
1955-56	768	259	509	33.7	66.3	7.06	2.38	4.68
1956-57	890	288	602	32.4	67.6	6.87	2.22	4.65
1957-58	1,045	327	718	31.3	68.7	7.83	2.45	5.38
1958-59	1,089	344	745	31.6	68.4	7.32	2.31	5.01
1959-60	1,216	378	838	31.1	68.9	7.76	2.41	5.35
1960-61	1,350	402	948	29.8	70.2	7.86	2.34	5.52
1961-62	1,543	449	1,094	29.1	70.9	8.48	2.47	6.01
1962-63	1,865	560	1,305	30.0	70.0	9.53	2.86	6.67
1963-64	2,325	693	1,632	29.8	70.2	10.34	3.08	7.26
1964-65	2,599	743	1,856	28.6	71.4	9.91	2.83	7.08
1965-66	2,922	734	2,188	25.1	74.9	10.56	2.65	7.91
1966-67	3,261	767	2,494	23.5	76.5	10.42	2.45	7.97
1967-68	3,456	780	2,676	22.6	77.4	9.43	2.13	7.30
1968-69	3,759	840	2,919	22.3	77.7	9.68	2.16	7.52
1969-70	4,200	963	3,237	22.9	77.1	9.82	2.25	7.57
1970-71	4,752	1,009	3,743	21.2	78.8	10.40	2.21	8.19
1971-72	5,575	1,171	4,404	21.0	79.0	11.39	2.39	9.00
1972-73	6,436	1,346	5,090	20.9	79.1	11.93	2.50	9.44
1973-74	7,389	1,552	5,837	21.0	79.0	11.26	2.37	8.90
1974-75	9,223	1,834	7,389	19.9	80.1	11.90	2.37	9.54
1975-76	11,182	2,493	8,689	22.3	77.7	13.43	2.99	10.43
1976-77	12,332	2,585	9,747	21.0	79.0	13.74	2.88	10.86
1977-78	13,237	2,680	10,557	20.2	79.8	13.03	2.64	10.39
1978-79	15,528	2,851	12,677	18.4	81.6	14.10	2.59	11.51
1979-80	17,683	3,096	14,587	17.5	82.5	14.63	2.56	12.07
1980-81	19,844	3,268	16,576	16.5	83.5	13.80	2.27	11.53
1981-82	24,142	4,133	20,009	17.1	82.9	14.32	2.45	11.87
1982-83	27,242	4,492	22,750	16.5	83.5	14.47	2.39	12.08
1983-84	31,525	4,907	26,618	15.6	84.4	14.36	2.24	12.13
1984-85	35,814	5,330	30,484	14.9	85.1	14.59	2.17	12.42
1985-86	43,267	6,252	37,015	14.4	85.6	15.56	2.25	13.32
1986-87	49,538	6,889	42,650	13.9	86.1	15.92	2.21	13.71
1987-88	56,977	7,483	49,493	13.1	86.9	16.08	2.11	13.97
1988-89	66,925	9,757	57,168	14.6	85.4	15.88	2.31	13.56
1989-90	77,693	11,165	66,528	14.4	85.6	15.98	2.30	13.68

Contd...

Year	Combined tax revenue* (3+4)	Direct taxes	Indirect taxes	Col. 3 as % of Col. 2	Col. 4 as % of Col. 2	Col. 2 as % of GDP	Col. 3 as % of GDP	Col. 4 as % of GDP
1	2	3	4	5	6	7	8	9
1990-91	87,722	12,260	75,462	14.0	86.0	15.43	2.16	13.27
1991-92	1,03,198	16,657	86,541	16.1	83.9	15.80	2.55	13.25
1992-93	1,14,166	19,387	94,779	17.0	83.0	15.26	2.59	12.66
1993-94	1,21,961	21,713	1,00,248	17.8	82.2	14.19	2.53	11.67
1994-95	1,47,849	28,878	1,18,971	19.5	80.5	14.60	2.85	11.75
1995-96	1,75,259	35,777	1,39,482	20.4	79.6	14.75	3.01	11.74
1996-97	2,01,056	41,061	1,59,995	20.4	79.6	14.69	3.00	11.69
1997-98	2,20,659	50,538	1,70,121	22.9	77.1	14.49	3.32	11.17
1998-99	2,33,017	49,119	1,83,898	21.1	78.9	13.38	2.82	10.56
1999-00	2,74,583	60,864	2,13,719	21.4	78.6	14.02	3.11	10.91
2000-01	3,05,320	71,762	2,33,558	23.5	76.5	14.49	3.40	11.08
2001-02	3,14,535	73,108	2,41,427	23.2	76.8	13.79	3.20	10.58
2002-03	3,56,277	87,365	2,68,912	24.5	75.5	14.54	3.57	10.98
2003-04	4,14,084	1,09,546	3,04,538	26.5	73.5	15.00	3.97	11.03
2004-05	4,94,370	1,37,093	3,57,277	27.7	72.3	15.81	4.38	11.43
2005-06	5,95,350	1,73,214	4,22,136	29.1	70.9	16.69	4.86	11.83
2006-07	6,99,135	2,12,804	4,86,331	30.4	69.6	16.95	5.16	11.79

* Total tax revenue of the Central and State Governments.

2005-06 = Revised estimates; 2006-07 = Budget estimates.

Note: The ratios of GDP since 1950-51 are with reference to new series GDP (Base: 1993-94) at current market prices.

Source: Rearranged data from Government of India, Ministry of Finance, *Indian Public Finance Statistics*, 2006-2007, Tables 1.7 and 1.8. Columns 5 and 6 calculations own.

Table 2: Gross Central Taxes, Breakdown between Direct and Indirect Taxes with Percentage Shares, and Tax-GDP Ratios: 1950-51 to 2006-07

(Rs. crore)

Year	Gross Central taxes*(3+4)	Direct taxes	Indirect taxes	Col. 3 as % of Col. 2	Col. 4 as % of Col. 2	Col. 2 as % of GDP	Col. 3 as % of GDP	Col. 4 as % of GDP
1	2	3	4	5	6	7	8	9
1950-51	405	176	229	43.4	56.6	4.08	1.77	2.31
1951-52	512	190	322	37.1	62.9	4.85	1.80	3.05
1952-53	445	186	259	41.8	58.2	4.29	1.79	2.50
1953-54	420	166	254	39.5	60.5	3.72	1.47	2.25
1954-55	455	161	294	35.4	64.6	4.26	1.51	2.75
1955-56	485	171	314	35.2	64.8	4.46	1.57	2.89
1956-57	570	194	376	34.0	66.0	4.40	1.50	2.90
1957-58	692	230	462	33.2	66.8	5.18	1.72	3.46
1958-59	701	238	463	34.0	66.0	4.71	1.60	3.11
1959-60	794	269	525	33.9	66.1	5.07	1.72	3.35
1960-61	895	292	603	32.6	67.4	5.21	1.70	3.51
1961-62	1,054	337	717	32.0	68.0	5.79	1.85	3.94
1962-63	1,285	423	862	32.9	67.1	6.57	2.16	4.41
1963-64	1,634	550	1,084	33.7	66.3	7.27	2.45	4.82
1964-65	1,821	600	1,221	32.9	67.1	6.95	2.29	4.66
1965-66	2,061	598	1,463	29.0	71.0	7.45	2.16	5.29
1966-67	2,307	657	1,650	28.5	71.5	7.37	2.10	5.27
1967-68	2,353	655	1,698	27.8	72.2	6.42	1.79	4.63
1968-69	2,510	698	1,812	27.8	72.2	6.47	1.80	4.67
1969-70	2,822	826	1,996	29.3	70.7	6.60	1.93	4.67
1970-71	3,206	869	2,337	27.1	72.9	7.02	1.90	5.12
1971-72	3,873	1,047	2,826	27.0	73.0	7.92	2.14	5.78
1972-73	4,505	1,233	3,272	27.4	72.6	8.35	2.29	6.07
1973-74	5,070	1,375	3,695	27.1	72.9	7.73	2.10	5.63
1974-75	6,322	1,650	4,672	26.1	73.9	8.16	2.13	6.03
1975-76	7,609	2,205	5,404	29.0	71.0	9.14	2.65	6.49
1976-77	8,271	2,328	5,943	28.1	71.9	9.22	2.59	6.62
1977-78	8,858	2,405	6,453	27.1	72.9	8.72	2.37	6.35
1978-79	10,525	2,528	7,997	24.0	76.0	9.56	2.30	7.26
1979-80	11,974	2,818	9,156	23.5	76.5	9.91	2.33	7.58
1980-81	13,179	2,997	10,182	22.7	77.3	9.17	2.08	7.08
1981-82	15,847	3,786	12,061	23.9	76.1	9.40	2.25	7.15
1982-83	17,696	4,139	13,557	23.4	76.6	9.40	2.20	7.20
1983-84	20,721	4,498	16,223	21.7	78.3	9.44	2.05	7.39
1984-85	23,471	4,798	18,673	20.4	79,6	9.56	1.95	7.61
1985-86	28,670	5,620	23,050	19.6	80.4	10.31	2.02	8.29
1986-87	32,838	6,236	26,602	19.0	81.0	10.55	2.00	8.55
1987-88	37,665	6,752	30,913	17.9	82.1	10.63	1.91	8.72
1988-89	44,474	8,830	35,644	19.9	80.1	10.55	2.09	8.46
1989-90	51,636	10,003	41,633	19.4	80.6	10.62	2.06	8.56

Contd...

Year	Gross Central taxes*(3+4)	Direct taxes	Indirect taxes	Col. 3 as % of Col. 2	Col. 4 as % of Col. 2	Col. 2 as % of GDP	Col. 3 as % of GDP	Col. 4 as % of GDP
1	2	3	4	5	6	7	8	9
1990-91	57,577	11,030	46,547	19.2	80.8	10.12	1.94	8.19
1991-92	67,361	15,353	52,008	22.8	77.2	10.31	2.35	7.96
1992-93	74,636	18,140	56,496	24.3	75.7	9.97	2.42	7.55
1993-94	75,742	20,299	55,443	26.8	73.2	8.82	2.36	6.45
1994-95	92,297	26,973	65,324	29.2	70.8	9.11	2.66	6.45
1995-96	1,11,224	33,564	77,660	30.2	69.8	9.36	2.83	6.54
1996-97	1,29,762	38,898	90,864	30.0	70.0	9.48	2.84	6.64
1997-98	1,39,220	48,282	90,938	34.7	65.3	9.14	3.17	5.97
1998-99	1,43,797	46,601	97,196	32.4	67.6	8.26	2.68	5.58
1999-00	1,71,752	57,960	1,13,792	33.7	66.3	8.77	2.96	5.81
2000-01	1,88,603	68,305	1,20,298	36.2	63.8	8.95	3.24	5.71
2001-02	1,87,060	69,197	1,17,863	37.0	63.0	8.20	3.03	5.17
2002-03	2,15,905	83,363	1,32,542	38.6	61.4	8.81	3.40	5.41
2003-04	2,54,348	1,05,091	1,49,257	41.3	58.9	9.21	3.81	5.41
2004-05	3,04,957	1,32,183	1,72,774	43.3	56.6	9.75	4.23	5.53
2005-06	3,70,141	1,67,341	2,02,800	45.2	54.8	10.38	4.69	5.69
2006-07	4,42,153	2,06,687	2,35,466	46.7	53.3	10.72	5.01	5.71

* Before transferring States' share in Central taxes.

2005-06 = Revised estimates; 2006-07 = Budget estimates.

Note: The ratios of GDP since 1950-51 are with reference to new series GDP (Base: 1993-94) at current market prices.

Source: Rearranged data from Government of India, Ministry of Finance, *Indian Public Finance Statistics*, 2006-2007, Tables 1.7 and 1.8. Columns 5 and 6 calculations own.

Table 3: Share of States in Central Taxes, Breakdown between Direct and Indirect Taxes with Percentage Shares, and Tax-GDP Ratios: 1950-51 to 2006-07

(Rs. crore)

Year	States' share in Central taxes (3+4)	Direct taxes	Indirect taxes	Col. 3 as % of Col. 2	Col. 4 as % of Col. 2	Col. 2 as % of GDP	Col. 3 as % of GDP	Col. 4 as % of GDP
1	2	3	4	5	6	7	8	9
1950-51	48	48	--	100.0	0.0	0.48	0.48	0.00
1951-52	53	53	--	100.0	0.0	0.50	0.50	0.00
1952-53	73	56	17	76.7	23.3	0.70	0.54	0.16
1953-54	73	58	15	79.5	20.5	0.65	0.51	0.13
1954-55	71	57	14	80.3	19.7	0.66	0.53	0.13
1955-56	74	57	17	77.0	23.0	0.68	0.52	0.16
1956-57	78	51	27	65.4	34.6	0.60	0.39	0.21
1957-58	116	76	40	65.5	34.5	0.87	0.57	0.30
1958-59	148	75	73	50.7	49.3	1.00	0.50	0.49
1959-60	152	79	73	52.0	48.0	0.97	0.50	0.47
1960-61	165	90	75	54.5	45.5	0.96	0.52	0.44
1961-62	179	98	81	54.7	45.3	0.98	0.54	0.45
1962-63	224	99	125	44.2	55.8	1.14	0.51	0.64
1963-64	260	124	136	47.7	52.3	1.16	0.55	0.60
1964-65	258	131	127	50.8	49.2	0.98	0.50	0.48
1965-66	276	130	146	47.1	52.9	1.00	0.47	0.53
1966-67	373	142	231	38.1	61.9	1.19	0.45	0.74
1967-68	416	181	235	43.5	56.5	1.14	0.49	0.64
1968-69	491	200	291	40.7	59.3	1.26	0.52	0.75
1969-70	621	300	321	48.3	51.7	1.45	0.70	0.75
1970-71	755	365	390	48.3	51.7	1.65	0.80	0.85
1971-72	945	470	475	49.7	50.3	1.93	0.96	0.97
1972-73	1,062	495	567	46.6	53.4	1.97	0.92	1.05
1973-74	1,170	539	631	46.1	53.9	1.78	0.82	0.96
1974-75	1,225	522	703	42.6	57.4	1.58	0.67	0.91
1975-76	1,599	742	857	46.4	53.6	1.92	0.89	1.03
1976-77	1,690	662	1,028	39.2	60.8	1.88	0.74	1.15
1977-78	1,798	685	1,113	38.1	61.9	1.77	0.67	1.10
1978-79	1,957	717	1,240	36.6	63.4	1.78	0.65	1.13
1979-80	3,406	876	2,530	25.7	74.3	2.82	0.72	2.09
1980-81	3,791	1,014	2,777	26.7	73.3	2.64	0.71	1.93
1981-82	4,274	1,034	3,240	24.2	75.8	2.53	0.61	1.92
1982-83	4,640	1,148	3,492	24.7	75.3	2.46	0.61	1.85
1983-84	5,245	1,188	4,057	22.7	77.3	2.39	0.54	1.85
1984-85	5,777	1,252	4,525	21.7	78.3	2.35	0.51	1.84
1985-86	7,490	1,865	5,625	24.9	75.1	2.69	0.67	2.02
1986-87	8,476	2,170	6,306	25.6	74.4	2.72	0.70	2.03
1987-88	9,597	2,595	7,002	27.0	73.0	2.71	0.73	1.98
1988-89	10,669	2,750	7,919	25.8	74.2	2.53	0.65	1.88

Contd...

Year	States' share in Central taxes (3+4)	Direct taxes	Indirect taxes	Col. 3 as % of Col. 2	Col. 4 as % of Col. 2	Col. 2 as % of GDP	Col. 3 as % of GDP	Col. 4 as % of GDP
1	2	3	4	5	6	7	8	9
1989-90	13,232	3,922	9,310	29.6	70.4	2.72	0.81	1.91
1990-91	14,535	4,121	10,414	28.4	71.6	2.56	0.72	1.83
1991-92	17,197	5,104	12,093	29.7	70.3	2.63	0.78	1.85
1992-93	20,522	6,057	14,465	29.5	70.5	2.74	0.81	1.93
1993-94	22,240	7,767	14,473	34.9	65.1	2.59	0.90	1.68
1994-95	24,843	8,560	16,283	34.5	65.5	2.45	0.85	1.61
1995-96	29,285	11,274	18,011	38.5	61.5	2.47	0.95	1.52
1996-97	35,061	13,516	21,545	38.5	61.5	2.56	0.99	1.57
1997-98	43,548	21,102	22,446	48.5	51.5	2.86	1.39	1.47
1998-99	39,145	14,480	24,665	37.0	63.0	2.25	0.83	1.42
1999-00	43,481	16,523	26,958	38.0	62.0	2.22	0.84	1.38
2000-01	51,945	18,655	33,290	35.9	64.1	2.46	0.89	1.58
2001-02	53,398	21,492	31,906	40.2	59.8	2.34	0.94	1.40
2002-03	56,122	21,473	34,649	38.3	61.7	2.29	0.88	1.41
2003-04	67,366	28,492	38,874	42.3	57.7	2.44	1.03	1.41
2004-05	80,159	36,828	43,331	45.9	54.1	2.56	1.18	1.39
2005-06	96,002	n.a.	n.a.	...	...	2.69	n.a.	n.a.
2006-07	1,14,948	55,437	59,511	48.2	51.8	2.79	1.34	1.44

2005-06 = Revised estimates; 2006-07 = Budget estimates.

Note: The ratios of GDP since 1950-51 are with reference to new series GDP (Base: 1993-94) at current market prices.

Source: Rearranged data from Government of India, Ministry of Finance, *Indian Public Finance Statistics*, 2006-2007, Tables 1.7 and 1.8. Columns 5 and 6 calculations own.

Table 4: Net Central Taxes, Breakdown between Direct and Indirect Taxes with Percentage Shares, and Tax-GDP Ratios: 1950-51 to 2006-07

(Rs. crore)

Year	Net Central taxes* (3+4)	Direct taxes	Indirect taxes	Col. 3 as % of Col. 2	Col. 4 as % of Col. 2	Col. 2 as % of GDP	Col. 3 as % of GDP	Col. 4 as % of GDP
1	2	3	4	5	6	7	8	9
1950-51	357	128	229	35.8	64.2	3.59	1.29	2.31
1951-52	459	137	322	29.8	70.2	4.34	1.30	3.05
1952-53	372	130	242	34.9	65.1	3.59	1.25	2.33
1953-54	347	108	239	31.1	68.9	3.08	0.96	2.12
1954-55	384	104	280	27.1	72.9	3.60	0.97	2.62
1955-56	411	114	297	27.7	72.3	3.78	1.05	2.73
1956-57	492	143	349	29.1	70.9	3.80	1.10	2.69
1957-58	576	154	422	26.7	73.3	4.31	1.15	3.16
1958-59	553	163	390	29.5	70.5	3.72	1.10	2.62
1959-60	642	190	452	29.6	70.4	4.10	1.21	2.88
1960-61	730	202	528	27.7	72.3	4.25	1.18	3.08
1961-62	875	239	636	27.3	72.7	4.81	1.31	3.50
1962-63	1,061	324	737	30.5	69.5	5.42	1.66	3.77
1963-64	1,374	426	948	31.0	69.0	6.11	1.89	4.22
1964-65	1,563	469	1,094	30.0	70.0	5.96	1.79	4.17
1965-66	1,785	468	1,317	26.2	73.8	6.45	1.69	4.76
1966-67	1,934	515	1,419	26.6	73.4	6.18	1.65	4.53
1967-68	1,937	474	1,463	24.5	75.5	5.29	1.29	3.99
1968-69	2,019	498	1,521	24.7	75.3	5.20	1.28	3.92
1969-70	2,201	526	1,675	23.9	76.1	5.15	1.23	3.92
1970-71	2,451	504	1,947	20.6	79.4	5.37	1.10	4.26
1971-72	2,928	577	2,351	19.7	80.3	5.98	1.18	4.80
1972-73	3,443	738	2,705	21.4	78.6	6.38	1.37	5.01
1973-74	3,900	836	3,064	21.4	78.6	5.94	1.27	4.67
1974-75	5,097	1,128	3,969	22.1	77.9	6.58	1.46	5.12
1975-76	6,010	1,463	4,547	24.3	75.7	7.22	1.76	5.46
1976-77	6,581	1,666	4,915	25.3	74.7	7.33	1.86	5.48
1977-78	7,060	1,720	5,340	24.4	75.6	6.95	1.69	5.26
1978-79	8,568	1,811	6,757	21.4	78.9	7.78	1.64	6.14
1979-80	8,568	1,942	6,626	22.7	77.3	7.09	1.61	5.48
1980-81	9,388	1,983	7,405	21.1	78.9	6.53	1.38	5.15
1981-82	11,573	2,752	8,821	23.8	76.2	6.86	1.63	5.23
1982-83	13,056	2,991	10,065	22.9	77.1	6.94	1.59	5.35
1983-84	15,476	3,310	12,166	21.4	78.6	7.05	1.51	5.54
1984-85	17,694	3,546	14,148	20.0	80.0	7.21	1.44	5.76
1985-86	21,180	3,755	17,425	17.7	82.3	7.62	1.35	6.27
1986-87	24,362	4,066	20,296	16.7	83.3	7.83	1.31	6.52
1987-88	28,068	4,157	23,911	14.8	85.2	7.92	1.17	6.75
1988-89	33,805	6,080	27,725	18.0	82.0	8.02	1.44	6.58
1989-90	38,404	6,081	32,323	15.8	84.2	7.90	1.25	6.65

Contd...

Year	Net Central taxes* (3+4)	Direct taxes	Indirect taxes	Col. 3 as % of Col. 2	Col. 4 as % of Col. 2	Col. 2 as % of GDP	Col. 3 as % of GDP	Col. 4 as % of GDP
1	2	3	4	5	6	7	8	9
1990-91	43,042	6,909	36,133	16.1	83.9	7.57	1.21	6.35
1991-92	50,164	10,249	39,915	20.4	79.6	7.68	1.57	6.11
1992-93	54,114	12,083	42,031	22.3	77.7	7.23	1.61	5.62
1993-94	53,502	12,532	40,970	23.4	76.6	6.23	1.46	4.77
1994-95	67,454	18,413	49,041	27.3	72.7	6.66	1.82	4.84
1995-96	81,939	22,290	59,649	27.2	72.8	6.90	1.88	5.02
1996-97	94,701	25,382	69,319	26.8	73.2	6.92	1.86	5.07
1997-98	95,672	27,180	68,492	28.4	71.6	6.28	1.79	4.50
1998-99	1,04,652	32,121	72,531	30.7	69.3	6.01	1.84	4.17
1999-00	1,28,271	41,437	86,834	32.3	67.7	6.55	2.12	4.43
2000-01	1,36,658	49,650	87,008	36.3	63.7	6.48	2.36	4.13
2001-02	1,33,662	47,705	85,957	35.7	64.3	5.86	2.09	3.77
2002-03	1,59,783	61,890	97,893	38.7	61.3	6.52	2.53	4.00
2003-04	1,86,982	76,599	1,10,382	41.0	59.0	6.77	2.78	4.00
2004-05	2,24,798	95,355	1,29,443	42.4	57.6	7.19	3.05	4.14
2005-06	2,74,139	n.a.	n.a.	...	...	7.69	n.a.	n.a.
2006-07	2,94,898	1,51,250	1,43,684	51.3	48.7	7.15	3.67	3.48

* After transferring States' share in Central taxes.

2005-06 = Revised estimates; 2006-07 = Budget estimates.

Note: The ratios of GDP since 1950-51 are with reference to new series GDP (Base: 1993-94) at current market prices.

Source: Rearranged data from Government of India, Ministry of Finance, *Indian Public Finance Statistics*, 2006-2007, Tables 1.7 and 1.8. Columns 5 and 6 calculations own.

Table 5: States' Own Taxes, Breakdown between Direct and Indirect Taxes with Percentage Shares, and Tax-GDP Ratios: 1950-51 to 2006-07

(Rs. crore)

Year	States' own taxes (3+4)	Direct taxes	Indirect taxes	Col. 3 as % of Col. 2	Col. 4 as % of Col. 2	Col. 2 as % of GDP	Col. 3 as % of GDP	Col. 4 as % of GDP
1	2	3	4	5	6	7	8	9
1950-51	222	55	167	24.7	75.3	2.23	0.55	1.68
1951-52	227	54	173	23.8	76.2	2.15	0.51	1.64
1952-53	233	66	167	28.3	71.7	2.25	0.64	1.61
1953-54	252	76	176	30.2	69.8	2.23	0.67	1.56
1954-55	265	79	186	29.8	70.2	2.48	0.74	1.74
1955-56	283	88	195	31.1	68.9	2.60	0.81	1.79
1956-57	320	94	226	29.4	70.6	2.47	0.73	1.75
1957-58	353	97	256	27.5	72.5	2.64	0.73	1.92
1958-59	388	106	282	27.3	72.7	2.61	0.71	1.90
1959-60	422	109	313	25.8	74.2	2.69	0.70	2.00
1960-61	455	110	345	24.2	75.8	2.65	0.64	2.01
1961-62	489	112	377	22.9	77.1	2.69	0.62	2.07
1962-63	580	137	443	23.6	76.4	2.96	0.70	2.26
1963-64	691	143	548	20.7	79.3	3.07	0.64	2.44
1964-65	778	143	635	18.4	81.6	2.97	0.55	2.42
1965-66	861	136	725	15.8	84.2	3.11	0.49	2.62
1966-67	954	110	844	11.5	88.5	3.05	0.35	2.70
1967-68	1,103	125	978	11.3	88.7	3.01	0.34	2.67
1968-69	1,249	142	1,107	11.4	88.6	3.22	0.37	2.85
1969-70	1,378	137	1,241	9.9	90.1	3.22	0.32	2.90
1970-71	1,546	140	1,406	9.1	90.9	3.38	0.31	3.08
1971-72	1,702	124	1,578	7.3	92.7	3.48	0.25	3.22
1972-73	1,931	113	1,818	5.8	94.2	3.58	0.21	3.37
1973-74	2,319	177	2,142	7.6	92.4	3.53	0.27	3.26
1974-75	2,901	184	2,717	6.3	93.7	3.74	0.24	3.51
1975-76	3,573	288	3,285	8.1	91.9	4.29	0.35	3.95
1976-77	4,061	257	3,804	6.3	93.7	4.53	0.29	4.24
1977-78	4,379	275	4,104	6.3	93.7	4.31	0.27	4.04
1978-79	5,003	323	4,680	6.5	93.5	4.54	0.29	4.25
1979-80	5,709	278	5,431	4.9	95.1	4.72	0.23	4.49
1980-81	6,665	271	6,394	4.1	95.9	4.64	0.19	4.45
1981-82	8,295	347	7,948	4.2	95.8	4.92	0.21	4.71
1982-83	9,546	353	9,193	3.7	96.3	5.07	0.19	4.88
1983-84	10,804	409	10,395	3.8	96.2	4.92	0.19	4.74
1984-85	12,343	532	11,811	4.3	95.7	5.03	0.22	4.81
1985-86	14,597	632	13,965	4.3	95.7	5.25	0.23	5.02
1986-87	16,701	653	16,048	3.9	96.1	5.37	0.21	5.16
1987-88	19,311	731	18,580	3.8	96.2	5.45	0.21	5.24
1988-89	22,452	928	21,524	4.1	95.9	5.33	0.22	5.11
1989-90	26,057	1,162	24,895	4.5	95.5	5.36	0.24	5.12
1990-91	30,145	1,230	28,915	4.1	95.9	5.30	0.22	5.08

Contd...

1991-92	35,837	1,304	34,533	3.6	96.4	5.49	0.20	5.29
1992-93	39,530	1,247	38,283	3.2	96.8	5.28	0.17	5.12
1993-94	46,219	1,414	44,805	3.1	96.9	5.38	0.16	5.21
1994-95	55,552	1,905	53,647	3.4	96.6	5.49	0.19	5.30
1995-96	64,034	2,213	61,822	3.5	96.5	5.39	0.19	5.20
1996-97	71,294	2,163	69,131	3.0	97.0	5.21	0.16	5.05
1997-98	81,439	2,256	79,183	2.8	97.2	5.35	0.15	5.20
1998-99	89,220	2,518	86,702	2.8	97.2	5.12	0.14	4.98
1999-00	1,02,831	2,904	99,927	2.8	97.2	5.25	0.15	5.10
2000-01	1,16,717	3,457	1,13,260	2.9	97.1	5.54	0.16	5.37
2001-02	1,27,475	3,911	1,23,564	3.1	96.9	5.59	0.17	5.42
2002-03	1,40,372	4,002	1,36,370	2.8	97.2	5.73	0.16	5.57
2003-04	1,59,736	4,455	1,55,281	2.8	97.2	5.79	0.16	5.63
2004-05	1,89,413	4,910	1,84,503	2.6	97.4	6.06	0.16	5.90
2005-06	2,25,209	5,873	2,19,336	2.6	97.4	6.31	0.16	6.15
2006-07	2,56,982	6,117	2,50,865	2.4	97.6	6.23	0.15	6.08

2005-06 = Revised estimates; 2006-07 = Budget estimates.

Note: The ratios of GDP since 1950-51 are with reference to new series GDP (Base: 1993-94) at current market prices.

Source: Rearranged data from Government of India, Ministry of Finance, *Indian Public Finance Statistics*, 2006-2007, Tables 1.7 and 1.8. Columns 5 and 6 calculations own.

Table 6: States' Total Tax Revenue, Breakdown between Direct and Indirect Taxes with Percentage Shares, and Tax-GDP Ratios: 1950-51 to 2006-07

(Rs. crore)

Year	States' total tax revenue* (3+4)	Direct taxes	Indirect taxes	Col. 3 as % of Col. 2	Col. 4 as % of Col. 2	Col. 2 as % of GDP	Col. 3 as % of GDP	Col. 4 as % of GDP
1	2	3	4	5	6	7	8	9
1950-51	270	103	167	38.1	61.9	2.72	1.04	1.68
1951-52	280	107	173	38.2	61.8	2.65	1.01	1.64
1952-53	306	122	184	39.9	60.1	2.95	1.18	1.78
1953-54	325	134	191	41.2	58.8	2.8	1.19	1.69
1954-55	336	136	200	40.5	59.5	3.15	1.27	1.87
1955-56	357	145	212	40.6	59.4	3.28	1.33	1.95
1956-57	398	145	253	36.4	63.6	3.07	1.12	1.95
1957-58	469	173	296	36.9	63.1	3.51	1.30	2.22
1958-59	536	181	355	33.8	66.2	3.60	1.22	2.39
1959-60	574	188	386	32.7	67.3	3.66	1.20	2.46
1960-61	620	200	420	32.3	67.7	3.61	1.17	2.45
1961-62	668	210	458	31.4	68.6	3.67	1.15	2.52
1962-63	804	236	568	29.4	70.6	4.11	1.21	2.90
1963-64	951	267	684	28.1	71.9	4.23	1.19	3.04
1964-65	1,036	274	762	26.4	73.6	3.95	1.05	2.91
1965-66	1,137	266	871	23.4	76.6	4.11	0.96	3.15
1966-67	1,327	252	1,075	19.0	81.0	4.24	0.80	3.43
1967-68	1,519	306	1,213	20.1	79.9	4.14	0.83	3.31
1968-69	1,740	342	1,398	19.7	80.3	4.48	0.88	3.60
1969-70	1,999	437	1,562	21.9	78.1	4.68	1.02	3.65
1970-71	2,301	505	1,796	21.9	78.1	5.04	1.11	3.93
1971-72	2,647	594	2,053	22.4	77.6	5.41	1.21	4.20
1972-73	2,993	608	2,385	20.3	79.7	5.55	1.13	4.42
1973-74	3,489	716	2,773	20.5	79.5	5.32	1.09	4.23
1974-75	4,126	706	3,420	17.1	82.9	5.33	0.91	4.41
1975-76	5,172	1,030	4,142	19.9	80.1	6.21	1.24	4.97
1976-77	5,751	919	4,832	16.0	84.0	6.41	1.02	5.38
1977-78	6,177	960	5,217	15.5	84.5	6.08	0.94	5.13
1978-79	6,960	1,040	5,920	14.9	85.1	6.32	0.94	5.38
1979-80	9,115	1,154	7,961	12.7	87.3	7.54	0.95	6.59
1980-81	10,456	1,285	9,171	12.3	87.7	7.27	0.89	6.38
1981-82	12,569	1,381	11,188	11.0	89.0	7.45	0.82	6.64
1982-83	14,186	1,501	12,685	10.6	89.4	7.54	0.80	6.74
1983-84	16,049	1,597	14,452	10.0	90.0	7.31	0.73	6.58
1984-85	18,120	1,784	16,336	9.9	90.1	7.38	0.73	6.65
1985-86	22,087	2,497	19,590	11.3	88.7	7.95	0.90	7.05
1986-87	25,177	2,823	22,354	11.2	88.8	8.09	0.91	7.18
1987-88	28,908	3,326	25,582	11.5	88.5	8.16	0.94	7.22
1988-89	33,121	3,678	29,443	11.1	88.9	7.86	0.87	6.98
1989-90	39,289	5,084	34,205	12.9	87.1	8.08	1.05	7.04

Contd...

1990-91	44,680	5,351	39,329	12.0	88.0	7.86	0.94	6.92
1991-92	53,034	6,408	46,626	12.1	87.9	8.12	0.98	7.14
1992-93	60,052	7,304	52,748	12.2	87.8	8.02	0.98	7.05
1993-94	68,459	9,181	59,278	13.4	86.6	7.97	1.07	6.90
1994-95	80,395	10,465	69,930	13.0	87.0	7.94	1.03	6.90
1995-96	93,320	13,487	79,833	14.4	85.6	7.86	1.14	6.72
1996-97	1,06,355	15,679	90,676	14.7	85.3	7.77	1.15	6.63
1997-98	1,24,987	23,358	1,01,629	18.7	81.3	8.21	1.53	6.67
1998-99	1,28,365	16,998	1,11,367	13.2	86.8	7.37	0.98	6.40
1999-00	1,46,312	19,427	1,26,885	13.3	86.7	7.47	0.99	6.48
2000-01	1,68,662	22,112	1,46,550	13.1	86.9	8.00	1.05	6.95
2001-02	1,80,873	25,403	1,55,470	14.0	86.0	7.93	1.11	6.81
2002-03	1,96,494	25,475	1,71,019	13.0	87.0	8.02	1.04	6.98
2003-04	2,27,102	32,947	1,94,155	14.5	85.5	8.23	1.19	7.03
2004-05	2,69,572	41,740	2,27,834	15.5	84.5	8.62	1.33	7.29
2005-06	3,21,211	n.a.	n.a.	...	...	9.00	n.a.	n.a.
2006-07	3,71,930	61,554	3,10,376	16.5	83.5	9.01	1.49	7.52

* States' share in Central taxes plus States' own taxes.

2005-06 = Revised estimates; 2006-07 = Budget estimates.

Note: The ratios of GDP since 1950-51 are with reference to new series GDP (Base: 1993-94) at current market prices.

Source: Rearranged data from Government of India, Ministry of Finance, *Indian Public Finance Statistics*, 2006-2007, Tables 1.7 and 1.8. Columns 5 and 6 calculations own.

Table 7: Income Tax (Including Corporation Tax) Collections*: 1950-51 to 2008-09

(Rs. crore)

Year	Gross Central taxes	Income tax	Col. 3 as % of Col. 2
1	2	3	4
1950-51	405	172	42.5
1951-52	415	185	36.1
1952-53	445	182	40.9
1953-54	420	161	38.3
1954-55	455	156	34.3
1955-56	485	165	34.0
1956-57	570	199	34.9
1957-58	692	215	31.1
1958-59	701	221	31.5
1959-60	794	250	31.5
1960-61	895	277	31.9
1961-62	1,054	316	30.0
1962-63	1,285	407	31.7
1963-64	1,634	533	32.6
1964-65	1,821	580	31.9
1965-66	2,061	576	27.9
1966-67	2,307	637	27.6
1967-68	2,353	636	27.0
1968-69	2,510	678	27.0
1969-70	2,822	801	28.4
1970-71	3,206	843	26.3
1971-72	3,873	1,009	26.1
1972-73	4,505	1,187	26.3
1973-74	5,070	1,328	26.2
1974-75	6,322	1,583	25.0
1975-76	7,609	2,076	27.3
1976-77	8,263	2,178	26.4
1977-78	8,858	2,223	25.1
1978-79	10,525	2,428	23.1
1979-80	11,974	2,731	22.8

Contd...

1980-81	13,179	2,816	21.4
1981-82	15,847	3,446	21.7
1982-83	17,696	3,755	21.2
1983-84	20,721	4,192	20.2
1984-85	23,471	4,484	19.1
1985-86	28,671	5,374	18.7
1986-87	32,837	6,038	18.4
1987-88	37,666	6,620	17.6
1988-89	44,474	8,648	19.4
1989-90	51,636	9,739	18.7
1990-91	57,577	10,606	18.4
1991-92	67,361	14,584	21.6
1992-93	74,636	16,787	22.5
1993-94	75,742	19,183	25.3
1994-95	92,297	25,847	28.0
1995-96	1,10,354	32,090	29.1
1996-97	1,28,762	36,798	28.6
1997-98	1,39,221	37,113	26.7
1998-99	1,43,797	44,764	31.1
1999-00	1,71,752	56,339	32.8
2000-01	1,88,603	67,460	35.8
2001-02	1,87,060	68,613	36.7
2002-03	2,16,266	82,038	37.9
2003-04	2,54,348	1,04,949	41.3
2004-05	3,04,958	1,31,948	43.3
2005-06	3,66,152	1,64,906	45.0
2006-07	4,73,512	2,19,411	46.3
2007-08	5,85,410	3,04,445	52.0
2008-09	6,87,715	3,64,675	53.0

*Before transferring States' share.

2007-08 = Revised estimates; 2008-09 = Budget estimates.

Source: Government of India, Ministry of Finance, *Explanatory Memorandum on the Budget of the Central Government;* and *Receipts Budget* (various years). Column 4 calculations own.

Table 8: Wealth Tax Revenue: 1957-58 to 2008-09

(Rs. crore)

Year	Yield	Year	Yield
1957-58	7	1983-84	93
1958-59	10	1984-85	107
1959-60	12	1985-86	153
1960-61	8	1986-87	174
1961-62	8	1987-88	101
1962-63	10	1988-89	122
1963-64	11	1989-90	179
1964-65	11	1990-91	231
1965-66	12	1991-92	307
1966-67	11	1992-93	468
1967-68	11	1993-94	154
1968-69	11	1994-95	105
1969-70	16	1995-96	74
1970-71	15	1996-97	78
1971-72	25	1997-98	113
1972-73	36	1998-99	162
1973-74	36	1999-00	133
1974-75	39	2000-01	132
1975-76	54	2001-02	135
1976-77	60	2002-03	154
1977-78	48	2003-04	136
1978-79	55	2004-05	145
1979-80	64	2005-06	250
1980-81	67	2006-07	240
1981-82	78	2007-08	315
1982-83	90	2008-09	325

An annual tax on net wealth was introduced in India with the enactment of the Wealth Tax Act, 1957 which came into force from April 1 of that year.

2007-08 = Revised estimates; 2008-09 = Budget estimates.

Source: Government of India, Ministry of Finance, *Explanatory Memorandum on the Budget of the Central Government:* and *Receipts Budget* (various years).

Table 9: Gift Tax Revenue: 1958-59 to 2005-06

(Rs. crore)

Year	Yield	Year	Yield
1958-59	1	1982-83	8
1959-60	1	1983-84	9
1960-61	1	1984-85	11
1961-62	1	1985-86	12
1962-63	1	1986-87	9
1963-64	1	1987-88	8
1964-65	2	1988-89	7
1965-66	2	1989-90	8
1966-67	2	1990-91	3
1967-68	1	1991-92	8
1968-69	2	1992-93	9
1969-70	2	1993-94	5
1970-71	2	1994-95	15
1971-72	4	1995-96	11
1972-73	4	1996-97	10
1973-74	5	1997-98	9
1974-75	5	1998-99	10
1975-76	5	1999-00	(-) 3
1976-77	6	2000-01	---
1977-78	6	2001-02	(-) 2
1978-79	6	2002-03	(-) 2
1979-80	7	2003-04	1
1980-81	7	2004-05	2
1981-82	8	2005-06	2

A tax on *inter vivos* gifts was imposed in India under the Gift Tax Act, 1958 which came into force on April 1 of that year. The Finance Minister in his 1998-99 budget discontinued the levy of gift tax on gifts made after September 30, 1998.

Source: Government of India, Ministry of Finance, *Explanatory Memorandum on the Budget of the Central Government:* and *Receipts Budget* (various years).

Table 10: Estate Duty* Revenue: 1954-55 to 2001-02

(Rs. crore)

Year	Yield	Year	Yield
1954-55	1	1978-79	13
1955-56	1	1979-80	14
1956-57	2	1980-81	16
1957-58	2	1981-82	20
1958-59	3	1982-83	20
1959-60	3	1983-84	26
1960-61	3	1984-85	24
1961-62	4	1985-86	23
1962-63	4	1986-87	14
1963-64	5	1987-88	8
1964-65	5	1988-89	6
1965-66	7	1989-90	4
1966-67	6	1990-91	3
1967-68	6	1991-92	3
1968-69	7	1992-93	1
1969-70	7	1993-94	...
1970-71	8	1994-95	1
1971-72	9	1995-96	1
1972-73	10	1996-97	1
1973-74	11	1997-98	1
1974-75	11	1998-99	---
1975-76	12	1999-00	(-) 1
1976-77	12	2000-01	---
1977-78	13	2001-02	1

*Estate duty was introduced in India in 1953 when the Estate Duty Act of that year imposed a duty on the capital value of all property passing on the death of any person on or after October 15, 1953. Estate Duty was abolished w.e.f. March 16, 1985. Yields for subsequent years represent collections on estates passing on deaths occurring before the abolition.

Source: Government of India, Ministry of Finance, *Explanatory Memorandum on the Budget of the Central Government:* and *Receipts Budget* (various years).

Table 11: Central Excise Collections*: 1950-51 to 2008-09

(Rs. crore)

Year	Gross Central taxes	Excise revenue	Col. 3 as % of Col. 2
1	2	3	4
1950-51	405	68	16.8
1951-52	512	79	15.4
1952-53	445	79	17.7
1953-54	420	92	21.9
1954-55	455	105	23.1
1955-56	485	142	29.3
1956-57	570	185	32.5
1957-58	692	268	38.7
1958-59	701	307	43.8
1959-60	794	354	44.6
1960-61	895	414	46.3
1961-62	1,054	482	45.7
1962-63	1,285	599	46.6
1963-64	1,634	730	44.7
1964-65	1,821	801	44.0
1965-66	2,061	898	43.6
1966-67	2,307	1,034	44.8
1967-68	2,353	1,148	48.8
1968-69	2,510	1,321	52.6
1969-70	2,822	1,524	54.0
1970-71	3,206	1,758	54.8
1971-72	3,873	2,061	53.2
1972-73	4,505	2,324	51.6
1973-74	5,070	2,602	51.3
1974-75	6,322	3,230	51.1
1975-76	7,609	3,845	50.5
1976-77	8,263	4,221	51.1
1977-78	8,858	4,448	50.2
1978-79	10,525	5,367	51.0
1979-80	11,974	6,011	50.2
1980-81	13,179	6,500	49.3

Contd...

1981-82	15,847	7,421	46.8
1982-83	17,696	8,059	45.5
1983-84	20,721	10,222	49.3
1984-85	23,471	11,151	47.5
1985-86	28,671	12,956	45.2
1986-87	32,837	14,470	44.1
1987-88	37,666	16,426	43.6
1988-89	44,474	18,841	42.4
1989-90	51,636	22,406	43.4
1990-91	57,577	24,514	42.6
1991-92	67,361	28,110	41.7
1992-93	74,636	30,832	41.3
1993-94	75,742	31,697	41.8
1994-95	92,297	37,347	40.5
1995-96	1,10,354	40,187	36.4
1996-97	1,28,762	45,008	34.9
1997-98	1,39,221	47,962	34.4
1998-99	1,43,797	53,246	37.0
1999-00	1,71,752	61,902	36.1
2000-01	1,88,603	68,526	36.3
2001-02	1,87,060	72,555	38.8
2002-03	2,16,266	82,310	38.1
2003-04	2,54,348	90,774	35.7
2004-05	3,04,958	99,125	32.5
2005-06	3,66,152	1,11,226	30.4
2006-07	4,73,512	1,17,613	24.8
2007-08	5,85,410	1,27,947	21.9
2008-09	6,87,715	1,37,874	20.0

*Before transferring States' Share.

2007-08 = Revised estimates; 2008-09 = Budget estimates.

Source: Government of India, Ministry of Finance, *Explanatory Memorandum on the Budget of the Central Government:* and *Receipts Budget* (various years). Column 4 calculations own.

Table 12: Revenue from Customs Duties: 1950-51 to 2008-09

(Rs. crore)

Year	Gross Central taxes	Customs revenue	Col. 3 as % of Col. 2
1		3	4
1950-51	405	157	38.8
1951-52	512	230	44.9
1952-53	445	172	38.7
1953-54	420	156	37.1
1954-55	455	182	40.0
1955-56	485	163	33.6
1956-57	570	170	29.8
1957-58	692	177	25.6
1958-59	701	135	19.3
1959-60	794	152	19.1
1960-61	895	170	19.0
1961-62	1,054	209	19.8
1962-63	1,285	246	19.1
1963-64	1,634	335	20.5
1964-65	1,821	397	21.8
1965-66	2,061	339	16.4
1966-67	2,307	585	25.4
1967-68	2,353	513	21.8
1968-69	2,510	446	17.8
1969-70	2,822	423	15.0
1970-71	3,206	524	16.3
1971-72	3,873	695	17.9
1972-73	4,505	857	19.0
1973-74	5,070	996	19.6
1974-75	6,322	1,332	21.1
1975-76	7,609	1,419	18.6
1976-77	8,263	1,554	18.8
1977-78	8,858	1,824	20.6
1978-79	10,525	2,423	23.0
1979-80	11,974	2,924	24.4
1980-81	13,179	3,409	25.9

Contd...

1981-82	15,847	4,300	27.1
1982-83	17,696	5,119	28.9
1983-84	20,721	5,583	26.9
1984-85	23,471	7,041	30.0
1985-86	28,671	9,526	33.2
1986-87	32,837	11,475	34.9
1987-88	37,666	13,702	36.4
1988-89	44,474	15,805	35.5
1989-90	51,636	18,036	34.9
1990-91	57,577	20,644	35.9
1991-92	67,361	22,257	33.0
1992-93	74,636	23,776	31.9
1993-94	75,742	22,193	29.3
1994-95	92,297	26,789	29.0
1995-96	1,10,354	35,757	32.4
1996-97	1,28,762	42,851	33.3
1997-98	1,39,221	40,193	28.9
1998-99	1,43,797	40,668	28.3
1999-00	1,71,752	48,419	28.2
2000-01	1,88,603	47,542	25.2
2001-02	1,87,060	40,268	21.5
2002-03	2,16,266	44,852	20.7
2003-04	2,54,348	48,629	19.1
2004-05	3,04,958	57,661	18.9
2005-06	3,66,152	65,067	17.8
2006-07	4,73,512	86,327	18.2
2007-08	5,85,410	1,00,766	17.2
2008-09	6,87,715	1,18,930	17.3

2007-08 = Revised estimates; 2008-09 = Budget estimates.

Source: Government of India, Ministry of Finance, *Explanatory Memorandum on the Budget of the Central Government:* and *Receipts Budget* (various years). Column 4 calculations own.

Table 13: Estimated Additional Resource Mobilisation through Taxation by the Central Government: Selected Years

(Rs. crore)

S. No.	Tax	1990-91	1991-92	1992-93	1993-94	1996-97	1997-98	1998-99	1999-2000	2000-2001
1.	Income tax. (including Corporation tax)	550	1429	895	---	912	---	2400	3100	6080
2.	Wealth tax	---	25	---	---	---	---	---	---	---
3.	Customs duties	835	-510	-2023	-3273	950	---	2748	1469	-1428
4.	Union excise duties	390	988	2211	-1249	760	---	4290	4765	3252
5.	Central sales tax Union Territory of Delhi	---	---	---	---	---	---	---	---	---
6.	Tax on foreign travel	---	---	---	---	---	---	---	---	---
7.	Interest tax	---	535	---	---	---	-600	---	---	-1000
8.	Stamp duty and excise duty on medical and toilet preparations in Union Territories	---	---	---	---	---	---	---	---	---
9.	Hotel receipts tax	---	---	---	---	---	---	---	---	---
10.	Expenditure Tax Act, 1987	---	150	-100	---	---	---	---	---	---
11.	Other taxes and duties	15	---	---	---	70	900	-233	---	---
12.	Total	1790	2617	983	-4522	2692	300	9205	9334	6904

Source: Rearranged data from Government of India, Ministry of Finance, *Indian Public Finance Statistics*, 2006-07, Table 5.1.

Table 14: Key Deficit Indicators of the Central Government: 1970-71 to 2008-09

(Rs. crore)

Year	Fiscal Deficit	Primary Deficit	Revenue Deficit
1970-71	1,408	803	(-) 163
1971-72	1,727	1,057	100
1972-73	2,179	1,403	15
1973-74	1,733	851	(-) 237
1974-75	2,302	1,301	(-) 765
1975-76	3,029	1,802	(-) 886
1976-77	3,802	2,314	(-) 298
1977-78	3,680	2,034	(-) 430
1978-79	5,710	3,726	(-) 292
1979-80	6,392	4,100	694
1980-81	8,299	5,695	2,037
1981-82	8,666	5,471	392
1982-83	10,627	6,689	1,308
1983-84	13,030	8,235	2,540
1984-85	17,416	11,442	4,225
1985-86	21,858	14,346	5,889
1986-87	26,342	17,096	7,777
1987-88	27,044	15,793	9,137
1988-89	30,923	16,645	10,515
1989-90	35,632	17,875	11,914
1990-91	44,632	23,134	18,562
1991-92	36,325	9,728	16,261
1992-93	40,173	9,098	18,574
1993-94	60,257	23,516	32,716
1994-95	57,703	13,644	31,029
1995-96	60,243	10,198	29,731
1996-97	66,733	7,255	32,654
1997-98	88,937	23,300	46,449
1998-99	1,13,349	35,466	66,976
1999-00	1,04,717	14,467	67,596
2000-01	1,18,816	19,502	85,234
2001-02	1,40,955	33,495	1,00,162

Contd...

2002-03	1,45,072	27,268	1,07,879
2003-04	1,23,272	(-) 816	98,262
2004-05	1,25,202	(-) 1,732	78,338
2005-06	1,46,435	13,805	92,299
2006-07	1,42,573	(-) 7,699	80,222
2007-08	1,43,653	(-) 28,318	63,488
2008-09	1,33,287	(-) 57,520	55,184

2007-08 = Revised estimates; 2008-09 = Budget estimates.

Sources: 1. Reserve Bank of India, *Handbook of Statistics on Indian Economy*, 2004-05, p. 169, Table 103; 2. Government of India, *Economic Survey*, 2006-07, p. 21, Table 2.2; 3. Government of India, Ministry of Finance, *Budget at a Glance*, 2008-09, p. 1.

Table 15: Composition of Revenue Budget of the Central Government, 2007-08

(Rs. crore)

Revenue receipts		**Revenue expenditure**	
Gross tax revenue, Of which	5,48,122	A. Revenue Non-Plan expenditure, of which	3,83,546
1. Corporation tax	1,68,401	1. Interest payment	1,58,995
2. Income tax	98,774	2. Defence	54,078
3. Customs duties	98,770	3. Major subsidies	54,330
4. Excise duties	1,30,220	B. Revenue Plan expenditure, of which	1,74,354
A. Net tax revenue*	4,03,832	1. Central Plan	1,28,727
B. Non-tax revenue, Of which	82,550	2. Central assistance for State Plans	45,627
1. Interest receipts	19,308	A+B Total revenue expenditure	5,57,900
2. Dividends and profits	33,925		
A+B Total revenue receipts	4,86,422		
Revenue deficit = 5,57,900 − 4,86,422 = 71,478			

* Net of States' share.

Source: Government of India, Ministry of Finance, *Budget at a Glance,* 2007-08.

Table 16: Composition of Capital Budget of the Central Government, 2007-08

(Rs. crore)

Capital receipts		Capital expenditure	
A. Non-debt receipts, Of which	43,151	A. Capital non-Plan expenditure, of which	91,875
1. Recoveries of loans	1,500	1. Defence	41,922
2. Miscellaneous capital receipts	41,651	2. Loans to public enterprises	767
B. Debt receipts to finance fiscal deficit, of which	1,50,948	B. Capital Plan expenditure, of which	30,746
1. Market loans	1,09,579	1. Central Plan	26,212
2. External assistance (net)	9,111	2. Central assistance for State Plans	4,534
3. State provident funds (net)	5,000	A+B Total capital expenditure	1,22,621
A+B Total capital receipts	1,94,099		

Source: Government of India, Ministry of Finance, *Budget at a Glance*, 2007-08.

Table 17: Summary Statement of the Central Government Budget, 2007-08

(Rs. crore)

Receipts		Expenditure	
1. Revenue receipts	4,86,422	4. Non-Plan expenditure	4,75,421
2. Capital receipts	1,94,099	4.1 On revenue account	3,83,546
2.1 Recoveries of loans	1,500	4.1.1 Interest payments	1,58,995
2.2 Other receipts	41,651	4.2 On capital account	91,875
2.3 Borrowings	1,50,948	5. Plan expenditure	2,05,100
3. Total receipts (1+2)	6,80,521	5.1 On revenue account	1,74,354
		5.2 On capital account	30,746
		6. Total revenue expenditure (4.1 + 5.1)	5,57,900
		7. Total capital expenditure (4.2 + 5.2)	1,22,621
		8. Total expenditure (6+7)	6,80,521
9. Revenue deficit = 71,478; (6 – 1)	10. Fiscal deficit = 1,50,948; [8 – (1+2.1+2.2)]	11. Primary deficit = – 8,047 (10 – 4.1.1)	

Source: Government of India, Ministry of Finance, *Budget at a Glance*, 2007-08.

Table 18: Revenue from Agricultural Income Tax Levied by State Governments: 1950-51 to 2006-07

(Rs. crore)

Year	Yield	Year	Yield
1950-51	3	1979-80	58
1951-52	4	1980-81	46
1952-53	4	1981-82	38
1953-54	4	1982-83	30
1954-55	5	1983-84	44
1955-56	8	1984-85	84
1956-57	8	1985-86	127
1957-58	8	1986-87	104
1958-59	8	1987-88	63
1959-60	9	1988-89	64
1960-61	10	1989-90	93
1961-62	9	1990-91	198
1962-63	10	1991-92	202
1963-64	9	1992-93	111
1964-65	11	1993-94	107
1965-66	10	1994-95	98
1966-67	11	1995-96	154
1967-68	12	1996-97	103
1968-69	10	1997-98	182
1969-70	14	1998-99	241
1970-71	11	1999-00	150
1971-72	13	2000-01	76
1972-73	12	2001-02	23
1973-74	12	2002-03	14
1974-75	14	2003-04	15
1975-76	29	2004-05	28
1976-77	35	2005-06	33
1977-78	62	2006-07	36
1978-79	80		

2005-06 = Revised estimates; 2006-07 = Budget estimates.

Sources: 1. Reserve Bank of India (a) *Report on Currency and Finance* and (b) *Supplement to Finances of State Governments* (various years); 2. Government of India, Ministry of Finance, *Indian Public Finance Statistics*, 2006-2007, Table 3.2.

Table 19: Land Revenue Collections of State Governments: 1950-51 to 2006-07

(Rs. crore)

Year	Yield	Year	Yield
1950-51	49	1979-80	152
1951-52	48	1980-81	146
1952-53	57	1981-82	205
1953-54	71	1982-83	189
1954-55	73	1983-84	213
1955-56	78	1984-85	282
1956-57	83	1985-86	353
1957-58	88	1986-87	382
1958-59	92	1987-88	447
1959-60	95	1988-89	594
1960-61	97	1989-90	690
1961-62	95	1990-91	607
1962-63	120	1991-92	636
1963-64	123	1992-93	617
1964-65	120	1993-94	732
1965-66	112	1994-95	1,141
1966-67	90	1995-96	1,326
1967-68	96	1996-97	1,074
1968-69	114	1997-98	1,090
1969-70	103	1998-99	1,031
1970-71	113	1999-00	1,070
1971-72	101	2000-01	1,377
1972-73	93	2001-02	1,717
1973-74	157	2002-03	1,722
1974-75	161	2003-04	2,156
1975-76	230	2004-05	2,531
1976-77	183	2005-06	3,198
1977-78	166	2006-07	3,332
1978-79	188		

2005-06 = Revised estimates; 2006-07 = Budget estimates.

Sources: 1. Reserve Bank of India (a) *Report on Currency and Finance* and (b) *Supplement to Finances of State Governments* (various years); 2. Government of India, Ministry of Finance, *Indian Public Finance Statistics*, 2006-2007, Table 3.2.

Table 20: Revenue from Sales Tax Levied by State Governments: 1950-51 to 2006-07

(Rs. crore)

Year	States' own tax revenue	Sales tax	Col. 3 as % of Col.2
1	2	3	4
1950-51	222	58	26.1
1951-52	227	59	26.0
1952-53	233	57	24.5
1953-54	252	66	26.2
1954-55	265	74	27.9
1955-56	283	82	29.0
1956-57	320	98	30.6
1957-58	353	117	33.1
1958-59	388	124	32.0
1959-60	422	137	32.5
1960-61	455	159	34.9
1961-62	489	181	37.0
1962-63	580	208	35.9
1963-64	691	268	38.8
1964-65	778	318	40.9
1965-66	861	368	42.7
1966-67	954	442	46.3
1967-68	1,103	508	46.1
1968-69	1,249	572	45.8
1969-70	1,378	657	47.7
1970-71	1,546	755	48.8
1971-72	1,702	826	48.5
1972-73	1,931	976	50.5
1973-74	2,319	1,143	49.3
1974-75	2,901	1,550	53.4
1975-76	3,573	1,944	54.4
1976-77	4,061	2,270	55.9
1977-78	4,379	2,414	55.1
1978-79	5,003	2,773	55.4
1979-80	5,709	3,211	56.2

Contd...

1980-81	6,665	3,888	58.3
1981-82	8,295	4,893	59.0
1982-83	9,546	5,496	57.6
1983-84	10,804	5,706	52.8
1984-85	12,343	7,060	57.2
1985-86	14,597	8,429	57.7
1986-87	16,701	9,640	57.7
1987-88	19,311	11,183	57.9
1988-89	22,452	13,120	58.4
1989-90	26,057	15,060	57.8
1990-91	30,145	17,667	58.6
1991-92	35,837	21,064	58.8
1992-93	39,530	23,349	59.1
1993-94	46,219	27,638	59.8
1994-95	55,552	33,154	59.7
1995-96	63,865	35,477	55.5
1996-97	71,294	41,896	58.8
1997-98	81,439	45,351	55.7
1998-99	89,220	49,250	55.2
1999-00	1,02,831	57,592	56.0
2000-01	1,16,717	68,386	58.6
2001-02	1,27,475	71,379	56.0
2002-03	1,40,372	79,425	56.6
2003-04	1,59,736	89,658	56.1
2004-05	1,89,413	1,10,597	58.4
2005-06	2,25,209	1,28,000	56.8
2006-07	2,56,982	1,51,099	58.8

2005-06 = Revised estimates; 2006-07 = Budget estimates.

Sources: 1. Reserve Bank of India (a) *Report on Currency and Finance* and (b) *Supplement to Finances of State Governments* (various years); 2. Government of India, Ministry of Finance, *Indian Public Finance Statistics*, 2006-2007, Table 3.2. Column 4 calculations own.

Table 21: Revenue from State Excise Duty: 1950-51 to 2006-07

(Rs. crore)

Year	Yield	Year	Yield
1950-51	48	1979-80	698
1951-52	49	1980-81	824
1952-53	46	1981-82	1,115
1953-54	45	1982-83	1,343
1954-55	45	1983-84	1,384
1955-56	45	1984-85	1,839
1956-57	46	1985-86	2,052
1957-58	46	1986-87	2,421
1958-59	47	1987-88	2,864
1959-60	50	1988-89	3,081
1960-61	53	1989-90	3,864
1961-62	59	1990-91	4,795
1962-63	63	1991-92	5,439
1963-64	73	1992-93	6,365
1964-65	84	1993-94	7,106
1965-66	96	1994-95	7,747
1966-67	109	1995-96	8,516
1967-68	131	1996-97	8,848
1968-69	159	1997-98	11,383
1969-70	174	1998-99	13,438
1970-71	194	1999-00	15,092
1971-72	234	2000-01	15,825
1972-73	279	2001-02	17,150
1973-74	354	2002-03	18,833
1974-75	387	2003-04	19,548
1975-76	435	2004-05	22,061
1976-77	505	2005-06	26,161
1977-78	570	2006-07	29,688
1978-79	583		

2005-06 = Revised estimates; 2006-07 = Budget estimates.

Sources: 1. Reserve Bank of India (a) *Report on Currency and Finance* and (b) *Supplement to Finances of State Governments* (various years); 2. Government of India, Ministry of Finance, *Indian Public Finance Statistics*, 2006-2007, Table 3.2.

Table 22: Revenue from Entertainment Tax Levied by State Governments: 1950-51 to 2006-07

(Rs. crore)

Year	Yield	Year	Yield
1950-51	---	1979-80	231
1951-52	6	1980-81	255
1952-53	6	1981-82	304
1953-54	6	1982-83	299
1954-55	6	1983-84	370
1955-56	7	1984-85	412
1956-57	9	1985-86	308
1957-58	9	1986-87	427
1958-59	11	1987-88	382
1959-60	11	1988-89	423
1960-61	13	1989-90	342
1961-62	15	1990-91	412
1962-63	18	1991-92	349
1963-64	23	1992-93	464
1964-65	25	1993-94	426
1965-66	29	1994-95	447
1966-67	35	1995-96	440
1967-68	26	1996-97	796
1968-69	43	1997-98	1,035
1969-70	50	1998-99	926
1970-71	58	1999-00	907
1971-72	63	2000-01	1,203
1972-73	77	2001-02	827
1973-74	100	2002-03	816
1974-75	125	2003-04	755
1975-76	150	2004-05	3,107
1976-77	175	2005-06	882
1977-78	181	2006-07	900
1978-79	205		

2005-06 = Revised estimates; 2006-07 = Budget estimates.

Sources: 1. Reserve Bank of India (a) *Report on Currency and Finance* and (b) *Supplement to Finances of State Governments* (various years); 2. Government of India, Ministry of Finance, *Indian Public Finance Statistics*, 2006-2007, Table 3.2.

Select Bibliography

Select Bibliography

Administrative Reforms Commission, *Report of the Study Team on Centre-State Relationships*, Vol. I, 1968.

Alejandro Foxley, Eduardo Aninat, and J.P. Arellano, *Redistributive Effects of Government Programmes - The Chilean Case* (Pergamon Press, 1979).

Alesina, Alberto and R. Perotti, "The Political Economy of Budget Deficits", *IMF Staff Papers*, 1995.

Aronson, Richard, *Public Finance* (New York: McGraw-Hill Book Company, 1985).

Bakshi, P.M., *The Constitution of India* (Delhi: Universal Law Publishing Co. Pvt. Ltd.).

Basu, Durga Das, *Introduction to the Constitution of India* (New Delhi: Prentice-Hall of India Private Ltd., 1987).

Brown, C.V. and Jackson, P.M., *Public Sector Economics* (Oxford: Martin Robertson and Co. Ltd., 1983).

Burkhead, Jesse, *Government Budgeting* (New York: John Wiley and Sons, 1956).

Caiden, Naomi and Wildavsky, Aaron, *Planning and Budgeting in Poor Countries* (New York: John Wiley and Sons, 1974).

Central Board of Excise and Customs, *Guide to MODVAT.*

Danziger, James, *Making Budgets* (London: Sage Publications, 1978).

Gyan Chand, *The Essentials of Federal Finance: A Contribution to the Problem of Financial Re-adjustment in India* (Humphrey Milford, Oxford University Press, 1930).

Government of India, *Report of the Indian Taxation Enquiry Committee*, 1924-25, Vol. I (President: Charles Todhunter).

——*Report of the Income Tax Investigation Commission* (Chairman: Srinivasa Varadachariar), 1948

——*Report of the Taxation Enquiry Commission* (Chairman: John Mathai) 1953-54, Vols. I, II and III.

——*Report of the Customs Reorganisation Committee,* (Chairman: F.C. Budhwar), 1957-58.

——*Report of the Direct Taxes Administration Enquiry Committee* (Chairman: Mahavir Tyagi) 1958-59.

——Central Excise Reorganisation Committee (Chairman: A.K. Chanda), 1963

——*Report of the Committee on Sales Tax* (Chairman: R.G. Saraiya), 1964.

——*Final Report on Rationalisation and Simplification of Tax Structure* (Chairman: S. Bhoothalingam), 1968.

——*Final Report of Direct Taxes Enquiry Committee* (Chairman: K.N. Wanchoo), December 1971.

——Ministry of Finance, *Report of the Committee on Taxation of Agricultural Wealth and Income* (Chairman: K. N. Raj), 1972.

——*Report of the Central Excise (Self-Removal Procedure) Review Committee* (Chairman: B. Venkatappiah), 1973.

——*Report of the Indirect Taxation Enquiry Committee* (Chairman: L.K. Jha), 1977, Part I.

——*Report of the Indirect Taxation Enquiry Committee* (Chairman: L. K. Jha), Part II, January 1978.

——*Final Report of Direct Tax Laws Committee* (Chairman: C.C. Chokshi), 1978.

——*Report of the Expert Committee on Tax Measures to Promote Employment* (Chairman: V.M. Dandekar), 1980.

——Economic Administrative Reforms Commission, *Report on Tax Administrations*, 1981-83.

——*Report of the Expert Committee on Replacement of Sales Tax by Additional Excise Duty* (Chairman: Kamlapati Tripathi), January 1983.

——*Aspects of the Black Economy in India,* March 1985.

——*Long Term Fiscal Policy* (December, 1985).

——*Report of the Technical Study Group on Central Excise Tariff* (Chairman: J. Datta) Part I, 1985.

——*Study Group on Taxation of Expenditure* (Final Report), 1987.

——*Report of the Commission on Centre-State Relations* (Chairman: R.S. Sarkaria), 1988, Part I.

——*Industrial Policy Statement, 1991.*

——*Interim Report of the Tax Reforms Committee* (Chairman: Raja Chelliah) December 1991.

——*Final Report of the Tax Reforms Committee* (Chairman: Raja Chelliah) Part I, 1992.

——*Advisory Group on Tax Policy and Tax Administration for the Tenth Plan* (Chairman: Parthasarathi Shome), 2001

——*Report of the Task Force on Direct Taxes* (Chairman: Vijay Kelkar), December 2002.

——*Report of the Task Force on Indirect Taxes* (Chairman: Vijay Kelkar),

December 2002.

——*White Paper on State-Level Value Added Tax* (Chairman: Asim Kumar Dasgupta), 2005.

——*Rationalisation of Customs and Excise Duties on Edible Oils and Oilseeds* (Chairman: Ashok Lahiri), 2006.

——*Five Year Plans.*

——*Budget Papers* (various years).

——*An Economic and Functional Classification of the Central Government Budget.*

——*Economic Survey* (various issues).

——*Reports of Finance Commissions.*

——*Indian Public Finance Statistics* (various issues).

—— *Constitution of India.*

——*Speeches of Union Finance Ministers, 1947-48 to 1984-85; Presenting Central Government Budgets.*

Lee, Robert and Johnson, Ronald, *Public Budgeting Systems* (Baltimore: University Park Press, 1977).

Lok Sabha Secretariat, New Delhi, *Abstracts on Parliamentary Procedures, 1986.*

Mark Krasnick, *Fiscal Federalism* (Toronto: University of Toronto Press, 1986).

Musgrave, Richard and Musgrave, Peggy, *Public Finance in Theory and Practice* (New York: McGraw-Hill Book Company, 1985).

Nicholas Kaldor, *Indian Tax Reform - Report of a Survey* (Government of India, Ministry of Finance, 1956).

Reserve Bank of India, *Report on Currency and Finance* (various years).

——*Handbook of Statistics on the Indian Economy* (various years).

——*Bulletins*

——*Occasional Papers*

——*Supplement on Finances of State Governments.*

Roy T. Gobin, "An Analysis of the System of Sales Taxation in Caribbean Market", *Public Finance*, Vol. XXXV, No. 2, 1980, pp. 272-73.

Shakdher, S.L., *The Budget and the Parliament* (New Delhi: National Publishing House, 1979).

Sury, M.M., Sales Tax in India Since 1938, *Journal of the Indian School of Political Economy*, Vol. 7, No. 1, January-March 1996.

——Excise Duties in India: 1894-1994, *Journal of the Indian School of Political Economy*, Vol. 6, No. 1, January-March 1994.

——Income Tax in India Since 1860, *Journal of the Indian School of Political*

Economy, Vol. 5, No. 1, January-March 1993.

——Centre-State Financial Relations in India: 1870-1990, *Journal of the Indian School of Political Economy*, Vol. 4, No. 1, January-March 1992.

——Tax Structure Developments in India: 1950-90, *Journal of the Indian School of Political Economy*, Vol. 3, No. 1, January-March 1991.

——India: Structure and Evaluation of the Income Tax System, *Asian-Pacific Tax and Investment Bulletin* (Singapore), Vol. 8, Nos. 2 and 3, 1990.

——Excise Concessions to Small Scale Industries in India: Some Issues, *Small Industry Bulletin for Asia and the Pacific* (United Nations, ESCAP, Bangkok), No. 22, 1987.

——India: Decline of Direct Taxes, *Bulletin for International Fiscal Documentation* (Amsterdam), Vol. 41, June 1987.

——Buoyancy and Elasticity of Union Excise Revenue in India: 1950-51 to 1080-81, *Margin*, Vol. 18, No. 1, October 1985.

United Nations, Department of Economic Affairs, *A Manual for Economic and Functional Classification of Government Transactions* (New York, 1958).

Wojthley, John and Ludwin, William, *Zero-Base Budgeting in State and Local Government* (New York: Praeger Publishers, 1979).

Indices

Name Index

Subject Index